THE
LIFE AND LETTERS
OF
WALTER H. PAGE

From a painting by P. A. LASZLO

Walter H. Page

THE
LIFE AND LETTERS OF
WALTER H. PAGE

BY
BURTON J. HENDRICK

GARDEN CITY   NEW YORK
DOUBLEDAY, PAGE & COMPANY
1925

PREFATORY NOTE

Among the many who have assisted in the preparation of this Biography especial acknowledgment is made to Mr. Irwin Laughlin, First Secretary and Counsellor of the London Embassy under Mr. Page. Mr. Page's papers show the high regard which he entertained for Mr. Laughlin's abilities and character, and the author similarly has found Mr. Laughlin's assistance indispensable. Mr. Laughlin has had the goodness to read the manuscript and make numerous suggestions, all for the purpose of reënforcing the accuracy of the narrative. The author gratefully remembers many long conversations with Viscount Grey of Fallodon, in which Anglo-American relations from 1913 to 1916 were exhaustively canvassed and many side-lights thrown upon Mr. Page's conduct of his difficult and delicate duties. The British Foreign Office most courteously gave the writer permission to examine a large number of documents in its archives bearing upon Mr. Page's ambassadorship and consented to the publication of several of the most important.

B. J. H.

CONTENTS

PART I

LIST OF ILLUSTRATIONS

PART I

ix

PART II

FACING PAGE

PART I

THE LIFE AND LETTERS OF WALTER H. PAGE

CHAPTER I

A RECONSTRUCTION BOYHOOD

I

THE earliest recollections of any man have great biographical interest, and this is especially the case with Walter Page, for not the least dramatic aspect of his life was that it spanned the two greatest wars in history. His last weeks in England Page spent at Sandwich, on the coast of Kent; every day and every night he could hear the pounding of the great guns in France, as the Germans were making their last desperate attempt to reach Paris or the Channel ports. His memories of his childhood days in America were similarly the sights and sounds of war. Page was a North Carolina boy; he has himself recorded the impression that the Civil War left upon his mind.

"One day," he writes, "when the cotton fields were white and the elm leaves were falling, in the soft autumn of the Southern climate wherein the sky is fathomlessly clear, the locomotive's whistle blew a much longer time than usual as the train approached Millworth. It did not stop at so small a station except when there was somebody to get off or to get on, and so long a blast meant that someone was coming. Sam and I ran down the avenue of elms to see who it was. Sam was my Negro companion,

1

philosopher, and friend. I was ten years old and Sam said that he was fourteen. There was constant talk about the war. Many men of the neighbourhood had gone away somewhere—that was certain; but Sam and I had a theory that the war was only a story. We had been fooled about old granny Thomas's bringing the baby and long ago we had been fooled also about Santa Claus. The war might be another such invention, and we sometimes suspected that it was. But we found out the truth that day, and for this reason it is among my clearest early recollections.

"For, when the train stopped, they put off a big box and gently laid it in the shade of the fence. The only man at the station was the man who had come to change the mail-bags; and he said that this was Billy Morris's coffin and that he had been killed in a battle. He asked us to stay with it till he could send word to Mr. Morris, who lived two miles away. The man came back presently and leaned against the fence till old Mr. Morris arrived, an hour or more later. The lint of cotton was on his wagon, for he was hauling his crop to the gin when the sad news reached him; and he came in his shirt sleeves, his wife on the wagon seat with him.

"All the neighbourhood gathered at the church, a funeral was preached and there was a long prayer for our success against the invaders, and Billy Morris was buried. I remember that I wept the more because it now seemed to me that my doubt about the war had somehow done Billy Morris an injustice. Old Mrs. Gregory wept more loudly than anybody else; and she kept saying, while the service was going on, 'It'll be my John next.' In a little while, sure enough, John Gregory's coffin was put off the train, as Billy Morris's had been, and I regarded her as a woman gifted with prophecy. Other coffins, too, were put off from time to time. About the war there could no longer be a doubt. And, a little later, its realities and horrors came nearer home to us, with swift, deep experiences.

"One day my father took me to the camp and parade ground ten miles away, near the capital. The General and the Governor sat on horses and the soldiers marched by them and the band played. They were going to the front. There surely must be a war at the front, I told Sam that night. Still more coffins were brought home, too, as the months and the years passed; and the women of the neighbourhood used to come and spend whole days with my mother, sewing for the soldiers. So precious became woollen cloth that every rag was saved and the threads were unravelled to be spun and woven into new fabrics. And they baked bread and roasted chickens and sheep and pigs and made cakes, all to go to the soldiers at the front."[1]

The quality that is uppermost in the Page stock, both in the past and in the present generation, is that of the builder and the pioneer. The ancestor of the North Carolina Pages was a Lewis Page, who, in the latter part of the eighteenth century, left the original American home in Virginia, and started life anew in what was then regarded as the less civilized country to the south. Several explanations have survived as to the cause of his departure, one being that his interest in the rising tide of Methodism had made him uncongenial to his Church of England relatives; in the absence of definite knowledge, however, it may safely be assumed that the impelling motive was that love of seeking out new things, of constructing a new home in the wilderness, which has never forsaken his

---

[1] From "The Southerner," Chapter I. The first chapter in this novel is practically autobiographical, though fictitious names have been used.

descendants. His son, Anderson Page, manifesting this same love of change, went farther south into Wake County, and acquired a plantation of a thousand acres about twelve miles north of Raleigh. He cultivated this estate with slaves, sending his abundant crops of cotton and tobacco to Petersburg, Virginia, a traffic that made him sufficiently prosperous to give several of his sons a college education. The son who is chiefly interesting at the present time, Allison Francis Page, the father of the future Ambassador, did not enjoy this opportunity. This fact in itself gives an insight into his character. While his brothers were grappling with Latin and Greek and theology—one of them became a Methodist preacher of the hortatory type for which the South is famous—we catch glimpses of the older man battling with the logs in the Cape Fear River, or penetrating the virgin pine forest, felling trees and converting its raw material to the uses of a growing civilization. Like many of the Page breed, this Page was a giant in size and in strength, as sound morally and physically as the mighty forests in which a considerable part of his life was spent, brave, determined, aggressive, domineering almost to the point of intolerance, deeply religious and abstemious—a mixture of the frontiersman and the Old Testament prophet. Walter Page dedicated one of his books[1] to his father, in words that accurately sum up his character and career. "To the honoured memory of my father, whose work was work that built up the commonwealth." Indeed, Frank Page —for this is the name by which he was generally known— spent his whole life in these constructive labours. He founded two towns in North Carolina, Cary and Aberdeen; in the City of Raleigh he constructed hotels and other buildings; his enterprising and restless spirit opened

[1] "The Rebuilding of Old Commonwealths." (1902.)

up Moore County—which includes the Pinehurst region; he scattered his logging camps and his sawmills all over the face of the earth; and he constructed a railroad through the pine woods that made him a rich man.

Though he was not especially versed in the learning of the schools, Walter Page's father had a mind that was keen and far-reaching. He was a pioneer in politics as he was in the practical concerns of life. Though he was the son of slave-holding progenitors and even owned slaves himself, he was not a believer in slavery. The country that he primarily loved was not Moore County or North Carolina, but the United States of America. In politics he was a Whig, which meant that, in the years preceding the Civil War, he was opposed to the extension of slavery and did not regard the election of Abraham Lincoln as a sufficient provocation for the secession of the Southern States. It is therefore not surprising that Walter Page, in the midst of the London turmoil of 1916, should have found his thoughts reverting to his father as he remembered him in Civil War days. That gaunt figure of America's time of agony proved an inspiration and hope in the anxieties that assailed the Ambassador. "When our Civil War began," wrote Page to Col. Edward M. House—the date was November 24, 1916, one of the darkest days for the Allied cause—"every man who had a large and firm grip on economic facts foresaw how it would end—not when but how. Young as I was, I recall a conversation between my father and the most distinguished judge of his day in North Carolina. They put down on one side the number of men in the Confederate States, the number of ships, the number of manufactures, as nearly as they knew, the number of skilled workmen, the number of guns, the aggregate of wealth and of possible production. On the other side they put down the best estimate they could make of all these things in the Northern States. The Northern States made two (or I shouldn't wonder if it were three) times as good a showing in men and resources as the Confederacy had. 'Judge,' said my father, 'this is the most foolhardy enterprise that man ever undertook.' But Yancey of Alabama was about that time making five-hour speeches to thousands of people all over the South, declaring that one Southerner could whip five Yankees, and the awful slaughter began and darkened our childhood and put all our best men where they would see the sun no more. Our people had at last to accept worse terms than they could have got at the beginning. This World War, even more than our Civil War, is an economic struggle. Put down on either side the same items that my father and the judge put down and add the items up. You will see the inevitable result."

If we are seeking an ancestral explanation for that moral ruggedness, that quick perception of the difference between right and wrong, that unobscured vision into men and events, and that deep devotion to America and to democracy which formed the fibre of Walter Page's being, we evidently need look no further than his father. But the son had qualities which the older man did not possess—an enthusiasm for literature and learning, a love of the beautiful in Nature and in art, above all a gentleness of temperament and of manner. These qualities he held in common with his mother. On his father's side Page was undiluted English; on his mother's he was French and English. Her father was John Samuel Raboteau, the descendant of Huguenot refugees who had fled from France on the Revocation of the Edict of Nantes; her mother was Esther Barclay, a member of a family which gave the name of Barclaysville to a small town half way between Raleigh and Fayetteville, North Carolina. It is a member of this tribe to whom Page once referred as the "vigorous Barclay who held her receptions to notable men in her bedroom during the years of her bedridden condition." She was the proprietor of the "Half Way House," a tavern located between Fayetteville and Raleigh; and in her old age she kept royal state, in the fashion which Page describes, for such as were socially entitled to this consideration. The most vivid impression which her present-day descendants retain is that of her fervent devotion to the Southern cause. She carried the spirit of secession to such an extreme that she had the gate to her yard painted to give a complete presentment of the Confederate Flag. Walter Page's mother, the granddaughter of this determined and rebellious lady, had also her positive quality, but in a somewhat more subdued form. She did not die until 1897, and so the recollection of her is fresh and vivid. As a mature woman she was undemonstrative and soft spoken; a Methodist of old-fashioned Wesleyan type, she dressed with a Quaker-like simplicity, her brown hair brushed flatly down upon a finely shaped head and her garments destitute of ruffles or ornamentation. The home which she directed was a home without playing cards or dancing or smoking or wine-bibbing or other worldly frivolities, yet the memories of her presence which Catherine Page has left are not at all austere. Duty was with her the prime consideration of life, and fundamental morals the first conceptions which she instilled in her children's growing minds, yet she had a quiet sense of humour and a real love of fun.

She had also strong likes and dislikes, and was not especially hospitable to men and women who fell under her disapproval. A small North Carolina town, in the years preceding and following the Civil War, was not a fruitful soil for cultivating an interest in things intellectual, yet those who remember Walter Page's mother remember her always with a book in her hand. She would read at her knitting and at her miscellaneous household duties, which were rather arduous in the straitened days that followed the war, and the books she read were always substantial ones. Perhaps because her son Walter was in delicate health, perhaps because his early tastes and temperament were not unlike her own, perhaps because he was her oldest surviving child, the fact remains that, of a family of eight, he was generally regarded as the child with whom she was especially sympathetic. The picture of mother and son in those early days is an altogether charming one. Page's mother was only twenty-four when he was born; she retained her youth for many years after that event, and during his early childhood, in appearance and manner, she was little more than a girl. When Walter was a small boy, he and his mother used to take long walks in the woods, sometimes spending the entire day, fishing along the brooks, hunting wild flowers, now and then pausing while the mother read pages of Dickens or of Scott. These experiences Page never forgot. Nearly all his letters to his mother—to whom, even in his busiest days in New York, he wrote constantly —have been accidentally destroyed, but a few scraps indicate the close spiritual bond that existed between the two. Always he seemed to think of his mother as young. Through his entire life, in whatever part of the world he might be, and however important was the work in which he might be engaged, Page never failed to write her a long and affectionate letter at Christmas.

"Well, I've gossiped a night or two"—such is the

conclusion of his Christmas letter of 1893, when Page was thirty-eight, with a growing family of his own—"till I've filled the paper—all such little news and less nonsense as most gossip and most letters are made of. But it is for you to read between the lines. That's where the love lies, dear mother. I wish you were here Christmas; we should welcome you as nobody else in the world can be welcomed. But wherever you are and though all the rest have the joy of seeing you, which is denied to me, never a Christmas comes but I feel as near you as I did years and years ago when we were young. (In those years *big* fish bit in old Wiley Bancom's pond by the railroad: they must have been two inches long!)—I would give a year's growth to have the pleasure of having you here. You may be sure that every one of my children along with me will look with an added reverence toward the picture on the wall that greets me every morning, when we have our little Christmas frolics—the picture that little Katharine points to and says 'That's my grandmudder.'—The years, as they come, every one, deepen my gratitude to you, as I better and better understand the significance of life and every one adds to an affection that was never small. God bless you.

"WALTER."

Such were the father and mother of Walter Hines Page; they were married at Fayetteville, North Carolina, July 5, 1849; two children who preceded Walter died in infancy. The latter was born at Cary, August 15, 1855. Cary was a small village which Frank Page had created; in honour of the founder it was for several years known as Page's Station; the father himself changed the name to Cary, as a tribute to a temperance orator who caused something of a commotion in the neighbourhood in the early seventies. Cary was not then much of a town and has not since become one; but it was placed amid the scene of important historical events. Page's home was almost the last stopping place of Sherman's army on its march through Georgia and the Carolinas, and the Confederacy came to an end, with Johnston's surrender of the last Confederate Army, at Durham, only fifteen miles from his native village. Walter, a boy of ten, his brother Robert, aged six, and the negro "companion" Tance—who figures as Sam in the extract quoted above—stood at the second-story window and watched Sherman's soldiers pass their house, in hot pursuit of General "Joe" Wheeler's cavalry. The thing that most astonished the children was the vast size of the army, which took all day to file by their home. They had never realized that either of the fighting forces could embrace such great numbers of men. Nor did the behaviour of the invading troops especially endear them to their unwilling hosts. Part of the cavalry encamped in the Page yard; their horses ate the bark off the mimosa trees; an army corps built its campfires under the great oaks, and cut their emblems on the trunks; the officers took possession of the house, a colonel making his headquarters in the parlour. Several looting cavalrymen ran their swords through the beds, probably looking for hidden silver; the hearth was torn up in the same feverish quest; angry at their failure, they emptied sacks of flour and scattered the contents in the bedrooms and on the stairs; for days the flour, intermingled with feathers from the bayonetted beds, formed a carpet all over the house. It is therefore perhaps not strange that the feelings which Walter entertained for Sherman's "bummers," despite his father's Whig principles, were those of most Southern communities. One day a kindly Northern soldier, sympathizing with the boy because of the small rations left for the local population, invited him to join the officers' mess at dinner. Walter drew proudly back.

"I'll starve before I'll eat with the Yankees," he said.

"I slept that night on a trundle bed by my mother's," Page wrote years afterward, describing these early scenes, "for her room was the only room left for the family, and we had all lived there since the day before. The dining room and the kitchen were now superfluous, because there was nothing more to cook or to eat. . . . A week or more after the army corps had gone, I drove with my father to the capital one day, and almost every mile of the journey we saw a blue coat or a gray coat lying by the road, with bones or hair protruding—the unburied and the forgotten of either army. Thus I had come to know what war was, and death by violence was among the first deep impressions made on my mind. My emotions must have been violently dealt with and my sensibilities blunted—or sharpened? Who shall say? The wounded and the starved straggled home from hospitals and from prisons. There was old Mr. Sanford, the shoemaker, come back again, with a body so thin and a step so uncertain that I expected to see him fall to pieces. Mr. Larkin and Joe Tatum went on crutches; and I saw a man at the post-office one day whose cheek and ear had been torn away by a shell. Even when Sam and I sat on the river-bank fishing, and ought to have been silent lest the fish swim away, we told over in low tones the stories that we had heard of wounds and of deaths and of battles.

"But there was the cheerful gentleness of my mother to draw my thoughts to different things. I can even now recall many special little plans that she made to keep my mind from battles. She hid the military cap that I had worn.   She bought from me my military buttons and put them away.   She would call me in and tell me pleasant stories of her own childhood.   She would put down her work to make puzzles with me, and she read gentle books to me and kept away from me all the stories of the war and of death that she could.   Whatever hardships befell her (and they must have been many) she kept a tender manner of resignation and of cheerful patience.

"After a while the neighbourhood came to life again. There were more widows, more sonless mothers, more empty sleeves and wooden legs than anybody there had ever seen before.   But the mimosa bloomed, the cotton was planted again, and the peach trees blossomed; and the barnyard and the stable again became full of life.   For, when the army marched away, they, too, were as silent as an old battlefield.   The last hen had been caught under the corn-crib by a 'Yankee' soldier, who had torn his coat in this brave raid.   Aunt Maria told Sam that all Yankees were chicken thieves whether they 'brung freedom or no.'

"Every year the cotton bloomed and ripened and opened white to the sun; for the ripening of the cotton and the running of the river and the turning of the mills make the thread not of my story only but of the story of our Southern land—of its institutions, of its misfortunes and of its place in the economy of the world; and they will make the main threads of its story, I am sure, so long as the sun shines on our white fields and the rivers run—a story that is now rushing swiftly into a happier narrative of a broader day.   The same women who had guided the spindles in war-time were again at their tasks—they at least were left; but the machinery was now old and worked ill.   Negro men, who had wandered a while looking for an invisible 'freedom,' came back and went to work on the farm from force of habit. They now received wages and bought their own food. That was the only apparent difference that freedom had brought them.

"My Aunt Katharine came from the city for a visit, my Cousin Margaret with her. Through the orchard, out into the newly ploughed ground beyond, back over the lawn which was itself bravely repairing the hurt done by horses' hoofs and tent-poles, and under the oaks, which bore the scars of camp-fires, we two romped and played gentler games than camp and battle. One afternoon, as our mothers sat on the piazza and saw us come loaded with apple-blossoms, they said something (so I afterward learned) about the eternal blooming of childhood and of Nature—how sweet the early summer was in spite of the harrying of the land by war; for our gorgeous pageant of the seasons came on as if the earth had been the home of unbroken peace."[1]

II

And so it was a tragic world into which this boy Page had been born. He was ten years old when the Civil War came to an end, and his early life was therefore cast in a desolate country. Like all of his neighbours, Frank Page had been ruined by the war. Both the Southern and Northern armies had passed over the Page territory; compared with the military depredations with which Page became familiar in the last years of his life, the Federal troops did not particularly misbehave, the attacks on hen roosts and the destruction of feather beds representing the extreme of their "atrocities"; but no country can entertain two great fighting forces without feeling the effects for a prolonged period. Life in this part of North Carolina again became reduced to its

[1] "The Southerner," Chapter I.

fundamentals. The old homesteads and the Negro huts were still left standing, and their interiors were for the most part unharmed, but nearly everything else had disappeared. Horses, cattle, hogs, livestock of all kinds had vanished before the advancing hosts of hungry soldiers; and there was one thing which was even more a rarity than these. That was money. Confederate veterans went around in their faded gray uniforms, not only because they loved them, but because they did not have the wherewithal to buy new wardrobes. Judges, planters, and other dignified members of the community became hack drivers from the necessity of picking up a few small coins. Page's father was more fortunate than the rest, for he had one asset with which to accumulate a little liquid capital; he possessed a fine peach orchard, which was particularly productive in the summer of 1865, and the Northern soldiers, who drew their pay in money that had real value, developed a weakness for the fruit. Walter Page, a boy of ten, used to take his peaches to Raleigh, and sell them to the "invader"; although he still disdained having companionable relations with the enemy, he was not above meeting them on a business footing; and the greenbacks and silver coin obtained in this way laid a new basis for the family fortunes.

Despite this happy windfall, life for the next few years proved an arduous affair. The horrors of reconstruction which followed the war were more agonizing than the war itself. Page's keenest inspiration in after life was democracy, in its several manifestations; but the form in which democracy first unrolled before his astonished eyes was a phase that could hardly inspire much enthusiasm. Misguided sentimentalists and more malicious politicians in the North had suddenly endowed the Negro with the ballot. In practically all Southern States that meant government by Negroes—or what was even worse, government by a combination of Negroes and the most vicious white elements, including that which was native to the soil and that which had imported itself from the North for this particular purpose. Thus the political vocabulary of Page's formative years consisted chiefly of such words as "scalawag," "carpet bagger," "regulator," "Union League," "Ku Klux Klan," and the like. The resulting confusion, political, social, and economic, did not completely amount to the destruction of a civilization, for underneath it all the old sleepy ante-bellum South still maintained its existence almost unchanged. The two most conspicuous and contrasting figures were the Confederate veteran walking around in a sleeveless coat and the sharp-featured New England school mar'm, armed with that spelling book which was overnight to change the African from a genial barbarian into an intelligent and conscientious social unit; but more persistent than these forces was that old dreamy, "unprogressive" Southland—the same country that Page himself described in an article on "An Old Southern Borough" which, as a young man, he contributed to the *Atlantic Monthly*. It was still the country where the "old-fashioned gentleman" was the controlling social influence, where a knowledge of Latin and Greek still made its possessor a person of consideration, where Emerson was a "Yankee philosopher" and therefore not important, where Shakespeare and Milton were looked upon almost as contemporary authors, where the Church and politics and the matrimonial history of friends and relatives formed the staple of conversation, and where a strong prejudice still existed against anything that resembled popular education. In the absence of more substantial employment, stump speaking, especially eloquent in praise of the South and its achievements in war, had become the leading industry.

"Wat." Page—he is still known by this name in his old home—was a tall, rangy, curly-headed boy, with brown hair and brown eyes, fond of fishing and hunting, not especially robust, but conspicuously alert and vital. Such of his old playmates as survive recall chiefly his keenness of observation, his contagious laughter, his devotion to reading and to talk. He was also given to taking long walks in the woods, frequently with the solitary companionship of a book. Indeed, his extremely efficient family regarded him as a dreamer and were not entirely clear as to what purpose he was destined to serve in a community which, above all, demanded practical men. Such elementary schools as North Carolina possessed had vanished in the war; the prevailing custom was for the better-conditioned families to join forces and engage a teacher for their assembled children. It was in such a primary school in Cary that Page learned the elementary branches, though his mother herself taught him to read and write. The boy showed such aptitude in his studies that his mother began to hope, though in no aggressive fashion, that he might some day become a Methodist clergyman; she had given him his middle name, "Hines," in honour of her favourite preacher—a kinsman. At the age of twelve Page was transferred to the Bingham School, then located at Mebane. This was the Eton of North Carolina, from both a social and an educational standpoint. It was a military school; the boys all dressed in gray uniforms built on the plan of the Confederate army; the hero constantly paraded before their imaginations was Robert E. Lee; discipline was rigidly military; more important, a high standard of honour was insisted upon. There was one thing a boy could not do at

Bingham and remain in the school; that was to cheat in class-rooms or at examinations. For this offence no second chance was given. "I cannot argue the subject," Page quotes Colonel Bingham saying to the distracted parent whose son had been dismissed on this charge, and who was begging for his reinstatement. "In fact, I have no power to reinstate your boy. I could not keep the honour of the school—I could not even keep the boys, if he were to return. They would appeal to their parents and most of them would be called home. They are the flower of the South, Sir!" And the social standards that controlled the thinking of the South for so many years after the war were strongly entrenched. "The son of a Confederate general," Page writes, "if he were at all a decent fellow, had, of course, a higher social rank at the Bingham School than the son of a colonel. There was some difficulty in deciding the exact rank of a judge or a governor, as a father; but the son of a preacher had a fair chance of a good social rating, especially of an Episcopalian clergyman. A Presbyterian preacher came next in rank. I at first was at a social disadvantage. My father had been a Methodist—that was bad enough; but he had had no military title at all. If it had become known among the boys that he had been a 'Union man'—I used to shudder at the suspicion in which I should be held. And the fact that my father had held no military title did at last become known!"

A single episode discloses that Page maintained his respect for the Bingham School to the end. In March, 1918, as American Ambassador, he went up to Harrow and gave an informal talk to the boys on the United States. His hosts were so pleased that two prizes were established to commemorate his visit. One was for an essay by Harrow boys on the subject: "The Drawing

Together of America and Great Britain by Common Devotion to a Great Cause." A similar prize on the same subject was offered to the boys of some American school, and Page was asked to select the recipient. He promptly named his old Bingham School in North Carolina.

It was at Bingham that Page gained his first knowledge of Greek, Latin, and mathematics, and he was an outstanding student in all three subjects. He had no particular liking for mathematics, but he could never understand why any one should find this branch of learning difficult; he mastered it with the utmost ease and always stood high. In two or three years he had absorbed everything that Bingham could offer and was ready for the next step. But political conditions in North Carolina now had their influence upon Page's educational plans. Under ordinary conditions he would have entered the State University at Chapel Hill; it had been a great head-quarters in ante-bellum days for the prosperous families of the South. But by the time that Page was ready to go to college the University had fallen upon evil days. The forces which then ruled the state, acting in accordance with the new principles of racial equality, had opened the doors of this, one of the most aristocratic of Southern institutions, to Negroes. The consequences may be easily imagined. The newly enfranchised blacks showed no inclination for the groves of Academe, and not a single representative of the race applied for matriculation. The outraged white population turned its back upon this new type of coeducation; in the autumn of 1872 not a solitary white boy made his appearance. The old university therefore closed its doors for lack of students and for the next few years it became a pitiable victim to the worst vices of the reconstruction era. Politicians were awarded the presidency and the professorships as political pap, and the resources of the place, in money and books, were scattered to the wind. Page had therefore to find his education elsewhere. The deep religious feelings of his family quickly settled this point. The young man promptly betook himself to the backwoods of North Carolina and knocked at the doors of Trinity College, a Methodist Institution then located in Randolph County. Trinity has since changed its abiding place to Durham and has been transformed into one of the largest and most successful colleges of the new South; but in those days a famous Methodist divine and journalist described it as "a college with a few buildings that look like tobacco barns and a few teachers that look as though they ought to be worming tobacco." Page spent something more than a year at Trinity, entering in the autumn of 1871, and leaving in December, 1872. A few letters, written from this place, are scarcely more complimentary than the judgment passed above. They show that the young man was very unhappy. One long letter to his mother is nothing but a boyish diatribe against the place. "I do not care a horse apple for Trinity's distinction," he writes, and then he gives the reasons for this juvenile contempt. His first report, he says, will soon reach home; he warns his mother that it will be unfavourable, and he explains that this bad showing is the result of a deliberate plot. The boys who obtain high marks, Page declares, secure them usually by cheating or through the partisanship of the professors; a high grade therefore really means that the recipient is either a humbug or a bootlicker. Page had therefore attempted to keep his reputation unsullied by aiming at a low academic record! The report on that three months' work, which still survives, discloses that Page's conspiracy against himself did not succeed, for his marks are all high. "Be sure to send him back" is the annotation on this document, indicating that Page had made a better impression on Trinity than Trinity had made on Page.

But the rebellious young man did not return. After Christmas, 1872, his schoolboy letters reveal him at Randolph-Macon College in Ashland, Va. Here again the atmosphere is Methodistical, but of a somewhat more genial type. "It was at Ashland that I first began to unfold," said Page afterward. "Dear old Ashland!" Dr. Duncan, the President, was a clergyman whose pulpit oratory is still a tradition in the South, but, in addition to his religious exaltation, he was an exceedingly lovable, companionable, and stimulating human being. Certainly there was no lack of the religious impulse. "We have a preacher president," Page writes his mother, "a preacher secretary, a preacher chaplain, and a dozen preacher students and three or more preachers are living here and twenty-five or thirty yet-to-be preachers in college!" In this latter class Page evidently places himself; at least he gravely writes his mother—he was now eighteen—that he had definitely made up his mind to enter the Methodist ministry. He had a close friend— Wilbur Fisk Tillett—who cherished similar ambitions, and Page one day surprised Tillett by suggesting that, at the approaching Methodist Conference, they apply for licensing as "local preachers" for the next summer. His friend dissuaded him, however, and henceforth Page concentrated on more worldly studies. In many ways he was the life of the undergraduate body. His desire for an immediate theological campaign was merely that passion for doing things and for self-expression which were always conspicuous traits. His intense ambition as a boy is still remembered in this sleepy little village. He read every book in the sparse college library; he talked to his college mates and his professors on every imaginable subject; he led his associates in the miniature parliament —the Franklin Debating Society—to which he belonged; he wrote prose and verse at an astonishing rate; he explored the country for miles around, making frequent pilgrimages to the birthplace of Henry Clay, which is the chief historical glory of Ashland, and to that Hanover Court House which was the scene of the oratorical triumph of Patrick Henry; he flirted with the pretty girls in the village, and even had two half-serious love affairs in rapid succession; he slept upon a hard mattress at night and imbibed more than the usual allotment of Greek, Latin, and mathematics in the daytime. One year he captured the Greek prize and the next the Sutherlin medal for oratory. With a fellow classicist he entered into a solemn compact to hold all their conversation, even on the most trivial topics, in Latin, with heavy penalties for careless lapses into English. Probably the linguistic result would have astonished Quintilian, but the experiment at least had a certain influence in improving the young man's Latinity. Another favourite dissipation was that of translating English masterpieces into the ancient tongue; there still survives among Page's early papers a copy of Bryant's "Waterfowl" done into Latin iambics. As to Page's personal appearance, a designation coined by a fellow student who afterward became a famous editor gives the suggestion of a portrait. He called him one of the "seven slabs" of the college. And, as always, the adjectives which his contemporaries chiefly use in describing Page are "alert" and "positive."

But Randolph-Macon did one great thing for Page. Like many small struggling Southern colleges it managed to assemble several instructors of real mental distinction. And at the time of Page's undergraduate life it possessed at least one great teacher. This was Thomas R. Price, afterward Professor of Greek at the University of Virginia and Professor of English at Columbia University in New York. Professor Price took one forward step that has given him a permanent fame in the history of Southern education. He found that the greatest stumbling block to teaching Greek was not the conditional mood, but the fact that his hopeful charges were not sufficiently familiar with their mother tongue. The prayer that was always on Price's lips, and the one with which he made his boys most familiar, was that of a wise old Greek: "O Great Apollo, send down the reviving rain upon our fields; preserve our flocks; ward off our enemies; and—build up our speech!" "It is irrational," he said, "absurd, almost criminal, to expect a young man, whose knowledge of English words and construction is scant and inexact, to put into English a difficult thought of Plato or an involved period of Cicero." Above all, it will be observed, Price's intellectual enthusiasm was the ancient tongue. A present-day argument for learning Greek and Latin is that thereby we improve our English; but Thomas R. Price advocated the teaching of English so that we might better understand the dead languages. To-day every great American educational institution has vast resources for teaching English literature; even in 1876, most American universities had their professors of English; but Price insisted on placing English on exactly the same footing as Greek and Latin. He himself became head of the new English school at Randolph-Macon; and Page himself at once became the favourite pupil. This distinguished scholar—a fine figure with an imperial beard that suggested the Confederate officer—used to have Page to tea at least twice a week and at these meetings the young man was first introduced in an understanding way to Shakespeare, Milton, Wordsworth, Tennyson, and the other writers who became the literary passions of his maturer life. And Price did even more for Page; he passed him on to another place and to another teacher who extended his horizon. Up to the autumn of 1876 Page had never gone farther North than Ashland; he was still a Southern boy, speaking with the Southern drawl, living exclusively the thoughts and even the prejudices of the South. His family's broad-minded attitude had prevented him from acquiring a too restricted view of certain problems that were then vexing both sections of the country; however, his outlook was still a limited one, as his youthful correspondence shows. But in October of the centennial year a great prospect opened before him.

III

Two or three years previously an eccentric merchant named Johns Hopkins had died, leaving the larger part of his fortune to found a college or university in Baltimore. Johns Hopkins was not an educated man himself and his conception of a new college did not extend beyond creating something in the nature of a Yale or Harvard in Maryland. By a lucky chance, however, a Yale graduate who was then the President of the University of California, Daniel Coit Gilman, was invited to come to Baltimore and discuss with the trustees his availability for the headship of the new institution. Dr. Gilman promptly informed his prospective employers that he would have no interest in associating himself with a new American college built upon the lines of those which then existed. Such a foundation would merely be a duplication of work already well done elsewhere and therefore a waste of money and effort. He proposed that this large endowment should be used, not for the erection of expensive architecture, but primarily for seeking out, in all parts of the world, the best professorial brains in certain approved branches of learning. In the same spirit he suggested that a similarly selective process be adopted in the choice of students: that only those American boys who had displayed exceptional promise should be admitted and that part of the university funds should be used to pay the expenses of twenty young men who, in undergraduate work at other colleges, stood head and shoulders above their contemporaries. The bringing together of these two sets of brains for graduate study would constitute the new university. A few rooms in the nearest dwelling house would suffice for headquarters. Dr. Gilman's scheme was approved; he became President on these terms; he gathered his faculty not only in the United States but in England, and he collected his first body of students, especially his first twenty fellows, with the same minute care.

It seems almost a miracle that an inexperienced youth in a little Methodist college in Virginia should have been chosen as one of these first twenty fellows, and it is a sufficient tribute to the impression that Page must have made upon all who met him that he should have won this great academic distinction. He was only twenty-one at the time—the youngest of a group nearly every member of which became distinguished in after life. He won a Fellowship in Greek. This in itself was a great good fortune; even greater was the fact that his new life brought him into immediate contact with a scholar of great genius and lovableness. Someone has said that America has produced four scholars of the very first rank—Agassiz in natural science, Whitney in philology, Willard Gibbs in physics, and Gildersleeve in Greek. It was the last of these who now took Walter Page in charge.

The atmosphere of Johns Hopkins was quite different from anything which the young man had previously known. The university gave a great shock to that part of the American community with which Page had spent his life by beginning its first session in October, 1876, without an opening prayer. Instead Thomas H. Huxley was invited from England to deliver a scientific address— an address which now has an honoured place in his collected works. The absence of prayer and the presence of so audacious a Darwinian as Huxley caused a tremendous excitement in the public prints, the religious press, and the evangelical pulpit. In the minds of Gilman and his abettors, however, all this was intended to emphasize the fact that Johns Hopkins was a real university, in which the unbiased truth was to be the only aim. And certainly this was the spirit of the institution. "Gentlemen, you must light your own torch," was the admonition of President Gilman, in his welcoming address to his twenty fellows; intellectual independence, freedom from the trammels of tradition, were thus to be the directing ideas. One of Page's associates was Josiah Royce, who afterward had a distinguished career in philosophy at Harvard. "The beginnings of Johns Hopkins," he afterward wrote, "was a dawn wherein it was bliss to be alive. The air was full of noteworthy work done by the older men of the place and of hopes that one might find a way to get a little working power one's self. One longed to be a doer of the word, not a hearer only, a creator of his own infinitesimal fraction of the product, bound in God's name to produce when the time came."

A choice group of five aspiring Grecians, of whom Page was one, periodically gathered around a long pine table in a second-story room of an old dwelling house on Howard Street, with Professor Gildersleeve at the head. The process of teaching was thus the intimate contact of mind with mind. Here in the course of nearly two years' residence, Page was led by Professor Gildersleeve into the closest communion with the great minds of the ancient world and gained that intimate knowledge of their written word which was the basis of his mental equipment. "Professor Gildersleeve, splendid scholar that he is!" he wrote to a friend in North Carolina. "He makes me grow wonderfully. When I have a chance to enjoy Æschylus as I have now, I go to work on those immortal pieces with a pleasure that swallows up everything." To the extent that Gildersleeve opened up the literary treasures of the past—and no man had a greater appreciation of his favourite authors than this fine humanist—Page's life was one of unalloyed delight. But there was another side to the picture. This little company of scholars was composed of men who aspired to no ordinary knowledge of Greek; they expected to devote their entire lives to the subject, to edit Greek texts, and to hold Greek chairs at the leading American universities. Such, indeed, has been the career of nearly all members of the group. The Greek tragedies were therefore read for other things than their stylistic and dramatic values. The sons of Germania then exercised a profound influence on American education; Professor Gildersleeve himself was a graduate of Göttingen, and the necessity of "settling hoti's business" was strong in his seminar. Gildersleeve was a writer of English who developed real style; as a Greek scholar, his fame rests chiefly upon his work in the field of historical syntax. He assumed that his students could read Greek as easily as they could read French, and the really important tasks he set them had to do with the most abstruse fields of philology. For work of this kind Page had little interest and less inclination. When Professor Gildersleeve would assign him the adverb πρίν, and direct him to study the peculiarities of its use from Homer down to the Byzantine writers, he found himself in pretty deep waters. Was it conceivable that a man could spend a lifetime in an occupation of this kind? By pursuing such studies Gildersleeve and his most advanced pupils uncovered many new facts about the language and even found hitherto unsuspected beauties; but Page's letters show that this sort of effort was extremely uncongenial. He fulminates against the "grammarians" and begins to think that perhaps, after all, a career of erudite scholarship is not the ideal existence. "Learn to look on me as a Greek drudge," he writes, "somewhere pounding into men and boys a faint hint of the beauty of old Greekdom. That's most probably what I shall come to before many years. I am sure that I have mistaken my lifework, if I consider Greek my lifework. In truth at times I am tempted to throw the whole thing away. . . . But without a home feeling in Greek literature no man can lay claim to high culture." So he would keep at it for three or four years and "then leave it as a man's work." Despite these despairing words Page acquired a living knowledge of Greek that was one of his choicest possessions through life. That he made a greater success than his self-depreciation would imply is evident from the fact that his Fellowship was renewed for the next year.

But the truth is that the world was tugging at Page more insistently than the cloister. "Speaking grammatically," writes Prof. E. G. Sihler, one of Page's fellow students of that time, in his "Confessions and Convictions of a Classicist," "Page was interested in that one of the main tenses which we call the Present." In his after life, amid all the excitements of journalism, Page could take a brief vacation and spend it with Ulysses by the sea; but actuality and human activity charmed him even more than did the heroes of the ancient world. He went somewhat into Baltimore society, but not extensively; he joined a club whose membership comprised the leading intellectual men of the town; probably his most congenial associations, however, came of the Saturday night meetings of the fellows in Hopkins Hall, where, over pipes and steins of beer, they passed in review all the questions of the day. Page was still the Southern boy, with the strange notions about the North and Northern people which were the inheritance of many years' misunderstandings. He writes of one fellow student to whom he had taken a liking. "He is that rare thing," he says, "a Yankee Christian gentleman." He particularly dislikes one of his instructors, but, as he explains, he is a native of Connecticut, and Connecticut, I suppose, is capable of producing any unholy human phenomenon." Speaking of a beautiful and well mannered Greek girl whom he had met. he writes: "The little creature might be taken for a Southern girl, but never for a Yankee. She has an easy manner and even an air of gentility about her that doesn't appear north of Mason and Dixon's Line. Indeed, however much the Southern race (I say race intentionally: Yankeedom is the home of another race from us) however much the Southern race owes its strength to Anglo-Saxon blood, it owes its beauty and gracefulness to the Southern climate and culture. Who says that we are not an improvement on the English? An improvement in a happy combination of mental graces and Saxon force?" This sort of thing is especially entertaining in the youthful Page, for it is precisely against this kind of complacency that, as a mature man, he directed his choicest ridicule. As an editor and writer

Allison Francis Page (1824-1899), father of Walter H. Page

Catherine Raboteau Page (1831–1897), Mother of
Walter H. Page

his energies were devoted to reconciling North and South, and Johns Hopkins itself had much to do with opening his eyes. Its young men and its professors were gathered from all parts of the country; a student, if his mind was awake, learned more than Greek and mathematics; he learned much about that far-flung nation known as the United States.

And Page did not confine his work exclusively to the curriculum. He writes that he is regularly attending a German Sunday School, not, however, from religious motives, but from a desire to improve his colloquial German. "Is this courting the Devil for knowledge?" he asks. And all this time he was engaging in a delightful correspondence—from which these quotations are taken —with a young woman in North Carolina, his cousin. About this time this cousin began spending her summers in the Page home at Cary; her great interest in books made the two young people good friends and companions. It was she who first introduced Page to certain Southern writers, especially Timrod and Sidney Lanier, and, when Page left for Johns Hopkins, the two entered into a compact for a systematic reading and study of the English poets. According to this plan, certain parts of Tennyson or Chaucer would be set aside for a particular week's reading; then both would write the impressions gained and the criticisms which they assumed to make, and send the product to the other. The plan was carried out more faithfully than is usually the case in such arrangements; a large number of Page's letters survive and give a complete history of his mental progress. There are lengthy disquisitions on Wordsworth, Browning, Byron, Shelley, Matthew Arnold, and the like. These letters also show that Page, as a relaxation from Greek roots and syntax, was indulging in poetic flights of his own; his efforts, which he encloses in his letters, are mainly imitations of the particular poet in whom he was at the moment interested. This correspondence also takes Page to Germany, in which country he spent the larger part of the summer of 1877. This choice of the Fatherland as a place of pilgrimage was probably merely a reflection of the enthusiasm for German educational methods which then prevailed in the United States, especially at Johns Hopkins. Page's letters are the usual traveller's descriptions of unfamiliar customs, museums, libraries, and the like; so far as enlarging his outlook was concerned the experience does not seem to have been especially profitable.

He returned to Baltimore in the autumn of 1877, but only for a few months. He had pretty definitely abandoned his plan of devoting his life to Greek scholarship. As a mental stimulus, as a recreation from the cares of life, his Greek authors would always be a first love, as they proved to be; but he had abandoned his early ambition of making them his everyday occupation and means of livelihood. Of course there was only one career for a man of his leanings, and, more and more, his mind was turning to journalism. For only one brief period did he again listen to the temptations of a scholar's existence. The university of his native state invited him to lecture in the summer school of 1878; he took Shakespeare for his subject, and made so great a success that there was some discussion of his settling down permanently at Chapel Hill in the chair of Greek. Had the offer definitely been made Page would probably have accepted, but difficulties arose. Page was no longer orthodox in his religious views; he had long outgrown dogma and could only smile at the recollection that he had once thought of becoming a clergyman. But a rationalist at the University of North Carolina in 1878 could hardly be endured. The offer, therefore, fortunately was not made. Afterward Page was much criticized for having left his native state at a time when it especially needed young men of his type. It may therefore be recorded that, if there were any blame at all, it rested upon North Carolina. He refers to his disappointment in a letter in February, 1879—a letter that proved to be a prophecy. "I shall some day buy a home," he says, "where I was not allowed to work for one, and be laid away in the soil that I love. I wanted to work for the old state; it had no need for it, it seems."

CHAPTER II

JOURNALISM

I

THE five years from 1878 to 1883 Page spent in various places, engaged, for the larger part of the time, in several kinds of journalistic work. It was his period of struggle and of preparation. Like many American public men he served a brief apprenticeship—in his case, a very brief one—as a pedagogue. In the autumn of 1878 he went to Louisville, Kentucky, and taught English for a year at the Boys' High School. But he presently found an occupation in this progressive city which proved far more absorbing. A few months before his arrival certain energetic spirits had founded a weekly paper, the *Age*, a journal which, they hoped, would fill the place in the Southern States which the very successful New York *Nation*, under the editorship of Godkin, was then occupying in the North. Page at once began contributing leading articles on literary and political topics to this publication; the work proved so congenial that he purchased—on notes—a controlling interest in the new venture and became its directing spirit. The *Age* was in every way a worthy enterprise; in the dignity of its make-up and the high literary standards at which it aimed it imitated the London *Spectator*. Perhaps Page obtained a thousand dollars' worth of fun out of his investment; if so, that represented his entire profit. He now learned a lesson which was emphasized in his after career as editor and publisher, and that was that the Southern States provided a poor market for books or periodicals. The net result of the proceeding was that, at the age of twenty-three, he found himself out of a job and considerably in debt.

He has himself rapidly sketched his varied activities of the next five years:

"After trying in vain," he writes, "to get work to do on any newspaper in North Carolina, I advertised for a job in journalism—any sort of a job. By a queer accident —a fortunate one for me—the owner of the St. Joseph, Missouri, *Gazette,* answered the advertisement. Why he did it, I never found out. He was in the same sort of desperate need of a newspaper man as I was in desperate need of a job. I knew nothing about him: he knew nothing about me. I knew nothing about newspaper work. I had done nothing since I left the University but teach English in the Louisville, Kentucky, High School for boys one winter and lecture at the summer school at Chapel Hill one summer. I made up my mind to go into journalism. But journalism didn't seem in any hurry to make up its mind to admit me. Not only did all the papers in North Carolina decline my requests for work, but such of them in Baltimore and Louisville as I tried said 'No.' So I borrowed $50 and set out to St. Joe, Missouri, where I didn't know a human being. I became a reporter. At first I reported the price of cattle—went to the stockyards, etc. My salary came near to paying my board and lodging, but it didn't quite do it. But I had a good time in St. Joe for somewhat more than a year. There were interesting people there. I came to know something about Western life. Kansas was across the river. I often went there. I came to know Kansas City, St. Louis—a good deal of the West. After a while I was made editor of the paper. What a rousing political campaign or two we had!

Then—I had done that kind of a job as long as I cared to. Every swashbuckling campaign is like every other one. Why do two? Besides, I knew my trade. I had done everything on a daily paper from stockyard reports to political editorials and heavy literary articles. In the meantime I had written several magazine articles and done other such jobs. I got leave of absence for a month or two. I wrote to several of the principal papers in Chicago, New York, and Boston and told them that I was going down South to make political and social studies and that I was going to send them my letters. I hoped they'd publish them.

"That's all I could say. I could make no engagement; they didn't know me. I didn't even ask for an engagement. I told them simply this: that I'd write letters and send them; and I prayed heaven that they'd print them and pay for them. Then off I went with my little money in my pocket—about enough to get to New Orleans. I travelled and I wrote. I went all over the South. I sent letters and letters and letters. All the papers published all that I sent them and I was rolling in wealth! I had money in my pocket for the first time in my life. Then I went back to St. Joe and resigned; for the (old) New York *World* had asked me to go to the Atlanta Exposition as a correspondent. I went. I wrote and kept writing. How kind Henry Grady was to me! But at last the Exposition ended. I was out of a job. I applied to the *Constitution*. No, they wouldn't have me. I never got a job in my life that I asked for! But all my life better jobs have been given me than I dared ask for. Well—I was at the end of my rope in Atlanta and I was trying to make a living in any honest way I could when one day a telegram came from the New York *World* (it was the old *World*, which was one of the best of the dailies in its literary quality) asking me to come to New York. I had never seen a man on the paper—had never been in New York except for a day when I landed there on a return voyage from a European trip that I took during one vacation when I was in the University. Then I went to New York straight and quickly. I had an interesting experience on the old *World*, writing literary matter chiefly, an editorial now and then, and I was frequently sent as a correspondent on interesting errands. I travelled all over the country with the Tariff Commission. I spent one winter in Washington as a sort of editorial correspondent while the tariff bill was going through Congress. Then, one day, the *World* was sold to Mr. Pulitzer and all the staff resigned. The character of the paper changed."

What better training could a journalist ask for than this? Page was only twenty-eight when these five years came to an end; but his life had been a comprehensive education in human contact, in the course of which he had picked up many things that were not included in the routine of Johns Hopkins University. From Athens to St. Joe, from the comedies of Aristophanes to the stockyards and political conventions of Kansas City—the transition may possibly have been an abrupt one, but it is not likely that Page so regarded it. For books and the personal relation both appealed to him, in almost equal proportions, as essentials to the fully rounded man. Merely from the standpoint of geography, Page's achievement had been an important one; how many Americans, at the age of twenty-eight, have such an extensive mileage to their credit? Page had spent his childhood—and his childhood only—in North Carolina; he had passed his youth in Virginia and Maryland; before he was twenty-three he had lived several months in Germany, and, on his return voyage, he had sailed by the white cliffs of England, and,

from the deck of his steamer, had caught glimpses of that
Isle of Wight which then held his youthful favourite Ten-
nyson. He had added to these experiences a winter in
Kentucky and a sojourn of nearly two years in Missouri.
His Southern trip, to which Page refers in the above, had
taken him through Tennessee, Mississippi, Alabama,
Georgia, and Louisiana; he had visited the West again in
1882, spending a considerable time in all the large cities,
Chicago, Omaha, Denver, Leadville, Salt Lake, and from
the latter point he had travelled extensively through
Mormondom. The several months spent in Atlanta had
given the young correspondent a glimpse into the new
South, for this energetic city embodied a Southern spirit
that was several decades removed from the Civil War.
After this came nearly two years in New York and Washington, where Page gained his first insight into Federal
politics; in particular, as a correspondent attached to the
Tariff Commission—an assignment that again started
him on his travels to industrial centres—he came into contact, for the first time, with the mechanism of framing the
great American tariff. And during this period Page was
not only forming a first-hand acquaintance with the passing scene, but also with important actors in it. The mere
fact that, on the St. Joseph *Gazette*, he succeeded Eugene
Field—"a good fellow named Page is going to take my
desk," said the careless poet, "I hope he will succeed to
my debts too"—always remained a pleasant memory.
He entered zealously into the life of this active community; his love of talk and disputation, his interest in politics,
his hearty laugh, his vigorous handclasp, his animation of
body and of spirit, and his sunny outlook on men and
events—these are the traits that his old friends in this
town, some of whom still survive, associate with the
juvenile editor. In his Southern trip Page called—self-

invited—upon Jefferson Davis and was cordially received. At Atlanta, as he records above, he made friends
with that chivalric champion of a resurrected South,
Henry Grady; here also he obtained fugitive glimpses
of a struggling and briefless lawyer, who, like Page, was
interested more in books and writing than in the hum-
drum of professional life, and who was then engaged
in putting together a brochure on *Congressional Government* which immediately gave him a national standing.
The name of this sympathetic acquaintance was Woodrow Wilson.

Another important event had taken place, for, at St.
Louis, on November 15, 1880, Page had married Miss
Willia Alice Wilson. Miss Wilson was the daughter of a
Scotch physician, Dr. William Wilson, who had settled
in Michigan, near Detroit, in 1832. When she was a
small child she went with her sister's family—her father
had died seven years before—to North Carolina, near
Cary; and she and Page had been childhood friends and
schoolmates. At the time of the wedding, Page was
editor of the St. Joseph *Gazette;* the fact that he had
attained this position, five months after starting at the
bottom, sufficiently discloses his aptitude for journalistic
work.

Page had now outgrown any Southern particularism
with which he may have started life. He no longer found
his country exclusively in the area south of the Potomac;
he had made his own the West, the North—New York,
Chicago, Denver, as well as Atlanta and Raleigh. It is
worth while insisting on this fact, for the cultivation of a
wide-sweeping Americanism and a profound faith in democracy became the qualities that will loom most largely in
his career from this time forward. It is necessary only to
read the newspaper letters which he wrote on his Southern

trip in 1881 to understand how early his mind seized this
new point of view. Many things which now fell under
his observant eye in the Southern States greatly irritated
him and with his characteristic impulsiveness he pictured
these traits in pungent phrase. The atmosphere of
shiftlessness that too generally prevailed in some localities;
the gangs of tobacco-chewing loafers assembled around railway stations; the listless Negroes that seemed to overhang
the whole country like a black cloud; the plantation man-
sions in a sad state of disrepair; the old unoccupied slave
huts overgrown with weeds; the unpainted and broken-down
fences; the rich soil that was crudely and wastefully cultivated with a single crop—the youthful social philosopher
found himself comparing these vestigia of a half-moribund
civilization with the vibrant cities of the North, the beautiful white and green villages of New England, and the
fertile prairie farms of the West. "Even the dogs,"
he said, "look old-fashioned." Oh, for a change in his
beloved South—a change of almost any kind! "Even
a heresy, if it be bright and fresh, would be a relief. You
feel as if you wished to see some kind of an effort put
forth, a discussion, a fight, a runaway, anything to make
the blood go faster." Wherever Page saw signs of a new
spirit—and he saw many—he recorded them with an
eagerness which showed his loyalty to the section of his
birth. The splitting up of great plantations into small
farms he put down as one of the indications of a new
day. A growing tendency to educate, not only the
white child, but the Negro, inspired a similar tribute.
But he rejoiced most over the decreasing bitterness of the
masses over the memories of the Civil War, and discovered, with satisfaction, that any remaining ill-feeling
was a heritage left not by the Union soldier, but by
the carpetbagger.

And one scene is worth preserving, for it illustrates not only the zeal of Page himself for the common country, but the changing attitude of the Southern people. It was enacted at Martin, Tennessee, on the evening of July 2, 1881. Page was spending a few hours in the village grocery, discussing things in general with the local yeomanry, when the telegraph operator came from the post office with rather more than his usual expedition and excitement. He was frantically waving a yellow slip which bore the news that President Garfield had been shot. Garfield had been an energetic and a successful general in the war and his subsequent course in Congress, where he had joined the radical Republicans, had not caused the South to look upon him as a friend. But these farmers responded to this shock, not like sectionalists, but like Americans. "Every man of them," Page records, "expressed almost a personal sorrow. Little was said of politics or of parties. Mr. Garfield was President of the United States—that was enough. A dozen voices spoke the great gratification that the assassin was not a Southern man. It was an affecting scene to see weather-beaten old countrymen so profoundly agitated—men who yesterday I should have supposed hardly knew and certainly did not seem to care who was President. The great centres of population, of politicians, and of thought may be profoundly agitated to-night, but no more patriotic sorrow and humiliation is felt anywhere by any men than by these old backwoods ex-Confederates."

Page himself was so stirred by the news that he ascended a cracker barrel, and made a speech to the assembled countrymen, preaching to responsive ears the theme of North and South, now reunited in a common sorrow. Thus, by the time he was twenty-six, Page, at any rate in respect to his Americanism, was a full-grown man.

II

A few years afterward Page had an opportunity of discussing this, his favourite topic, with the American whom he most admired.   Perhaps the finest thing in the career of Grover Cleveland was the influence which he exerted upon young men.   After the sordid political transactions of the reconstruction period and after the orgy of partisanship which had followed the Civil War, this new figure, acceding to the Presidency in 1885, came as an inspiration to millions of zealous and intelligent young college-bred Americans. One of the first to feel the new spell was Walter Page; Mr. Cleveland was perhaps the most important influence in forming his public ideals.   Of everything that Cleveland represented—civil service reform; the cleansing of politics, state and national; the reduction in the tariff; a foreign policy which, without degenerating into truculence, manfully upheld the rights of American citizens; a determination to curb the growing pension evil; the doctrine that the Government was something to be served and not something to be plundered—Page became an active and brilliant journalistic advocate.   It was therefore a great day in his life when, on a trip to Washington in the autumn of 1885, he had an hour's private conversation with President Cleveland, and it was entirely characteristic of Page that he should make the conversation take the turn of a discussion of the so-called Southern question.

"In the White House at Washington," Page wrote about this visit, "is an honest, plain, strong man, a man of wonderfully broad information and of most uncommon industry.   He has always been a Democrat.   He is a distinguished lawyer and a scholar on all public questions. He is as frank and patriotic and sincere as any man that ever won the high place he holds. Within less than a year he has done so well and so wisely that he has disappointed his enemies and won their admiration. He is as unselfish as he is great. He is one of the most industrious men in the world. He rises early and works late and does not waste his time—all because his time is now not his own but the Republic's, whose most honoured servant he is. I count it among the most inspiring experiences in my life that I had the privilege, at the suggestion of one of his personal friends, of talking with him one morning about the complete reuniting of the two great sections of our Republic by his election. I told him, and I know I told him the truth, when I said that every young man in the Southern States who, without an opportunity to share either the glory or the defeat of the late Confederacy, had in spite of himself suffered the disadvantages of the poverty and oppression that followed war, took new hope for the full and speedy realization of a complete union, of unparalleled prosperity and of broad thinking and noble living from his elevation to the Presidency. I told him that the men of North Carolina were not only patriotic but ambitious as well; and that they were Democrats and proud citizens of the State and the Republic not because they wanted offices or favours, but because they loved freedom and wished the land that had been impoverished by war to regain more than it had lost. 'I have not called, Mr. President, to ask for an office for myself or for anybody else,' I remarked; 'but to have the pleasure of expressing my gratification, as a citizen of North Carolina, at the complete change in political methods and morals that I believe will date from your Administration.' He answered that he was glad to see all men who came in such a spirit and did not come to beg—especially young men of the South of to-day; and he talked and encouraged me to talk freely as if he had been as small a man as I am, or I as great a man as he is.

"From that day to this it has been my business to watch every public act that he does, to read every public word he speaks, and it has been a pleasure and a benefit to me (like the benefit that a man gets from reading a great history—for he is making a great history) to study the progress of his Administration; and at every step he seems to me to warrant the trust that the great Democratic party put in him."

The period to which Page refers in this letter repre-sented the time when he was making a serious and harass-ing attempt to establish himself in his chosen profession in his native state. He went south for a short visit after resigning his place on the New York *World,* and several admirers in Raleigh persuaded him to found a new paper, which should devote itself to preaching the Cleveland ideals, and, above all, to exerting an influence on the development of a new Southern spirit. No task could have been more grateful to Page and there was no place in which he would have better liked to under-take it than in the old state which he loved so well. The result was the *State Chronicle* of Raleigh, practically a new paper, which for a year and a half proved to be the most unconventional and refreshing influence that North Carolina had known in many a year. Necessarily Page found himself in conflict with his environment. He had little interest in the things that then chiefly interested the state, and North Carolina apparently had little in-terest in the things that chiefly occupied the mind of the youthful journalist. Page was interested in Cleveland,

in the reform of the civil service; the Democrats of North
Carolina little appreciated their great national leader
and were especially hostile to his belief that service to a
party did not in itself establish a qualification for public
office.   Page was interested in uplifting the common
people, in helping every farmer to own his own acres, and
in teaching the most modern and scientific way of cultivating them; he was interested in giving every boy and
girl at least an elementary education, and in giving a
university training to such as had the aptitude and the
ambition to obtain it; he believed in industrial training
—and in these things the North Carolina of those days
had little concern.   Page even went so far as to take an
open stand for the pitiably neglected black man: he insisted that he should be taught to read and write, and
instructed in agriculture and the manual trades.   A man
who advocated such revolutionary things in those days
was accused—and Page was so accused—of attempting to
promote the "social equality" of the two races.   Page
also declaimed in favour of developing the state indus-
trially; he called attention to the absurdity of sending
Southern cotton to New England spinning mills, and he
pointed out the boundless but unworked natural resources
of the state, in minerals, forests, waterpower, and lands.
North Carolina, he informed his astonished compatriots,
had once been a great manufacturing colony; why could
the state not become one again?   But the matter in which
the buoyant editor and his constituents found themselves
most at variance was the spirit that controlled North
Carolina life.   It was a spirit that found comfort for its
present poverty and lack of progress in a backward look
at the greatness of the state in the past and the achievements of its sons in the Civil War.   Though Page believed
that the Confederacy had been a ghastly error, and though

he abhorred the institution of slavery and attributed to it all the woes, economic and social, from which his section suffered, he rendered that homage to the soldiers of the South which is the due of brave, self-sacrificing and conscientious men; yet he taught that progress lay in regarding the four dreadful years of the Civil War as the closed chapter of an unhappy and mistaken history and in hastening the day when the South should resume its place as a living part of the great American democracy. All manifestations of a contrary spirit he ridiculed in language which was extremely readable but which at times outraged the good conservative people whom he was attempting to convert. He did not even spare the one figure which was almost a part of the Southerner's religion, the Confederate general, especially that particular type who used his war record as a stepping stone to public office, and whose oratory, colourful and turgid in its celebrations of the past, Page regarded as somewhat unrelated, in style and matter, to the realities of the present. The image-breaking editor even asserted that the Daughters of the Confederacy were not entirely a helpful influence in Southern regeneration; for they, too, were harping always upon the old times and keeping alive sectional antagonisms and hatreds. This he regarded as an unworthy occupation for high-minded Southern women, and he said so, sometimes in language that made him very unpopular in certain circles.

Altogether it was a piquant period in Page's life. He found that he had suddenly become a "traitor" to his country and that his experiences in the North had completely "Yankeeized" him. Even in more mature days, Page's pen had its javelin-like quality; and in 1884, possessed as he was of all the fury of youth, he never hesitated to return every blow that was rained upon his head. As

Walter H. Page in 1876, when he was a Fellow of Johns Hopkins
University, Baltimore, Md.

Basil L. Gildersleeve, Professor of Greek, Johns Hopkins University, 1876-1915

a matter of fact he had a highly enjoyable time. The *State Chronicle* during his editorship is one of the most cherished recollections of older North Carolinians to-day. Even those who hurled the liveliest epithets in his direction have long since accepted the ideas for which Page was then contending; "the only trouble with him," they now ruefully admit, "was that he was forty years ahead of his time." They recall with satisfaction the satiric accounts which Page used to publish of Democratic Conventions—solemn, long-winded, frock-coated, white-necktied affairs that displayed little concern for the reform of the tariff or of the civil service, but an energetic interest in pensioning Confederate veterans and erecting monuments to the Southern heroes of the Civil War. One editorial is joyfully recalled, in which Page referred to a public officer who was distinguished for his dignity and his family tree, but not noted for any animated administration of his duties, as "Thothmes II." When this bewildered functionary searched the Encyclopædia and learned that "Thothmes II" was an Egyptian king of the XVIIIth dynasty, whose dessicated mummy had recently been disinterred from the hot sands of the desert, he naturally stopped his subscription to the paper. The metaphor apparently tickled Page, for he used it in a series of articles which have become immortal in the political annals of North Carolina. These have always been known as the "Mummy letters." They furnished a vivid but rather aggravating explanation for the existing backwardness and chauvinism of the commonwealth. All the trouble, it seems, was caused by the "mummies." "It is an awfully discouraging business," Page wrote, "to undertake to prove to a mummy that it is a mummy. You go up to it and say, 'Old fellow, the Egyptian dynasties crumbled several thousand years ago:

you are a fish out of water. You have by accident or the
Providence of God got a long way out of your time. This
is America.' The old thing grins that grin which death
set on its solemn features when the world was young; and
your task is so pitiful that even the humour of it is gone.
Give it up."

Everything great in North Carolina, Page declared, belonged to a vanished generation. "Our great lawyers, great
judges, great editors, are all of the past. . . . In
the general intelligence of the people, in intellectual force
and in cultivation, we are doing nothing. We are not
doing or getting more liberal ideas, a broader view of this
world. . . . The presumptuous powers of ignorance,
heredity, decayed respectability and stagnation that control public action and public expression are absolutely
leading us back intellectually."

But Page did more than berate the mummified aristocracy which, he declared, was driving the best talent and
initiative from the state; he was not the only man in
Raleigh who expressed these unpopular views; at that time,
indeed, he was the centre and inspiration of a group of
young progressive spirits who held frequent meetings to devise ways of starting the state on the road to a new existence. Page then, as always, exercised a great fascination
over young men. The apparently merciless character of
his ridicule might at first convey the idea of intolerance;
the fact remains, however, that he was the most tolerant
of men; he was almost deferential to the opinions of others,
even the shallow and the inexperienced; and nothing delighted him more than an animated discussion. His
liveliness of spirits, his mental and physical vitality, the
constant sparkle of his talk, the sharp edge of his humour,
naturally drew the younger men to his side. The result
was the organization of the Wautauga Club, a gathering

which held monthly meetings for the discussion of ways and means of improving social and educational conditions in North Carolina. The very name gives the key to its mental outlook. The Wautauga colony was one of the last founded in North Carolina—in the extreme west, on a plateau of the Great Smoky Mountains; it was always famous for the energy and independence of its people. The word "Wautauga" therefore suggested the breaker of tradition; and it provided a stimulating name for Page's group of young spiritual and economic pathfinders. The Wautauga Club had a brief existence of a little more than two years, the period practically covering Page's residence in the state; but its influence is an important fact at the present time. It gave the state ideas that afterward caused something like a revolution in its economic and educational status. The noblest monument to its labours is the State College in Raleigh, an institution which now has more than a thousand students, for the most part studying the mechanic arts and scientific agriculture. To this one college most North Carolinians to-day attribute the fact that their state in appreciable measure is realizing its great economic and industrial opportunities. From it in the last thirty years thousands of young men have gone: in all sections of the commonwealth they have caused the almost barren acres to yield fertile and diversified crops; they have planted everywhere new industries; they have unfolded unsuspected resources and everywhere created wealth and spread enlightenment. This institution is a direct outcome of Page's brief sojourn in his native state nearly forty years ago. The idea originated in his brain; the files of the *State Chronicle* tell the story of his struggle in its behalf; the activities of the Wautauga Club were largely concentrated upon securing its establishment.

The State College was a great victory for Page, but final success did not come until three years after he had left the state. For a year and a half of hard newspaper work convinced Page that North Carolina really had no permanent place for him. The *Chronicle* was editorially a success: Page's articles were widely quoted, not only in his own state but in New England and other parts of the Union. He succeeded in stirring up North Carolina and the South generally, but popular support for the *Chronicle* was not forthcoming in sufficient amount to make the paper a commercial possib lity. Reluctantly and sadly Page had to forego his hope of playing an active part in rescuing his state from the disasters of the Civil War. Late in the summer of 1885, he again left for the North, which now became his permanent home.

III

And with this second sojourn in New York Page's opportunity came. The first two years he spent in newspaper work, for the most part with the *Evening Post*, but, one day in November, 1887, a man whom he had never seen came into his office and unfolded a new opportunity. Two years before a rather miscellaneous group had launched an ambitious literary undertaking. This was a monthly periodical, which, it was hoped, would do for the United States what such publications as the *Fortnightly* and the *Contemporary* were doing for England. The magazine was to have the highest literary quality and to be sufficiently dignified to attract the finest minds in America as contributors; its purpose was to exercise a profound influence in politics, literature, science, and art. The projectors had selected for this publication a title that was almost perfection—the *Forum*—but this, after nearly two years' experimentation, represented about the limit of their achievement. The *Forum* had hardly made an impression on public thought and had attracted very few readers, although it had lost large sums of money for its progenitors. These public-spirited gentlemen now turned to Page as the man who might rescue them from their dilemma and achieve their purpose. He accepted the engagement, first as manager and presently as editor, and remained the guiding spirit of the *Forum* for eight years, until the summer of 1895.

That the success of a publication is the success of its editors, and not of its business managers and its "backers," is a truth that ought to be generally apparent; never has this fact been so eloquently illustrated as in the case of the *Forum* under Page. Before his accession it had had not the slightest importance; for the period of his editorship it is doubtful if any review published in English exercised so great an influence, and certainly none ever obtained so large a circulation. From almost nothing the *Forum*, in two or three years, attracted 30,000 subscribers—something without precedent for a publication of this character. It had accomplished this great result simply because of the vitality and interest of its contents. The period covered was an important one, in the United States and Europe; it was the time of Cleveland's second administration in this country, and of Gladstone's fourth administration in England; it was a time of great controversy and of a growing interest in science, education, social reform and a better political order. All these great matters were reflected in the pages of the *Forum*, whose list of contributors contained the most distinguished names in all countries. Its purpose, as Page explained it, was "to provoke discussion about subjects of contemporary interest, in which the magazine is not a partisan, but merely the instrument." In the highest sense, that is, its purpose was journalistic; practically everything that it printed was related to the thought and the action of the time. So insistent was Page on this programme that his pages were not "closed" until a week before the day of issue. Though the *Forum* dealt constantly in controversial subjects it never did so in a narrow-minded spirit; it was always ready to hear both sides of a question and the magazine "debate," in which opposing writers handled vigorously the same theme, was a constant feature.

Page, indeed, represented a new type of editor. Up to that time this functionary had been a rather solemn, inaccessible high priest; he sat secluded in his sanctuary, and weeded out from the mass of manuscripts dumped upon his desk the particular selections which seemed to be most suited to his purpose. To solicit contributions would have seemed an entirely undignified proceeding; in all cases contributors must come to him. According to Page, however, "an editor must know men and be out among men." His system of "making up" the magazine at first somewhat astounded his associates. A month or two in advance of publication day he would draw up his table of contents. This, in its preliminary stage, amounted to nothing except a list of the main subjects which he aspired to handle in that number. It was a hope, not a performance. The subjects were commonly suggested by the happenings of the time—an especially outrageous lynching, the trial of a clergyman for heresy, a new attack upon the Monroe Doctrine, the discovery of a new substance such as radium, the publication of an epoch-making book. Page would then fix upon the inevitable men who could write most readably and most authoritatively upon these topics, and "go after" them. Sometimes he would write one of his matchless

editorial letters; at other times he would make a personal visit; if necessary, he would use any available friends
in a wire-pulling campaign. At all odds he must "get"
his man; once he had fixed upon a certain contributor
nothing could divert him from the chase. Nor did the
negotiations cease after he had "landed" his quarry. He
had his way of discussing the subject with his proposed
writer, and he discussed it from every possible point of
view. He would take him to lunch or to dinner; in his
quiet way he would draw him out, find whether he really
knew much about the subject, learn the attitude that he
was likely to take, and delicately slip in suggestions of
his own. Not infrequently this preliminary interview
would disclose that the much sought writer, despite
appearances, was not the one who was destined for that
particular job; in this case Page would find some way of
shunting him in favour of a more promising candidate.
But Page was no mere chaser of names; there was nothing
of the literary tuft-hunter about his editorial methods.
He liked to see such men as Theodore Roosevelt, Woodrow
Wilson, William Graham Sumner, Charles W. Eliot,
Frederic Harrison, Paul Bourget, and the like upon his
title page—and here these and many other similarly
distinguished authors appeared—but the greatest name
could not attain a place there if the letter press that followed were unworthy. Indeed Page's habit of throwing
out the contributions of the great, after paying a stiff
price for them, caused much perturbation in his counting
room. One day he called in one of his associates.

"Do you see that waste basket?" he asked, pointing
to a large receptacle filled to overflowing with manuscripts. "All our Cleveland articles are there!"

He had gone to great trouble and expense to obtain
a series of six articles from the most prominent publicists

and political leaders of the country on the first year of
Mr. Cleveland's second administration.   It was to be the
"feature" of the number then in preparation.

"There isn't one of them," he declared, "who has got
the point.   I have thrown them all away and I am going
to try to write something myself."

And he spent a couple of days turning out an article
which aroused great public interest.   When Page commissioned an article, he meant simply that he would pay
full price for it; whether he would publish it depended
entirely upon the quality of the material itself.   But
Page was just as severe upon his own writings as upon
those of other men.   He wrote occasionally—always under
a nom-de-plume; but he had great difficulty in satisfy-
ing his own editorial standards.   After finishing an article
he would commonly send for one of his friends and read
the result.

"That is superb!" this admiring associate would sometimes say.

In response Page would take the manuscript and,
holding it aloft in two hands, tear it into several bits, and
throw the scraps into the waste basket.

"Oh, I can do better than that," he would laugh and in
another minute he was busy rewriting the article, from
beginning to end.

Page retired from the editorship of the *Forum* in 1895.
The severance of relations was half a comedy, half a
tragedy.   The proprietors had only the remotest relation
to literature; they had lost much money in the enterprise
before Page became editor and only the fortunate accident
of securing his services had changed their losing venture
into a financial success.   In a moment of despair, before the
happier period had arrived, they offered to sell the property to Page and his friends.   Page quickly assembled a

new group to purchase control, when, much to the amazement of the old owners, the *Forum* began to make money.
Instead of having a burden on their hands, the proprietors
suddenly discovered that they had a gold mine. They
therefore refused to deliver their holdings and an inevitable struggle ensued for control. Page could edit a magazine and turn a shipwrecked enterprise into a profitable
one; but, in a tussle of this kind, he was no match for the
shrewd business men who owned the property. When the
time came for counting noses Page and his friends found
themselves in a minority. Of course his resignation as
editor necessarily followed this little unpleasantness.
And just as inevitably the *Forum* again began to lose
money, and soon sank into an obscurity from which it has
never emerged.

The *Forum* had established Page's reputation as an
editor, and the competition for his services was lively.
The distinguished Boston publishing house of Houghton,
Mifflin & Company immediately invited him to become
a part of their organization. When Horace E. Scudder,
in 1898, resigned the editorship of the *Atlantic Monthly*,
Page succeeded him. Thus Page became the successor of
James Russell Lowell, James T. Fields, William D. Howells,
and Thomas Bailey Aldrich as the head of this famous
periodical. This meant that he had reached the top of
his profession. He was now forty-three years old.

No American publication had ever had so brilliant a
history. Founded in 1857, in the most flourishing period
of the New England writers, its pages had first published
many of the best essays of Emerson, the second series of
the Biglow papers as well as many other of Lowell's
writings, poems of Longfellow and Whittier, such great
successes as Holmes's "Autocrat of the Breakfast Table,"
Mrs. Howe's "Battle Hymn of the Republic," and the

early novels of Henry James.   If America had a literature, the *Atlantic* was certainly its most successful periodical exponent.   Yet, in a sense, the *Atlantic,* by the time Page succeeded to the editorship, had become the victim of its dazzling past.   Its recent editors had lived too exclusively in their back numbers.   They had conducted the magazine too much for the restricted audience of Boston and New England.   There was a time, indeed, when the business office arranged the subscribers in two classes—"Boston" and "foreign"; "Boston" representing their local adherents, and "foreign" the loyal readers who lived in the more benighted parts of the United States. One of its editors had been heard to boast that he never solicited a contribution; it was not his business to be a literary drummer!   Let the truth be fairly spoken: when Page made his first appearance in the *Atlantic* office, the magazine was unquestionably on the decline. Its literary quality was still high; the momentum that its great contributors had given it was still keeping the publication alive; entrance into its columns still represented the ultimate ambition of the aspiring American writer; but it needed a new spirit to insure its future. What it required was the kind of editing that had suddenly made the *Forum* one of the greatest of English-written reviews.   This is the reason why the canny Yankee proprietors had reached over to New York and grasped Page as quickly as the capitalists of the *Forum* let him slip between their fingers.

Page's sense of humour discovered a certain ironic aspect in his position as the dictator of this famous New England magazine.   The fact that his manner was impatiently energetic and somewhat startling to the placid atmosphere of Park Street was not the thing that really signified its break with its past.   But here was a Southerner firmly entrenched in a headquarters that had long been sacred to the New England abolitionists. One of the first sights that greeted Page, as he came into the office, was the angular and spectacled countenance of William Lloyd Garrison, gazing down from a steel engraving on the wall. One of Garrison's sons was a colleague, and the anterooms were frequently cluttered with dusky gentlemen patiently waiting for interviews with this benefactor of their race. Page once was careless enough to inform Mr. Garrison that "one of your niggers" was waiting outside for an audience. "I very much regret, Mr. Page," came the answer, "that you should insist on spelling 'Negro' with two 'g's'." Despite the mock solemnity of this rebuke, perennial good-nature and raillery prevailed between the son of Garrison and his disrespectful but ever sympathetic Southern friend. Indeed, one of Page's earliest performances was to introduce a spirit of laughter and genial coöperation into a rather solemn and self-satisfied environment. Mr. Mifflin, the head of the house, even formally thanked Page "for the hearty human way in which you take hold of life." Mr. Ellery Sedgwick, the present editor of the *Atlantic*, has described the somewhat disconcerting descent of Page upon the editorial sanctuary of James Russell Lowell:

"Were a visitant from another sphere to ask me for the incarnation of those qualities we love to call American, I should turn to a familiar gallery of my memory and point to the living portrait that hangs there of Walter Page. A sort of foursquareness, bluntness, it seemed to some; an uneasy, often explosive energy; a disposition to underrate fine drawn nicenesses of all sorts; ingrained Yankee common sense, checking his vaulting enthusiasm; enormous self-confidence, impatience of failure—all of these were in him; and he was besides affectionate to a fault, devoted to his country, his family, his craft—a strong, bluff, tender man.

"Those were the decorous days of the old tradition, and Page's entrance into the 'atmosphere' of Park Street has taken on the dignity of legend. There were all kinds of signs and portents, as the older denizens will tell you. Strange breezes floated through the office, electric emanations, and a pervasive scent of tobacco, which—so the local historian says—had been unknown in the vicinity since the days of Walter Raleigh, except for the literary aroma of Aldrich's quarantined sanctum upstairs. Page's coming marked the end of small ways. His first requirement was, in lieu of a desk, a table that might have served a family of twelve for Thanksgiving dinner. No one could imagine what that vast, polished tableland could serve for until they watched the editor at work. Then they saw. Order vanished and chaos reigned. Huge piles of papers, letters, articles, reports, books, pamphlets, magazines, congregated themselves as if by magic. To work in such confusion seemed hopeless, but Page eluded the congestion by the simple expedient of moving on. He would light a fresh cigar, give the editorial chair a hitch, and begin his work in front of a fresh expanse of table, with no clutter of the past to disturb the new day's litter.

"The motive power of his work was enthusiasm. Never was more generous welcome given to a newcomer than Page held out to the successful manuscript of an unknown. I remember, though I heard the news second hand at the time, what a day it was in the office when the first manuscript from the future author of 'To Have and To Hold,' came in from an untried Southern girl. He walked up and down, reading paragraphs aloud and slapping the crisp manuscript to enforce his commendation. To take a humbler instance, I recall the words of over generous praise with which he greeted the first paper I ever sent to an editor quite as clearly as I remember the monstrous effort which had brought it into being. Sometimes he would do a favoured manuscript the honour of taking it out to lunch in his coat-pocket, and an associate vividly recalls eggs, coffee, and pie in a near-by restaurant, while, in a voice that could be heard by the remotest lunchers, Page read passages which many of them were too startled to appreciate. He was not given to overrating, but it was not in his nature to understate. 'I tell you,' said he, grumbling over some unfortunate proof-sheets from Manhattan, 'there isn't one man in New York who can write English—not from the Battery to Harlem Heights.' And if the faults were moral rather than literary, his disapproval grew in emphasis. There is more than tradition in the tale of the Negro who, presuming on Page's deep interest in his race, brought to his desk a manuscript copied word for word from a published source. Page recognized the deception, and seizing the rascal's collar with a firm editorial grip, rejected the poem, and ejected the poet, with an energy very invigorating to the ancient serenities of the office.

"Page was always effervescent with ideas. Like an editor who would have made a good fisherman, he used to say that you had to cast a dozen times before you could get a strike. He was forever in those days sending out ideas and suggestions and invitations to write. The result was electric, and the magazine became with a suddenness (of which only an editor can appreciate the wonder) a storehouse of animating thoughts. He avoided the mistake common to our craft of editing a magazine for the immediate satisfaction of his colleagues. 'Don't write for the office,' he would say. 'Write for outside,' and so his magazine became a living thing. His phrase suggests one special gift that Page had, for which his profession should do him especial honour. He was able, quite beyond the powers of any man of my acquaintance, to put compendiously into words the secrets of successful editing. It was capital training just to hear him talk. 'Never save a feature,' he used to say. 'Always work for the next number. Forget the others. Spend everything just on that.' And to those who know, there is divination in the principle. Again he understood instinctively that to write well a man must not only have something to say, but must long to say it. A highly intelligent representative of the coloured race came to him with a philosophic essay. Page would have none of it. 'I know what you are thinking of,' said Page. 'You are thinking of the barriers we set up against you, and the handicap of your lot. If you will write what it feels like to be a Negro, I will print that.' The result was a paper which has seemed to me the most moving expression of the hopeless hope of the race I know of.

"Page was generous in his coöperation. He never drew a rigid line about his share in any enterprise, but gave and took help with each and all. A lover of good English, with an honest passion for things tersely said, Page esteemed good journalism far above any second-rate manifestation of more pretentious forms; but many of us will regret that he was not privileged to find some outlet for his energies in which aspiration for real literature might have played an ampler part. For the literature of the past Page had great respect, but his interest was ever in the present and the future. He was forever fulminating against bad writing, and hated the ignorant and slipshod work of the hack almost as much as he despised the sham of the man who affected letters, the dabbler and the poetaster. His taste was for the roast beef of literature, not for the side dishes and the trimmings, and his appreciation of the substantial work of others was no surer than his instinct for his own performance. He was an admirable writer of exposition, argument, and narrative—solid and thoughtful, but never dull. . . . I came into close relations with him and from him I learned more of my profession than from any one I have ever known. Scores of other men would say the same."

But the fact that a new hand had seized the *Atlantic* was apparent in other places than in the *Atlantic* office itself. One of Page's contributors of the *Forum* days, Mr. Courtney DeKalb, happened to be in St. Louis when the first number of the magazine under its new editor made its appearance. Mr. DeKalb had been out of the country for some time and knew nothing of the change. Happening accidentally to pick up the *Atlantic*, the table of contents caught his eye. It bore the traces of an unmistakable hand. Only one man, he said to himself, could assemble such a group as that, and above all, only Page could give such an enticing turn of the titles. He therefore sat down and wrote his old friend congratulating him on his accession to the *Atlantic Monthly*. The change that now took place was indeed a conspicuous, almost a startling one. The *Atlantic* retained all its old literary flavour, for to its traditions Page was as much devoted as the highest caste Bostonian; it still gave up much of its space to a high type of fiction, poetry, and reviews of contemporary literature, but every number contained also an assortment of articles which celebrated the prevailing activities of men and women in all worth-while fields of effort. There were discussions of present-day politics, and these even became personal dissections of presidential candidates; there were articles on the racial characters of the American population: Theodore Roosevelt was permitted to discuss the New York police; Woodrow Wilson to pass in review the several elements that made the Nation; Booker T. Washington to picture the awakening of the Negro; John Muir to enlighten Americans upon a national beauty and wealth of which they had been woefully ignorant, their forests; William Allen White to describe certain aspects of his favourite Kansas; E. L. Godkin to review the dangers and the hopes of American democracy; Jacob Riis to tell about the Battle with the Slum; and W. G. Frost to reveal for the first time the archaic civilization of the Kentucky mountaineers. This subject always appealed to Page's democratic instincts. Mr. Frost's theme was that these Kentucky mountaineers were really Elizabethan survivals; that their dialect, their ballads, their habits were really a case of arrested development; that by studying them present-day Americans could get a picture of their distant forbears. The author gave vitality to this subject by his title, which has ever since been quoted as a masterpiece, "Our Contemporary Ancestors"

There were those who were offended by Page's willingness to seek inspiration on the highways and byways and even in newspapers, for not infrequently he would find hidden away in a corner an idea that would result in valuable magazine matter. On one occasion at least this practice had important literary consequences. One day he happened to read that a Mrs. Robert Hanning had died in Toronto, the account casually mentioning the fact that Mrs. Hanning was the youngest sister of Thomas Carlyle. Page handed this clipping to a young assistant, and told him to take the first train to Canada. The editor could easily divine that a sister of Carlyle, expatriated for forty-six years on this side of the Atlantic, must have received a large number of letters from her brother, and it was safe to assume that they had been carefully preserved. Such proved to be the fact; and a new volume of Carlyle letters, of somewhat more genial character than the other collections, was the outcome of this visit.[1] And another fruit of this journalistic habit was "The Memoirs of a Revolutionist," by Prince Peter Kropotkin. In 1897 the great Russian nihilist was lecturing in Boston. Page met him, learned from his own lips his story, and persuaded him to put it in permanent form. This willingness of Page to admit such a revolutionary person into the pages of the *Atlantic* caused some excitement in conventional circles. In fact, it did take some courage, but Page never hesitated; the man was of heroic mould, he had a great story to tell, he wielded an engaging pen, and his purposes were high-minded. A great book of memoirs was the result.

Mr. Sedgwick refers above to Page's editorial fervour when Miss Mary Johnston's "Prisoners of Hope" first fell out of the blue sky into his Boston office. Page's joy was not less keen because the young author was a Virginia girl, and because she had discovered that the early period of Virginia history was a field for romance. When, a few months afterward, Page was casting about for an *Atlantic* serial, Miss Johnston and this Virginia field seemed to be an especially favourable prospect. "Prisoners of Hope" had been published as a book and had made a good success, but Miss Johnston's future still lay ahead of her. With Page to think meant to act, and so, instead of writing a formal letter, he at once jumped on a train for Birmingham, Alabama, where Miss Johnston

[1] "Letters of Thomas Carlyle to his Youngest Sister." Edited by Charles Townsend Copeland. Houghton, Mifflin & Company, 1899.

was then living. "I remember quite distinctly that first meeting," writes Miss Johnston. "The day was rainy. Standing at my window I watched Mr. Page—a characteristic figure, air and walk—approach the house. When a few minutes later I met him he was simplicity and kindliness itself. This was my first personal contact with publishers (my publishers) or with editors of anything so great as the *Atlantic*. My heart beat! But he was friendly and Southern. I told him what I had done upon a new story. He was going on that night. Might he take the manuscript with him and read it upon the train? It might—he couldn't say positively, of course—but it might have serial possibilities. I was only too glad for him to have the manuscript. I forget just how many chapters I had completed. But it was not quite in order. Could I get it so in a few hours? In that case he would send a messenger for it from the hotel. Yes, I could. Very good! A little further talk and he left with a strong handshake. Three or four hours later he had the manuscript and took it with him from Birmingham that night."

Page's enterprising visit had put into his hands the half-finished manuscript of a story, "To Have and to Hold," which, when printed in the *Atlantic*, more than doubled its circulation, and which, when made into a book, proved one of the biggest successes since "Uncle Tom's Cabin."

Page's most independent stroke in his *Atlantic* days came with the outbreak of the Spanish-American War. Boston was then the headquarters of a national mood which has almost passed out of popular remembrance. Its spokesmen called themselves anti-imperialists. The theory back of their protest was that the American declaration of war on Spain was not only the wanton attack of a great bully upon a feeble little country: it was something that was bound to have deplorable consequences. The United States was breaking with its past and engaging in European quarrels; as a consequence of the war it would acquire territories and embark on a career of "imperialism." Page was impatient at this kind of twaddle. He declared that the Spanish War was a "necessary act of surgery for the health of civilization." He did not believe that a nation, simply because it was small, should be permitted to maintain indefinitely a human slaughter house at the door of the United States. The *Atlantic* for June, 1898, gave the so-called anti-imperialists a thrill of horror. On the cover appeared the defiantly flying American flag; the first article was a vigorous and approving presentation of the American case against Spain; though this was unsigned, its incisive style at once betrayed the author. The *Atlantic* had printed the American flag on its cover during the Civil War; but certain New Englanders thought that this latest struggle, in its motives and its proportions, was hardly entitled to the distinction. Page declared, however, that the Spanish War marked a new period in history; and he endorsed the McKinley Administration, not only in the war itself, but in its consequences, particularly the annexation of the Philippine Islands.

Page greatly enjoyed life in Boston and Cambridge. The *Atlantic* was rapidly growing in circulation and in influence, and the new friends that its editor was making were especially to his taste. He now had a family of four children, three boys and one girl—and their bringing up and education, as he said at this time, constituted his real occupation. So far as he could see, in the summer of 1899, he was permanently established in life. But larger events in the publishing world now again pulled him back to New York.

CHAPTER III

"THE FORGOTTEN MAN"

I

IN JULY, 1899, the publishing community learned that financial difficulties were seriously embarrassing the great house of Harper. For nearly a century this establishment had maintained a position almost of preëminence among American publishers. Three generations of Harpers had successively presided over its destinies; its magazines and books had become almost a household necessity in all parts of the United States, and its authors included many of the names most celebrated in American letters. The average American could no more associate the idea of bankruptcy with this great business than with the federal Treasury itself. Yet this incredible disaster had virtually taken place. At this time the public knew nothing of the impending ruin; the fact was, however, that, in July, 1899, the banking house of J. P. Morgan & Company practically controlled this property. This was the situation which again called Page to New York.

In the preceding year Mr. S. S. McClure, whose recent success as editor and publisher had been little less than a sensation, had joined forces with Mr. Frank N. Doubleday, and organized the new firm of Doubleday & McClure. This business was making rapid progress; and that it would soon become one of the leading American publishing houses was already apparent. It was perhaps not unnatural, therefore, that Mr. J. Pierpont Morgan, scanning the horizon for the men who might rescue the

Harper concern from approaching disaster, should have had his attention drawn to Mr. McClure and Mr. Doubleday. "The failure of Harper & Brothers," Mr. Morgan said in a published statement, "would be a national calamity." One morning, therefore, a member of the Harper firm called upon Mr. McClure. Without the slightest hesitation he unfolded the Harper situation to his astonished contemporary. The solution proposed was more astonishing still. This was that Mr. Doubleday and Mr. McClure should amalgamate their young and vigorous business with the Harper enterprise and become the active managers of the new corporation. Both Mr. McClure and Mr. Doubleday were comparatively young men, and the magnitude of the proposed undertaking at first rather staggered them. It was as though a small independent steel maker should suddenly be invited to take over the United States Steel Corporation. Mr. McClure, characteristically impetuous and daring, wished to accept the invitation outright; Mr. Doubleday, however, suggested a period of probation. The outcome was that the two men offered to take charge of Harper & Brothers for a few months, and then decide whether they wished to make the association a permanent one. One thing was immediately apparent; Messrs. Doubleday and McClure, able as they were, would need the help of the best talent available in the work that lay ahead. The first man to whom they turned was Page, who presently left Boston and took up his business abode at Franklin Square. The rumble of the elevated road was somewhat distracting after the four quiet years in Park Street, but the new daily routine was not lacking in interest. The Harper experiment, however, did not end as Mr. Morgan had hoped. After a few months Messrs. Doubleday, Page and McClure withdrew, and left the work of rescue to be performed by Mr. George Harvey, who, curiously enough, succeeded Page, twenty-one years afterward, in an even more important post—that of ambassador to the Court of St. James's. The one important outcome of the Harper episode, so far as Page was concerned, was the forming of a close business and personal association with Mr. Frank N. Doubleday. As soon as the two men definitely decided not to assume the Harper responsibility, therefore, they joined forces and founded the firm of Doubleday, Page & Company. Page now had the opportunity which he had long wished for; the mere editing of magazines, even magazines of such an eminent character as the *Forum* and the *Atlantic Monthly*, could hardly satisfy his ambition; he yearned to possess something which he could call his own, at least in part.

The life of an editor has its unsatisfactory aspect, unless the editor himself has an influential ownership in his periodical. Page now found his opportunity to establish a monthly magazine which he could regard as his own in both senses. He was its untrammelled editor, and also, in part, its proprietor. All editors and writers will sympathize with the ideas expressed in a letter written about this time to Page's friend, Mr. William Roscoe Thayer, already distinguished as the historian of Italian unity and afterward to win fame as the biographer of Cavour and John Hay. When the first number of the *World's Work* appeared Mr. Thayer wrote, expressing a slight disappointment that its leading tendency was journalistic rather than literary and intellectual. "When you edited the *Forum*," wrote Mr. Thayer, "I perceived that no such talent for editing had been seen in America before, and when, a little later, you rejuvenated the *Atlantic*, making it for a couple of years the best periodical printed in English, I felt that you had a great mission before you

as evoker and editor of the best literary work and weight-
iest thought on important topics of our foremost men."
He had hoped to see a magnified *Atlantic*, and the new
publication, splendid as it was, seemed to be of rather
more popular character than the publications with which
Page had previously been associated. Page met this
challenge in his usual hearty fashion.

To William Roscoe Thayer

34 Union Square East, New York,
December 5, 1900.

My dear Thayer:

The *World's Work* has brought me nothing so good as
your letter of yesterday. When Mrs. Page read it,
she shouted "Now that's it!" For "it" read "truth,"
and you will have her meaning and mine. My thanks
you may be sure you have, in great and earnest abun-
dance.

You surprise me in two ways—(1) that you think as
well of the magazine as you do. If it have half the force
and earnestness that you say it has, how happy I shall be,
for then it will surely bring something to pass. The
other way in which you surprise me is by the flattering
things that you say about my conduct of the *Atlantic*.
Alas! it was not what you in your kind way say—no,
no.

Of course the *World's Work* is not yet by any means what
I hope to make it. But it has this incalculable advantage
(to me) over every other magazine in existence: it is mine
(mine and my partners', i. e., partly mine), and I shall not
work to build up a good piece of machinery and then
be turned out to graze as an old horse is. This of course,
is selfish and personal—not wholly selfish either, I think.
I threw down the *Atlantic* for this reason: (Consider the

history of its editors) Lowell[1] complained bitterly that he was never rewarded properly for the time and work he did; Fields was (in a way) one of its owners; it was sold out from under Howells, etc., etc. I might (probably should) have been at the mercy completely of owners some day who would have dismissed me for a younger man. Nearly all hired editors suffer this fate. My good friends in Boston were sincere in thinking that my day of doom would never come; but they didn't offer me any guarantee—part ownership, for instance; and the years go swiftly. I could afford, of my own volition, to leave the *Atlantic*. I couldn't afford to take permanently the risks that a hired editor must take. Nor should I ever again have turned my hand to such a task except on a magazine of my own. I should have sought other employment. There are many easier and better and more influential things to do—yet; ten years hence I might have been too old. Harry Houghton[2] has an old horse thirty years old. I used to see him grazing sometimes and hear his master's self-congratulatory explanation of his own kindness to that faithful beast. In the office of Houghton, Mifflin & Company there is an old man whom I used to see every day—pensioned, grazing. Then I would go home and see four bright children. Three of them are now away from home at school; and the four cost a pretty penny to educate. My income had been the same for ten years—or very nearly the same. If I was a "magic" editor, I confess I didn't see the magic; and there is no power under Heaven or in it that can prove to me that I ought to keep on making magazines as a hired man—without the common

---

[1] A memorandum of an old *Atlantic* balance sheet discloses that James Russell Lowell's salary as editor was $1,500 a year.

[2] A member of the firm of Houghton, Mifflin & Company.

security of permanent service for lack of which nearly all my predecessors lost their chance.

But this is not all, nor half. A man ought to express himself, ought to live his own life, say his own little say, before silence comes. The "say" may be bad—a mere yawp, and silence might be more becoming. But the same argument would make a man dissatisfied with his own nose if it happened to be ugly. It's *his* nose, and he must content himself. So it's *his* yawp and he must let it go.

I'm not going to make the new magazine my own megaphone—you may be sure of that. It will nevertheless contain my general interpretation of things, in which I swear I do believe! The first thing, of course, is to establish it. Then it can be shaped more nearly into what I wish it to become. If it seem unmannerly, aggressive, I know no other way to make it heard. If it died, then the game would be up. Well, we seem to have established it at once. It promises not to cost us a penny of investment.

Now, the magazines need new topics. They have all threshed over old straw for many years. There is *one* new subject, to my thinking worth all the old ones: the new impulse in American life, the new feeling of nationality, our coming to realize ourselves. To my mind there is greater promise in democracy than men of any preceding period ever dared dream of—aggressive democracy—growth by action. Our writers (the few we have) are yet in the pre-democratic era. When men's imaginations lay hold on the things that already begin to appear above the horizon, we shall have something worth reading. At present I can do no more than bawl out, "See! here are new subjects." One of these days somebody will come along who can write about them. I have started out without a writer. Fiske is under contract, James would give nothing more to the *Atlantic*, you were ill (I thank Heaven you are no longer so) the second- and third-rate essayists have been bought by mere Wall Street publishers. Beyond these are the company of story tellers and beyond them only a dreary waste of dead-level unimaginative men and women. I can (soon) get all that I could ever have got in the *Atlantic* and new ones (I know they'll come) whom I could never have got there.

You'll see—within a year or two—by far a better magazine than I have ever made; and you and I will differ in nothing unless you feel despair about the breakdown of certain democratic theories, which I think were always mere theories. Let 'em go! The real thing, which is life' and action, is better.

Heartily and always your grateful friend,

WALTER H. PAGE.

Thus the fact that Page's new magazine was intended for a popular audience was not the result of accident, but of design. It represented a periodical plan which had long been taking shape in Page's mind. The things that he had been doing for the *Forum* and the *Atlantic* he aspired to do for a larger audience than that to which publications of this character could appeal. Scholar though Page was, and lover of the finest things in literature that he had always been, yet this sympathy and interest had always lain with the masses. Perhaps it is impossible to make literature democratic, but Page believed that he would be genuinely serving the great cause that was nearest his heart if he could spread wide the facts of the modern world, especially the facts of America, and if he could clothe the expression in language which, while always dignified and even "literary," would still be sufficiently touched with the vital, the picturesque, and the "human," to make his new publication appeal to a wide audience of intelligent, everyday Americans. It was thus part of his general programme of improving the status of the average man, and it formed a logical part of his philosophy of human advancement. For the only acceptable measure of any civilization, Page believed, was the extent to which it improved the condition of the common citizen. A few cultured and university-trained men at the top; a few ancient families living in luxury; a few painters and poets and statesmen and generals; these things, in Page's view, did not constitute a satisfactory state of society; the real test was the extent to which the masses participated in education, in the necessities and comforts of existence, in the right of self-evolution and self-expression, in that "equality of opportunity," which, Page never wearied of repeating, "was the basis of social progress." The mere right to vote and to hold office was not democracy; parliamentary majorities and political caucuses were not democracy—at the best these things were only details and not the most important ones; democracy was the right of every man to enjoy, in accordance with his aptitudes of character and mentality, the material and spiritual opportunities that nature and science had placed at the disposition of mankind. This democratic creed had now become the dominating interest of Page's life. From this time on it consumed all his activities. His new magazine set itself first of all to interpret the American panorama from this point of view; to describe the progress that the several parts of the country were making in the several manifestations of democracy— education, agriculture, industry, social life, politics— and the importance that Page attached to them was practically in the order named. Above all it concerned itself with the men and women who were accomplishing most in the definite realization of this great end.

And now also Page began to carry his activities far beyond mere print.   In his early residence in New York, from 1885 to 1895, he had always taken his part in public movements; he had been a vital spirit in the New York Reform Club, which was engaged mainly in advocating the Cleveland tariff; he had always shown a willingness to experiment with new ideas; at one time he had mingled with Socialists and he had been quite captivated by the personal and literary charm of Henry George.   After 1900, however, Page became essentially a public man, though not in the political sense.   His work as editor and writer was merely one expression of the enthusiasms that occupied his mind.   From 1900 until 1913, when he left for England, life meant for him mainly an effort to spread the democratic ideal, as he conceived it; concretely it represented a constant campaign for improving the fundamental opportunities and the everyday social advantages of the masses.

II

Inevitably the condition of the people in his own homeland enlisted Page's sympathy, for he had learned of their necessities at first hand.   The need of education had powerfully impressed him even as a boy.   At twenty-three he began writing articles for the Raleigh *Observer*, and practically all of them were pleas for the education of the Southern child.   His subsequent activities of this kind, as editor of the *State Chronicle*, have already been described.   The American from other parts of the country is rather shocked when he first learns of the backwardness of education in the South a generation ago.   In any real sense there was no publicly supported system for training the child.   A few wretched hovels, scattered through a sparsely settled country, served as school houses; a few uninspiring and neglected women, earning perhaps $50 or $75 a year, did weary duty as teachers; a few groups of anemic and listless children, attending school for only forty days a year—such was the preparation for life which most Southern states gave the less fortunate of their citizens. The glaring fact that emphasized the outcome of this official carelessness was an illiteracy, among white men and women, of 26 per cent. Among the Negroes it was vastly larger.

The first exhortation to reform came from the Wautauga Club, which Page had organized in Raleigh in 1884. After Page had left his native state, other men began preaching the same crusade. Perhaps the greatest of those advocates whom the South loves to refer to as "educational statesmen" was Dr. Charles D. McIver, of Greensboro, N. C. McIver's personality and career had an heroic quality all their own. Back in the 'eighties McIver and Edwin A. Alderman, now President of the University of Virginia, endured all kinds of hardships and buffetings in the cause of popular education; they stumped the state, much like political campaigners, preaching the strange new gospel in mountain cabin, in village church, at the cart's tail—all in an attempt to arouse their lethargic countrymen to the duty of laying a small tax to save their children from illiteracy. Some day the story of McIver and Alderman will find its historian; when it does, he will learn that, in those dark ages, one of their greatest sources of inspiration was Walter Page. McIver, a great burly boy, physically and intellectually, so full of energy that existence for him was little less than an unending tornado, so full of zeal that any other occupation than that of training the neglected seemed a trifling with life, so sleepless in his efforts that, at the age of forty-five, he one day dropped dead while travelling on a railroad train; Alderman, a man of finer culture, quieter in his methods, an orator of polish and restraint, but an advocate vigorous in the prosecution of the great end; and Page, living faraway in the North, but pumping his associates full of courage and enthusiasm—these were the three guardsmen of this new battle for the elevation of the white and black men of the South. McIver's great work was the State Normal College for Women, which, amid unparallelled difficulties, he founded for teaching the teachers of the new Southern generation. It was at this institution that Page, in 1897, delivered the address which gave the cause of Southern education that one thing which is worth armies to any struggling reform—a phrase; and it was a phrase that lived in the popular mind and heart and summed up, in a way that a thousand speeches could never have done, the great purpose for which the best people in the state were striving.

His editorial gift for title-making now served Page in good stead. "The Forgotten Man," which was the heading of his address, immediately passed into the common speech of the South and even at this day inevitably appears in all discussions of social progress. It was again Page's familiar message of democracy, of improving the condition of the everyday man, woman, and child; and the message, as is usually the case in all incitements to change, involved many unpleasant facts. Page had first of all to inform his fellow Southerners that it was only in the South that "The Forgotten Man" was really an outstanding feature. He did not exist in New England, in the Middle States, in the Mississippi Valley, or in the West, or existed in these regions to so slight an extent that he was not a grave menace to society. But in the South the situation was quite different. And for this fact the explanation was found in history. The South certainly could not fix the blame upon Nature. In natural wealth —in forests, mines, quarries, rich soil, in the unlimited power supplied by water courses—the Southern States formed perhaps the richest region in the country. These things North Carolina and her sister communities had not developed; more startling still, they had not developed a source of wealth that was infinitely greater than all these combined; they had not developed their men and their women. The Southern States represented the purest "Anglo-Saxon" strain in the United States; to-day in North Carolina only one person in four hundred is of "foreign stock," and a voting list of almost any town contains practically nothing except the English and Scotch names that were borne by the original settlers. Yet here democracy, in any real sense, had scarcely obtained a footing. The region which had given Thomas Jefferson and George Washington to the world was still, in the year 1897, organized upon an essentially aristocratic basis. The conception of education which prevailed in the most hidebound aristocracies of Europe still ruled south of the Potomac. There was no acceptance of that fundamental American doctrine that education was the function of the state. It was generally regarded as the luxury of the rich and the socially high placed; it was certainly not for the poor; and it was a generally accepted view that those who enjoyed this privilege must pay for it out of their own pockets. Again Page returned to the "mummy" theme —the fact that North Carolina, and the South generally, were too much ruled by "dead men's" hands. The state was controlled by a "little aristocracy, which, in its social and economic character, made a failure and left a stubborn crop of wrong social notions behind it—

especially about education." The chief backward influences were the stump and the pulpit. "From the days of King George to this day, the politicians of North Carolina have declaimed against taxes, thus laying the foundation of our poverty. It was a misfortune for us that the quarrel with King George happened to turn upon the question of taxation—so great was the dread of taxation that was instilled into us." What had the upper classes done for the education of the average man? The statistics of illiteracy, the deplorable economic and social conditions of the rural population—and most of the population of North Carolina was rural—furnished the answer.

Thus the North Carolina aristocracy had failed in education and the failure of the Church had been as complete and deplorable. The preachers had established preparatory schools for boys and girls, but these were under the control of sects; and so education was either a class or an ecclesiastical concern. "The forgotten man remained forgotten. The aristocratic scheme of education had passed him by. To a less extent, but still to the extent of hundreds of thousands, the ecclesiastical scheme had passed him by." But even the education which these institutions gave was inferior. Page told his North Carolina audience that the University of which they were so proud did not rank with Harvard, Yale, Princeton, and other universities of the North. The state had not produced great scholars nor established great libraries. In the estimation of publishers North Carolina was unimportant as a book market. "By any test that may be made, both these systems have failed even with the classes that they appealed to." The net result was that "One in every four was wholly forgotten"—that is, was unable to read and write. And the worst of it all was that the victim of this neglect was not disturbed over his situation. "The forgotten man was content to be forgotten. He became not only a dead weight, but a definite opponent of social progress. He faithfully heard the politician on the stump praise him for virtues that he did not have. The politicians told him that he lived in the best state in the Union; told him that the other politicians had some hare-brained plan to increase his taxes, told him as a consolation for his ignorance how many of his kinsmen had been killed in the war, told him to distrust any one who wished to change anything. What was good enough for his fathers was good enough for him. Thus the 'forgotten man' became a dupe, became thankful for being neglected. And the preacher told him that the ills and misfortunes of this life were blessings in disguise, that God meant his poverty as a means of grace, and that if he accepted the right creed all would be well with him. These influences encouraged inertia. There could not have been a better means to prevent the development of the people."

Even more tragic than these "forgotten men" were the "forgotten women." "Thin and wrinkled in youth from ill-prepared food, clad without warmth or grace, living in untidy houses, working from daylight till bedtime at the dull round of weary duties, the slaves of men of equal slovenliness, the mothers of joyless children—all uneducated if not illiterate." "This sight," Page told his hearers, "every one of you has seen, not in the countries whither we send missionaries, but in the borders of the State of North Carolina, in this year of grace."

"Our civilization," he declared, "has been a failure." Both the politicians and the preacher had failed to lift the masses. "It is a time for a wiser statesmanship and a more certain means of grace." He admitted that there had been recent progress in North Carolina, owing largely to the work of McIver and Alderman, but taxes for educational purposes were still low. What was the solution? "A public school system generously supported by public sentiment and generously maintained by both state and local taxation, is the only effective means to develop the forgotten man and even more surely the only means to develop the forgotten woman. . . ." "If any beggar for a church school oppose a local tax for schools or a higher school tax, take him to the huts of the forgotten women and children, and in their hopeless presence remind him that the church system of education has not touched tens of thousands of these lives and ask him whether he thinks it wrong that the commonwealth should educate them. If he think it wrong ask him and ask the people plainly, whether he be a worthy preacher of the gospel that declares one man equal to another in the sight of God? . . . The most sacred thing in the commonwealth and to the commonwealth is the child, whether it be your child or the child of the dull-faced mother of the hovel. The child of the dull-faced mother may, as you know, be the most capable child in the state. . . . Several of the strongest personalities that were ever born in North Carolina were men whose very fathers were unknown. We have all known two such, who held high places in Church and State. President Eliot said a little while ago that the ablest man that he had known in his many years' connection with Harvard University was the son of a brick mason."

In place of the ecclesiastical creed that had guided North Carolina for so many generations Page proposed his creed of democracy. He advised that North Carolina commit this to memory and teach it to its children. It was as follows:

"I believe in the free public training of both the hands and the mind of every child born of woman.

"I believe that by the right training of men we add to the wealth of the world. All wealth is the creation of man, and he creates it only in proportion to the trained uses of the community; and the more men we train the more wealth everyone may create.

"I believe in the perpetual regeneration of society, and in the immortality of democracy and in growth everlasting."

Thus Page nailed his theses upon the door of his native state, and mighty was the reverberation. In a few weeks Page's Greensboro address had made its way all over the Southern States, and his melancholy figure, "the forgotten man" had become part of the indelible imagery of the Southern people. The portrait etched itself deeply into the popular consciousness for the very good reason that its truth was pretty generally recognized. The higher type of newspaper, though it winced somewhat at Page's strictures, manfully recognized that the best way of meeting his charge was by setting to work and improving conditions. The fact is that the better conscience of North Carolina welcomed this eloquent description of unquestioned evils; but the gentlemen whom Page used to stigmatize as "professional Southerners"— the men who commercialized class and sectional prejudice to their own political and financial or ecclesiastical profit —fell foul of this "renegade," this "Southern Yankee" this sacrilegious "intruder" who had dared to visit his old home and desecrate its traditions and its religion. This clerical wrath was kindled into fresh flame when Page, in an editorial in his magazine, declared that these same preachers, ignoring their real duties, were content "to herd their women and children around the stagnant pools of theology." For real religion Page had the deepest reverence, and he had great respect also for the robust evangelical preachers whose efforts had contributed so much to the opening up of the frontier. In his Greensboro address Page had given these men high praise. But for the assiduous idolaters of stratified dogma he entertained a contempt which he was seldom at pains to conceal. North Carolina had many clergymen of the more progressive type; these men chuckled at Page's vigorous characterization of the brethren, but those against whom it had been aimed raged with a fervour that was almost unchristian. This clerical excitement, however, did not greatly disturb the philosophic Page. The hubbub lasted for several years—for Page's Greensboro speech was only the first of many pronouncements of the same kind—but he never publicly referred to the attacks upon him. Occasionally in letters to his friends he would good-naturedly discuss them. "I have had several letters," he wrote to Professor Edwin Mims, of Trinity College, North Carolina, "about an 'excoriation' (Great Heavens! What a word!) that somebody in North Carolina has been giving me. I never read these things and I don't know what it's all about—nor do I care. But perhaps you'll be interested in a letter that I wrote an old friend (a lady) who is concerned about it. I enclose a copy of it. I shall never notice any 'excoriator.' But if you wish to add to the gaiety of nations, give this copy to some newspaper and let it loose in the state—if you care to do so. We must have patience with these puny and peevish brethren. They've been trained to a false view of life. Heaven knows I bear them no ill-will."

The letter to which Page referred follows:

My dear Friend:

I have your letter saying that some of the papers in North Carolina are again "jumping on" me. I do not know which they are, and I am glad that you did not tell me. I had heard of it before. A preacher wrote me the other day that he approved of every word of an "excoriation" that some religious editor had given me. A kindly Christian act—wasn't it, to send a stranger word that you were glad that he had been abused by a religious editor? I wrote him a gentle letter, telling him that I hoped he'd have a long and happy life preaching a gospel of friendliness and neighbourliness and good-will, and that I cared nothing about "excoriations." Why should he, then, forsake his calling and take delight in disseminating personal abuse?

And why do you not write me about things that I really care for in the good old country—the budding trees, the pleasant weather, news of old friends, gossip of good people—cheerful things? I pray you, don't be concerned about what any poor whining soul may write about me. I don't care for myself: I care only for him; for the writer of personal abuse always suffers from it—never the man abused.

I haven't read what my kindly clerical correspondent calls an "excoriation" for ten years, and I never shall read one if I know what it is beforehand. Why should I or anybody read such stuff? I can't find time to do half the positive things that I should like to do for the broadening of my own character and for the encouragement of others. Why should I waste a single minute in such a negative and cheerless way as reading anybody's personal abuse of anybody else—least of all myself?

These silly outbursts never reach me and they never can; and they, therefore, utterly fail, and always will fail, of their aim; yet, my dear friend, there is nevertheless a serious side to such folly. For it shows the need of education, education, education. The religious editor and the preacher who took joy in his abuse of me have such a starved view of life that they cannot themselves, perhaps, ever be educated into kindliness and dignity of thought. But their children may be—must be. Think of beautiful children growing up in a home where "excoriating" people who differ with you is regarded as a manly Christian exercise! It is pitiful beyond words. There is no way to lift up life that is on so low a level except by the free education of all the people. Let us work for that and, when the growlers are done growling and forgotten, better men will remember us with gratitude.

I felt greatly complimented and pleased to receive an invitation the other day to attend the North Carolina Teachers' Assembly in June. I have many things to do in June, but I am going—going with great pleasure. I hope to see you there. I know of no other company of people that I should be so glad to meet. They are doing noble work—the most devoted and useful work in this whole wide world. They are the true leaders of the people. I often wish that I were one of them. They inspire me as nobody else does. They are the army of our salvation.

Write me what they are doing. Write me about the wonderful educational progress. And write me about the peach trees and the budding imminence of spring; and about the children who now live all day outdoors and grow brown and plump. And never mind that queer sect, "The Excoriators." They and their stage thunder will be forgotten to-morrow. Meantime let us live and work for things nobler than any controversies, for things that are larger than the poor mission of any sect; and let us have charity and a patient pity for those that think they serve God by abusing their fellow-men. I wish I saw some way to help them to a broader and a higher life.

Faithfully yours,

WALTER H. PAGE.

III

That Page should have little interest in "excoriators" at the time this letter was written—in April, 1902—was not surprising, for his educational campaign and that of his friends was now bearing fruit. "Write me about the wonderful educational progress," he says to this correspondent; and, indeed, the change that was coming over North Carolina and the South generally seemed to be tinged with the miraculous. The "Forgotten Man" and the "Forgotten Woman" were rapidly coming into their own. Two years after the delivery of Page's Greensboro address, a small group of educational enthusiasts met at Capon Springs, West Virginia, to discuss the general situation in the South. The leader of this little gathering was Robert C. Ogden, a great New York merchant who for many years had been President of the Board of Hampton Institute. Out of this meeting grew the Southern Educational Conference, which was little more than an annual meeting for advertising broadcast the educational needs of the South. Each year Mr. Ogden chartered a railroad train; a hundred or so of the leading editors, lawyers, bankers, and the like became his guests; the train moved through the Southern States, pausing now and then to investigate some particular institution or locality; and at some Southern city, such as Birmingham or Atlanta or Winston-Salem, a stop of several days would be made, a public building engaged, and long meetings held. In all these proceedings Page was an active figure, as he became in the Southern Education Board, which directly resulted from Mr. Ogden's public spirited excursions. Like the Conference, the Southern Education Board was a purely missionary organization, and its most active worker was Page himself. He was constantly speaking and writing on his favourite subject; he printed article after article, not only in his own magazine, but in the *Atlantic*, in the *Outlook*, and in a multitude of newspapers, such as the Boston *Transcript*, the New York *Times*, and the Kansas City *Star*. And always through his writings, and, indeed, through his life, there ran, like the motif of an opera, that same perpetual plea for "the forgotten man"—the need of uplifting the backward masses through training, both of the mind and of the hand.

The day came when this loyal group had other things to work with than their voices and their pens; their efforts had attracted the attention of Mr. John D. Rockefeller, who brought assistance of an extremely substantial character. In 1902 Mr. Rockefeller organized the General Education Board. Of the ten members six were taken from the Southern Education Board; other members represented general educational movements and especially the Baptist interests to which Mr. Rockefeller had been contributing for years. In a large sense, therefore, especially in its membership, the General Education Board was a development of the Ogden organization; but it was much broader in its sweep, taking under its view the entire nation and all forms of educational effort. It immediately began to concern itself with the needs of the South. In 1902 Mr. Rockefeller gave this new corporation $1,000,000; in 1905 he gave it $10,000,000; in 1907 he astonished the Nation by giving $32,000,000, and, in 1909, another $10,000,000; the whole making a total of $53,000,000,

Walter H. Page (1899), from a photograph taken when he was
editor of the *Atlantic Monthly*

Dr. Wallace Buttrick, President of the General Education Board

the largest sum ever given by a single man, up to that time, for social or philanthropic purposes. The General Education Board now became the chief outside interest of Page's life. He was made a member of the Executive Committee, faithfully attended all its sessions, and participated intimately in every important plan. All such bodies have their decorative members and their working members; Page belonged emphatically in the latter class. Not only was he fertile in suggestions, but his ready mind could give almost any proposal its proper emphasis and clearly set forth its essential details. Between Page and Dr. Buttrick, Secretary and now President of the Board, a close personal intimacy grew up. Dr. Buttrick moved to Teaneck Road, Englewood, where Page had his home, and many a long evening did the two men spend together, many a long walk did they take in the surrounding country, always discussing education, especially Southern education. A letter to the present writer from Dr. Abraham Flexner, the present Secretary of the Board, perhaps sums up the matter. "Page was one of the real educational statesmen of this country," says Dr. Flexner, "probably the greatest that we have had since the Civil War."

And this Rockefeller support came at a time when that movement known as the "educational awakening" had started in the South. In 1900 North Carolina elected its greatest governor since the Civil War—Charles B. Aycock. A much repeated anecdote attributes Lincoln's detestation of slavery to a slave auction that he witnessed as a small boy; Aycock's first zeal as an educational reformer had an origin that was even more pathetic, for he always carried in his mind his recollection of his own mother signing an important legal document with a cross. As a young man fresh from the university Aycock also

came under the influence of Page. An old letter, preserved among Page's papers, dated February 26, 1886,
discloses that he was a sympathizing reader of the
"mummy" controversy; when the brickbats began flying
in Page's direction Aycock wrote, telling Page that
"fully three fourths of the people are with you and wish
you Godspeed in your effort to awaken better work,
greater activity, and freer opinion in the state." And
now under Aycock's governorship North Carolina began
to tackle the educational problem with a purpose. School
houses started up all over the state at the rate of one a
day—many of them beautiful, commodious, modern structures, in every way the equals of any in the North or
West; high schools, normal schools, trade schools made
their appearance wherever the need was greatest; and
in other parts of the South the response was similarly
energetic. The reform is not yet complete, but the
description that Page gave of Southern education in
1897, accurate in all its details as it was then, has now
become ancient history.

IV

And in occupations of this kind Page passed his years
of maturity. His was not a spectacular life; his family
for the most part still remained his most immediate
interest; the daily round of an editor has its imaginative
quality, but in the main it was for Page a quiet, even a
cloistered existence; the work that an editor does, the
achievements that he can put to his credit, are usually
anonymous; and the American public little understood
the extent to which Page was influencing many of the
most vital forces of his time. The business association
that he had formed with Mr. Doubleday turned out
most happily. Their publishing house, in a short time,

attained a position of great influence and prosperity. The two men, on both the personal and the business side, were congenial and complementary; and the love that both felt for country life led to the establishment of a publishing and printing plant of unusual beauty. In Garden City, Long Island, a great brick structure was built, somewhat suggestive in its architecture of Hampton Court, surrounded by pools and fountains, Italian gardens, green walks and pergolas, gardens blooming in appropriate seasons with roses, peonies, rhododendrons, chrysanthemums, and the like, and parks of evergreen, fir, cedar, and more exotic trees and shrubs. Certainly fate could have designed no more fitting setting for Page's favourite activities than this. In assembling authors, in instigating the writing of books, in watching the achievements and the tendencies of American life, in the routine of editing his magazine—all this in association with partners whose daily companionship was a delight and a stimulation—Page spent his last years in America.

Page's independence as an editor, sufficiently indicated in the days of his vivacious youth, became even more emphatic in his maturer years. In his eyes, merely inking over so many pages of good white paper was not journalism; conviction, zeal, honesty—these were the important points. Almost on the very day that his appointment as Ambassador to Great Britain was announced his magazine published an editorial from his pen, which contained not especially complimentary references to his new chief, Mr. Bryan, the Secretary of State; naturally the newspapers found much amusement in these few sentences; but the thing was typical of Page's whole career as an editor. He held to the creed that an editor should divorce himself entirely from prejudices, animosities, and predilections; this seems an obvious, even a trite thing to say, yet there are so few men who can leave personal considerations aside in writing of men and events that it is worth while pointing out that Page was such a man. When his firm was planning to establish its magazine, his partner, Mr. Doubleday, was approached by a New York politician of large influence but shady reputation who wished to be assured that it would reflect correct political principles. "You should see Mr. Page about that," was the response. "No, this is a business matter," the insinuating gentleman went on, and then he proceeded to show that about twenty-five thousand subscribers could be obtained if the publication preached orthodox standpat doctrine. "I don't think you had better see Mr. Page," said Mr. Doubleday, dismissing his caller.

Many incidents which illustrate this independence could be given; one will suffice. In 1907 and 1908, Page's magazine published the "Random Reminiscences of John D. Rockefeller." While the articles were appearing, the Hearst newspapers obtained a large number of letters that, some years before, had passed between Mr. John D. Archbold, President of the Standard Oil Company and one of Mr. Rockefeller's business associates from the earliest days, and a well known Senator of the United States. These letters uncovered one of the gravest scandals that had ever involved an American public man; they instantaneously destroyed the Senator's political career and hastened his death. They showed that this brilliant man had been obtaining large sums of money from the Standard Oil Company while he was filling the post of United States Senator and that at the same time he was receiving suggestions from Mr. Archbold about pending legislation. Mr. Rockefeller was not personally involved, for he had retired from active busi-

ness many years before these things had been done; but
the Standard Oil Company, with which his name was
intimately associated, was involved and in a way that
seemed to substantiate the worst charges that had been
made against it. At this time Page, as a member of the
General Education Board, was doing his part in helping
to disperse the Rockefeller millions for public purposes;
his magazine was publishing Mr. Rockefeller's reminiscences; there are editors who would have felt a certain
embarrassment in commenting on the Archbold transaction. Page, however, did not hesitate. Mr. Archbold, hearing that he intended to treat the subject fully,
asked him to come and see him. Page replied that he
would be glad to have Mr. Archbold call upon him.
The two men were brought together by friendly intermediaries in a neutral place; but the great oil magnate's
explanation of his iniquities did not satisfy Page. The
November, 1908, issue of the magazine contained, in one
section, an interesting chapter by Mr. Rockefeller, describing the early days of the Standard Oil Company, and,
in another, ten columns by Page, discussing the Archbold
disclosures in language that was discriminating and well
tempered, but not at all complimentary to Mr. Archbold
or to the Standard Oil Company.

Occasionally Page was summoned for services of a
public character. Thus President Roosevelt, whose friendship he had enjoyed for many years, asked him to
serve upon his Country Life Commission—a group of
men called by the President to study ways of improving the surroundings and extending the opportunities of American farmers. Page's interest in Negro
education led to his appointment to the Jeanes Board.
He early became an admirer of Booker Washington, and
especially approved his plan for uplifting the Negro

by industrial training. One of the great services that Page rendered literature was his persuasion of Washington to write that really great autobiography, "Up from Slavery," and another biography in a different field, for which he was responsible, was Miss Helen Keller's "Story of My Life." And only once, amid these fine but not showy activities, did Page's life assume anything in the nature of the sensational. This was in 1909, when he published his one effort at novel writing, "The Southerner." To write novels had been an early ambition with Page; indeed his papers disclose that he had meditated several plans of this kind; but he never seriously settled himself to the task until the year 1906. In July of that year the *Atlantic Monthly* began publishing a serial entitled "The Autobiography of a Southerner Since the Civil War," by Nicholas Worth. The literary matter that appeared under this title most readers accepted as veracious though anonymous autobiography. It related the life adventures of a young man, born in the South, of parents who had had little sympathy with the Confederate cause, attempting to carve out his career in the section of his birth and meeting opposition and defeat from the prejudices with which he constantly found himself in conflict. The story found its main theme and background in the fact that the Southern States were so exclusively living in the memories of the Civil War that it was impossible for modern ideas to obtain a foothold. "I have sometimes thought," said the author, and this passage may be taken as embodying the leading point of the narrative, "that many of the men who survived that unnatural war unwittingly did us a greater hurt than the war itself. It gave everyone of them the intensest experience of his life and ever afterward he referred every other experience to this. Thus

it stopped the thought of most of them as an earthquake
stops a clock. The fierce blow of battle paralyzed the
mind. Their speech was a vocabulary of war, their
loyalties were loyalties, not to living ideas or duties, but
to old commanders and to distorted traditions. They
were dead men, most of them, moving among the living
as ghosts; and yet, as ghosts in a play, they held the
stage." In another passage the writer names the "ghosts"
which are chiefly responsible for preventing Southern
progress. They are three: "The Ghost of the Confederate dead, the Ghost of religious orthodoxy, the Ghost
of Negro domination." Everywhere the hero finds his
progress blocked by these obstructive wraiths of the past.
He seeks a livelihood in educational work—becomes a local
superintendent of Public Instruction, and loses his place
because his religious views are unorthodox, because he
refuses to accept the popular estimate of Confederate
statesmen, and because he hopes to educate the black
child as well as the white one. He enters politics and
runs for public office on the platform of the new day, is
elected, and then finds himself counted out by political
ringsters. Still he does not lose faith, and finally settles
down in the management of a cotton mill, convinced that
the real path of salvation lies in economic effort. This
mere skeleton of a story furnishes an excuse for rehearsing again the ideas that Page had already made familiar
in his writings and in his public addresses. This time
the lesson is enlivened by the portrayal of certain typical characters of the post-bellum South. They are
all there—the several types of Negro, ranging all the
way from the faithful and philosophic plantation re-
tainer to the lazy "'Publican" office-seeker; the political colonel, to whom the Confederate veterans and
the "fair daughters of the South (God bless 'em)" are

the mainstays of "civerlerzation" and indispensable in-
strumentalities in the game of partisan politics; the evangelical clergymen who cared more for old-fashioned creeds
than for the education of the masses; the disreputable editor who specialized in Negro crime and constantly preached
the doctrine of the "white man's country"; the Southern
woman who, innocently and sincerely and even charm-
ingly, upheld the ancient tradition and the ancient feud.
On the other hand, Page's book portrays the buoyant
enthusiast of the new day, the reformer who was seeking
to establish a public school system and to strengthen
the position of woman; and, above all, the quiet, hard-
working industrialist who cared nothing for stump speaking but much for cotton mills, improved methods of
farming, the introduction of diversified crops, the tidying
up of cities and the country.

These chapters, extensively rewritten, were published
as a book in 1909. Probably Page was under no illusion
that he had created a real romance when he described
his completed work as a "novel." The *Atlantic* autobiography had attracted wide attention, and the identification of the author had been immediate and accurate.
Page's friends began calling his house on the telephone and
asking for "Nicholas" and certain genial spirits addressed
him in letters as "Marse Little Nick"—the name under
which the hero was known to the old Negro family servant, Uncle Ephraim—perhaps the best drawn character
in the book. Page's real purpose in calling the book a
"novel" therefore, was to inform the public that the
story, so far as its incidents and most of its characters
were concerned, was pure fiction. Certain episodes, such
as those describing the hero's early days, were, in the
main, veracious transcripts from Page's own life, but the
rest of the book bears practically no relation to his career.

The fact that he spent his mature years in the North, editing magazines and publishing, whereas Nicholas Worth spends his in the South, engaged in educational work and in politics and industry, settles this point. The characters, too, are rather types than specific individuals, though one or two of them, particularly Professor Billy Bain, who is clearly Charles D. McIver, may be accepted as fairly accurate portraits. But as a work of fiction "The Southerner" can hardly be considered a success; the love story is too slight, the women not well done, most of the characters rather personified qualities than flesh and blood people. Its strength consists in the picture that it gives of the so-called "Southern problem," and especially of the devastating influence of slavery. From this standpoint the book is an autobiography, for the ideas and convictions it presents had formed the mental life of Page from his earliest days.

And these were the things that hurt. Yet the stories of the anger caused by "The Southerner" have been much exaggerated. It is said that a certain distinguished Southern senator declared that, had he known that Page was the author of "The Southerner," he would have blocked his nomination as Ambassador to Great Britain; certain Southern newspapers also severely denounced the volume; even some of Page's friends thought that it was a little unkind in spots; yet as a whole the Southern people accepted it as a fair, and certainly as an honest, treatment of a very difficult subject. Possibly Page was a little hard upon the Confederate veteran, and did not sufficiently portray the really pathetic aspects of his character; any shortcomings of this sort are due, not to any failing in sympathy, but to the fact that Page's zeal was absorbingly concentrated upon certain glaring abuses. And as to the accuracy of his vision in these respects there could be no question. The volume was a welcome antidote to the sentimental Southern novels that had contented themselves with glorifying a vanished society which, when the veil is stripped, was not heroic in all its phases, for it was based upon an institution so squalid as human slavery, and to those even more pernicious books which, by luridly portraying the unquestioned vices of reconstruction and the frightful consequences which resulted from giving the Negro the ballot, simply aroused useless passions and made the way out of the existing wilderness still more difficult. So the best public opinion, North and South, regarded "The Southerner," and decided that Page had performed a service to the section of his birth in writing it. Indeed the fair-minded and intelligent spirit with which the best elements in the South received "The Southerner" in itself demonstrated that this great region had entered upon a new day.

V

Nor was Page's work for the South yet ended. In the important five years from 1905 to 1910 he performed two services of an extremely practical kind. In 1906 the problem of Southern education assumed a new phase. Dr. Wallace Buttrick, the Secretary of the General Education Board, had now decided that the fundamental difficulty was economic. By that time the Southern people had revised their original conception that education was a private and not a public concern; there was now a general acceptance of the doctrine that the mental and physical training of every child, white and black, was the responsibility of the state; Aycock's campaign had worked such a popular revolution on this subject that no politician who aspired to public office would dare to take a contrary view. Yet the economic difficulty still remained. The South was poor; whatever might be the general desire, the taxable resources were not sufficient to support such a comprehensive system of popular instruction as existed in the North and West. Any permanent improvement must therefore be based upon the strengthening of the South's economic position. Essentially the task was to build up Southern agriculture, which for generations had been wasteful, unintelligent and consequently unproductive. Such a far-reaching programme might well appall the most energetic reformer, but Dr. Buttrick set to work. He saw little light until his attention was drawn to a quaint and philosophic gentleman—a kind of bucolic Ben Franklin —who was then obscurely working in the cotton lands of Louisiana, making warfare on the boll weevil in a way of his own. At that time Dr. Seaman A. Knapp had made no national reputation; yet he had evolved a plan for redeeming country life and making American farms more fruitful that has since worked marvellous results. There was nothing especially sensational about its details. Dr. Knapp had made the discovery in relation to farms that the utilitarians had long since made with reference to other human activities: that the only way to improve agriculture was not to talk about it, but to go and do it. During the preceding fifty years agricultural colleges had sprung up all over the United States—Dr. Knapp had been president of one himself; practically every Southern state had one or more; agricultural lecturers covered thousands of miles annually telling their yawning audiences how to farm; these efforts had scattered broadcast much valuable information about the subject, but the difficulty lay in inducing the farmers to apply it. Dr. Knapp had a new method. He selected a particular farmer and persuaded him to work his fields for a period according to methods which he prescribed. He told his pupil how to plough, what seed to plant, how to space his rows, what fertilizers to use, and the like. If a selected acreage yielded a profitable crop which the farmer could sell at an increased price Dr. Knapp had sufficient faith in human nature to believe that that particular farmer would continue to operate his farm on the new method and that his neighbours, having this practical example of growing prosperity, would imitate him.

Such was the famous "Demonstration Work" of Dr. Seaman A. Knapp; this activity is now a regular branch of the Department of Agriculture, employing thousands of agents and spending not far from $18,000,000 a year. Its application to the South has made practically a new and rich country, and it has long since been extended to other regions. When Dr. Buttrick first met Knapp, however, there were few indications of this splendid future. He brought Dr. Knapp North and exhibited him to Page. This was precisely the kind of man who appealed to Page's sympathies. His mind was always keenly on the scent for the new man—the original thinker who had some practical plan for uplifting humankind and making life more worth while. And Dr. Knapp's mission was one that had filled most of his thoughts for many years; its real purpose was the enrichment of country life. Page therefore took to Dr. Knapp with a mighty zest. He supported him on all occasions; he pled his cause with great eloquence before the General Education Board, whose purse strings were liberally unloosed in behalf of the Knapp work; in his writings, in speeches, in letters, in all forms of public advocacy, he insisted that Dr. Knapp had found the solution of the agricultural problem. The fact is that Page regarded Knapp as one of the greatest men of the time. His feeling came out with character-

istic intensity on the occasion of the homely reformer's
funeral. "The exercises," Page once told a friend, "were
held in a rather dismal little church on the outskirts of
Washington. The day was bleak and chill, the attend-
ants were few—chiefly officials of the Department of
Agriculture. The clergyman read the service in the most
perfunctory way. Then James Wilson, the Secretary of
Agriculture, spoke formally of Dr. Knapp as a faithful
servant of the Department who always did well what he
was told to do, commending his life in an altogether commonplace fashion. By that time my heart was pretty hot.
No one seemed to divine that in the coffin before them
was the body of a really great man, one who had hit upon a fruitful idea in American agriculture—an idea that
was destined to cover the nation and enrich rural life
immeasurably." Page was so moved by this lack of appreciation, so full of sorrow at the loss of one of his
dearest friends, that, when he rose to speak, his apprais-
ment took on a certain indignation. Their dead associate,
Page declared, would outrank the generals and the politicians who received the world's plaudits, for he had devoted his life to a really great purpose; his inspiration had
been the love of the common people, his faith, his sympathy had all been expended in an effort to brighten the
life of the too frequently neglected masses. Page's address on this occasion was entirely extemporaneous; no
record of it was ever made, but those who heard it still
carry the memory of an eloquent and fiery outburst that
placed Knapp's work in its proper relation to American
history and gave an unforgettable picture of a patient,
idealistic, achieving man whose name will loom large in
the future.

During this same period Page, always on the outlook for the exceptional man, made another discovery

which has had world-wide consequences. As a member of President Roosevelt's Country Life Commission Page became one of the committee assigned to investigate conditions in the Southern States. The sanitarian of this commission was Dr. Charles W. Stiles, a man who held high rank as a zoölogist, and who, as such, had for many years done important work with the Department of Agriculture. Page had hardly formed Dr. Stiles's acquaintance before he discovered that, at that time, he was a man of one idea. And this one idea had for years brought upon his head much good-natured ridicule. For Dr. Stiles had his own explanation for much of the mental and physical sluggishness that prevailed in the rural sections of the Southern States. Yet he could not mention this without exciting uproarious laughter— even in the presence of scientific men. Several years previously Dr. Stiles had discovered that a hitherto unclassified species of a parasite popularly known as the hookworm prevailed to an astonishing extent in all the Southern States. The pathological effects of this creature had long been known; it localized in the intestines, there secreted a poison that destroyed the red blood corpuscles, and reduced its victims to a deplorable state of anæmia, making them constantly ill, listless, mentally dull—in every sense of the word useless units of society. The encouraging part of this discovery was that the patients could quickly be cured and the hookworm eradicated by a few simple improvements in sanitation. Dr. Stiles had long been advocating such a campaign as an indispensable preliminary to improving Southern life. But the humorous aspect of the hookworm always interfered with his cause; the microbe of laziness had at last been found!

It was not until Dr. Stiles, in the course of this Southern trip, cornered Page in a Pullman car, that he finally found an attentive listener. Page, of course, had his preliminary laugh, but then the hookworm began to work on his imagination. He quickly discovered that Dr. Stiles was no fool; and before the expedition was finished, he had become a convert and, like most converts, an extremely zealous one. The hookworm now filled his thoughts as completely as it did those of his friend; he studied it, he talked about it; and characteristically he set to work to see what could be done. How much Southern history did the thing explain? Was it not forces like this, and not statesmen and generals, that really controlled the destinies of mankind? Page's North Carolina country people had for generations been denounced as "crackers," and as "hill-billies," but here was the discovery that the great mass of them were ill—as ill as the tuberculosis patients in the Adirondacks. Free these masses from the enervating parasite that consumed all their energies—for Dr. Stiles had discovered that the disease afflicted the great majority of the rural classes—and a new generation would result. Naturally the cause strongly touched Page's sympathies. He laid the case before the ever sympathetic Dr. Buttrick, but here again progress was slow. By hard hammering, however, he half converted Dr. Buttrick, who, in turn, took the case of the hookworm to his old associate, Dr. Frederick T. Gates. What Page was determined to obtain was a million dollars or so from Mr. John D. Rockefeller, for the purpose of engaging in deadly warfare upon this pest. This was the proper way to produce results: first persuade Dr. Buttrick, then induce him to persuade Dr. Gates, who, if convinced, had ready access to the great treasure house. But Dr. Gates also began to smile; even the combined eloquence of Page and Dr. Buttrick could not move him. So the reform marked time until one day Dr. Buttrick,

Dr. Gates, and Dr. Simon Flexner, the Director of the Rockefeller Institute, happened to be fellow travellers—again on a Pullman car.

"Dr. Flexner," said Dr. Buttrick—this for the benefit of his incredulous friend—"what is the scientific standing of Dr. Charles W. Stiles?"

"Very, very high," came the immediate response, and at this Dr. Gates pricked up his ears. Yet the subsequent conversation disclosed that Dr. Flexner was unfamiliar with the Stiles hookworm work. He, too, smiled at the idea, but, like Page his smile was not one of ridicule.

"If Dr. Stiles believes this," was his dictum, "it is something to be taken most seriously."

As Dr. Flexner is probably the leading medical scientist in the United States, his judgment at once lifted the hookworm issue to a new plane. Dr. Gates ceased laughing and events now moved rapidly. Mr. Rockefeller gave a million dollars to a sanitary commission for the eradication of the hookworm in the Southern States, and of this Page became a charter member. In this way an enterprise that is the greatest sanitary and health reform of modern times had its beginnings. So great was the success of the Hookworm Commission in the South, so many thousands were almost daily restored to health and usefulness, that Mr. Rockefeller extended its work all over the world—to India, Egypt, China, Australia, to all sections that fall within the now accurately located "hookworm belt." Out of it grew the great International Health Commission, also endowed with unlimited millions of Rockefeller money, which is engaged in stamping out disease and promoting medical education in all quarters of the globe. Dr. Stiles and Page's associates on the General Education Board attribute the origin of this work to the simple fact that Page, great humourist that he was, could temper his humour with intelligence, and could therefore perceive the point at which a joke ceased to be a joke and actually concealed a truth of the most far-reaching importance to mankind.

Page enjoyed the full results of this labour one night in the autumn of 1913, when Dr. Wickliffe Rose, the head of the International Health Board, came to London to discuss the possibility of beginning hookworm work in the British Empire, especially in Egypt and India. Page, as Ambassador, arranged a dinner at the Marlborough Club, attended by the leading medical scientists of the kingdom and several members of the Cabinet. Dr. Rose's description of his work made a deep impression. He was informed that the British Government was only too ready to coöperate with the Health Board. When the discussion was ended the Right Honourable Lewis Harcourt, the Secretary of State for the Colonies, concluded an eloquent address with these words:

"The time will come when we shall look back on this evening as the beginning of a new era in British colonial administration."

CHAPTER IV

THE WILSONIAN ERA BEGINS

I

IT WAS Page's interest in the material and spiritual elevation of the masses that first directed his attention to the Presidential aspirations of Woodrow Wilson. So much history has been made since 1912 that the public questions which then stirred the popular mind have largely passed out of recollection. Yet the great rallying cry of that era was democracy, spelled with a small "d." In the fifty years since the Civil War only one Democratic President had occupied the White House. The Republicans' long lease of power had produced certain symptoms which their political foes now proceeded to describe as great public abuses. The truth of the matter, of course, is that neither political virtue nor political depravity was the exclusive possession of either of the great national organizations. The Republican party, especially under the enlightened autocracy of Roosevelt, had started such reforms as conservation, the improvement of country life, the regulation of the railroads, and the warfare on the trusts, and had shown successful interest in such evidences of the new day as child labour laws, employer's liability laws, corrupt practice acts, direct primaries and the popular election of United States Senators—not all perhaps wise as methods, but all certainly inspired with a new conception of democratic government. Roosevelt also had led in the onslaught on that corporation influence which, after all, constituted the great

problem of American politics. But Mr. Taft's administration had impressed many men, and especially Page, as
a discouraging slump back into the ancient system. Page
was never blind to the inadequacies of his own party;
the three campaigns of Bryan and his extensive influence
with the Democratic masses at times caused him deep
despair; that even the corporations had extended their
tentacles into the ranks of Jefferson was all too obvious
a fact; yet the Democratic party at that time Page
regarded as the most available instrument for embodying in legislation and practice the new things in which
he most believed. Above all, the Democratic party in
1912 possessed one asset to which the Republicans could
lay no claim—a new man, a new leader, the first statesman who had crossed its threshold since Grover Cleveland.

Like many scholarly Americans, Page had been charmed
by the intellectual brilliancy of Woodrow Wilson. The
utter commonplaceness of much of what passes for political thinking in this country had for years discouraged
him. American political life may have possessed energy,
character, even greatness; but it was certainly lacking in
distinction. It was this new quality that Wilson
brought, and it was this that attracted thousands of
cultivated Americans to his standard, irrespective of
party. The man was an original thinker; he exercised the
priceless possession of literary style. He entertained;
he did not weary; even his temperamental deficiencies,
which were apparent to many observers in 1912, had
at least the advantage that attaches to the interesting and
the unusual.

What Page and thousands of other public-spirited men
saw in Wilson was a leader of fine intellectual gifts who
was prepared to devote his splendid energies to making

life more attractive and profitable to the "Forgotten Man." Here was the opportunity then, to embody in one imaginative statesman all the interest which for a generation had been accumulating in favour of the democratic revival. At any rate, after thirty years of Republican half-success and half-failure, here was the chance for a new deal. Amid a mob of shopworn public men, here was one who had at least the charm of novelty.

Page had known Mr. Wilson for thirty years, and all this time the Princeton scholar had seemed to him to be one of the most helpful influences at work in the United States. As already noted Page had met the future President when he was serving a journalistic apprenticeship in Atlanta, Georgia. Wilson was then spending his days in a dingy law office and was putting to good use the time consumed in waiting for the clients who never came by writing that famous book on "Congressional Government" which first lifted his name out of obscurity. This work, the product of a man of twenty-nine, was perhaps the first searching examination to which the American Congressional system had ever been subjected. It brought Wilson a professorship at the newly established Bryn Mawr College and drew to him other growing minds like Page's. "Watch that man!" was Page's admonition to his friends. Wilson then went into academic work and Page plunged into the exactions of daily and periodical journalism, but Page's papers show that the two men had kept in touch with each other during the succeeding thirty years. These papers include a collection of letters from Woodrow Wilson, the earliest of which is dated October 30, 1885, when the future President was beginning his career at Bryn Mawr. He was eager to come to New York, Wilson said, and discuss with Page "half a hundred

topics" suggested by "Congressional Government." The
atmosphere at Bryn Mawr was evidently not stimulating.
"Such a talk would give me a chance to let off some of the
enthusiasm I am just now painfully stirring up in enforced
silence." The *Forum* and the *Atlantic Monthly*, when
Page was editor, showed many traces of his interest in
Wilson, who was one of his most frequent contributors.
When Wilson became President of Princeton, he occasionally called upon his old *Atlantic* friend for advice. He
writes to Page on various matters—to ask for suggestions
about filling a professorship or a lectureship; and there
are also references to the difficulties Wilson is having with
the Princeton trustees.

Page's letters also portray the new hopes with which
Wilson inspired him. One of his best loved correspondents was Henry Wallace, editor of *Wallace's Farmer*, a
homely and genial Rooseveltian. Page was one of those
who immensely admired Roosevelt's career; but he regarded him as a man who had finished his work, at least
in domestic affairs, and whose great claim upon posterity
would be as the stimulator of the American conscience.
"I see you are coming around to Wilson," Page writes,
"and in pretty rapid fashion. I assure you that that is
the solution of the problem. I have known him since we
were boys, and I have been studying him lately with a
great deal of care. I haven't any doubt but that is the
way out. The old labels 'Democrat' and 'Republican'
have ceased to have any meaning, not only in my mind
and in yours, but I think in the minds of nearly all the
people. Don't you feel that way?"

The campaign of 1912 was approaching its end when
this letter was written; and no proceeding in American
politics had so aroused Page's energies. He had himself
played a part in Wilson's nomination. He was one of the

first to urge the Princeton President to seize the great opportunity that was rising before him.   These suggestions were coming from many sources in the summer of 1910; Mr. Wilson was about to retire from the Presidency of Princeton; the movement had started to make him Governor of New Jersey, and it was well understood that this was merely intended as the first step to the White House. But Mr. Wilson was himself undecided; to escape the excitement of the moment he had retired to a country house at Lyme, Connecticut.   In this place, in response to a letter, Page now sought him out.   His visit was a plea that Mr. Wilson should accept his proffered fate; the Governorship of New Jersey, then the Presidency, and the opportunity to promote the causes in which both men believed.

"But do you think I can do it, Page?" asked the hesitating Wilson.

"I am sure you can": and then Page again, with his customary gusto, launched into his persuasive argument. His host at one moment would assent; at another present the difficulties; it was apparent that he was having trouble in reaching a decision.   To what extent Page's conversation converted him the record does not disclose; it is apparent, however, that when, in the next two years, difficulties came, his mind seemed naturally to turn in Page's direction.   Especially noticeable is it that he appeals to Page for help against his fool friends.   An indiscreet person in New Jersey is booming Mr. Wilson for the Presidency; the activity of such a man inevitably brings ridicule upon the object of his attention; cannot Page find some kindly way of calling him off?   Mr. Wilson asks Page's advice about a campaign manager, and incidentally expresses his own aversion to a man of "large calibre" for this engagement.   There were occasional conferences with Mr. Wilson on his Presidential prospects, one of which took place at Page's New York apartment. Page was also the man who brought Mr. Wilson and Colonel House together; this had the immediate result of placing the important state of Texas on the Wilson side, and, as its ultimate consequence, brought about one of the most important associations in the history of American politics. Page had known Colonel House for many years and was the advocate who convinced the sagacious Texan that Woodrow Wilson was the man. Wilson also acquired the habit of referring to Page men who offered themselves to him as volunteer workers in his cause. "Go and see Walter Page" was his usual answer to this kind of an approach. But Page was not a collector of delegates to nominating conventions; not his the art of manipulating these assemblages in the interest of a favoured man; yet his services to the Wilson cause, while less demonstrative, were almost as practical. His talent lay in exposition; and he now took upon himself the task of spreading Wilson's fame. In his own magazine and in books published by his firm, in letters to friends, in personal conferences, he set forth Wilson's achievements. Page also persuaded Wilson to make his famous speechmaking trip through the Western States in 1911 and this was perhaps his largest definite contribution to the Wilson campaign. It was in the course of this historic pilgrimage that the American masses obtained their first view of a previously too-much hidden figure.

On election day Page wrote the President-elect a letter of congratulation which contains one item of the greatest interest. When the time came for the new President to deliver his first message to Congress, he surprised the country by abandoning the usual practice of sending a long written communication to be droned out by a reading clerk to a yawning company of legislators. He appeared in person and read the document himself. As President Harding has followed his example it seems likely that this innovation, which certainly represents a great improvement over the old routine, has become the established custom. The origin of the idea therefore has historic value.

To Woodrow Wilson

Garden City, N. Y.
Election Day, 1912. [Nov. 5]

My dear Mr. President-elect:

Before going into town to hear the returns, I write you my congratulations. Even if you were defeated, I should still congratulate you on putting a Presidential campaign on a higher level than it has ever before reached since Washington's time. Your grip became firmer and your sweep wider every week. It was inspiring to watch the unfolding of the deep meaning of it and to see the people's grasp of the main idea. It was fairly, highly, freely, won, and now we enter the Era of Great Opportunity. It is hard to measure the extent or the thrill of the new interest in public affairs and the new hope that you have aroused in thousands of men who were becoming hopeless under the long-drawn-out reign of privilege.

To the big burden of suggestions that you are receiving, may I add these small ones?

1. Call Congress in extra session mainly to revise the tariff and incidentally to prepare the way for rural credit societies.

Mr. Taft set the stage admirably in 1909 when he promptly called an extra session; but then he let the villain run the play. To get the main job in hand at once will be both dramatic and effective and it will save time. Moreover, it will give you this great tactical advantage—you can the better keep in line those who have debts or doubts before you have answered their importunities for offices and for favours.

The time is come when the land must be developed by the new agriculture and farming made a business. This calls for money. Every acre will repay a reasonable loan on long time at a fair interest rate, and group-borrowing develops the men quite as much as the men will develop the soil. It saved the German Empire and is remaking Italy. And this is the proper use of much of the money that now flows into the reach of the credit barons. This building up of farm life will restore the equilibrium of our civilization and, besides, will prove to be one half the solution of our currency and credit problem. . . .

2. Set your trusted friends immediately to work, every man in the field he knows best, to prepare briefs for you on such great subjects and departments as the Currency, the Post Office, Conservation, Rural Credit, the Agricultural Department, which has the most direct power for good to the most people—to make our farmers as independent as Denmark's and to give our best country folk the dignity of the old-time English gentleman —this expert, independent information to compare with your own knowledge and with official reports.

3. The President reads (or speaks) his Inaugural to the people. Why not go back to the old custom of himself delivering his Messages to Congress? Would that not restore a feeling of comradeship in responsibility and make the Legislative branch feel nearer to the Executive? Every President of our time has sooner or later got away with Congress.

I cannot keep from saying what a new thrill of hope and tingle of expectancy I feel—as of a great event about to happen for our country and for the restoration of popular government; for you will keep your rudder true.

Most heartily yours,

WALTER H. PAGE.

To Governor Wilson,
Princeton, N. J.

Page was one of the first of Mr. Wilson's friends to discuss with the President-elect the new legislative programme. The memorandum which he made of this interview shows how little any one, in 1912, appreciated the tremendous problems that Mr. Wilson would have to face. Only domestic matters then seemed to have the slightest importance. Especially significant is the fact that even at this early date, Page was chiefly impressed by Mr. Wilson's "loneliness."

Memorandum dated November 15, 1912

To use the Government, especially the Department of Agriculture and the Bureau of Education, to help actively in the restoration of country life—that's the great chance for Woodrow Wilson, ten days ago elected President. Precisely how well he understands this chance, how well, for example, he understands the grave difference between the Knapp Demonstration method of teaching farmers and the usual Agricultural College method of lecturing to them, and what he knows about the rising movement for country schools of the right sort, and agricultural credit societies—how all this great constructive problem of Country Life lies in his mind, who knows? I do not. If I do not know, who does know? The political managers who have surrounded him these six months have now done their task. *They* know nothing of this Big Chance and Great Outlook. And for the moment they have left him alone. In two days he will go to Bermuda for a month to rest and to meditate. He ought to meditate on this Constructive programme. It seemed my duty to go and tell him about it. I asked for an interview and he telegraphed to go to-day at five o'clock.

Arthur and I drove in the car and reached Princeton just before five—a beautiful drive of something less than four hours from New York. Presently we arrived at the Wilson house.

"The Governor is engaged," I was informed by the man who opened the door. "He can see nobody. He is going away to-morrow."

"I have an appointment with him," said I, and I gave him my card.

"I know he can't see anybody."

"Will you send my card in?"

We waited at the door till the maid took it in and returned to say the Governor would presently come down.

The reception room had a desk in the corner, and on a row of chairs across the whole side of the room were piles of unopened letters. It is a plain, modestly but decently furnished room, such as you would expect to find in the modest house of a professor at Princeton. During his presidency of the college, he had lived in the President's house in the college yard. This was his own house of his professorial days.

"Hello, Page, come out here: I am glad to see you." There he stood in a door at the back of the room, which led to his library and work room. "Come back here."

"In the best of all possible worlds, the right thing does sometimes happen," said I.

"Yes."

"And a great opportunity."

He smiled and was cordial and said some pleasant words. But he was weary. "I have cobwebs in my head." He was not depressed but oppressed—rather shy, I thought, and I should say rather lonely. The campaign noise and the little campaigners were hushed and gone. There were no men of companionable size about him, and the Great Task lay before him. The Democratic party has not brought forward large men in public life during its long term of exclusion from the Government; and the newly elected President has had few opportunities and a very short time to make acquaintances of a continental kind. This little college town, this little hitherto corrupt state, are both small.

I went at my business without delay. The big country-life idea, the working of great economic forces to put its vitalization within sight, the coming equilibrium by the restoration of country life—all coincident with his coming into the Presidency. His Administration must fall in with it, guide it, further it. The chief instruments are the Agricultural Department, the Bureau of Education, and the power of the President himself to bring about Rural Credit Societies and similar organized helps. He quickly saw the difference between Demonstration Work by the Agricultural Department and the plan to vote large sums to agricultural colleges and to the states to build up schools.

"Who is the best man for Secretary of Agriculture?"

I ought to have known, but I didn't. For who is?

"May I look about and answer your question later?"

"Yes, I will thank you."

"I wish to find the very best men for my Cabinet, regardless of consequences. I do not forget the party as an instrument of government, and I do not wish to do violence to it. But I must have the best men in the

Nation "—with a very solemn tone as he sat bolt upright, with a stern look on his face, and a lonely look.

I told him my idea of the country school that must be and talked of the Bureau of Education. He saw quickly and assented to all my propositions.

And then we talked somewhat more conservatively of Conservation, about which he knows less.

I asked if he would care to have me make briefs about the Agricultural Department, the Bureau of Education, the Rural Credit Societies, and Conservation. "I shall be very grateful, if it be not too great a sacrifice."

I had gained that permission, which (if he respect my opinion) ought to guide him somewhat toward a real understanding of how the Government may help toward our Great Constructive Problem.

I gained also the impression that he has no sympathy with the idea of giving government grants to schools and agricultural colleges—a very distinct impression.

I had been with him an hour and had talked (I fear) too much. But he seemed hearty in his thanks. He came to the front door with me, insisted on helping me on with my coat, envied me the motor-car drive in the night back to New York, spoke to eight or ten reporters who had crowded into the hall for their interview—a most undignified method, it seemed to me, for a President-elect to reach the public; I stepped out on the muddy street, and, as I walked to the Inn, I had the feeling of the man's oppressive loneliness as he faced his great task. There is no pomp of circumstance, nor hardly dignity in this setting, except the dignity of his seriousness and his loneliness.

There was a general expectation that Page would become a member of President Wilson's Cabinet, and the place for which he seemed particularly qualified was the Secretaryship of Agriculture. The smoke of battle had hardly passed away, therefore, when Page's admirers began bringing pressure to bear upon the President-elect. There was probably no man in the United States who had such completely developed views about this Department as Page; and it is not improbable that, had circumstances combined to offer him this position, he would have accepted it. But fate in matters of this sort is sometimes kinder than a man's friends. Page had a great horror of anything which suggested office-seeking, and the campaign which now was started in his interest greatly embarrassed him. He wrote Mr. Wilson, disclaiming all responsibility and begging him to ignore these misguided efforts. As the best way of checking the movement, Page now definitely answered Mr. Wilson's question: Who was the best man for the Agricultural Department? It is interesting to note that the candidate whom Page nominated in this letter—a man who had been his friend for many years and an associate on the Southern Education Board—was the man whom Mr. Wilson chose.

To Woodrow Wilson

Garden City, N. Y.
November 27, 1912.

MY DEAR WILSON:

I send you (wrongly, perhaps, when you are trying to rest) the shortest statement that I could make about the demonstration field-work of the Department of Agriculture. This is the best tool yet invented to shape country life. Other (and shorter) briefs will be ready in a little while.

You asked me who I thought was the best man for Secre-

tary of Agriculture.   Houston,[1] I should say, of the men
that I know.   You will find my estimate of him in the
little packet of memoranda.   Van Hise[2] may be as good or
even better if he be young in mind and adaptable enough.
But he seems to me a man who may already have done
his big job.

I answer the other questions you asked at Princeton
and I have taken the liberty to send some memoranda
about a few other men—on the theory that every friend
of yours ought now to tell you with the utmost frankness
about the men he knows, of whom you may be thinking.

The building up of the countryman is the big constructive job of our time.   When the countryman comes
to his own, the town man will no longer be able to tax,
and to concentrate power, and to bully the world.

Very heartily yours,

WALTER H. PAGE.

To Henry Wallace

Garden City, N. Y.

11 March, 1913.

MY DEAR UNCLE HENRY:

What a letter yours is!   By George! we must get on the
job, you and I, of steering the world—get on it a little
more actively.   Else it may run amuck.   We have
frightful responsibilities in this matter.   The subject
weighs the more deeply and heavily on me because I am
just back from a month's vacation in North Carolina,
where I am going to build me a winter and old-age bunga-
low.   No; you would be disappointed if you went out of

---

[1]Mr. David F. Houston, ex-President of the University of Texas, and in 1912
Chancellor of the Washington University of St. Louis.

[2]Charles R. Van Hise, President of the University of Wisconsin.

your way to see my boys. Moreover, they are now
merely clearing land. They sold out the farm they put
in shape, after two years' work, for just ten times what
it had cost, and they are now starting another one *de
novo*. About a year hence, they'll have something to
show. And next winter, when my house is built down
there, I want you to come and see me and see that country. I'll show you one of the most remarkable farmers'
clubs you ever saw and many other interesting things as
well—many, very many. I'm getting into this farm
business in dead earnest. That's the dickens of it: how
can I do my share in our partnership to run the universe
if I give my time to cotton-growing problems? It's a
tangled world.

Well, bless your soul! You and the younger Wallaces
(my regards to every one of them) and Poe[1]—you are all
very kind to think of me for that difficult place—too difficult by far, for me. Besides, it would have cost me my
life. If I were to go into public life, I should have had
to sell my whole interest here. This would have meant
that I could never make another dollar. More than that,
I'd have thrown away a trade that I've learned and gone
at another one that I know little about—a bad change,
surely. So, you see, there never was anything serious
in this either in my mind or in the President's. Arthur
hit it off right one day when somebody asked him:

"Is your father going to take the Secretaryship of
Agriculture?"

He replied: "Not seriously."

Besides, the President didn't ask me! He knew too
much for that.

But he did ask me who would be a good man and I
said "Houston." You are not quite fair to him in your

---

[1]Clarence Poe, editor of *The Progressive Farmer*.

Charles D. McIver of Greensboro, North Carolina, a
leader in the cause of Southern Education

Woodrow Wilson in 1912

editorial. He does know—knows much and well and is the strongest man in the Cabinet—in promise. The farmers don't yet know him: that's the only trouble. Give him a chance.

I've "put it up" to the new President and to the new Secretary to get on the job immediately of *organizing country life.* I've drawn up a scheme (a darned good one, too) which they have. I have good hope that they'll get to it soon and to the thing that we have all been working toward. I'm very hopeful about this. I told them both last week to get their minds on this before the wolves devour them. Don't you think it better to work with the Government and to try to steer it right than to go off organizing other agencies?

God pity our new masters! The President is all right. He's sound, earnest, courageous. But his party! I still have some muscular strength. In certain remote regions they still break stones in the road by hand. Now I'll break stones before I'd have a job at Washington now. I spent four days with them last week—the new crowd. They'll try their best. I think they'll succeed. But, if they do succeed and survive, they'll come out of the' scrimmage bleeding and torn. We've got to stand off and run 'em, Uncle Henry. That's the only hope I see for the country. Don't damn Houston, then, beforehand. He's a real man. Let's get on the job and tell 'em how.

Now, when you come East, come before you need to get any of your meetings and strike a bee-line for Garden City; and don't be in a hurry when you get here. If a Presbyterian meeting be necessary for your happiness, I'll drum up one on the Island for you. And, of course, you must come to my house and pack up right and get your legs steady sometime before you sail—you and Mrs. Wallace: will she not go with you?

In the meantime, don't be disgruntled. We can steer the old world right, if you'll just keep your shoulder to the wheel. We'll work it all out here in the summer and verify it all (including your job of setting the effete kingdoms of Europe all right)—we'll verify it all next winter down in North Carolina. I think things have got such a start that they'll keep going in some fashion, till we check up the several items, political, ethical, agricultural, journalistic, and international. God bless us all!

Most heartily always yours,

WALTER H. PAGE.

Though Mr. Wilson did not offer Page the Agricultural Department, he much desired to have him in his Cabinet, and had already decided upon him for a post which the new President probably regarded as more important— the Interior. The narrow margin with which Page escaped this responsibility illustrates again the slender threads upon which history is constructed. The episode is also not without its humorous side. For there was only one reason why Page did not enter the Cabinet as Secretary of the Interior; and that is revealed in the above letter to "Uncle Henry"; he was so busy planning his new house in the sandhills of North Carolina that, while cabinets were being formed and great decisions taken, he was absent from New York. A short time before the inauguration, Mr. Wilson asked Colonel House to arrange a meeting with Page in the latter's apartment. Mr. Wilson wished to see him on a Saturday; the purpose was to offer him the Secretaryship of the Interior. Colonel House called up Page's office at Garden City and was informed that he was in North Carolina. Colonel House then telegraphed asking Page to start north immediately, and suggesting the succeeding Monday as a good time for the interview. A reply was at once received from Page that he was on his way.

Meanwhile certain of Mr. Wilson's advisers had heard of the plan and were raising objections. Page was a Southerner; the Interior Department has supervision over the pension bureau, with its hundreds of thousands of Civil War veterans as pensioners; moreover, Page was an outspoken enemy of the whole pension system and had led several "campaigns" against it. The appointment would never do! Mr. Wilson himself was persuaded that it would be a mistake.

"But what are we going to do about Page?" asked Colonel House. "I have summoned him from North Carolina on important business. What excuse shall I give for bringing him way up here?"

But the President-elect was equal to the emergency.

"Here's the cabinet list," he drily replied. "Show it to Page. Tell him these are the people I have about decided to appoint and ask him what he thinks of them. Then he will assume that we summoned him to get his advice."

When Page made his appearance, therefore, Colonel House gave him the list of names and solemnly asked him what he thought of them. The first name that attracted Page's attention was that of Josephus Daniels, as Secretary of the Navy. Page at once expressed his energetic dissent.

"Why, don't you think he is Cabinet timber?" asked Colonel House.

"Timber!" Page fairly shouted. "He isn't a splinter! Have you got a time table? When does the next train leave for Princeton?"

In a couple of hours Page was sitting with Mr. Wilson,

earnestly protesting against Mr. Daniels's appointment. But Mr. Wilson said that he had already offered Mr. Daniels the place.

II

About the time of Wilson's election a great calamity befell one of Page's dearest friends. Dr. Edwin A. Alderman, the President of the University of Virginia, one of the pioneer educational forces in the Southern States, and for years an associate of Page on the General Education Board, was stricken with tuberculosis. He was taken to Saranac, and here a patient course of treatment happily restored him to health. One of the dreariest aspects of such an experience is its tediousness and loneliness. Yet the maintenance of one's good spirits and optimism is an essential part of the treatment. And it was in this work that Page now proved an indispensable aid to the medical men. As soon as Dr. Alderman found himself stretched out, a weak and isolated figure, cut off from those activities and interests which had been his inspiration for forty years, with no companions except his own thoughts and a few sufferers like himself, letters began to arrive with weekly regularity from the man whom he always refers to as "dear old Page." The gayety and optimism of these letters, the lively comments which they passed upon men and things, and their wholesome and genial philosophy, were largely instrumental, Dr. Alderman has always believed, in his recovery. Their effect was so instant and beneficial that the physicians asked to have them read to the other patients, who also derived abounding comfort and joy from them. The whole episode was one of the most beautiful in Page's life, and brings out again that gift for friendship which was perhaps his finest quality. For this reason it is a calamity that most of these letters have not been preserved. The few that have survived are interesting not only in themselves; they reveal Page's innermost thoughts on the subject of Woodrow Wilson. That he admired the new President is evident, yet these letters make it clear that, even in 1912 and 1913, there was something about Mr. Wilson that caused him to hesitate, to entertain doubts, to wonder how, after all, the experiment was to end.

To Edwin A. Alderman

Garden City, L. I.
December 31, 1912.

MY DEAR ED ALDERMAN:

I have a new amusement, a new excitement, a new study, as you have and as we all have who really believe in democracy—a new study, a new hope, and sometimes a new fear; and its name is Wilson. I have for many years regarded myself as an interested, but always a somewhat detached, outsider, believing that the demo-cratic idea was real and safe and lifting, if we could ever get it put into action, contenting myself ever with such patches of it as time and accident and occasion now and then sewed on our gilded or tattered garments. But now it is come—the real thing; at any rate a man somewhat like us, whose thought and aim and dream are our thought and aim and dream. That's enormously exciting! I didn't suppose I'd ever become so interested in a general proposition or in a governmental hope.

Will he do it? Can he do it? Can anybody do it? How can we help him do it? Now that the task is on him, does he really understand? Do I understand him and he me? There's a certain unreality about it.

The man himself—I find that nobody quite knows him

now. Alas! I wonder if he quite knows himself. Temperamentally very shy, having lived too much alone and far too much with women (how I wish two of his daughters were sons!) this Big Thing having descended on him before he knew or was quite prepared for it, thrust into a whirl of self-seeking men even while he is trying to think out the theory of the duties that press, knowing the necessity of silence, surrounded by small people—well, I made up my mind that his real friends owed it to him and to what we all hope for, to break over his reserve and to volunteer help. He asks for conferences with official folk —only, I think. So I began to write memoranda about those subjects of government about which I know something and have opinions and about men who are or who may be related to them. It has been great sport to set down in words without any reserve precisely what you think. It is imprudent, of course, as most things worth doing are. But what have I to lose, I who have my life now planned and laid out and have got far beyond the reach of gratitude or hatred or praise or blame or fear of any man? I sent him some such memoranda. Here came forthwith a note of almost abject thanks. I sent more. Again, such a note—written in his own hand. Yet not a word of what he thinks. The Sphinx was garrulous in comparison. Then here comes a mob of my good friends crying for office for me. So I sent a ten-line note, by the hand of my secretary, saying that this should not disturb my perfect frankness nor (I knew it would not) his confidence. Again, a note in his own hand, of perfect understanding and with the very glow of gratitude. And he talks—generalities to the public. Perhaps that's all he can talk now. Wise? Yes. But does he know the men about him? Does he really know men? Nobody knows. Thus 'twixt fear and hope I see—suspense. I'll swear I can't doubt, I can't believe. Whether it is going to work out or not—whether he or anybody can work it out of the haze of theory—nobody knows; and nobody's speculation is better than mine and mine is worthless.

This is the game, this is the excitement, this is the doubthope and the hopedoubt. I send this word about it to you (I could and would to nobody else: you're snow-bound, you see, and don't write much and don't see many people: restrain your natural loquacity!) But for the love of heaven tell me if you see any way *very clearly*. It's a kind of misty dream to me.

I ask myself why should I concern myself about it? Of course the answer's easy and I think creditable: I do profoundly hold this democratic faith and believe that it can be worked into action among men; and it may be I shall yet see it done. That's the secret of my interest. But when this awful office descends on a man, it oppresses him, changes him, you are not quite so sure of him, you doubt whether he knows himself or you in the old way.

And I find among men the very crudest ideas of government or of democracy. They have not thought the thing out. They hold no ordered creed of human organization or advancement. They leave all to chance and think, when they think at all, that chance determines it. And yet the Great Hope persists, and I think I have grown an inch by it.

I wonder how it seems, looked at from the cold mountains of Lake Saranac?

It's the end of the year. Mrs. Page and I (alone!) have been talking of democracy, of these very things I've written. The bell-ringing and the dancing and the feasting are not, on this particular year, to our liking.

We see all our children gone—half of them to nests of their own building, the rest on errands of their own pleasure, and we are left, young yet, but the main job of life behind us! We're going down to a cottage in southern North Carolina (with our own cook and motor car, praise God!) for February, still further to think this thing out and incidentally to build us a library, in which we'll live when we can. That, for convention's sake, we call a Vacation.

Your brave note came to-day. Of course, you'll "get" 'em—those small enemies. The gain of twelve pounds tells the story. The danger is, your season of philosophy and reverie will be too soon ended. Don't fret; the work and the friends will be here when you come down. There's many a long day ahead; and there may not be so many seasons of rest and meditation. You are the only man I know who has time enough to think out a clear answer to this: "What ought to be done with Bryan?" What *can* be done with Bryan? When you find the answer, telegraph it to me.

I've a book or two more to send you. If they interest you, praise the gods. If they bore you, fling 'em in the snow and think no worse of me. You can't tell what a given book may be worth to a given man in an unknown mood. They've become such a commodity to me that I thank my stars for a month away from them when I may come at 'em at a different angle and really need a few old ones—Wordsworth, for instance. When you get old enough, you'll wake up some day with the feeling that the world is much more beautiful than it was when you were young, that a landscape has a closer meaning, that the sky is more companionable, that outdoor colour and motion are more splendidly audacious and beautifully rhythmical than you had ever thought. That's true. The gently snow-clad little pines out my window are more to me than the whole Taft Administration. They'll soon be better than the year's dividends. And the few great craftsmen in words who can confirm this feeling—they are the masters you become grateful for. Then the sordidness of the world lies far beneath you and your great democracy is truly come—the democracy of Nature. To be akin to a tree, in this sense, is as good as to be akin to a man. I have a grove of little long-leaf pines down in the old country and I know they'll have some consciousness of me after all men have forgotten me: I've saved 'em, and they'll sing a century of gratitude if I can keep 'em saved. Joe Holmes gave me a dissertation on them the other day. He was down there "on a little Sunday jaunt" of forty miles—the best legs and the best brain that ever worked together in one anatomy.

A conquering New Year—that's what you'll find, begun before this reaches you, carrying all good wishes from

Yours affectionately,
W. H. P.

To Edwin A. Alderman

Garden City, New York,
January 26, 1913.

MY DEAR ED ALDERMAN:

This has been "Board"[1] week, as you know. The men came from all quarters of the land, and we had a good time. New work is opening; old work is going well; the fellowship ran in good tide—except that everybody asked everybody else: "What do you know about Alderman?" Everybody who had late news of you gave

---

[1]The reference is to the meeting of the Southern and the General Education Boards.

a good report. The Southern Board formally passed a resolution to send affectionate greetings to you and high hope and expectation, and I was commissioned to frame the message. This is it. I shall write no formal resolution, for that wasn't the spirit of it. The fellows all asked me, singly and collectively, to send their love. And we don't put that sort of a message under *whereases* and *wherefores*. There they were, every one of them, except Peabody and Bowie. Mr. Ogden in particular was anxious for his emphatic remembrance and good wishes to go. The dear old man is fast passing into the last stage of his illness and he knows it and he soon expects the end, in a mood as brave and as game as he ever was. I am sorry to tell you he suffers a good deal of pain.

What a fine thing to look back over—this Southern Board's work! Here was a fine, zealous merchant twenty years ago, then fifty-seven years old, who saw this big job as a modest layman. If he had known more about "Education" or more about "the South, bygawd, sir!" he'd never have had the courage to tackle the job. But with the bravery of ignorance, he turned out to be the wisest man on that task in our generation. He has united every real, good force, and he showed what can be done in a democracy even by one zealous man. I've sometimes thought that this is possibly the wisest single piece of work that I have ever seen done—*wisest*, not smartest. I don't know what can be done when he's gone. His phase of it is really done. But, if another real leader arise, there will doubtless be another phase.

The General Board doesn't find much more college-endowing to do. We made only one or two gifts. But we are trying to get the country school task rightly focussed. We haven't done it yet; but we will. Buttrick and Rose will work it out. I wish to God I could throw down my practical job and go at it with 'em. Darned if I couldn't get it going! though *I* say it, as shouldn't. And we are going pretty soon to begin with the medical colleges; that, I think, is good—very.

But the most efficient workmanlike piece of organization that my mortal eyes have ever seen is Rose's hookworm work. We're going soon to organize country life in a sanitary way, the county health officer being the biggest man on the horizon. Stiles has moved his marine hospital and his staff to Wilmington, North Carolina, and he and the local health men are quietly going to make New Hanover the model county for sanitary condition and efficiency. You'll know what a vast revolution that denotes!—And Congress seems likely to charter the big Rockefeller Foundation, which will at once make five millions available for chasing the hookworm off the face of the earth. Rose will spread himself over Honduras, etc., etc., and China, and India! This does literally beat the devil; for, if the hookworm isn't the devil, what is?

I'm going to farming. I've two brothers and two sons, all young and strong, who believe in the game. We have land without end, thousands of acres; engines to pull stumps, to plough, to plant, to reap. The nigger go hang! A white boy with an engine can outdo a dozen of 'em. Cotton and corn for staple crops; peaches, figs, scuppernongs, vegetables, melons for incidental crops; God's good air in North Carolina; good roads, too—why, man, Moore County has authorized the laying out of a strip of land along all highways to be planted in shrubbery and fruit trees and kept as a park, so that you will motor for 100 miles through odorous bloom in spring!—I mean I am going down there to-morrow for a month, one day for golf at Pinehurst, the next day for clearing land with an oil locomotive, ripping up stumps! Every day for life out-of-doors and every night, too. I'm going to grow dasheens. You know what a dasheen is? It's a Trinidad potato, which keeps and tastes like a sweet potato stuffed with chestnuts. There are lots of things to learn in this world.

God bless us all, old man. It's a pretty good world, whether seen from the petty excitements of reforming the world and dreaming of a diseaseless earth in New York, or from the stump-pulling recreation of a North Carolina wilderness.

Health be with you!

W. H. P.

To Edwin A. Alderman

Garden City, L. I.
March 10, 1913.

MY DEAR ED ALDERMAN:

I'm home from a month of perfect climate in the sandhills of North Carolina, where I am preparing a farm and building a home at least for winter use; and I had the most instructive and interesting month of my life there. I believe I see, even in my life-time, the coming of a kind of man and a kind of life that shall come pretty near to being the model American citizen and the model American way to live. Half of it is climate; a fourth of it occupation; the other fourth, companionship. And the climate (with what it does) is three fourths companionship.

Then I came to Washington and saw Wilson made President—a very impressive experience indeed. The future —God knows; but I believe in Wilson very thoroughly. Men fool him yet. Men fool us all. He has already made some mistakes. But he's sound. And, if we have moral courage enough to beat back the grafters, little and big—I mean if we, the people, will vote two years and four years hence, to keep them back, I think that we shall now really work toward a democratic government. I have a stronger confidence in government now as an instrument of human progress than I have ever had before. And I find it an exhilarating and exciting experience.

I have seen many of your good friends in North Carolina, Virginia, and Washington. How we all do love you, old man! Don't forget that, in your successful fight. And, with my affectionate greetings to Mrs. Alderman, ask her to send me the news of your progress.

Always affectionately yours,
WALTER H. PAGE.

To Edwin A. Alderman

On the *Baltic*, New York to Liverpool,
May 19, 1913.

MY DEAR ED ALDERMAN:

It was the best kind of news I heard of you during my last weeks at home—every day of which I wished to go to Briarcliff to see you. At a distance, it seems absurd to say that it was impossible to go. But it was. I set down five different days in my calendar for this use; and somehow every one of them was taken. Two were taken by unexpected calls to Washington. Another was taken by my partners who arranged a little good-bye dinner. Another was taken by the British Ambassador—and so on. Absurd—of course it was absurd, and I feel now as if it approached the criminal. But every stolen day I said, "Well, I'll find another." But another never came.

But good news of you came by many hands and mouths. My congratulations, my cheers, my love, old man. Now when you do take up work again, don't take up all the work. Show the fine virtue called self-restraint. We work too much and too hard and do too many things even when we are well. There are three titled Englishmen who sit at the table with me on this ship—one a former Lord Mayor of London, another a peer, and the third an M. P. Damn their self-sufficiencies! They do excite my envy. *They* don't shoulder the work of the world: they shoulder the world and leave the work to be done by somebody else. Three days' stories and political discussion with them have made me wonder why the devil I've been so industrious all my life. They know more than I know; they are richer than I am; they have been about the world more than I have; they are far more influential than I am; and yet one of them asked me to-day if George Washington was a born American! I said to him, "Where the devil do you suppose he came from—Hades?" And he laughed at himself as heartily as the rest of us laughed at him, and didn't care a hang!

If that's British, I've a mind to become British; and, the point is, you must, too. Work is a curse. There was some truth in that old doctrine. At any rate a little of it must henceforth go a long way with you.

A sermon? Yes. But, since it's a good one, I know you'll forgive me; for it is preached in love, my dear boy, and accompanied with the hearty and insistent hope that you'll write to me.

Affectionately,

WALTER PAGE.

This last letter apparently anticipates the story. A few weeks before it was written President Wilson had succeeded in carrying out his determination to make Page an important part of his Administration. One morning Page's telephone rang and Colonel House's well-known and well-modulated voice came over the wire.

"Good morning, Your Excellency," was his greeting.

"What the devil are you talking about?" asked Page.

Then Colonel House explained himself. The night before, he said, he had dined at the White House. In a pause of the conversation the President had quietly remarked:

"I've about made up my mind to send Walter Page to England. What do you think of that?"

Colonel House thought very well of it indeed and the result of his conversation was this telephone call, in which he was authorized to offer Page the Ambassadorship to Great Britain.

CHAPTER V

ENGLAND BEFORE THE WAR

THE London Embassy is the greatest diplomatic gift at the disposal of the President, and, in the minds of the American people, it possesses a glamour and an historic importance all its own. Page came to the position, as his predecessors had come, with a sense of awe; the great traditions of the office; the long line of distinguished men, from Thomas Pinckney to Whitelaw Reid, who had filled it; the peculiar delicacy of the problems that then existed between the two countries; the reverent respect which Page had always entertained for English history, English literature, and English public men—all these considerations naturally quickened the new ambassador's imagination and, at the same time, made his arrival in England a rather solemn event. Yet his first days in London had their grotesque side as well. He himself has recorded his impressions, and, since they contain an important lesson for the citizens of the world's richest and most powerful Republic, they should be preserved. When the ambassador of practically any other country reaches London, he finds waiting for him a spacious and beautiful embassy, filled with a large corps of secretaries and servants—everything ready, to the minutest detail, for the beginning of his labours. He simply enters these elaborate state-owned and state-supported quarters and starts work. How differently the mighty United States welcomes its ambassadors let Page's memorandum tell:

The boat touched at Queenstown, and a mass of Irish reporters came aboard and wished to know what I thought of Ireland. Some of them printed the important announcement that I was quite friendly to Ireland! At Liverpool was Mr. Laughlin,[1] Chargé d' Affaires in London since Mr. Reid's death, to meet me, and of course the consul, Mr. Washington. . . . On our arrival in London, Laughlin explained that he had taken quarters for me at the Coburg Hotel, whither we drove, after having fought my way through a mob of reporters at the station. One fellow told me that since I left New York the papers had published a declaration by me that I meant to be very "democratic" and would under no conditions wear "knee breeches"; and he asked me about that report. I was foolish enough to reply that the existence of an ass in the United States ought not necessarily to require the existence of a corresponding ass in London. He printed that! I never knew the origin of this "knee breeches" story.

That residence at the Coburg Hotel for three months was a crowded and uncomfortable nightmare. The indignity and inconvenience—even the humiliation—of an ambassador beginning his career in an hotel, especially during the Court season, and a green ambassador at that! I hope I may not die before our Government does the conventional duty to provide ambassadors' residences.

The next morning I went to the Chancery (123, Victoria Street) and my heart sank. I had never in my life been in an American Embassy. I had had no business with them in Paris or in London on my previous visits. In fact I had never been in any embassy except the British Embassy at Washington. But the moment I

---

[1]Mr. Irwin Laughlin, first secretary of the American Embassy in London.

entered that dark and dingy hall at 123, Victoria Street, between two cheap stores—the same entrance that the dwellers in the cheap flats above used—I knew that Uncle Sam had no fit dwelling there. And the Ambassador's room greatly depressed me—dingy with twenty-nine years of dirt and darkness, and utterly undignified. And the rooms for the secretaries and attachés were the little bedrooms, kitchen, etc., of that cheap flat; that's all it was. For the place we paid $1,500 a year. I did not understand then and I do not understand yet how Lowell, Bayard, Phelps, Hay, Choate, and Reid endured that cheap hole. Of course they stayed there only about an hour a day; but they sometimes saw important people there. And, whether they ever saw anybody there or not, the offices of the United States Government in London ought at least to be as good as a common lawyer's office in a country town in a rural state of our Union. Nobody asked for anything for an embassy: nobody got anything for an embassy. I made up my mind in ten minutes that I'd get out of this place.[1]

At the Coburg Hotel, we were very well situated; but the hotel became intolerably tiresome. Harold Fowler and Frank and I were there until W. A. W. P.[2] and Kitty[3] came (and Frances Clark came with them). Then we were just a little too big a hotel party. Every morning I drove down to the old hole of a Chancery and remained about two hours. There wasn't very much work to do; and my main business was to become acquainted with the work and with people—to find myself with reference to

[1] In about a year Page moved the Chancery to the present satisfactory quarters at No. 4 Grosvenor Gardens.

[2] Mrs. Walter H. Page.

[3] Miss Katharine A. Page, the Ambassador's daughter.

this task, with reference to official life and to London life in general.

Every afternoon people came to the hotel to see me—some to pay their respects and to make life pleasant, some out of mere curiosity, and many for ends of their own. I confess that on many days nightfall found me completely worn out. But the evenings seldom brought a chance to rest. The social season was going at its full gait; and the new ambassador (any new ambassador) would have been invited to many functions. A very few days after my arrival, the Duchess of X invited Frank and me to dinner. The powdered footmen were the chief novelty of the occasion for us. But I was much confused because nobody introduced anybody to anybody else. If a juxtaposition, as at the dinner table, made an introduction imperative, the name of the lady next you was so slurred that you couldn't possibly understand it.

Party succeeded party. I went to them because they gave me a chance to become acquainted with people.

But very early after my arrival, I was of course summoned by the King. I had presented a copy of my credentials to the Foreign Secretary (Sir Edward Grey) and the real credentials—the original in a sealed envelope—I must present to His Majesty. One morning the King's Master of the Ceremonies, Sir Arthur Walsh, came to the hotel with the royal coaches, four or five of them, and the richly caparisoned grooms. The whole staff of the Embassy must go with me. We drove to Buckingham Palace, and, after waiting a few moments, I was ushered into the King's presence. He stood in one of the drawing rooms on the ground floor looking out on the garden. There stood with him in uniform Sir Edward Grey. I entered and bowed. He shook my hand, and I spoke my little piece of three or four sentences.

He replied, welcoming me and immediately proceeded to express his surprise and regret that a great and rich country like the United States had not provided a residence for its ambassadors. "It is not fair to an ambassador," said he; and he spoke most earnestly.

I reminded him that, although the lack of a home was an inconvenience, the trouble or discomfort that fell on an ambassador was not so bad as the wrong impression which I feared was produced about the United States and its Government, and I explained that we had had so many absorbing domestic tasks and, in general, so few absorbing foreign relations, that we had only begun to develop what might be called an international consciousness.

Sir Edward was kind enough the next time I saw him to remark that I did that very well and made a good impression on the King.

I could now begin my ambassadorial career proper— call on the other ambassadors and accept invitations to dinners and the like.

I was told after I came from the King's presence that the Queen would receive me in a few minutes. I was shown upstairs, the door opened, and there in a small drawing room, stood the Queen alone—a pleasant woman, very royal in appearance. The one thing that sticks in my memory out of this first conversation with her Majesty was her remark that she had seen only one man who had been President of the United States—Mr. Roosevelt. She hoped he was well. I felt moved to remark that she was not likely to see many former Presidents because the office was so hard a task that most of them did not long survive.

"I'm hoping that office will not soon kill the King," she said.

In time Page obtained an entirely adequate and dignified house at 6 Grosvenor Square, and soon found that the
American Ambassadorship had compensations which were
hardly suggested by his first glimpse of the lugubrious
Chancery. He brought to this new existence his plastic
and inquisitive mind, and his mighty gusto for the interesting and the unusual; he immensely enjoyed his meetings with the most important representatives of all types
of British life. The period of his arrival marked a crisis in British history; Mr. Lloyd George was supposed to be
taxing the aristocracy out of existence; Mr. Asquith was
accused of plotting the destruction of the House of Lords;
the tide of liberalism, even of radicalism, was running
high, and, in the judgment of the conservative forces,
England was tottering to its fall; the gathering mob was
about to submerge everything that had made it great.
And the Irish question had reached another crisis with
the passage of the Home Rule Bill, which Sir Edward
Carson was preparing to resist with his Irish "volunteers."

All these matters formed the staple of talk at dinner
tables, at country houses and at the clubs; and Page found
constant entertainment in the variegated pageant. There
were important American matters to discuss with the
Foreign Office—more important than any that had arisen
in recent years—particularly Mexico and the Panama
Tolls. Before these questions are considered, however,
it may be profitable to print a selection from the many
letters which Page wrote during his first year, giving his
impressions of this England which he had always loved
and which a closer view made him love and admire still
more. These letters have the advantage of presenting a
frank and yet sympathetic picture of British society and
British life as it was just before the war.

To Frank N. Doubleday

The Coburg Hotel,
Carlos Place, Grosvenor Square,
London, W.

DEAR EFFENDI:[1]

You can't imagine the intensity of the party feeling here. I dined to-night in an old Tory family. They had just had a "division" an hour or two before in the House of Lords on the Home Rule Bill. Six Lords were at the dinner and their wives. One was a Duke, two were Bishops, and the other three were Earls. They expect a general "bust-up." If the King does so and so, off with the King! That's what they fear the Liberals will do. It sounds very silly to me; but you can't exaggerate their fear. The Great Lady, who was our hostess, told me, with tears in her voice, that she had suspended all social relations with the Liberal leaders.

At lunch—just five or six hours before—we were at the Prime Minister's, where the talk was precisely on the other side. Gladstone's granddaughter was there and several members of the Cabinet.

Somehow it reminds me of the tense days of the slavery controversy just before the Civil War.

Yet in the everyday life of the people, you hear nothing about it. It is impossible to believe that the ordinary man cares a fig!

Good-night. You don't care a fig for this. But I'll get time to write you something interesting in a little while.

Yours,

W. H. P.

---

[1] "Effendi" is the name by which Mr. F. N. Doubleday, Page's partner, is known to his intimates. It is obviously suggested by the initials of his name.

To Herbert S. Houston

American Embassy
London
Sunday, 24 Aug., 1913.

DEAR H. S. H.:

. . . You know there's been much discussion of the decadence of the English people. I don't believe a word of it. They have an awful slum, I hear, as everybody knows, and they have an idle class. Worse, from an equal-opportunity point-of-view, they have a very large servant-class, and a large class that depends on the no-bility and the rich. All these are economic and social drawbacks. But they have always had all these—ex-cept that the slum has become larger in modern years. And I don't see or find any reason to believe in the theory of decadence. The world never saw a finer lot of men than the best of their ruling class. You may search the world and you may search history for finer men than Lord Morley, Sir Edward Grey, Mr. Harcourt, and other members of the present Cabinet. And I meet such men everywhere—gently bred, high-minded, physically fit, intellectually cultivated, patriotic. If the devotion to old forms and the inertia which makes any change al-most impossible strike an American as out-of-date, you must remember that in the grand old times of England, they had all these things and had them worse than they are now. I can't see that the race is breaking down or giving out. Consider how their political morals have been pulled up since the days of the rotten boroughs; consider how their court-life is now high and decent, and think what it once was. British trade is larger this year than it ever was, Englishmen are richer then they ever were and more of them are rich. They write and speak and play cricket, and govern, and fight as well as they have ever done—excepting, of course, the writing of Shakespeare.

Another conclusion that is confirmed the more you see of English life is their high art of living. When they make their money, they stop money-making and cultivate their minds and their gardens and entertain their friends and do all the high arts of living—to perfection. Three days ago a retired soldier gave a garden-party in my honour, twenty-five miles out of London. There was his historic house, a part of it 500 years old; there were his ten acres of garden, his lawn, his trees; and they walk with you over it all; they sit out-of-doors; they serve tea; they take life rationally; they talk pleasantly (not jocularly, nor story-telling); they abhor the smart in talk or in conduct; they have gentleness, cultivation, the best manners in the world; and they are genuine. The hostess has me take a basket and go with her while she cuts it full of flowers for us to bring home; and, as we walk, she tells the story of the place. She is a tenant-for-life; it is entailed. Her husband was wounded in South Africa. Her heir is her nephew. The home, of course, will remain in the family forever. No, they don't go to London much in recent years: why should they? But they travel a month or more. They give three big tea-parties—one when the rhododendrons bloom and the others at stated times. They have friends to stay with them half the time, perhaps—sometimes parties of a dozen. England never had a finer lot of folk than these. And you see them everywhere. The art of living sanely they have developed to as high a level, I think, as you will find at any time in any land.

The present political battle is fiercer than you would ever guess. The Lords feel that they are sure to be

robbed: they see the end of the ordered world. Chaos
and confiscation lie before them. Yet that, too, has
nearly always been so. It was so in the Reform Bill days.
Lord Morley said to me the other day that when all the
abolitions had been done, there would be fewer things
abolished than anybody hopes or fears, and that there
would be the same problems in some form for many
generations. I'm beginning to believe that the Englishman has always been afraid of the future—that's what's
keeps him so alert. They say to me: "You have frightful
things happen in the United States—your Governor of
New York,[1] your Thaw case, your corruption, etc., etc.;
and yet you seem sure and tell us that your countrymen
feel sure of the safety of your government." In the
newspaper comments on my Southampton[2] speech the
other day, this same feeling cropped up; the American
Ambassador assures us that the note of hope is the dominant note of the Republic—etc., etc. Yes, they are
dull, *in a way*—not dull, so much as steady; and yet
they have more solid sense than any other people.

It's an interesting study—the most interesting in the
world. The genuineness of the courtesy, the real kindness and the hospitality of the English are beyond praise
and without limit. In this they show a strange contra-
diction to their dickering habits in trade and their "unc-
tuous rectitude" in stealing continents. I know a place
in the world now where they are steadily moving their
boundary line into other people's territory. I guess they
really believe that the earth belongs to them.

Sincerely,
W. H. P.

---

[1] A reference to William Sulzer, Governor of New York, who at this time was
undergoing impeachment.

[2] See Chapter VIII, page 258.

To Arthur W. Page[1]

Gordon Arms Hotel, Elgin, Scotland.
September 6, 1913.

DEAR ARTHUR:

Your mother and Kitty[2] and I are on our way to see Andy.[3] Had you any idea that to motor from London to Skibo means driving more than eight hundred miles? Our speedometer now shows more than seven hundred and we've another day to go—at least one hundred and thirty miles. And we haven't even had a tire accident. We're having a delightful journey—only this country yields neither vegetables nor fruits, and I have to live on oatmeal. They spell it p-o-r-r-i-d-g-e, and they call it pŭruge. But they beat all creation as carnivorous folk. We stayed last night at a beautiful mountain hotel at Braemar (the same town whereat Stevenson wrote "Treasure Island") and they had nine kinds of meat for dinner and eggs in three ways, and no vegetables but potatoes. But this morning we struck the same thin oatbread that you ate at Grandfather Mountain.

I've never understood the Scotch. I think they are, without doubt, the most capable race in the world—away from home. But how they came to be so and how they keep up their character and supremacy and keep breeding true needs explanation. As you come through the country, you see the most monotonous and dingy little houses and thousands of robust children, all dirtier than niggers. In the fertile parts of the country, the fields are beautifully cultivated—for Lord This-and-T'Other who lives in London and comes up here in sum-

[1]The Ambassador's son.

[2]Miss Katharine A. Page.

[3]Mr. Andrew Carnegie.

mer to collect his rents and to shoot. The country people
seem desperately poor. But they don't lose their ro-
bustness. In the solid cities—the solidest you ever saw,
all being of granite—such as Edinburgh and Aberdeen,
where you see the prosperous class, they look the sturdiest
and most independent fellows you ever saw. As they
grow old they all look like blue-bellied Presbyterian
elders. Scotch to the marrow—everybody and everything seem—bare knees alike on the street and in the
hotel with dress coats on, bagpipes—there's no sense in
these things, yet being Scotch they live forever. The
first men I saw early this morning on the street in front
of the hotel were two weather-beaten old chaps, with
gray beards under their chins. "Guddddd Murrrrn-
inggggg, Andy," said one. "Guddddd murrninggggg,
Sandy," said the other; and they trudged on. They'd
dethrone kings before they'd shave differently or drop
their burrs and gutturals or cover their knees or cease
lying about the bagpipe. And you can't get it out of
the blood. Your mother[1] becomes provoked when I say
these things, and I shouldn't wonder if you yourself
resent them and break out quoting Burns. Now the
Highlands can't support a population larger than the
mountain counties of Kentucky. Now your Kentucky
feud is a mere disgrace to civilization. But your High-
land feud is celebrated in song and story. Every clan
keeps itself together to this day by its history and by its
plaid. At a turn in the road in the mountains yesterday,
there stood a statue of Rob Roy painted every stripe to
life. We saw his sword and purse in Sir Walter's house
at Abbotsford. The King himself wore the kilt and one
of the plaids at the last court ball at Buckingham Palace,
and there is a man who writes his name and is called

---

[1]Mrs. Walter H. Page is the daughter of a Scotchman from Ayrshire.

"The Macintosh of Macintosh," and that's a prouder title than the King's. A little handful of sheep-stealing bandits got themselves immortalized and heroized, and they are now all Presbyterian elders. They got *their* church "established" in Scotland, and when the King comes to Scotland, by Jehoshaphat! he is obliged to become a Presbyterian. Yet your Kentucky feudist— poor devil—he comes too late. The Scotchman has pre- empted that particular field of glory. And all such com- parisons make your mother fighting mad. . . .

Affectionately,   W. H. P.

To the President

American Embassy, London.
October 25, 1913.

DEAR MR. PRESIDENT:

I am moved once in a while to write you privately, not about any specific piece of public business, but only, if I can, to transmit something of the atmosphere of the work here. And, since this is meant quite as much for your amusement as for any information it may carry, don't read it "in office hours."

The future of the world belongs to us. A man needs to live here, with two economic eyes in his head, a very little time to become very sure of this. Everybody will see it presently. These English are spending their capital, and it is their capital that continues to give them their vast power. Now what are we going to do with the leadership of the world presently when it clearly falls into our hands?[1] And how can we use the English for the highest uses of democracy?

[1]The astonishing thing about Page's comment on the leadership of the United States—if it would only take this leadership—is that these letters were written in 1913, a year before the outbreak of the war, and eight years before the Washing- ton Disarmament Conference of 1921–22.

You see their fear of an on-sweeping democracy in their social treatment of party opponents. A Tory lady told me with tears that she could no longer invite her Liberal friends to her house: "I have lost them—they are robbing us, you know." I made the mistake of saying a word in praise of Sir Edward Grey to a duke. "Yes, yes, no doubt an able man; but you must understand, sir, that I don't train with that gang." A bishop explained to me at elaborate length why the very monarchy is doomed unless something befalls Lloyd George and his programme. Every dinner party is made up with strict reference to the party politics of the guests. Sometimes you imagine you see something like civil war; and money is flowing out of the Kingdom into Canada in the greatest volume ever known and I am told that a number of old families are investing their fortunes in African lands.

These and such things are, of course, mere chips which show the direction the slow stream runs. The great economic tide of the century flows our way. *We* shall have the big world questions to decide presently. Then we shall need world policies; and it will be these old-time world leaders that we shall then have to work with, more closely than now.

The English make a sharp distinction between the American people and the American Government—a distinction that they are conscious of and that they themselves talk about. They do not think of our *people* as foreigners. I have a club book on my table wherein the members are classified as British, Colonial, American, and Foreign—quite unconsciously. But they do think of our Government as foreign, and as a frontier sort of thing without good manners or good faith. This distinction presents the big task of implanting here a real respect for our Government. People often think to compliment the American Ambassador by assuming that he is better than his Government and must at times be ashamed of it. Of course the Government never does this—never—but persons in unofficial life; and I have sometimes hit some hard blows under this condescending provocation. This is the one experience that I have found irritating. They commiserate me on having a Government that will not provide an Ambassador's residence—from the King to my servants. They talk about American lynchings. Even the *Spectator*, in an early editorial about you, said that we should now see what stuff there is in the new President by watching whether you would stop lynchings. They forever quote Bryce on the badness of our municipal government. They pretend to think that the impeachment of governors is common and ought to be commoner. One delicious M. P. asked me: "Now, since the Governor of New York is impeached, who becomes Vice-President?"[1] Ignorance, unfathomable ignorance, is at the bottom of much of it; if the Town Treasurer of Yuba Dam gets a $100 "rake off" on a paving contract, our city government is a failure.

I am about to conclude that our yellow press does us more harm abroad than at home, and many of the American correspondents of the English papers send exactly the wrong news. The whole governing class of England has a possibly exaggerated admiration for the American people and something very like contempt for the American Government.

---

[1] Just what this critical Briton had in mind, in thinking that the removal of a New York governor created a vacancy in the Vice-Presidency, is not clear. Possibly, however, he had a cloudy recollection of the fact that Theodore Roosevelt, after serving as Governor of New York State, became Vice-President, and may have concluded from this that the two offices were held by the same man.

If I make it out right two causes (in addition to their ignorance) of their dislike of our Government are (1) its lack of manners in the past, and (2) its indiscretions of publicity about foreign affairs. We ostentatiously stand aloof from their polite ways and courteous manners in many of the every-day, ordinary, unimportant dealings with them—aloof from the common amenities of long-organized political life. . . . .

Not one of these things is worth mentioning or remembering. But generations of them have caused our Government to be regarded as thoughtless of the fine little acts of life—as rude. The more I find out about diplomatic customs and the more I hear of the little-big troubles of others, the more need I find to be careful about details of courtesy.

Thus we are making as brave a show as becomes us. I no longer dismiss a princess after supper or keep the whole diplomatic corps waiting while I talk to an interesting man till the Master of Ceremonies comes up and whispers: "Your Excellency, I think they are waiting for you to move." But I am both young and green, and even these folk forgive much to green youth, if it show a willingness to learn.

But our Government, though green, isn't young enough to plead its youth. It is time that it, too, were learning Old World manners in dealing with Old World peoples. I do not know whether we need a Bureau, or a Major-Domo, or a Master of Ceremonies at Washington, but we need somebody to prompt us to act as polite as we really are, somebody to think of those gentler touches that we naturally forget. Some other governments have such officers—perhaps all. The Japanese, for instance, are newcomers in world politics. But this Japanese Ambassador and his wife here never miss a trick; and they come across the square and ask us how to do it! All the other governments, too, play the game of small courtesies to perfection—the French, of course, and the Spanish and—even the old Turk.

Another reason for the English distrust of our Government is its indiscretions in the past of this sort: one of our Ministers to Germany, you will recall, was obliged to resign because the Government at Washington inadvertently published one of his confidential despatches; Griscom saved his neck only by the skin, when he was in Japan, for a similar reason. These things travel all round the world from one chancery to another and all governments know them. Yesterday somebody in Washington talked about my despatch summarizing my talk with Sir Edward Grey about Mexico, and it appeared in the papers here this morning that Sir Edward had told me that the big business interests were pushing him hard. This I sent as only *my* inference. I had at once to disclaim it. This leaves in his mind a doubt about our care for secrecy. They have monstrous big doors and silent men in Downing Street; and, I am told, a stenographer sits behind a big screen in Sir Edward's room while an Ambassador talks![1] I wonder if my comments on certain poets, which I have poured forth there to provoke his, are preserved in the archives of the British Empire. The British Empire is surely very welcome to them. I have twice found it useful, by the way, to bring up Wordsworth

[1]For years this idea of the stenographer back of a screen in the Foreign Office has been abroad, but it is entirely unfounded. Several years ago a Foreign Secretary, perhaps Lord Salisbury, put a screen behind his desk to keep off the draughts and from this precaution the myth arose that it shielded a stenographer who took a complete record of ambassadorial conversations. After an ambassador leaves, the Foreign Secretary, however, does write out the important points in the conversation. Copies are made and printed, and sent to the King, the Prime Minister, the British Ambassador in the country to which the interview relates, and occasionally to others. All these records are, of course, carefully preserved in the archives of the Foreign Office.

when he has begun to talk about Panama tolls. Then your friend Canon Rawnsley[1] has, without suspecting it, done good service in diplomacy.

The newspaper men here, by the way, both English and American, are disposed to treat us fairly and to be helpful. The London *Times*, on most subjects, is very friendly, and I find its editors worth cultivating for their own sakes and because of their position. It is still the greatest English newspaper. Its general friendliness to the United States, by the way, has started a rumour that I hear once in a while—that it is really owned by Americans—nonsense yet awhile. To the fairness and helpfulness of the newspaper men there are one or two exceptions, for instance, a certain sneaking whelp who writes for several papers. He went to the Navy League dinner last night at which I made a little speech. When I sat down, he remarked to his neighbour, with a yawn, "Well, nothing in it for me. The Ambassador, I am afraid, said nothing for which I can demand his recall." They, of course, don't care thrippence about me; it's you they hope to annoy.

Then after beating them at their own game of daily little courtesies, we want a fight with them—a good stiff fight about something wherein we are dead right, to remind them sharply that we have sand in our craw.[2] I pray every night for such a fight; for they like fighting men. Then they'll respect our Government as they already respect us—if we are dead right.

But I've little hope for a fight of the right kind with Sir Edward Grey. He is the very reverse of insolent—

---

[1] The Rev. Hardwicke Drummond Rawnsley, the well-known Vicar of Crosthwaite, Keswick, poet and student of Wordsworth. President Wilson, who used occasionally to spend his vacation in the Lake region, was one of his friends.

[2] It is perhaps unnecessary to say that the Ambassador was thinking only of a diplomatic "fight."

fair, frank, sympathetic, and he has so clear an understanding of our real character that he'd yield anything
that his party and Parliament would permit. He'd make
a good American with the use of very little sandpaper.
Of course I know him better than I know any other
member of the Cabinet, but he seems to me the best-
balanced man of them all.

I can assure you emphatically that the tariff act[1] does
command their respect and is already having an amazing
influence on their opinion of our Government. Lord
Mersey, a distinguished law lord and a fine old fellow of
the very best type of Englishman, said to me last Sunday,
"I wish to thank you for stopping half-way in reducing
your tariff; that will only half ruin us." A lady of a
political family (Liberal) next whom I sat at dinner the
other night (and these women know their politics as no
class of women among us do) said: "Tell me something
about your great President. We hadn't heard much
about him nor felt his hand till your tariff bill passed.
He seems to have real power in the Government. You
know we do not always know who has power in your
Government." Lord Grey, the one-time Governor-
General of Canada, stopped looking at the royal wedding
presents the other evening long enough to say: "The
United States Government is waking up—waking up."

I sum up these atmospheric conditions—I do not presume to call them by so definite a name as recommendations:

We are in the international game—not in its Old World
intrigues and burdens and sorrows and melancholy, but
in the inevitable way to leadership and to cheerful mastery

[1]The Underwood Bill revising the tariff "downward" became a law October,
1913. It was one of the first important measures of the new Wilson Administration

in the future; and everybody knows that we are in it but us. It is a sheer blind habit that causes us to continue to try to think of ourselves as aloof. They think in terms of races here, and we are of their race, and we shall become the strongest and the happiest branch of it.

While we play the game with them, we shall play it better by playing it under their long-wrought-out rules of courtesy in everyday affairs.

We shall play it better, too, if our Government play it quietly—except when the subject demands publicity. I have heard that in past years the foreign representatives of our Government have reported too few things and much too meagrely. I have heard since I have been here that these representatives become timid because Washington has for many a year conducted its foreign business too much in the newspapers; and the foreign governments themselves are always afraid of this.

Meantime I hardly need tell you of my appreciation of such a chance to make so interesting a study and to enjoy so greatly the most interesting experience, I really believe, in the whole world. I only hope that in time I may see how to shape the constant progression of incidents into a constructive course of events; for we are soon coming into a time of big changes.

Most heartily yours,

WALTER H. PAGE.

To David F. Houston[1]

American Embassy, London [undated].

DEAR HOUSTON:

You're doing the bigger job: as the world now is, there is no other job so big as yours or so well worth doing; but I'm having more fun. I'm having more fun than any-

[1]Secretary of Agriculture in President Wilson's Cabinet.

body else anywhere. It's a large window you look through on the big world—here in London; and, while I am for the moment missing many of the things that I've most cared about hitherto (such as working for the countryman, guessing at American public opinion, coffee that's fit to drink, corn bread, sunshine, and old faces) big new things come on the horizon. Yet a man's personal experiences are nothing in comparison with the large job that our Government has to do in its Foreign Relations. I'm beginning to begin to see what it is. The American people are taken most seriously here. I'm sometimes almost afraid of the respect and even awe in which they hold us. But the American Government is a mere joke to them. They don't even believe that we ourselves believe in it. We've had no foreign policy, no continuity of plan, no matured scheme, no settled way of doing things and we seem afraid of Irishmen or Germans or some "element" when a chance for real action comes. I'm writing to the President about this and telling him stories to show how it works.

We needn't talk any longer about keeping aloof. If Cecil Spring Rice would tell you the complaints he has already presented and if you saw the work that goes on here—more than in all the other posts in Europe—you'd see that all the old talk about keeping aloof is Missouri buncombe. We're very much "in," but not frankly in.

I wish you'd keep your eye on these things in cabinet meetings. The English and the whole English world are ours, if we have the courtesy to take them—fleet and trade and all; and we go on pretending we are afraid of "entangling alliances." What about disentangling alliances?

We're in the game. There's no use in letting a few wild Irish or cocky Germans scare us. We need courtesy and frankness, and the destinies of the world will be in our hands. They'll fall there anyhow after we are dead; but I wish to see them come, while my own eyes last. Don't you?

Heartily yours,

W. H. P.

To Robert N. Page[1]

London, December 22, 1913.

MY DEAR BOB:

. . . We have a splendid, big old house—not in any way pretentious—a commonplace house in fact for fashionable London and the least showy and costly of the Embassies. But it does very well—it's big and elegantly plain and dignified. We have fifteen servants in the house. They do just about what seven good ones would do in the United States, but they do it a great deal better. They pretty nearly run themselves and the place. The servant question is admirably solved here. They divide the work according to a fixed and unchangeable system and they do it remarkably well—in their own slow English way. We simply let them alone, unless something important happens to go wrong. Katharine simply tells the butler that we'll have twenty-four people to dinner to-morrow night and gives him a list of them. As they come in, the men at the door address every one correctly—Your Lordship or Your Grace, or what not. When they are all in, the butler comes to the reception room and announces dinner. We do the rest. As every man goes out, the butler asks him if he'll have a glass of water or of grog or a cigar; he calls his car, puts him in it, and that's the end of it. Bully good plan. But in the United States that butler, whose wages are less than the ramshackle nigger I had at Garden City to keep the place

---

[1] Of Aberdeen, North Carolina, the Ambassador's brother.

neat, would have a business of his own. But here he is a sort of duke downstairs. He sits at the head of the servants' table and orders them around and that's worth more than money to an Old World servile mind.

The "season" doesn't begin till the King comes back and Parliament opens, in February. But every kind of club and patriotic and educational organization is giving its annual dinner now. I've been going to them and making after-dinner speeches to get acquainted and also to preach into them some little knowledge of American ways and ideals. They are very nice—very. You could not suggest or imagine any improvement in their kindness and courtesy. They do all these things in some ways better than we. They have more courtesy. They make far shorter speeches. But they do them all too much alike. Still they do get much pleasure out of them and much instruction too.

Then we are invited to twice as many private dinners and luncheons as we can attend. At these, these people are at their best. But it is yet quite confusing. A sea of friendly faces greets you—you can't remember the names. Nobody ever introduces anybody to anybody; and if by accident anybody ever tries, he simply says—"Uh-o-oh-Lord Xzwwxkmpt." You couldn't understand it if you had to be hanged.

But we are untangling some of this confusion and coming to make very real and very charming friends.

About December 20, everybody who is anybody leaves London. They go to their country places for about a fortnight or they go to the continent. Almost everything stops. It has been the only dull time at the Embassy that I've had. Nothing is going on now. But up to two days ago, it kept a furious gait. I'm glad of a little rest.

Dealing with the Government doesn't present **the**

difficulties that I feared. Sir Edward Grey is in the main responsible for the ease with which it is done. He is a frank and fair and truthful man. You will find him the day after to-morrow precisely where you left him the day before yesterday. We get along very well indeed. I think we should get along if we had harder tasks one with the other. And the English people are even more friendly than the Government. You have no idea of their respect for the American Nation. Of course there is much ignorance, sometimes of a surprising sort. Very many people, for instance, think that all the Americans are rich. A lady told me the other night how poor she is—she is worth only $1,250,000—"nothing like all you Americans." She was quite sincere. In fact the wealth of the world (and the poverty, too) is centred here in an amazing way. You can't easily take it in—how rich or how many rich English families there are. They have had wealth for generation after generation, and the surprising thing is, they take care of it. They spend enormously—seldom ostentatiously—but they are more than likely to add some of their income every year to their principal. They have better houses in town and in the country than I had imagined. They spend vast fortunes in making homes in which they expect to live forever—generation after generation.

To an American democrat the sad thing is the servile class. Before the law the chimney sweep and the peer have exactly the same standing. They have worked that out with absolute justice. But there it stops. The serving class is what we should call abject. It does not occur to them that they might ever become—or that their descendants might ever become—ladies and gentlemen.

The "courts" are a very fine sight. The diplomatic

ladies sit on a row of seats on one side the throne room, the Duchesses on a row opposite. The King and Queen sit on a raised platform with the royal family. The Ambassadors come in first and bow and the King shakes hands with them. Then come the forty or more Ministers—no shake for them. In front of the King are a few officers in gaudy uniform, some Indians of high rank (from India) and the court officials are all round about, with pages who hold up the Queen's train. Whenever the Queen and King move, two court officials back before them, one carrying a gold stick and the other a silver stick.

The ladies to be presented come along. They curtsy to the King, then to the Queen, and disappear in the rooms farther on. The Ambassadors (all in gaudy uniforms but me) stand near the throne—stand through the whole performance. One night after an hour or two of ladies coming along and curtsying and disappearing, I whispered to the Spanish Ambassador, "There must be five hundred of these ladies." "U-m," said he, as he shifted his weight to the other foot, "I'm sure there are five thousand!" When they've all been presented, the King and Queen go into a room where a stand-up supper is served. The royalty and the diplomatic folks go into that room, too; and their Majesties walk around and talk with whom they please. Into another and bigger room everybody else goes and gets supper. Then we all flock back to the throne room; and preceded by the backing courtiers, their Majesties come out into the floor and bow to the Ambassadors, then to the Duchesses, then to the general diplomatic group and they go out. The show is ended. We come downstairs and wait an hour for our car and come home about midnight. The uniforms on the men and the jewels on the ladies (by the ton) and their trains—all this makes a very brilliant spectacle. The American Ambassador and his Secretaries and the Swiss and the Portuguese are the only ones dressed in citizens' clothes.

At a levee, the King receives only gentlemen. Here they come in all kinds of uniforms. If you are not entitled to wear a uniform, you have a dark suit, knee breeches, and a funny little tin sword. I'm going to adopt the knee breeches part of it for good when I go home—golf breeches in the day time and knee breeches at night. You've no idea how nice and comfortable they are—though it is a devil of a lot of trouble to put 'em on. Of course every sort of man here but the Americans wears some sort of decorations around his neck or on his stomach, at these functions. For my part, I like it—here. The women sparkle with diamonds, the men strut; the King is a fine man with a big bass voice and he talks very well and is most agreeable; the Queen is very gracious; the royal ladies (Queen Victoria's daughters, chiefly) are nice; you see all the big Generals and all the big Admirals and the great folk of every sort—fine show.

You've no idea how much time and money they spend on shooting. The King has been shooting most of the time for three months. He's said to be a very good shot. He has sent me, on different occasions, grouse, a haunch of venison, and pheasants.

But except on these occasions, you never think about the King. The people go about their business as if he didn't exist, of course. They begin work much later than we do. You'll not find any of the shops open till about ten o'clock. The sun doesn't shine except once in a while and you don't know it's daylight till about ten. You know the House of Commons has night sessions always. Nobody is in the Government offices, except clerks and secretaries, till the afternoon. We dine at eight, and, when we have a big dinner, at eight thirty.

I like these people (most of 'em) immensely. They are very genuine and frank, good fighters and folk of our own sort—after you come to know them. At first they have no manners and don't know what to do. But they warm up to you later. They have abundant wit, but much less humour than we. And they know how to live.

Except that part of life which is ministered to in mechanical ways, they resist conveniences. They don't really like bathrooms yet. They prefer great tin tubs, and they use bowls and pitchers when a bathroom is next door. The telephone—Lord deliver us!—I've given it up. They know nothing about it. (It is a government concern, but so are the telegraph and the post office, and they are remarkably good and swift.) You can't buy a newspaper on the street, except in the afternoon. Cigar-stores are as scarce as hen's teeth. Barber-shops are all "hairdressers"—dirty and wretched beyond description. You can't get a decent pen; their newspapers are as big as tablecloths. In this aquarium in which we live (it rains every day) they have only three vegetables and two of them are cabbages. They grow all kinds of fruit in hothouses, and (I can't explain this) good land in admirable cultivation thirty miles from London sells for about half what good corn land in Iowa brings. Lloyd George has scared the land-owners to death.

Party politics runs so high that many Tories will not invite Liberals to dinner. They are almost at the point of civil war. I asked the Prime Minister the other day how he was going to prevent war. He didn't give any clear answer. During this recess of Parliament, though there's no election pending, all the Cabinet are all the

time going about making speeches on Ireland. They talk
to me about it.

"What would you do?"

"Send 'em all to the United States," say I.

"No, no."

They have had the Irish question three hundred years
and they wouldn't be happy without it. One old Tory
talked me deaf abusing the Liberal Government.

"You do this way in the United States—hate one another, don't you?"

"No," said I, "we live like angels in perfect harmony
except a few weeks before election."

"The devil you do! You don't hate one another?
What do you do for enemies? I couldn't get along without enemies to swear at."

If you think it's all play, you fool yourself; I mean this
job. There's no end of the work. It consists of these
parts: Receiving people for two hours every day, some on
some sort of business, some merely "to pay respects,"
attending to a large (and exceedingly miscellaneous)
mail; going to the Foreign Office on all sorts of errands;
looking up the oddest assortment of information that
you ever heard of; making reports to Washington on all
sorts of things; then the so-called social duties—giving
dinners, receptions, etc., and attending them. I hear the
most important news I get at so-called social functions.
Then the court functions; and the meetings and speeches!
The American Ambassador must go all over England and
explain every American thing. You'd never recover from
the shock if you could hear me speaking about Education,
Agriculture, the observance of Christmas, the Navy, the
Anglo-Saxon, Mexico, the Monroe Doctrine, Co-educa-
tion, Woman Suffrage, Medicine, Law, Radio-Activity,
Flying, the Supreme Court, the President as a Man of

letters, Hookworm, the Negro—just get down the Encyclopædia and continue the list. I've done this every
week-night for a month, hand running, with a few afternoon performances thrown in! I have missed only one
engagement in these seven months; and that was merely
a private luncheon. I have been late only once. I
have the best chauffeur in the world—he deserves credit
for much of that. Of course, I don't get time to read
a book. In fact, I can't keep up with what goes on at
home. To read a newspaper eight or ten days old, when
they come in bundles of three or four—is impossible.'
What isn't telegraphed here, I miss; and that means I
miss most things.

I forgot, there are a dozen other kinds of activities, such
as American marriages, which they always want the Ambassador to attend; getting them out of jail, when they
are jugged (I have an American woman on my hands now,
whose four children come to see me every day); looking
after the American insane; helping Americans move the
bones of their ancestors; interpreting the income-tax law;
receiving medals for Americans; hearing American fid-
dlers, pianists, players; sitting for American sculptors and
photographers; sending telegrams for property owners in
Mexico; reading letters from thousands of people who
have shares in estates here; writing letters of introduction;
getting tickets to the House Gallery; getting seats in the
Abbey; going with people to this and that and t'other;
getting tickets to the races, the art-galleries, the House of
Lords; answering fool questions about the United States
put by Englishmen. With a military attaché, a naval
attaché, three secretaries, a private secretary, two automobiles, Alice's private secretary, a veterinarian, an im-
migration agent, consuls everywhere, a despatch agent,
lawyers, doctors, messengers—they keep us all busy. A

woman turned up dying the other day. I sent for a big
doctor. She got well. As if that wasn't enough, both
the woman and the doctor had to come and thank me
(fifteen minutes each). Then each wrote a letter! Then
there are people who are going to have a Fair here; others
who have a Fair coming on at San Francisco; others at
San Diego; secretaries and returning and outgoing diplomats come and go (lunch for 'em all); niggers come up
from Liberia; Rhodes Scholars from Oxford; Presidential
candidates to succeed Huerta; people who present books;
women who wish to go to court; Jews who are excited
about Rumania; passports, passports to sign; peace committees about the hundred years of peace; opera singers
going to the United States; artists who have painted some
American's portrait—don't you see? I haven't said a
word about reporters and editors: the city's full of them.

A Happy New Year.

Affectionately,   WAT.

To Ralph W. Page[1]

London, December 23, 1913.

DEAR RALPH:

. . . The game is pretty much as it has been. I
can't think of any new kinds of things to write you. The
old kinds simply multiply and repeat themselves. But we
are beginning now really to become acquainted, and some
life friendships will grow out of our experience. And
there's no doubt about its being instructive. I get
glimpses of the way in which great governments deal with
one another, in ways that our isolated, and, therefore,
safe government seldom has any experience of. For
instance, one of the Lords of the Admiralty told me the
other night that he never gets out of telephone reach of

---

[1] Of Pinehurst, North Carolina, the Ambassador's eldest son.

the office—not even half an hour. "The Admiralty," said he, "never sleeps." He has a telephone by his bed which he can hear at any moment in the night. I don't believe that they really expect the German fleet to attack them any day or night. But they would not be at all surprised if it did so to-night. They talk all the time of the danger and of the probability of war; they don't expect it; but most wars have come without warning, and they are all the time prepared to begin a fight in an hour.

They talk about how much Germany must do to strengthen her frontier against Russia and her new frontier on the Balkan States. They now have these problems in hand and therefore they are for the moment not likely to provoke a fight. But they might.

It is all pitiful to see them thinking forever about danger and defense. The controversy about training boys for the army never ends. We don't know in the United States what we owe to the Atlantic Ocean—safe separation from all these troubles. . . .

But I've often asked both Englishmen and Americans in a dining room where there were many men of each country, whether they could look over the company and say which were English and which were Americans. Nobody can tell till—they begin to talk.

The ignorance of the two countries, each of the other, is beyond all belief. A friend of Kitty's—an American—received a letter from the United States yesterday. The maid noticed the stamp, which had the head of George Washington on it. Every stamp in this kingdom bears the image of King George. She asked if the American stamp had on it the head of the American Ambassador! I've known far wiser people to ask far more foolish questions.

Affectionately,
W. H. P.

To Mrs. Ralph W. Page

London, Christmas-is-coming, 1913.

MY DEAR LEILA:

. . . Her work [Mrs. Walter H. Page's] is all the work of going and receiving and—of reading. She reads incessantly and enormously; and, when she gets tired, she goes to bed. That's all there is about it. Lord! I wish I could. But, when I get tired, I have to go and make another speech. They think the American Ambassador has omniscience for a foible and oratory as a pastime.

In some ways my duties are very instructive. We get different points of view on many things, some better than we had before had, some worse. For instance, life is pretty well laid out here in water-tight compartments; and you can't let a stream in from one to another without danger of sinking the ship. Four reporters have been here to-day because Mr. and Mrs. Sayre[1] arrived this morning. Every one of 'em asked the same question, "Who met them at the station?" That's the chief thing they wished to know. When I said "I did"—that fixed the whole thing on the highest peg of dignity. They could classify the whole proceeding properly, and they went off happy. Again: You've got to go in to dinner in the exact order prescribed by the constitution; and, if you avoid that or confuse that, you'll never be able to live it down. And so about Government, Literature, Art—everything. Don't you forget your water-tight compartments. If you do, you are gone! They have the same toasts at every public dinner. One is to "the guests." Now you needn't say a word about the guests

---

[1] Mr. and Mrs. Francis B. Sayre, son-in-law and daughter of President Wilson, at that time on their honeymoon trip in Europe.

when you respond. But they've been having toasts to the guests since the time of James I and they can't change it. They had me speak to "the guests" at a club last night, when they wanted me to talk about Mexico! The winter has come—the winter months at least. But they have had no cold weather—not so cold as you have in Pinehurst. But the sun has gone out to sea—clean gone. We never see it. A damp darkness (semi-darkness at least) hangs over us all the time. But we manage to feel our way about.

A poor photograph goes to you for Xmas—a poor thing enough surely. But you get Uncle Bob[1] busy on the job of paying for an Ambassador's house. Then we'll bring Christmas presents home for you. What a game we are playing, we poor folks here, along with Ambassadors whose governments pay them four times what ours pays. But we don't give the game away, you bet! We throw the bluff with a fine, straight poker face.

Affectionately,

W. H. P.

To Frank N. Doubleday and Others

London, Sunday, December 28, 1913.

My dear Comrades:

I was never one of those abnormal creatures who got Christmas all ready by the Fourth of July. The true spirit of the celebration has just now begun to work on me —three days late. In this respect the spirit is very like Christmas plum-pudding. Moreover, we've just got the patriotic fervour flowing at high tide this morning. This is the President's birthday. We've put up the Stars and

---

[1] Mr. Robert N. Page, the Ambassador's brother, was at this time a Congressman from North Carolina.

Stripes on the roof; and half an hour ago the King's Master of Ceremonies drove up in a huge motor car and, being shown into my presence in the state drawing room, held his hat in his hand and (said he):

"Your Excellency: I am commanded by the King to express to you His Majesty's congratulations on the birthday of the President, to wish him a successful administration and good health and long life and to convey His Majesty's greetings to Your Excellency: and His Majesty commands me to express the hope that you will acquaint the President with His Majesty's good wishes."

Whereto I made just as pretty a little speech as your 'umble sarvant could. Then we sat down, I called in Mrs. Page and my secretary and we talked like human beings.

Having worked like the devil, upon whom, I imagine, at this bibulous season many heavy duties fall—having thus toiled for two months—the international docket is clean, I've got done a round of twenty-five speeches (O Lord!) I've slept three whole nights, I've made my dinner-calls— you see I'm feeling pretty well, in this first period of quiet life I've yet found in this Babylon. Praise Heaven! they go off for Christmas. Everything's shut up tight. The streets of London are as lonely and as quiet as the road to Oyster Bay while the Oyster is in South America. It's about as mild here as with you in October and as damp as Sheepshead's Bay in an autumn storm. But such people as you meet complain of the c-o-l-d—the c-o-l-d; and they run into their heatless houses and put on extra waistcoats and furs and throw shawls over their knees and curse Lloyd George and enjoy themselves. They are a great people—even without mint juleps in summer or eggnog in winter; and I like them. The old gouty Lords curse the Americans for the decline of drinking. And you can't live among them without laughing yourself to death and admiring them, too. It's a fine race to be sprung from.

All this field of international relations—you fellows regard it as a bore. So it used to be before my entrance into the game! But it's everlastingly interesting. Just to give him a shock, I asked the Foreign Secretary the other day what difference it would make if the Foreign Offices were all to go out of business and all the Ambassadors were to be hanged. He thought a minute and said: "Suppose war kept on in the Balkans, the Russians killed all their Jews, Germany took Holland and sent an air-fleet over London, the Japanese landed in California, the English took all the oil-wells in Central and South America and——"

"Good Lord!" said I, "do you and I prevent all these calamities? If so, we don't get half the credit that is due us—do we?"

You could ask the same question about any group or profession of men in the world; and on a scratch, I imagine that any of them would be missed less than they think. But the realness and the bigness of the job here in London is simply oppressive. We don't even know what it is in the United States and, of course, we don't go about doing it right. If we did, we shouldn't pick up a green fellow on the plain of Long Island and send him here: we'd train the most capable male babies we have from the cradle. But this leads a long way.

As I look back over these six or seven months, from the pause that has come this week, I'm bound to say (being frank, not to say vain) that I had the good fortune to do one piece of work that was worth the effort and worth coming to do—about that infernal Mexican situation. An abler man would have done it better; but, as it was, I did it; and I have a most appreciative letter about it from the President.

By thunder, he's doing *his* job, isn't he? Whether you like the job or not, you've got to grant that. When I first came over here, I found a mild curiosity about Wilson—only mild. But now they sit up and listen and ask most eager questions. He has impressed his personality most strongly on the governing class here.

W. H. P.

The following memorandum, found among Page's papers, was incorporated, virtually in the same words, in letters to the President:

American Embassy, London
[May 11, 1914.]

The King of Denmark (I always think of Hamlet) having come to make his royal kinsman of these Isles a visit, his royal kinsman to-night gave a state dinner at the palace whereto the Ambassadors of the eight Great Powers were, of course, invited. Now I don't know how other kings do, but I'm willing to swear by King George for a job of this sort. The splendour of the thing is truly regal and the friendliness of it very real and human; and the company most uncommon. Of course the Ambassadors and their wives were there, the chief rulers of the Empire and men and women of distinction and most of the royal family. The dinner and the music and the plate and the decorations and the jewels and the uniforms—all these were regal; but there is a human touch about it that seems almost democratic.

All for His Majesty of Denmark, a country with fewer people and less wealth than New Jersey. This whole royal game is most interesting. Lloyd George and H. H. Asquith and John Morley were there, all in white knee

breeches of silk, and swords and most gaudy coats—these
that are the radicals of the Kingdom, in literature and in
action.   Veterans of Indian and South African wars stood
on either side of every door and of every stairway, dressed
as Sir Walter Raleigh dressed, like so many statues, never
blinking an eye.   Every person in the company is printed,
in all the papers, with every title he bears.   Crowds lined
the streets in front of the palace to see the carriages go
in and to guess who was in each.   To-morrow the Diplomatic Corps calls on King Christian and to-morrow night
King George commands us to attend the opera as his
guests.

Whether it's the court, or the honours and the orders and
all the social and imperial spoils, that keep the illusion up,
or whether it is the Old World inability to change anything, you can't ever quite decide.   In Defoe's time they
put pots of herbs on the desks of every court in London
to keep the plague off.   The pots of herbs are yet put
on every desk in every court room in London.   Several
centuries ago somebody tried to break into the Bank of
England.   A special guard was detached—a little company of soldiers—to stand watch at night.   The bank has
twice been moved and is now housed in a building that
would stand a siege; but that guard, in the same uniform
goes on duty every night.   Nothing is ever abolished,
nothing ever changed.   On the anniversary of King
Charles's execution, his statue in Trafalgar Square is
covered with flowers.   Every month, too, new books
appear about the mistresses of old kings—as if they, too,
were of more than usual interest: I mean serious, historical books.   From the King's palace to the humblest house
I've been in, there are pictures of kings and queens.   In
every house, too (to show how nothing ever changes), the
towels are folded in the same peculiar way.   In every

grate in the kingdom the coal fire is laid in precisely the same way. There is not a salesman in any shop on Piccadilly who does not, in the season, wear a long-tail coat. Everywhere they say a second grace at dinner—not at the end—but before the dessert, because two hundred years ago they dared not wait longer lest the parson be under the table: the grace is said to-day *before* dessert! I tried three months to persuade my "Boots" to leave off blacking the soles of my shoes under the instep. He simply couldn't do it. Every "Boots" in the Kingdom does it. A man of learning had an article in an afternoon paper a few weeks ago which began thus: "It is now universally conceded by the French and the Americans that the decimal system is a failure," and he went on to concoct a scheme for our money that would be more "rational" and "historical." In this hot debate about Ulster a frequent phrase used is, "Let us see if we can't find the right formula to solve the difficulty"; their whole lives are formulas. Now may not all the honours and garters and thistles and O. M.'s and K. C. B.'s and all manner of gaudy sinecures be secure, only because they can't abolish anything? My servants sit at table in a certain order, and Mrs. Page's maid wouldn't yield her precedence to a mere housemaid for any mortal consideration—any more than a royal person of a certain rank would yield to one of a lower rank. A real democracy is as far off as doomsday. So you argue, till you remember that it is these same people who made human liberty possible—to a degree—and till you sit day after day and hear them in the House of Commons, mercilessly pounding one another. Then you are puzzled. Do they keep all these outworn things because they are incapable of changing anything, or do these outworn burdens keep them from becoming able to change anything? I daresay it works both ways. Every venerable ruin, every outworn custom, makes the King more secure; and the King gives veneration to every ruin and keeps respect for every outworn custom.

Praise God for the Atlantic Ocean! It is the geographical foundation of our liberties. Yet, as I've often written, there are men here, real men, ruling men, mighty men, and a vigorous stock.

A civilization, especially an old civilization, isn't an easy nut to crack. But I notice that the men of vision keep their thought on us. They never forget that we are 100 million strong and that we dare do new things; and they dearly love to ask questions about—Rockefeller! Our power, our adaptability, our potential wealth they never forget. They'll hold fast to our favour for reasons of prudence as well as for reasons of kinship. And, whenever we choose to assume the leadership of the world, they'll grant it—gradually—and follow loyally. They cannot become French, and they dislike the Germans. They must keep in our boat for safety as well as for comfort.

Yours heartily,

WALTER H. PAGE.

The following extracts are made from other letters and memoranda written at this time:

. . . To-night I had a long talk with the Duchess of X, a kindly woman who spends much time and money in the most helpful "uplift" work; that's the kind of woman she is.

Now she and the Duke are invited to dine at the French Ambassador's to-morrow night. "If the Duke went into any house where there was any member of this Government," said she, "he'd turn and walk out again. We

thought we'd better find out who the French Ambassador's guests are. We didn't wish to ask him nor to have
correspondence about it. Therefore the Duke sent his
Secretary quietly to ask the Ambassador's Secretary—
before we accepted."

This is now a common occurrence. We had Sir Edward
Grey to dinner a little while ago and we had to make sure
we had no Tory guests that night.

This same Duchess of X sat in the Peeresses' gallery of
the House of Lords to-night till 7 o'clock. "I had to sit in
plain sight of the wives of two members of the Cabinet
and of the wife and daughter of the Prime Minister. I
used to know them," she said, "and it was embarrassing."

Thus the revolution proceeds. For that's what it is.

. . . On the other hand the existing order is the
most skilfully devised machinery for perpetuating itself
that has ever grown up among civilized men. Did you
ever see a London directory? It hasn't names al-
phabetically; but one section is "Tradesmen," another
"The City," etc., etc., and another "The Court." Any
one who has ever been presented at Court is in the
"Court" section, and you must sometimes look in several
sections to find a man. Yet everybody so values these
distinctions that nobody complains of the inconvenience.
When the Liberal party makes Liberals Peers in order to
have Liberals in the House of Lords, lo! they soon turn
Conservative after they get there. The system perpetu-
ates itself and stifles the natural desire for change that
most men in a state of nature instinctively desire in order
to assert their own personalities. . . .

. . . All this social life which engages us at this
particular season, sets a man to thinking. The mass of

the people are very slow—almost dull; and the privileged are most firmly entrenched. The really alert people are the aristocracy. They see the drift of events. "What is the pleasantest part of your country to live in?" Dowager Lady X asked me on Sunday, more than half in earnest. "My husband's ancestors sat in the House of Lords for six hundred years. My son sits there now—a dummy. They have taken all power from the Lords; they are taxing us out of our lands; they are saving the monarchy for destruction last. England is of the past—all is going. God knows what is coming." . . .

. . . And presently the presentations come. Lord! how sensible American women scramble for this privilege! It royally fits a few of them. Well, I've made some rules about presentations myself, since it's really a sort of personal perquisite of the Ambassador. One rule is, I don't present any but handsome women. Pretty girls: that's what you want when you are getting up a show. Far too many of ours come here and marry Englishmen. I think I shall make another rule and exact a promise that after presentation they shall go home. But the American women do enliven London. . . .

That triumph with the tariff is historic. I wrote to the President: "Score one!" And I have been telling the London writers on big subjects, notably the editor of the *Economist*, that this event, so quiet and undramatic, will mark a new epoch in the trade history of the world. . . . This island is a good breeding place for men whose children find themselves and develop into real men in freer lands. All that is needed to show the whole world that the future is ours is just this sort of an act of self-confidence. You know the old story of the Negro who saw a ghost—"Git outen de way, Mr. Rabbit, and let somebody come who *kin* run!" Score one! We're making History, and these people here know it. The trade of the world, or as much of it as is profitable, we may take as we will. The over-taxed, under-productive, army-burdened men of the Old World—alas! I read a settled melancholy in much of their statesmanship and in more of their literature. The most cheerful men in official life here are the High Commissioners of Canada, Australia, New Zealand, and such fellows who know what the English race is doing and can do freed from uniforms and heavy taxes and class feeling and such like. . . .

. . . The two things that this island has of eternal value are its gardens and its men. Nature sprinkles it almost every day and holds its moisture down so that every inch of it is forever green; and somehow men thrive as the lawns do—the most excellent of all races for progenitors. You and I[1] can never be thankful enough that our ancestors came of this stock. Even those that have stayed have cut a wide swath, and they wield good scythes yet. But I have moods when I pity them—for their dependence, for instance, on a navy (2 keels to 1) for their very bread and meat. They frantically resent conveniences. They build their great law court building (the architecture ecclesiastical) so as to provide an entrance hall of imposing proportions which they use once a year; and to get this fine hall they have to make their court rooms, which they must use all the time, dark and small and inaccessible. They think as much of that once-a-year ceremony of opening their courts as they think of the even justice that they dispense; somehow they feel that the justice depends on the ceremony.

[1]This is from a letter to President Wilson.

This moss that has grown all over their lives (some of it very pretty and most of it very comfortable—it's soft and warm) is of no great consequence—except that they think they'd die if it were removed. And this state of mind gives us a good key to their character and habits. What are we going to do with this England and this Empire, presently, when economic forces unmistakably put the leadership of the race in our hands? How can we lead it and use it for the highest purposes of the world and of democracy? We can do what we like if we go about it heartily and with good manners (any man prefers to yield to a gentleman rather than to a rustic) and throw away—gradually—our isolating fears and alternate boasting and bashfulness. "What do we most need to learn from you?" I asked a gentle and bejewelled nobleman the other Sunday, in a country garden that invited confidences. "If I may speak without offence, modesty." A commoner in the company, who had seen the Rocky Mountains, laughed, and said: "No; see your chance and take it: that's what we did in the years when we made the world's history." . . .

CHAPTER VI

"POLICY" AND "PRINCIPLE" IN MEXICO

I

THE last days of February, 1913, witnessed one of those sanguinary scenes in Mexico which for generations had accompanied changes in the government of that distracted country. A group of revolutionists assailed the feeble power of Francisco Madero and virtually imprisoned that executive and his forces in the Presidential Palace. The Mexican army, whose most influential officers were General Blanquet and General Victoriano Huerta, was hastily summoned to the rescue of the Government; instead of relieving the besieged officials, however, these generals turned their guns upon them, and so assured the success of the uprising. The speedy outcome of these transactions was the assassination of President Madero and the seizure of the Presidency by General Huerta. Another outcome was the presentation to Page of one of the most delicate problems in the history of Anglo-American relations.

At almost any other time this change in the Mexican succession would have caused only a momentary disturbance. There was nothing new in the violent overthrow of government in Latin-America; in Mexico itself no president had ever risen to power except by revolution. The career of Porfirio Diaz, who had maintained his authority for a third of a century, had somewhat obscured this fundamental fact in Mexican politics, but Diaz had dominated Mexico for seven presidential terms, not because his methods differed from the accepted methods of his country, but because he was himself an executive of great force and a statesman of genius, and could successfully hold his own against any aspiring antagonist. The civilized world, including the United States, had long since become reconciled to this situation as almost a normal one. In recognizing momentarily successful adventurers, Great Britain and the United States had never considered such details as justice or constitutionalism: the legality of the presidential title had never been the point at issue; the only question involved was whether the successful aspirant actually controlled the country, whether he had established a state of affairs that approximately represented order, and whether he could be depended upon to protect life and property. During the long dictatorship of Porfirio Diaz, however, certain events had taken place which had awakened the minds of Americans to the possibility of a new international relationship with all backward peoples. The consequences of the Spanish War had profoundly impressed Page. This conflict had left the United States a new problem in Cuba and the Philippines. Under the principles that for generations had governed the Old World there would have been no particular difficulty in meeting this problem. The United States would have candidly annexed the islands, and exploited their resources and their peoples; we should have concerned ourselves little about any duties that might be owed to the several millions of human beings who inhabited them. Indeed, what other alternatives were there?

One was to hand the possessions back to Spain, who in a four hundred years' experiment had demonstrated her unfitness to govern them; another was to give the islands their independence, which would have meant merely an indefinite continuance of anarchy. It is one of the greatest triumphs of American statesmanship that it discovered a more satisfactory solution. Essentially, the new plan was to establish in these undeveloped and politically undisciplined regions the fundamental conditions that may make possible the ultimate creation of democratic, self-governing states. It was recognized that constitutions and election ballots in themselves did not necessarily imply a democratic order. Before these there must come other things that were far more important, such as popular education, scientific agriculture, sanitation, public highways, railroads, and the development of the resources of nature. If the backward peoples of the world could be schooled in such a preliminary apprenticeship, the time might come when the intelligence and the conscience of the masses would be so enlightened that they could be trusted with independence. The labour of Leonard Wood in Cuba, and of other Americans in the Philippines, had apparently pointed the way to the only treatment of such peoples that was just to them and safe for mankind.

With the experience of Cuba and the Philippines as a guide, it is not surprising that the situation in Mexico appealed to many Americans as opening a similar opportunity to the United States. The two facts that outstood all others were that Mexico, in her existing condition of popular ignorance, could not govern herself, and that the twentieth century could not accept indefinitely a condition of disorder and bloodshed that had apparently satisfied the nineteenth. The basic difficulty in this American republic was one of race and of national character. The fact that was constantly overlooked was that Mexico was not a Caucasian country: it was a great shambling Indian Republic. Of its 15,000,000 people less

than 3,000,000 were of unmixed white blood, about 35 per
cent. were pure Indian, and the rest represented varying
mixtures of white and aboriginal stock. The masses had
advanced little in civilization since the days of Cortez.
Eighty per cent. were illiterate; their lives for the most
part were a dull and squalid routine; protection against
disease was unknown; the agricultural methods were
most primitive; the larger number still spoke the native
dialects which had been used in the days of Montezuma;
and over good stretches of the country the old tribal
régime still represented the only form of political organization. The one encouraging feature was that these
Mexican Indians, backward as they might be, were far
superior to the other native tribes of the North American Continent; in ancient times, they had developed
a state of society far superior to that of the traditional
Redskin. Nevertheless, it was true that the progress of
Mexico in the preceding fifty years had been due almost entirely to foreign enterprise. By 1913, about 75,000 Americans were living in Mexico as miners, engineers, merchants,
and agriculturists; American investments amounted to
about $1,200,000,000—a larger sum than that of all the
other foreigners combined. Though the work of European
countries, particularly Great Britain, was important, yet
Mexico was practically an economic colony of the United
States. Most observers agree that these foreign activities
had not only profited the foreigners, but that they had
greatly benefited the Mexicans themselves. The enterprise of Americans had disclosed enormous riches, had
given hundreds of thousands employment at very high
wages, had built up new Mexican towns on modern American lines, had extended the American railway system
over a large part of the land, and had developed street
railways, electric lighting, and other modern necessities

in all sections of the Republic. The opening up of Mexican oil resources was perhaps the most typical of these achievements, as it was certainly the most adventurous. Americans had created this, perhaps the greatest of Mexican industries, and in 1913, these Americans owned nearly 80 per cent. of Mexican oil. Their success had persuaded several Englishmen, the best known of whom was Lord Cowdray, to enter this same field. The activities of the Americans and the British in oil had an historic significance which was not foreseen in 1913, but which assumed the greatest importance in the World War; for the oil drawn from these Mexican fields largely supplied the Allied fleets and thus became an important element in the defeat of the Central Powers. In 1913, however, American and British oil operators were objects of general suspicion in both continents. They were accused of participating too actively in Mexican politics and there were those who even held them responsible for the revolutionary condition of the country. One picturesque legend insisted that the American oil interests looked with jealous hostility upon the great favours shown by the Diaz Administration to Lord Cowdray's company, and that they had instigated the Madero revolution in order to put in power politicians who would be more friendly to themselves. The inevitable complement to this interpretation of events was a prevailing suspicion that the Cowdray interests had promoted the Huerta revolt in order to turn the tables on "Standard Oil," to make safe the "concessions" already obtained from Diaz and to obtain still more from the new Mexican dictator.

To determine the truth in all these allegations, which were freely printed in the American press of the time, would demand more facts than are at present available; yet it is clear that these oil and other "concessions" presented the perpetual Mexican problem in a new and difficult light. The Wilson Administration came into power a few days after Huerta had seized the Mexican Government. The first difficulty presented to the State Department was to determine its attitude toward this usurper.

A few days after President Wilson's inauguration Mr. Irwin Laughlin, then Chargé d'Affaires in London—this was several weeks before Page's arrival—was instructed to ask the British Foreign Office what its attitude would be in regard to the recognition of President Huerta. Mr. Laughlin informed the Foreign Office that he was not instructed that the United States had decided on any policy, but that he felt sure it would be to the advantage of both countries to follow the same line. The query was not an informal one; it was made in definite obedience to instructions and was intended to elicit a formal commitment. The unequivocal answer that Mr. Laughlin received was that the British Government would not recognize Huerta, either formally or tacitly.

Mr. Laughlin sent his message immediately to Washington, where it apparently made a favourable impression. The Administration then let it be known that the United States would not recognize the new Mexican régime. Whether Mr. Wilson would at this time have taken such a position, irrespective of the British attitude, is not known, but at this stage of the proceedings Great Britain and the United States were standing side by side.

About three weeks afterward Mr. Laughlin heard that the British Foreign Office was about to recognize Huerta. Naturally the report astonished him; he at once called again on the Foreign Office, taking with him the despatch that he had recently sent to Washington. Why had the British Government recognized Huerta when it had given definite assurances to Washington that it had no intention

of doing so?   The outcome of the affair was that Sir Cecil
Spring Rice, British Ambassador in Washington, was instructed to inform the State Department that Great
Britain had changed its mind.   France, Germany, Spain,
and most other governments followed the British example
in recognizing the new President of Mexico.

It is thus apparent that the initial mistake in the Huerta
affair was made by Great Britain.   Its action produced
the most unpleasant impression upon the new Administration.   Mr. Wilson, Mr. Bryan, and their associates in
the cabinet easily found an explanation that was satisfactory to themselves and to the political enthusiasms
upon which they had come into power.   They believed
that the sudden change in the British attitude was the result of pressure from British commercial interests which
hoped to profit from the Huerta influence.   Lord Cowdray was a rich and powerful Liberal; he had great concessions in Mexico which had been obtained from President Diaz; it was known that Huerta aimed to make his
dictatorship a continuation of that of Diaz, to rule Mexico
as Diaz had ruled it, that is, by force, and to extend a
welcoming hand to foreign capitalists.   An important consideration was that the British Navy had a contract with
the Cowdray Company for oil, which was rapidly becoming indispensable as a fuel for warships, and this fact
necessarily made the British Government almost a champion of the Cowdray interests.   It was not necessary to
believe all the rumours that were then afloat in the American press to conclude that a Huerta administration would
be far more acceptable to the Cowdray Company than
any headed by one of the military chieftains who were
then disputing the control of Mexico.   Mr. Wilson and
Mr. Bryan believed that these events proved that certain
"interests," similar to the "interests" which, in their view,

had exercised so baleful an influence on American politics, were also active in Great Britain. The Wilson election in 1912 had been a protest against the dominance of "Wall Street" in American politics; Mr. Bryan's political stock-in-trade for a generation had consisted of little except a campaign against these forces; naturally, therefore, the suspicion that Great Britain was giving way to a British "Standard Oil" was enough to arm these statesmen against the Huerta policy, and to intensify that profound dislike of Huerta himself that was soon to become almost an obsession.

With this as a starting point President Wilson presently formulated an entirely new principle for dealing with Latin-American republics. There could be no permanent order in these turbulent countries and nothing approaching a democratic system until the habit of revolution should be checked. One of the greatest encouragements to revolution, said the President, was the willingness of foreign governments to recognize any politician who succeeded in seizing the executive power. He therefore believed that a refusal to recognize any government "founded upon violence" would exercise a wholesome influence in checking this national habit; if Great Britain and the United States and the other powers would set the example by refusing to have any diplomatic dealings with General Huerta, such an unfriendly attitude would discourage other forceful intriguers from attempting to repeat his experiment. The result would be that the decent elements in Mexico and other Latin-American countries would at last assert themselves, establish a constitutional system, and select their governments by constitutional means. At the bottom of the whole business were, in the President's and Mr. Bryan's opinion, the "concession" seekers, the "exploiters," who were constantly obtaining advantages at the hands of these corrupt governments and constantly stirring up revolutions for their financial profit.   The time had now come to end the whole miserable business.   "We are closing one chapter in the history of the world," said Mr. Wilson, "and opening another of unimaginable significance. . . . It is a very perilous thing to determine the foreign policy of a nation in the terms of material interests. . . . We have seen such material interests threaten constitutional freedom in the United States.   Therefore we will now know how to sympathize with those in the rest of America who have to contend with such powers, not only within their borders, but from outside their borders."

In this way General Huerta, who, in his own eyes, was merely another in the long succession of Mexican revolutionary chieftains, was translated into an epochal figure in the history of American foreign policy; he became a symbol in Mr. Wilson's new scheme of things—the representative of the order which was to come to an end, the man who, all unwittingly, was to point the new way not only in Mexico, but in all Latin-American countries. The first diplomatic task imposed upon Page therefore was one that would have dismayed a more experienced ambassador.   This was to persuade Great Britain to retrace its steps, to withdraw its recognition of Huerta, and to join hands with the United States in bringing about his downfall.   The new ambassador sympathized with Mr. Wilson's ideas to a certain extent; the point at which he parted company with the President's Mexican policy will appear in due course.   He therefore began zealously to preach the new Latin-American doctrine to the British Foreign Office, with results that appear in his letters of this period.

American Embassy, London,
Oct. 25, 1913.

DEAR MR. PRESIDENT:

About this wretched Mexican business I have read columns and columns of comment and turned every conceivable phase of it back and forth in my mind; and I have not seen or heard even an allusion to any moral principle involved or a word of concern for the Mexican people. It is all about who is the stronger, Huerta or some other bandit, and about the necessity of order for the sake of financial interests. Nobody gives us credit for any moral purpose. Nobody recalls our giving Cuba to the Cubans or our pledge to the Philippine Islands. But there is reference to the influence of the Standard Oil Company on the American policy.

This illustrates the complete divorce of European politics from fundamental morals, and it shocks even a man who already knew of this divorce.

In my last talk with Sir Edward Grey I drove this home by emphasizing with all my might the impossibility of your giving primary heed even to any American business interests in Mexico—even the immorality of your doing so: there are many things that come before business and there are some things that come before order. I used American business interests because of course I could not speak openly to him of British commercial interests and his own Government. I am sure he drew the inevitable inference. But not even from him came a word about the moral foundation of government or about the welfare of the Mexican people. These things are not in the European ruling vocabulary.

Still I cannot get rid of the feeling that when this Government recognized Huerta it did not foresee the consequences. I have been trying to find a way whereby they may now avoid repeating this mistake and save their face. I have telegraphed one such plan to Mr. Bryan, if you and he should approve of it—to put it to Sir Edward Grey as squarely and as hard as may be prudent that one way lies a friendly act to us and that the other way lies an unfriendly. I think we can force him to show his hand. It's a wretched business, and the low level of European statecraft is—sad. It leaves to us the task of pulling the world up.—

Very heartily yours,
WALTER H. PAGE.

To the President.

P. S.

But it is possible to extract some fun even from this sordid affair. The Prime Minister came up to me at the Royal wedding reception the other day and said:

"What do you infer from the latest news from Mexico?" (The Huerta coup d'etat in arresting the deputies).

"Several things."

"Tell me the most important inference you draw."

"The danger of prematurely making up one's mind about a Mexican adventurer."

"Ah!" and he moved on.

W. H. P.

To the President

American Embassy, London,
Nov. 22, 1913.

DEAR MR. PRESIDENT:

. . . About the obligations and inferences of democracy, they are dense. They are slow to see what good will come of ousting Huerta unless we know beforehand who will succeed him. Sir Edward Grey is not dense— very far from it—but in this matter even he is slow fully to understand the new policy. The Lord knows I've told him plainly over and over again and, I fear, even preached to him. At first he couldn't see the practical nature of so "idealistic" a programme. I explained to him how the policy that we all too easily have followed for a long time of recognizing any sort of adventurer in Latin-America had, of course, simply encouraged revolutions; that you had found something better than any mere policy, namely, a principle; that policies change but principles do not. His sympathy and his friendliness are beyond any possible question. But Egypt and India, rather than Cuba, are in his mind. He said one day with a smile that it might take two centuries to bring the Mexicans to self-government. "Well," said I, "the United States will be here for two centuries." He still sees no escape from armed intervention.—But he is learning. And many men are seeing the new idea. (I wonder if you are conscious how new it is and how incredible to the Old World mind?) and they express sincere admiration for "your brave new President." A wave of friendliness to the United States swept over the Kingdom when the Prime Minister took his stand in his Guildhall speech. Such hitherto unusual experiences as these are almost common now: At a dinner of the Titmarsh Club—a little group of Thackeray enthusiasts, to which I belong— Courtney, the editor of *The Fortnightly Review*, proposed your health in a capital little speech. The very next night at the big dinner of the largest of the guilds—successful business men—your health was given most heartily; and when I arose to speak they cheered longer than I had ever heard a British dinner-audience cheer. There is, among the people (the Shipping people excepted) a positive and definite enthusiasm for the United States.—But they are simply dense about any sort of government for "dependencies" or backward people, but their own. I have a neighbor who spent many years as an administrator in India. He has talked me deaf about the foolishness of any other plan of dealing with Mexico than by the sword. He is wholly friendly but wholly incredulous. And for old-time Toryism gone to seed, commend me to *The Spectator*. Not a glimmering of the idea has entered Strachey's head: I doubt if it ever does. The London *Times*, however, now sees it very clearly. Their editors have had much talk with me and they have written good leaders out of our conversations. . . .

The upshot of it all so far is that this Government and this people feel that there is a new hand at the helm in Washington; and we can drive them hard, if need be; for they will not risk losing our friendship. I have the utmost confidence in Sir Edward, but not in the same degree in all his cabinet associates—on a pinch. I have discovered that infallibility, wherever she live, dwells not in Downing Street: they make many mistakes. In this Mexican business they have made two bad blunders—recognizing Huerta (they see that now) and sending Carden, who lacks political imagination amazingly (they may be brought to see that if he makes another "break.")

And I never expected to have the holy joy of putting the British Government through an elementary course in the meaning of Democracy!

Yours, Mr. President, with congratulations on the historic Wilson doctrine—no more territory, no more tyrants, no stealing of American governments by concessions or financial obligations (that's fixed now: no successor can set aside a righteous principle once clearly formulated)— Yours most heartily and faithfully.

WALTER H. PAGE.

To the President.

Occasionally Page discussed with Sir Edward Grey an alternative American policy which was in the minds of most people at that time:

Memorandum

. . . The foregoing I wrote before this Mexican business took its present place. I can't get away from the feeling that the English simply do not and will not believe in any unselfish public action—further than the keeping of order. They have a mania for order, sheer order, order for the sake of order. They can't see how anything can come in any one's thought before order or how anything need come afterward. Even Sir Edward Grey jocularly ran me across our history with questions like this:

"Suppose you have to intervene, what then?"

"Make 'em vote and live by their decisions."

"But suppose they will not so live?"

"We'll go in again and make 'em vote again."

"And keep this up 200 years?" asked he.

"Yes," said I. "The United States will be here two hundred years and it can continue to shoot men for that little space till they learn to vote and to rule themselves."

I have never seen him laugh so heartily. Shooting men into self-government! Shooting them into orderliness—he comprehends that; and that's all right. But that's as far as his habit of mind goes. At Sheffield last night, when I had to make a speech, I explained "idealism" (they always quote it) in Government. They listened attentively and even eagerly. Then they came up and asked if I really meant that Government should concern itself with idealistic things—beyond keeping order. Ought they to do so in India?—I assure you they don't think beyond order. A nigger lynched in Mississippi offends them more than a tyrant in Mexico.

To Edward M. House

London, November 2, 1913.

DEAR HOUSE:

I've been writing to the President that the Englishman has a mania for order, order for order's sake, and for— trade. He has reduced a large part of the world to order. He is the best policeman in creation; and—he has the policeman's ethics! Talk to him about character as a basis of government or about a moral basis of government in any outlying country, he'll think you daft. Bah! what matter who governs or how he governs or where he got his authority or how, so long as he keeps order. He won't see anything else. The lesson of our dealing with Cuba is lost on him. He doesn't believe *that*. We may bring this Government in line with us on Mexico. But in this case and in general, the moral uplift of government must be forced by us—I mean government in outlying countries.

Mexico is only part of Central America, and the only way we can ever forge a Central and South American policy that will endure is *this* way, precisely, by saying that your momentarily successful adventurer can't count on us anywhere; the man that rules must govern for the governed. Then we have a policy; and nobody else has that policy. This Mexican business is worth worlds to us—to establish this.

We may have a diplomatic fight here; and I'm ready! Very ready on this, for its own sake and for reasons that follow, to wit:

Extraordinary and sincere and profound as is the respect of the English for the American people, they hold the American Government in contempt. It shifts and doesn't keep its treaty, etc., etc.—They are right, too. But they need to feel the hand that now has the helm.

But one or two things have first to be got out of the way. That Panama tolls is the worst. We are dead wrong in that, as we are dead right on the Mexican matter. If it were possible (I don't know that it is) for the President to say (quietly, not openly) that he agrees with us—if he do—then the field would be open for a fight on Mexico; and the reënforcement of our position would be incalculable.

Then we need in Washington some sort of Bureau or Master of Courtesies for the Government, to do and to permit us to do those little courtesies that the English spend half their time in doing—this in the course of our everyday life and intercourse. For example: When I was instructed to inform this Government that our fleet would go to the Mediterranean, I was instructed also to say that they mustn't trouble to welcome us—don't pay no 'tention to us! Well, that's what they live for in times of peace—ceremonies. We come along and say, "We're comin' but, hell! don't kick up no fuss over us, we're from Missouri, we are!" And the Briton shrugs his shoulders and says, "Boor!" These things are happening all the time. Of course no one nor a dozen nor a hundred count; but generations of 'em have counted badly. A Government without manners.

If I could outdo these folk at their game of courtesy, and could keep our treaty faith with 'em, then I could lick 'em into the next century on the moral aspects of the Mexican Government, and make 'em look up and salute every time the American Government is mentioned. See?—Is there any hope?—Such is the job exactly. And you know what it would lead to—even in our lifetime—

to the leadership of the world: and we should presently be considering how we may best use the British fleet, the British Empire, and the English race for the betterment of mankind.

Yours eagerly,

W. H. P.

A word of caution is necessary to understand Page's references to the British democracy. That the parliamentary system is democratic in the sense that it is responsive to public opinion he would have been the first to admit. That Great Britain is a democracy in the sense that the suffrage is general is also apparent. But, in these reflections on the British commonwealth, the Ambassador was thinking of his old familiar figure, the "Forgotten Man"—the neglected man, woman, and child of the masses. In an address delivered, in June, 1914, before the Royal Institution of Great Britain, Page gave what he regarded as the definition of the American ideal. "The fundamental article in the creed of the American democracy—you may call it the fundamental dogma if you like—is the unchanging and unchangeable resolve that every human being shall have his opportunity for his utmost development—his chance to become and to do the best that he can." Democracy is not only a system of government—"it is a scheme of society." Every citizen must have not only the suffrage, he must likewise enjoy the same advantages as his neighbour for education, for social opportunity, for good health, for success in agriculture, manufacture, finance, and business and professional life. The country that most successfully opened all these avenues to every boy or girl, exclusively on individual merit, was in Page's view the most democratic. He believed that the United States did this

more completely than Great Britain or any other country;
and therefore he believed that we were far more democratic. He had not found in other countries the splendid
phenomenon presented by America's great agricultural
region. "The most striking single fact about the United
States is, I think, this spectacle, which, so far as I know,
is new in the world: On that great agricultural area are
about seven million farms of an average size of about 140
acres, most of which are tilled by the owners themselves,
a population that varies greatly, of course, in its thrift
and efficiency, but most of which is well housed, in houses
they themselves own, well clad, well fed, and a population
that trains practically all its children in schools maintained by public taxation." It was some such vision as
this that Page hoped to see realized ultimately in Mexico. And some such development as this would make
Mexico a democracy. It was his difficulty in making
the British see the Mexican problem in this light that
persuaded him that, in this comprehensive meaning of
the word, the democratic ideal had made an inappreciable
progress in Europe—and even in Great Britain itself.

II

These letters are printed somewhat out of their chrono-
logical order because they picture definitely the two
opposing viewpoints of Great Britain and the United
States on Mexico and Latin-America generally. Here,
then, was the sharp issue drawn between the Old World
and the New—on one side the dreary conception of outlying countries as fields to be exploited for the benefit of
"investors," successful revolutionists to be recognized in
so far as they promoted such ends, and no consideration
to be shown to the victims of their rapacity; and the
new American idea, the idea which had been made reality

in Cuba and the Philippines, that the enlightened and successful nations stood something in the position of trustees to such unfortunate lands and that it was their duty to lead them along the slow pathway of progress and democracy. So far the Wilsonian principle could be joyfully supported by the Ambassador. Page disagreed with the President, however, in that he accepted the logical consequences of this programme. His formula of "shooting people into self-government," which had so entertained the British Foreign Secretary, was a characteristically breezy description of the alternative that Page, in the last resort, was ready to adopt, but which President Wilson and Secretary Bryan persistently refused to consider. Page was just as insistent as the Washington Administration that Huerta should resign and that Great Britain should assist the United States in accomplishing his dethronement, and that the Mexican people should have a real opportunity of setting up for themselves. He was not enough of an "idealist," however, to believe that the Mexicans, without the assistance of their powerful neighbours, could succeed in establishing a constitutional government. In early August, 1913, President Wilson sent Mr. John Lind, ex-Governor of Minnesota, to Mexico as his personal representative. His mission was to invite Huerta to remove himself from Mexican politics, and to permit the Mexican people to hold a presidential election at which Huerta would himself agree not to be a candidate. Mr. Lind presented these proposals on August 15th, and President Huerta rejected every one of them with a somewhat disconcerting promptitude.

That Page was prepared to accept the consequences of this failure appears in the following letter. The lack of confidence which it discloses in Secretary Bryan was a

feeling that became stronger as the Mexican drama unfolded.

To Edward M. House

London, August 25, 1913.

MY DEAR HOUSE:

. . . If you find a chance, get the substance of this
memorandum into the hands of two men: the President
and the Secretary of Agriculture. Get 'em in Houston's
at once—into the President's whenever the time is ripe.
I send the substance to Washington and I send many
other such things. But I never feel sure that they reach
the President. The most confidential letter I have
written was lost in Washington, and there is pretty good
testimony that it reached the Secretary's desk. He does
not acknowledge the important things, but writes me
confidentially to inquire if the office of the man who
attends to the mail pouches (the diplomatic and naval
despatches in London)[1] is not an office into which he
might put a Democrat.—But I keep at it. It would be
a pleasure to know that the President knows what I
am trying to do. . . .

Yours heartily,

WALTER H. PAGE.

Following is the memorandum:

In October the provisional recognition of Huerta by
England will end. Then this Government will be free.
Then is the time for the United States to propose to
England joint intervention merely to reduce this turbu-
lent scandal of a country to order—on an agreement, of
course, to preserve the territorial integrity of Mexico.
It's a mere police duty that all great nations have to do—
as they did in the case of the Boxer riots in China. Of

---

[1]See the Appendix (at end of Vol. II) for this episode in detail.

course Germany and France, etc., ought to be invited—
on the same pledge: the preservation of territorial integrity. If Germany should come in, she will thereby
practically acknowledge the Monroe Doctrine, as England
has already done. If Germany stay out, then she can't
complain. England and the United States would have
only to announce their intention: there'd be no need to
fire a gun. Besides settling the Mexican trouble, we'd
gain much—having had England by our side in a praiseworthy enterprise. That, and the President's visit[1]
would give the world notice to whom it belongs, and
cause it to be quiet and to go about its proper business of
peaceful industry.

Moreover, it would show all the Central and South
American States that we don't want any of their territory,
that we will not let anybody else have any, but that they,
too, must keep orderly government or the great Nations
of the earth, will, at our bidding, forcibly demand quiet in
their borders. I believe a new era of security would come
in all Spanish America. Investments would be safer,
governments more careful and orderly. And—we would
not have made any entangling alliance with anybody. All
this would prevent perhaps dozens of little wars. It's
merely using the English fleet and ours to make the world
understand that the time has come for orderliness and
peace and for the honest development of backward, turbulent lands and peoples.

If you don't put this through, tell me what's the
matter with it. I've sent it to Washington after talking
and being talked to for a month and after the hardest
kind of thinking. Isn't this constructive? Isn't it using

---

[1]There was a suggestion, which the Ambassador endorsed, that President Wilson
should visit England to accept, in the name of the United States, Sulgrave Manor,
the ancestral home of the Washingtons. See Chapter IX, page 274.

196 THE LIFE AND LETTERS OF WALTER H. PAGE

the great power lying idle about the world, to do the thing that most needs to be done?

Colonel House presented this memorandum to the President, but events sufficiently disclosed that it had no influence upon his Mexican policy. Two days after it was written Mr. Wilson went before Congress, announced that the Lind Mission had failed, and that conditions in Mexico had grown worse. He advised all Americans to leave the country, and declared that he would lay an embargo on the shipment of munitions—an embargo that would affect both the Huerta forces and the revolutionary groups that were fighting them.

Meanwhile Great Britain had taken another step that made as unpleasant an impression on Washington as had the recognition of Huerta. Sir Lionel Edward Gresley Carden had for several years been occupying British diplomatic posts in Central America, in all of which he had had disagreeable social and diplomatic relations with Americans. Sir Lionel had always shown great zeal in promoting British commercial interests, and, justly or unjustly, had acquired the fame of being intensely anti-American. From 1911 to 1913 Carden had served as British Minister to Cuba; here his anti-Americanism had shown itself in such obnoxious ways that Mr. Knox, Secretary of State under President Taft, had instructed Ambassador Reid to bring his behaviour to the attention of the British Foreign Office. These representations took practically the form of requesting Carden's removal from Cuba. Perhaps the unusual relations that the United States bore toward Cuba warranted Mr. Knox in making such an approach; yet the British refused to see the matter in that light; not only did they fail to displace Carden, but they knighted him—the traditional British way of defending a faithful public servant who has been attacked. Sir Lionel Carden refused to mend his ways; he continued to indulge in what Washington regarded as anti-American propaganda; and a second time Secretary Knox intimated that his removal would be acceptable to this country, and a second time this request was refused. With this preliminary history of Carden as a background, and with the British-American misunderstanding over Huerta at its most serious stage, the emotions of Washington may well be imagined when the news came, in July, 1913, that this same gentleman had been appointed British Minister to Mexico. If the British Government had ransacked its diplomatic force to find the one man who would have been most objectionable to the United States, it could have made no better selection. The President and Mr. Bryan were pretty well persuaded that the "oil concessionaires" were dictating British-Mexican policy, and this appointment translated their suspicion into a conviction. Carden had seen much service in Mexico; he had been on the friendliest terms with Diaz; and the newspapers openly charged that the British oil capitalists had dictated his selection. All these assertions Carden and the oil interests denied; yet Carden's behaviour from the day of his appointment showed great hostility to the United States. A few days after he had reached New York, on his way to his new post, the New York *World* published an interview with Carden in which he was reported as declaring that President Wilson knew nothing about the Mexican situation and in which he took the stand that Huerta was the man to handle Mexico at this crisis. His appearance in the Mexican capital was accompanied by other highly undiplomatic publications. In late October President Huerta arrested all his enemies in the Mexican Congress, threw them into jail, and proclaimed himself dictator. Washington was much displeased that Sir Lionel Carden should have selected the day of these high-handed proceedings to present to Huerta his credentials as minister; in its sensitive condition, the State Department interpreted this act as a reaffirmation of that recognition that had already caused so much confusion in Mexican affairs.

Carden made things worse by giving out more newspaper interviews, a tendency that had apparently grown into a habit. "I do not believe that the United States recognizes the seriousness of the situation here. . . . I see no reason why Huerta should be displaced by another man whose abilities are yet to be tried. . . . Safety in Mexico can be secured only by punitive and remedial methods, and a strong man;"—such were a few of the reflections that the reporters attributed to this astonishing diplomat. Meanwhile, the newspapers were filled with reports that the British Minister was daily consorting with Huerta, that he was constantly strengthening that chieftain's backbone in opposition to the United States and that he was obtaining concessions in return for this support. To what extent these press accounts rested on fact cannot be ascertained definitely at this time; yet it is a truth that Carden's general behaviour gave great encouragement to Huerta and that it had the deplorable effect of placing Great Britain and the United States in opposition. The interpretation of the casual reader was that Great Britain was determined to seat Huerta in the Presidency against the determination of the United States to keep him out. The attitude of the Washington cabinet was almost bitter at this time against the British Government. "There is a feeling here," wrote Secretary Lane to Page, "that England is playing a game unworthy of her."

The British Government promptly denied the authenticity of the Carden interview, but that helped matters little, for the American public insisted on regarding such denials as purely diplomatic. Something of a storm against Carden arose in England itself, where it was believed that his conception of his duties was estranging two friendly countries. Probably the chief difficulty was that the British Foreign Office could see no logical sequence in the Washington policy. Put Huerta out—yes, by all means: but what then? Page's notes of his visit to Sir Edward Grey a few days after the latest Carden interview confirm this:

I have just come from an hour's talk with Grey about Mexico. He showed me his telegram to Carden, asking about Carden's reported interview criticizing the United States, and Carden's flat denial. He showed me another telegram to Carden about Huerta's reported boast that he would have the backing of London, Paris, and Berlin against the United States, in which Grey advised Carden that British policy should be to keep aloof from Huerta's boasts and plans. Carden denied that Huerta made such a boast in his statement to the Diplomatic Corps. Grey wishes the President to know of these telegrams.

Talk then became personal and informal. I went over the whole subject again, telling how the Press and people of the United States were becoming critical of the British Government; that they regarded the problem as wholly American; that they resented aid to Huerta, whom they regarded as a mere tyrant; that they suspected British interests of giving financial help to Huerta; that many newspapers and persons refused to believe Carden's denial; that the President's policy was not academic but was the only policy that would square with American ideals and that it was unchangeable. I cited our treatment of Cuba. I explained again that I was talking unofficially and giving him only my own interpretation of the people's mood. He asked, if the British Government should withdraw the recognition of Huerta, what would happen.

"In my opinion," I replied, "he would collapse."

"What would happen then—worse chaos?"

"That is impossible," I said. "There is no worse chaos than deputies in jail, the dictatorial doubling of the tariff, the suppression of opinion, and the practical banishment of independent men. If Huerta should fall, there is hope that suppressed men and opinion will set up a successful government."

"Suppose that fail," he asked—"what then?"

I replied that, in case of continued and utter failure, the United States might feel obliged to repeat its dealings with Cuba and that the continued excitement of opinion in the United States might precipitate this.

Grey protested that he knew nothing of what British interests had done or were doing, that he wished time to think the matter out and that he was glad to await the President's communication. He thanked me cordially for my frank statements and declared that he understood perfectly their personal nature. I impressed him with the seriousness of American public opinion.

The last thing that the British Government desired at this time was a serious misunderstanding with the United States, on Mexico or any other matter. Yet the Mexican situation, in early November, 1913, clearly demanded a complete cleaning up. The occasion soon presented itself. Sir William Tyrrell, the private secretary of Sir Edward Grey sailed, in late October, for the United

States. The purpose of his visit was not diplomatic, but Page evidently believed that his presence in the United States offered too good an opportunity to be lost.

To Edward M. House

Newton Hall, Newton, Cambridge.
Sunday, October 26, 1913.

DEAR HOUSE:

Sir William Tyrrell, the secretary of Sir Edward Grey— himself, I think, an M. P.—has gone to the United States to visit his friend, Sir Cecil Spring Rice. He sailed yesterday, going first to Dublin, N. H., thence with the Ambassador to Washington. He has never before been to the United States, and he went off in high glee, alone, to see it. He's a good fellow, a thoroughly good fellow, and he's an important man. He of course has Sir Edward's complete confidence, but he's also a man on his own account. I have come to reckon it worth while to get ideas that I want driven home into his head. It's a good head and a good place to put good ideas.

The Lord knows you have far too much to do; but in this juncture I should count it worth your while to pay him some attention. I want him to get the President's ideas about Mexico, good and firm and hard. They are so far from altruistic in their politics here that it would be a good piece of work to get our ideas and aims into this man's head. His going gives you and the President and everybody a capital chance to help me keep our good American-English understanding.

Whatever happen in Mexico, I'm afraid there will be a disturbance of the very friendly feeling between the American people and the English. I am delivering a series of well-thought-out discourses to Sir Edward—

with what effect, I don't know.   If the American press could be held in a little, that would be as good as it is impossible.

I'm now giving the Foreign Office the chance to refrain from more premature recognizing.

Very hastily yours,
WALTER H. PAGE.

Sir William Tyrrell, to whom Page refers so pleasantly, was one of the most engaging men personally in the British Foreign Office, as well as one of the most influential.   Though he came to America on no official mission to our Government, he was exceptionally qualified to discuss Mexico and other pending questions with the Washington Administration.   He had an excellent background, and a keen insight into the human aspects of all problems, but perhaps his most impressive physical trait was a twinkling eye, as his most conspicuous mental quality was certainly a sense of humour. Constant association with Sir Edward Grey had given his mind a cast not dissimilar to that of his chief—a belief in ordinary decency in international relations, an enthusiasm for the better ordering of the world, a sincere admiration for the United States and a desire to maintain British-American friendship.   In his first encounter with official Washington Sir William needed all that sense of the ludicrous with which he is abundantly endowed. This took the form of a long interview with Secretary Bryan on the foreign policy of Great Britain.   The Secretary harangued Sir William on the wickedness of the British Empire, particularly in Egypt and India and in Mexico.   The British oil men, Mr. Bryan declared, were nothing but the "paymasters" of the British Cabinet.

"You are wrong," replied the Englishman, who saw

that the only thing to do on an occasion of this kind was to refuse to take the Secretary seriously. "Lord Cowdray hasn't money enough. Through a long experience with corruption the Cabinet has grown so greedy that Cowdray hasn't the money necessary to reach their price."

"Ah," said Mr. Bryan, triumphantly, accepting Sir William's bantering answer as made in all seriousness. "Then you admit the charge."

From this he proceeded to denounce Great Britain in still more unmeasured terms. The British, he declared, had only one interest in Mexico, and that was oil. The Foreign Office had simply handed its Mexican policy over to the "oil barons" for predatory purposes.

"That's just what the Standard Oil people told me in New York," the British diplomat replied. "Mr. Secretary, you are talking just like a Standard Oil man. The ideas that you hold are the ones which the Standard Oil is disseminating. You are pursuing the policy which they have decided on. Without knowing it you are promoting the interest of Standard Oil."

Sir William saw that it was useless to discuss Mexico with Mr. Bryan—that the Secretary was not a thinker but an emotionalist. However, despite their differences, the two men liked each other and had a good time. As Sir William was leaving, he bowed deferentially to the Secretary of State and said:

"You have stripped me naked, Mr. Secretary, but I am unashamed."

With President Wilson, however, the Englishman had a more satisfactory experience. He was delighted by the President's courtesy, charm, intelligence, and conversational powers. The impression which Sir William obtained of the American President on this occasion remained with him for several years and was itself an

important element in British-American relations after the
outbreak of the World War.   And the visit was a profitable one for Mr. Wilson, since he obtained a clear understanding of the British policy toward Mexico.   Sir William
succeeded in persuading the President that the so-called
oil interests were not dictating the policy of Sir Edward
Grey.   That British oil men were active in Mexico was apparent; but they were not using a statesman of so high a
character as Sir Edward Grey for their purposes and would
not be able to do so.   The British Government entertained
no ambitions in Mexico that meant unfriendliness to the
United States.   In no way was the policy of Great Britain
hostile to our own.   In fact, the British recognized the predominant character of the American interest in Mexico and
were willing to accept any policy in which Washington
would take the lead.   All it asked was that British property and British lives be protected; once these were
safeguarded Great Britain was ready to stand aside and let
the United States deal with Mexico in its own way.

The one disappointment of this visit was that Sir
William Tyrrell was unable to obtain from President
Wilson any satisfactory statement of his Mexican policy.

"When I go back to England," said the Englishman,
as the interview was approaching an end, "I shall be
asked to explain your Mexican policy.   Can you tell me
what it is?"

President Wilson looked at him earnestly and said, in
his most decisive manner:

"I am going to teach the South American Republics to
elect good men!"

This was excellent as a purpose, but it could hardly be
regarded as a programme.

"Yes," replied Sir William, "but, Mr. President, I
shall have to explain this to Englishmen, who, as you

know, lack imagination. They cannot see what is the difference between Huerta, Carranza, and Villa."

The only answer he could obtain was that Carranza was the best of the three and that Villa was not so bad as he had been painted. But the phrase that remained with the British diplomat was that one so characteristically Wilsonian: "I propose to teach the South American Republics to elect good men." In its attitude, its phrasing, it held the key to much Wilson history.

Additional details of this historic interview are given in Colonel House's letters:

From Edward M. House

145 East 35th Street,
New York City.
November 4, 1913.

DEAR PAGE:

Your cablegram, telling me of the arrival of Sir William Tyrrell on the *Imperator*, was handed me on my way to the train as I left for Washington.

The President talked with me about the Mexican situation and it looks as if something positive will be done in a few days unless Huerta abdicates.

It is to be the policy of this Administration henceforth not to recognize any Central American government that is not formed along constitutional lines. Anything else would be a makeshift policy. As you know, revolutions and assassinations in order to obtain control of governments are instituted almost wholly for the purpose of loot and when it is found that these methods will not bring the desired results, they will cease.

The President also feels strongly in regard to foreign financial interests seeking to control those unstable governments through concessions and otherwise. This, too, he is determined to discourage as far as it is possible to do so.

This was a great opportunity for England and America to get together. You know how strongly we both feel upon this subject and I do not believe that the President differed greatly from us, but the recent actions of the British Government have produced a decided irritation, which to say the least is unfortunate.

Faithfully yours,
E. M. House.

145 East 35th Street,
New York City.
November 14, 1913.

DEAR PAGE:

Things have happened quickly since I last wrote to you.

I went to Washington Monday night as the guest of the Bryans. They have been wanting me to come to them and I thought this a good opportunity.

I talked the Mexican situation out thoroughly with him and one of your dispatches came while I was there. I found that he was becoming prejudiced against the British Government, believing that their Mexican policy was based purely upon commercialism, that they were backing Huerta quietly at the instance of Lord Cowdray, and that Cowdray had not only already obtained concessions from the Huerta Government, but expected to obtain others. Sir Lionel Carden was also all to the bad.

I saw the President and his views were not very different from those of Mr. Bryan. I asked the President to permit me to see Sir William Tyrrell and talk to him frankly and to attempt to straighten the tangle out. He gave me a free hand.

I lunched with Sir William at the British Embassy although Sir Cecil Spring Rice was not well enough to be present. I had a long talk with Sir William after lunch and found that our suspicions were unwarranted and that we could get together without any difficulty whatever.

I told him very frankly what our purpose was in Mexico and that we were determined to carry it through if it was within our power to do so. That being so I suggested that he get his government to coöperate cordially with ours rather than to accept our policy reluctantly.

I told him that you and I had dreamed of a sympathetic alliance between the two countries and that it seemed to me that this dream might come true very quickly because of the President and Sir Edward Grey. He expressed a willingness to coöperate freely and I told him I would arrange an early meeting with the President. I thought it better to bring the President into the game rather than Mr. Bryan. I told him of the President's attitude upon the Panama toll question but I touched upon that lightly and in confidence, preferring for the President himself to make his own statement.

I left the Bryans in the morning of the luncheon with Sir William, intending to take an afternoon train for New York, but the President wanted me to stay with him at the White House over night and meet Sir William with him at half past nine the following morning. He was so tired that I did not have the heart to urge a meeting that night.

From half past nine until half past ten the President and Sir William repeated to each other what they had said separately to me, and which I had given to each, and then the President elaborated upon the toll question much to the satisfaction of Sir William.

He explained the matter in detail and assured him of his entire sympathy and purpose to carry out our treaty obligations, both in the letter and the spirit.

Sir William was very happy after the interview and when the President left us he remained to talk to me and to express his gratification. He cleared up in the President's mind all suspicion, I think, in regard to concessions and as to the intentions and purposes of the British Government. He assured the President that his government would work cordially with ours and that they would do all that they could to bring about joint pressure through Germany and France for the elimination of Huerta.

We are going to give them a chance to see what they can do with Huerta before moving any further. Sir William thinks that if we are willing to let Huerta save his face he can be got out without force of arms.

Sir William said that if foreign diplomats could have heard our conversation they would have fallen in a faint; it was so frankly indiscreet and undiplomatic. I did not tell him so, but I had it in the back of my mind that where people wanted to do right and had the power to carry out their intentions there was no need to cloak their thoughts in diplomatic language.

All this makes me very happy for it looks as if we are in sight of the promised land.

I am pleased to tell you of the compliments that have been thrown at you by the President, Mr. Bryan, and Sir William. They were all enthusiastic over your work in London and expressed the keenest appreciation of the way in which you have handled matters. Sir William told me that he did not remember an American Ambassador that was your equal.

Faithfully yours,

E. M. HOUSE.

So far as a meeting between a British diplomat and the President of the United States could solve the Mexican problem, that problem was apparently solved. The dearest wish of Mr. Wilson, the elimination of Huerta, seemed to be approaching realization, now that he had persuaded Great Britain to support him in this enterprise. Whether Sir William Tyrrell, or Sir Edward Grey, had really become converted to the President's "idealistic" plans for Mexico is an entirely different question. At this time there was another matter in which Great Britain's interest was even greater than in Mexico. These letters have already contained reference to tolls on the Panama Canal. Colonel House's letter shows that the President discussed this topic with Sir William Tyrrell and gave him assurances that this would be settled on terms satisfactory to Great Britain. It cannot be maintained that that assurance was really the consideration which paved the way to an understanding on Huerta. The conversation was entirely informal; indeed, it could not be otherwise, for Sir William Tyrrell brought no credentials; there could be no definite bargain or agreement, but there is little question that Mr. Wilson's friendly disposition toward British shipping through the Panama Canal made it easy for Great Britain to give him a free hand in Mexico.

A few days after this White House interview Sir Lionel Carden performed what must have been for him an uncongenial duty. This loquacious minister led a procession of European diplomats to General Huerta, formally advised that warrior to yield to the American demands and withdraw from the Presidency of Mexico. The delegation informed the grim dictator that their governments were supporting the American policy and Sir Lionel brought him the unwelcome news that he could not depend upon British support. About the same time Premier Asquith made conciliatory remarks on Mexico at the Guildhall banquet. He denied that the British Government had undertaken any policy "deliberately opposed to that of the United States. There is no vestige of foundation for such a rumour." These events changed the atmosphere at Washington, which now became almost as cordial to Great Britain as it had for several months been suspicious.

To Edward M. House

London, November 15, 1913.

DEAR HOUSE:

All's well here. The whole trouble was caused not here but in Mexico City; and that is to be remedied yet. And it will be! For the moment it is nullified. But you need give yourself no concern about the English Government or people, in the long run. It is taking them some time to see the vast difference between acting by a principle and acting by what they call a "policy." They and we ourselves too have from immemorial time been recognizing successful adventurers, and they didn't instantly understand this new "idealistic" move; they didn't know the man at the helm! I preached many sermons to our friend, I explained the difference to many private groups, I made after-dinner speeches leading right up to the point—as far as I dared, I inspired many newspaper articles; and they see it now and have said it and have made it public; and the British people are enthusiastic as far as they understand it.

And anybody concerned here understands the language that the President speaks now. You mustn't forget that in all previous experiences in Latin America we ourselves have been as much to blame as anybody else. Now we have a clear road to travel, a policy based on character to follow forever—a new era. Our dealing with Cuba was a new chapter in the history of the world. Our dealing with Mexico is Chapter II of the same Revelation. Tell em this in Washington.

The remaining task will be done too and I think pretty soon. For that I need well-loaded shells. I'll supply the gunpowder.

And don't you concern yourself about the English. They're all right—a little slow, but all right.

Heartily yours,

WALTER H. PAGE.

To Edward M. House

Newtimber Place, Hassocks, Sussex,
Sunday, November 23, 1913.

DEAR HOUSE:

Your letter telling me about Tyrrell and the President brought me great joy. Tyrrell is in every way a square fellow, much like his Chief; and, you may depend on it, they are playing fair—in their slow way. They always think of India and of Egypt—never of Cuba. Lord! Lord! the fun I've had, the holy joy I am having (I never expected to have such exalted and invigorating felicity) in delivering elementary courses of instruction in democracy to the British Government. Deep down at the bottom, they don't know what Democracy means. Their Empire is in the way. Their centuries of land-stealing are in the way. Their unsleeping watchfulness of British commerce is in the way. "You say you'll shoot men into self-government," said Sir Edward. "Doesn't that strike you as comical?" And I answered, "It is comical only to the Briton and to others who have associated shooting with subjugation. We associate shooting with freedom." Half this blessed Sunday at this country house I have been ramming the idea down the throat of the Lord Chancellor.[1] *He* sees it, too, being a Scotchman.   I take the members of the Government, as I get the chance or can make it, and go over with them the A B C of the President's principle: no territorial annexation; no trafficking with tyrants; no stealing of American governments by concession or financial thimble-rigging.   They'll not recognize another Huerta—they're sick of that.   And they'll not endanger our friendship. They didn't see the idea in the beginning.   Of course the real trouble has been in Mexico City—Carden.   They don't know yet just what he did.   But they will, if *I* can find out.   I haven't yet been able to make them tell me at Washington.   Washington is a deep hole of silence toward ambassadors.   By gradual approaches, I'm going to prove that Carden can do—and in a degree has already done—as much harm as Bryce did good—and all about a paltry few hundreds of million dollars' worth of oil.   What the devil does the oil or the commerce of Mexico or the investments there amount to in comparison with the close friendship of the two nations? Carden can't be good long: he'll break out again presently.   He has no political imagination.   That's a rather common disease here, too.   Few men have.   It's good fun.   I'm inviting the Central and South American Ministers to lunch with me, one by one, and I'm incidentally loading them up.   I have all the boys in the Embassy full of zeal and they are tackling the Secretaries of the Central and South American legations.   We've got a *principle* now to deal by with them.   They'll see after a while.

English people are all right, too—except the Doctrinaires.   They write much rank ignorance.   But the learned men learn things last of all.

---

[1]Viscount Haldane, Lord High Chancellor of Great Britain since 1912.

I thank you heartily for your good news about Tyrrell, about the President (but I'm sorry he's tired: make him quit eating meat and play golf); about the Panama tolls; about the Currency Bill (my love to McAdoo); about my own little affairs.—We are looking with the very greatest pleasure to the coming of the young White House couple. I've got two big dinners for them—Sir Edward, the Lord Chancellor, a duchess or two, some good folk, Ruth Bryan, a couple of ambassadors, etc., etc., etc. Then we'll take 'em to a literary speaking-feast or two, have 'em invited to a few great houses; then we'll give 'em another dinner, and then we'll get a guide for them to see all the reforming institutions in London, to their hearts' content—lots of fun.

Lots of fun: I got the American Society for its Thanksgiving dinner to invite the Lord Chancellor to respond to a toast to the President. He's been to the United States lately and he is greatly pleased. So far, so good. Then I came down here—where he, too, is staying. After five or six hours' talk about everything else he said, "By the way, your countrymen have invited me," etc., etc. "Now what would be appropriate to talk about?" Then I poured him full of the New Principle as regards Central and South America; for, if he will talk on that, what he says will be reported and read on both continents. He's a foxy Scot, and he didn't say he would, but he said that he'd consider it. "Consider it" means that he will confer with Sir Edward. I'm beginning to learn their vocabulary. Anyhow the Lord Chancellor is in line.

It's good news you send always. Keep it up—keep it up. The volume of silence that I get is oppressive. You remember the old nigger that wished to pick a quarrel with another old nigger? Nigger No. 1 swore and stormed at nigger No. 2, and kept on swearing and storming, hoping to provoke him. Nigger No. 2 said not a word, but kept at his work. Nigger No. 1 swore and stormed more. Nigger No. 2 said not a word. Nigger No. 1 frothed still more. Nigger No. 2, still silent. Nigger No. 1 got desperate and said: "Look here, you kinky-headed, flat-nosed, slab-footed nigger, I warns you 'fore God, don't you keep givin' me none o' your damned silence!"   I wish you'd tell all my friends that story.

Always heartily yours,

WALTER H. PAGE.

CHAPTER VII

PERSONALITIES OF THE MEXICAN PROBLEM

PAGE'S remarks about the "trouble in Mexico City" and the "remaining task" refer, of course, to Sir Lionel Carden. "As I make Carden out," he wrote about this time, "he's a slow-minded, unimaginative, commercial Briton, with as much nimbleness as an elephant. British commerce is his deity, British advantage his duty and mission; and he goes about his work with blunt dullness and ineptitude. That's his mental calibre as I read him—a dull, commercial man."

Although Sir Lionel Carden had been compelled to harmonize himself with the American policy, Page regarded his continued presence in Mexico City as a standing menace to British-American relations. He therefore set himself to accomplish the minister's removal. The failure of President Taft's attempt to obtain Carden's transfer from Havana, in 1912, showed that Page's new enterprise was a delicate and difficult one; yet he did not hesitate.

The part that the wives of diplomats and statesmen play in international relations is one that few Americans understand. Yet in London, the Ambassador's wife is almost as important a person as the Ambassador himself. An event which now took place in the American Embassy emphasized this point. A certain lady, well known in London, called upon Mrs. Page and gave her a message on Mexican affairs for the Ambassador's benefit. The purport was that the activities of certain British commercial interests in Mexico, if not checked, would produce a serious situation between Great Britain and the United States. The lady in question was herself a sincere worker for Anglo-American amity, and this was the motive that led her to take an unusual step.

"It's all being done for the benefit of one man," she said.

The facts were presented in the form of a memorandum, which Mrs. Page copied and gave the Ambassador. This, in turn, Page sent to President Wilson.

To Edward M. House

London, November 26, 1913.

DEAR HOUSE:

Won't you read the enclosed and get it to the President? It is somewhat extra-official but it is very confidential, and I have a special reason for wishing it to go through your hands. Perhaps it will interest you.

The lady that wrote it is one of the very best-informed women I know, one of those active and most influential women in the high political society of this Kingdom, at whose table statesmen and diplomats meet and important things come to pass. . . .

I am sure she has no motive but the avowed one. She has taken a liking to Mrs. Page and this is merely a friendly and patriotic act.

I had heard most of the things before as gossip—never before as here put together by a responsible hand.

Mrs. Page went to see her and, as evidence of our appreciation and safety, gave the original back to her. We have kept no copy, and I wish this burned, if you please. It would raise a riot here, if any breath of it were to get out, that would put bedlam to shame.

Lord Cowdray has been to see me for four successive days. I have a suspicion (though I don't know) that, instead of his running the Government, the Government has now turned the tables and is running him. His government contract is becoming a bad thing to sleep with. He told me this morning that he (through Lord Murray) had withdrawn the request for any concession in Colombia.[1] I congratulated him. "That, Lord Cowdray, will save you as well as some other people I know a good deal of possible trouble." I have explained to him the whole New Principle *in extenso*, "so that you may see clearly where the line of danger runs." Lord! how he's changed! Several weeks ago when I ran across him accidentally he was humorous, almost cynical. Now he's very serious. I explained to him that the only thing that had kept South America from being parcelled out as Africa has been is the Monroe Doctrine and the United States behind it. He granted that.

"In Monroe's time," said I, "the only way to take a part of South America was to take land. Now finance has new ways of its own!"

"Perhaps," said he.

"Right there," I answered, "where you put your 'perhaps,' I put a danger signal. That, I assure you, you will read about in the histories as 'The Wilson Doctrine'!"

You don't know how easy it all is with our friend and leader in command. I've almost grown bold. You feel steady ground beneath you. They are taking to their tents.

"What's going to happen in Mexico City?"

---

[1]This was another manifestation of British friendliness. When the American excitement was most acute, it became known that British capitalists had secured oil concessions in Colombia. At the demand of the British Government they gave them up.

"A peaceful tragedy, followed by emancipation."

"And the great industries of Mexico?"

"They will not have to depend on adventurers' fa vours!"

"But in the meantime, what?"

"Patience, looking towards justice!"

Yours heartily and in health (you bet!)

W. H. P.

From Edward M. House

145 East 35th Street,
New York City.
December 12, 1913.

DEAR PAGE:

Your budget under dates, November 15th, 23rd, and 26th came to me last week, just after the President had been here. I saved the letters until I went to Washington, from which place I have just returned.

The President has been in bed for nearly a week and Doctor Grayson permitted no one to see him but me. Yesterday before I left he was feeling so well that I asked him if he did not want to feel better and then I read him your letters. Mrs. Wilson was present.

I cannot tell you how pleased he was. He laughed repeatedly at the different comments you made and he was delighted with what you had to say concerning Lord Cowdray. We do not love him for we think that between Cowdray and Carden a large part of our troubles in Mexico has been made. Your description of his attitude at the beginning and his present one pleased us much.

After I had read the confidential letter the President said "now let me see if I have the facts." He then recited them in consecutive order just as the English lady had written them, almost using the same phrases, showing the well-trained mind that he has. I then dropped the letter in the grate.

He enjoyed heartily the expression "Washington is a deep hole of silence towards ambassadors," and again "The volume of silence that I get is oppressive," and of course the story apropos of this last remark.

I was with him for more than an hour and he was distinctly better when I left. I hated to look at him in bed for I could not help realizing what his life means to the Democratic Party, to the Nation and almost to the world.

Of course you know that I only read your letters to him. Mr. Bryan was my guest on Wednesday and I returned to Washington with him but I made no mention of our correspondence and I never have. The President seems to like our way of doing things and further than that I do not care.

Upon my soul I do not believe the President could be better pleased than he is with the work you are doing.

Faithfully yours,
E. M. HOUSE.

From now on the Ambassador exerted a round-about pressure—the method of "gradual approach" already referred to—upon the Foreign Office for Carden's removal. An extract from a letter to the President gives a hint concerning this method:

I have already worked upon Sir Edward's mind about his Minister to Mexico as far as I could. Now that the other matter is settled and while Carden is behaving, I go at it. Two years ago Mr. Knox made a bad blunder in protesting against Carden's "anti-Americanism" in Cuba. Mr. Knox sent Mr. Reid no definite facts nor even

accusations to base a protest on. The result was a failure
—a bad failure. I have again asked Mr. Bryan for all
the definite reports he has heard about Carden. That
man, in my judgment, has caused nine tenths of the
trouble here.

Naturally Page did not ask the Minister's removal
directly—that would have been an unpardonable blunder. His meetings during this period with Sir Edward
were taking place almost every day, and Carden, in
one way or another, kept coming to the front in their
conversation. Sir Edward, like Page, would sacrifice
much in the cause of Anglo-American relations; Page
would occasionally express his regret that the British Minister to Mexico was not a man who shared
their enthusiasm on this subject; in numerous other ways
the impression was conveyed that the two countries
could solve the Mexican entanglement much better if a
more congenial person represented British interests in
the Southern Republic. This reasoning evidently produced the desired results. In early January, 1914, a
hint was unofficially conveyed to the American Ambassador that Carden was to be summoned to London for
a "conversation" with Sir Edward Grey, and that his
return to Mexico would depend upon the outcome of that
interview. There was a likelihood that, in future, Sir
Lionel Carden would represent the British Empire in
Brazil.

This news, sent in discreet cipher to Washington, delighted the Administration. "It is fine about Carden,"
wrote Colonel House on January 10th. "I knew you had
done it when I saw it in the papers, but I did not know just
how. You could not have brought it about in a more
diplomatic and effectual way."

And the following came from the President:

From President Wilson

Pass Christian,
January 6, 1914.

MY DEAR PAGE:

I have your letter of December twenty-first, which I have greatly enjoyed.

Almost at the very time I was reading it, the report came through the Associated Press from London that Carden was to be transferred immediately to Brazil. If this is true, it is indeed a most fortunate thing and I feel sure it is to be ascribed to your tactful and yet very plain representations to Sir Edward Grey. I do not think you realize how hard we worked to get from either Lind or O'Shaughnessy[1] definite items of speech or conduct which we could furnish you as material for what you had to say to the Ministers about Carden. It simply was not obtainable. Everything that we got was at second or third hand. That he was working against us was too plain for denial, and yet he seems to have done it in a very astute way which nobody could take direct hold of. I congratulate you with all my heart on his transference.

I long, as you do, for an opportunity to do constructive work all along the line in our foreign relations, particularly with Great Britain and the Latin-American states, but surely, my dear fellow, you are deceiving yourself in supposing that constructive work is not now actually going on, and going on at your hands quite as much as at ours. The change of attitude and the growing ability to understand what we are thinking about and purposing on the part of the official circle in London is directly attributable

[1] Mr. Nelson O'Shaughnessy, Chargé d'Affaires in Mexico.

to what you have been doing, and I feel more and more grateful every day that you are our spokesman and interpreter there. This is the only possible constructive work in foreign affairs, aside from definite acts of policy.

So far as the policy is concerned, you may be sure I will strive to the utmost to obtain both a repeal of the discrimination in the matter of tolls and a renewal of the arbitration treaties, and I am not without hope that I can accomplish both at this session. Indeed this is the session in which these things must be done if they are to be done at all.

Back of the smile which came to my face when you spoke of the impenetrable silence of the State Department toward its foreign representatives lay thoughts of very serious concern. We must certainly manage to keep our foreign representatives properly informed. The real trouble is to conduct genuinely confidential correspondence except through private letters, but surely the thing can be changed and it will be if I can manage it.

We are deeply indebted to you for your kindness and generous hospitality to our young folks[1] and we have learned with delight through your letters and theirs of their happy days in England.

With deep regard and appreciation,

Cordially and faithfully yours,

WOODROW WILSON.

HON. WALTER H. PAGE,
American Embassy,
London, England.

Yet for the American Ambassador the experience was not one of unmixed satisfaction. These letters have contained references to the demoralized condition of the

----

[1] Mr. and Mrs. Francis B. Sayre.

State Department under Mr. Bryan and the succeeding ones will contain more; the Carden episode portrayed the stupidity and ignorance of that Department at their worst. By commanding Carden to cease his anti-American tactics and to support the American policy the Foreign Office had performed an act of the utmost courtesy and consideration to this country. By quietly "promoting" the same minister to another sphere, several thousand miles away from Mexico and Washington, it was now preparing to eliminate all possible causes of friction between the two countries. The British, that is, had met the wishes of the United States in the two great matters that were then making serious trouble—Huerta and Carden. Yet no government, Great Britain least of all, wishes to be placed in the position of moving its diplomats about at the request of another Power. The whole deplorable story appears in the following letter.

To Edward M. House

January 8th, 1914.

MY DEAR HOUSE:

Two days ago I sent a telegram to the Department saying that I had information from a private, *unofficial* source that the report that Carden would be transferred was true, and from another source that Marling would succeed him. The Government here has given out nothing. I know nothing from official sources. Of course the only decent thing to do at Washington was to sit still till this Government should see fit to make an announcement. But what do they do? Give my telegram to the press! It appears here almost verbatim in this morning's *Mail.*—I have to make an humiliating explanation to the Foreign Office. This is the third time I've had to make such an humiliating explanation to Sir Edward. It's getting a little monotonous. He's getting tired, and so am I. They now deny at the Foreign Office that anything has been decided about Carden, and this meddling by us (as they look at it) will surely cause a delay and may even cause a change of purpose.

That's the practical result of their leaking at Washington. On a previous occasion they leaked the same way. When I telegraphed a remonstrance, they telegraphed back to me that the leak had been *here!* That was the end of it—except that I had to explain to Sir Edward the best I could. And about a lesser matter, I did the same thing a third time, in a conversation. Three times this sort of thing has happened.—On the other hand, the King's Master of Ceremonies called on me on the President's Birthday and requested for His Majesty that I send His Majesty's congratulations. Just ten days passed before a telegraphic answer came! The very hour it came, I was myself making up an answer for the President that I was going to send, to save our face.

Now, I'm trying with all my might to do this job. I spend all my time, all my ingenuity, all my money at it. I have organized my staff as a sort of Cabinet. We meet every day. We go over everything conceivable that we may do or try to do. We do good team work. I am not sure but I doubt whether these secretaries have before been taken into just such a relation to their chief. They are enthusiastic and ambitious and industrious and— *safe.* There's no possibility of any leak. We arrange our dinners with reference to the possibility of getting information and of carrying points. Mrs. Page gives and accepts invitations with the same end in view. We're on the job to the very limit of our abilities.

And I've got the Foreign Office in such a relation that

they are frank and friendly. (I can't keep 'em so, if this sort of thing goes on.)

Now the State Department seems (as it touches us) to be utterly chaotic—silent when it ought to respond, loquacious when it ought to be silent. There are questions that I have put to it at this Government's request to which I can get no answer.

It's hard to keep my staff enthusiastic under these conditions. When I reached the Chancery this morning, they were in my room, with all the morning papers marked, on the table, eagerly discussing what we ought to do about this publication of my dispatch. The enthusiasm and buoyancy were all gone out of them. By their looks they said, "Oh! what's the use of our bestirring ourselves to send news to Washington when they use it to embarrass us?"—While we are thus at work, the only two communications from the Department to-day are two letters from two of the Secretaries about—presenting "Democratic" ladies from Texas and Oklahoma at court! And Bryan is now lecturing in Kansas.

Since I began to write this letter, Lord Cowdray came here to the house and stayed two and a half hours, talking about possible joint intervention in Mexico. Possibly he came from the Foreign Office. I don't know whether to dare send a despatch to the State Department, telling what he told me, for fear they'd leak. And to leak this— Good Lord! Two of the Secretaries were here to dinner, and I asked them if I should send such a despatch. They both answered instantly: "No, sir, don't dare: *write* it to the President." I said: "No, I have no right to bother the President with regular business nor with frequent letters." To that they agreed; but the interesting and somewhat appalling thing is, they're actually afraid to have a confidential despatch go to the State Department.

I see nothing to do but to suggest to the President to put somebody in the Department who will stay there and give intelligent attention to the diplomatic telegrams and letters—some conscientious assistant or clerk. For I hear mutterings, somewhat like these mutterings of mine, from some of the continental embassies.—The whole thing is disorganizing and demoralizing beyond description.

All these and more are *my* troubles. I'll take care of them. But remember what I am going to write on the next sheet. For here may come a trouble for *you:*

Mrs. Page has learned something more about Secretary Bryan's proposed visit here in the spring. He's coming to talk his peace plan which, you know, is a sort of grape-juice arbitration—a distinct step backward from a real arbitration treaty. Well, if he comes with *that,* when you come to talk about reducing armaments, you'll wish you'd never been born. Get your ingenuity together, then, and prevent that visit.[1]

Not the least funny thing in the world is—Senator X turned up to-day. As he danced around the room begging everybody's pardon (nobody knew what for) he complimented everybody in sight, explained the forged letter, dilated on state politics, set the Irish question on the right end, cleared Bacon[2] of all hostility to me, declined tea because he had insomnia and explained just how it works to keep you awake, danced more and declared himself happy and bowed himself out—well pleased. He's as funny a cuss as I've seen in many a day. Lord Cowdray, who was telling Mexican woes to Katharine in the corner, looked up and asked, "Who's the little

---

[1]Colonel House succeeded in preventing it.

[2]Senator Augustus O. Bacon, of Georgia who was reported to nourish ill-feeling toward Page for his authorship of " The Southerner."

dancing gentleman?" Suppose X had known he was dancing for—Lord Cowdray's amusement, what do y' suppose he'd 've thought? There are some strange combinations in our house on Mrs. Page's days at home. Cowdray has, I am sure, lost (that is, failed to make) a hundred million dollars that he had within easy reach by this Wilson Doctrine, but he's game. He doesn't lie awake. He's a dead-game sport, and he knows he's knocked out in that quarter and he doesn't squeal. His experiences will serve us many a good turn in the future— as a warning. I rather like him. He eats out of my hand in the afternoon and has one of his papers jump on me in the morning. Some time in the twenty-four hours, he must attain about the normal temperature—say about noon. He admires the President greatly—sincerely. Force meets force, you see. With the President behind me I could really enjoy Cowdray centuries after X had danced himself into oblivion.

By the way, Cowdray said to me to-day: "Whatever the United States and Great Britain agree on the world must do." He's right. (1) The President must come here, perhaps in his second term; (2) these two Governments must enter a compact for peace and for gradual disarmament. Then we can go about our business for (say) a hundred years.

Heartily,

W. H. P.

In spite of the continued pressure of the United States and the passive support of its anti-Huerta policy by Great Britain, the Mexican usurper refused to resign. President Wilson now began to espouse the interests of Villa and Carranza. His letters to Page indicate that he took these men at their own valuation, believed that they were sincere patriots working for the cause of

"democracy" and "constitutionalism" and that their triumph would usher in a day of enlightenment and progress
for Mexico. It was the opinion of the Foreign Office
that Villa and Carranza were worse men than Huerta
and that any recognition of their revolutionary activities
would represent no moral gain.

From the President

The White House, Washington,
May 18, 1914.

My dear Page:

. . . As to the attitude of mind on that side of the
water toward the Constitutionalists, it is based upon prejudices which cannot be sustained by the facts. I am enclos-
ing a copy of an interview by a Mr. Reid[1] which appeared
in one of the afternoon papers recently and which sums up
as well as they could be summed up my own conclusions
with regard to the issues and the personnel of the pending contest in Mexico. I can verify it from a hundred
different sources, most of them sources not in the least
touched by predilections for such men as our friends in
London have supposed Carranza and Villa to be.

Cordially and faithfully yours,
Woodrow Wilson.

Hon. Walter H. Page,
U. S. Embassy,
London, England.

The White House, Washington,
June 1, 1914.

My dear Page:

. . . The fundamental thing is that they (British
critics of Villa) are all radically mistaken. There has

---

[1]Probably an error for John Reed, at that time a newspaper correspondent in
Mexico—afterward well known as a champion of the Bolshevist régime in Russia.

been less disorder and less danger to life where the Constitutionalists have gained control than there has been where Huerta is in control. I should think that if they are getting correct advices from Tampico, people in England would be very much enlightened by what has happened there. Before the Constitutionalists took the place there was constant danger to the oil properties and to foreign residents. Now there is no danger and the men who felt obliged to leave the oil wells to their Mexican employees are returning, to find, by the way, that their Mexican employees guarded them most faithfully without wages, and in some instances almost without food. I am told that the Constitutionalists cheered the American flag when they entered Tampico.

I believe that Mexico City will be much quieter and a much safer place to live in after the Constitutionalists get there than it is now. The men who are approaching and are sure to reach it are much less savage and much more capable of government than Huerta.

These, I need not tell you, are not fancies of mine but conclusions I have drawn from facts which are at last becoming very plain and palpable, at least to us on this side of the water. If they are not becoming plain in Great Britain, it is because their papers are not serving them with the truth. Our own papers were prejudiced enough in all conscience against Villa and Carranza and everything that was happening in the north of Mexico, but at last the light is dawning on them in spite of themselves and they are beginning to see things as they really are. I would be as nervous and impatient as your friends in London are if I feared the same things that they fear, but I do not. I am convinced that even Zapata would restrain his followers and leave, at any rate, all foreigners and all foreign property untouched if he were the first to enter Mexico City.

Cordially and faithfully yours,

WOODROW WILSON.

HON. WALTER H. PAGE,
American Embassy,
London, England.

On this issue, however, the President and his Ambassador to Great Britain permanently disagreed. The events which took place in April, 1914—the insult to the American flag at Tampico, the bombardment and capture of Vera Cruz by American forces—made stronger Page's conviction, already set forth in this correspondence, that there was only one solution of the Mexican problem.

To Edward M. House

April 27, 1914.

DEAR HOUSE:

. . . And, as for war with Mexico—I confess I've had a continually growing fear of it for six months. I've no confidence in the Mexican leaders—none of 'em. We shall have to Cuba-ize the country, which means thrashing 'em first—I fear, I fear, I fear; and I feel sorry for us all, the President in particular. It's inexpressibly hard fortune for him. I can't tell you with what eager fear we look for despatches every day and twice a day hurry to get the newspapers. All England believes we've got to fight it out.

Well, the English are with us, you see. Admiral Cradock, I understand, does not approve our policy, but he stands firmly with us whatever we do. The word to stand firmly with us has, I am very sure, been passed along the whole line—naval, newspaper, financial, dip-

lomatic.   Carden won't give us any more trouble during
the rest of his stay in Mexico.   The yellow press's abuse
of the President and me has actually helped us here.

Heartily yours,

W. H. P.

CHAPTER VIII

HONOUR AND DISHONOUR IN PANAMA

IN THE early part of January, 1914, Colonel House
wrote Page, asking whether he would consider favourably an offer to enter President Wilson's Cabinet, as
Secretary of Agriculture. Mr. David F. Houston, who
was then most acceptably filling that position, was also
an authority on banking and finance; the plan was to
make him governor of the new Federal Reserve Board,
then in process of formation, and to transfer Page to the
vacant place in the Cabinet. The proposal was not
carried through, but Page's reply took the form of a review of his ambassadorship up to date, of his vexations,
his embarrassments, his successes, and especially of the
very important task which still lay before him. There
were certain reasons, it will appear, why he would have
liked to leave London; and there was one impelling reason
why he preferred to stay. From the day of his arrival
in England, Page had been humiliated, and his work had
been constantly impeded, by the almost studied neglect
with which Washington treated its diplomatic service.
The fact that the American Government provided no
official residence for its Ambassador, and no adequate
financial allowance for maintaining the office, had made
his position almost an intolerable one. All Page's predecessors for twenty-five years had been rich men who
could advance the cost of the Embassy from their own
private purses; to meet these expenses, however, Page
had been obliged to encroach on the savings of a life-

time, and such liberality on his part necessarily had its
limitations.

To Edward M. House

London, England,
February 13, 1914.

MY DEAR HOUSE:

. . . Of course I am open to the criticism of having
taken the place at all. But I was both uninformed and
misinformed about the cost as well as about the frightful
handicap of having no Embassy. It's a kind of scandal
in London and it has its serious effect. Everybody talks
about it all the time: "Will you explain to me why it is
that your great Government has no Embassy: it's very
odd!" "What a frugal Government you have!" "It's a
damned mean outfit, your American Government." Mrs.
Page collapses many an evening when she gets to her room.
"If they'd only quit talking about it!" The other Ambassadors, now that we're coming to know them fairly well,
commiserate us. It's a constant humiliation. Of course
this aspect of it doesn't worry me much—I've got hard-
ened to it. But it is a good deal of a real handicap, and
it adds that much dead weight that a man must overcome; and it greatly lessens the respect in which our
Government and its Ambassador are held. If I had
known this fully in advance, I should not have had the
courage to come here. Now, of course, I've got used
to it, have discounted it, and can "bull" it through—
could "bull" it through if I could afford to pay the bill.
But I shouldn't advise any friend of mine to come here
and face this humiliation without realizing precisely what
it means—wholly apart, of course, from the cost of
it. . . .

My dear House, on the present basis much of the diplomatic business is sheer humbug. It will always be so till we have our own Embassies and an established position in consequence. Without a home or a house or a fixed background, every man has to establish his own position for himself; and unless he be unusual, this throws him clean out of the way of giving emphasis to the right things. . . .

As for our position, I think I don't fool myself. The job at the Foreign Office is easy because there is no real trouble between us, and because Sir Edward Grey is pretty nearly an ideal man to get on with. I think he likes me, too, because, of course, I'm straightforward and frank with him, and he likes the things we stand for. Outside this official part of the job, of course, we're commonplace—a successful commonplace, I hope. But that's all. We don't know how to try to be anything but what we naturally are. I dare say we are laughed at here and there about this and that. Sometimes I hear criticisms, now and then more or less serious ones. Much of it comes of our greenness; some of it from the very nature of the situation. Those who expect to find us brilliant are, of course, disappointed. Nor are we *smart*, and the smart set (both American and English) find us uninteresting. But we drive ahead and keep a philosophical temper and simply do the best we can, and, you may be sure, a good deal of it. It *is* laborious. For instance, I've made two trips lately to speak before important bodies, one at Leeds, the other at Newcastle, at both of which, in different ways, I have tried to explain the President's principle in dealing with Central American turbulent states—and, incidentally, the American ideals of government. The audiences see it, approve it, applaud it. The newspaper editorial writers never quite go the length—it involves a denial of the divine right of the British Empire; at least they fear so. The fewest possible Englishmen really understand our governmental aims and ideals. I have delivered unnumbered and innumerable little speeches, directly or indirectly, about them; and they seem to like them. But it would take an army of oratorical ambassadors a lifetime to get the idea into the heads of them all. In some ways they are incredibly far back in mediævalism—incredibly.

If I have to leave in the fall or in December, it will be said and thought that I've failed, unless there be some reason that can be made public. I should be perfectly willing to tell the reason—the failure of the Government to make it financially possible. I've nothing to conceal —only definite amounts. I'd never say what it has cost —only that it costs more than I or anybody but a rich man can afford. If then, or in the meantime, the President should wish me to serve elsewhere, *that* would, of course, be a sufficient reason for my going.

Now another matter, with which I shall not bother the President—he has enough to bear on that score. It was announced in one of the London papers the other day that Mr. Bryan would deliver a lecture here, and probably in each of the principal European capitals, on Peace. Now, God restrain me from saying, much more from doing, anything rash. But if I've got to go home at all, I'd rather go before he comes. It'll take years for the American Ambassadors to recover what they'll lose if he carry out this plan. They now laugh at him here. Only the President's great personality saves the situation in foreign relations. Of course the public here doesn't know how utterly unorganized the State Department is— how we can't get answers to important questions, and how they publish most secret despatches or allow them to leak out. But "bad breaks" like this occur. Mr. Z, of the 100-years'-Peace Committee,[1] came here a week ago, with a letter from Bryan to the Prime Minister! Z told me that this 100-year business gave a chance to bind the nations together that ought not to be missed. Hence Bryan had asked him to take up the relations of the countries with the Prime Minister! Bryan sent a telegram to Z to be read at a big 100-year meeting here. As for the personal indignity to me—I overlook that. I don't think he means it. But if he doesn't mean it, what does he mean? That's what the Prime Minister asks himself. Fortunately Mr. Asquith and I get along mighty well. He met Bryan once, and he told me with a smile that he regarded him as "a peculiar product of your country." But the Secretary is always doing things like this. He dashes off letters of introduction to people asking me to present them to Mr. Asquith, Mr. Lloyd George, etc.

In the United States we know Mr. Bryan. We know his good points, his good services, his good intentions. We not only tolerate him; we like him. But when he comes here as "the American Prime Minister"[2]—good-bye, John! All that we've tried to do to gain respect for our Government (as they respect our great nation) will disappear in one day. Of course they'll feel obliged to give him big official dinners, etc. And——

Now you'd just as well abandon your trip if he comes; and (I confess) I'd rather be gone. No member of another government ever came here and lectured. T. R. did it as a private citizen, and even then he split the heavens asunder.[3] Most Englishmen will regard it as a

---

[1] The Committee to celebrate the centennial of the signing of the Treaty of Ghent, which ended the War of 1812. The plan to make this an elaborate commemoration of a 100 years' peace between the English-speaking peoples was upset by the outbreak of the World War.

[2] This was the designation Mr. Bryan's admirers sometimes gave him.

[3] The reference is to President Roosevelt's speech at the Guildhall in June, 1910.

piece of effrontery. Of course, I'm not in the least concerned about mere matters of taste. It's only the bigger
effects that I have in mind in *queering* our Government in
their eyes. He must be kept at home on the Mexican
problem, or some other.

Yours faithfully,

WALTER H. PAGE.

P. S. But, by George, it's a fine game! This Government and ours are standing together all right, especially
since the President has taken hold of our foreign relations
himself. With such a man at the helm at home, we can
do whatever we wish to do with the English, as I've often
told you. (But it raises doubts every time the shoe-
string necktie, broad-brimmed black hat, oratorical, old-
time, River Platte kind of note is heard.) We've come
a long way in a year—a very joyful long way, full of
progress and real understanding; there's no doubt about
that. A year ago they knew very well the failure that
had saddled them with the tolls trouble and the failure
of arbitration, and an unknown President had just come
in. Presently an unknown Ambassador arrived. Mexico
got worse; would we not recognize Huerta? They send
Carden. We had nothing to say about the tolls—simply
asked for time. They were very friendly; but our slang
phrase fits the situation—"nothin' doin'." They declined
San Francisco.[1] Then presently they began to see some
plan in Mexico; they began to see our attitude on the
tolls; they began to understand our attitude toward concessions and governments run for profit; they began dimly
to see that Carden was a misfit; the Tariff Bill passed;
the Currency Bill; the President loomed up; even the

[1]This refers to the declination of the British Government to be represented at
the San Francisco world exhibition, held in 1915.

Ambassador, they said, really believed what he preached; he wasn't merely making pretty, friendly speeches.—Now, when we get this tolls job done, we've got 'em where we can do any proper and reasonable thing we want. It's been a great three quarters of a year—immense, in fact. No man has been in the White House who is so regarded since Lincoln; in fact, they didn't regard Lincoln while he lived.

Meantime, I've got to be more or less at home. The Prime Minister dines with me, the Foreign Secretary, the Archbishop, the Colonial Secretary—all the rest of 'em; the King talks very freely; Mr. Asquith tells me some of his troubles; Sir Edward is become a good personal friend; Lord Bryce warms up; the Lord Chancellor is chummy; and so it goes.

So you may be sure we are all in high feather after all; and the President's (I fear exaggerated) appreciation of what I've done is very gratifying indeed. I've got only one emotion about it all—gratitude; and gratitude begets eagerness to go on. Of course I can do future jobs better than I have done any past ones.

There are two shadows in the background—not disturbing, but shadows none the less:

1. The constant reminder that the American Ambassador's homeless position (to this Government and to this whole people) shows that the American Government and the American people know nothing about foreign relations and care nothing—regard them as not worth buying a house for. This leaves a doubt about any continuity of any American policy. It even suggests a sort of fear that we don't really care.

The other is (2) the dispiriting experience of writing and telegraphing about important things and never hearing a word concerning many of them, and the consequent fear of some dead bad break in the State Department. The clubs are full of stories of the silly and incredible things that are *said* to happen there.

After all, these are old troubles. They are not new—neither of them. And we are the happiest group you ever saw.

W. H. P.

Page's letters of this period contain many references to his inability to maintain touch with the State Department. His letters remained unacknowledged, his telegrams unanswered; and he was himself left completely in the dark as to the plans and opinions at Washington.

To Edward M. House

February 28, 1914.

DEAR HOUSE:

. . . *Couldn't the business with Great Britain be put into Moore's*[1] *hands?* It is surely important enough at times to warrant separate attention—or (I might say) attention. You know, after eight or nine months of this sort of thing, the feeling grows on us all here that perhaps many of our telegrams and letters may not be read by anybody at all. You begin to feel that they may not be deciphered or even opened. Then comes the feeling (for a moment), why send any more? Why do anything but answer such questions as come now and then? Corresponding with Nobody—can you imagine how that feels?—What the devil *do* you suppose does become of the letters and telegrams that I send, from which and about which I never hear a word? As a mere matter of curiosity I should like to know who receives them and what he does with them!

---

[1]John Bassett Moore, at that time the very able counsellor of the State Department.

I've a great mind some day to send a despatch saying that an earthquake has swallowed up the Thames, that a suffragette has kissed the King, and that the statue of Cromwell has made an assault on the House of Lords—just to see if anybody deciphers it.

After the Civil War an old fellow in Virginia was tired of the world. He'd have no more to do with it. He cut a slit in a box in his house and nailed up the box. Whenever a letter came for him, he'd read the postmark and say "Baltimore—Baltimore—there isn't anybody in Baltimore that I care to hear from." Then he'd drop the letter unopened through the slit into the box. "Philadelphia? I have no friend in Philadelphia"—into the box, unopened. When he died, the big box was nearly full of unopened letters. When I get to Washington again, I'm going to look for a big box that must now be nearly full of my unopened letters and telegrams.

W. H. P.

The real reason why the Ambassador wished to remain in London was to assist in undoing a great wrong which the United States had done itself and the world. Page was attempting to perform his part in introducing new standards into diplomacy. His discussions of Mexico had taken the form of that "idealism" which he was apparently having some difficulty in persuading British statesmen and the British public to accept. He was doing his best to help bring about that day when, in Gladstone's famous words, "the idea of public right would be the governing idea" of international relations. But while the American Ambassador was preaching this new conception, the position of his own country on one important matter was a constant impediment to his efforts. Page was continually confronted by the fact that the

United States, high-minded as its foreign policy might pretend to be, was far from "idealistic" in the observance of the treaty that it had made with Great Britain concerning the Panama Canal. There was a certain embarrassment involved in preaching unselfishness in Mexico and Central America at a time when the United States was practising selfishness and dishonesty in Panama. For, in the opinion of the Ambassador and that of most other dispassionate students of the Panama treaty, the American policy on Panama tolls amounted to nothing less.

To one unskilled in legal technicalities, the Panama controversy involved no great difficulty. Since 1850 the United States and Great Britain had had a written understanding upon the construction of the Panama Canal. The Clayton-Bulwer Treaty, which was adopted that year, provided that the two countries should share equally in the construction and control of the proposed waterway across the Isthmus. This idea of joint control had always rankled in the United States, and in 1901 the American Government persuaded Great Britain to abrogate the Clayton-Bulwer Treaty and agree to another—the Hay-Pauncefote—which transferred the rights of ownership and construction exclusively to this country. In consenting to this important change, Great Britain had made only one stipulation. "The Canal," so read Article III of the Convention of 1901, "shall be free and open to the vessels of commerce and war of all nations observing these rules, on terms of entire equality, so that there shall be no discrimination against any such nation, or its citizens or subjects, in respect of the conditions or charges of traffic, or otherwise." It would seem as though the English language could utter no thought more clearly than this. The agreement said, not inferentially, but in

so many words, that the "charges" levied on the ships
of "all nations" that used the Canal should be the same.
The history of British-American negotiations on the subject of the Canal had always emphasized this same point.
All American witnesses to drawing the Treaty have testified that this was the American understanding. The
correspondence of John Hay, who was Secretary of
State at the time, makes it clear that this was the agreement. Mr. Elihu Root, who, as Secretary of War, sat
next to John Hay in the Cabinet which authorized the
treaty, has taken the same stand. The man who conducted the preliminary negotiations with Lord Salisbury,
Mr. Henry White, has emphasized the same point. Mr.
Joseph H. Choate, who, as American Ambassador to
Great Britain in 1901, had charge of the negotiations,
has testified that the British and American Governments
"meant what they said and said what they meant."

In the face of this solemn understanding, the American
Congress, in 1912, passed the Panama Canal Act, which
provided that "no tolls shall be levied upon vessels engaged in the coastwise trade of the United States." A
technical argument, based upon the theory that "all
nations" did not include the United States, and that,
inasmuch as this country had obtained sovereign rights
upon the Isthmus, the situation had changed, persuaded
President Taft to sign this bill. Perhaps this line of
reasoning satisfied the legal consciences of President
Taft and Mr. Knox, his Secretary of State, but it really
cut little figure in the acrimonious discussion that ensued. Of course, there was only one question involved;
that was as to whether the exemption violated the Treaty.
This is precisely the one point that nearly all the con-
troversialists avoided. The statement that the United
States had built the Canal with its own money and its

own genius, that it had achieved a great success where other nations had achieved a great failure, and that it had the right of passing its own ships through its own highway without assessing tolls—this was apparently argument enough. When Great Britain protested the exemption as a violation of the Treaty, there were not lacking plenty of elements in American politics and journalism to denounce her as committing an act of high-handed impertinence, as having intruded herself in matters which were not properly her concern, and as having attempted to rob the American public of the fruits of its own enterprise. That animosity to Great Britain, which is always present in certain parts of the hyphenated population, burst into full flame.

Clear as were the legal aspects of the dispute, the position of the Wilson Administration was a difficult one. The Irish-American elements, which have specialized in making trouble between the United States and Great Britain, represented a strength to the Democratic Party in most large cities. The great mass of Democratic Senators and Congressmen had voted for the exemption bill. The Democratic platform of 1912 had endorsed this same legislation. This declaration was the handiwork of Senator O'Gorman, of New York State, who had long been a leader of the anti-British crusade in American politics. More awkward still, President Wilson, in the course of his Presidential campaign, had himself spoken approvingly of free tolls for American ships. The probability is that, when the President made this unfortunate reference to this clause in the Democratic programme, he had given the matter little personal investigation; it must be held to his credit that, when the facts were clearly presented to him, his mind quickly grasped the real point at issue—that it was not a matter of commercial advantage or disadvantage, but one simply of national honour, of whether the United States proposed to keep its word or to break it.

Page's contempt for the hair-drawn technicalities of lawyers was profound, and the tortuous effort to make the Hay-Pauncefote Treaty mean something quite different from what it said, inevitably moved him to righteous wrath. Before sailing for England he spent several days in the State Department studying the several questions that were then at issue between his country and Great Britain. A memorandum contains his impressions of the free tolls contention:

"A little later I went to Washington again to acquaint myself with the business between the United States and Great Britain. About that time the Senate confirmed my appointment, and I spent a number of days reading the recent correspondence between the two governments. The two documents that stand out in my memory are the wretched lawyer's note of Knox about the Panama tolls (I never read a less sincere, less convincing, more purely artificial argument) and Bryce's brief reply, which did have the ring of sincerity in it. The diplomatic correspondence in general seemed to me very dull stuff, and, after wading through it all day, on several nights as I went to bed the thought came to me whether this sort of activity were really worth a man's while."

Anything which affected British shipping adversely touched Great Britain in a sensitive spot; and Page had not been long in London before he perceived the acute nature of the Panama situation. In July, 1913, Col. Edward M. House reached the British capital. A letter of Page's to Sir Edward Grey gives such a succinct description of this new and influential force in American public life that it is worth quoting:

To Sir Edward Grey

Coburg Hotel, London.
[No date.]

DEAR SIR EDWARD:

There is an American gentleman in London, the like of whom I do not know. Mr. Edward M. House is his name. He is "the silent partner" of President Wilson—that is to say, he is the most trusted political adviser and the nearest friend of the President. He is a private citizen, a man without personal political ambition, a modest, quiet, even shy fellow. He helps to make Cabinets, to shape policies, to select judges and ambassadors and suchlike merely for the pleasure of seeing that these tasks are well done.

He is suffering from over-indulgence in advising, and he has come here to rest. I cannot get him far outside his hotel, for he cares to see few people. But he is very eager to meet you.

I wonder if you would do me the honour to take luncheon at the Coburg Hotel with me, to meet him either on July 1, or 3, or 5—if you happen to be free? I shall have only you and Mr. House.

Very sincerely yours,
WALTER H. PAGE.

The chief reason why Colonel House wished to meet the British Foreign Secretary was to bring him a message from President Wilson on the subject of the Panama tolls. The three men—Sir Edward, Colonel House, and Mr. Page—met at the suggested luncheon on July 3rd.

Colonel House informed the Foreign Secretary that President Wilson was now convinced that the Panama Act violated the Hay-Pauncefote Treaty and that he intended to use all his influence to secure its repeal.   The matter, the American urged, was a difficult one, since it would be necessary to persuade Congress to pass a law acknowledging its mistake.   The best way in which Great Britain could aid in the process was by taking no public action. If the British should keep protesting or discussing the subject acrimoniously in the press and Parliament, such a course would merely reënforce the elements that would certainly oppose the President.   Any protests would give them the opportunity to set up the cry of "British dictation," and a change in the Washington policy would subject it to the criticism of having yielded to British pressure.   The inevitable effect would be to defeat the whole proceeding.   Colonel House therefore suggested that President Wilson be left to handle the matter in his own way and in his own time, and he assured the British statesman that the result would be satisfactory to both countries.   Sir Edward Grey at once saw that Colonel House's statement of the matter was simply common sense, and expressed his willingness to leave the Panama matter in the President's hands.

Thus, from July 3, 1913, there was a complete understanding between the British Government and the Washington Administration on the question of the tolls.   But neither the British nor the American public knew that President Wilson had pledged himself to a policy of repeal. All during the summer and fall of 1913 this matter was as generally discussed in England as was Mexico. Everywhere the Ambassador went—country houses, London dinner tables, the colleges and the clubs— he was constantly confronted with what was universally

regarded as America's great breach of faith.   How deeply
he felt in the matter his letters show.

To Edward M. House

August 25, 1913.

DEAR HOUSE:

. . . The English Government and the English
people without regard to party—I hear it and feel it
everywhere—are of one mind about this: they think we
have acted dishonourably.   They really think so—it
isn't any mere political or diplomatic pretense.   We
made a bargain, they say, and we have repudiated it.
If it were a mere bluff or game or party contention—
that would be one thing.   We could "bull" it through
or live it down.   But they look upon it as we look upon
the repudiation of a debt by a state.   Whatever the
arguments by which the state may excuse itself, we never
feel the same toward it—never quite so safe about it.
They say, "You are a wonderful nation and a wonderful
people.   We like you.   But your Government is not a
government of honour.   Your honourable men do not
seem to get control."   You can't measure the damage
that this does us.   Whatever the United States may
propose till this is fixed and forgotten will be regarded
with a certain hesitancy.   They will not fully trust the
honour of our Government.   They say, too, "See, you've
preached arbitration and you propose peace agreements,
and yet you will not arbitrate this: you know you are
wrong, and this attitude proves it."   Whatever Mr.
Hay might or could have done, he made a bargain.   The
Senate ratified it.   We accepted it.   Whether it were a
good bargain or a bad one, we ought to keep it.   The
English feeling was shown just the other week when
Senator Root received an honourary degree at Oxford.

The thing that gave him fame here was his speech on this treaty.[1] There is no end of ways in which they show their feeling and conviction.

Now, if in the next regular session the President takes a firm stand against the ship subsidy that this discrimination gives, couldn't Congress be carried to repeal this discrimination? For this economic objection also exists.

No Ambassador can do any very large constructive piece of work so long as this suspicion of the honour of our Government exists. Sir Edward Grey will take it up in October or November. If I could say then that the President will exert all his influence for this repeal— that would go far. If, when he takes it up, I can say nothing, it will be practically useless for me to take up any other large plan. This is the most important thing for us on the diplomatic horizon.

Memorandum

Dornoch, Scotland,
September 10, 1913.

I am spending ten or more of the dog days visiting the Englishman and the Scotchman in their proper setting— their country homes—where they show themselves the best of hosts and reveal their real opinions. There are, for example, in the house where I happen to be to-day, the principals of three of the Scotch universities, and a Member of Parliament, and an influential editor.

They have, of course—I mean all the educated folk I meet—the most intelligent interest in American affairs, and they have an unbounded admiration for the American people—their energy, their resourcefulness, their wealth,

[1]Mr. Root's masterly speech on Panama tolls was made in the United States Senate, January 21, 1913.

their economic power and social independence. I think that no people ever really admired and, in a sense, envied another people more. They know we hold the keys of the future.

But they make a sharp distinction between our people and our Government. They are sincere, God-fearing people who speak their convictions. They cite Tammany, the Thaw case, Sulzer, the Congressional lobby, and sincerely regret that a democracy does not seem to be able to justify itself. I am constantly amazed and sometimes dumbfounded at the profound effect that the yellow press (including the American correspondents of the English papers) has had upon the British mind. Here is a most serious journalistic problem, upon which I have already begun to work seriously with some of the editors of the better London papers. But it is more than a journalistic problem. It becomes political. To eradicate this impression will take years of well-planned work. I am going to make this the subject of one of the dozen addresses that I must deliver during the next six months —"The United States as an Example of Honest and Honourable Government."

And everywhere—in circles the most friendly to us, and the best informed—I receive commiseration because of the dishonourable attitude of our Government about the Panama Canal tolls. This, I confess, is hard to meet. We made a bargain—a solemn compact—and we have broken it. Whether it were a good bargain or a bad one, a silly one or a wise one; that's far from the point. Isn't it? I confess that this bothers me. . . .

And this Canal tolls matter stands in the way of everything. It is in their minds all the time—the minds of all parties and all sections of opinion. They have no respect for Mr. Taft, for they remember that he might have vetoed the bill; and they ask, whenever they dare, what you will do about it. They hold our Government in shame so long as this thing stands.

As for the folly of having made such a treaty—that's now passed. As for our unwillingness to arbitrate it—that's taken as a confession of guilt. . . .

We can command these people, this Government, this tight island, and its world-wide empire; they honour us, they envy us, they see the time near at hand when we shall command the capital and the commerce of the world if we unfetter our mighty people; they wish to keep very close to us. But they are suspicious of our Government because, they contend, it has violated its faith. Is it so or is it not?

Life meantime is brimful of interest; and, despite this reflex result of the English long-blunder with Ireland (how our sins come home to roost), the Great Republic casts its beams across the whole world and I was never so proud to be an American democrat, as I see it light this hemisphere in a thousand ways.

WALTER H. PAGE.

The story of Sir William Tyrrell's[1] visit to the White House in November, 1913, has already been told. On this occasion, it will be recalled, not only was an agreement reached on Mexico, but President Wilson also repeated the assurances already given by Colonel House on the repeal of the tolls legislation. Now that Great Britain had accepted the President's leadership in Mexico, the time was approaching when President Wilson might be expected to take his promised stand on Panama

---

[1]Ante: page 202.

tolls. Yet it must be repeated that there had been no
definite diplomatic bargain. But Page was exerting all
his efforts to establish the best relations between the two
countries on the basis of fair dealing and mutual respect.
Great Britain had shown her good faith in the Mexican
matter; now the turn of the United States had come.

To the President

London, 6 Grosvenor Square,
January 8, 1914.

DEAR MR. PRESIDENT:

We've travelled a long way since this Mexican trouble
began—a long way with His Majesty's Government.
When your policy was first flung at 'em, they showed
at best a friendly incredulity: what! set up a moral
standard for government in Mexico? Everybody's mind
was then fixed merely on the restoring of order—the safety
of investments. They thought of course our army
would go down in a few weeks. I recall that Sir Edward Grey asked me one day if you would not consult
the European governments about the successor to Huerta,
speaking of it as a problem that would come up next
week. And there was much unofficial talk about joint
intervention.

Well, they've followed a long way. They apologized
for Carden (that's what the Prime Minister's speech was);
they ordered him to be more prudent. Then the real
meaning of concessions began to get into their heads.
They took up the dangers that lurked in the Government's contract with Cowdray for oil; and they pulled
Cowdray out of Colombia and Costa Rica—granting the
application of the Monroe Doctrine to concessions that
might imperil a country's autonomy. Then Sir Edward

asked me if you would not consult him about such concessions—a long way had been travelled since his other question! Lord Haldane made the Thanksgiving speech that I suggested to him. And now they have transferred Carden. They've done all we asked and more; and, more wonderful yet, they've come to understand what we are driving at.

As this poor world goes, all this seems to me rather handsomely done. At any rate, it's square and it's friendly.

Now in diplomacy, as in other contests, there must be give and take; it's our turn.

If you see your way clear, it would help this Liberal Government (which needs help) and would be much appreciated if, before February 10th, when Parliament meets, you could say a public word friendly to our keeping the Hay-Pauncefote Treaty—on the tolls. You only, of course, can judge whether you would be justified in doing so. I presume only to assure you of the most excellent effect it would have here. If you will pardon me for taking a personal view of it, too, I will say that such an expression would cap the climax of the enormously heightened esteem and great respect in which recent events and achievements have caused you to be held here. It would put the English of all parties in the happiest possible mood toward you for whatever subsequent dealings may await us. It was as friendly a man as Kipling who said to me the night I spent with him: "You know your great Government, which does many great things greatly, does *not* lie awake o' nights to keep its promises."

It's our turn next, whenever you see your way clear.

Most heartily yours,

WALTER H. PAGE.

From Edward M. House

145 East 35th Street,
New York City.
January 24, 1914.

DEAR PAGE:

I was with the President for twenty-four hours and we went over everything thoroughly.

He decided to call the Senate Committee on Foreign Relations to the White House on Monday and tell them of his intentions regarding Panama tolls. We discussed whether it would be better to see some of them individually, or to take them collectively. It was agreed that the latter course was better. It was decided, however, to have Senator Jones poll the Senate in order to find just how it stood before getting the Committee together.

The reason for this quick action was in response to your letter urging that something be done before the 10th of February. . . .

Faithfully yours,
E. M. HOUSE.

On March 5th the President made good his promise by going before Congress and asking the two Houses to repeal that clause in the Panama legislation which granted preferential treatment to American coastwise shipping. The President's address was very brief and did not discuss the matter in the slightest detail. Mr. Wilson made the question one simply of national honour. The exemption, he said, clearly violated the Hay-Pauncefote Treaty and there was nothing left to do but to set the matter right. The part of the President's address that aroused the greatest interest was the conclusion:

"I ask this of you in support of the foreign policy of

the Administration. I shall not know how to deal with other matters of even greater delicacy and nearer consequence, if you do not grant it to me in ungrudging measure."

The impression that this speech made upon the statesman who then presided over the British Foreign office is evident from the following letter that he wrote to the Ambassador in Washington.

Sir Edward Grey to Sir C. Spring Rice

Foreign Office,
March 13, 1914.

SIR:

In the course of a conversation with the American Ambassador to-day, I took the opportunity of saying how much I had been struck by President Wilson's Message to Congress about the Panama Canal tolls. When I read it, it struck me that, whether it succeeded or failed in accomplishing the President's object, it was something to the good of public life, for it helped to lift public life to a higher plane and to strengthen its morale.

I am, &c.,

E. GREY.

Two days after his appearance before Congress the President wrote to his Ambassador:

From the President

The White House, Washington,
March 7, 1914.

MY DEAR PAGE:

I have your letters of the twenty-second and twenty-fourth of February and I thank you for them most warmly. Happily, things are clearing up a little in the matters which have embarrassed our relations with Great Britain, and I hope that the temper of public opinion is in fact changing there, as it seems to us from this distance to be changing.

Your letters are a lamp to my feet. I feel as I read that their analysis is searching and true.

Things over here go on a tolerably even keel. The prospect at this moment for the repeal of the tolls exemption is very good indeed. I am beginning to feel a considerable degree of confidence that the repeal will go through, and the Press of the country is certainly standing by me in great shape.

My thoughts turn to you very often with gratitude and affectionate regard. If there is ever at any time anything specific you want to learn, pray do not hesitate to ask it of me directly, if you think best.

Carden was here the other day and I spent an hour with him, but I got not even a glimpse of his mind. I showed him all of mine that he cared to see.

With warmest regards from us all,

Faithfully yours,
Woodrow Wilson.

The debate which now took place in Congress proved to be one of the stormiest in the history of that body. The proceeding did not prove to be the easy victory that the Administration had evidently expected. The struggle was protracted for three months; and it signalized Mr. Wilson's first serious conflict with the Senate—that same Senate which was destined to play such a vexatious and destructive rôle in his career. At this time, however, Mr. Wilson had reached the zenith of his control over the law-making bodies. It was early in his Presidential term, and in these early days Senators are likely to be careful about quarrelling with the White House—especially the Senators who are members of the President's political party. In this struggle, moreover, Mr. Wilson had the intelligence and the character of the Senate largely on his side, though, strangely enough, his strongest supporters were Republicans and his bitterest opponents were Democrats. Senator Root, Senator Burton, Senator Lodge, Senator Kenyon, Senator McCumber, all Republicans, day after day and week after week upheld the national honour; while Senators O'Gorman, Chamberlain, Vardaman, and Reed, all members of the President's party, just as persistently led the fight for the baser cause. The debate inspired an outburst of Anglophobia which was most distressing to the best friends of the United States and Great Britain. The American press, as a whole, honoured itself by championing the President, but certain newspapers made the debate an occasion for unrestrained abuse of Great Britain, and of any one who believed that the United States should treat that nation honestly. The Hearst organs, in cartoon and editorial page, shrieked against the ancient enemy. All the well-known episodes and characters in American history—Lexington, Bunker Hill, John Paul Jones, Washington, and Franklin—were paraded as arguments against the repeal of an illegal discrimination. Petitions from the Ancient Order of Hibernians and other Irish societies were showered upon Congress—in almost unending procession they clogged the pages of the *Congressional Record;* public meetings were held in New York and elsewhere denouncing an administration that disgraced the country by "truckling" to Great Britain. The President was accused of seeking an Anglo-American Alliance and of sacrificing American shipping to the glory of British trade, while the history of our diplomatic rela tions was surveyed in detail for the purpose of proving that Great Britain had broken every treaty she had ever made. In the midst of this deafening hubbub the quiet voice of Senator McCumber—"we are too big in national power to be too little in national integrity"—and that of Senator Root, demolishing one after another the pettifogging arguments of the exemptionists, demonstrated that, after all, the spirit and the eloquence that had given the Senate its great fame were still influential forces in that body.

In all this excitement, Page himself came in for his share of hard knocks. Irish meetings "resolved" against the Ambassador as a statesman who "looks on English claims as superior to American rights," and demanded that President Wilson recall him. It has been the fate of practically every American ambassador to Great Britain to be accused of Anglomania. Lowell, John Hay, and Joseph H. Choate fell under the ban of those elements in American life who seem to think that the main duty of an American diplomat in Great Britain is to insult the country of which he has become the guest. In 1895 the House of Representatives solemnly passed a resolution censuring Ambassador Thomas F. Bayard for a few sentiments friendly to Great Britain which he had uttered at a public banquet. That Page was no undiscriminating idolater of Great Britain these letters have abundantly revealed. That he had the profoundest respect for the British character and British institutions has been made just as clear. With Page this was no sudden enthusiasm; the conviction that British conceptions of liberty and government and British ideals of life represented the fine flower of human progress was one that he felt deeply. The fact that these fundamentals had had the opportunity of even freer develop-

ment in America he regarded as most fortunate both for
the United States and for the world.   He had never concealed his belief that the destinies of mankind depended
more upon the friendly coöperation of the United States
and Great Britain than upon any other single influence.
He had preached this in public addresses, and in his
writings for twenty-five years preceding his mission to
Great Britain.   But the mere fact that he should hold
such convictions and presume to express them as American
Ambassador apparently outraged those same elements
in this country who railed against Great Britain in this
Panama Tolls debate.

On August 16, 1913, the City of Southampton, England, dedicated a monument in honour of the *Mayflower*
Pilgrims—Southampton having been their original point
of departure for Massachusetts.   Quite appropriately
the city invited the American Ambassador to deliver an
address on this occasion; and quite appropriately the
Ambassador acknowledged the debt that Americans of
to-day owed to the England that had sent these adventurers to lay the foundations of new communities on
foreign soil.   Yet certain historic truths embodied in
this very beautiful and eloquent address aroused considerable anger in certain parts of the United States.
"Blood," said the Ambassador, "carries with it that
particular trick of thought which makes us all English
in the last resort.   .   .   .   And Puritan and Pilgrim
and Cavalier, different yet, are yet one in that they are
English still.   And thus, despite the fusion of races and
of the great contributions of other nations to her 100 millions of people and to her incalculable wealth, the United
States is yet English-led and English-ruled."   This was
merely a way of phrasing a great historic truth—that
overwhelmingly the largest element in the American

population is British in origin[1]; that such vital things as its speech and its literature are English; and that our political institutions, our liberty, our law, our conceptions of morality and of life are similarly derived from the British Isles. Page applied the word "English" to Americans in the same sense in which that word is used by John Richard Green, when he traces the history of the English race from a German forest to the Mississippi Valley and the wilds of Australia. But the anti-British elements on this side of the water, taking "English-led and English-ruled" out of its context, misinterpreted the phrase as meaning that the American Ambassador had approvingly called attention to the fact that the United States was at present under the political control of Great Britain! Senator Chamberlain of Oregon presented a petition from the *Staatsverband Deutschsprechender Vereine von Oregon*, demanding the Ambassador's removal, while the Irish-American press and politicians became extremely vocal.

Animated as was this outburst, it was mild compared with the excitement caused by a speech that Page made while the Panama debate was raging in Congress. At a dinner of the Associated Chambers of Commerce, in early March, the Ambassador made a few impromptu remarks. The occasion was one of good fellowship and good humour, and Page, under the inspiration of the occasion, indulged in a few half-serious, half-jocular references to the Panama Canal and British-American good-feeling, which, when inaccurately reported, caused a great disturbance in the England-baiting press. "I

---

[1] This is the fact that is too frequently lost sight of in current discussions of the melting pot. In the *Atlantic Monthly* for August, 1920, Mr. William S. Rossiter, for many years chief clerk of the United States Census and a statistician of high standing, shows that, of the 95,000,000 white people of the United States, 55,000-000 trace their origin to England, Scotland, and Wales.

would not say that we constructed the Panama Canal
even for you," he said, "for I am speaking with great
frankness and not with diplomatic indirection. We
built it for reasons of our own. But I will say that it
adds to the pleasure of that great work that you will
profit by it. You will profit most by it, for you have
the greatest carrying trade." A few paragraphs on the
Monroe Doctrine, which practically repeated President
Wilson's Mobile speech on that subject, but in which
Mr. Page used the expression, "we prefer that European
Powers shall acquire no more territory on this continent,"
alarmed those precisians in language, who pretended to
believe that the Ambassador had used the word "prefer"
in its literal sense, and interpreted the sentence to mean
that, while the United States would "prefer" that
Europe should not overrun North and South America, it
would really raise no serious objection if Europe did so.

Senator Chamberlain of Oregon, who by this time had
apparently become the Senatorial leader of the anti-Page
propaganda, introduced a resolution demanding that the
Ambassador furnish the Senate a complete copy of this
highly pro-British outgiving. The copy was furnished
forthwith—and with that the tempest subsided.

To the President

American Embassy, London,
March 18, 1914.

DEAR MR. PRESIDENT:

About this infernal racket about my poor speech, I think
I have telegraphed you all there is to say. I infer that,
as a dying phase of the fuss, they are raising a controversy
over certain words and phrases. The speech was not
written out, but on the Panama part of it I made notes as
the preceding speakers paid us very handsome compli-

ments.   When you telegraphed for the text, I secured a
fairly good stenographic report, which had obvious errors
here and there.   I corrected it—nowhere changing the
fundamental meaning—to correspond with my notes, with
my own recollection of what I had said and with my very
clear and obvious meaning.   I cannot swear, neither can
anybody else, that every word and phrase in any report is
precisely as I spoke it.   But the speech as I sent it to you
is, I believe, as nearly verbally correct as it can now be
got;[1] and I know I spoke it with the meaning thereby conveyed and everybody so understands it.   They paid us
more fulsome (or emphatic and effusive) compliments than
I paid them; and I spoke that part of the speech in answer
to their compliments.   We were all in a very friendly
humour—thanks, in great measure, to your Message
spoken to Congress on the tolls question and to the great
pleasure that this has given here.

While what I said was not to the slightest degree "truckling to British opinion" and was, as I conceive it, every
word true, it is true also that I committed a fault in being
betrayed by the friendly and complimentary atmosphere
into mentioning at all a subject under fierce controversy.
In that I did wrong; and, if I have your pardon for this
offence, I shall try to avoid repeating it.   I shall hereafter
write out my speeches and turn every phrase over beforehand to see if any of them lend themselves to misconstruc-
tion.   That's a lot of work, but it seems necessary.   Of
course even then intonations and methods of delivery are
quite as full of meaning as adjectives and adverbs and
qualifying phrases.   Then, too, I shall make fewer
speeches.   Hitherto I have accepted only a very small part
of the invitations I have received; but I shall decline more.

---

[1] I have telegraphed a slight change in the phraseology of one passage, out of
deference to stenographers—no real change of meaning.   W. H. P.'s Note.

Right or wrong, the American Ambassador here is put
in a class by himself and given liberties that European
Ambassadors have never taken and are denied by their
armed and jealous governments. The American is not
regarded as a foreigner nor even as a stranger—a position
that, of course, has dangers, as my tactical mistake proves.
For when the Irishman becomes rampant on two continents and attacks the government on each side of the ocean,
all these unusual facts are forgotten—it is forgotten that I
was talking with business men—not a politician among
them except the Prime Minister, who was a guest—and
that all that was said by everybody was said and heard
from a commercial point of view, with no dream of any
political bearings of any speech or sentiment or compliment. That does not lessen my blunder; but it does seem
to me that the Irish and the Confederates (witness the
fellow who said in Congress that a part of your "bargain"
was to pay the British holders of repudiated Southern
State bonds!) have gone clean daft. Well, it is through
this sort of mire that a real foreign policy must be constructed. We had sunk to the bottom of foreign dis-
esteem. They had little respect for our Gov't here till
you put in the arbitration treaties for renewal and delivered your tolls message.

Then the atmosphere cleared up amazingly. I lunched
with Sir Edward Grey the other day and for the third
time he spoke of the "high ground" of your message.
He said that that utterance set a high example for all
rulers and public servants—"it moves higher the motives
of action of us all." Then he added with a laugh, "It
doesn't make so much difference now whether the President succeeds immediately or not. He has set us all a
great example." In talking about my poor speech, by
the way, he remarked that it wouldn't get me into trouble

at this end.   Then he said (which is very true) that he was much criticized for "bowing too low to the Americans." Then we each bowed to the other.   (Think what a photograph that would make for our crazy friends, he and I bowing to one another!)

It's a part of the insane furor—this irony of fate and imprudence on my part—that the reputation I have made here—so far as I have made any—is for plain speaking to the British—plainer and franker than any recent ambassador, and that now I should be accused of truckling to them.   Willard (of Spain) was with me at the speech and he said as we drove home, "I admire your frankness is slapping them good naturedly in the face.   Well as they take it, it is yet a slap."

I am greatly distressed lest this incident embarrass you. I heartily hope not.   Of course they are merely using me as a club to hit you; and I am sorry that I unwittingly lent myself to so ignoble a use.   I was taking too literally your parting advice—"Go, and be yourself"—and too literally the friendly atmosphere and attitude of that company of British masters of commerce, who perfectly understood my independent, frank, and friendly manner and speech.

Yours very heartily,
WALTER H. PAGE.

The only editorial comment I have seen here is a paragraph in the *Pall Mall* that I am being punished by the Irish and the yellow press for daring to be courteous.
To the President.

Apparently this episode had caused little perturbation in the White House.   Such a disturbance was precisely the kind of thing which President Wilson would naturally regard with contempt.

A final letter from the President satisfactorily closed the episode. The incident was chiefly important for its disclosure of certain currents in American life that were afterward to exercise a malevolent influence on a much greater and more destructive scale. The journals especially virulent in their attacks on Page for Anglomania, were published in the German language, and the politicians who most sought to turn the proceeding to personal account were those to whom the cultivation of the German vote was an industry zealously pursued. In a way this Anglophobia in the German sections of our population was something new. It is apparent now that German-Americans, in lifting their voices thus raucously against the Anglo-Saxon, were merely reproducing in this country a state of mind that, ever since the Boer war, had been one of the chief emotions of the Fatherland. The manifestation was therefore a portent.

From the President

The White House, Washington,
March 25, 1914.

MY DEAR PAGE:

Thank you for your little note of March thirteenth.[1] You may be sure that none of us who knew you or read the speech felt anything but admiration for it. It is very astonishing to me how some Democrats in the Senate themselves bring these artificial difficulties on the Administration, and it distresses me not a little. Mr. Bryan read your speech yesterday to the Cabinet, who greatly enjoyed it. It was at once sent to the Senate and I hope will there be given out for publication in full.

I want you to feel constantly how I value the intelligent

---

[1]The Ambassador's letter is dated March 18th.

and effective work you are doing in London. I do not know what I should do without you.

The fight is on now about the tolls, but I feel perfectly confident of winning in the matter, though there is not a little opposition in Congress—more in the House, it strangely turns out, where a majority of the Democrats originally voted against the exemption, than in the Senate, where a majority of the Democrats voted for it. The vicissitudes of politics are certainly incalculable.

With the warmest regard, in necessary haste,

WOODROW WILSON.

From the President

The White House, Washington,
April 2, 1914.

MY DEAR PAGE:

Please do not distress yourself about that speech. I think with you that it was a mistake to touch upon that matter while it was right hot, because any touch would be sure to burn the finger; but as for the speech itself, I would be willing to subscribe to every bit of it myself, and there can be no rational objection to it. We shall try to cool the excited persons on this side of the water and I think nothing further will come of it. In the meantime, pray realize how thoroughly and entirely you are enjoying my confidence and admiration.

Your letter about Cowdray and Murray was very illuminating and will be very serviceable to me. I have come to see that the real knowledge of the relations between countries in matters of public policy is to be gained at country houses and dinner tables, and not in diplomatic correspondence; in brief, that when we know the men and the currents of opinion, we know more than foreign ministers can tell us; and your letters give me, in a thoroughly dignified way, just the sidelights that are necessary to illuminate the picture. I am heartily obliged to you.

All unite with me in the warmest regards as always.

In haste,

Faithfully yours,

WOODROW WILSON.

HON. WALTER H. PAGE,
  American Embassy,
    London, England.

A note of a conversation with Sir Edward Grey touches the same point: "April 1, 1914. Sir Edward Grey recalled to me to-day that he had waited for the President to take up the Canal tolls controversy at his convenience. 'When he took it up at his own time to suit his own plans, he took it up in the most admirable way possible.' This whole story is too good to be lost. If the repeal of the tolls clause passes the Senate, I propose to make a speech in the House of Commons on 'The Proper Way for Great Governments to Deal with One Another,' and use this experience.

"Sir Edward also spoke of being somewhat 'depressed' by the fierce opposition to the President on the tolls question—the extent of Anglophobia in the United States.

"Here is a place for a campaign of education—Chautauqua and whatnot.

"The amount of Anglophobia *is* great. But I doubt if it be as great as it seems; for it is organized and is very vociferous. If you collected together or thoroughly organized all the people in the United States who have birthmarks on their faces, you'd be 'depressed' by the number of them."

Nothing could have more eloquently proved the truth of this last remark than the history of this Panama bill itself. After all the politicians in the House and Senate had filled pages of the *Congressional Record* with denunciations of Great Britain—most of it intended for the entertainment of Irish-Americans and German-Americans in the constituencies—the two Houses proceeded to the really serious business of voting. The House quickly passed the bill by 216 to 71, and the Senate by 50 to 35. Apparently the amount of Anglophobia was not portentous, when it came to putting this emotion to the test of counting heads. The bill went at once to the President, was signed—and the dishonour was atoned for.

Mr. and Mrs. Page were attending a ball in Buckingham Palace when the great news reached London. The gathering represented all that was most distinguished in the official and diplomatic life of the British capital. The word was rapidly passed from guest to guest, and the American Ambassador and his wife soon found themselves the centre of a company which could hardly restrain itself in expressing its admiration for the United States. Never in the history of the country had American prestige stood so high as on that night. The King and the Prime Minister were especially affected by this display of fair-dealing in Washington. The slight commercial advantage which Great Britain had obtained was not the thought that was uppermost in everybody's mind. The thing that really moved these assembled statesmen and diplomats was the fact that something new had appeared in the history of legislative chambers. A great nation had committed an outrageous wrong—that was something that had happened many times before in all countries. But the unprecedented thing was that this same nation had exposed its fault boldly to the world—had lifted up its hands and cried, "We have sinned!" and then had publicly undone its error. Proud as Page had always been of his country, that moment was perhaps the most triumphant in his life. The action of Congress emphasized all that he had been saying of the ideals of the United States, and gave point to his arguments that justice and honour and right, and not temporary selfish interest, should control the foreign policy of any nation which really claimed to be enlightened. The general feeling of Great Britain was perhaps best expressed by the remark made to Mrs. Page, on this occasion, by Lady D——:

"The United States has set a high standard for all nations to live up to. I don't believe that there is any other nation that would have done it."

One significant feature of this great episode was the act of Congress in accepting the President's statement that the repeal of the Panama discrimination was a necessary preliminary to the success of American foreign policy. Mr. Wilson's declaration, that, unless this legislation should be repealed, he would not "know how to deal with other matters of even greater delicacy and nearer consequence" had puzzled Congress and the country. The debates show the keenest curiosity as to what the President had in mind. The newspapers turned the matter over and over, without obtaining any clew to the mystery. Some thought that the President had planned to intervene in Mexico, and that the tolls legislation was the consideration demanded by Great Britain for a free hand in this matter. But this correspondence has already demolished that theory. Others thought that Japan was in some way involved—but that explanation also failed to satisfy.

Congress accepted the President's statement trustfully and blindly, and passed the asked-for legislation. Up to the present moment this passage in the Presidential message has been unexplained. Page's papers, however, disclose what seems to be a satisfactory solution to the mystery. They show that the President and Colonel House and Page were at this time engaged in a negotiation of the utmost importance. At the very time that the tolls bill was under discussion Colonel House was making arrangements for a visit to Great Britain, France, and Germany, the purpose of which was to bring these nations to some kind of an understanding that would prevent a European war. This evidently was the great business that could not be disclosed at the time and for which the repeal of the tolls legislation was the necessary preliminary.

CHAPTER IX
AMERICA TRIES TO PREVENT THE EUROPEAN WAR

PAGE'S mind, from the day of his arrival in England, had been filled with that portent which was the most outstanding fact in European life. Could nothing be done to prevent the dangers threatened by European militarism? Was there no way of forestalling the war which seemed every day to be approaching nearer? The dates of the following letters, August, 1913, show that this was one of the first ideas which Page presented to the new Administration.

To Edward M. House

Aug. 28, 1913.

MY DEAR HOUSE:

. . . Everything is lovely and the goose hangs high. We're having a fine time. Only, only, only—I do wish to do something constructive and lasting. Here are great navies and armies and great withdrawals of men from industry—an enormous waste. Here are kings and courts and gold lace and ceremonies which, without producing anything, require great cost to keep them going. Here are all the privileges and taxes that this state of things implies—every one a hindrance to human progress. We are free from most of these. We have more people and more capable people and many times more territory than both England and Germany; and we have more *potential* wealth than all Europe. They know that.

270

They'd like to find a way to escape. The Hague pro-grammes, for the most part, just lead them around a circle in the dark back to the place where they started. Somebody needs to *do* something. If we could find some friendly use for these navies and armies and kings and things—in the service of humanity—they'd follow us. We ought to find a way to use them in cleaning up the tropics under our leadership and under our code of ethics—that everything must be done for the good of the tropical peoples and that nobody may annex a foot of land. They want a job. Then they'd quit sitting on their haunches, growling at one another.

I wonder if we couldn't serve notice that the land-stealing game is forever ended and that the cleaning up of backward lands is now in order—for the people that live there; and then invite Europe's help to make the tropics as healthful as the Panama Zone?

There's no future in Europe's vision—no long look ahead. They give all their thought to the immediate danger. Consider this Balkan War; all European energy was spent merely to keep the Great Powers at peace. The two wars in the Balkans have simply impoverished the people—left the world that much worse than it was before. Nobody has considered the well-being or the future of those peoples nor of their land. The Great Powers are mere threats to one another, content to check, one the other! There can come no help to the progress of the world from this sort of action—no step forward.

Work on a world-plan. Nothing but blue chips, you know. Is it not possible that Mexico may give an enter-ing wedge for this kind of thing?

Heartily yours,

WALTER H. PAGE.

In a memorandum, written about the same time, Mr. Page explains his idea in more detail:

Was there ever greater need than there is now of a first-class mind unselfishly working on world problems? The ablest ruling minds are engaged on domestic tasks. There is no world-girdling intelligence at work in government. On the continent of Europe, the Kaiser is probably the foremost man. Yet he cannot think far beyond the provincial views of the Germans. In England, Sir Edward Grey is the largest-visioned statesman. All the Europeans are spending their thought and money in watching and checkmating one another and in maintaining their armed and balanced *status quo*.

A way must be found out of this stagnant watching. Else a way will have to be fought out of it; and a great European war would set the Old World, perhaps the whole world, back a long way; and thereafter, the present armed watching would recur; we should have gained nothing. It seems impossible to talk the Great Powers out of their fear of one another or to "Hague" them out of it. They'll never be persuaded to disarm. The only way left seems to be to find some common and useful work for these great armies to do. Then, perhaps, they'll *work* themselves out of their jealous position. Isn't this sound psychology?

To produce a new situation, the vast energy that now spends itself in maintaining armies and navies must find a new outlet. Something new must be found for them to do, some great unselfish task that they can do together.

Nobody can lead in such a new era but the United States.

May there not come such a chance in Mexico—to clean out bandits, yellow fever, malaria, hookworm—all to make the country healthful, safe for life and investment, and for orderly self-government at last? What we did in Cuba might thus be made the beginning of a new epoch in history—conquest for the sole benefit of the conquered, worked out by a sanitary reformation. The new sanitation will reclaim all tropical lands; but the work must be first done by military power—probably from the outside.

May not the existing military power of Europe conceivably be diverted, gradually, to this use? One step at a time, as political and financial occasions arise? As presently in Mexico?

This present order must change. It holds the Old World still. It keeps all parts of the world apart, in spite of the friendly cohesive forces of trade and travel. It keeps back self-government and the progress of man.

And the tropics cry out for sanitation, which is at first an essentially military task.

A strange idea this may have seemed in August, 1913, a year before the outbreak of the European war; yet the scheme is not dissimilar to the "mandatory" principle, adopted by the Versailles Peace Conference as the only practical method of dealing with backward peoples. In this work, as in everything that would help mankind on its weary way to a more efficient and more democratic civilization, Page regarded the United States, Great Britain, and the British Dominions as inevitable partners. Anything that would bring these two nations into a closer coöperation he looked upon as a step making for human advancement. He believed that any opportunity of sweeping away misconceptions and prejudices and of impressing upon the two peoples their common mission should be eagerly seized by the statesmen of the two countries. And circumstances at this particular

moment, Page believed, presented a large opportunity of
this kind. It is one of the minor ironies of modern
history that the United States and Great Britain should
have selected 1914 as a year for a great peace celebration.
That year marked the one hundredth anniversary of the
signing of the Treaty of Ghent, which ended the War of
1812, and in 1913 comprehensive plans had already been
formed for observing this impressive centennial. The
plan was to make it more than the mere observance of a
hundred years of peaceful intercourse; it was the intention to use the occasion to emphasize the fundamental
identity of American and British ideals and to lay the
foundation of a permanent understanding and friendship. The erection of a monument to Abraham Lincoln
at Westminster—a plan that has since been realized—
was one detail of this programme. Another was the restoration of Sulgrave Manor, the English country seat of
the Washingtons, and its preservation as a place where
the peoples of both countries could share their common
traditions. Page now dared to hope that President
Wilson might associate himself with this great purpose to
the extent of coming to England and accepting this
gift in the name of the American nation. Such a Presidential visit, he believed, would exercise a mighty influence in forestalling a threatening European war.
The ultimate purpose, that is, was world peace—precisely the same motive that led President Wilson, in 1919,
to make a European pilgrimage.

This idea was no passing fancy with Page: it was with
him a favourite topic of conversation. Such a presidential visit, he believed, would accomplish more than any
other influences in dissipating the clouds that were
darkening the European landscape. He would elaborate
the idea at length in discussions with his intimates.

"What I want," he would say, "is to have the President of the United States and the King of England stand up side by side and let the world take a good look at them!"

To Edward M. House

August 25, 1913.

. . . I wrote him (President Wilson) my plan—a mere outline. He'll only smile now. But when the tariff and the currency and Mexico are off his hands, and when he can be invited to come and deliver an oration on George Washington next year at the presentation of the old Washington homestead here, he may be " pushed over." You do the pushing. Mrs. Page has invited the young White House couple to visit us on their honeymoon.[1] Encourage that and that may encourage the larger plan later. Nothing else would give such a friendly turn to the whole world as the President's coming here. The old Earth would sit up and rub its eyes and take notice to whom it belongs. This visit might prevent an English-German war and an American-Japanese war, by this mere show of friendliness. It would be one of the greatest occasions of our time. Even at my little speeches, they "whoop it up!" What would they do over the President's!

But at that time Washington was too busy with its domestic programme to consider such a proposal seriously. "Your two letters," wrote Colonel House in reply, "have come to me and lifted me out of the rut of things and given me a glimpse of a fair land. What you are thinking of and what you want this Administration to do is

---

[1] Mr. and Mrs. Francis B. Sayre, son-in-law and daughter of President Wilson.

beyond the power of accomplishment for the moment. My desk is covered with matters of no lasting importance, but which come to me as a part of the day's work, and which must be done if I am to help lift the load that is pressing upon the President. It tells me better than anything else what he has to bear, and how utterly futile it is for him to attempt such problems as you present."

From the President

MY DEAR PAGE:

. . . As for your suggestion that I should myself visit England during my term of office, I must say that I agree with all your arguments for it, and yet the case against the President's leaving the country, particularly now that he is expected to exercise a constant leadership in all parts of the business of the government, is very strong and I am afraid overwhelming. It might be the beginning of a practice of visiting foreign countries which would lead Presidents rather far afield.

It is a most attractive idea, I can assure you, and I turn away from it with the greatest reluctance.

We hear golden opinions of the impression you are making in England, and I have only to say that it is just what I had expected.

Cordially and faithfully yours,
WOODROW WILSON.

HON. WALTER H. PAGE,
    American Embassy,
      London, England.

In December, however, evidently Colonel House's mind had turned to the general subject that had so engaged that of the Ambassador.

Walter H. Page, from a photograph taken a few years before he
became American Ambassador to Great Britain

The British Foreign Office, Downing Street

From Edward M. House

145 East 35th Street,
New York City.
December 13th, 1913.

DEAR PAGE:

In my budget of yesterday I did not tell you of the suggestion which I made to Sir William Tyrrell when he was here, and which I also made to the President.

It occurred to me that between us all we might bring about the naval holiday which Winston Churchill has proposed. My plan is that I should go to Germany in the spring and see the Kaiser, and try to win him over to the thought that is uppermost in our mind and that of the British Government.

Sir William thought there was a good sporting chance of success. He offered to let me have all the correspondence that had passed between the British and German governments upon this question so that I might be thoroughly informed as to the position of them both. He thought I should go directly to Germany without stopping in England, and that Gerard should prepare the Kaiser for my coming, telling him of my relations with the President. He thought this would be sufficient without any further credentials.

In other words, he would do with the Kaiser what you did with Sir Edward Grey last summer.

I spoke to the President about the matter and he seemed pleased with the suggestion; in fact, I might say, he was enthusiastic. He said, just as Sir William did, that it would be too late for this year's budget; but he made a suggestion that he get the Appropriations Committee to incorporate a clause, permitting him to eliminate certain parts of the battleship budget in the event that other nations declared for a naval holiday. So this will be done and will further the plan.

Now I want to get you into the game. If you think it advisable, take the matter up with Sir William Tyrrell and then with Sir Edward Grey, or directly with Sir Edward, if you prefer, and give me the benefit of your advice and conclusions.

Please tell Sir William that I lunched at the Embassy with the Spring Rices yesterday, and had a satisfactory talk with both Lady Spring Rice and Sir Cecil.

Faithfully yours,
E. M. House.

It is apparent from Page's letters that the suggestion now contained in Colonel House's communication would receive a friendly hearing. The idea that Colonel House suggested was merely the initial stage of a plan which soon took on more ambitious proportions. At the time of Sir William Tyrrell's American visit, the Winston Churchill proposal for a naval holiday was being actively discussed by the British and the American press. In one form or another it had been figuring in the news for nearly two years. Viscount Haldane, in the course of his famous visit to Berlin in February, 1912, had attempted to reach some understanding with the German Government on the limitation of the German and the British fleets. The Agadir crisis of the year before had left Europe with a bad state of nerves, and there was a general belief that only some agreement on shipbuilding could prevent a European war. Lord Haldane and von Tirpitz spent many hours discussing the relative sizes of the two navies, but the discussions led to no definite under-

standing. In March, 1913, Mr. Churchill, then First
Lord of the Admiralty, took up the same subject in a
different form. In this speech he first used the words
"naval holiday," and proposed that Germany and Great
Britain should cease building first-class battleships for one
year, thus giving the two nations a breathing space, during
which time they might discuss their future plans in the hope
of reaching a permanent agreement. The matter lagged
again until October 18, 1913, when, in a speech at Manchester, Mr. Churchill placed his proposal in this form: "Now,
we say to our great neighbour, Germany, 'If you will put off
beginning your two ships for twelve months from the ordinary date when you would have begun them, we will put off
beginning our four ships, in absolute good faith, for exactly the same period.'" About the same time Premier
Asquith made it clear that the Ministry was back of the
suggested programme. In Germany, however, the "naval holiday" soon became an object of derision. The
official answer was that Germany had a definite naval
law and that the Government could not entertain any
suggestion of departing from it. Great Britain then
answered that, for every keel Germany laid down, the
Admiralty would lay down two. The outcome, therefore, of this attempt at friendship was that the two nations
had been placed farther apart than ever.

The dates of this discussion, it will be observed, almost
corresponded with the period covered by the Tyrrell
visit to America. This fact, and Page's letters of this
period, had apparently implanted in Colonel House's mind
an ambition for definite action. He now proposed that
President Wilson should take up the broken threads of
the rapprochement and attempt to bring them together
again. From this, as will be made plain, the plan developed into something more comprehensive. Page's

ideas on the treatment of backward nations had strongly
impressed both the President and Colonel House. The
discussion on Mexico which had just taken place between the American and the British Governments seemed
to have developed ideas that could have a much wider
application. The fundamental difficulties in Mexico
were not peculiar to that country nor indeed to Latin-
America. Perhaps the most prolific cause of war among
the more enlightened countries was that produced by the
jealousies and antagonisms which were developed by their
contacts with unprogressive peoples—in the Balkans, the
Ottoman Empire, Asia, and the Far East. The method
of dealing with such peoples, which the United States
had found so successful in Cuba and the Philippines, had
proved that there was just one honourable way of dealing
with the less fortunate and more primitive races in all
parts of the world. Was it not possible to bring the
greatest nations, especially the United States, Great
Britain, and Germany, to some agreement on this question, as well as on the question of disarmament? This
once accomplished, the way could be prepared for joint
action on the numerous other problems which were then
threatening the peace of the world. The League of
Nations was then not even a phrase, but the plan that
was forming in Colonel House's mind was at least some
scheme for permanent international coöperation. For
several years Germany had been the nation which had
proved the greatest obstacle to such international friendliness and arbitration. The Kaiser had destroyed both
Hague Conferences as influential forces in the remaking of
the world; and in the autumn of 1913 he had taken on a
more belligerent attitude than ever. If this attempt to establish a better condition of things was to succeed, Germany's coöperation would be indispensable. This is the

reason why Colonel House proposed first of all to visit Berlin.

From Edward M. House

145 East 35th Street,
New York City.
January 4th, 1914.

DEAR. PAGE:

. . . Benj. Ide Wheeler[1] took lunch with me the other day. He is just back from Germany and he is on the most intimate terms with the Kaiser. He tells me he often takes dinner with the family alone, and spends the evening with them.

I know, now, the different Cabinet officials who have the Kaiser's confidence and I know his attitude toward England, naval armaments, war, and world politics in general.

Wheeler spoke to me very frankly and the information he gave me will be invaluable in the event that my plans carry. The general idea is to bring about a sympathetic understanding between England, Germany, and America, not only upon the question of disarmament, but upon other matters of equal importance to themselves, and to the world at large.

It seems to me that Japan should come into this pact, but Wheeler tells me that the Kaiser feels very strongly upon the question of Asiatics. He thinks the contest of the future will be between the Eastern and Western civilizations. . . .

Your friend always,
E. M. HOUSE.

By January 4, 1914, the House-Wilson plan had thus grown into an Anglo-American-German "pact," to deal

---

[1] Ex-President of the University of California, Roosevelt Professor at the University of Berlin, 1909–10.

not only with "disarmament, but other matters of equal importance to themselves and to the world at large." Page's response to this idea was consistent and characteristic. He had no faith in Germany and believed that the existence of Kaiserism was incompatible with the extension of the democratic ideal. Even at this early time—eight months before the outbreak of the World War—he had no enthusiasm for anything in the nature of an alliance, or a "pact," that included Germany as an equal partner. He did, however, have great faith in the coöperation of the English-speaking peoples as a force that would make for permanent peace and international justice. In his reply to Colonel House, therefore, Page fell back at once upon his favourite plan for an understanding between the United States, Great Britain, and the British colonies. That he would completely sympathize with the Washington aspiration for disarmament was to be expected.

To Edward M. House

January 2, 1914.

MY DEAR HOUSE:

You have set my imagination going. I've been thinking of this thing for months, and now you've given me a fresh start. It can be worked out somehow—doubtless, not in the form that anybody may at first see; but experiment and frank discussion will find a way.

As I think of it, turning it this way and that, there always comes to me just as I am falling to sleep this reflection: the English-speaking peoples now rule the world in all essential facts. They alone and Switzerland have permanent free government. In France there's freedom—but for how long? In Germany and Austria —hardly. In the Scandinavian States—yes, but they are small and exposed as are Belgium and Holland. In the big secure South American States—yes, it's coming. In Japan—? Only the British lands and the United States have secure liberty. They also have the most treasure, the best fighters, the most land, the most ships—the future in fact.

Now, because George Washington warned us against alliances, we've gone on as if an alliance were a kind of smallpox. Suppose there were—let us say for argument's sake—the tightest sort of an alliance, offensive and defensive, between all Britain, colonies and all, and the United States—what would happen? Anything we'd say would go, whether we should say, "Come in out of the wet," or, "Disarm." That might be the beginning of a real world-alliance and union to accomplish certain large results—disarmament, for instance, or arbitration —dozens of good things.

Of course, we'd have to draw and quarter the O'Gormans.[1] But that ought to be done anyhow in the general interest of good sense in the world. We could force any nation into this "trust" that we wanted in it.

Isn't it time we tackled such a job frankly, fighting out the Irish problem once for all, and having done with it?

I'm not proposing a programme. I'm only thinking out loud. I see little hope of doing anything so long as we choose to be ruled by an obsolete remark made by George Washington.

W. H. P.

January 11, 1914.

. . . But this armament flurry is worth serious thought. Lloyd George gave out an interview, seeming to imply the necessity of reducing the navy programme.

---

[1] James A. O'Gorman was the anti-British Senator from New York State at this time working hard against the repeal of the Panama tolls discrimination.

The French allies of the British went up in the air! They raised a great howl. Churchill went to see them, to soothe them. They would not be soothed. Now the Prime Minister is going to Paris—ostensibly to see his daughter off to the Riviera. Nobody believes that reason. They say he's going to smooth out the French. Meantime the Germans are gleeful.

And the British Navy League is receiving money and encouraging letters from British subjects, praying greater activity to keep the navy up. You touch the navy and you touch the quick—that's the lesson. It's an enormous excitement that this small incident has caused.

W. H. P.

To Edward M. House

London, February 24, 1914.

My DEAR HOUSE:

You'll be interested in these pamphlets by Sir Max Waechter, who has opened an office here and is spending much money to "federate" Europe, and to bring a lessening of armaments. I enclose also an article about him from the *Daily Telegraph*, which tells how he has interviewed most of the Old World monarchs. Get also, immediately, the new two-volume life of Lord Lyons, Minister to the United States during the Civil War, and subsequently Ambassador to France. You will find an interesting account of the campaign of about 1870 to reduce armaments, when old Bismarck dumped the whole basket of apples by marching against France. You know I sometimes fear some sort of repetition of that experience. Some government (probably Germany) will see bankruptcy staring it in the face and the easiest way out will seem a great war. Bankruptcy before a war would be ignominious; after a war, it could be charged to

"Glory." It'll take a long time to bankrupt England. It's unspeakably rich; they pay enormous taxes, but they pay them out of their incomes, not out of their principal, except their inheritance tax. That looks to me as if it came out of the principal. . . .

I hope you had a good time in Texas and escaped some cold weather. This deceptive sort of winter here is grippe-laden. I've had the thing, but I'm now getting over it. . . .

This Benton[1]-Mexican business is causing great excitement here.

Always heartily yours,
W. H. P.

P. S. There's nothing like the President. By George! the passage of the arbitration treaty (renewal) almost right off the bat, and apparently the tolls discrimination coming presently to its repeal! Sir Edward Grey remarked to me yesterday: "Things are clearing up!" I came near saying to him: "Have you any miracles in mind that you'd like to see worked?" Wilson stock is at a high premium on this side of the water in spite of the momentary impatience caused by Benton's death.

W. H. P.

From Edward M. House

145 East 35th Street,
New York City.
April 19th, 1914.

DEAR PAGE:

I have had a long talk with Mr. Laughlin.[2] At first he thought I would not have more than one chance in a

---

[1] In February, 1915, William S. Benton, an English subject who had spent the larger part of his life in Mexico, was murdered in the presence of Francisco Villa.

[2] Mr. Irwin Laughlin, first secretary of the American Embassy in London; at this time spending a few weeks in the United States.

million to do anything with the Kaiser, but after talking with him further, he concluded that I would have a fairly good sporting chance. I have about concluded to take it.

If I can do anything, I can do it in a few days. I was with the President most of last week. . . .

He spoke of your letters to him and to me as being classics, and said they were the best letters, as far as he knew, that any one had ever written. Of course you know how heartily I concur in this. He said that sometime they should be published.

The President is now crystallizing his mind in regard to the Federal Reserve Board, and if you are not to remain in London, then he would probably put Houston on the Board and ask you to take the Secretaryship of Agriculture.

You have no idea the feeling that is being aroused by the tolls question. The Hearst papers are screaming at all of us every day. They have at last honoured me with their abuse. . . .

With love and best wishes, I am,

Faithfully yours,

E. M. HOUSE.

From Edward M. House

145 East 35th Street,
New York City.
April 20th, 1914.

DEAR PAGE:

. . . . It is our purpose to sail on the *Imperator*, May 16th, and go directly to Germany. I expect to be there a week or more, but Mrs. House will reach London by the 1st or 2nd of June. . . .

Our friend¹ in Washington thinks it is worth while for

¹ Obviously President Wilson.

me to go to Germany, and that determines the matter. The press is shrieking to-day over the Mexican situation, but I hope they will be disappointed. It is not the intention to do anything further for the moment than to blockade the ports, and unless some overt act is made from the North, our troops will not cross the border.

Your friend always,

E. M. HOUSE.

To Edward M. House

London, April 27, 1914.

MY DEAR HOUSE:

Of course you decided wisely to carry out your original Berlin plan, and you ought never to have had a moment's hesitation, if you did have any hesitation. I do not expect you to produce any visible or immediate results. I hope I am mistaken in this. But you know that the German Government has a well-laid progressive plan for shipbuilding for a certain number of years. I believe that the work has, in fact, already been arranged for. But that has nothing to do with the case. You are going to see what effect you can produce on the mind of a man. Perhaps you will never know just what effect you will produce. Yet the fact that you are who you are, that you make this journey for this especial purpose, that you are everlastingly right—these are enough.

Moreover, you can't ever tell results, nor can you afford to make your plans in this sort of high work with the slightest reference to probable results. That's the bigness and the glory of it. Any ordinary man can, on any ordinary day, go and do a task, the favourable results of which may be foreseen. *That's* easy. The big thing is to go confidently to work on a task, the results of which nobody can possibly foresee—a task so vague and improbable of definite results that small men hesitate. It is in this spirit that very many of the biggest things in history have been done. Wasn't the purchase of Louisiana such a thing? Who'd ever have supposed that that could have been brought about? I applaud your errand and I am eagerly impatient to hear the results. When will *you* get here? I assume that Mrs. House will not go with you to Berlin. No matter so you both turn up here for a good long stay.

I've taken me a little bit of a house about twenty miles out of town whither we are going in July as soon as we can get away from London. I hope to stay down there till far into October, coming up to London about thrice a week. That's the dull season of the year. It's a charming little country place—big enough for you to visit us. . . .

From Edward M. House

An Bord des Dampfers *Imperator*
den May 21, 1914.

Hamburg-Amerika Linie

DEAR PAGE:

Here we are again. The Wallaces[1] land at Cherbourg, Friday morning, and we of course go on to Berlin. I wish I might have the benefit of your advice just now, for the chances for success in this great adventure are slender enough at best. The President has done his part in the letter I have with me, and it is clearly up to me to do mine. . . .

Faithfully yours,
E. M. HOUSE.

---

[1] Mr. Hugh C. Wallace, afterward Ambassador to France, and Mrs. Wallace. Mr. and Mrs. Wallace accompanied Mr. and Mrs. House on this journey.

It will be observed that Colonel House had taken the advice of Sir William Tyrrell, and had sailed directly to Germany on a German ship—the *Imperator*. Ambassador Gerard had made preparations for his reception in Berlin, and the American soon had long talks with Admiral von Tirpitz, Falkenhayn, Von Jagow, Solf, and others. Von Bethmann-Hollweg's wife died almost on the day of his arrival in Berlin, so it was impossible for him to see the Chancellor—the man who would have probably been the most receptive to these peace ideas. All the leaders of the government, except Von Tirpitz, gave Colonel House's proposals a respectful if somewhat cynical hearing. Von Tirpitz was openly and demonstratively hostile. The leader of the German Navy simply bristled with antagonism at any suggestion for peace or disarmament or world coöperation. He consumed a large part of the time which Colonel House spent with him denouncing England and all its works. Hatred of the "Island Kingdom" was apparently the consuming passion of his existence. On the whole, Von Tirpitz thus made no attempt to conceal his feeling that the purpose of the House mission was extremely distasteful to him. The other members of the Government, while not so tactlessly hostile, were not particularly encouraging. The usual objections to disarmament were urged—the fear of other Powers, the walled-in state of Germany, the vigilant enemies against which it was necessary constantly to be prepared and watchful. Even more than the unsympathetic politeness of the German Cabinet the general atmosphere of Berlin was depressing to Colonel House. The militaristic oligarchy was absolutely in control. Militarism possessed not only the army, the navy, and the chief officers of state, but the populace as well. One almost trivial circumstance has left a lasting impression on Colonel House's mind. Ambassador Gerard took him out one evening for a little relaxation. Both Mr. Gerard and Colonel House were fond of target shooting and the two men sought one of the numerous rifle galleries of Berlin. They visited gallery after gallery, but could not get into one. Great crowds lined up at every place, waiting their turns at the target; it seemed as though every able-bodied man in Berlin was spending all his time improving his marksmanship. But this was merely a small indication of the atmosphere of militarism which prevailed in the larger aspects of life. Colonel House found himself in a strange place to preach international accord for the ending of war!

He had come to Berlin not merely to talk with the Cabinet heads; his goal was the Kaiser himself. But he perceived at once a persistent opposition to his plan. As he was the President's personal representative, and carried a letter from the President to the Kaiser, an audience could not be refused—indeed, it had already been duly arranged; but there was a quiet opposition to his consorting with the "All Highest" alone. It was not usual, Colonel House was informed, for His Imperial Majesty to discuss such matters except in the presence of a representative of the Foreign Office. Germany had not yet recovered from the shock which the Emperor's conversation with certain foreign correspondents had given the nation. The effects were still felt of the famous interviews of October 28, 1908, which, when published in the London *Telegraph*, had caused the bitterest resentment in Great Britain. The Kaiser had given his solemn word that he would indulge in no more indiscretions of this sort, and a private interview with Colonel House was regarded by his advisers as a possible infraction of that promise. But the American would not be denied. He

knew that an interview with a third person present would
be simply time thrown away since his message was intended for the Kaiser's own ears; and ultimately his persistence succeeded. The next Monday would be June
1st—a great day in Germany. It was the occasion of the
Schrippenfest, a day which for many years had been set
aside for the glorification of the German Army. On that
festival, the Kaiser entertained with great pomp representative army officers and representative privates, as
well as the diplomatic corps and other distinguished
foreigners. Colonel House was invited to attend the
Kaiser's luncheon on that occasion, and was informed that,
after this function was over, he would have an opportunity of having a private conversation with His Majesty.

The affair took place in the palace at Potsdam. The
militarism which Colonel House had felt so oppressively
in Berlin society was especially manifest on this occasion.
There were two luncheon parties—that of the Kaiser
and his officers and guests in the state dining room, and
that of the selected private soldiers outside. The Kaiser
and the Kaiserin spent a few moments with their humbler
subjects, drinking beer with them and passing a few com-
radely remarks; they then proceeded to the large dining
hall and took their places with the gorgeously caparisoned
and bemedalled chieftains of the German Army. The
whole proceeding has an historic interest, in that it was
the last Schrippenfest held. Whether another will ever
be held is problematical, for the occasion was an inevitable
part of the trappings of Hohenzollernism. Despite the
gravity of the occasion, Colonel House's chief memory
of this function is slightly tinged with the ludicrous. He
had spent the better part of a lifetime attempting to
rid himself of his military title, but uselessly. He was
now embarrassed because these solemn German officers

persisted in regarding him as an important part of the American Army, and in discussing technical and strategical problems. The visitor made several attempts to explain that he was merely a "geographical colonel"— that the title was constantly conferred in an informal sense on Americans, especially Southerners, and that the handle to his name had, therefore, no military significance. But the round-faced Teutons stared at his explanation in blank amazement; they couldn't grasp the point at all, and continued to ask his opinion of matters purely military.

When the lunch was finished, the Kaiser took Colonel House aside, and the two men withdrew to the terrace, out of earshot of the rest of the gathering. However, they were not out of sight. For nearly half an hour the Kaiser and the American stood side by side upon the terrace, the German generals, at a respectful distance, watching the proceeding, resentful, puzzled, curious as to what it was all about. The quiet demeanour of the American "Colonel," his plain citizen's clothes, and his almost impassive face, formed a striking contrast to the Kaiser's dazzling uniform and the general scene of military display. Two or three of the generals and admirals present were in the secret, but only two or three; the mass of officers watching this meeting little guessed that the purpose of House's visit was to persuade the Kaiser to abandon everything for which the Schrippenfest stood; to enter an international compact with the United States and Great Britain for reducing armaments, to reach an agreement about trade and the treatment of backward peoples, and to form something of a permanent association for the preservation of peace. The one thing which was apparent to the watchers was that the American was only now and then saying a brief word, but that the Kaiser was, as usual, doing a vast amount of talking. His speech rattled on with the utmost animation, his arms were constantly gesticulating, he would bring one fist down into his palm to register an emphatic point, and enforce certain ideas with a menacing forefinger. At times Colonel House would show slight signs of impatience and interrupt the flow of talk. But the Kaiser was clearly absorbed in the subject under discussion. His entourage several times attempted to break up the interview. The Court Chamberlain twice gingerly approached and informed His Majesty that the Imperial train was waiting to take the party back to Berlin. Each time the Kaiser, with an angry gesture, waved the interrupter away. Despairing of the usual resources, the Kaiserin was sent with the same message. The Kaiser did not treat her so summarily, but he paid no attention to the request, and continued to discuss the European situation with the American.

The subject that had mainly aroused the Imperial warmth was the "Yellow Peril." For years this had been an obsession with the Kaiser, and he launched into the subject as soon as Colonel House broached the purpose of his visit. There could be no question of disarmament, the Kaiser vehemently declared, as long as this danger to civilization existed. "We white nations should join hands," he said, "to oppose Japan and the other yellow nations, or some day they will destroy us."

It was with difficulty that Colonel House could get His Majesty away from this subject. Whatever topic he touched upon, the Kaiser would immediately start declaiming on the dangers that faced Europe from the East. His insistence on this accounted partly for the slight signs of impatience which the American showed. He feared that all the time allotted for the interview would be devoted to discussing the Japanese. About another nation, the Kaiser showed almost as much alarm as he did about Japan, and that was Russia. He spoke contemptuously of France and Great Britain as possible enemies, for he apparently had no fear of them. But the size of Russia and the exposed eastern frontier of Germany seemed to appal him. How could Germany join a peace pact, and reduce its army, so long as 175,000,000 Slavs threatened them from this direction?

Another matter that the Kaiser discussed with derision was Mr. Bryan's arbitration treaty. Practically all the great nations had already ratified this treaty except Germany. The Kaiser now laughed at the treaties and pooh-poohed Bryan. Germany, he declared, would never accept such an arbitration plan. Colonel House had particular cause to remember this part of the conversation three years afterward, when the United States declared war on Germany. The outstanding feature of the Bryan treaty was the clause which pledged the high contracting parties not to go to war without taking a breathing spell of one year in which to think the matter over. Had Germany adopted this treaty, the United States, in April, 1917, after Germany had presented a *casus belli* by resuming unrestricted submarine warfare, could not have gone to war. We should have been obliged to wait a year, or until April, 1918, before engaging in hostilities. That is, an honourable observance of this Bryan treaty by the United States would have meant that Germany would have starved Great Britain into surrender, and crushed Europe with her army. Had the Kaiser, on this June afternoon, not notified Colonel House that Germany would not accept this treaty, but, instead, had notified him that he would accept it, William II might now be sitting on the throne of a victorious Germany, with Europe for a footstool.

Despite the Kaiser's hostile attitude toward these details, his general reception of the President's proposals
was not outwardly unfriendly. Perhaps he was sincere,
perhaps not; yet the fact is that he manifested more
cordiality to this somewhat vague "get-together" proposal than had any of his official advisers. He encouraged
Colonel House to visit London, talk the matter over with
British statesmen, and then return to Berlin.

"The last thing," he said, "that Germany wants is
war. We are getting to be a great commercial country.
In a few years Germany will be a rich country, like England and the United States. We don't want a war to
interfere with our progress."

Any peace suggestion that was compatible with German
safety, he said, would be entertained. Yet his parting
words were not reassuring.

"Every nation in Europe," he said, "has its bayonets
pointed at Germany. But——"—and with this he gave
a proud and smiling glance at the glistening representatives of his army gathered on this brilliant occasion—
"we are ready!"

Colonel House left Berlin, not particularly hopeful;
the Kaiser impressed him as a man of unstable nervous
organization—as one who was just hovering on the border-
land of insanity. Certainly, this was no man to be en-
trusted with such powers as the American had witnessed
that day at Potsdam. Dangerous as the Kaiser was,
however, he did not seem to Colonel House to be as great
a menace to mankind as were his military advisers. The
American came away from Berlin with the conviction
that the most powerful force in Germany was the militaristic clique, and second, the Hohenzollern dynasty.
He has always insisted that this represented the real
precedence in power. So long as the Kaiser was obedient

to the will of militarism, so long could he maintain his standing. He was confident, however, that the militaristic oligarchy was determined to have its will, and would dethrone the Kaiser the moment he showed indications of taking a course that would lead to peace. Colonel House was also convinced that this militaristic oligarchy was determined on war. The coolness with which it listened to his proposals, the attempts it made to keep him from seeing the Kaiser alone, its repeated efforts to break up the conversation after it had begun, all pointed to the inevitable tragedy. The fact that the Kaiser expressed a wish to discuss the matter again, after Colonel House had sounded London, was the one hopeful feature of an otherwise discouraging experience, and accounts for the tone of faint optimism in his letters describing the visit.

From Edward M. House

Embassy of the United States of America,
Berlin,
May 28, 1914.

DEAR PAGE:

. . . I have done something here already—not much, but enough to open negotiations with London. I lunch with the Kaiser on Monday. I was advised to avoid Admiral von Tirpitz as being very unsympathetic. However, I went directly at him and had a most interesting talk. He is a forceful fellow. Von Jagow is pleasant but not forceful. I have had a long talk with him. The Chancellor's wife died last week so I have not got in touch with him. I will write you more fully from Paris. My address there will be Hotel Ritz.

Hastily,
E. M. H.

From Edward M. House

Hotel Ritz, 15, Place Vendôme, Paris.
June 3, 1914.

DEAR PAGE:

I had a satisfactory talk with the Kaiser on Monday. I have now seen everyone worthwhile in Germany except the Chancellor. I am ready now for London. Perhaps you had better prepare the way. The Kaiser knows I am to see them, and I have arranged to keep him in touch with results—if there are any. We must work quickly after I arrive, for it may be advisable for me to return to Germany, and I am counting on sailing for home July 15th or 28th. . . . I am eager to see you and tell you what I know.

Yours,

E. M. H.

Colonel House left that night for Paris, but there the situation was a hopeless one. France was not thinking of a foreign war; it was engrossed with its domestic troubles. There had been three French ministries in two weeks; and the trial of Madame Caillaux for the murder of Gaston Calmette, editor of the Paris *Figaro*, was monopolizing all the nation's capacity for emotion. Colonel House saw that it would be a waste of energy to take up his mission at Paris—there was no government stable enough to make a discussion worth while. He therefore immediately left for London.

The political situation in Great Britain was almost as confused as that in Paris. The country was in a state approaching civil war on the question of Home Rule for Ireland; the suffragettes were threatening to dynamite the Houses of Parliament; and the eternal struggle between the Liberal and the Conservative elements was raging with unprecedented virulence. A European war was far from everybody's mind. It was this utter inability to grasp the realities of the European situation which proved the main impediment to Colonel House's work in England. He met all the important people—Mr. Asquith, Mr. Lloyd George, Sir Edward Grey, and others. With them he discussed his "pact" proposal in great detail.

Naturally, ideas of this sort were listened to sympathetically by statesmen of the stamp of Asquith, Grey, and Lloyd George. The difficulty, however, was that none of these men apprehended an immediate war. They saw no necessity of hurrying about the matter. They had the utmost confidence in Prince Lichnowsky, the German Ambassador in London, and Von Bethmann-Hollweg, the German Chancellor. Both these men were regarded by the Foreign Office as guarantees against a German attack; their continuance in their office was looked upon as an assurance that Germany entertained no immediately aggressive plans. Though the British statesmen did not say so definitely, the impression was conveyed that the mission on which Colonel House was engaged was an unnecessary one—a preparation against a danger that did not exist. Colonel House attempted to persuade Sir Edward Grey to visit the Kiel regatta, which was to take place in a few days, see the Kaiser, and discuss the plan with him. But the Government feared that such a visit would be very disturbing to France and Russia. Already Mr. Churchill's proposal for a "naval holiday" had so wrought up the French that a hurried trip to France by Mr. Asquith had been necessary to quiet them; the consternation that would have been caused in Paris by the presence of Sir Edward Grey at Kiel can only be imagined. The fact that the British statesmen entertained so little apprehension of a German attack may possibly be a reflection on their judgment; yet Colonel House's visit has great historical value, for the experience afterward convinced him that Great Britain had had no part in bringing on the European war, and that Germany was solely responsible. It certainly should have put the Wilson Administration right on this all-important point, when the great storm broke.

The most vivid recollection which the British statesmen whom Colonel House met retain of his visit, was his consternation at the spirit that had confronted him everywhere in Germany. The four men most interested— Sir Edward Grey, Sir William Tyrrell, Mr. Page, and Colonel House—met at luncheon in the American Embassy a few days after President Wilson's emissary had returned from Berlin. Colonel House could talk of little except the preparations for war which were manifest on every hand.

"I feel as though I had been living near a mighty electric dynamo," Colonel House told his friends. "The whole of Germany is charged with electricity. Everybody's nerves are tense. It needs only a spark to set the whole thing off."

The "spark" came two weeks afterward with the assassination of the Archduke Ferdinand.

"It is all a bad business," Colonel House wrote to Page when war broke out, "and just think how near we came to making such a catastrophe impossible! If England had moved a little faster and had let me go back to Germany, the thing, perhaps, could have been done."

To which Page at once replied:

"No, no, no—no power on earth could have prevented it. The German militarism, which is *the* crime of the last fifty years, has been working for this for twenty-five years. It is the logical result of their spirit and enterprise and doctrine. It *had* to come. But, of course, they chose the wrong time and the wrong issue. Militarism has no judgment. Don't let your conscience be worried. You did all that any mortal man could do. But nobody could have done anything effective.

"We've got to see to it that this system doesn't grow up again. That's all."

CHAPTER X

THE GRAND SMASH

IN THE latter part of July the Pages took a small house at Ockham, in Surrey, and here they spent the fateful week that preceded the outbreak of war. The Ambassador's emotions on this event are reflected in a memorandum written on Sunday, August 2nd—a day that was full of negotiations, ultimatums, and other precursors of the approaching struggle.

> Bachelor's Farm, Ockham, Surrey.
> Sunday, August 2, 1914.

The Grand Smash is come. Last night the German Ambassador at St. Petersburg handed the Russian Government a declaration of war. To-day the German Government asked the United States to take its diplomatic and consular business in Russia in hand. Herrick, our Ambassador in Paris, has already taken the German interests there.

It is reported in London to-day that the Germans have invaded Luxemburg and France.

Troops were marching through London at one o'clock this morning. Colonel Squier[1] came out to luncheon. He sees no way for England to keep out of it. There is no way. If she keep out, Germany will take Belgium and Holland, France would be betrayed, and England would be accused of forsaking her friends.

---

[1]At this time American military attaché.

People came to the Embassy all day to-day (Sunday), to learn how they can get to the United States—a rather hard question to answer. I thought several times of going in, but Greene and Squier said there was no need of it. People merely hoped we might tell them what we can't tell them.

Returned travellers from Paris report indescribable confusion—people unable to obtain beds and fighting for seats in railway carriages.

It's been a hard day here. I have a lot (not a big lot either) of routine work on my desk which I meant to do. But it has been impossible to get my mind off this Great Smash. It holds one in spite of one's self. I revolve it and revolve it—of course getting nowhere.

It will revive our shipping. In a jiffy, under stress of a general European war, the United States Senate passed a bill permitting American registry to ships built abroad. Thus a real emergency knocked the old Protectionists out, who had held on for fifty years! Correspondingly the political parties here have agreed to suspend their Home Rule quarrel till this war is ended. Artificial structures fall when a real wind blows.

The United States is the only great Power wholly out of it. The United States, most likely, therefore, will be able to play a helpful and historic part at its end. It will give President Wilson, no doubt, a great opportunity. It will probably help us politically and it will surely help us economically.

The possible consequences stagger the imagination. Germany has staked everything on her ability to win primacy. England and France (to say nothing of Russia) really ought to give her a drubbing. If they do not, this side of the world will henceforth be German. If they do flog Germany, Germany will for a long time be in discredit.

I walked out in the night a while ago. The stars are bright, the night is silent, the country quiet—as quiet as peace itself. Millions of men are in camp and on warships. Will they all have to fight and many of them die—to untangle this network of treaties and alliances and to blow off huge debts with gunpowder so that the world may start again?

A hurried picture of the events of the next seven days is given in the following letter to the President:

To the President

London, Sunday, August 9, 1914.

DEAR MR. PRESIDENT:

God save us! What a week it has been! Last Sunday I was down here at the cottage I have taken for the summer—an hour out of London—uneasy because of the apparent danger and of what Sir Edward Grey had told me. During the day people began to go to the Embassy, but not in great numbers—merely to ask what they should do in case of war. The Secretary whom I had left in charge on Sunday telephoned me every few hours and laughingly told funny experiences with nervous women who came in and asked absurd questious. Of course, we all knew the grave danger that war might come but nobody could by the wildest imagination guess at what awaited us. On Monday I was at the Embassy earlier than I think I had ever been there before and every member of the staff was already on duty. Before breakfast time the place was filled—packed like sardines. This was two days before war was declared. There was no chance to talk to individuals, such was the jam. I got on a chair and explained that I had already telegraphed to Washington—on Saturday—suggesting the sending of money and ships, and asking them to be patient. I made a speech to them several times during the day, and kept the Secretaries doing so at intervals. More than 2,000 Americans crowded into those offices (which are not large) that day. We were kept there till two o'clock in the morning. The Embassy has not been closed since.

Mr. Kent of the Bankers Trust Company in New York volunteered to form an American Citizens' Relief Committee. He and other men of experience and influence organized themselves at the Savoy Hotel. The hotel gave the use of nearly a whole floor. They organized themselves quickly and admirably and got information about steamships and currency, etc. We began to send callers at the Embassy to this Committee for such information. The banks were all closed for four days. These men got money enough—put it up themselves and used their English banking friends for help—to relieve all cases of actual want of cash that came to them. Tuesday the crowd at the Embassy was still great but smaller. The big space at the Savoy Hotel gave them room to talk to one another and to get relief for immediate needs. By that time I had accepted the volunteer services of five or six men to help us explain to the people—and they have all worked manfully day and night. We now have an orderly organization at four places: The Embassy, the Consul-General's Office, the Savoy, and the American Society in London, and everything is going well. Those two first days, there was, of course, great confusion. Crazy men and weeping women were imploring and cursing and demanding—God knows it was bedlam turned loose. I have been called a man of the greatest genius for an emergency by some, by others a damned fool, by others every epithet between these extremes. Men shook English banknotes in my face and demanded United States money and swore our Government and its agents ought all to be shot. Women expected me to hand them steamship tickets home. When some found out that they could not get tickets on the transports (which they assumed would sail the next day) they accused me of favouritism. These absurd experiences will give you a hint of the panic. But now it has worked out all right, thanks to the Savoy Committee and other helpers.

Meantime, of course, our telegrams and mail increased almost as much as our callers. I have filled the place with stenographers, I have got the Savoy people to answer certain classes of letters, and we have caught up. My own time and the time of two of the secretaries has been almost wholly taken with governmental problems; hundreds of questions have come in from every quarter that were never asked before. But even with them we have now practically caught up—it has been a wonderful week!

Then the Austrian Ambassador came to give up his Embassy—to have me take over his business. Every detail was arranged. The next morning I called on him to assume charge and to say good-bye, when he told me that he was not yet going! That was a stroke of genius by Sir Edward Grey, who informed him that Austria had not given England cause for war. That *may* work out, or it may not. Pray Heaven it may! Poor Mensdorff, the Austrian Ambassador, does not know where he is. He is practically shut up in his guarded Embassy, weeping and waiting the decree of fate.

Then came the declaration of war, most dramatically.

Tuesday night, five minutes after the ultimatum had expired, the Admiralty telegraphed to the fleet "Go." In a few minutes the answer came back "Off." Soldiers began to march through the city going to the railway stations. An indescribable crowd so blocked the streets about the Admiralty, the War Office, and the Foreign Office, that at one o'clock in the morning I had to drive in my car by other streets to get home.

The next day the German Embassy was turned over to me. I went to see the German Ambassador at three o'clock in the afternoon. He came down in his pajamas, a crazy man. I feared he might literally go mad. He is of the anti-war party and he had done his best and utterly failed. This interview was one of the most pathetic experiences of my life. The poor man had not slept for several nights. Then came the crowds of frightened Germans, afraid that they would be arrested. They besieged the German Embassy and our Embassy. I put one of our naval officers in the German Embassy, put the United States seal on the door to protect it, and we began business there, too. Our naval officer has moved in—sleeps there. He has an assistant, a stenographer, a messenger: and I gave him the German automobile and chauffeur and two English servants that were left there. He has the job well in hand now, under my and Laughlin's supervision. But this has brought still another new lot of diplomatic and governmental problems—a lot of them. Three enormous German banks in London have, of course, been closed. Their managers pray for my aid. Howling women come and say their innocent German husbands have been arrested as spies. English, Germans, Americans—everybody has daughters and wives and invalid grandmothers alone in Germany. In God's name, they ask, what can I do for them? Here come stacks of letters sent under the impression that I can send them to Germany. But the German business is already well in hand and I think that that will take little of my own time and will give little trouble. I shall send a report about it in detail to the Department the very first day I can find time to write it. In spite of the effort of the English Government to remain at peace with Austria, I fear I shall yet have the Austrian Embassy too. But I can attend to it.

Now, however, comes the financial job of wisely using the $300,000 which I shall have to-morrow. I am using Mr. Chandler Anderson as counsel, of course. I have appointed a Committee—Skinner, the Consul-General, Lieut.-Commander McCrary of our Navy, Kent of the Bankers Trust Company, New York, and one other man yet to be chosen—to advise, after investigation, about every proposed expenditure. Anderson has been at work all day to-day drawing up proper forms, etc., to fit the Department's very excellent instructions. I have the feeling that more of that money may be wisely spent in helping to get people off the continent (except in France, where they seem admirably to be managing it, under Herrick) than is immediately needed in England. All this merely to show you the diversity and multiplicity of the job.

I am having a card catalogue, each containing a sort of who's who, of all Americans in Europe of whom we hear. This will be ready by the time the *Tennessee*[1] comes. Fifty or more stranded Americans—men and women—are doing this work free.

I have a member of Congress[2] in the general reception

---

[1]The American Government, on the outbreak of war, sent the U. S. S. *Tennessee* to Europe, with large supplies of gold for the relief of stranded Americans.

[2]The late Augustus P. Gardner, of Massachusetts.

room of the Embassy answering people's questions—three other volunteers as well.

We had a world of confusion for two or three days. But all this work is now well organized and it can be continued without confusion or cross purposes. I meet committees and lay plans and read and write telegrams from the time I wake till I go to bed. But, since it is now all in order, it is easy. Of course I am running up the expenses of the Embassy—there is no help for that: but the bill will be really exceedingly small because of the volunteer work—for awhile. I have not and shall not consider the expense of whatever it seems absolutely necessary to do—of other things I shall always consider the expense most critically. Everybody is working with everybody else in the finest possible spirit. I have made out a sort of military order to the Embassy staff, detailing one man with clerks for each night and forbidding the others to stay there till midnight. None of us slept more than a few hours last week. It was not the work that kept them after the first night or two, but the sheer excitement of this awful cataclysm. All London has been awake for a week. Soldiers are marching day and night; immense throngs block the streets about the government offices. But they are all very orderly. Every day Germans are arrested on suspicion; and several of them have committed suicide. Yesterday one poor American woman yielded to the excitement and cut her throat. I find it hard to get about much. People stop me on the street, follow me to luncheon, grab me as I come out of any committee meeting—to know my opinion of this or that—how can they get home? Will such-and-such a boat fly the American flag? Why did I take the German Embassy? I have to fight my way about and rush to an automobile. I have had to buy me a second one to keep

No. 6 Grosvenor Square, the American Embassy under Mr. Page

Irwin Laughlin, Secretary of the American Embassy at London,
1912–1917, Counsellor 1916–1919

up the racket. Buy?—no—only bargain for it, for I have not any money. But everybody is considerate, and that makes no matter for the moment. This little cottage in an out-of-the-way place, twenty-five miles from London, where I am trying to write and sleep, has been found by people to-day, who come in automobiles to know how they may reach their sick kinspeople in Germany. I have not had a bath for three days: as soon as I got in the tub, the telephone rang an "urgent" call!

Upon my word, if one could forget the awful tragedy, all this experience would be worth a lifetime of commonplace. One surprise follows another so rapidly that one loses all sense of time: it seems an age since last Sunday.

I shall never forget Sir Edward Grey's telling me of the ultimatum—while he wept; nor the poor German Ambassador who has lost in his high game—almost a demented man; nor the King as he declaimed at me for half-an-hour and threw up his hands and said, "My God, Mr. Page, what else could we do?" Nor the Austrian Ambassador's wringing his hands and weeping and crying out, "My dear Colleague, my dear Colleague."

Along with all this tragedy come two reverend American peace delegates who got out of Germany by the skin of their teeth and complain that they lost all the clothes they had except what they had on. "Don't complain," said I, "but thank God you saved your skins." Everybody has forgotten what war means—forgotten that folks get hurt. But they are coming around to it now. A United States Senator telegraphs me: "Send my wife and daughter home on the first ship." Ladies and gentlemen filled the steerage of that ship—not a bunk left; and his wife and daughter are found three days later sitting in a swell hotel waiting for

me to bring them stateroom tickets on a silver tray! One
of my young fellows in the Embassy rushes into my office
saying that a man from Boston, with letters of introduction from Senators and Governors and Secretaries,
et al., was demanding tickets of admission to a picture
gallery, and a secretary to escort him there.

"What shall I do with him?"

"Put his proposal to a vote of the 200 Americans in
the room and see them draw and quarter him."

I have not yet heard what happened. A woman writes
me four pages to prove how dearly she loves my sister
and invites me to her hotel—five miles away—"please
to tell her about the sailing of the steamships." Six
American preachers pass a resolution unanimously "urging our Ambassador to telegraph our beloved, peace-
loving President to stop this awful war"; and they come
with simple solemnity to present their resolution. Lord
save us, what a world!

And this awful tragedy moves on to—what? We
do not know what is really happening, so strict is the
censorship. But it seems inevitable to me that Germany
will be beaten, that the horrid period of alliances and
armaments will not come again, that England will gain
even more of the earth's surface, that Russia may next
play the menace; that all Europe (as much as survives)
will be bankrupt; that relatively we shall be immensely
stronger financially and politically—there must surely
come many great changes—very many, yet undreamed
of. Be ready; for you will be called on to compose this
huge quarrel. I thank Heaven for many things—first,
the Atlantic Ocean; second, that you refrained from war
in Mexico; third, that we kept our treaty—the canal
tolls victory, I mean. Now, when all this half of the
world will suffer the unspeakable brutalization of war,

we shall preserve our moral strength, our political powers, and our ideals.

God save us!

W. H. P.

Vivid as is the above letter, it lacks several impressive details. Probably the one event that afterward stood out most conspicuously in Page's mind was his interview with Sir Edward Grey, the Foreign Secretary. Sir Edward asked the American Ambassador to call Tuesday afternoon; his purpose was to inform him that Great Britain had sent an ultimatum to Germany. By this time Page and the Foreign Secretary had established not only cordial official relations but a warm friendship. The two men had many things in common; they had the same general outlook on world affairs, the same ideas of justice and fair dealing, the same belief that other motives than greed and aggrandizement should control the attitude of one nation to another. The political tendencies of both men were idealistic; both placed character above everything else as the first requisite of a statesman; both hated war, and looked forward to the time when more rational methods of conducting international relations would prevail. Moreover, their purely personal qualities had drawn Sir Edward and Page closely together. A common love of nature and of out-of-door life had made them akin; both loved trees, birds, flowers, and hedgerows; the same intellectual diversions and similar tastes in reading had strengthened the tie. "I could never mention a book I liked that Mr. Page had not read and liked too," Sir Edward Grey once remarked to the present writer, and the enthusiasm that both men felt for Wordsworth's poetry in itself formed a strong bond of union. The part that the American Ambassador had played in the repeal of the Panama discrimination had also made a great impression upon this British statesman —a man to whom honour means more in international dealings than any other consideration. "Mr. Page is one of the finest illustrations I have ever known," Grey once said, "of the value of character in a public man." In their intercourse for the past year the two men had grown accustomed to disregard all pretense of diplomatic technique; their discussions had been straightforward man-to-man talks; there had been nothing suggestive of pose or finesse, and no attempts at cleverness —merely an effort to get to the bottom of things and to discover a common meeting ground. The Ambassador, moreover, represented a nation for which the Foreign Secretary had always entertained the highest respect and even affection, and he and Page could find no happier common meeting-ground than an effort to bring about the closest coöperation between the two countries. Sir Edward, far-seeing statesman that he was, had already appreciated, even amid the exciting and engrossing experiences through which he was then passing, the critical and almost determining part which the United States was destined to play in the war, and he had now sent for the American Ambassador because he believed that the President was entitled to a complete explanation of the momentous decision which Great Britain had just made.

The meeting took place at three o'clock on Tuesday afternoon, August 4th—a fateful date in modern history. The time represented the interval which elapsed between the transmission of the British ultimatum to Germany and the hour set for the German reply. The place was that same historic room in the Foreign Office where so many interviews had already taken place and where so many were to take place in the next four years. As

Page came in, Sir Edward, a tall and worn and rather pallid figure, was standing against the mantelpiece; he greeted the Ambassador with a grave handshake and the two men sat down. Overwrought the Foreign Secretary may have been, after the racking week which had just passed, but there was nothing flurried or excited in his manner; his whole bearing was calm and dignified, his speech was quiet and restrained, he uttered not one bitter word against Germany, but his measured accents had a sureness, a conviction of the justice of his course, that went home in almost deadly fashion. He sat in a characteristic pose, his elbows resting on the sides of his chair, his hands folded and placed beneath his chin, the whole body leaning forward eagerly and his eyes searching those of his American friend. The British Foreign Secretary was a handsome and an inspiring figure. He was a man of large, but of well knit, robust, and slender frame, wiry and even athletic; he had a large head, surmounted with dark brown hair, slightly touched with gray; a finely cut, somewhat rugged and bronzed face, suggestive of that out-of-door life in which he had always found his greatest pleasure; light blue eyes that shone with straightforwardness and that on this occasion were somewhat pensive with anxiety; thin, ascetic lips that could smile in the most confidential manner or close tightly with grimness and fixed purpose. He was a man who was at the same time shy and determined, elusive and definite, but if there was one note in his bearing that predominated all others, it was a solemn and quiet sincerity. He seemed utterly without guile and magnificently simple.

Sir Edward at once referred to the German invasion of Belgium.

"The neutrality of Belgium," he said, and there was

the touch of finality in his voice, "is assured by treaty. Germany is a signatory power to that treaty. It is upon such solemn compacts as this that civilization rests. If we give them up, or permit them to be violated, what becomes of civilization? Ordered society differs from mere force only by such solemn agreements or compacts. But Germany has violated the neutrality of Belgium. That means bad faith. It means also the end of Belgium's independence. And it will not end with Belgium. Next will come Holland, and, after Holland, Denmark. This very morning the Swedish Minister informed me that Germany had made overtures to Sweden to come in on Germany's side. The whole plan is thus clear. This one great military power means to annex Belgium, Holland, and the Scandinavian states and to subjugate France."

Sir Edward energetically rose; he again stood near the mantelpiece, his figure straightened, his eyes were fairly flashing—it was a picture, Page once told me, that was afterward indelibly fixed in his mind.

"England would be forever contemptible," Sir Edward said, "if it should sit by and see this treaty violated. Its position would be gone if Germany were thus permitted to dominate Europe. I have therefore asked you to come to tell you that this morning we sent an ultimatum to Germany. We have told Germany that, if this assault on Belgium's neutrality is not reversed, England will declare war."

"Do you expect Germany to accept it?" asked the Ambassador.

Sir Edward shook his head.

"No. Of course everybody knows that there will be war."

There was a moment's pause and then the Foreign Secretary spoke again:

"Yet we must remember that there are two Germanys. There is the Germany of men like ourselves—of men like Lichnowsky and Jagow. Then there is the Germany of men of the war party. The war party has got the upper hand."

At this point Sir Edward's eyes filled with tears.

"Thus the efforts of a lifetime go for nothing. I feel like a man who has wasted his life."

"This scene was most affecting," Page said afterward. "Sir Edward not only realized what the whole thing meant, but he showed that he realized the awful responsibility for it."

Sir Edward then asked the Ambassador to explain the situation to President Wilson; he expressed the hope that the United States would take an attitude of neutrality and that Great Britain might look for "the courtesies of neutrality" from this country. Page tried to tell him of the sincere pain that such a war would cause the President and the American people.

"I came away," the Ambassador afterward said, "with a sort of stunned sense of the impending ruin of half the world."[1]

The significant fact in this interview is that the British Foreign Secretary justified the attitude of his country exclusively on the ground of the violation of a treaty. This is something that is not yet completely understood in the United States. The participation of Great Britain in this great continental struggle is usually regarded as having been inevitable, irrespective of the German invasion of Belgium; yet the fact is that, had Germany not invaded Belgium, Great Britain would not have declared war, at least at this critical time. Sir Edward

---

[1]The materials on which this account is based are a memorandum of the interview made by Sir Edward Grey, now in the archives of the British Foreign Office, a similar memorandum made by Page, and a detailed description given verbally by Page to the writer.

came to Page after a week's experience with a wavering cabinet. Upon the general question of Britain's participation in a European war the Asquith Ministry had been by no means unanimous. Probably Mr. Asquith himself and Mr. Lloyd George would have voted against taking such a step. It is quite unlikely that the cabinet could have carried a majority of the House of Commons on this issue. But the violation of the Belgian treaty changed the situation in a twinkling. The House of Commons at once took its stand in favour of intervention. All members of the cabinet, excepting John Morley and John Burns, who resigned, immediately aligned themselves on the side of war. In the minds of British statesmen the violation of this treaty gave Britain no choice. Germany thus forced Great Britain into the war, just as, two and a half years afterward, the Prussian war lords compelled the United States to take up arms. Sir Edward Grey's interview with the American Ambassador thus had great historic importance, for it makes this point clear. The two men had recently had many discussions on another subject in which the violation of a treaty was the great consideration—that of Panama tolls—and there was a certain appropriateness in this explanation of the British Foreign Secretary that precisely the same point had determined Great Britain's participation in the greatest struggle that has ever devastated Europe.

Inevitably the question of American mediation had come to the surface in this trying time. Several days before Page's interview with Grey, the American Ambassador, acting in response to a cablegram from Washington, had asked if the good offices of the United States could be used in any way. "Sir Edward is very appreciative of our mood and willingness," Page wrote in reference to this visit. "But they don't want peace on the continent—the ruling classes do not. But they will want it presently and then our opportunity will come. Ours is the only great government in the world that is not in some way entangled. Of course I'll keep in daily touch with Sir Edward and with everybody who can and will keep me informed."

This was written about July 27th; at that time Austria had sent her ultimatum to Serbia but there was no certainty that Europe would become involved in war. A demand for American mediation soon became widespread in the United States; the Senate passed a resolution requesting the President to proffer his good offices to that end. On this subject the following communications were exchanged between President Wilson and his chief adviser, then sojourning at his summer home in Massachusetts. Like Mr. Tumulty, the President's Secretary, Colonel House usually addressed the President in terms reminiscent of the days when Mr. Wilson was Governor of New Jersey. Especially interesting also are Colonel House's references to his own trip to Berlin and the joint efforts made by the President and himself in the preceding June to forestall the war which had now broken out.

Edward M. House to the President

Pride's Crossing (Mass.),
August 3, 1914. [Monday.]

THE PRESIDENT,
The White House, Washington, D. C.
DEAR GOVERNOR:
Our people are deeply shocked at the enormity of this general European war, and I see here and there regret that you did not use your good offices in behalf of peace.

If this grows into criticism so as to become noticeable I believe everyone would be pleased and proud that you had anticipated this world-wide horror and had done all that was humanly possible to avert it.

The more terrible the war becomes, the greater credit it will be that you saw the trend of events long before it was seen by other statesmen of the world.

Your very faithful,
E. M. HOUSE.

P. S. The question might be asked why negotiations were only with Germany and England and not with France and Russia. This, of course, was because it was thought that Germany would act for the Triple Alliance and England for the Triple Entente.[1]

The President to Edward M. House

The White House,
Washington, D. C.
August 4th, 1914. [Tuesday.]

EDWARD M. HOUSE,
Pride's Crossing, Mass.

Letter of third received. Do you think I could and should act now and if so how?

WOODROW WILSON.

Edward M. House to the President

[Telegram]

Pride's Crossing, Mass.
August 5th, 1914. [Wednesday.]

THE PRESIDENT,
The White House, Washington, D. C.

Olney[2] and I agree that in response to the Senate reso-

---

[1]Colonel House, of course, is again referring to his experience in Berlin and London, described in the preceding chapter.

[2]Richard Olney, Secretary of State in the Cabinet of President Cleveland, who was a neighbour of Colonel House at his summer home, and with whom the latter apparently consulted

lution it would be unwise to tender your good offices at this time. We believe it would lessen your influence when the proper moment arrives. He thinks it advisable that you make a direct or indirect statement to the effect that you have done what was humanly possible to compose the situation before this crisis had been reached. He thinks this would satisfy the Senate and the public in view of your disinclination to act now upon the Senate resolution. The story might be told to the correspondents at Washington and they might use the expression "we have it from high authority."

He agrees to my suggestion that nothing further should be done now than to instruct our different ambassadors to inform the respective governments to whom they are accredited, that you stand ready to tender your good offices whenever such an offer is desired.

Olney agrees with me that the shipping bill[1] is full of lurking dangers.

E. M. HOUSE.

For some reason, however, the suggested statement was not made. The fact that Colonel House had visited London, Paris, and Berlin six weeks before the outbreak of war, in an effort to bring about a plan for disarmament, was not permitted to reach the public ear. Probably the real reason why this fact was concealed was that its publication at that time would have reflected so seriously upon Germany that it would have been regarded as "un-neutral." Colonel House, as already described, had found Germany in a most belligerent frame of mind, its army "ready," to use the Kaiser's own word, for an immediate spring at France; on the other hand he had

---

[1] This is the bill passed soon after the outbreak of war admitting foreign built ships to American registry. Subsequent events showed that it was "full of lurking dangers."

found Great Britain in a most pacific frame of mind, entirely unsuspicious of Germany, and confident that the European situation was daily improving.   It is interesting now to speculate on the public sensation that would have been caused had Colonel House's account of his visit to Berlin been published at that exciting time.

Page's telegrams and letters show that any suggestion at mediation would have been a waste of effort.   The President seriously forebore, but the desire to mediate was constantly in his mind for the next few months, and he now interested himself in laying the foundations of future action.   Page was instructed to ask for an audience with King George and to present the following document:

From the President of the United States to His Majesty the King

SIR:

As official head of one of the Powers signatory to the Hague Convention, I feel it to be my privilege and my duty under Article 3 of that Convention to say to your Majesty, in a spirit of most earnest friendship, that I should welcome an opportunity to act in the interest of European peace either now or at any time that might be thought more suitable as an occasion, to serve your Majesty and all concerned in a way that would afford me lasting cause for gratitude and happiness.

WOODROW WILSON.

This, of course, was not mediation, but a mere expression of the President's willingness to mediate at any time that such a tender from him, in the opinion of the warring Powers, would serve the cause of peace.   Identically the same message was sent to the American Ambassadors at the capitals of all the belligerent Powers for presentation to the heads of state. Page's letter of August 9th, printed above, refers to the earnestness and cordiality with which King George received him and to the freedom with which His Majesty discussed the situation.

In this exciting week Page was thrown into intimate contact with the two most pathetic figures in the diplomatic circle of London—the Austrian and the German Ambassadors. To both of these men the war was more than a great personal sorrow: it was a tragedy. Mensdorff, the Austrian Ambassador, had long enjoyed an intimacy with the British royal family. Indeed he was a distant relative of King George, for he was a member of the family of Saxe-Coburg-Gotha, a fact which was emphasized by his physical resemblance to Prince Albert, the consort of Queen Victoria. Mensdorff was not a robust man, physically or mentally, and he showed his consternation at the impending war in most unrestrained and even unmanly fashion. As his government directed him to turn the Austrian Embassy over to the American Ambassador, it was necessary for Page to call and arrange the details. The interview, as Page's letter indicates, was little less than a paroxysm of grief on the Austrian's part. He denounced Germany and the Kaiser; he paraded up and down the room wringing his hands; he could be pacified only by suggestions from the American that perhaps something might happen to keep Austria out of the war. The whole atmosphere of the Austrian Embassy radiated this same feeling. "Austria has no quarrel with England," remarked one of Mensdorff's assistants to one of the ladies of the American Embassy; and this sentiment was the general one in Austrian diplomatic circles. The disinclination of both Great Britain and

Austria to war was so great that, as Page relates, for several days there was no official declaration.

Even more tragical than the fate of the Austrian Ambassador was that of his colleague, the representative of the German Emperor. It was more tragical because Prince Lichnowsky represented the power that was primarily responsible, and because he had himself been an unwilling tool in bringing on the cataclysm. It was more profound because Lichnowsky was a man of deeper feeling and greater moral purpose than his Austrian colleague, and because for two years he had been devoting his strongest energies to preventing the very calamity which had now become a fact. As the war went on Lichnowsky gradually emerged as one of its finest figures; the pamphlet which he wrote, at a time when Germany's military fortunes were still high, boldly placing the responsibility upon his own country and his own Kaiser, was one of the bravest acts which history records. Through all his brief Ambassadorship Lichnowsky had shown these same friendly traits. The mere fact that he had been selected as Ambassador at this time was little less than a personal calamity. His appointment gives a fair measure of the depths of duplicity to which the Prussian system could descend. For more than fourteen years Lichnowsky had led the quiet life of a Polish country gentleman; he had never enjoyed the favour of the Kaiser; in his own mind and in that of his friends his career had long since been finished; yet from this retirement he had been suddenly called upon to represent the Fatherland at the greatest of European capitals. The motive for this elevation, which was unfathomable then, is evident enough now. Prince Lichnowsky was known to be an Anglophile; everything English—English literature, English country life, English public men—had for

him an irresistible charm; and his greatest ambition as
a diplomat had been to maintain the most cordial relations between his own country and Great Britain. This
was precisely the type of Ambassador that fitted into the
Imperial purpose at that crisis. Germany was preparing
energetically but quietly for war; it was highly essential
that its most formidable potential foe, Great Britain,
should be deceived as to the Imperial plans and lulled into
a sense of security. The diabolical character of Prince
Lichnowsky's selection for this purpose was that, though
his mission was one of deception, he was not himself a
party to it and did not realize until it was too late that he
had been used merely as a tool. Prince Lichnowsky was
not called upon to assume a mask; all that was necessary
was that he should simply be himself. And he acquitted
himself with great success. He soon became a favourite
in London society; the Foreign Office found him always
ready to coöperate in any plan that tended to improve
relations between the two countries. It will be remembered that, when Colonel House returned to London
from his interview with the Kaiser in June, 1914, he
found British statesmen incredulous about any trouble
with Germany. This attitude was the consequence of
Lichnowsky's work. The fact is that relations between
the two countries had not been so harmonious in twenty
years. All causes of possible friction had been adjusted.
The treaty regulating the future of the Bagdad Railroad,
the only problem that clouded the future, had been
initialled by both the British and the German Foreign
Offices and was about to be signed at the moment when
the ultimatums began to fly through the air. Prince
Lichnowsky was thus entitled to look upon his ambassadorship as one of the most successful in modern history,
for it had removed all possible cause of war.

And then suddenly came the stunning blow. For several days Lichnowsky's behaviour was that of an irresponsible person. Those who came into contact with him found his mind wandering and incoherent. Page describes the German Ambassador as coming down and receiving him in his pajamas; he was not the only one who had that experience, for members of the British Foreign Office transacted business with this most punctilious of diplomats in a similar condition of personal disarray. And the dishabille extended to his mental operations as well.

But Lichnowsky's and Mensdorff's behaviour merely portrayed the general atmosphere that prevailed in London during that week. This atmosphere was simply hysterical. Among all the intimate participants, however, there was one man who kept his poise and who saw things clearly. That was the American Ambassador. It was certainly a strange trick which fortune had played upon Page. He had come to London with no experience in diplomacy. Though the possibility of such an outbreak as this war had been in every man's consciousness for a generation, it had always been as something certain yet remote; most men thought of it as most men think of death—as a fatality which is inevitable, but which is so distant that it never becomes a reality. Thus Page, when he arrived in London, did not have the faintest idea of the experience that awaited him. Most people would have thought that his quiet and studious and unworldly life had hardly prepared him to become the representative of the most powerful neutral power at the world's capital during the greatest crisis of modern history. To what an extent that impression was justified the happenings of the next four years will disclose; it is enough to point out in this place that in one respect at least the war found the American Ambassador well prepared. From the instant hostilities began his mind seized the significance of it all. "Mr. Page had one fine qualification for his post," a great British statesman once remarked to the present writer. "From the beginning he saw that there was a right and a wrong to the matter. He did not believe that Great Britain and Germany were equally to blame. He believed that Great Britain was right and that Germany was wrong. I regard it as one of the greatest blessings of modern times that the United States had an ambassador in London in August, 1914, who had grasped this overwhelming fact. It seems almost like a dispensation of Providence."

It is important to insist on this point now, for it explains Page's entire course as Ambassador. The confidential telegram which Page sent directly to President Wilson in early September, 1914, furnishes the standpoint from which his career as war Ambassador can be understood:

Confidential to the President

September 11, 3 A. M.
No. 645.

Accounts of atrocities are so inevitably a part of every war that for some time I did not believe the unbelievable reports that were sent from Europe, and there are many that I find incredible even now. But American and other neutral observers who have seen these things in France and especially in Belgium now convince me that the Germans have perpetrated some of the most barbarous deeds in history. Apparently credible persons relate such things without end.

Those who have violated the Belgian treaty, those who have sown torpedoes in the open sea, those who have dropped bombs on Antwerp and Paris indiscriminately with the idea of killing whom they may strike, have taken to heart Bernhardi's doctrine that war is a glorious occupation.   Can any one longer disbelieve the completely barbarous behaviour of the Prussians?[1]

PAGE.

¹This is a cipher message, and, in accordance with the rules of the State Department in the publication of such documents, it is paraphrased.   The same rule is observed in the publication of all cipher telegrams in these volumes.

CHAPTER XI

ENGLAND UNDER THE STRESS OF WAR

THE months following the outbreak of the war were busy ones for the American Embassy in London. The Embassies of all the great Powers with which Great Britain was contending were handed over to Page, and the citizens of these countries—Germany, Austria, Turkey—who found themselves stranded in England, were practically made his wards. It is a constant astonishment to his biographer that, during all the labour and distractions of this period, Page should have found time to write long letters describing the disturbing scene. There are scores of them, all penned in the beautiful copper-plate handwriting that shows no signs of excitement or weariness, but is in itself an evidence of mental poise and of the sure grip which Page had upon the evolving drama. From the many sent in these autumn and early winter months the following selections are made:

To Edward M. House

September 22nd, 1914.

MY DEAR HOUSE:

When the day of settlement comes, the settlement must make sure that the day of militarism is done and can come no more. If sheer brute force is to rule the world, it will not be worth living in. If German bureaucratic brute force could conquer Europe, presently it would try to conquer the United States; and we should all go back to the era of war as man's chief industry and back to the domination of kings by divine right. It seems to me, therefore, that the Hohenzollern idea must perish—be utterly strangled in the making of peace.

Just how to do this, it is not yet easy to say. If the German defeat be emphatic enough and dramatic enough, the question may answer itself—how's the best way to be rid of the danger of the recurrence of a military bureaucracy? But in any event, this thing must be killed forever—somehow. I think that a firm insistence on this is the main task that mediation will bring. The rest will be corollaries of this.

The danger, of course, as all the world is beginning to fear, is that the Kaiser, after a local victory—especially if he should yet take Paris—will propose peace, saying that he dreads the very sight of blood—propose peace in time, as he will hope, to save his throne, his dynasty, his system. That will be a dangerous day. The horror of war will have a tendency to make many persons in the countries of the Allies accept it. All the peace folk in the world will say "Accept it!" But if he and his throne and his dynasty and his system be saved, in twenty-five years the whole job must be done over again.

We are settling down to a routine of double work and to an oppression of gloom. Dead men, dead men, maimed men, the dull gray dread of what may happen next, the impossibility of changing the subject, the monotony of gloom, the consequent dimness of ideals, the overworking of the emotions and the heavy bondage of thought—the days go swiftly: that's one blessing.

The diplomatic work proper brings fewer difficulties than you would guess. New subjects and new duties come with great rapidity, but they soon fall into formulas —at least into classes. We shall have no sharp crises nor grave difficulties so long as our Government and this Government keep their more than friendly relations. I see Sir Edward Grey almost every day. We talk of many things—all phases of one vast wreck; and all the clear-cut points that come up I report by telegraph. To-day the talk was of American cargoes in British ships and the machinery they have set up here for fair settlement. Then of Americans applying for enlistment in Canadian regiments. "If sheer brute force conquer Europe," said he, "the United States will be the only country where life will be worth living; and in time you will have to fight against it, too, if it conquer Europe." He spoke of the letter he had just received from the President, and he asked me many sympathetic questions about you also and about your health. I ventured to express some solicitude for him.

"How much do you get out now?"

"Only for an automobile drive Sunday afternoon."

This from a man who is never happy away from nature and is at home only in the woods and along the streams. He looks worn.

I hear nothing but satisfaction with our neutrality tight-rope walk. I think we are keeping it here, by close attention to our work and by silence.

Our volunteer and temporary aids are doing well— especially the army and navy officers. We now occupy three work-places: (1) the over-crowded embassy; (2) a suite of offices around the corner where the ever-lengthening list of inquiries for persons is handled and where an army officer pays money to persons whose friends have deposited it for them with the Government in Washington—just now at the rate of about $15,000 a day; and (3) two great rooms at the Savoy Hotel, where the admirable relief committee (which meets all trains that bring people from the continent) gives aid to the needy and helps people to get tickets home. They have this week helped about 400 with more or less money—after full investigation.

At the Embassy a secretary remains till bed-time, which generally means till midnight; and I go back there for an hour or two every night.

The financial help we give to German and Austrian subjects (poor devils) is given, of course, at their embassies, where we have men—our men—in charge. Each of these governments accepted my offer to give our Ambassadors (Gerard and Penfield) a sum of money to help Americans if I would set aside an equal sum to help their people here. The German fund that I thus began with was $50,000; the Austrian, $25,000. All this and more will be needed before the war ends.—All this activity is kept up with scrupulous attention to the British rules and regulations. In fact, we are helping this Government much in the management of these "alien enemies," as they call them.

I am amazed at the good health we all keep with this big volume of work and the long hours. Not a man nor a woman has been ill a day. I have known something about work and the spirit of good work in other organizations of various sorts; but I never saw one work in better spirit than this. And remember, most of them are volunteers.

The soldiers here complained for weeks in private about the lethargy of the people—the slowness of men to enlist. But they seemed to me to complain with insufficient reason. For now they come by thousands. They do need more men in the field, and they may conscript them, but I doubt the necessity. But I run across such incidents as these: I met the Dowager Countess of D— yesterday —a woman of 65, as tall as I and as erect herself as a soldier, who might be taken for a woman of 40, prematurely gray. "I had five sons in the Boer War. I have three in this war. I do not know where any one of them is." Mrs. Page's maid is talking of leaving her. "My two brothers have gone to the war and perhaps I ought to help their wives and children." The Countess and the maid are of the same blood, each alike unconquerable. My chauffeur has talked all day about the naval battle in which five German ships were lately sunk.[1] He reminded me of the night two months ago when he drove Mrs. Page and me to dine with Sir John and Lady Jellicoe—Jellicoe now, you know, being in command of the British fleet.

This Kingdom has settled down to war as its one great piece of business now in hand, and it is impossible, as the busy, burdensome days pass, to pick out events or impressions that one can be sure are worth writing. For instance a soldier—a man in the War Office—told me to-day that Lord Kitchener had just told him that the war may last for several years. That, I confess, seems to me very improbable, and (what is of more importance) it is not the notion held by most men whose judgment I respect. But all the military men say it will be long. It would take several years to kill that vast horde of Germans, but it will not take so long to starve them out. Food here is practically as cheap as it was three months ago and the sea routes are all open to England and practically all closed to Germany. The ultimate result, of course, will be Germany's defeat. But the British are now going about the business of war as if they knew they would continue it indefinitely. The grim efficiency of their work even in small details was illustrated to-day by the Government's informing us that a German handy man, whom the German Ambassador left at his Embassy, with the English Govern-

[1] Evidently the battle of Heligoland Bight of August 28, 1914.

ment's consent, is a spy—that he sends verbal messages to Germany by women who are permitted to go home, and that they have found letters written by him sewed in some of these women's undergarments! This man has been at work there every day under the two very good men whom I have put in charge there and who have never suspected him. How on earth they found this out simply passes my understanding. Fortunately it doesn't bring any embarrassment to us; he was not in our pay and he was left by the German Ambassador with the British Government's consent, to take care of the house. Again, when the German Chancellor made a statement two days ago about the causes of the war, in a few hours Sir Edward Grey issued a statement showing that the Chancellor had misstated every important historic fact.—The other day a commercial telegram was sent (or started) by Mr. Bryan for some bank or trading concern in the United States, managed by Germans, to some correspondent of theirs in Germany. It contained the words, "Where is Harry?" The censor here stopped it. It was brought to me with the explanation that "Harry" is one of the most notorious of German spies—whom they would like to catch. The English were slow in getting into full action, but now they never miss a trick, little or big.

The Germans have far more than their match in resources and in shrewdness and—in character. As the bloody drama unfolds itself, the hollow pretence and essential barbarity of Prussian militarism become plainer and plainer: there is no doubt of that. And so does the invincibility of this race. A well-known Englishman told me to-day that his three sons, his son-in-law, and half his office men are in the military service, "where they belong in a time like this." The lady who once so sharply criticized this gentleman to Mrs. Page has a son and a brother in the army in France. It makes you take a fresh grip on your eyelids to hear either of these talk. In fact the strain on one's emotions, day in and day out, makes one wonder if the world is real—or is this a vast dream? From sheer emotional exhaustion I slept almost all day last Sunday, though I had not for several days lost sleep at all. Many persons tell me of their similar experiences. The universe seems muffled. There is a ghostly silence in London (so it seems); and only dim street lights are lighted at night. No experience seems normal. A vast organization is working day and night down town receiving Belgian refugees. They become the guests of the English. They are assigned to people's homes, to boarding houses, to institutions. They are taking care of them—this government and this people are. I do not recall when one nation ever did another whole nation just such a hospitable service as this. You can't see that work going on and remain unmoved. An old woman who has an income of $15 a week decided that she could live on $7.50. She buys milk with the other $7.50 and goes to meet every train at one of the big stations with a basket filled with baby bottles, and she gives milk to every hungry-looking baby she sees. Our American committeeman, Hoover, saw her in trouble the other day and asked her what was the matter. She explained that the police would no longer admit her to the platform because she didn't belong to any relief committee. He took her to headquarters and said: "Do you see this good old lady? She puts you and me and everybody else to shame—do you understand?" The old lady now gets to the platform. Hoover himself gave $5,000 for helping stranded Americans and he goes to the trains to meet them, while the war has stopped his big business and his big income. This is a sample of the noble American end of the story.

These are the saving class of people to whom life becomes a bore unless they can help somebody. There's just such a fellow in Brussels—you may have heard of him, for his name is Whitlock. Stories of his showing himself a man come out of that closed-up city every week. To a really big man, it doesn't matter whether his post is a little post, or a big post but, if I were President, I'd give Whitlock a big post. There's another fellow somewhere in Germany—a consul—of whom I never heard till the other day. But people have taken to coming in my office —English ladies—who wish to thank "you and your great government" for the courage and courtesy of this consul.[1] Stories about him will follow. Herrick, too, in Paris, somehow causes Americans and English and even Guatemalans who come along to go out of their way to say what he has done for them. Now there is a quality in the old woman with the baby bottles, and in the consul and in Whitlock and Hoover and Herrick and this English nation which adopts the Belgians—a quality that is invincible. When folk like these come down the road, I respectfully do obeisance to them. And—it's this kind of folk that the Germans have run up against. I thank Heaven I'm of their race and blood.

The whole world is bound to be changed as a result of this war. If Germany should win, our Monroe Doctrine would at once be shot in two, and we should have to get "out of the sun." The military party is a party of conquest—absolutely. If England wins, as of course she will, it'll be a bigger and a stronger England, with no strong enemy in the world, with her Empire knit closer than ever—India, Canada, Australia, New Zealand, South Africa, Egypt; under obligations to and in alliance with

---

[1]The reference in all probability is to Mr. Charles L. Hoover, at that time American Consul at Carlsbad.

Russia! England will not need our friendship as much as she now needs it; and there may come governments here that will show they do not. In any event, you see, the world will be changed. It's changed already: witness Bernstorff[1] and Münsterberg[2] playing the part once played by Irish agitators!

All of which means that it is high time we were constructing a foreign service. First of all, Congress ought to make it possible to have half a dozen or more permanent foreign under-secretaries—men who, after service in the Department, could go out as Ministers and Ambassadors; it ought generously to reorganize the whole thing. It ought to have a competent study made of the foreign offices of other governments. Of course it ought to get room to work in. Then it ought at once to give its Ambassadors and Ministers homes and dignified treatment. We've got to play a part in the world whether we wish to or not. Think of these things.

The blindest great force in this world to-day is the Prussian War Party—blind and stupid.—Well, and the most weary man in London just at this hour is

Your humble servant,
W. H. P.

but he'll be all right in the morning.

To Arthur W. Page

[Undated][3]

DEAR ARTHUR:

. . . I recall one night when we were dining at Sir John Jellicoe's, he told me that the Admiralty never slept —that he had a telephone by his bed every night.

[1]German Ambassador in Washington.

[2]Professor of Psychology at Harvard University, whose openly expressed pro-Germanism was making him exceedingly unpopular in the United States.

[3]Evidently written in the latter part of September, 1914.

"Did it ever ring?" I asked.

"No; but it will."

You begin to see pretty clearly how English history has been made and makes itself. This afternoon Lady S—— told your mother of her three sons, one on a warship in the North Sea, another with the army in France, and a third in training to go. "How brave you all are!" said your mother, and her answer was: "They belong to their country; we can't do anything else." One of the daughters-in-law of the late Lord Salisbury came to see me to find out if I could make an inquiry about her son who was reported "missing" after the battle of Mons. She was dry-eyed, calm, self-restrained—very grateful for the effort I promised to make; but a Spartan woman would have envied her self-possession. It turned out that her son was dead.

You hear experiences like these almost every day. These are the kinds of women and the kinds of men that have made the British Empire and the English race. You needn't talk of decadence. All their great qualities are in them here and now. I believe that half the young men who came to Katharine's[1] dances last winter and who used to drop in at the house once in a while are dead in France already. They went as a matter of course. This is the reason they are going to win. Now these things impress you, as they come to you day by day.

There isn't any formal social life now—no dinners, no parties. A few friends dine with a few friends now and then very quietly. The ladies of fashion are hospital nurses and Red Cross workers, or they are collecting socks and blankets for the soldiers. One such woman told your mother to-day that she went to one of the recruiting camps every day and taught the young fellows

[1]Miss Katharine A. Page, the Ambassador's daughter.

what colloquial French she could.   Every man, woman, and child seems to be doing something.   In the ordinary daily life, we see few of them: everybody is at work somewhere.

We live in a world of mystery: nothing can surprise us. The rumour is that a servant in one of the great families sent word to the Germans where the three English cruisers[1] were that German submarines blew up the other day. Not a German in the Kingdom can earn a penny.   We're giving thousands of them money at the German Embassy to keep them alive.   Our Austrian Embassy runs a soup kitchen where it feeds a lot of Austrians.   Your mother went around there the other day and they showed that they thought they owe their daily bread to her.   One day she went to one of the big houses where the English receive and distribute the thousands of Belgians who come here, poor creatures, to be taken care of.   One old woman asked your mother in French if she were a princess.   The lady that was with your mother answered, "Une Grande Dame."   That seemed to do as well.

This government doesn't now let anybody carry any food away.   But to-day they consented on condition I'd receive the food (for the Belgians) and consign it to Whitlock.   This is their way of keeping it out of German hands --have the Stars and Stripes, so to speak, to cover every bag of flour and of salt.   That's only one of 1,000 queer activities that I engage in.   I have a German princess's[2] jewels in our safe—$100,000 worth of them in my keeping; I have an old English nobleman's check for $40,000 to be sent to men who have been building a house for his daugh-

---

[1] The *Hogue*, the *Cressy*, and the *Aboukir* were torpedoed by a German submarine September 22, 1914.   This exploit first showed the world the power of the submarine.

[2] Princess Lichnowsky, wife of the German Ambassador to Great Britain.

ter in Dresden—to be sent as soon as the German Government agrees not to arrest the lady for debt. I have sent Miss Latimer[1] over to France to bring an Austrian baby eight months old whose mother will take it to the United States and bring it up an American citizen! The mother can't go and get it for fear the French might detain her; I've got the English Government's permission for the family to go to the United States. Harold[2] is in Belgium, trying to get a group of English ladies home who went there to nurse wounded English and Belgians and whom the Germans threaten to kidnap and transport to German hospitals—every day a dozen new kinds of jobs.

London is weird and muffled and dark and, in the West End, deserted. Half the lamps are not lighted, and the upper half of the globes of the street lights are painted black—so the Zeppelin raiders may not see them. You've no idea what a strange feeling it gives one. The papers have next to no news. The 23rd day of the great battle is reported very much in the same words as the 3rd day was. Yet nobody talks of much else. The censor erases most of the matter the correspondents write. We're in a sort of dumb as well as dark world. And yet, of course, we know much more here than they know in any other European capital.

Memorandum

[Undated.]

When England, France, and Russia agreed the other day not to make peace separately, that cooked the Kaiser's goose. They'll wear him out. Since England thus has Frenchmen and Russians bound, the Allies are strength-

---

[1]Private Secretary to Mrs. Page.

[2]Mr. Harold Fowler, the Ambassador's Secretary.

ened at their only weak place. That done, England is now going in deliberately, methodically, patiently to do the task. Even a fortnight ago, the people of this Kingdom didn't realize all that the war means to them. But the fever is rising now. The wounded are coming back, the dead are mourned, and the agony of hearing only that such-and-such a man is missing—these are having a prodigious effect. The men I meet now say in a matter-of-fact way: "Oh, yes! we'll get 'em, of course; the only question is, how long it will take us and how many of us it will cost. But no matter, we'll get 'em."

Old ladies and gentlemen of the high, titled world now begin by driving to my house almost every morning while I am at breakfast. With many apologies for calling so soon and with the fear that they interrupt me, they ask if I can make an inquiry in Germany for "my son," or "my nephew"—"he's among the missing." They never weep; their voices do not falter; they are brave and proud and self-restrained. It seems a sort of matter-of-course to them. Sometimes when they get home, they write me polite notes thanking me for receiving them. This morning the first man was Sir Dighton Probyn of Queen Alexandra's household—so dignified and courteous that you'd hardly have guessed his errand. And at intervals they come all day. Not a tear have I seen yet. They take it as a part of the price of greatness and of empire. You guess at their grief only by their reticence. They use as few words as possible and then courteously take themselves away. It isn't an accident that these people own a fifth of the world. Utterly unwarlike, they outlast anybody else when war comes. You don't get a sense of fighting here—only of endurance and of high resolve. Fighting is a sort of incident in the struggle to keep their world from German domination. . . .

To Edward M. House

October 11, 1914.

DEAR HOUSE:

There is absolutely nothing to write. It's war, war, war all the time; no change of subject; and, if you changed with your tongue, you couldn't change in your thought; war, war, war—"for God's sake find out if my son is dead or a prisoner"; rumours—they say that two French generals were shot for not supporting French, and then they say only one; and people come who have helped take the wounded French from the field and they won't even talk, it is so horrible; and a lady says that her own son (wounded) told her that when a man raised up in the trench to fire, the stench was so awful that it made him sick for an hour; and the poor Belgians come here by the tens of thousands, and special trains bring the English wounded; and the newspapers tell little or nothing—every day's reports like the preceding days'; and yet nobody talks about anything else.

Now and then the subject of its settlement is mentioned—Belgium and Serbia, of course, to be saved and as far as possible indemnified; Russia to have the Slav-Austrian States and Constantinople; France to have Alsace-Lorraine, of course; and Poland to go to Russia; Schleswig-Holstein and the Kiel Canal no longer to be German; all the South-German States to become Austrian and none of the German States to be under Prussian rule; the Hohenzollerns to be eliminated; the German fleet, or what is left of it, to become Great Britain's; and the German colonies to be used to satisfy such of the Allies as clamour for more than they get.

Meantime this invincible race is doing this revolutionary task marvellously—volunteering; trying to buy arms in the United States (a Pittsburgh manufacturer is now here trying to close a bargain with the War Office!);[1] knitting socks and mufflers; taking in all the poor Belgians; stopping all possible expenditure; darkening London at night; doing every conceivable thing to win as if they had been waging this war always and meant to do nothing else for the rest of their lives—and not the slightest doubt about the result and apparently indifferent how long it lasts or how much it costs.

Every aspect of it gets on your nerves. I can't keep from wondering how the world will seem after it is over— Germany (that is, Prussia and its system) cut out like a cancer; England owning still more of the earth; Belgium— all the men dead; France bankrupt; Russia admitted to the society of nations; the British Empire entering on a new lease of life; no great navy but one; no great army but the Russian; nearly all governments in Europe bankrupt; Germany gone from the sea—in ten years it will be difficult to recall clearly the Europe of the last ten years. And the future of the world more than ever in our hands!

We here don't know what you think or what you know at home; we haven't yet any time to read United States newspapers, which come very, very late; nobody writes us real letters (or the censor gets 'em, perhaps!); and so the war, the war, the war is the one thing that holds our minds.

We have taken a house for the Chancery[2]—almost the size of my house in Grosvenor Square—for the same sum as rent that the landlord proposed hereafter to charge us for the old hole where we've been for twenty-nine years. For the first time Uncle Sam has a decent place

---

[1] Probably a reference to Mr. Charles M. Schwab, President of the Bethlehem Steel Company, who was in London at this time on this errand.

[2] No. 4 Grosvenor Gardens.

in London. We've five times as much room and ten times as much work. Now—just this last week or two—I get off Sundays: that's doing well. And I don't now often go back at night. So, you see, we've much to be thankful for.—Shall we insure against Zeppelins? That's what everybody's asking. I told the Spanish Ambassador yesterday that I am going to ask the German Government for instructions about insuring their Embassy here!

Write and send some news. I saw an American to-day who says he's going home to-morrow. "Cable me," said I, "if you find the continent where it used to be."

Faithfully yours,

WALTER H. PAGE.

P. S. It is strange how little we know what you know on your side and just what you think, what relative value you put on this and what on that. There's a new sort of loneliness sprung up because of the universal absorption in the war.

And I hear all sorts of contradictory rumours about the effect of the German crusade in the United States. Oh well, the world has got to choose whether it will have English or German domination in Europe; that's the single big question at issue. For my part I'll risk the English and then make a fresh start ourselves to outstrip them in the spread of well-being; in the elevation of mankind of all classes; in the broadening of democracy and democratic rule (which is the sheet-anchor of all men's hopes just as bureaucracy and militarism are the destruction of all men's hopes); in the spread of humane feeling and action; in the growth of human kindness; in the tender treatment of women and children and the old; in literature, in art; in the abatement of suffering; in great changes in economic conditions which discourage poverty; and in science which gives us new leases on life and new tools and wider visions.   These are *our* world tasks, with England as our friendly rival and helper.   God bless us.

W. H. P.

To Arthur W. Page

London, November 6, 1914.

DEAR ARTHUR:

Those excellent photographs, those excellent apples, those excellent cigars—thanks.   I'm thinking of sending Kitty[1] over again.   They all spell and smell and taste of home—of the U. S. A.   Even the messenger herself seems Unitedstatesy, and that's a good quality, I assure you.   She's told us less news than you'd think she might for so long a journey and so long a visit; but that's the way with us all.   And, I dare say, if it were all put together it would make a pretty big news-budget.   And luckily for us (I often think we are among the luckiest families in the world) all she says is quite cheerful.   It's a wonderful report she makes of County Line[2]—the country, the place, the house, and its inhabitants.   Maybe, praise God, I'll see it myself some day—it and them.

But—but—I don't know when and can't guess out of this vast fog of war and doom.   The worst of it is nobody knows just what is happening.   I have, for an example, known for a week of the blowing up of a British dreadnaught[3]—thousands of people know it privately—and yet it isn't published!   Such secrecy makes you fear there may be other and even worse secrets.   But I don't really

---

[1]Miss Katharine A. Page had just returned from a visit to the United States.

[2]Mr. Arthur W. Page's country home on Long Island.

[3]Evidently the *Audacious*, sunk by mine off the North of Ireland. October 27, 1914.

believe there are. What I am trying to say is, so far as news (and many other things) go, we are under a military rule.

It's beginning to wear on us badly. It presses down, presses down, presses down in an indescribable way. All the people you see have lost sons or brothers; mourning becomes visible over a wider area all the time; people talk of nothing else; all the books are about the war; ordinary social life is suspended—people are visibly growing older. And there are some aspects of it that are incomprehensible. For instance, a group of American and English military men and correspondents were talking with me yesterday—men who have been on both sides—in Germany and Belgium and in France—and they say that the Germans in France alone have had 750,000 men killed. The Allies have lost 400,000 to 500,000. This in France only. Take the other fighting lines and there must already be a total of 2,000,000 killed. Nothing like that has ever happened before in the history of the world. A flood or a fire or a wreck which has killed 500 has often shocked all mankind. Yet we know of this enormous slaughter and (in a way) are not greatly moved. I don't know of a better measure of the brutalizing effect of war—it's bringing us to take a new and more inhuman standard to measure events by.

As for any political or economic reckoning—that's beyond any man's ability yet. I see strings of incomprehensible figures that some economist or other now and then puts in the papers, summing up the loss in pounds sterling. But that means nothing because we have no proper measure of it. If a man lose $10 or $10,000 we can grasp that. But when nations shoot away so many million pounds sterling every day—that means nothing to me. I do know that there's going to be no money on this side the world for a long time to buy American securities. The whole world is going to be hard up in consequence of the bankruptcy of these nations, the inestimable destruction of property, and the loss of productive men. I fancy that such a change will come in the economic and financial readjustment of the world as nobody can yet guess at.—Are Americans studying these things? It is not only South-American trade; it is all sorts of manufacturers; it is financial influence—if we can quit spending and wasting, and husband our earnings. There's no telling the enormous advantages we shall gain if we are wise.

The extent to which the German people have permitted themselves to be fooled is beyond belief. As a little instance of it, I enclose a copy of a letter that Lord Bryce gave me, written by an English woman who did good social work in her early life—a woman of sense—and who married a German merchant and has spent her married life in Germany. She is a wholly sincere person. This letter she wrote to a friend in England and—she believes every word of it. If she believes it, the great mass of the Germans believe similar things. I have heard of a number of such letters—sincere, as this one is. It gives a better insight into the average German mind than a hundred speeches by the Emperor.

This German and Austrian diplomatic business involves an enormous amount of work. I've now sent one man to Vienna and another to Berlin to straighten out almost hopeless tangles and lies about prisoners and such things and to see if they won't agree to swap more civilians detained in each country. On top of these, yesterday came the Turkish Embassy! Alas, we shall never see old Tewfik[1] again! This business begins briskly to-day

[1]Tewfik Pasha, the very popular Turkish Ambassador to Great Britain.

with the detention of every Turkish consul in the British Empire.   Lord!   I dread the missionaries; and I know they're coming now.   This makes four embassies.   We put up a sign, "The American Embassy," on every one of them.   Work?   We're worked to death.   Two nights ago I didn't get time to read a letter or even a telegram that had come that day till 11 o'clock at night. For on top of all these Embassies, I've had to become Commissary-General to feed 6,000,000 starving people in Belgium; and practically all the food must come from the United States.   You can't buy food for export in any country in Europe.   The devastation of Belgium defeats the Germans.—I don't mean in battle but I mean in the after-judgment of mankind.   They cannot recover from that half as soon as they may recover from the economic losses of the war.   The reducing of those people to starvation—that will stick to damn them in history, whatever they win or whatever they lose.

When's it going to end?   Everybody who ought to know says at the earliest next year—next summer.   Many say in two years.   As for me, I don't know.   I don't see how it can end soon.   Neither can lick the other to a frazzle and neither can afford to give up till it is completely licked.   This way of living in trenches and fighting a month at a time in one place is a new thing in warfare. Many a man shoots a cannon all day for a month without seeing a single enemy.   There are many wounded men back here who say they haven't seen a single German. When the trenches become so full of dead men that the living can't stay there longer, they move back to other trenches.   So it goes on.   Each side has several more million men to lose.   What the end will be—I mean when it will come, I don't see how to guess.   The Allies are obliged to win; they have more food and more money, and in the long run, more men.   But the German fighting machine is by far the best organization ever made—not the best men, but the best organization; and the whole German people believe what the woman writes whose letter I send you.   It'll take a long time to beat it.

Affectionately,
W. H. P.

The letter that Page inclosed, and another copy of which was sent to the President, purported to be written by the English wife of a German in Bremen.   It was as follows:

It is very difficult to write, more difficult to believe that what I write will succeed in reaching you.   My husband insists on my urging you—it is not necessary I am sure—to destroy the letter and all possible indications of its origin, should you think it worth translating.   The letter will go by a business friend of my husband's to Holland, and be got off from there.   For our business with Holland is now exceedingly brisk as you may understand.   Her neutrality is most precious to us.[1]

Well, I have of course a divided mind.   I think of those old days in Liverpool and Devonshire—how far off they seem!   And yet I spent all last year in England.   It was in March last when I was with you and we talked of the amazing treatment of your army—I cannot any longer call it *our* army—by ministers crying for the resignation of its officers and eager to make their humiliation an election cry!   How far off that seems, too!   Let me tell you that it was the conduct of your ministers, Churchill especially, that made people here so confident that your

---

[1] Germany was conducting her trade with the neutral world largely through Dutch and Danish ports.

Government could not fight. It seemed impossible that Lloyd George and his following could have the effrontery to pose as a "war" cabinet; still more impossible that any sane people could trust them if they did! Perhaps you may remember a talk we had also in March about Matthew Arnold whom I was reading again during my convalescence at Sidmouth. You said that "Friendship's Garland" and its Arminius could not be written now. I disputed that and told you that it was still true that your Government talked and "gassed" just as much as ever, and were wilfully blind to the fact that your power of action was wholly unequal to your words. As in 1870 so now. Nay, worse, your rulers have always known it perfectly well, but refused to see it or to admit it, because they wanted office and knew that to say the truth would bring the radical vote in the cities upon their poor heads. It is the old hypocrisy, in the sense in which Germans have always accused your nation: alas! and it is half my nation too. You pride yourselves on "Keeping your word" to Belgium. But you pride yourselves also, not so overtly just now, on always refusing to prepare yourselves to keep that word in *deed*. In the first days of August you knew, absolutely and beyond all doubt, that you could do nothing to make good your word. You had not the moral courage to say so, and, having said so, to act accordingly and to warn Belgium that your promise was "a scrap of paper," and effectively nothing more. It *is* nothing more, and has proved to be nothing more, but you do not see that your indelible disgrace lies just in this, that you unctuously proclaim that you are keeping your word when all the time you know, you have always known, that you refused utterly and completely to take the needful steps to enable you to translate word into action. Have you not torn up your "scrap of paper" just as effectively as Germany has? As my husband puts it: England gave Belgium a check, a big check, and gave it with much ostentation, but took care that there should be no funds to meet it! Trusting to your check Belgium finds herself bankrupt, sequestrated, blotted out as a nation. But I know England well enough to foresee that English statesmen, with our old friend, the Manchester *Guardian*, which we used to read in years gone by, will always quote with pride how they "guaranteed" the neutrality of Belgium.

As to the future. You cannot win. A nation that has prided itself on making no sacrifice for political power or even independence must pay for its pride. Our house here in Bremen has lately been by way of a centre for naval men, and to a less extent, for officers of the neighbouring commands. They are absolutely confident that they will land ten army corps in England before Christmas. It is terrible to know what they mean to go for. They mean to destroy. Every town which remotely is concerned with war material is to be annihilated. Birmingham, Bradford, Leeds, Newcastle, Sheffield, Northampton are to be wiped out, and the men killed, ruthlessly hunted down. The fact that Lancashire and Yorkshire have held aloof from recruiting is not to save them. The fact that Great Britain is to be a Reichsland will involve the destruction of inhabitants, to enable German citizens to be planted in your country in their place. German soldiers hope that your poor creatures will resist, as patriots should, but they doubt it very much. For resistance will facilitate the process of clearance. Ireland will be left independent, and its harmlessness will be guaranteed by its inevitable civil war.

You may wonder, as I do sometimes, whether this hatred of England is not unworthy, or a form of mental disease. But you must know that it is at bottom not hatred but contempt; fierce, unreasoning scorn for a country that pursues money and ease, from aristocrat to trade-unionist labourer, when it has a great inheritance to defend. I feel bitter, too, for I spent half my life in your country and my dearest friends are all English still; and yet I am deeply ashamed of the hypocrisy and make-believe that has initiated your national policy and brought you down. Now, one thing more. England is, after all, only a stepping stone. From Liverpool, Queenstown, Glasgow, Belfast, we shall reach out across the ocean. I firmly believe that within a year Germany will have seized the new Canal and proclaimed its defiance of the great Monroe Doctrine. We have six million Germans in the United States, and the Irish-Americans behind them. The Americans, believe me, are *as a nation* a cowardly nation, and will never fight organized strength except in defense of their own territories. With the Nova Scotian peninsula and the Bermudas, with the West Indies and the Guianas we shall be able to dominate the Americas. By our possession of the entire Western European seaboard America can find no outlet for its products except by our favour. Her finance is in German hands, her commercial capitals, New York and Chicago, are in reality German cities. It is some years since my father and I were in New York. But my opinion is not very different from that of the forceful men who have planned this war—that with Britain as a base the control of the American continent is under existing conditions the task of a couple of months.

I remember a conversation with Doctor Dohrn, the head of the great biological station at Naples, some four or five years ago. He was complaining of want of adequate subventions from Berlin. "Everything is wanted for the Navy," he said. "And what really does Germany want with such a navy?" I asked. "She is always saying that she certainly does not regard it as a weapon against England." At that Doctor Dohrn raised his eyebrows. "But you, *gnädige Frau*, are a German?" "Of course." "Well, then, you will understand me when I say with all the seriousness I can command that this fleet of ours is intended to deal with smugglers on the shores of the Island of Rügen." I laughed. He became graver still. "The ultimate enemy of our country is America;[1] and I pray that I may see the day of an alliance between a beaten England and a victorious Fatherland against the bully of the Americas." Well, Germany and Austria were never friends until Sadowa had shown the way. Oh! if your country, which in spite of all I love so much, would but "see things clearly and see them whole."

Bremen, September 25, 1914.

To Ralph W. Page[2]

London, Sunday, November 15, 1914.

DEAR RALPH:

You were very good to sit down in Greensboro', or anywhere else, and to write me a fine letter. Do that often. You say there's nothing to do now in the Sandhills. Write us letters: that's a fair job!

God save us, we need 'em. We need anything from the sane part of the world to enable us to keep our balance. One of the commonest things you hear about now is the insanity of a good number of the poor fellows who come back from the trenches as well as of a good many

---

[1] Mr. Irwin Laughlin, first secretary of the American Embassy in London, furnishes this note: "This statement about America was made to me more than once in Germany, between 1910 and 1912, by German officers, military and naval."

[2] Of Pinehurst, North Carolina, the Ambassador's oldest son.

Belgians. The sights and sounds they've experienced un-hinge their reason. If this war keep up long enough—and it isn't going to end soon—people who have had no sight of it will go crazy, too—the continuous thought of it, the inability to get away from it by any device what-ever—all this tells on us all. Letters, then, plenty of them—let 'em come.

You are in a peaceful land. The war is a long, long way off. You suffer nothing worse than a little idleness and a little poverty. They are nothing. I hope (and believe) that you get enough to eat. Be content, then. Read the poets, improve a piece of land, play with the baby, learn golf. That's the happy and philosophic and fortunate life in these times of world-madness.

As for the continent of Europe—forget it. We have paid far too much attention to it. It has ceased to be worth it. And now it's of far less value to us—and will be for the rest of your life—than it has ever been before. An ancient home of man, the home, too, of beautiful things—buildings, pictures, old places, old traditions, dead civili-zations—the place where man rose from barbarism to civilization—it is now bankrupt, its best young men dead, its system of politics and of government a failure, its social structure enslaving and tyrannical—it has little help for us. The American spirit, which is the spirit that con-cerns itself with making life better for the whole mass of men—that's at home at its best with us. The whole future of the race is in the new countries—our country chiefly. This grows on one more and more and more. The things that are best worth while are on our side of the ocean. And we've got all the bigger job to do because of this violent demonstration of the failure of continental Europe. It's gone on living on a false basis till its ele-ments got so mixed that it has simply blown itself to pieces. It is a great convulsion of nature, as an earth-quake or a volcano is. Human life there isn't worth what a yellow dog's life is worth in Moore County. Don't bother yourself with the continent of Europe any more—except to learn the value of a real democracy and the benefits it can confer precisely in proportion to the extent to which men trust to it. Did you ever read my Ad-dress delivered before the Royal Institution of Great Britain?[1] I enclose a copy. Now that's my idea of the very milk of the word. To come down to daily, deadly things—this upheaval is simply infernal. Parliament opened the other day and half the old lords that sat in their robes had lost their heirs and a larger part of the members of the House wore khaki. To-morrow they will vote $1,125,000,000 for war purposes. They had already voted $500,000,000. They'll vote more, and more, and more, if necessary. They are raising a new army of 2,000,-000 men. Every man and every dollar they have will go if necessary. That's what I call an invincible people. The Kaiser woke up the wrong passenger. But for fifty years the continent won't be worth living on. My heavens! what bankruptcy will follow death!

Affectionately,
W. H. P.

To Frank C. Page[2]

Sunday, December 20th, 1914.

DEAR OLD MAN:

I envy both you and your mother[3] your chance to make plans for the farm and the house and all the rest of it and

---

[1] On June 12, 1914. The title of the address was "Some Aspects of the American Democracy."

[2] The Ambassador's youngest son.

[3] Mrs. W. H. Page was at this time spending a few weeks in the United States.

to have one another to talk to. And, most of all, you are where you can now and then change the subject. You can guess somewhat at our plight when Kitty and I confessed to one another last night that we were dead tired and needed to go to bed early and to stay long. She's sleeping yet, the dear kid, and I hope she'll sleep till lunch time. There isn't anything the matter with us but the war; but that's enough, Heaven knows. It's the worst ailment that has ever struck me. Then, if you add to that this dark, wet, foggy, sooty, cold, penetrating climate— you ought to thank your stars that you are not in it. I'm glad your mother's out of it, as much as we miss her; and miss her? Good gracious! there's no telling the hole her absence makes in all our life. But Kitty is a trump, true blue and dead game, and the very best company you can find in a day's journey. And, much as we miss your mother, you mustn't weep for us; we are having some fun and are planning more. I could have no end of fun with her if I had any time. But to work all day and till bedtime doesn't leave much time for sport.

The farm—the farm—the farm—it's yours and Mother's to plan and make and do with as you wish. I shall be happy whatever you do, even if you put the roof in the cellar and the cellar on top of the house.

If you have room enough (16×10 plus a fire and a bath are enough for me), I'll go down there and write a book. If you haven't it, I'll go somewhere else and write a book. I don't propose to be made unhappy by any house or by the lack of any house nor by anything whatsoever.

All the details of life go on here just the same. The war goes as slowly as death because it *is* death, death to millions of men. We've all said all we know about it to one another a thousand times; nobody knows anything else; nobody can guess when it will end; nobody has any doubt about how it will end, unless some totally improbable and unexpected thing happens, such as the falling out of the Allies, which can't happen for none of them can afford it; and we go around the same bloody circle all the time. The papers never have any news; nobody ever talks about anything else; everybody is tired to death; nobody is cheerful; when it isn't sick Belgians, it's aeroplanes; and when it isn't aeroplanes, it's bombarding the coast of England. When it isn't an American ship held up, it's a fool American-German arrested as a spy; and when it isn't a spy it's a liar who *knows* the Zeppelins are coming tonight. We don't know anything; we don't believe anybody; we should be surprised at nothing; and at 3 o'clock I'm going to the Abbey to a service in honour of the 100 years of peace! The world has all got itself so jumbled up that the bays are all promontories, the mountains are all valleys, and earthquakes are necessary for our happiness. We have disasters for breakfast; mined ships for luncheon; burned cities for dinner; trenches in our dreams, and bombarded towns for small talk.

Peaceful seems the sandy landscape where you are, glad the very blackjacks, happy the curs, blessed the sheep, interesting the chin-whiskered clodhopper, innocent the fool darkey, blessed the mule, for it knows no war. And you have your mother—be happy, boy; you don't know how much you have to be thankful for.

Europe is ceasing to be interesting except as an example of how-not-to-do-it. It has no lessons for us except as a warning. When the whole continent has to go fighting— every blessed one of them—once a century, and half of them half the time between and all prepared even when they are not fighting, and when they shoot away all their money as soon as they begin to get rich a little and everybody else's money, too, and make the whole world poor, and when they kill every third or fourth generation of the best men and leave the worst to rear families, and have to start over afresh every time with a worse stock—give me Uncle Sam and his big farm. We don't need to catch any of this European life. We can do without it all as well as we can do without the judges' wigs and the court costumes. Besides, I like a land where the potatoes have some flavour, where you can buy a cigar, and get your hair cut and have warm bathrooms.

Build the farm, therefore; and let me hear at every stage of that happy game. May the New Year be the best that has ever come for you!

Affectionately,
W. H. P.

CHAPTER XII

"WAGING NEUTRALITY"

I

THE foregoing letters sufficiently portray Page's attitude toward the war; they also show the extent to which he suffered from the daily tragedy. The great burdens placed upon the Embassy in themselves would have exhausted a physical frame that had never been particularly robust; but more disintegrating than these was the mental distress—the constant spectacle of a civilization apparently bent upon its own destruction. Indeed there were probably few men in Europe upon whom the war had a more depressing effect. In the first few weeks the Ambassador perceptibly grew older; his face became more deeply lined, his hair became grayer, his body thinner, his step lost something of its quickness, his shoulders began to stoop, and his manner became more and more abstracted. Page's kindness, geniality, and consideration had long since endeared him to all the embassy staff, from his chief secretaries to clerks and doormen; and all his associates now watched with affectionate solicitude the extent to which the war was wearing upon him. "In those first weeks," says Mr. Irwin Laughlin, Page's most important assistant and the man upon whom the routine work of the Embassy largely fell, "he acted like a man who was carrying on his shoulders all the sins and burdens of the world. I know no man who seemed to realize so poignantly the misery and sorrow of it all. The sight of an England which he loved bleeding to death in defence of the things in which he most believed was a grief that seemed to be sapping his very life."

Page's associates, however, noted a change for the better after the Battle of the Marne. Except to his most intimate companions he said little, for he represented a nation that was "neutral"; but the defeat of the Germans added liveliness to his step, gave a keener sparkle to his eye, and even brought back some of his old familiar gaiety of spirit. One day the Ambassador was lunching with Mr. Laughlin and one or two other friends.

"We did pretty well in that Battle of the Marne, didn't we?" he said.

"Isn't that remark slightly unneutral, Mr. Ambassador?" asked Mr. Laughlin.

At this a roar of laughter went up from the table that could be heard for a considerable distance.

About this same time Page's personal secretary, Mr. Harold Fowler, came to ask the Ambassador's advice about enlisting in the British Army. To advise a young man to take a step that might very likely result in his death was a heavy responsibility, and the Ambassador refused to accept it. It was a matter that the Secretary could settle only with his own conscience. Mr. Fowler decided his problem by joining the British Army; he had a distinguished career in its artillery and aviation service as he had subsequently in the American Army. Mr. Fowler at once discovered that his decision had been highly pleasing to his superior.

"I couldn't advise you to do this, Harold," Page said, placing his hand on the young man's shoulder, "but now that you've settled it yourself I'll say this—if I were a young man like you and in your circumstances, I should enlist myself."

Yet greatly as Page abhorred the Prussians and greatly

as his sympathies from the first day of the war were enlisted on the side of the Allies, there was no diplomat in
the American service who was more "neutral" in the
technical sense. "Neutral!" Page once exclaimed.
"There's nothing in the world so neutral as this embassy.
Neutrality takes up all our time." When he made this
remark he was, as he himself used to say, "the German
Ambassador to Great Britain." And he was performing
the duties of this post with the most conscientious fidelity.
These duties were onerous and disagreeable ones and were
made still more so by the unreasonableness of the German
Government. Though the American Embassy was car-
ing for the more than 70,000 Germans who were then
living in England and was performing numerous other
duties, the Imperial Government never realized that Page
and the Embassy staff were doing it a service. With
characteristic German tactlessness the German Foreign
Office attempted to be as dictatorial to Page as though he
had been one of its own junior secretaries. The business
of the German Embassy in London was conducted with
great ability; the office work was kept in the most ship-
shape condition; yet the methods were American methods
and the Germans seemed aggrieved because the routine
of the Imperial bureaucracy was not observed. With
unparallelled insolence they objected to the American
system of accounting—not that it was unsound or did
not give an accurate picture of affairs—but simply that
it was not German. Page quietly but energetically
informed the German Government that the American diplomatic service was not a part of the German organization, that its bookkeeping system was American, not
German, that he was doing this work not as an obligation
but as a favour, and that, so long as he continued to do it,
he would perform the duty in his own way. At this the

Imperial Government subsided. Despite such annoy-
ances Page refused to let his own feelings interfere with
the work. The mere fact that he despised the Germans
made him over-scrupulous in taking all precautions that
they obtained exact justice. But this was all that the
German cause in Great Britain did receive. His administration of the German Embassy was faultless in its
technique, but it did not err on the side of over-enthu-
siasm.

His behaviour throughout the three succeeding years
was entirely consistent with his conception of "neutrality." That conception, as is apparent from the letters
already printed, was not the Wilsonian conception.
Probably no American diplomat was more aggrieved at
the President's definition of neutrality than his Ambassador to Great Britain. Page had no quarrel with
the original neutrality proclamation; that was purely a
routine governmental affair, and at the time it was issued
it represented the proper American attitude. But the
President's famous emendations filled him with astonishment and dismay. "We must be impartial in thought
as well as in action," said the President on August 19th,[1]
"we must put a curb upon our sentiments as well as upon
every transaction that might be construed as a prejudice
of one party to the prejudice of another." Page was
prepared to observe all the traditional rules of neutrality,
to insist on American rights with the British Government,
and to do full legal justice to the Germans, but he declined to abrogate his conscience where his personal
judgment of the rights and wrongs of the conflict were
concerned. "Neutrality," he said in a letter to his
brother, Mr. Henry A. Page, of Aberdeen, N. C., "is a

---

[1]In a letter addressed to "My fellow Countrymen" and presented to the Senate
by Mr. Chilton.

quality of government—an artificial unit. When a war comes a government must go in it or stay out of it. It must make a declaration to the world of its attitude. That's all that neutrality is. A government can be neutral, but no *man* can be."

"The President and the Government," Page afterward wrote, "in their insistence upon the moral quality of neutrality, missed the larger meaning of the war. It is at bottom nothing but the effort of the Berlin absolute monarch and his group to impose their will on as large a part of the world as they can overrun. The President started out with the idea that it was a war brought on by many obscure causes—economic and the like; and he thus missed its whole meaning. We have ever since been dealing with the chips which fly from the war machine and have missed the larger meaning of the conflict. Thus we have failed to render help to the side of Liberalism and Democracy, which are at stake in the world."

Nor did Page think it his duty, in his private communications to his Government and his friends, to maintain that attitude of moral detachment which Mr. Wilson's pronouncement had evidently enjoined upon him. It was not his business to announce his opinions to the world, for he was not the man who determined the policy of the United States; that was the responsibility of the President and his advisers. But an ambassador did have a certain rôle to perform. It was his duty to collect information and impressions, to discover what important people thought of the United States and of its policies, and to send forward all such data to Washington. According to Page's theory of the Ambassadorial office, he was a kind of listening post on the front of diplomacy, and he would have grievously failed had he not done his best to keep headquarters informed. He did not regard it as

"loyalty" merely to forward only that kind of material
which Washington apparently preferred to obtain; with
a frankness which Mr. Wilson's friends regarded as almost ruthless, Page reported what he believed to be the
truth. That this practice was displeasing to the powers
of Washington there is abundant evidence. In early
December, 1914, Colonel House was compelled to transmit a warning to the American Ambassador at London.
"The President wished me to ask you to please be more
careful not to express any unneutral feeling, either by
word of mouth, or by letter and not even to the State
Department. He said that both Mr. Bryan and Mr.
Lansing had remarked upon your leaning in that direction and he thought that it would materially lessen
your influence. He feels very strongly about this."

Evidently Page did not regard his frank descriptions of
England under war as expressing unneutral feeling; at any
rate, as the war went on, his letters, even those which he
wrote to President Wilson, became more and more outspoken. Page's resignation was always at the President's disposal; the time came, as will appear, when it
was offered; so long as he occupied his post, however,
nothing could turn him from his determination to make
what he regarded as an accurate record of events. This
policy of maintaining an outward impartiality, and, at
the same time, of bringing pressure to bear on Washington
in behalf of the Allies, he called "waging neutrality."

Such was the mood in which Page now prepared to
play his part in what was probably the greatest diplomatic drama in history. The materials with which this
drama concerned itself were such apparently lifeless subjects as ships and cargoes, learned discourses on such
abstract matters as the doctrine of continuous voyage,
effective blockade, and conditional contraband; yet the

struggle, which lasted for three years, involved the greatest issue of modern times—nothing less than the survival of those conceptions of liberty, government, and society which make the basis of English-speaking civilization. To the newspaper reader of war days, shipping difficulties signified little more than a newspaper headline which he hastily read, or a long and involved lawyer's note which he seldom read at all—or, if he did, practically never understood. Yet these minute and neglected controversies presented to the American Nation the greatest decision in its history. Once before, a century ago, a European struggle had laid before the United States practically the same problem. Great Britain fought Napoleon, just as it had now been compelled to fight the Hohenzollern, by blockade; such warfare, in the early nineteenth century, led to retaliations, just as did the maritime warfare in the recent conflict, and the United States suffered, in 1812, as in 1914, from what were regarded as the depredations of both sides. In Napoleon's days France and Great Britain, according to the international lawyers, attacked American commerce in illegal ways; on strictly technical grounds this infant nation had an adequate cause of war against both belligerents; but the ultimate consequence of a very confused situation was a declaration of war against Great Britain. Though an England which was ruled by a George III or a Prince Regent—an England of rotten boroughs, of an ignorant and oppressed peasantry, and of a social organization in which caste was almost as definitely drawn as in an Oriental despotism—could hardly appeal to the enthusiastic democrat as embodying all the ideals of his system, yet the England of 1800 did represent modern progress when compared with the mediæval autocracy of Napoleon. If we take this broad view, therefore, we must admit that, in 1812, we fought on the side of darkness and injustice against the forces that were making for enlightenment. The war of 1914 had not gone far when the thinking American foresaw that it would present to the American people precisely this same problem. What would the decision be? Would America repeat the experience of 1812, or had the teachings of a century so dissipated hatreds that it would be able to exert its influence in a way more worthy of itself and more helpful to the progress of mankind?

There was one great difference, however, between the position of the United States in 1812 and its position in 1914. A century ago we were a small and feeble nation, of undeveloped industries and resources and of immature character; our entrance into the European conflict, on one side or the other, could have little influence upon its results, and, in fact, it influenced it scarcely at all; the side we fought against emerged triumphant. In 1914, we had the greatest industrial organization and the greatest wealth of any nation and the largest white population of any country except Russia; the energy of our people and our national talent for success had long been the marvel of foreign observers. It mattered little in 1812 on which side the United States took its stand; in 1914 such a decision would inevitably determine the issue. Of all European statesmen there was one man who saw this point with a definiteness which, in itself, gives him a clear title to fame. That was Sir Edward Grey. The time came when a section of the British public was prepared almost to stone the Foreign Secretary in the streets of London, because they believed that his "subservience" to American trade interests was losing the war for Great Britain; his tenure of office was a constant struggle with British naval and military chiefs who asserted that the Foreign Office, in its efforts to maintain harmonious relations with America, was hamstringing the British fleet, was rendering almost impotent its control of the sea, and was thus throwing away the greatest advantage which Great Britain possessed in its life and death struggle. "Some blight has been at work in our Foreign Office for years," said the *Quarterly Review*, "steadily undermining our mastery of the sea."

"The fleet is not allowed to act," cried Lord Charles Beresford in Parliament; the Foreign Office was constantly interfering with its operations. The word "traitor" was not infrequently heard; there were hints that pro-Germanism was rampant and that officials in the Foreign Office were drawing their pay from the Kaiser. It was constantly charged that the navy was bringing in suspicious cargoes only to have the Foreign Office order their release. "I fight Sir Edward about stopping cargoes," Page wrote to Colonel House in December, 1914; "literally fight. He yields and promises this or that. This or that doesn't happen or only half happens. I know why. The military ministers balk him. I inquire through the back door and hear that the Admiralty and the War Office of course value American good-will, but they'll take their chances of a quarrel with the United States rather than let copper get to Germany. The cabinet has violent disagreements. But the military men yield as little as possible. It was rumoured the other day that the Prime Minister threatened to resign; and I know that Kitchener's sister told her friends, with tears in her eyes, that the cabinet shamefully hindered her brother."

These criticisms unquestionably caused Sir Edward great unhappiness, but this did not for a moment move him from his course. His vision was fixed upon a much greater purpose. Parliamentary orators might rage because the British fleet was not permitted to make indiscriminate warfare on commerce, but the patient and far-seeing British Foreign Secretary was the man who was really trying to win the war. He was one of the few Englishmen who, in August, 1914, perceived the tremendous extent of the struggle in which Great Britain had engaged. He saw that the English people were facing the greatest crisis since William of Normandy, in 1066, subjected their island to foreign rule. Was England to become the "Reichsland" of a European monarch, and was the British Empire to pass under the sway of Germany? Proud as Sir Edward Grey was of his country, he was modest in the presence of facts; and one fact of which he early became convinced was that Great Britain could not win unless the United States was ranged upon its side. Here was the country—so Sir Edward reasoned—that contained the largest effective white population in the world; that could train armies larger than those of any other nation; that could make the most munitions, build the largest number of battleships and merchant vessels, and raise food in quantities great enough to feed itself and Europe besides. This power, the Foreign Secretary believed, could determine the issue of the war. If Great Britain secured American sympathy and support, she would win; if Great Britain lost this sympathy and support, she would lose. A foreign policy that would estrange the United States and perhaps even throw its support to Germany would not only lose the war to Great Britain, but it would be perhaps the blackest crime in history, for it would mean the collapse of that British-American coöperation, and the destruction of those British-American ideals and institutions which are the

greatest facts in the modern world. This conviction
was the basis of Sir Edward's policy from the day that
Great Britain declared war. Whatever enemies he might
make in England, the Foreign Secretary was determined
to shape his course so that the support of the United
States would be assured to his country. A single illustration shows the skill and wisdom with which he pursued
this great purpose.

Perhaps nothing in the early days of the war enraged
the British military chiefs more than the fact that cotton
was permitted to go from the United States to Germany.
That Germany was using this cotton in the manufacture
of torpedoes to sink British ships and of projectiles to kill
British soldiers in trenches was well known; nor did many
people deny that Great Britain had the right to put
cotton on the contraband list. Yet Grey, in the pursuit
of his larger end, refused to take this step. He knew
that the prosperity of the Southern States depended
exclusively upon the cotton crop. He also knew that the
South had raised the 1914 crop with no knowledge that a
war was impending and that to deny the Southern planters their usual access to the German markets would all
but ruin them. He believed that such a ruling would immediately alienate the sympathy of a large section of the
United States and make our Southern Senators and Congressmen enemies of Great Britain. Sir Edward was also
completely informed of the extent to which the German-
Americans and the Irish-Americans were active and he
was familiar with the aims of American pacifists. He believed that declaring cotton contraband at this time would
bring together in Congress the Southern Senators and
Congressmen, the representatives of the Irish and the
German causes and the pacifists, and that this combination would exercise an influence that would be disastrous

to Great Britain. Two dangers constantly haunted Sir Edward's mind at this time. One was that the enemies of Great Britain would assemble enough votes in Congress to place an embargo upon the shipment of munitions from this country. Such an embargo might well be fatal to Great Britain, for at this time she was importing munitions, especially shells, in enormous quantities from the United States. The other was that such pressure might force the Government to convoy American cargoes with American warships. Great Britain then could stop the cargoes only by attacking our cruisers, and to attack a cruiser is an act of war. Had Congress taken either one of these steps the Allies would have lost the war in the spring of 1915. At a cabinet meeting held to consider this question, Sir Edward Grey set forth this view and strongly advised that cotton should not be made contraband at that time.[1] The Cabinet supported him and events justified the decision. Afterward, in Washington, several of the most influential Senators informed Sir Edward that this action had averted a great crisis.

This was the motive, which, as will appear as the story of our relations with Great Britain progresses, inspired the Foreign Secretary in all his dealings with the United States. His purpose was to use the sea power of Great Britain to keep war materials and foodstuffs out of Germany, but never to go to the length of making an unbridgeable gulf between the United States and Great Britain. The American Ambassador to Great Britain completely sympathized with this programme. It was Page's business to protect the rights of the United States, just as it was Grey's to protect the rights of Great Britain.

---

[1]This was in October, 1914. In August, 1915, when conditions had changed, cotton was declared contraband.

Both were vigilant in protecting such rights, and animated differences between the two men on this point were not infrequent. Great Britain did many absurd and high-handed things in intercepting American cargoes, and Page was always active in "protesting" when the basis for the protest actually existed. But on the great overhanging issue the two men were at one. Like Grey, Page believed that there were more important things involved than an occasional cargo of copper or of oil cake. The American Ambassador thought that the United States should protect its shipping interests, but that it should realize that maritime law was not an exact science, that its principles had been modified by every great conflict in which the blockade had been an effective agency, and that the United States itself, in the Civil War, had not hesitated to make such changes as the changed methods of modern transportation had required. In other words he believed that we could safeguard our rights in a way that would not prevent Great Britain from keeping war materials and foodstuffs out of Germany. And like Sir Edward Grey, Page was obliged to contend with forces at home which maintained a contrary view. In this early period Mr. Bryan was nominally Secretary of State, but the man who directed the national policy in shipping matters was Robert Lansing, then counsellor of the Department. It is somewhat difficult to appraise Mr. Lansing justly, for in his conduct of his office there was not the slightest taint of malice. His methods were tactless, the phrasing of his notes lacked deftness and courtesy, his literary style was crude and irritating; but Mr. Lansing was not anti-British, he was not pro-German; he was nothing more nor less than a lawyer. The protection of American rights at sea was to him simply a "case" in which he had been retained as counsel for the plaintiff. As a good lawyer it was his business to score as many points as possible for his client and the more weak joints he found in the enemy's armour the better did he do his job. It was his duty to scan the law books, to look up the precedents, to examine facts, and to prepare briefs that would be unassailable from a technical standpoint. To Mr. Lansing this European conflict was the opportunity of a lifetime. He had spent thirty years studying the intricate problems that now became his daily companions. His mind revelled in such minute details as ultimate destination, the continuous voyage as applied to conditional contraband, the searching of cargoes upon the high seas, belligerent trading through neutral ports, war zones, orders in council, and all the other jargon of maritime rights in time of war. These topics engrossed him as completely as the extension of democracy and the significance of British-American coöperation engrossed all the thoughts of Page and Grey.

That Page took this larger view is evident from the communications which he now began sending to the President. One that he wrote on October 15, 1914, is especially to the point. The date is extremely important; so early had Page formulated the standards that should guide the United States and so early had he begun his work of attempting to make President Wilson understand the real nature of the conflict. The position which Page now assumed was one from which he never departed.

Cipher Telegram to the President

In this great argument about shipping I cannot help being alarmed because we are getting into deep water uselessly. The Foreign Office has yielded unquestioningly to all our requests and has shown the sincerest wish to meet all our suggestions, so long as it is not called upon to admit war materials into Germany. It will not give way to us in that. We would not yield it if we were in their place. Neither would the Germans. England will risk a serious quarrel or even hostilities with us rather than yield. You may look upon this as the final word.

Since the last lists of contraband and conditional contraband were published, such materials as rubber and copper and petroleum have developed entirely new uses in war. The British simply will not let Germany import them. Nothing that can be used for war purposes in Germany now will be used for anything else. Representatives of Spain, Holland, and all the Scandinavian states agree that they can do nothing but acquiesce and file protests and claims, and they admit that Great Britain has the right to revise the list of contraband. This is not a war in the sense in which we have hitherto used that word. It is a world-clash of systems of government, a struggle to the extermination of English civilization or of Prussian military autocracy. Precedents have gone to the scrap heap. We have a new measure for military and diplomatic action. Let us suppose that we press for a few rights to which the shippers have a theoretical claim. The American people gain nothing and the result is friction with this country; and that is what a very small minority of the agitators in the United States would like. Great Britain can any day close the Channel to all shipping or can drive Holland to the enemy and blockade her ports.

Let us take a little farther view into the future. If Germany win, will it make any difference what position Great Britain took on the Declaration of London? The Monroe Doctrine will be shot through. We shall have to have a great army and a great navy. But suppose that

England win. We shall then have an ugly academic dispute with her because of this controversy. Moreover,
we shall not hold a good position for helping to compose
the quarrel or for any other service.

The present controversy seems here, where we are close
to the struggle, academic. It seems to us a petty matter
when it is compared with the grave danger we incur of
shutting ourselves off from a position to be of some service
to civilization and to the peace of mankind.

In Washington you seem to be indulging in a more or
less theoretical discussion. As we see the issue here, it is
a matter of life and death for English-speaking civilization.
It is not a happy time to raise controversies that can be
avoided or postponed. We gain nothing, we lose every
chance for useful coöperation for peace. In jeopardy also
are our friendly relations with Great Britain in the sorest
need and the greatest crisis in her history. I know that
this is the correct view. I recommend most earnestly
that we shall substantially accept the new Order in Council or acquiesce in it and reserve whatever rights we may
have. I recommend prompt information be sent to the
British Government of such action. I should like to inform Grey that this is our decision.

So far as our neutrality obligations are concerned, I do
not believe that they require us to demand that Great
Britain should adopt for our benefit the Declaration of
London. Great Britain has never ratified it, nor have
any other nations except the United States. In its
application to the situation presented by this war it is
altogether to the advantage of Germany.

I have delayed to write you this way too long. I have
feared that I might possibly seem to be influenced by
sympathy with England and by the atmosphere here.
But I write of course solely with reference to our own

country's interest and its position after the reorganization of Europe.

Anderson[1] and Laughlin[2] agree with me emphatically.

WALTER H. PAGE.

II

The immediate cause of this protest was, as its context shows, the fact that the State Department was insisting that Great Britain should adopt the Declaration of London as a code of law for regulating its warfare on German shipping. Hostilities had hardly started when Mr. Bryan made this proposal; his telegram on this subject is dated August 7, 1914. "You will further state," said Mr. Bryan, "that this Government believes that the acceptance of these laws by the belligerents would prevent grave misunderstandings which may arise as to the relations between belligerents and neutrals. It therefore hopes that this inquiry may receive favourable consideration." At the same time Germany and the other belligerents were asked to adopt this Declaration.

The communication was thus more than a suggestion; it was a recommendation that was strongly urged. According to Page this telegram was the first great mistake the American Government made in its relations with Great Britain. In September, 1916, the Ambassador prepared for President Wilson a memorandum which he called "Rough notes toward an explanation of the British feeling toward the United States." "Of recent years," he said, "and particularly during the first year of the present Administration, the British feeling toward the United States was most friendly and cordial. About

---

[1] Mr. Chandler P. Anderson, of New York, at this time advising the American Embassy on questions of international law.

[2] Mr. Irwin Laughlin, first secretary of the Embassy.

the time of the repeal of the tolls clause in the Panama Act, the admiration and friendliness of the whole British public (governmental and private) reached the highest point in our history.   In considering the change that has taken place since, it is well to bear this cordiality in mind as a starting point.   When the war came on there was at first nothing to change this attitude.   The hysterical hope of many persons that our Government might protest against the German invasion of Belgium caused some feeling of disappointment, but thinking men did not share it; and, if this had been the sole cause of criticism of us, the criticism would have died out.   The unusually high regard in which the President—and hence our Government—was then held was to a degree new.   The British had for many years held the people of the United States in high esteem: they had not, as a rule, so favourably regarded the Government at Washington, especially in its conduct of foreign relations.   They had long regarded our Government as ignorant of European affairs and amateurish in its cockiness.   When I first got to London I found evidence of this feeling, even in the most friendly atmosphere that surrounded us.   Mr. Bryan was looked on as a joke.   They forgot him—rather, they never took serious notice of him.   But, when the Panama tolls incident was closed, they regarded the President as his own Foreign Secretary; and thus our Government as well as our Nation came into this high measure of esteem.

"The war began.   We, of course, took a neutral attitude, wholly to their satisfaction.   But we at once interfered—or tried to interfere—by insisting on the Declaration of London, which no Great Power but the United States (I think) had ratified and which the British House of Lords had distinctly rejected.   That Declaration would probably have given a victory to Germany if the

Allies had adopted it. In spite of our neutrality we insisted vigorously on its adoption and aroused a distrust in our judgment. Thus we started in wrong, so far as the British Government is concerned."

The rules of maritime warfare which the American State Department so disastrously insisted upon were the direct outcome of the Hague Conference of 1907. That assembly of the nations recognized, what had long been a palpable fact, that the utmost confusion existed in the operations of warring powers upon the high seas. About the fundamental principle that a belligerent had the right, if it had the power, to keep certain materials of commerce from reaching its enemy, there was no dispute. But as to the particular articles which it could legally exclude there were as many different ideas as there were nations. That the blockade, a term which means the complete exclusion of cargoes and ships from an enemy's ports, was a legitimate means of warfare, was also an accepted fact, but as to the precise means in which the blockade could be enforced there was the widest difference of opinion. The Hague Conference provided that an attempt should be made to codify these laws into a fixed system, and the representatives of the nations met in London in 1908, under the presidency of the Earl of Desart, for this purpose. The outcome of their two months' deliberations was that document of seven chapters and seventy articles which has ever since been known as the Declaration of London. Here at last was the thing for which the world had been waiting so long—a complete system of maritime law for the regulation of belligerents and the protection of neutrals, which would be definitely binding upon all nations because all nations were expected to ratify it.

But the work of all these learned gentlemen was thrown away. The United States was the only party to the negotiations that put the stamp of approval upon its labours. All other nations declined to commit themselves. In Great Britain the Declaration had an especially interesting course. In that country it became a football of party politics. The Liberal Government was at first inclined to look upon it favourably; the Liberal House of Commons actually ratified it. It soon became apparent, however, that this vote did not represent the opinion of the British public. In fact, few measures have ever aroused such hostility as this Declaration, once its details became known. For more than a year the hubbub against it filled the daily press, the magazines, the two Houses of Parliament and the hustings; Rudyard Kipling even wrote a poem denouncing it. The adoption of the Declaration, these critics asserted, would destroy the usefulness of the British fleet. In many quarters it was described as a German plot—as merely a part of the preparations which Germany was making for world conquest. The fact is that the Declaration could not successfully stand the analysis to which it was now mercilessly submitted; the House of Lords rejected it, and this action met with more approbation than had for years been accorded the legislative pronouncements of that chamber. The Liberal House of Commons was not in the least dissatisfied with this conclusion, for it realized that it had made a mistake and it was only too happy to be permitted to forget it.

When the war broke out there was therefore no single aspect of maritime law which was quite so odious as the Declaration of London. Great Britain realized that she could never win unless her fleet were permitted to keep contraband out of Germany and, if necessary, completely to blockade that country. The two greatest conflicts of the nineteenth century were the European struggle with Napoleon and the American Civil War. In both the blockade had been the decisive element, and that this great agency would similarly determine events in this even greater struggle was apparent. What enraged the British public against any suggestion of the Declaration was that it practically deprived Great Britain of this indispensable means of weakening the enemy. In this Declaration were drawn up lists of contraband, non-contraband, and conditional contraband, and all of these, in English eyes, worked to the advantage of Germany and against the advantage of Great Britain. How absurd this classification was is evident from the fact that airplanes were not listed as absolute contraband of war. Germany's difficulty in getting copper was one of the causes of her collapse; yet the Declaration put copper for ever on the non-contraband list; had this new code been adopted, Germany could have imported enormous quantities from this country, instead of being compelled to reinforce her scanty supply by robbing housewives of their kitchen utensils, buildings of their hardware, and church steeples of their bells. Germany's constant scramble for rubber formed a diverting episode in the struggle; there are indeed few things so indispensable in modern warfare; yet the Declaration included rubber among the innocent articles and thus opened up to Germany the world's supply. But the most serious matter was that the Declaration would have prevented Great Britain from keeping foodstuffs out of the Fatherland.

When Mr. Bryan, therefore, blandly asked Great Britain to accept the Declaration as its code of maritime warfare, he was asking that country to accept a document which Great Britain, in peace time, had repudiated and which would, in all probability, have caused that country to lose the war. The substance of this request was bad enough, but the language in which it was phrased made, matters much worse. It appears that only the intervention of Colonel House prevented the whole thing from becoming a tragedy.

From Edward M. House

115 East 53rd Street,
New York City.
October 3, 1914.

HIS EXCELLENCY,
  The American Ambassador, London, England.

DEAR PAGE:

  . . . I have just returned from Washington where I was with the President for nearly four days. He is looking well and is well. Sometimes his spirits droop, but then, again, he is his normal self.

  I had the good fortune to be there at a time when the discussion of the Declaration of London had reached a critical stage. Bryan was away and Lansing, who had not mentioned the matter to Sir Cecil,[1] prepared a long communication to you which he sent to the President for approval. The President and I went over it and I strongly urged not sending it until I could have a conference with Sir Cecil. I had this conference the next day without the knowledge of any one excepting the President, and had another the day following. Sir Cecil told me that if the dispatch had gone to you as written and you had shown it to Sir Edward Grey, it would almost have been a declaration of war; and that if, by any chance, the newspapers had got hold of it as they so often get things from our State Department, the greatest panic would have prevailed. He said it would have been the Venezuela incident magnified by present conditions.

  At the President's suggestion, Lansing then prepared a

---

[1] Sir Cecil Spring Rice, British Ambassador at Washington.

cablegram to you. This, too, was objectionable and the President and I together softened it down into the one you received.

Faithfully yours,
E. M. HOUSE.

In justice to Mr. Lansing, a passage in a later letter of Colonel House must be quoted: "It seems that Lansing did not write the particular dispatch to you that was objected to. Someone else prepared it and Lansing rather too hastily submitted it to the President, with the result you know."

This suppressed communication is probably for ever lost, but its tenor may perhaps be gathered from instructions which were actually sent to the Ambassador about this time. After eighteen typewritten pages of not too urbanely expressed discussion of the Declaration of London and the general subject of contraband, Page was instructed to call the British Government's attention to the consequences which followed shipping troubles in previous times. It is hard to construe this in any other way than as a threat to Great Britain of a repetition of 1812:

Confidential. You will not fail to impress upon His Excellency[1] the gravity of the issues which the enforcement of the Order in Council seems to presage, and say to him in substance as follows:

It is a matter of grave concern to this Government that the particular conditions of this unfortunate war should be considered by His Britannic Majesty's Government to be such as to justify them in advancing doctrines and advocating practices which in the past aroused strong opposition on the part of the Government of the United

[1] Sir Edward Grey.

States, and bitter feeling among the American people. This Government feels bound to express the fear, though it does so reluctantly, that the publicity, which must be given to the rules which His Majesty's Government announce that they intend to enforce, will awaken memories of controversies, which it is the earnest desire of the United States to forget or to pass over in silence. . . .

Germany, of course, promptly accepted the Declaration, for the suggestion fitted in perfectly with her programme; but Great Britain was not so acquiescent. Four times was Page instructed to ask the British Government to accede unconditionally, and four times did the Foreign Office refuse. Page was in despair. In the following letter he notified Colonel House that if he were instructed again to move in this matter he would resign his ambassadorship.

To Edward M. House

American Embassy, London,
October 22, 1914.

DEAR HOUSE:

This is about the United States and England. Let's get that settled before we try our hands at making peace in Europe.

One of our greatest assets is the friendship of Great Britain, and our friendship is a still bigger asset for her, and she knows it and values it. Now, if either country should be damfool enough to throw this away because old Stone[1] roars in the Senate about something that hasn't happened, then this crazy world would be completely mad

---

[1] Senator William J. Stone, perhaps the leading spokesman of the pro-German cause in the United States Senate. Senator Stone represented Missouri, a state with a large German-American element.

all round, and there would be no good-will left on earth at all.

The case is plain enough to me. England is going to keep war-materials out of Germany as far as she can. We'd do it in her place. Germany would do it. Any nation would do it. That's all she has declared her intention of doing. And, if she be let alone, she'll do it in a way to give *us* the very least annoyance possible; for she'll go any length to keep our friendship and good will. And *she has not confiscated a single one of our cargoes even of unconditional contraband.* She has stopped some of them and bought them herself, but confiscated not one. All right; what do we do? We set out on a comprehensive plan to regulate the naval warfare of the world and we up and ask 'em all, "Now, boys, all be good, damn you, and agree to the Declaration of London."

"Yah," says Germany, "if England will."

Now Germany isn't engaged in naval warfare to count, and she never even paid the slightest attention to the Declaration all these years. But she saw that it would hinder England and help her now, by forbidding England to stop certain very important war materials from reaching Germany. "Yah," said Germany. But England said that her Parliament had rejected the Declaration in times of peace and that she could now hardly be expected to adopt it in the face of this Parliamentary rejection. But, to please us, she agreed to adopt it with only two changes.

Then Lansing to the bat:

"No, no," says Lansing, "you've got to adopt it all."

Four times he's made me ask for its adoption, the last time coupled with a proposition that if England would adopt it, she might issue a subsequent proclamation saying that, since the Declaration is contradictory, she will construe it her own way, and the United States will raise no objection!

Then he sends eighteen pages of fine-spun legal arguments (not all sound by any means) against the sections of the English proclamations that have been put forth, giving them a strained and unfriendly interpretation.

In a word, England has acted in a friendly way to us and will so act, if we allow her. But Lansing, instead of trusting to her good faith and reserving all our rights under international law and usage, imagines that he can force her to agree to a code that the Germans now agree to because, in Germany's present predicament, it will be especially advantageous to Germany. Instead of trusting her, he assumes that she means to do wrong and proceeds to try to bind her in advance. He hauls her up and tries her in court—that's his tone.

Now the relations that I have established with Sir Edward Grey have been built up on frankness, fairness and friendship. I can't have relations of any other sort nor can England and the United States have relations of any other sort. This is the place we've got to now. Lansing seems to assume that the way to an amicable agreement is through an angry controversy.

Lansing's method is the trouble. He treats Great Britain, to start with, as if she were a criminal and an opponent. That's the best way I know to cause trouble to American shipping and to bring back the good old days of mutual hatred and distrust for a generation or two. If that isn't playing into the hands of the Germans, what would be? And where's the "neutrality" of this kind of action?

See here: If we let England go on, we can throw the whole responsibility on her and reserve all our rights under international law and usage and claim damages (and get

'em) for every act of injury, if acts of injury occur; and
we can keep her friendship and good-will. Every other
neutral nation is doing that. Or we can insist on regulating all naval warfare and have a quarrel and refer it to a
Bryan-Peace-Treaty Commission and claim at most the
selfsame damages with a less chance to get 'em. We can
get damages without a quarrel; or we can have a quarrel
and probably get damages. Now, why, in God's name,
should we provoke a quarrel?

The curse of the world is little men who for an imagined
small temporary advantage throw away the long growth
of good-will nurtured by wise and patient men and who
cannot see the lasting and far greater future evil they do.
Of all the years since 1776 this great war-year is the worst
to break the 100 years of our peace, or even to ruffle it.
I pray you, good friend, get us out of these incompetent
lawyer-hands.

Now about the peace of Europe. Nothing can yet be
done, perhaps nothing now can ever be done by us. The
Foreign Office doubts our wisdom and prudence since
Lansing came into action. The whole atmosphere is
changing. One more such move and they will conclude
that Dernburg and Bernstorff have seduced us—without
our knowing it, to be sure; but their confidence in our
judgment will be gone. God knows I have tried to keep
this confidence intact and our good friendship secure.
But I have begun to get despondent over the outlook since
the President telegraphed me that Lansing's proposal
would settle the matter. I still believe he did not understand it—he couldn't have done so. Else he could not
have approved it. But that tied my hands. If Lansing
again brings up the Declaration of London—after four
flat and reasonable rejections—I shall resign. I will not
be the instrument of a perfectly gratuitous and ineffective

insult to this patient and fair and friendly government and people who in my time have done us many kindnesses and never an injury but Carden,[1] and who sincerely try now to meet our wishes. It would be too asinine an act ever to merit forgiveness or ever to be forgotten. I should blame myself the rest of my life. It would grieve Sir Edward more than anything except this war. It would knock the management of foreign affairs by this Administration into the region of sheer idiocy. I'm afraid any peace talk from us, as it is, would merely be whistling down the wind. If we break with England—not on any case or act of violence to our shipping—but on a useless discussion, in advance, of general principles of conduct during the war—just for a discussion—we've needlessly thrown away our great chance to be of some service to this world gone mad. If Lansing isn't stopped, that's what he will do. Why doesn't the President see Spring Rice? Why don't you take him to see him?

Good night, my good friend. I still have hope that the President himself will take this in hand.

Yours always,

W. H. P.

The letters and the cablegrams which Page was sending to Colonel House and the State Department at this time evidently ended the matter. By the middle of October the two nations were fairly deadlocked. Sir Edward Grey's reply to the American proposal had been an acceptance of the Declaration of London with certain modifications. For the list of contraband in the Declaration he had submitted the list already adopted by Great Britain in its Order in Council, and he had also rejected that article which made it impossible for Great Britain

---

[1]See Chapter VII.

to apply the doctrine of "continuous voyage" to conditional contraband. The modified acceptance, declared Mr. Lansing, was a practical rejection—as of course it was, and as it was intended to be. So the situation remained for several exciting weeks, the State Department insisting on the Declaration in full, precisely as the legal luminaries had published it five years before, the Foreign Office courteously but inflexibly refusing to accede. Only the cordial personal relations which prevailed between Grey and Page prevented the crisis from producing the most disastrous results. Finally, on October 17th, Page proposed by cable an arrangement which he hoped would settle the matter. This was that the King should issue a proclamation accepting the Declaration with practically the modifications suggested above, and that a new Order in Council should be issued containing a new list of contraband. Sir Edward Grey was not to ask the American Government to accept this proclamation; all that he asked was that Washington should offer no objections to it. It was proposed that the United States at the same time should publish a note withdrawing its suggestion for the adoption of the Declaration, and explaining that it proposed to rest the rights of its citizens upon the existing rules of international law and the treaties of the United States. This solution was accepted. It was a defeat for Mr. Lansing, of course, but he had no alternative. The relief that Page felt is shown in the following memorandum,[1] written soon after the tension had ceased:

"That insistence on the Declaration entire came near to upsetting the whole kettle of fish. It put on me the task of insisting on a general code—which would have

---

[1] This memorandum, considerably revised, was included in a letter to the President.

prevented the British from putting on their contraband
list, several of the most important war materials—accompanied by a proposal that would have angered every neutral nation through which supplies can possibly reach
Germany and prevented this Government from making
friendly working arrangements with them; and after Sir
Edward Grey had flatly declined for these reasons, I had
to continue to insist. I confess it did look as if we were determined to dictate to him how he should conduct the war
—and in a way that distinctly favoured the Germans.

"I presented every insistence; for I should, of course,
not have been excusable if I had failed in any case vigorously to carry out my instructions. But every time I
plainly saw matters getting worse and worse; and I should
have failed of my duty also if I had not so informed the
President and the Department. I can conceive of no
more awkward situation for an Ambassador or for any
other man under Heaven. I turned the whole thing over
in my mind backward and forward a hundred times every
day. For the first time in this stress and strain, I lost
my appetite and digestion and did not know the day of
the week nor what month it was—seeing the two governments rushing toward a very serious clash, which would
have made my mission a failure and done the Administration much hurt, and have sowed the seeds of bitterness
for generations to come.

"One day I said to Anderson (whose assistance is in
many ways invaluable): 'Of course nobody is infallible—
least of all we. Is it possible that we are mistaken? You
and Laughlin and I, who are close to it all, are absolutely
agreed. But may there not be some important element in
the problem that we do not see? Summon and nurse
every doubt that you can possibly muster up of the cor-
rectness of our view, put yourself on the defensive. recall

every mood you may have had of the slightest hesitation, and tell me to-morrow of every possible weak place there may be in our judgment and conclusions.' The next day Anderson handed me seventeen reasons why it was unwise to persist in this demand for the adoption of the Declaration of London. Laughlin gave a similar opinion. I swear I spent the night in searching every nook and corner of my mind and I was of the same opinion the next morning. There was nothing to do then but the most unwelcome double duty: (1) Of continuing to carry out instructions, at every step making a bad situation worse and running the risk of a rupture (which would be the only great crime that now remains uncommitted in the world); and (2) of trying to persuade our own Government that this method was the wrong method to pursue. I know it is not my business to make policies, but I conceive it to be my business to report when they fail or succeed. Now if I were commanded to look throughout the whole universe for the most unwelcome task a man may have, I think I should select this. But, after all, a man has nothing but his own best judgment to guide him; and, if he follow that and fail—that's all he *can* do. I do reverently thank God that we gave up that contention. We *may* have trouble yet, doubtless we shall, but it will not be trouble of our own making, as that was.

"Tyrrell[1] came into the reception room at the Foreign Office the day after our withdrawal, while I was waiting to see Sir Edward Grey, and he said: 'I wish to tell you personally—just privately between you and me—how infinite a relief it is to us all that your Government has withdrawn that demand. We couldn't accept it; our refusal was not stubborn nor pig-headed: it was a physical necessity in order to carry on the war with any hope of success.'

[1] Private secretary to Sir Edward Grey.

Then, as I was going out, he volunteered this remark: 'I make this guess—that that programme was not the work of the President but of some international prize court enthusiast (I don't know who) who had failed to secure the adoption of the Declaration when parliaments and governments could discuss it at leisure and who hoped to jam it through under the pressure of war and thus get his prize court international.' I made no answer for several reasons, one of which is, I do not know whose programme it was. All that I know is that I have here, on my desk at my house, a locked dispatch book half full of telegrams and letters insisting on it, which I do not wish (now at least) to put in the Embassy files, and the sight of which brings the shuddering memory of the worst nightmare I have ever suffered.

"Now we can go on, without being a party to any general programme, but in an independent position vigorously stand up for every right and privilege under law and usage and treaties; and we have here a government that we can deal with frankly and not (I hope) in a mood to suspect us of wishing to put it at a disadvantage for the sake of a general code or doctrine. A land and naval and air and submarine battle (the greatest battle in the history of the belligerent race of man) within 75 miles of the coast of England, which hasn't been invaded since 1066 and is now in its greatest danger since that time; and this is no time I fear, to force a great body of doctrine on Great Britain. God knows I'm afraid some American boat will run on a mine somewhere in the Channel or the North Sea. There's war there as there is on land in Germany. Nobody tries to get goods through on land on the continent, and they make no complaints that commerce is stopped. Everybody tries to ply the Channel and the North Sea as usual, both of which have German and English mines and torpedo craft and submarines almost as thick as batteries along the hostile camps on land. The British Government (which now issues marine insurance) will not insure a British boat to carry food to Holland en route to the starving Belgians; and I hear that no government and no insurance company will write insurance for anything going across the North Sea. I wonder if the extent and ferocity and danger of this war are fully realized in the United States?

"There is no chance yet effectively to talk of peace.[1] The British believe that their civilization and their Empire are in grave danger. They are drilling an army of a million men here for next spring; more and more troops come from all the Colonies, where additional enlistments are going on. They feel that to stop before a decisive result is reached would simply be provoking another war, after a period of dread such as they have lived through the last ten years; a large and increasing proportion of the letters you see are on black-bordered paper and this whole island is becoming a vast hospital and prisoners' camp— all which, so far from bringing them to think of peace, urges them to renewed effort; and all the while the bitterness grows.

"The Straus incident[1] produced the impression here that it was a German trick to try to shift the responsibility of continuing the war, to the British shoulders. Mr. Sharp's bare mention of peace in Paris caused the French censor to forbid the transmission of a harmless interview; and our insistence on the Declaration left, for the time being at least, a distinct distrust of our judgment and perhaps even of our good-will. It was suspected—I am

[1]The reference is to an attempt by Germany to start peace negotiations in September, 1914, after the Battle of the Marne. This is described in the next chapter.

sure—that the German influence in Washington had unwittingly got influence over the Department. The atmosphere (toward me) is as different now from what it was a week ago as Arizona sunshine is from a London fog, as much as to say, 'After all, perhaps, you don't *mean* to try to force us to play into the hands of our enemies!' "

III

And so this crisis was passed; it was the first great service that Page had rendered the cause of the Allies and his own country. Yet shipping difficulties had their more agreeable aspects. Had it not been for the fact that both Page and Grey had an understanding sense of humour, neutrality would have proved a more difficult path than it actually was. Even amid the tragic problems with which these two men were dealing there was not lacking an occasional moment's relaxation into the lighter aspect of things. One of the curious memorials preserved in the British Foreign Office is the cancelled $15,000,000 check with which Great Britain paid the *Alabama* claims. That the British should frame this memento of their great diplomatic defeat and hang it in the Foreign Office is an evidence of the fact that in statesmanship, as in less exalted matters, the English are excellent sportsmen. The real justification of the honour paid to this piece of paper, of course, is that the settlement of the *Alabama* claims by arbitration signalized a great forward step in international relations and did much to heal a century's troubles between the United States and Great Britain. Sir Edward Grey used frequently to call Page's attention to this document. It represented the amount of money, then considered large, which Great Britain had paid the United States for the depredations on American shipping for which she was responsible during the Civil War.

One day the two men were discussing certain detentions of American cargoes—high-handed acts which, in Page's opinion, were unwarranted. Not infrequently, in the heat of discussion, Page would get up and pace the floor. And on this occasion his body, as well as his mind, was in a state of activity. Suddenly his eye was attracted by the framed Alabama check. He leaned over, peered at it intensely, and then quickly turned to the Foreign Secretary:

"If you don't stop these seizures, Sir Edward, some day you'll have your entire room papered with things like that!"

Not long afterward Sir Edward in his turn scored on Page. The Ambassador called to present one of the many State Department notes. The occasion was an embarrassing one, for the communication was written in the Department's worst literary style. It not infrequently happened that these notes, in the form in which Page received them, could not be presented to the British Government; they were so rasping and undiplomatic that Page feared that he would suffer the humiliation of having them returned, for there are certain things which no self-respecting Foreign Office will accept. On such occasions it was the practice of the London Embassy to smooth down the language before handing the paper to the Foreign Secretary. The present note was one of this kind; but Page, because of his friendly relations with Grey, decided to transmit the communication in its original shape.

Sir Edward glanced over the document, looked up, and remarked, with a twinkle in his eye,—

"This reads as though they thought that they are still talking to George the Third."

The roar of laughter that followed was something quite

unprecedented amid the thick and dignified walls of the Foreign Office.

One of Page's most delicious moments came, however, after the Ministry of Blockade had been formed, with Lord Robert Cecil in charge. Lord Robert was high minded and conciliatory, but his knowledge of American history was evidently not without its lapses. One day, in discussing the ill-feeling aroused in the United States by the seizure of American cargoes, Page remarked banteringly:

"You must not forget the Boston Tea Party, Lord Robert."

The Englishman looked up, rather puzzled.

"But you must remember, Mr. Page, that I have never been in Boston. I have never attended a tea party there."

It has been said that the tact and good sense of Page and Grey, working sympathetically for the same end, avoided many an impending crisis. The trouble caused early in 1915 by the ship *Dacia* and the way in which the difficulty was solved, perhaps illustrate the value of this coöperation at its best. In the early days of the War Congress passed a bill admitting foreign ships to American registry. The wisdom and even the "neutrality" of such an act were much questioned at the time. Colonel House, in one of his early telegrams to the President, declared that this bill "is full of lurking dangers." Colonel House was right. The trouble was that many German merchant ships were interned in American harbours, fearing to put to sea, where the watchful British warships lay waiting for them. Any attempt to place these vessels under the American flag, and to use them for trade between American and German ports, would at once cause a crisis with the Allies, for such a paper change in ownership would be altogether too transparent. Great Britain viewed this legislation with disfavour, but did not think it politic to protest such transfers generally; Spring Rice contented himself with informing the State Department that his government would not object so long as this changed status did not benefit Germany. If such German ships, after being transferred to the American flag, engaged in commerce between American ports and South American ports, or other places remotely removed from the Fatherland, Great Britain would make no difficulty. The *Dacia*, a merchantman of the Hamburg-America line, had been lying at her wharf in Port Arthur, Texas, since the outbreak of the war. In early January, 1915, she was purchased by Mr. E. N. Breitung, of Marquette, Michigan. Mr. Breitung caused great excitement in the newspapers when he announced that he had placed the *Dacia* under American registry, according to the terms of this new law, had put upon her an American crew, and that he proposed to load her with cotton and sail for Germany. The crisis had now arisen which the well-wishers of Great Britain and the United States had so dreaded. Great Britain's position was a difficult one. If it acquiesced, the way would be opened for placing under American registry all the German and Austrian ships that were then lying unoccupied in American ports and using them in trade between the United States and the Central Powers. If Great Britain seized the *Dacia*, then there was the likelihood that this would embroil her with the American Government—and this would serve German purposes quite as well.

Sir Cecil Spring Rice, the British Ambassador at Washington, at once notified Washington that the *Dacia* would be seized if she sailed for a German port. The cotton which she intended to carry was at that time not contraband, but the vessel itself was German and was thus subject to apprehension as enemy property. The seriousness of this position was that technically the *Dacia* was now an American ship, for an American citizen owned her, she carried an American crew, she bore on her flagstaff the American flag, and she had been admitted to American registry under a law recently passed by Congress. How could the United States sit by quietly and permit this seizure to take place? When the *Dacia* sailed on January 23rd the excitement was keen; the voyage had obtained a vast amount of newspaper advertising, and the eyes of the world were fixed upon her. German sympathizers attributed the attitude of the American Government in permitting the vessel to sail as a "dare" to Great Britain, and the fact that Great Britain had announced her intention of taking up this "dare" made the situation still more tense.

When matters had reached this pass Page one day dropped into the Foreign Office.

"Have you ever heard of the British fleet, Sir Edward?" he asked.

Grey admitted that he had, though the question obviously puzzled him.

"Yes," Page went on musingly. "We've all heard of the British fleet. Perhaps we have heard too much about it. Don't you think it's had too much advertising?"

The Foreign Secretary looked at Page with an expression that implied a lack of confidence in his sanity.

"But have you ever heard of the French fleet?" the American went on. "France has a fleet too, I believe."

Sir Edward granted that.

"Don't you think that the French fleet ought to have a little advertising?"

"What on earth are you talking about?"

"Well," said Page, "there's the *Dacia*. Why not let the French fleet seize it and get some advertising?"

A gleam of understanding immediately shot across Grey's face. The old familiar twinkle came into his eye.

"Yes," he said, "why not let the Belgian royal yacht seize it?"

This suggestion from Page was one of the great inspirations of the war. It amounted to little less than genius. By this time Washington was pretty wearied of the *Dacia*, for mature consideration had convinced the Department that Great Britain had the right on its side. Washington would have been only too glad to find a way out of the difficult position into which it had been forced, and this Page well understood. But this government always finds itself in an awkward plight in any controversy with Great Britain, because the hyphenates raise such a noise that it has difficulty in deciding such disputes upon their merits. To ignore the capture of this ship by the British would have brought all this hullabaloo again about the ears of the Administration. But the position of France is entirely different; the memories of Lafayette and Rochambeau still exercise a profound spell on the American mind; France does not suffer from the persecution of hyphenate populations, and Americans will stand even outrages from France without getting excited. Page knew that if the British seized the *Dacia*, the cry would go up in certain quarters for immediate war, but that, if France committed the same crime, the guns of the adversary would be spiked. It was purely a case of sentiment and "psychology." And so the event proved. His suggestion was at once acted on; a French cruiser went out into the Channel, seized the offending ship, took it into port, where a French prize court promptly condemned it. The proceeding did not cause even a ripple of hostility. The *Dacia* was sold to Frenchmen, rechristened the *Yser* and put to work in the Mediterranean trade. The episode was closed in the latter part of 1915 when a German submarine torpedoed the vessel and sent it to the bottom.

Such was the spirit which Page and Sir Edward Grey brought to the solution of the shipping problems of 1914–1917. There is much more to tell of this great task of "waging neutrality," and it will be told in its proper place. But already it is apparent to what extent these two men served the cause of English-speaking civilization. Neither would quibble or uphold an argument which he thought unjust, even though his nation might gain in a material sense, and neither would pitch the discussion in any other key than forbearance and mutual accommodation and courtliness. For both men had the same end in view. They were both thinking, not of the present, but of the coming centuries. The coöperation of the two nations in meeting the dangers of autocracy and Prussian barbarism, in laying the foundations of a future in which peace, democracy, and international justice should be the directing ideas of human society— such was the ultimate purpose at which these two statesmen aimed. And no men have ever been more splendidly justified by events. The Anglo-American situation of 1914 contained dangers before which all believers in real progress now shudder. Had Anglo-American diplomacy been managed with less skill and consideration, the United States and Great Britain would have become involved in a quarrel beside which all their previous differences would have appeared insignificant. Mutual hatreds and hostilities would have risen that would have prevented the entrance of the United States into the war on the side of the Allies. It is not inconceivable that the history of 1812 would have been repeated, and that the men and resources of this country might have been used to support purposes which have always been hateful to the American conscience. That the world was saved from this calamity is owing largely to the fact that Great Britain had in its Foreign Office a man who was always solving temporary irritations with his eyes constantly fixed upon a great goal, and that the United States had as ambassador in London a man who had the most exalted view of the mission of his country, who had dedicated his life to the worldwide spread of the American ideal, and who believed that an indispensable part of this work was the maintenance of a sympathetic and helpful coöperation with the English-speaking peoples.

CHAPTER XIII

GERMANY'S FIRST PEACE DRIVES

THE Declaration of London was not the only problem that distracted Page in these early months of the war. Washington's apparent determination to make peace also added to his daily anxieties. That any attempt to end hostilities should have distressed so peace-loving and humanitarian a statesman as Page may seem surprising; it was, however, for the very reason that he was a man of peace that these Washington endeavours caused him endless worry. In Page's opinion they indicated that President Wilson did not have an accurate understanding of the war. The inspiring force back of them, as the Ambassador well understood, was a panic-stricken Germany. The real purpose was not a peace, but a truce; and the cause which was to be advanced was not democracy but Prussian absolutism. Between the Battle of the Marne and the sinking of the *Lusitania* four attempts were made to end the war; all four were set afoot by Germany. President Wilson was the man to whom the Germans appealed to rescue them from their dilemma. It is no longer a secret that the Germans at this time regarded their situation as a tragic one; the success that they had anticipated for forty years had proved to be a disaster. The attempt to repeat the great episodes of 1864, 1866, and 1870, when Prussia had overwhelmed Denmark, Austria, and France in three brief campaigns, had ignominiously failed. Instead of beholding a conquered Europe at her feet, Germany awoke from her illusion to find

398

herself encompassed by a ring of resolute and powerful foes. The fact that the British Empire, with its immense resources, naval, military, and economic, was now leading the alliance against them, convinced the most intelligent Germans that the Fatherland was face to face with the greatest crisis in its history.

Peace now became the underground Germanic programme. Yet the Germans did not have that inexorable respect for facts which would have persuaded them to accept terms to which the Allies could consent. The military oligarchy were thinking not so much of saving the Fatherland as of saving themselves; a settlement which would have been satisfactory to their enemies would have demanded concessions which the German people, trained for forty years to expect an unparalleled victory, would have regarded as a defeat. The collapse of the militarists and of Hohenzollernism would have ensued. What the German oligarchy desired was a peace which they could picture to their deluded people as a triumph, one that would enable them to extricate themselves at the smallest possible cost from what seemed a desperate position, to escape the penalties of their crimes, to emerge from their failure with a Germany still powerful, both in economic resources and in arms, and to set to work again industriously preparing for a renewal of the struggle at a more favourable time. If negotiations resulted in such a truce, the German purpose would be splendidly served; even if they failed, however, the gain for Germany would still be great. Germany could appear as the belligerent which desired peace and the Entente could perhaps be manœuvred into the position of the side responsible for continuing the war. The consideration which was chiefly at stake in these tortuous proceedings was public opinion in the United States. Americans do not yet understand the extent to which their country was regarded as the determining power. Both the German and the British Foreign Offices clearly understood, in August, 1914, that the United States, by throwing its support, especially its economic support, to one side or the other, could settle the result. Probably Germany grasped this point even more clearly than did Great Britain, for, from the beginning, she constantly nourished the hope that she could embroil the United States and Great Britain—a calamity which would have given victory to the German arms. In every German move there were thus several motives, and one of the chief purposes of the subterranean campaigns which she now started for peace was the desire of putting Britain in the false light of prolonging the war for aggressive purposes, and thus turning to herself that public opinion in this country which was so outspoken on the side of the Allies. Such public opinion, if it could be brought to regard Germany in a tolerant spirit, could easily be fanned into a flame by the disputes over blockades and shipping, and the power of the United States might thus be used for the advancement of the Fatherland. On the other hand, if Germany could obtain a peace which would show a profit for her tremendous effort, then the negotiations would have accomplished their purpose.

Conditions at Washington favoured operations of this kind. Secretary Bryan was an ultra-pacifist; like men of one idea, he saw only the fact of a hideous war, and he was prepared to welcome anything that would end hostilities. The cessation of bloodshed was to him the great purpose to be attained: in the mind of Secretary Bryan it was more important that the war should be stopped than that the Allies should win. To President Wilson the European disaster appeared to be merely a selfish struggle for power, in which both sides were almost equally to blame. He never accepted Page's obvious interpretation that the single cause was Germany's determination to embark upon a war of world conquest. From the beginning, therefore, Page saw that he would have great difficulty in preventing intervention from Washington in the interest of Germany, yet this was another great service to which he now unhesitatingly directed his efforts.

The Ambassador was especially apprehensive of these peace moves in the early days of September, when the victorious German armies were marching on Paris. In London, as in most parts of the world, the capture of the French capital was then regarded as inevitable. September 3, 1914, was one of the darkest days in modern times. The population of Paris was fleeing southward; the Government had moved its headquarters to Bordeaux; and the moment seemed to be at hand when the German Emperor would make his long anticipated entry into the capital of France. It was under these circumstances that the American Ambassador to Great Britain sent the following cablegram directly to the President:

To the President

American Embassy, London,
Sep. 3, 4 A. M.

Everybody in this city confidently believes that the Germans, if they capture Paris, will make a proposal for peace, and that the German Emperor will send you a message declaring that he is unwilling to shed another drop of blood. Any proposal that the Kaiser makes will be simply the proposal of a conqueror. His real purpose will be to preserve the Hohenzollern dynasty and the imperial bureaucracy. The prevailing English judgment is that, if Germany be permitted to stop hostilities, the war will have accomplished nothing. There is a determination here to destroy utterly the German bureaucracy, and Englishmen are prepared to sacrifice themselves to any extent in men and money. The preparations that are being made here are for a long war; as I read the disposition and the character of Englishmen they will not stop until they have accomplished their purpose. There is a general expression of hope in this country that neither the American Government nor the public opinion of our country will look upon any suggestion for peace as a serious one which does not aim, first of all, at the absolute destruction of the German bureaucracy.

From such facts as I can obtain, it seems clear to me that the opinion of Europe—excluding of course, Germany—is rapidly solidifying into a severe condemnation of the German Empire. The profoundest moral judgment of the world is taking the strongest stand against Germany and German methods. Such incidents as the burning of Louvain and other places, the slaughter of civilian populations, the outrages against women and children—outrages of such a nature that they cannot be printed, but which form a matter of common conversation everywhere—have had the result of arousing Great Britain to a mood of the grimmest determination.

PAGE.

This message had hardly reached Washington when the peace effort of which it warned the President began to take practical form. In properly estimating these manœuvres it must be borne in mind that German diplomacy always worked underground and that it approached its negotiations in a way that would make the other side appear as taking the initiative. This was a phase of German diplomatic technique with which every European Foreign Office had long been familiar. Count Bern-storff arrived in the United States from Germany in the latter part of August, evidently with instructions from his government to secure the intercession of the United States. There were two unofficial men in New York who were ideally qualified to serve the part of intermediaries. Mr. James Speyer had been born in New York; he had received his education at Frankfort-on-the-Main, Germany, and had spent his apprenticeship also in the family banking house in that city. As the head of an American banking house with important German affiliations, his interests and sympathies were strong on the side of the Fatherland; indeed, he made no attempt to conceal his strong pro-Germanism.

Mr. Oscar S. Straus had been born in Germany; his father had been a German revolutionist of 'Forty-eight; like Carl Schurz, Abraham Jacobi, and Franz Sigel, he had come to America to escape Prussian militarism and the Prussian autocracy, and his children had been educated in a detestation of the things for which the German Empire stood. Mr. Oscar Straus was only two years old when he was brought to this country, and he had given the best evidences of his Americanism in a distinguished public career. Three times he had served the United States as Ambassador to Turkey; he had filled the post of Secretary of Commerce and Labour in President Roosevelt's cabinet, and had held other important public commissions. Among his other activities, Mr. Straus had played an important part in the peace movement of the preceding quarter of a century and he had been a member of the Permanent Court of Arbitration at The Hague. Mr. Straus was on excellent terms with the German, the British, and the French ambassadors at Washington. As far back as 1888, when he was American

Minister at Constantinople, Bernstorff, then a youth, was an attaché at the German Embassy; the young German was frequently at the American Legation and used to remind Mr. Straus, whenever he met him in later years, how pleasantly he remembered his hospitality. With Sir Cecil Spring Rice, the British Ambassador, and M. Jules Jusserand, the French Ambassador, Mr. Straus had also become friendly in Constantinople and in Washington. This background, and Mr. Straus's well-known pro-British sentiments, would have made him a desirable man to act as a liaison agent between the Germans and the Allies, but there were other reasons why this ex-ambassador would be useful at this time. Mr. Straus had been in Europe at the outbreak of the war; he had come into contact with the British statesmen in those exciting early August days; in particular he had discussed all phases of the conflict with Sir Edward Grey, and before leaving England, he had given certain interviews which the British statesmen declared had greatly helped their cause in the United States. Of course, the German Government knew all about these activities.

On September 4th, Mr. Straus arrived at New York on the *Mauretania*. He had hardly reached this country when he was called upon the telephone by Mr. Speyer, a friend of many years' standing. Count Bernstorff, the German Ambassador, Mr. Speyer said, was a guest at his country home, Waldheim, at Scarboro, on the Hudson; Mr. Speyer was giving a small, informal dinner the next evening, Saturday, September 5th, and he asked Mr. and Mrs. Straus to come. The other important guests were Mr. Frank A. Vanderlip, president of the National City Bank, and Mrs. Vanderlip. Mr. Straus accepted the invitation, mentally resolving that he would not discuss the war himself, but merely listen. It would

certainly have been a difficult task for any man to avoid
this subject on this particular evening; the battle of the
Marne was raging and the thoughts of two continents
were centered on the tremendous events then taking place
in France. That this gathering around Mr. Speyer's
dinner table should have taken place on the evening of
September 5, the day that the Germans suddenly stopped
their progress towards Paris, and began retreating, the
British and the French armies in pursuit, gives it an additional interest, though it is not likely that this change in
the fortunes of Germany could have been known to
Count Bernstorff and the other guests.

Of course the war became the immediate topic of discussion. Count Bernstorff at once plunged into the
usual German point of view—that Germany did not want
war in the first place, that the Entente had forced the
issue, and the like.

"The Emperor and the German Government stood
for peace," he said.

Naturally, a man who had spent a considerable part of
his life promoting the peace cause pricked up his ears at
this statement.

"Does that sentiment still prevail in Germany?"
asked Mr. Straus.

"Yes," replied the German Ambassador.

"Would your government entertain a proposal for
mediation now?" asked Mr. Straus.

"Certainly," Bernstorff promptly replied. He hastened to add, however, that he was speaking unofficially.
He had had no telegraphic communication from Berlin
for five days, and therefore could not definitely give the
attitude of his government. But he was quite sure that
the Kaiser would be glad to have President Wilson take
steps to end the war.

The possibility that he might play a part in bringing hostilities to a close now occurred to Mr. Straus. He had come to the dinner determined to avoid the subject altogether, but Count Bernstorff had precipitated the issue in a way that left the American no option. Certainly Mr. Straus would have been derelict if he had not reported this conversation to the high quarters for which Count Bernstorff had evidently intended it.

"That is a very important statement you have made, Mr. Ambassador," said Mr. Straus, measuring every word. "May I make use of it?"

"Yes."

"May I use it in any way I choose?"

"You may," replied Bernstorff.

Mr. Straus saw in this acquiescent mood a chance to appeal directly to President Wilson.

"Do you object to my laying this matter before our government?"

"No, I do not."

Mr. Straus glanced at his watch; it was 10:15 o'clock.

"I think I shall go to Washington at once—this very night. I can get the midnight train."

Mr. Speyer, who has always maintained that this proceeding was casual and in no way promoted by himself and Bernstorff, put in a word of caution.

"I would sleep on it," he suggested.

But, in a few moments, Mr. Straus was speeding in his automobile through Westchester County in the direction of the Pennsylvania Station. He caught the express, and, the next morning, which was Sunday the sixth, he was laying the whole matter before Secretary Bryan at the latter's house. Naturally, Mr. Bryan was overjoyed at the news; he at once summoned Bernstorff from New York to Washington, and went over the suggestion personally. The German Ambassador repeated the statements which he had made to Mr. Straus—always guardedly qualifying his remarks by saying that the proposal had not come originally from him but from his American friend. Meanwhile Mr. Bryan asked Mr. Straus to discuss the matter with the British and French ambassadors.

The meeting took place at the British Embassy. The two representatives of the Entente, though only too glad to talk the matter over, were more skeptical about the attitude of Bernstorff than Mr. Bryan had been.

"Of course, Mr. Straus," said Sir Cecil Spring Rice, "you know that this dinner was arranged purposely so that the German Ambassador could meet you?"

Mr. Straus demurred at this statement, but the Englishman smiled.

"Do you suppose," Sir Cecil asked, "that any ambassador would make such a statement as Bernstorff made to you without instructions from his government?"

"You and M. Jusserand," replied the American, "have devoted your whole lives to diplomacy with distinguished ability and you can therefore answer that question better than I."

"I can assure you," replied M. Jusserand, "that no ambassador under the German system would dare for a moment to make such a statement without being authorized to do so."

"The Germans," added Sir Cecil, "have a way of making such statements unofficially and then denying that they have ever made them."

Both the British and French ambassadors, however, thought that the proposal should be seriously considered.

"If it holds out one chance in a hundred of lessening

the length of the war, we should entertain it," said Ambassador Jusserand.

"I certainly hope that you will entertain it cordially," said Mr. Straus.

"Not cordially—that is a little too strong."

"Well, sympathetically?"

"Yes, sympathetically," said M. Jusserand, with a smile.

These facts were at once cabled to Page, who took the matter up with Sir Edward Grey. A despatch from the latter to the British Ambassador in Washington gives a splendid summary of the British attitude on such approaches at this time.

Sir Edward Grey to Sir Cecil Spring Rice

Foreign Office,
September 9, 1914.

SIR:

The American Ambassador showed me to-day a communication that he had from Mr. Bryan. It was to the effect that Mr. Straus and Mr. Speyer had been talking with the German Ambassador, who had said that, though he was without instructions, he thought that Germany might be disposed to end the war by mediation. This had been repeated to Mr. Bryan, who had spoken to the German Ambassador, and had heard the same from him. Mr. Bryan had taken the matter up, and was asking direct whether the German Emperor would accept mediation if the other parties who were at war would do the same.

The American Ambassador said to me that this information gave him a little concern. He feared that, coming after the declaration that we had signed last week with France and Russia about carrying on the war in common,[1] the peace parties in the United States might be given the impression that Germany was in favour of peace, and that the responsibility for continuing the war was on others.

I said that the agreement that we had made with France and Russia was an obvious one; when three countries were at war on the same side, one of them could not honourably make special terms for itself and leave the others in the lurch. As to mediation, I was favourable to it in principle, but the real question was: On what terms could the war be ended? If the United States could devise anything that would bring this war to an end and prevent another such war being forced on Europe I should welcome the proposal.

The Ambassador said that before the war began I had made suggestions for avoiding it, and that these suggestions had been refused.

I said that this was so, but since the war began there were two further considerations to be borne in mind: We were fighting to save the west of Europe from being dominated by Prussian militarism; Germany had prepared to the day for this war, and we could not again have a great military power in the middle of Europe preparing war in this way and forcing it upon us; and the second thing was that cruel wrong had been done to Belgium, for which there should be some compensation. I had no indication whatever that Germany was prepared to make any reparation to Belgium, and, while repeating that in principle I was favourable to mediation, I could see nothing to do but to wait for the reply of the German Emperor to the question that Mr. Bryan had put to him

---

[1] On September 5, 1914, Great Britain, France, and Russia signed the Pact of London, an agreement which bound the three powers of the Entente to make war and peace as a unit. Each power specifically pledged itself not to make a separate peace.

and for the United States to ascertain on what terms Germany would make peace if the Emperor's reply was favourable to mediation.

The Ambassador made it quite clear that he regarded what the German Ambassador had said as a move in the game. He agreed with what I had said respecting terms of peace, and that there seemed no prospect at present of Germany being prepared to accept them.

I am, &c.,

E. GREY.

A letter from Page to Colonel House gives Page's interpretation of this negotiation:

To Edward M. House

London, September 10, 1914.

MY DEAR HOUSE:

A rather serious situation has arisen: The Germans of course thought that they would take Paris. They were then going to propose a conqueror's terms of peace, which they knew would not be accepted. But they would use their so-called offer of peace purely for publicity purposes. They would say, "See, men of the world, we want peace; we offer peace; the continuance of this awful war is not our doing." They are using Hearst for this purpose. I fear they are trying to use so good a man as Oscar Straus. They are fooling the Secretary.

Every nation was willing to accept Sir Edward Grey's proposals but Germany. She was bent on a war of conquest. Now she's likely to get licked—lock, stock and barrel. She is carrying on a propaganda and a publicity campaign all over the world. The Allies can't and won't accept any peace except on the condition that German militarism be uprooted. They are not going to live again under that awful shadow and fear. They say truly that life on such terms is not worth living. Moreover, if Germany should win the military control of Europe, she would soon—that same war-party—attack the United States. The war will not end until this condition can be imposed—that there shall be no more militarism.

But in the meantime, such men as Straus (a good fellow) may be able to let (by helping) the Germans appear to the Peace people as really desiring peace. Of course, what they want is to save their mutton.

And if we begin mediation talk now on that basis, we shall not be wanted when a real chance for mediation comes. If we are so silly as to play into the hands of the German-Hearst publicity bureau, our chance for real usefulness will be thrown away.

Put the President on his guard.

W. H. P.

In the latter part of the month came Germany's reply. One would never suspect, when reading it, that Germany had played any part in instigating the negotiation. The Kaiser repeated the old charges that the Entente had forced the war on the Fatherland, that it was now determined to annihilate the Central Powers and that consequently there was no hope that the warring countries could agree upon acceptable terms for ending the struggle.

So ended Germany's first peace drive, and in the only possible way that it could end. But the Washington administration continued to be most friendly to mediation. A letter of Colonel House's, dated October 4, 1914, possesses great historical importance. It was written after a detailed discussion with President Wilson, and it indicates not only the President's desire to bring the struggle to a close, but it describes in some detail the principles which the President then regarded as essential to a permanent peace. It furnishes the central idea of the presidential policy for the next four years; indeed, it contains the first statement of that famous "Article X" of the Covenant of the League of Nations which was Mr. Wilson's most important contribution to that contentious document. This was the article which pledges the League "to respect and preserve as against external aggression the territorial integrity and existing political independence" of all its members; it was the article which, more than any other, made the League obnoxious to Americans, who interpreted it as an attempt to involve them perpetually in the quarrels of Europe; and it was the one section of the Treaty of Versailles which was most responsible for the rejection of that document by the United States Senate. There are other suggestions in Colonel House's letter which apparently bore fruit in the League Covenant. It is somewhat astonishing that a letter of Colonel House's, written as far back as October 3, 1914, two months after the outbreak of the war, should contain "Article X" as one of the essential terms of peace, as well as other ideas afterward incorporated in that document, accompanied by an injunction that Page should present the suggestion to Sir Edward Grey:

From Edward M. House

115 East 53rd Street,
New York City.
October 3rd, 1914.

DEAR PAGE:

Frank [the Ambassador's son] has just come in and has given me your letter of September 22nd[1] which is of ab-

¹Published in Chapter XI, page 327.

sorbing interest.   You have never done anything better than this letter, and some day, when you give the word, it must be published.   But in the meantime, it will repose in the safe deposit box along with your others and with those of our great President.

I have just returned from Washington where I was with the President for nearly four days.   He is looking well and is well.   Sometimes his spirits droop, but then again, he is his normal self.

Before I came from Prides[1] I was fearful lest Straus, Bernstorff, and others would drive the President into doing something unwise.   I have always counselled him to remain quiet for the moment and let matters unfold themselves further.   In the meantime, I have been conferring with Bernstorff, with Dumba,[2] and, of course, Spring Rice.   The President now wants me to keep in touch with the situation, and I do not think there is any danger of any one on the outside injecting himself into it unless Mr. Bryan does something on his own initiative.

Both Bernstorff and Dumba say that their countries are ready for peace talks, but the difficulty is with England.   Sir Cecil says their statements are made merely to place England in a false position.

The attitude, I think, for England to maintain is the one which she so ably put forth to the world.   That is, peace must come only upon condition of disarmament and must be permanent.   I have a feeling that Germany will soon be willing to discuss terms.   I do not agree that Germany has to be completely crushed and that terms must be made either in Berlin or London.   It is manifestly against England's interest and the interest of

---

[1] Colonel House's summer home in Massachusetts.

[2] Ambassador from Austria-Hungary to the United States.

Europe generally for Russia to become the dominating military force in Europe, just as Germany was. The dislike which England has for Germany should not blind her to actual conditions. If Germany is crushed, England cannot solely write the terms of peace, but Russia's wishes must also largely prevail.

With Russia strong in militarism, there is no way by which she could be reached. Her government is so constituted that friendly conversations could not be had with her as they might be had even with such a power as Germany, and the world would look forward to another cataclysm and in the not too distant future.

When peace conversations begin, at best, they will probably continue many months before anything tangible comes from them. England and the Allies could readily stand on the general proposition that only enduring peace will satisfy them and I can see no insuperable obstacle in the way.

The Kaiser did not want war and was not responsible for it further than his lack of foresight which led him to build up a formidable engine of war which later dominated him. Peace cannot be made until the war party in Germany find that their ambitions cannot be realized, and this, I think, they are beginning to know.

When the war is ended and the necessary territorial alignments made, it seems to me, the best guaranty of peace could be brought by every nation in Europe guaranteeing the territorial integrity of every other nation.[1] By confining the manufacture of arms to the governments themselves and by permitting representatives of all nations to inspect, at any time, the works.[2]

---

[1] This, with certain modifications is Article 10 of the Covenant of the League of Nations.

[2] There is a suggestion of these provisions in Article 8 of the League Covenant.

Then, too, all sources of national irritation should be removed so what at first may be a sore spot cannot grow into a malignant disease.[1] It will not be too difficult, I think, to bring about an agreement that will insure permanent peace, provided all the nations of Europe are honest in their desire for it.

I am writing this to you with the President's knowledge and consent and with the thought that it will be conveyed to Sir Edward. There is a growing impatience in this country because of this war and there is constant pressure upon the President to use his influence to bring about normal conditions. He does not wish to do anything to irritate or offend any one of the belligerent nations, but he has an abiding faith in the efficacy of open and frank discussion between those that are now at war.

As far as I can see, no harm can be done by a dispassionate discussion at this stage, even though nothing comes of it. In a way, it is perhaps better that informal and unofficial conversations are begun and later the principals can take it up themselves.

I am sure that Sir Edward is too great a man to let any prejudices deter him from ending, as soon as possible, the infinite suffering that each day of war entails.

Faithfully yours,

E. M. HOUSE.

It is apparent that the failure of this first attempt at mediation discouraged neither Bernstorff nor the Washington administration. Colonel House was constantly meeting the German and the British Ambassadors; he was also, as his correspondence shows, in touch with Zimmermann, the German Under Foreign Secretary. The German desire for peace grew stronger in the autumn

---

[1] Article 11 of the League Covenant reflects the influence of this idea.

and winter of 1914–1915, as the fact became more and more clear that Great Britain was summoning all her resources for the greatest effort in her history, as the stalemate on the Aisne more and more impressed upon the German chieftains the impossibility of obtaining any decision against the French Army, and as the Russians showed signs of great recuperation after the disaster of Tannenberg. By December 4th Washington had evidently made up its mind to move again.

From Edward M. House

115 East 53rd Street,
New York City,
December 4th, 1914.

DEAR PAGE:

The President desires to start peace parleys at the very earliest moment, but he does not wish to offend the sensibilities of either side by making a proposal before the time is opportune. He is counting upon being given a hint, possibly through me, in an unofficial way, as to when a proffer from him will be acceptable.

Pressure is being brought upon him to offer his services again, for this country is suffering, like the rest of the neutral world, from the effects of the war, and our people are becoming restless.

Would you mind conveying this thought delicately to Sir Edward Grey and letting me know what he thinks?

Would the Allies consider parleys upon a basis of indemnity for Belgium and a cessation of militarism? If so, then something may be begun with the Dual Alliance.

I have been told that negotiations between Russia and Japan were carried on several months before they agreed to meet at Portsmouth. The havoc that is being wrought in human lives and treasure is too great to permit racial feeling or revenge to enter into the thoughts of those who govern the nations at war.

I stand ready to go to Germany at any moment in order to sound the temper of that government, and I would then go to England as I did last June.

This nation would not look with favour upon a policy that held nothing but the complete annihilation of the enemy.

Something must be done sometime, by somebody, to initiate a peace movement, and I can think of no way, at the moment, than the one suggested.

I will greatly appreciate your writing me fully and freely in regard to this phase of the situation.

Faithfully yours,

E. M. HOUSE.

To this Page immediately replied:

To Edward M. House

December 12th, 1914.

MY DEAR HOUSE:

The English rulers have no feeling of vengeance. I have never seen the slightest traces of that. But they are determined to secure future safety. They will not have this experience repeated if they can help it. They realize now that they have been living under a sort of fear—or dread—for ten years: they sometimes felt that it was bound to come some time and then at other times they could hardly believe it. And they will spend all the men and all the money they have rather than suffer that fear again or have that danger. Now, if anybody could fix a basis for the complete restoration of Belgium, so far as restoration is possible, and for the elimination of militarism, I am sure the *English* would talk on that basis.

But there are two difficulties—Russia wouldn't talk till she has Constantinople, and I haven't found anybody who can say exactly what you mean by the "elimination of militarism." Disarmament? England will have her navy to protect her incoming bread and meat. How, then, can she say to Germany, "You can't have an army"?

You say the Americans are becoming "restless." The plain fact is that the English people, and especially the English military and naval people, don't care a fig what the Americans think and feel. They say, "We're fighting their battle, too—the battle of democracy and freedom from bureaucracy—why don't they come and help us in our life-and-death struggle?" I have a drawer full of letters saying this, not one of which I have ever answered. The official people never say that of course— nor the really responsible people, but a vast multitude of the public do. This feeling comes out even in the present military and naval rulers of this Kingdom—comes indirectly to me. A part of the public, then, and the military part of the Cabinet, don't longer care for American opinion and they resent even such a reference to peace as the President made in his Message to Congress.[1] But the civil part of the Cabinet and the responsible and better part of the public do care very much. The President's intimation about peace, however, got no real response here. They think he doesn't understand the meaning of the war. They don't want war; they are not a warlike people. They don't hate the Germans. There is no feeling of vengeance. They constantly say: "Why

---

[1]From the President's second message to Congress, December 8, 1914: "It is our dearest present hope that this character and reputation may presently, in God's providence, bring us an opportunity, such as has seldom been vouchsafed any nation, to counsel and obtain peace in the world and reconciliation and a healing settlement of many a matter that has cooled and interrupted the friendship of nations."

do the Germans hate us? We don't hate them." But, since Germany set out to rule the world and to conquer Great Britain, they say, "We'll all die first." That's "all there is to it." And they will all die unless they can so fix things that this war cannot be repeated. Lady K—, as kindly an old lady as ever lived, said to me the other day: "A great honour has come to us. Our son has been killed in battle, fighting for the safety of England."

Now, the question which nobody seems to be able to answer is this: How can the military party and the military spirit of Germany be prevented from continuing to prepare for the conquest of Great Britain and from going to work to try it again? That implies a change in the form, spirit, and control of the German Empire. If they keep up a great army, they will keep it up with that end more or less in view. If the military party keeps in power, they will try it again in twenty-five or forty years. This is all that the English care about or think about.

They don't see how it is to be done themselves. All they see yet is that they must show the Germans that they can't whip Great Britain. If England wins decisively the English hope that somehow the military party will be overthrown in Germany and that the Germans, under peaceful leadership, will go about their business—industrial, political, educational, etc.—and quit dreaming of and planning for universal empire and quit maintaining a great war-machine, which at some time, for some reason, must attack somebody to justify its existence. This makes it difficult for the English to make overtures to or to receive overtures from this military war-party which now *is* Germany. But, if it be possible so completely to whip the war party that it will somehow be thrown out of power at home—that's the only way they now see out of it. To patch up a peace, leaving the

German war party in power, they think, would be only to invite another war.

If you can get over this point, you can bring the English around in ten minutes. But they are not going to take any chances on it. Read English history and English literature about the Spanish Armada or about Napoleon. They are acting those same scenes over again, having the same emotions, the same purpose: nobody must invade or threaten England. "If they do, we'll spend the last man and the last shilling. We value," they say truly, "the good-will and the friendship of the United States more than we value anything except our own freedom, but we'll risk even that rather than admit copper to Germany, because every pound of copper prolongs the war."

There you are. I've blinked myself blind and talked myself hoarse to men in authority—from Grey down—to see a way out—without keeping this intolerable slaughter up to the end. But they stand just where I tell you.

And the horror of it no man knows. The news is suppressed. Even those who see it and know it do not realize it. Four of the crack regiments of this kingdom --regiments that contained the flower of the land and to which it was a distinction to belong—have been practically annihilated, one or two of them annihilated twice. Yet their ranks are filled up and you never hear a murmur. Presently it'll be true that hardly a title or an estate in England will go to its natural heir—the heir has been killed. Yet, not a murmur; for England is threatened with invasion. They'll all die first. It will presently be true that more men will have been killed in this war than were killed before in all the organized wars since the Christian era began. The English are willing and eager to stop it if things can be so fixed that there will be no military power in Europe that wishes or prepares to attack and invade England.

I've had many one-hour, two-hour, three-hour talks with Sir Edward Grey. He sees nothing further than I have written. He says to me often that if the United States could see its way to cease to protest against stopping war materials from getting into Germany, they could end the war more quickly—all this, of course, informally; and I say to him that the United States will consider any proposal you will make that does not infringe on a strict neutrality. Violate a rigid neutrality we will not do. And, of course, he does not ask that. I give him more trouble than all the other neutral Powers combined; they all say this. And, on the other side, his war-lord associates in the Cabinet make his way hard.

So it goes—God bless us, it's awful. I never get away from it—war, war, war every waking minute, and the worry of it; and I see no near end of it. I've had only one thoroughly satisfactory experience in a coon's age, and this was this: Two American ships were stopped the other day at Falmouth. I telegraphed the captains to come here to see me. I got the facts from them—all the facts. I telephoned Sir Edward that I wished to see him at once. I had him call in one of his ship-detaining committee. I put the facts on the table. I said, "By what right, or theory of right, or on what excuse, are those ships stopped? They are engaged in neutral commerce. They fly the American flag." One of them was released that night—no more questions asked. The other was allowed to go after giving bond to return a lot of kerosene which was loaded at the bottom of the ship.

If I could get facts, I could do many things. The State Department telegraphs me merely what the shipper says —a partial statement. The British Government tells me (after infinite delay) another set of facts. The British Government says, "We're sorry, but the Prize Court must decide." Our Government wires a dissertation on International Law—Protest, protest: (I've done nothing else since the world began!) One hour with a sensible ship captain does more than a month of cross-wrangling with Government Departments.

I am trying my best, God knows, to keep the way as smooth as possible; but neither government helps me. Our Government merely sends the shipper's ex-parte statement. This Government uses the Navy's excuse. . . .

At present, I can't for the life of me see a way to peace, for the one reason I have told you. The Germans wish to whip England, to invade England. They started with their army toward England. Till that happened England didn't have an army. But I see no human power that can give the English now what they are determined to have—safety for the future—till some radical change is made in the German system so that they will no longer have a war-party any more than England has a war-party. England surely has no wish to make conquest of Germany. If Germany will show that she has no wish to make conquest of England, the war would end to-morrow.

What impresses me through it all is the backwardness of all the Old World in realizing the true aims of government and the true methods. I can't see why any man who has hope for the progress of mankind should care to live anywhere in Europe. To me it is all infinitely sad. This dreadful war is a logical outcome of their condition, their thought, their backwardness. I think I shall never care to see the continent again, which of course is committing suicide and bankruptcy. When my natural term of service is done here, I shall go home with more joy than you can imagine. That's the only home for a man who wishes his horizon to continue to grow wider. All this for you and me only—nobody else.

Heartily yours,

WALTER H. PAGE.

Probably Page thought that this statement of the case —and it was certainly a masterly statement—would end any attempt to get what he regarded as an unsatisfactory and dangerous peace. But President Wilson could not be deterred from pressing the issue. His conviction was firm that this winter of 1914–1915 represented the most opportune time to bring the warring nations to terms, and it was a conviction from which he never departed. After the sinking of the *Lusitania* the Administration gazed back regretfully at its frustrated attempts of the preceding winter, and it was inclined to place the responsibility for this failure upon Great Britain and France. "The President's judgment," wrote Colonel House on August 4, 1915, three months after the *Lusitania* went down, "was that last autumn was the time to discuss peace parleys, and we both saw present possibilities. War is a great gamble at best, and there was too much at stake in this one to take chances. I believe if one could have started peace parleys in November, we could have forced the evacuation of both France and Belgium, and finally forced a peace which would have eliminated militarism on land and sea. The wishes of the Allies were heeded with the result that the war has now fastened itself upon the vitals of Europe and what the end may be is beyond the knowledge of man."

This shows that the efforts which the Administration was making were not casual or faint-hearted, but that they represented a most serious determination to bring hostilities to an end. This letter and the correspondence which now took place with Page also indicate the general terms upon which the Wilson Administration believed that the mighty differences could be composed. The ideas which Colonel House now set forth were probably more the President's than his own; he was merely the intermediary in their transmission. They emphasized Mr. Wilson's conviction that a decisive victory on either side would be a misfortune for mankind. As early as August, 1914, this was clearly the conviction that underlay all others in the President's interpretation of events. His other basic idea was that militarism should come to an end "on land and sea"; this could mean nothing except that Germany was expected to abandon its army and that Great Britain was to abandon its navy.

From Edward M. House

115 East 53rd Street,
New York City.
January 4th, 1915.

DEAR PAGE:

I believe the Dual Alliance is thoroughly ready for peace and I believe they would be willing to agree upon terms England would accept provided Russia and France could be satisfied.

They would, in my opinion, evacuate both Belgium and France and indemnify the former, and they would, I think, be willing to begin negotiations upon a basis looking to permanent peace.

It would surprise me if the Germans did not come out in the open soon and declare that they have always been for peace, that they are for peace now, and that they are willing to enter into a compact which would insure peace for all time; that they have been misrepresented and maligned and that they leave the entire responsibility for the continuation of the war with the Allies.

If they should do this, it would create a profound impression, and if it was not met with sympathy by the Allies, the neutral sentiment, which is now almost wholly against the Germans, would veer toward them.

Will you not convey this thought to Sir Edward and let me know what he says?

The President is willing and anxious for me to go to England and Germany as soon as there is anything tangible to go on, and whenever my presence will be welcome. The Germans have already indicated this feeling but I have not been able to get from Spring Rice any expression from his Government.

As I told you before, the President does not wish to offend the sensibilities of any one by premature action, but he is, of course, enormously interested in initiating at least tentative conversations.

Will you not advise me in regard to this?

Faithfully yours,

E. M. HOUSE.

From Edward M. House

115 East 53rd Street,
New York City.
January 18, 1915.

DEAR PAGE:

The President has sent me a copy of your confidential dispatch No. 1474, January 15th.

The reason you had no information in regard to what General French mentioned was because no one knew of it outside of the President and myself and there was no safe way to inform you.

As a matter of fact, there has been no direct proposal

made by anybody. I have had repeated informal talks with the different ambassadors and I have had direct communication with Zimmermann, which has led the President and me to believe that peace conversations may be now initiated in an unofficial way.

This is the purpose of my going over on the *Lusilania*, January 30th. When I reach London I will be guided by circumstances as to whether I shall go next to France or Germany.

The President and I find that we are going around in a circle in dealing with the representatives in Washington, and he thinks it advisable and necessary to reach the principals direct. When I explain just what is in the President's mind, I believe they will all feel that it was wise for me to come at this time.

I shall not write more fully for the reason I am to see you so soon.

I am sending this through the kindness of Sir Horace Plunkett.

Faithfully yours,

E. M. HOUSE.

P. S. We shall probably say, for public consumption, that I am coming to look into relief measures, and see what further can be done. Of course, no one but you and Sir Edward must know the real purpose of my visit.

Why was Colonel House so confident that the Dual Alliance was prepared at this time to discuss terms of peace? Colonel House, as his letter shows, was in communication with Zimmermann, the German Under Foreign Secretary. But a more important approach had just been made, though information bearing on this had not been sent to Page. The Kaiser had asked President Wilson to transmit to Great Britain a suggestion for making peace on the basis of surrendering Belgium and of paying for its restoration. It seems incredible that the Ambassador should not have been told of this, but Page learned of the proposal from Field Marshal French, then commanding the British armies in the field, and this accounts for Colonel House's explanation that, "the reason you had no information, in regard to what General French mentioned was because no one knew of it outside of the President and myself and there was no safe way to inform you." Page has left a memorandum which explains the whole strange proceeding—a paper which is interesting not only for its contents, but as an illustration of the unofficial way in which diplomacy was conducted in Washington at this time:

Field Marshal Sir John French, secretly at home from his command of the English forces in France, invited me to luncheon. There were his especially confidential friend Moore, the American who lives with him, and Sir John's private secretary. The military situation is this: a trench stalemate in France. Neither army has made appreciable progress in three months. Neither can advance without a great loss of men. Neither is whipped. Neither can conquer. It would require a million more men than the Allies can command and a very long time to drive the Germans back across Belgium. Presently, if the Russians succeed in driving the Germans back to German soil, there will be another trench stalemate there. Thus the war wears a practically endless outlook so far as military operations are concerned. Germany has plenty of men and plenty of food for a long struggle yet; and, if she use all the copper now in domestic use in the Empire, she will probably have also plenty of ammunition for a long struggle. She is not nearly at the end of her rope either in a military or an economic sense.

What then? The Allies are still stronger—so long as they hold together as one man. But is it reasonable to assume that they can? And, even if they can, is it worth while to win a complete victory at such a cost as the lives of practically all the able-bodied men in Europe? But can the Allies hold together as one man for two or three or four years? Well, what are we going to do? And here came the news of the lunch. General French informed me that the President had sent to England, at the request of the Kaiser, a proposal looking toward peace, Germany offering to give up Belgium and to pay for its restoration.

"This," said Sir John, "is their fourth proposal."

"And," he went on, "if they will restore Belgium and give Alsace-Lorraine to France and Constantinople will go to Russia, I can't see how we can refuse it."

He scouted the popular idea of "crushing out militarism" once for all. It would be desirable, even if it were not necessary, to leave Germany as a first-class power. We couldn't disarm her people forever. We've got to leave her and the rest to do what they think they must do; and we must arm ourselves the best we can against them.

Now—did General French send for me and tell me this just for fun and just because he likes me? He was very eager to know my opinion whether this peace offer were genuine or whether it was a trick of the Germans to—publish it later and thereby to throw the blame for continuing the war on England?

It occurs to me as possible that he was directed to tell me what he told, trusting to me, in spite of his protestations of personal confidence, etc., to get it to the President. Assuming that the President sent the Kaiser's message to the King, this may be a suggested informal answer—that if the offer be extended to give France and Russia what they want, it will be considered, etc. This may or may not be true. Alas! the fact that I know nothing about the offer has no meaning; for the State Department never informs me of anything it takes up with the British Ambassador in Washington. Well, I'll see.

These were therefore the reasons why Colonel House had decided to go to Europe and enter into peace negotiations with the warring powers. Colonel House was wise in taking all possible precautions to conceal the purpose of this visit. His letter intimates that the German Government was eager to have him cross the ocean on this particular mission; it discloses, on the other hand, that the British Government regarded the proposed negotiations with no enthusiasm. Sir Edward Grey and Mr. Asquith would have been glad to end hostilities on terms that would permanently establish peace and abolish the vices which were responsible for the war, and they were ready to welcome courteously the President's representative and discuss the situation with him in a fair-minded spirit. But they did not believe that such an enterprise could serve a useful purpose. Possibly the military authorities, as General French's remarks to Page may indicate, did not believe that either side could win a decisive victory, but this was not the belief of the British public itself. The atmosphere in England at that time was one of confidence in the success of British arms and of suspicion and distrust of the British Government. A strong expectation prevailed in the popular mind, that the three great Powers of the Entente would at an early date destroy the menace which had enshrouded Europe for forty years, and there was no intention of giving Germany a breathing spell during which she could regenerate her forces to resume the onslaught.

In the winter of 1915 Great Britain was preparing for the naval attack on the Dardanelles, and its success was regarded as inevitable. Page had an opportunity to observe the state of optimism which prevailed in high British circles. In March of 1915 he was visiting the Prime Minister at Walmer Castle; one afternoon Mr. Asquith took him aside, informed him of the Dardanelles preparations and declared that the Allies would have possession of Constantinople in two weeks. The Prime Minister's attitude was not one of hope; it was one of confidence. The capture of Constantinople, of course, would have brought an early success to the allied army on all fronts.[1] This was the mood that was spurring on the British public to its utmost exertions, and, with such a determination prevailing everywhere, a step in the direction of peace was the last thing that the British desired; such a step could have been interpreted only as an attempt to deprive the Allies of their victory and as an effort to assist Germany in escaping the consequences of her crimes. Combined with this stout popular resolve, however, there was a lack of confidence in the Asquith ministry. An impression was broadcast that it was pacifist, even "defeatist," in its thinking, and that it harboured a weak humanitarianism which was disposed to look gently even upon the behaviour of the Prussians. The masses suspected that the ministry would welcome a peace with Germany which would mean little more than a cessation of hostilities and which would leave the great problems of the war unsolved. That this opinion was unjust, that, on the contrary, the British Foreign Office was steadily resisting all attempts to end the

---

[1] The opening of the Dardanelles would have given Russian agricultural products access to the markets of the world and thus have preserved the Russian economic structure. It would also have enabled the Entente to munition the Russian Army. With a completely equipped Russian Army in the East and the Entente Army in the West, Germany could not long have survived the pressure.

war on an unsatisfactory basis, Page's correspondence, already quoted, abundantly proves, but this unreasoning belief did prevail and it was an important element in the situation.   This is the reason why the British Cabinet regarded Colonel House's visit at that time with positive alarm.   It feared that, should the purpose become known, the British public and press would conclude that the Government had invited a peace discussion.   Had any such idea seized the popular mind in February and March, 1915, a scandal would have developed which would probably have caused the downfall of the Asquith Ministry. "Don't fool yourself about peace," Page writes to his son Arthur, about this time.   "If any one should talk about peace, or doves, or ploughshares here, they'd shoot him."

Colonel House reached London early in February and was soon in close consultation with the Prime Minister and Sir Edward Grey.   He made a great personal success; the British statesmen gained a high regard for his disinterestedness and his general desire to serve the cause of decency among nations; but he made little progress in his peace plans, simply because the facts were so discouraging and so impregnable.   Sir Edward repeated to him what he had already said to Page many times: that Great Britain was prepared to discuss a peace that would really safeguard the future of Europe, but was not prepared to discuss one that would merely reinstate the régime that had existed before 1914.   The fact that the Germans were not ready to accept such a peace made discussion useless.   Disappointed at this failure, Colonel House left for Berlin.   His letters to Page show that the British judgment of Germany was not unjust and that the warnings which Page had sent to Washington were based on facts:

From Edward M. House

Embassy of the United States of America,
Berlin, Germany,
March 20, 1915.

DEAR PAGE:

I arrived yesterday morning and I saw Zimmermann[1] almost immediately. He was very cordial and talked to me frankly and sensibly.

I tried to bring about a better feeling toward England, and told him how closely their interests touched at certain points. I also told him of the broad way in which Sir Edward was looking at the difficult problems that confronted Europe, and I expressed the hope that this view would be reciprocated elsewhere, so that, when the final settlement came, it could be made in a way that would be to the advantage of mankind.

The Chancellor is out of town for a few days and I shall see him when he returns. I shall also see Ballin, Von Gwinner, and many others. I had lunch yesterday with Baron von Wimpsch who is a very close friend of the Emperor.

Zimmermann said that it was impossible for them to make any peace overtures, and he gave me to understand that, for the moment, even what England would perhaps consent to now, could not be accepted by Germany, to say nothing of what France had in mind.

I shall hope to establish good relations here and then go somewhere and await further developments. I even doubt whether more can be done until some decisive military result is obtained by one or other of the belligerents.

[1]German Under Foreign Secretary.

I will write further if there is any change in the situation. I shall probably be here until at least the 27th.

Faithfully yours,
E. M. House.

From Edward M. House

Embassy of the United States of America,
Berlin, Germany.
March 26, 1915.

Dear Page:

While I have accomplished here much that is of value, yet I leave sadly disappointed that no direct move can be made toward peace.

The Civil Government are ready, and upon terms that would at least make an opening. There is also a large number in military and naval circles that I believe would be glad to begin parleys, but the trouble is mainly with the people. It is a very dangerous thing to permit a people to be misled and their minds inflamed either by the press, by speeches, or otherwise.

In my opinion, no government could live here at this time if peace was proposed upon terms that would have any chance of acceptance. Those in civil authority that I have met are as reasonable and fairminded as their counterparts in England or America, but, for the moment, they are impotent.

I hear on every side the old story that all Germany wants is a permanent guaranty of peace, so that she may proceed upon her industrial career undisturbed.

I have talked of the second convention,[1] and it has been cordially received, and there is a sentiment here, as well as

---

[1] It was the Wilson Administration's plan that there should be two peace gatherings, one of the belligerents to settle the war, and the other of belligerents and neutrals, to settle questions of general importance growing out of the war. This latter is what Colonel House means by "the second convention."

elsewhere, to make settlement upon lines broad enough to prevent a recurrence of present conditions.

There is much to tell you verbally, which I prefer not to write.

Faithfully yours,

E. M. HOUSE.

Colonel House's next letter is most important, for it records the birth of that new idea which afterward became a ruling thought with President Wilson and the cause of almost endless difficulties in his dealings with Great Britain. The "new phase of the situation" to which he refers is "the Freedom of the Seas" and this brief note to Page, dated March 27, 1915, contains the first reference to this idea on record. Indeed, it is evident from the letter itself that Colonel House made this notation the very day the plan occurred to him.

From Edward M. House

Embassy of the United States of America,
Berlin, Germany.
March 27, 1915.

DEAR PAGE:

I have had a most satisfactory talk with the Chancellor. After conferring with Stovall,[1] Page,[2] and Willard,[3] I shall return to Paris and then to London to discuss with Sir Edward a phase of the situation which promises results.

I did not think of it until to-day and have mentioned it to both the Chancellor and Zimmermann, who have received it cordially, and who join me in the belief that it may be the first thread to bridge the chasm.

---

[1]Mr. Pleasant A. Stovall, American Minister to Switzerland.

[2]Mr. Thomas Nelson Page, American Ambassador to Italy.

[3]Mr. Joseph E. Willard, American Ambassador to Spain.

I am writing hastily, for the pouch is waiting to be closed.

Faithfully yours,

E. M. HOUSE.

The "freedom of the seas" was merely a proposal to make all merchant shipping, enemy and neutral, free from attack in time of war. It would automatically have ended all blockades and all interference with commerce. Germany would have been at liberty to send all her merchant ships to sea for undisturbed trade with all parts of the world in war time as in peace, and, in future, navies would be used simply for fighting. Offensively, their purpose would be to bombard enemy fortifications, to meet enemy ships in battle, and to convoy ships which were transporting troops for the invasion of enemy soil; defensively, their usefulness would consist in protecting the homeland from such attacks and such invasions. Perhaps an argument can be made for this new rule of warfare, but it is at once apparent that it is the most startling proposal brought forth in modern times in the direction of disarmament. It meant that Great Britain should abandon that agency of warfare with which she had destroyed Napoleon, and with which she expected to destroy Germany in the prevailing struggle—the blockade. From a defensive standpoint, Colonel House's proposed reform would have been a great advantage to Britain, for an honourable observance of the rule would have insured the British people its food supply in wartime. With Great Britain, however, the blockade has been historically an offensive measure: it is the way in which England has always made war. Just what reception this idea would have had with official London, in April, 1915, had Colonel House been able to present it as his own proposal, is not clear, but the Germans, with characteristic stupidity, prevented the American from having a fair chance. The Berlin Foreign Office at once cabled to Count Bernstorff and Bernhard Dernburg —the latter a bovine publicity agent who was then promoting the German cause in the American press—with instructions to start a "propaganda" in behalf of the "freedom of the seas." By the time Colonel House reached London, therefore, these four words had been adorned with the Germanic label. British statesmen regarded the suggestion as coming from Germany and not from America, and the reception was worse than cold.

And another horror now roughly interrupted President Wilson's attempts at mediation. Page's letters have disclosed that he possessed almost a clairvoyant faculty of foreseeing approaching events. The letters of the latter part of April and of early May contain many forebodings of tragedy. "Peace? Lord knows when!" he writes to his son Arthur on May 2nd. "The blowing up of a liner with American passengers may be the prelude. I almost expect such a thing." And again on the same date: "If a British liner full of American passengers be blown up, what will Uncle Sam do? That's what's going to happen."

"We all have the feeling here," the Ambassador writes on May 6th, "that more and more frightful things are about to happen."

The ink on those words was scarcely dry when a message from Queenstown was handed to the American Ambassador. A German submarine had torpedoed and sunk the *Lusitania* off the Old Head of Kinsale, and one hundred and twenty-four American men, women, and children had been drowned.

PART II

Sir Edward Grey (now Viscount Grey of Fallodon), Secretary of
State for Foreign Affairs, 1905-1916

THE LIFE AND LETTERS OF WALTER H. PAGE

CHAPTER XIV

THE "LUSITANIA"—AND AFTER

I

THE news of the *Lusitania* was received at the American Embassy at four o'clock on the afternoon of May 7, 1915. At that time preparations were under way for a dinner in honour of Colonel and Mrs. House; the first *Lusitania* announcement declared that only the ship itself had been destroyed and that all the passengers and members of the crew had been saved; there was, therefore, no good reason for abandoning this dinner.

At about seven o'clock, the Ambassador came home; his manner showed that something extraordinary had taken place; there were no outward signs of emotion, but he was very serious. The first news, he now informed Mrs. Page, had been a mistake; more than one thousand men, women, and children had lost their lives, and more than one hundred of these were American citizens. It was too late to postpone the dinner but that affair was one of the most tragic in the social history of London. The Ambassador was constantly receiving bulletins from his Chancery, and these, as quickly as they were received, he read to his guests. His voice was quiet and subdued; there were no indications of excitement in his manner or in that of his friends, and hardly of suppressed emotion.

The atmosphere was rather that of dumb stupefaction. The news seemed to have dulled everyone's capacity for thought and even for feeling. If any one spoke, it was in whispers. Afterward, in the drawing room, this same mental state was the prevailing one; there was little denunciation of Germany and practically no discussion as to the consequences of the crime; everyone's thought was engrossed by the harrowing and unbelievable facts which the Ambassador was reading from the little yellow slips that were periodically brought in. An irresistible fascination evidently kept everybody in the room; the guests stayed late, eager for every new item. When they finally left, one after another, their manner was still abstracted and they said their good-nights in low voices. There were two reasons for this behaviour. The first was that the Ambassador and his guests had received the details of the greatest infamy which any supposedly civilized state had perpetrated since the massacre of Saint Bartholomew. The second was the conviction that the United States would at once declare war on Germany.

On this latter point several of the guests expressed their ideas and one of the most shocked and outspoken was Colonel House. For a month the President's personal representative had been discussing with British statesmen possible openings for mediation, but all his hopes in this direction now vanished. That President Wilson would act with the utmost energy Colonel House took for granted. This act, he evidently believed, left the United States no option. "We shall be at war with Germany within a month," he declared.

The feeling that prevailed in the Embassy this evening was the one that existed everywhere in London for several days. Emotionally the event acted like an anæsthetic. This was certainly the condition of all Americans associated with the American Embassy, especially Page himself. A day or two after the sinking the Ambassador went to Euston Station, at an early hour in the morning, to receive the American survivors. The hundred or more men and women who shambled from the train made a listless and bedraggled gathering. Their grotesque clothes, torn and unkempt—for practically none had had the opportunity of obtaining a change of dress—their expressionless faces, their lustreless eyes, their uncertain and bewildered walk, faintly reflected an experience such as comes to few people in this world. The most noticeable thing about these unfortunates was their lack of interest in their surroundings; everything had apparently been reduced to a blank; the fact that practically none made any reference to their ordeal, or could be induced to discuss it, was a matter of common talk in London. And something of this disposition now became noticeable in Page himself. He wrote his dispatches to Washington in an abstracted mood; he went through his duties almost with the detachment of a sleep-walker; like the *Lusitania* survivors, he could not talk much at that time about the scenes that had taken place off the coast of Ireland. Yet there were many indications that he was thinking about them, and his thoughts, as his letters reveal, were concerned with more things than the tragedy itself. He believed that his country was now face to face with its destiny. What would Washington do?

Page had a characteristic way of thinking out his problems. He performed his routine work at the Chancery in the daytime, but his really serious thinking he did in his own room at night. The picture is still a vivid one in the recollection of his family and his other intimates. Even at this time Page's health was not good, yet he frequently spent the evening at his office in Grosvenor

Gardens, and when the long day's labours were finished, he would walk rather wearily to his home at No. 6 Grosvenor Square. He would enter the house slowly—and his walk became slower and more tired as the months went by—go up to his room and cross to the fireplace, so apparently wrapped up in his own thoughts that he hardly greeted members of his own family. A wood fire was kept burning for him, winter and summer alike; Page would put on his dressing gown, drop into a friendly chair, and sit there, doing nothing, reading nothing, saying nothing —only thinking. Sometimes he would stay for an hour; not infrequently he would remain till two, three, or four o'clock in the morning; occasions were not unknown when his almost motionless figure would be in this same place at daybreak. He never slept through these nights, and he never even dozed; he was wide awake, and his mind was silently working upon the particular problem that was uppermost in his thoughts. He never rose until he had solved it or at least until he had decided upon a course of action. He would then get up abruptly, go to bed, and sleep like a child. The one thing that made it possible for a man of his delicate frame, racked as it was by anxiety and over work, to keep steadily at his task, was the wonderful gift which he possessed of sleeping.

Page had thought out many problems in this way. The tension caused by the sailing of the *Dacia*, in January, 1915, and the deftness with which the issue had been avoided by substituting a French for a British cruiser, has already been described. Page discovered this solution on one of these all-night self-communings. It was almost two o'clock in the morning that he rose, said to himself, "I've got it!" and then went contentedly to bed. And during the anxious months that followed the *Lusitania*, the *Arabic*, and those other outrages which have now taken their place in history, he spent night after night turning the matter over in his mind. But he found no way out of the humiliations presented by the policy of Washington.

"Here we are swung loose in time," he wrote to his son Arthur, a few days after the first *Lusitania* note had been sent to Germany, "nobody knows the day or the week or the month or the year—and we are caught on this island, with no chance of escape, while the vast slaughter goes on and seems just beginning, and the degradation of war goes on week by week; and we live in hope that the United States will come in, as the only chance to give us standing and influence when the reorganization of the world must begin. (Beware of betraying the word 'hope'!) It has all passed far beyond anybody's power to describe. I simply go on day by day into unknown experiences and emotions, seeing nothing before me very clearly and remembering only dimly what lies behind. I can see only one proper thing: that all the world should fall to and hunt this wild beast down.

"Two photographs of little Mollie[1] on my mantelpiece recall persons and scenes and hopes unconnected with the war: few other things can. Bless the baby, she couldn't guess what a sweet purpose she serves."

The sensations of most Americans in London during this crisis are almost indescribable. Washington's failure promptly to meet the situation affected them with astonishment and humiliation. Colonel House was confident that war was impending, and for this reason he hurried his preparations to leave England; he wished to be in the United States, at the President's side, when the declaration was made. With this feeling about Mr. Wilson,

---
[1] The Ambassador's granddaughter.

Colonel House received a fearful shock a day or two after the *Lusitania* had gone down: while walking in Piccadilly, he caught a glimpse of one of the famous sandwich men, bearing a poster of an afternoon newspaper. This glaring broadside bore the following legend: "We are too proud to fight—Woodrow Wilson." The sight of that placard was Colonel House's first intimation that the President might not act vigorously. He made no attempt to conceal from Page and other important men at the American Embassy the shock which it had given him. Soon the whole of England was ringing with these six words; the newspapers were filled with stinging editorials and cartoons, and the music halls found in the Wilsonian phrase materials for their choicest jibes. Even in more serious quarters America was the subject of the most severe denunciation. No one felt these strictures more poignantly than President Wilson's closest confidant. A day or two before sailing home he came into the Embassy greatly depressed at the prevailing revulsion against the United States. "I feel," Colonel House said to Page, "as though I had been given a kick at every lamp post coming down Constitution Hill." A day or two afterward Colonel House sailed for America.

II

And now came the period of distress and of disillusionment. Three *Lusitania* notes were sent and were evasively answered, and Washington still seemed to be marking time. The one event in this exciting period which gave Page satisfaction was Mr. Bryan's resignation as Secretary of State. For Mr. Bryan personally Page had a certain fondness, but as head of the State Department the Nebraska orator had been a cause of endless vexation. Many of Page's letters, already printed, bear evidence of the utter demoralization which existed in this branch of the Administration and this demoralization became especially glaring during the *Lusitania* crisis. No attempt was made even at this momentous period to keep the London Embassy informed as to what was taking place in Washington; Page's letters and cablegrams were, for the most part, unacknowledged and unanswered, and the American Ambassador was frequently obliged to obtain his information about the state of feeling in Washington from Sir Edward Grey. It must be said, in justice to Mr. Bryan, that this carelessness was nothing particularly new, for it had worried many ambassadors before Page. Readers of Charles Francis Adams's correspondence meet with the same complaints during the Civil War; even at the time of the *Trent* crisis, when for a fortnight Great Britain and the United States were living on the brink of war, Adams was kept entirely in the dark about the plans of Washington.[1] The letters of John Hay show a similar condition during his brief ambassadorship to Great Britain in 1897–1898.[2]

But Mr. Bryan's incumbency was guilty of diplomatic vices which were peculiarly its own. The "leaks" in the State Department, to which Page has already referred, were constantly taking place; the Ambassador would send the most confidential cipher dispatches to his superior, cautioning the Department that they must be held inviolably secret, and then he would pick up the London newspapers the next morning and find that everything had been cabled from Washington. To most readers, the informal method of conducting foreign business, as it is disclosed in these letters, probably comes as something of

[1] "A Cycle of Adams Letters, 1861–1865," edited by Worthington Chauncey Ford. Vol. I, p. 84.

[2] "The Life and Letters of John Hay," by William Roscoe Thayer. Vol. II, p. 166.

a shock. Page is here discovered discussing state matters, not in correspondence with the Secretary of State,
but in private unofficial communications to the President, and especially to Colonel House—the latter at that
time not an official person at all. All this, of course,
was extremely irregular and, in any properly organized
State Department, it would have been even reprehensible.
But the point is that there was no properly organized
State Department at that time, and the impossibility of
conducting business through the regular channels compelled Page to adopt other means. "There is only one
way to reform the State Department," he informed Colonel House at this time. "That is to raze the whole building, with its archives and papers, to the ground, and begin
all over again."

This state of affairs in Washington explains the curious
fact that the real diplomatic history of the United States
and Great Britain during this great crisis is not to be found
in the archives of the State Department, for the official
documents on file there consist of the most routine telegrams, which are not particularly informing, but in the
Ambassador's personal correspondence with the President,
Colonel House, and a few other intimates. The State
Department did not have the first requisite of a properly
organized foreign office, for it could not be trusted with
confidential information. The Department did not tell
Page what it was doing, but it apparently told the whole
world what Page was doing. It is an astonishing fact that
Page could not write and cable the most important details, for he was afraid that they would promptly be given
to the reporters.

"I shall not send another confidential message to the
State Department," Page wrote to Colonel House,

September 15, 1914; "it's too dangerous. Time and time again now the Department has leaked. Last week, I sent a dispatch and I said in the body of it, *'this is confidential and under no condition to be given out or made public, but to be regarded as inviolably secret.'* The very next morning it was telegraphed from Washington to the London newspapers. Bryan telegraphed me that he was sure it didn't get out from the Department and that he now had so fixed it that there could be no leak. He's said that at least four times before. The Department swarms with newspaper men, I hear. But whether it does or not the leak continues. I have to go with my tail between my legs and apologize to Sir Edward Grey and to do myself that shame and to do my very best to keep his confidence— against these unnecessary odds. The only way to be safe is to do the job perfunctorily, to answer the questions the Department sends and to do nothing on your own account. That's the reason so many of our men do their jobs in that way—or *one* reason and a strong one. We can never have an alert and energetic and powerful service until men can trust the Department and until they can get necessary information from it. I wrote the President that of course I'd go on till the war ended and all the questions growing out of it were settled, and that then he must excuse me, if I must continue to be exposed to this danger and humiliation. In the meantime, I shall send all my confidential matter in private letters to him."

Page did not regard Mr. Bryan's opinions and attitudes as a joke: to him they were a serious matter and, in his eyes, Bryan was most interesting as a national menace. He regarded the Secretary as the extreme expression of an irrational sentimentalism that was in danger of undermining the American character, especially as the kind of thought he represented was manifest in many phases of American life.   In a moment of exasperation, Page gave expression to this feeling in a letter to his son:

To Arthur W. Page

London, June 6, 1915.

DEAR ARTHUR:

. . . We're in danger of being feminized and fad-ridden—grape juice (God knows water's good enough: why grape juice?); pensions; Christian Science; peace cranks; efficiency-correspondence schools; aid-your-memory; women's clubs; co-this and co-t'other and coddling in general; Billy Sunday; petticoats where breeches ought to be and breeches where petticoats ought to be; white livers and soft heads and milk-and-water;—I don't want war: nobody knows its horrors or its degradations or its cost.   But to get rid of hyphenated degenerates perhaps it's worth while, and to free us from 'isms and soft folk.   That's the domestic view of it.   As for being kicked by a sauerkraut caste—O Lord, give us backbone!

Heartily yours,

W. H. P.

In the bottom of this note, Page has cut a notch in the paper and against it he has written: "This notch is the place to apply a match to this letter."

"Again and ever I am reminded," Page also wrote in reference to Bryan's resignation, "of the danger of having to do with cranks.   A certain orderliness of mind and conduct seems essential for safety in this short life.   Spiritualists, bone-rubbers, anti-vivisectionists, all sort of anti's in fact, those who have fads about education or fads against it, Perfectionists, Daughters of the Dove of Peace, Sons of the Roaring Torrent, itinerant peace-

mongers—all these may have a real genius among them
once in forty years; but to look for an exception to the
common run of yellow dogs and damfools among them is
like opening oysters with the hope of finding pearls.   It's
the common man we want and the uncommon common
man when we can find him—never the crank.   This is
the lesson of Bryan."

At one time, however, Mr. Bryan's departure seemed
likely to have important consequences for Page.   Colonel
House and others strongly urged the President to call him
home from London and make him Secretary of State.
This was the third position in President Wilson's Cabinet
for which Page had been considered.   The early plans
to make him Secretary of the Interior or Secretary of
Agriculture have already been described.   Of all cabinet
posts, however, the one that would have especially attracted him would have been the Department of State.
But President Wilson believed that the appointment of an
Ambassador at one of the belligerent capitals, especially
of an Ambassador whose sympathies for the Allies were
so pronounced as were Page's, would have been an "unneutral" act, and, therefore, Colonel House's recommendation was not approved.

From Edward M. House

Roslyn, Long Island,
June 25th, 1915.

DEAR PAGE:
The President finally decided to appoint Lansing to
succeed Mr. Bryan.   In my opinion, he did wisely, though
I would have preferred his appointing you.
The argument against your appointment was the fact
that you are an Ambassador at one of the belligerent

capitals. The President did not think it would do, and from what I read, when your name was suggested I take it there would have been much criticism. I am sorry—sorrier than I can tell you, for it would have worked admirably in the general scheme of things.

However, I feel sure that Lansing will do the job, and that you will find your relations with him in every way satisfactory.

The President spent yesterday with me and we talked much of you. He is looking well and feeling so.

I read the President your letter and he enjoyed it as much as I did.

I am writing hastily, for I am leaving for Manchester, Massachusetts, where I shall be during July and August.

Your sincere friend,
E. M. HOUSE.

III

But, in addition to the *Lusitania* crisis, a new terror now loomed on the horizon. Page's correspondence reveals that Bryan had more reasons than one for his resignation; he was now planning to undertake a self-appointed mission to Europe for the purpose of opening peace negotiations entirely on his own account.

From Edward M. House

Manchester, Massachusetts,
August 12th, 1915.

DEAR PAGE:

The Bryans have been stopping with the X's. X writes me that Bryan told him that he intended to go to Europe soon and try peace negotiations. He has Lloyd George in mind in England, and it is then his purpose to go to Germany.

I take it he will want credentials from the President which, of course, he will not want to give, but just what he will feel obliged to give is another story. I anticipated this when he resigned. I knew it was merely a matter of time when he would take this step.

He may find encouragement in Germany, for he is in high favour now in that quarter. It is his purpose to oppose the President upon the matter of "preparedness," and, from what we can learn, it will not be long before there will be open antagonism between the Administration and himself.

It might be a good thing to encourage his going to Europe. He would probably come back a sadder and wiser man. I take it that no one in authority in England would discuss the matter seriously with him, and, in France, I do not believe he could even get a hearing.

Please let me have your impressions upon this subject.

I wish I could be near you to-day for there are so many things I could tell that I cannot write.

Your friend,
E. M. House.

To Edward M. House

American Embassy, London [Undated].

DEAR HOUSE:

Never mind about Bryan. Send him over here if you wish to get rid of him. He'll cut no more figure than a tar-baby at a Negro camp-meeting. If he had come while he was Secretary, I should have jumped off London Bridge and the country would have had one ambassador less. But I shall enjoy him now. You see some peace crank from the United States comes along every week— some crank or some gang of cranks. There've been two this week. Ever since the Daughters of the Dove of

Peace met at The Hague, the game has become popular in America; and I haven't yet heard that a single one has been shot—so far. I think that some of them are likely soon to be hanged, however, because there are signs that they may come also from Germany. The same crowd that supplies money to buy labour-leaders and the press and to blow up factories in the United States keeps a good supply of peace-liars on tap. It'll be fun to watch Bryan perform and never suspect that anybody is lying to him or laughing at him; and he'll go home convinced that he's done the job and he'll let loose doves all over the land till they are as thick as English sparrows. Not even the President could teach him anything permanently. He can do no harm on this side the world. It's only your side that's in any possible danger; and, if I read the signs right, there's a diminishing danger there.

No, there's never yet come a moment when there was the slightest chance of peace. Did the Emperor not say last year that peace would come in October, and again this year in October? Since he said it, how can it come?

The ambitions and the actions of men, my friend, are determined by their antecedents, their surroundings, and their opportunities—the great deeds of men before them whom consciously or unconsciously they take for models, the codes they are reared by, and the chances that they think they see. These influences shaped Alexander and Cæsar, and they shaped you and me. Now every monarch on the Continent has behind him the Napoleonic example. "Can I do that?" crosses the mind of every one. Of course every one thinks of himself as doing it beneficently—for the good of the world. Napoleon, himself, persuaded himself of his benevolent intentions, and the devil of it was he persuaded other people also. Now the only monarch in Europe in our time who thought he had a

chance is your friend in Berlin. When he told you last
year (1914) that of course he didn't want war, but that he
was "ready," that's what he meant. A similar ambition,
of course, comes into the mind of every professional
soldier of the continent who rises to eminence. In Berlin
you have both—the absolute monarch and the military
class of ambitious soldiers and their fighting machine.
Behind these men walks the Napoleonic ambition all the
time, just as in the United States we lie down every night
in George Washington's feather-bed of no entangling
alliances.

Then remember, too, that the German monarchy is a
cross between the Napoleonic ambition and its inheritance
from Frederick the Great and Bismarck. I suppose the
three damnedest liars that were ever born are these
three—old Frederick, Napoleon, and Bismarck—not, I
take it, because they naturally loved lying, but because
the game they played constantly called for lying. There
was no other way to play it: they *had* to fool people all the
time. You have abundant leisure—do this: Read the
whole career of Napoleon and write down the startling
and exact parallels that you will find there to what is
happening to-day. The French were united and patriotic,
just as the Germans now are. When they invaded other
people's territory, they said they were attacked and that
the other people had brought on war. They had their
lying diplomats, their corruption funds; they levied money
on cities and states; they took booty; and they were God's
elect. It's a wonderful parallel—not strangely, because
the game is the same and the moral methods are the same.
Only the tools are somewhat different—the submarine, for
example. Hence the *Lusitania* disaster (not disavowed,
you will observe), the *Arabic* disaster, the propaganda,
underground and above, in the United States. And

there'll be more.   The Napoleonic Wars were about eleven years long.   I fancy that we shall have war and wars from this attempt to dominate Europe, for perhaps as long a period.   The Balkans can't be quieted by this war only, nor Russia and Italy perhaps.   And Germany may have a series of earthquakes herself—internal explosions. Then Poland and perhaps some of the Scandinavian States.   Nobody can tell.

I cannot express my admiration of the President's management, so far at least, of his colossal task of leading us right.   He has shown his supreme wisdom up to this point and I have the profoundest confidence in his judgment.   But I hope he doesn't fool himself about the future; I'm sure he doesn't.   I see no possible way for us to keep out, because I know the ignorance and falseness of the German leaders.   They'll drown or kill more Americans—on the sea and in America.   They *may* at last even attack one of our own passenger ships, or do something that will dramatically reveal them to the whole American people.   Then, of course, the tune will be called.   It's only a question of time; and I am afraid the war will last long enough to give them time.   An early peace is all that can prevent them from driving us at last into war; and I can see no chance of an early peace.   You had as well prepare as fast as the condition of public opinion will permit.

There could be no better measure of the immeasurable moral advance that the United States has made over Europe than the incredulity of our people.   They simply can't comprehend what the Napoleonic legend can do, nor the low political morality of the Continent—of Berlin in particular.   Hence they don't believe it.   We have gone on for 100 years working might and main to better our condition and the condition of people about us—the greatest effort made by the largest number of people since the world began to further the mood and the arts of peace. There is no other such chapter in human history as our work for a hundred years. Yet just a hundred years ago the Capitol at Washington was burned by—a political oligarchy in the freest country of Europe—as damnable an atrocity as you will find in history. The Germans are a hundred years behind the English in political development and political morality.

So, let Willum J. come. He can't hurt Europe—nor help it; and you can spare him. Let all the Peace-gang come. You can spare *them*, too; and they can do no harm here. Let somebody induce Hoke Smith to come, too. You have hit on a great scheme—friendly deportation.

And Bryan won't be alone. Daughters of the Dove of Peace and Sons of the Olive Branch come every week. The latest Son came to see me to-day. He said that the German Chancellor told him that he wanted peace— wants it now and wants it bad, and that only one thing stood in the way—if England would agree not to take Belgium, Germany would at once make peace! This otherwise sensible American wanted me to take him to see Sir Edward to tell him this, and to suggest to him to go over to Holland next week to meet the German Chancellor and fix it up. A few days ago a pious preacher chap (American) who had come over to "fix it all up," came back from France and called on me. He had seen something in France—he was excited and he didn't quite make it clear what he had seen; but he said that if they'd only let him go home safely and quickly he'd promise not to mention peace any more—did I think the American boats *entirely* safe?—So, you see, I do have some fun even in these dark days.

Yours heartily,

W. H. PAGE.

IV

This letter discloses that Page was pinning his faith in President Wilson, and that he still had confidence in the President's determination to uphold the national honour. Page was not one of those who thought that the United States should declare war immediately after the *Lusitania*. The President's course, in giving Germany a chance to make amends, and to disavow the act, met with his approval, and he found, also, much to admire in Mr. Wilson's first *Lusitania* note. His judgment in this matter was based first of all upon the merits of the case; besides this, his admiration for Mr. Wilson as a public man was strong. To think otherwise of the President would have been a great grief to the Ambassador and to differ with his chief on the tremendous issue of the war would have meant for Page the severance of one of the most cherished associations of his life. The interest which he had shown in advocating Wilson's presidential candidacy has already been set forth; and many phases of the Wilson administration had aroused his admiration. The President's handling of domestic problems Page regarded as a masterpiece in reconciling statesmanship with practical politics, and his energetic attitude on the Panama Tolls had introduced new standards into American foreign relations. Page could not sympathize with all the details of the Wilsonian Mexican policy, yet he saw in it a high-minded purpose and a genuine humanitarianism. But the outbreak of war presented new aspects of Mr. Wilson's mind. The President's attitude toward the European struggle, his conception of "neutrality," and his failure to grasp the meaning of the conflict, seemed to Page to show a lack of fundamental statesmanship; still his faith in Wilson was deep-seated, and he did not abandon hope that the

President could be brought to see things as they really were. Page even believed that he might be instrumental in his conversion.

But in the summer and autumn of 1915 one agony followed another. The "too proud to fight" speech was in Page's mind nothing less than a tragedy. The president's first *Lusitania* note for a time restored the Ambassador's confidence; it seemed to show that the President intended to hold Germany to that "strict accountability" which he had threatened. But Mr. Wilson's course now presented new difficulties to his Ambassador. Still Page believed that the President, in his own way and in his own time, would find a path out of his dilemma that would protect the honour and the safety of the United States. If any of the Embassy subordinates became impatient over the procedure of Washington, he did not find a sympathetic listener in the Ambassador. The whole of London and of Europe might be resounding with denunciations of the White House, but Page would tolerate no manifestations of hostility in his presence. "The problem appears different to Washington than it does to us," he would say to his confidants. "We see only one side of it; the President sees all sides. If we give him all the facts, he will decide the thing wisely." Englishmen with whom the Ambassador came into contact soon learned that they could not become flippant or critical about Mr. Wilson in his presence; he would resent the slightest hostile remark, and he had a way of phrasing his rebukes that usually discouraged a second attempt. About this time Page began to keep closely to himself, and to decline invitations to dinners and to country houses, even those with which he was most friendly. The reason was that he could not meet Englishmen and Englishwomen, or even Americans who were resident in England, on his old easy familiar terms; he knew the ideas which everybody entertained about his country, and he knew also what they were saying, when he was not among them; the restraint which his presence necessarily put upon his friends produced an uncongenial atmosphere, and the Ambassador therefore gave up, for a time, those distractions which had ordinarily proved such a delightful relief from his duties. For the first time since he had come to England he found himself a solitary man. He even refused to attend the American Luncheon Club in London because, in speeches and in conversation, the members did not hesitate to assail the Wilson policies.

Events, however, eventually proved too strong for the most devoted supporter of President Wilson. After the *Arabic* and the *Hesperian*, Page's official intimates saw signs that the Ambassador was losing confidence in his old friend. He would discuss Mr. Wilson occasionally, with those secretaries, such as Mr. Laughlin, in whom his confidence was strongest; his expressions, however, were never flippant or violent. That Page could be biting as well as brilliant in his comments on public personages his letters abundantly reveal, yet he never exercised his talent for sarcasm or invective at the expense of the White House. He never forgot that Mr. Wilson was President and that he was Ambassador; he would still defend the Administration; and he even now continued to find consolation in the reflection that Mr. Wilson was living in a different atmosphere and that he had difficulties to confront of which a man in London could know nothing. The Ambassador's emotion was rather one of disappointment and sorrow, mingled with anxiety as to the plight into which his country was being led. As to his duty in this situation, however, Page never hesitated. In his relations with his Embassy and with the

British world he maintained this non-critical attitude; but in his letters to President Wilson and Colonel House, he was describing the situation, and expressing his convictions, with the utmost freedom and frankness. In both these attitudes Page was consistent and absolutely loyal. It was his duty to carry out the Wilson instructions and he had too high a conception of the Ambassadorial office to show to the world any unfavourable opinions he may have held about his country's course. His duty to his post made it just as imperative that he set forth to the President the facts exactly as they were. And this the Ambassador now proceeded to do. For the mere ornamental dignities of an Ambassadorship Page cared nothing; he was wasting his health in his duties and exhausting his private resources; much as he loved the English and congenial as were his surroundings, the fear of being recalled for "disloyalty" or insubordination never influenced him. The letters which he now wrote to Colonel House and to President Wilson himself are probably without parallel in the diplomatic annals of this or of any other country. In them he told the President precisely what Englishmen thought of him and of the extent to which the United States was suffering in European estimation from the Wilson policy. His boldness sometimes astounded his associates. One day a friend and adviser of President Wilson's came into the Ambassador's office just as Page had finished one of his communications to Washington.

"Read that!" the Ambassador said, handing over the manuscript to his visitor.

As the caller read, his countenance displayed the progressive stages of his amazement. When he had finished, his hands dropped helplessly upon his knees.

"Is that the way you write to the President?" he gasped.

"Of course," Page replied, quietly. "Why not? Why shouldn't I tell him the truth? That is what I am here for."

"There is no other person in the world who dare talk to him like that!" was the reply.

This is unquestionably the fact. That President Wilson did not like people about him whose views were opposed to his own is now no secret, and during the period when his policy was one of the great issues of the world there was probably no one except Page who intruded upon his solitude with ideas that so abruptly disagreed with the opinions of the White House. The letters which Page wrote Colonel House were intended, of course, for the President himself, and practically all of them Colonel House read aloud to the head of the nation. The two men would closet themselves in the old cabinet room on the second floor of the White House—that same room in which Lincoln had met his advisers during Civil War days; and here Colonel House would quietly read the letters in which Page so mercilessly portrayed the situation as it appeared in English and European eyes. The President listened impassively, giving no sign of approval or disapproval, and hardly, at times, of much interest. In the earlier days, when Page's letters consisted of pictures of English life and English men, and colourful descriptions of England under the stress of war, the President was vastly entertained; he would laugh loudly at Page's wit, express his delight at his graphic and pungent style and feel deeply the horrors of war as his Ambassador unfolded them. "I always found Page compelling on paper," Mr. Wilson remarked to Mr. Laughlin, during one of the latter's visits to Washington. "I could never resist him—I get more information from his letters than from any other single source. Tell him to keep it up." It was during this period that the President used occasionally to read Page's letters to the Cabinet, expressing his great appreciation of their charm and historical importance. "The President quoted from one of the Ambassador's letters to the Cabinet to-day," a member of the Cabinet wrote to Mrs. Page in February, 1915. "'Some day,' the President said, 'I hope that Walter Page's letters will be published. They are the best letters I have ever read. They make you feel the atmosphere in England, understand the people, and see into the motives of the great actors.'" The President repeated this statement many times, and his letters to Page show how greatly he enjoyed and profited from this correspondence. But after the sinking of the *Lusitania* and the *Arabic* his attitude toward Page and his letters changed.

He now found little pleasure or satisfaction in the Page communications. When Mr. Wilson found that one of his former confidants had turned out to be a critic, that man instantaneously passed out of his life. And this was now Page's fate; the friendship and associations of forty years were as though they had never been. Just why Mr. Wilson did not recall his Ambassador is a question that has puzzled Page's friends. He would sometimes refer to him as a man who was "more British than the British," as one who had been taken completely captive by British blandishments, but he never came to the point of dismissing him. Perhaps he did not care to face the public scandal that such an act would have caused; but a more plausible reason is that Page, despite the causes which he had given for irritation, was indispensable to him. Page's early letters had furnished the President ideas which had taken shape in Wilson's policies, and, disagreeable as the communications now became, there are evidences that they influenced the solitary statesman in the White House, and that they had much to do in finally forcing Mr. Wilson into the war. The alternative question, as to why Page did not retire when he found himself so out of sympathy with the President, will be sufficiently answered in subsequent chapters; at present it may be said that he did resign and only consented to remain at the urgent request of Washington. In fact, all during 1915 and 1916, there seemed to be a fear in Washington that Page would definitely abandon the London post. On one occasion, when the newspapers published rumours to this effect, Page received an urgent despatch from Mr. Lansing. The message came at a time—the date was October 26, 1915—when Page was especially discouraged over the Washington policy. "Representatives of the press," said Mr. Lansing, "have repeated rumours that you are planning to resign. These have been brought to the President's attention, and both he and I have denied them. Still these rumours persist, and they cause both the President and me great anxiety. We cannot believe that they are well founded.

"In view of the fact that they are so persistent, we have thought it well to inform you of them and to tell you how earnestly we hope that they are baseless. We trust that you will set both our minds at rest."

If Page had ever had any compunction about addressing the President in blunt phrases these expressions certainly convinced him that he was a free agent.

Yet Page himself at times had his doubts as to the value of this correspondence. He would frequently discuss the matter with Mr. Laughlin. "That's a pretty harsh letter," he would say. "I don't like to talk that way to the President, yet it doesn't express half what I feel."

"It's your duty to tell the President the real state of affairs," Mr. Laughlin would urge.

"But do you suppose it does any good?" Page would ask.

"Yes, it's bound to, and whether it does or not, it's your business to keep him informed."

If in these letters Page seems to lay great stress on the judgment of Great Britain and Europe on American policy, it must be remembered that that was his particular province. One of an Ambassador's most important duties is to transmit to his country the public opinion of the country to which he is accredited. It was Page's place to tell Washington what Great Britain thought of it; it was Washington's business to formulate policy, after giving due consideration to this and other matters.

To Edward M. House

July 21, 1915.

DEAR HOUSE:

I enclose a pamphlet in ridicule of the President. I don't know who wrote it, for my inquiries so far have brought no real information. I don't feel like sending it to him. I send it to you—to do with as you think best. This thing alone is, of course, of no consequence. But it is symptomatic. There is much feeling about the slowness with which he acts. One hundred and twenty people (Americans) were drowned on the *Lusitania* and we are still writing notes about it—to the damnedest pirates that ever blew up a ship. Anybody who knows the Germans knows, of course, that they are simply playing for time, that they are not going to "come down," that Von Tirpitz is on deck, that they'd just as lief have war with us as not —perhaps had rather—because they don't want any large nation left fresh when the war ends. They'd like to have the whole world bankrupt. There is a fast growing feeling here, therefore, that the American Government is pusillanimous —dallies with 'em, is affected by the German propaganda, etc., etc. Of course, such a judgment is not fair.

It is formed without knowing the conditions in the United States.   But I think you ought to realize the strength of this sentiment.   No doubt before you receive this, the President will send something to Germany that will amount to an ultimatum and there will be at least a momentary change of sentiment here.   But looking at the thing in a long-range way, we're bound to get into the war. For the Germans will blow up more American travellers without notice.   And by dallying with them we do not change the ultimate result, but we take away from ourselves the spunk and credit of getting in instead of being kicked and cursed in.   We've got to get in: they won't play the game in any other way.   I have news direct from a high German source in Berlin which strongly confirms this. . . .

It's a curious thing to say.   But the only solution that I see is another *Lusitania* outrage, which would force war.

W. H. P.

P. S.   The London papers every day say that the President will send a strong note, etc.   And the people here say, "Damn notes: hasn't he written enough?"   Writing notes hurts nobody—changes nothing.   The Washington correspondents to the London papers say that Burleson, the Attorney-General, and Daniels are Bryan men and are holding the President back.

The prophecy contained in this letter was quickly fulfilled.   A week or two after Colonel House had received it, the *Arabic* was sunk with loss of American life.

Page was taking a brief holiday with his son Frank in Rowsley, Derbyshire, when this news came.   It was telegraphed from the Embassy.

"That settles it," he said to his son.   "They have sunk the *Arabic*.   That means that we shall break with Germany and I've got to go back to London."

To Edward M. House

American Embassy, London, August 23, 1915.

DEAR HOUSE:

The sinking of the *Arabic* is the answer to the President and to your letter to me. And there'll be more such answers. You said to me one day after you had got back from your last visit to Berlin: "They are impossible." I think you told the truth, and surely you know your German and you know your Berlin—or you did know them when you were here.

The question is not what we have done for the Allies, not what any other neutral country has done or has failed to do—such comparisons, I think, are far from the point. The question is when the right moment arrives for us to save our self-respect, our honour, and the esteem and fear (or the contempt) in which the world will hold us.

Berlin has the Napoleonic disease. If you follow Napoleon's career—his excuses, his evasions, his inventions, the wild French enthusiasm and how he kept it up—you will find an exact parallel. That becomes plainer every day. Europe may not be wholly at peace in five years— may be ten.

Hastily and heartily,

W. H. P.

I have your note about Willum J. . . . Crank once, crank always. My son, never tie up with a crank. W. H. P.

To Edward M. House

London, September 2nd, 1915.

DEAR HOUSE:

You write me about pleasing the Allies, the big Ally in particular. That doesn't particularly appeal to me. We don't owe them anything. There's no obligation. I'd never confess for a moment that we are under any obligation to any of them nor to anybody. I'm not out to "please" anybody, as a primary purpose: that's not my game nor my idea—nor yours either. As for England in particular, the account was squared when she twice sent an army against us—in her folly—especially the last time when she burnt our Capitol. There's been no obligation since. The obligation is on the other foot. We've set her an example of what democracy will do for men, an example of efficiency, an example of freedom of opportunity. The future is ours, and she may follow us and profit by it. Already we have three white English-speaking men to every two in the British Empire: we are sixty per cent. of the Anglo-Saxons in the world. If there be any obligation to please, the obligation is on her to please us. And she feels and sees it now.

My point is not that, nor is it what we or any other neutral nation has done or may do—Holland or any other. This war is the direct result of the over-polite, diplomatic, standing-aloof, bowing-to-one-another in gold lace, which all European nations are guilty of in times of peace— castes and classes and uniforms and orders and such folderol, instead of the proper business of the day. Every nation in Europe knew that Germany was preparing for war. If they had really got together—not mere Hague Sunday-school talk and resolutions—but had really got together for business and had said to Germany, "The moment you fire a shot, we'll all fight against you; we have so many millions of men, so many men-of-war, so many billions of money; and we'll increase all these if you do not change your system and your building-up of armies"—then there would have been no war.

My point is not sentimental.   It is:

(1) We must maintain our own self-respect and safety.   If we submit to too many insults, *that* will in time bring Germany against us.   We've got to show at some time that we don't believe, either, in the efficacy of Sunday-School resolves for peace—that we are neither Daughters of the Dove of Peace nor Sons of the Olive Branch, and

(2) About nagging and forever presenting technical legal points as lawyers do to confuse juries—the point is the point of efficiency.   If we do that, we can't carry our main points.   I find it harder and harder to get answers now to important questions because we ask so many unimportant and nagging ones.

I've no sentiment—perhaps not enough.   My gushing days are gone, if I ever had 'em.   The cutting-out of the "100 years of peace" oratory, etc., etc., was one of the blessings of the war.   But we must be just and firm and preserve our own self-respect and keep alive the fear that other nations have of us; and we ought to have the courage to make the Department of State more than a bureau of complaints.   We must learn to say "No" even to a Gawdamighty independent American citizen when he asks an improper or impracticable question.   Public opinion in the United States consists of something more than the threats of Congressmen and the bleating of newspapers; it consists of the judgment of honourable men on courageous and frank actions—a judgment that cannot be made up till action is taken.

Heartily yours,

W. H. P.

To Edward M. House

American Embassy, London, Sept. 8, 1915.
(This is not prudent.   It is only true—nothing more.)
DEAR HOUSE:

I take it for granted that Dumba[1] is going, of course. But I must tell you that the President is being laughed at by our best friends for his slowness in action.   I hardly ever pick up a paper without seeing some sarcastic remark.   I don't mean they expect us to come into the war. They only hoped we would be as good as our word— would regard another submarine attack on a ship carrying Americans as an unfriendly act and would send Bernstorff home.   Yet the *Arabic* and now the *Hesperian* have had no effect in action.   Bernstorff's personal *note to Lansing,*[2] *even as far as it goes, does not bind his Government.*

The upshot of all this is that the President is fast losing in the minds of our best friends here all that he gained by his courageous stand on the Panama tolls.   They feel that if he takes another insult—keeps taking them—and is satisfied with Bernstorff's personal word, which is proved false in four days—he'll take anything.   And the British will pay less attention to what we say.   That's inevitable.   If the American people and the President accept the *Arabic* and the *Hesperian* and do nothing to Dumba till the Government here gave out his letter, which the State Department had (and silently held) for

---

[1] On September 6th, certain documents seriously compromising Dr. Constantin Dumba, Austro-Hungarian Ambassador to the United States, were published in the British press.   They disclosed that Dr. Dumba was fomenting strikes in the United States and conducting other intrigues.   The American Government gave Dr. Dumba his passports on September 17th.

[2] On August 26th, Count Bernstorff gave a pledge to the United States Government, that, in future, German submarines would not attack liners without warning.   This promise was almost immediately violated.

several days—then nobody on this side the world will pay much heed to anything we say hereafter.

This, as I say, doesn't mean that these (thoughtful) people wish or expect us to go to war. They wish only that we'd prove ourselves as good as the President's word. That's the conservative truth; we're losing influence more rapidly than I supposed it were possible.

Dumba's tardy dismissal will not touch the main matter, which is the rights of neutrals at sea, and keeping our word in action.

Yours sincerely,

W. H. P.

P. S. They say it's Mexico over again—watchful waiting and nothing doing. And the feeling grows that Bryan has really conquered, since his programme seems to prevail.

To Edward M. House

London, Tuesday night, Sept. 8, 1915.

DEAR HOUSE:

The Germans seem to think it a good time to try to feel about for peace. They have more to offer now than they may have again. That's all. A man who seriously talks peace now in Paris or in London on any terms that the Germans will consider, would float dead that very night in the Seine or in the Thames. The Germans have for the time being "done-up" the Russians; but the French have shells enough to plough the German trenches day and night (they've been at it for a fortnight now); Joffre has been to see the Italian generalissimo; and the English destroy German submarines now almost as fast as the Germans send them out. I am credibly told that several weeks ago a group of Admiralty men who are in the secret had a little dinner to celebrate the destruction of the 50th submarine.

While this is going on, you are talking on your side of the water about a change in German policy! The only change is that the number of submarines available becomes smaller and smaller, and that they wish to use Uncle Sam's broad, fat back to crawl down on when they have failed.

Consequently, they are laughing at Uncle Sam here— it comes near to being ridicule, in fact, for seeming to jump at Bernstorff's unfrank assurances. And, as I have telegraphed the President, English opinion is— well, it is very nearly disrespectful. Men say here (I mean our old friends) that with no disavowal of the *Lusitania*, the *Falaba*, the *Gulflight*, or the *Arabic* or of the *Hesperian*, the Germans are "stuffing" Uncle Sam, that Uncle Sam is in the clutches of the peace-at-any-price public opinion, that the United States will suffer any insult and do nothing. I hardly pick up a paper that does not have a sarcastic paragraph or cartoon. We are on the brink of convincing the English that we'll not act, whatever the provocation. By the English, I do not mean the lighter, transitory public opinion, but I mean the thoughtful men who do not wish us or expect us to fire a gun. They say that the American democracy, since Cleveland's day, has become a mere agglomeration of different races, without national unity, national aims, and without courage or moral qualities. And (I deeply regret to say) the President is losing here the high esteem he won by his Panama tolls repeal. They ask, why on earth did he raise the issue if under repeated provocation he is unable to recall Gerard or to send Bernstorff home? The *Hesperian* follows the *Arabic;* other "liners" will follow the *Hesperian*, if the Germans have submarines.

And, when Sackville-West[1] was promptly sent home for answering a private citizen's inquiry about the two political parties, Dumba is (yet awhile) retained in spite of a far graver piece of business. There is a tone of sad disappointment here—not because the most thoughtful men want us in the war (they don't), but because for some reason, which nobody here understands, the President, having taken a stand, seems unable to do anything.

All this is a moderate interpretation of sorrowful public opinion here. And the result will inevitably be that they will pay far less heed to anything we may hereafter say. In fact men now say here every day that the American democracy has no opinion, can form no opinion, has no moral quality, and that the word of its President never gets as far as action even of the mildest form. The atmosphere is very depressing. And this feeling has apparently got beyond anybody's control. I've even heard this said: "The voice of the United States is Mr. Wilson's: its actions are controlled by Mr. Bryan."

So, you see, the war will go on a long long time. So far as English opinion is concerned, the United States is useful to make ammunition and is now thought of chiefly in this connection. Less and less attention is paid to what we say. Even the American telegrams to the London papers have a languid tone.

Yet recent revelations have made it clearer than ever that the same qualities that the English accuse us of having are in them and that these qualities are directly to blame for this war. I recall that when I was in Germany a few weeks, six years ago, I became convinced that

[1]Sir Lionel Sackville-West was British Minister to the United States from 1881 to 1888. In the latter year a letter was published which he had written to an American citizen of British origin, the gist of which was that the reëlection of President Cleveland would be of advantage to British interests. For this gross interference in American domestic affairs, President Cleveland immediately handed Sir Lionel his passports. The incident ended his diplomatic career.

Germany had prepared to fight England; I didn't know
when, but I did know that was what the war-machine had
in mind. Of course, I had no opportunities to find out
anything in particular. You were told practically that
same thing by the Kaiser, before the war began. "We
are ready," said he. Of course the English feared it and
Sir Edward put his whole life into his effort to prevent it.
The day the war began, he told me with tears that it
seemed that his life had been wasted—that his life work
had gone for naught.—Nobody could keep from wondering why England didn't——

(Here comes a parenthesis. Word came to me a little
while ago that a Zeppelin was on its way to London.
Such a remark doesn't arouse much attention. But just
as I had finished the fifth line above this, Frank and Mrs.
Page came in and challenged me to play a game of cards
before we should go to bed. We sat down, the cards
were dealt, and bang! bang!—with the deep note of an
explosion. A third, a fourth shot. We went into the
street. There the Zeppelin was revealed by a searchlight
—sailing along. I think it had probably dropped its
bombs; but the aircraft guns were cracking away at it.
Some of them shot explosive projectiles to find the range.
Now and then one such explosive would almost reach the
Zeppelin, but it was too high for them and it sailed away,
the air guns doing their ineffectual best. I couldn't see
whether airplanes were trying to shoot it or not. The
searchlight revealed the Zeppelin but nothing else.—
While we were watching this battle in the air, the maids
came down from the top of the house and went into the
cellar. I think they've already gone back. You can't
imagine how little excitement it caused. It produces
less fright than any other conceivable engine of war.
We came back as soon as the Zeppelin was out of sight

and the firing had ceased; we played our game of cards; and here I am writing you the story—all within about half an hour.—There was a raid over London last night, too, wherein a dozen or two women and children and a few men were killed. I haven't the slightest idea what harm this raid to-night has done. For all I know it may not be all done. But of all imaginable war-experiences this seems the most futile. It interrupted a game of cards for twenty minutes!)

Now—to go on with my story: I have wondered ever since the war began why the Allies were not better pre-pared—especially England on land. England has just one *big* land gun—no more. Now it has turned out, as you have doubtless read, that the British Government were as good as told by the German Government that Germany was going to war pretty soon—this in 1912 when Lord Haldane[1] was sent to make friends with Germany.

The only answer he brought back was a proposition that England should in any event remain neutral—stand aside while Germany whipped Russia and France. This insulting proposal was kept secret till the other day. Now, why didn't the British Cabinet inform the people and get ready? They were afraid the English people wouldn't believe it and would accuse them of fomenting war. The English people were making money and pur-suing their sports. Probably they wouldn't have be-lieved it. So the Liberal Cabinet went on in silence, knowing that war was coming, but not exactly when it was coming, and they didn't make even a second big gun.

---

[1] In this passage the Ambassador touches on one of the bitterest controversies of the war. In order completely to understand the issues involved and to obtain Lord Haldane's view, the reader should consult the very valuable book recently published by Lord Haldane: "Before the War." Chapter II tells the story of Lord Haldane's visit to the Kaiser, and succeeding chapters give the reasons why the creation of a huge British army in preparation for the war was not a simple matter.

Now here was the same silence in this "democracy" that they now complain of in ours. Rather an interesting and discouraging parallel—isn't it? Public opinion has turned Lord Haldane out of office because he didn't tell the public what he declares they wouldn't have believed. If the English had raised an army in 1912, and made a lot of big guns, Austria would not have trampled Serbia in the earth. There would have been no war now; and the strong European Powers might have made then the same sort of protective peace-insurance combine that they will try to make after this war is ended. Query: A democracy's inability to *act*—how much is this apparently inherent quality of a democracy to blame for this war and for—other things?

When I am asked every day "Why the United States doesn't *do* something—send Dumba and Bernstorff home?"—Well, it is not the easiest question in the world to answer.

Yours heartily,
W. H. P.

P. S. This is the most comical of all worlds: While I was writing this, it seems the maids went back upstairs and lighted their lights without pulling their shades down —they occupy three rooms, in front. The doorbell rang furiously. Here were more than half a dozen policemen and special constables—must investigate! "One light would be turned on, another would go out; another one on!"—etc., etc. Frank tackled them, told 'em it was only the maids going to bed, forgetting to pull down the shades. Spies and signalling were in the air! So, in the morning, I'll have to send over to the Foreign Office and explain. The Zeppelin did more "frightfulness" than I had supposed, after all. Doesn't this strike you as comical?

W. H. P.

Friday, September 10, 1915.

P. S.   The news is just come that Dumba is dismissed. That will clear the atmosphere—a little, but only a little. Dumba committed a diplomatic offence. The German Government has caused the death of United States citizens, has defied us, has declared it had changed its policy and yet has gone on with the same old policy. Besides, Bernstorff has done everything that Dumba did except employ Archibald, which was a mere incident of the game. The President took a strong stand: they have disregarded it—no apology nor reparation for a single boat that has been sunk. Now the English opinion of the Germans is hardly a calm, judicial opinion—of course not. There may be facts that have not been made known. There must be good reasons that nobody here can guess, why the President doesn't act in the long succession of German acts against us. *But I tell you with all solemnity that British opinion and the British Government have absolutely lost their respect for us and their former high estimate of the President. And that former respect is gone for good unless he acts now very quickly.*[1] They will pay nothing more than formal and polite attention to anything we may hereafter say. This is not resentful. They don't particularly care for us to get into the war. Their feeling (I mean among our best old friends) is not resentful. It is simply sorrowful. They had the highest respect for our people and our President. The Germans defy us; we sit in silence. They conclude here that we'll submit to anything from anybody. We'll write strong notes—nothing more.

I can't possibly exaggerate the revulsion of feeling. Members of the Government say (in private, of course) that we'll submit to any insult. The newspapers refuse

[1]The italics are Page's.

to publish articles which attempt to make the President's silence reasonable. "It isn't defensible," they say, "and they would only bring us thousands of insulting letters from our readers." I can't think of a paper nor of a man who has a good word to say for us—except, perhaps, a few Quaker peace-at-any-price people. And our old friends are disappointed and sorrowful. They feel that we have dropped out of a position of influence in the world.

I needn't and can't write more. Of course there are more important things than English respect. But the English think that every Power has lost respect for us— the Germans most of all. And (unless the President acts very rigorously and very quickly) we'll have to get along a long time without British respect.

W. H. P.

P. S. The last Zeppelin raid—which interrupted the game of cards—killed more than twenty persons and destroyed more than seven million dollars' worth of private business property—all non-combatants'!

W. H. P.

To Edward M. House

21st of September, 1915.

DEAR HOUSE:
The insulting cartoon that I enclose (destroy it without showing it) is typical of, I suppose, five hundred that have appeared here within a month. This represents the feeling and opinion of the average man. They say we wrote brave notes and made courageous demands, to none of which a satisfactory reply has come, but only more outrages and no guarantee for the future. Yet we will not even show our displeasure by sending Berns-

torff home. We've simply "gone out," like a snuffed candle, in the regard and respect of the vast volume of British opinion. (The last *Punch* had six ridiculing allusions to our "fall.")

It's the loneliest time I've had in England. There's a tendency to avoid me.

They can't understand here the continued declaration in the United States that the British Government is trying to take our trade—to use its blockade and navy with the direct purpose of giving British trade profit out of American detentions. Of course, the Government had no such purpose and has done no such thing—with any such purpose. It isn't thinking about trade but only about war.

The English think they see in this the effect on our Government and on American opinion of the German propaganda. I have had this trade-accusation investigated half a dozen times—the accusation that this Government is using its military power for its own trade advantage to our detriment: it simply isn't true. They stop our cargoes, not for their advantage, but wholly to keep things from the enemy. Study our own trade reports.

In a word, our importers are playing (so the English think) directly into the hands of the Germans. So matters go on from bad to worse.

Bryce[1] is very sad. He confessed to me yesterday the utter hopelessness of the two people's ever understanding one another.

The military situation is very blue—very blue. The general feeling is that the long war will begin next March and end—nobody dares predict.

W. H. P.

---

[1]Viscount Bryce, author of "The American Commonwealth" and British Ambassador to the United States, 1907–1913.

P. S. There's not a moral shadow of a doubt (1) that the commander of the submarine that sunk the *Arabic* is dead—although he makes reports to his government! nor (2) that the *Hesperian* was torpedoed. The State Department has a piece of the torpedo.

V

"Incidents occur nearly every day," Page wrote in the autumn of 1915, "which reveal the feeling that the Germans have taken us in. Last week one of our naval men, Lieutenant McBride, who has just been ordered home, asked the Admiralty if he might see the piece of metal found on the deck of the *Hesperian*. Contrary to their habit, the British officer refused. 'Take my word for it,' he said. 'She was torpedoed. Why do you wish to investigate? Your country will do nothing—will accept any excuse, any insult and—do nothing.' When McBride told me this, I went at once to the Foreign Office and made a formal request that this metal should be shown to our naval attaché, who (since Symington is with the British fleet and McBride has been ordered home) is Lieutenant Towers. Towers was sent for and everything that the Admiralty knows was shown to him and I am sending that piece of metal by this mail. But to such a pass has the usual courtesy of a British naval officer come. There are many such instances of changed conduct. They are not hard to endure or to answer and are of no consequence in themselves but only for what they denote. They're a part of war's bitterness. But my mind runs ahead and I wonder how Englishmen will look at this subject five years hence, and it runs afield and I wonder how the Germans will regard it. A sort of pro-German American newspaper correspondent came along the other day from the German headquarters; and he told me that one of the German generals remarked to him: 'War with America? Ach no! Not war. If trouble should come, we'd send over a platoon of our policemen to whip your little army.' (He didn't say just how he'd send 'em.)"

Page's letters to the President were just as frank as those to Colonel House:

To the President

American Embassy, London, Oct. 5, 1915.
DEAR MR. PRESIDENT:

I have two letters that I have lately written to you but which I have not sent because they utterly lack good cheer. After reading them over, I have not liked to send them. Yet I should fail of my duty if I did not tell you bad news as well as good.

The high esteem in which our Government was held when the first *Lusitania* note to Germany was sent seems all changed to indifference or pity—not hatred or hostility, but a sort of hopeless and sad pity. That ship was sunk just five months ago; the German Government (or its Ambassador) is yet holding conversations about the principle involved, making "concessions" and promises for the future, and so far we have done nothing to hold the Germans to accountability.[1] In the meantime their submarine fleet has been so reduced that probably the future will take care of itself and we shall be used as a sort of excuse for their failure. This is what the English think and say; and they explain our failure to act by concluding that the peace-at-any-price sentiment dominates the Government and paralyzes it. They have now, I think, given up hope that we will ever take any action.

---

[1] In a communication sent February 10, 1915, President Wilson warned the German Government that he would hold it to a "strict accountability" for the loss of American lives by illegal submarine attack.

So deeply rooted (and, I fear, permanent) is this feeling that every occurrence is made to fit into and to strengthen this supposition.   When Dumba was dismissed, they said: "Dumba, merely the abject tool of German intrigue. Why not Bernstorff?"   When the Anglo-French loan[1] was oversubscribed, they said: "The people's sympathy is most welcome, but their Government is paralyzed." Their respect has gone—at least for the time being.

It is not that they expect us to go to war: many, in fact, do not wish us to.   They expected that we would be as good as our word and hold the Germans to accountability. Now I fear they think little of our word.   I shudder to think what our relations might be if Sir Edward Grey were to yield to another as Foreign Minister, as, of course, he must yield at some time.

The press has less to say than it had a few weeks ago. *Punch*, for instance, which ridiculed and pitied us in six cartoons and articles in each of two succeeding numbers, entirely forgets us this week.   But they've all said their say.   I am, in a sense, isolated—lonely in a way that I have never before been.   I am not exactly avoided, I hope, but I surely am not sought.   They have a polite feeling that they do not wish to offend me and that to make sure of this the safest course is to let me alone. There is no mistaking the great change in the attitude of men I know, both in official and private life.

It comes down and comes back to this—that for five months after the sinking of the *Lusitania* the Germans are yet playing with us, that we have not sent Bernstorff home, and hence that we will submit to any rebuff or any indignity.   It is under these conditions—under this judgment of us—that we now work—the English respect for

---

[1] A reference to the Anglo-French loan for $500,000,000, placed in the United States in the autumn of 1915.

our Government indefinitely lessened and instead of the old-time respect a sad pity. I cannot write more.

Heartily yours,

WALTER H. PAGE.

"I have authoritatively heard," Page cables to President Wilson in early September, "of a private conversation between a leading member of the Cabinet and a group of important officials all friendly to us in which all sorrowfully expressed the opinion that the United States will submit to any indignity and that no effect is now to be hoped for from its protests against unlawful submarine attacks or against anything else. The inactivity of our Government, or its delay, which they assume is the same as inactivity, is attributed to domestic politics or to the lack of national, consciousness or unity.

"No explanation has appeared in the British press of our Government's inactivity or of any regret or promise of reparation by Germany for the sinking of the *Lusitania*, the *Falaba*, the *Gulflight*, the *Nebraskan*, the *Arabic*, or the *Hesperian*, nor any explanation of a week's silence about the Dumba letter; and the conclusion is drawn that, in the absence of action by us, all these acts have been practically condoned.

"I venture to suggest that such explanations be made public as will remove, if possible, the practically unanimous conclusion here that our Government will permit these and similar future acts to be explained away. I am surprised almost every hour by some new evidence of the loss of respect for our Government, which, since the sinking of the *Arabic*, has become so great as to warrant calling it a complete revulsion of English feeling toward the United States. There is no general wish for us to enter the war, but there is genuine sorrow that we are thought to submit to any indignity, especially after having taken a firm stand. I conceive I should be lacking in duty if I did not report this rapid and unfortunate change in public feeling, which seems likely to become permanent unless facts are quickly made public which may change it."

There are many expressions of such feelings in Page's communications of this time. They brought only the most perfunctory acknowledgment from the White House. On January 3, 1916, Page sent the President a mass of clippings from the British press, all criticizing the Wilson Administration in unrestrained terms. In his comment on these, he cables the President:

"Public opinion, both official and unofficial, is expressed by these newspaper comments, with far greater restraint than it is expressed in private conversation. Ridicule of the Administration runs through the programmes of the theatres; it inspires hundreds of cartoons; it is a staple of conversation at private dinners and in the clubs. The most serious class of Englishmen, including the best friends of the United States, feel that the Administration's reliance on notes has reduced our Government to a third- or fourth-rate power. There is even talk of spheres of German influence in the United States as in China. No government could fall lower in English opinion than we shall fall if more notes are sent to Austria or to Germany. The only way to keep any shred of English respect is the immediate dismissal without more parleying of every German and Austrian official at Washington. Nobody here believes that such an act would provoke war.

"I can do no real service by mincing matters. My previous telegrams and letters have been purposely restrained as this one is. We have now come to the parting of the ways. If English respect be worth preserving at all, it can be preserved only by immediate action. Any other course than immediate severing of diplomatic relations with both Germany and Austria will deepen the English opinion into a conviction that the Administration was insincere when it sent the *Lusilania* notes and that its notes and protests need not be taken seriously on any subject. And English opinion is allied opinion. The Italian Ambassador[1] said to me, 'What has happened? The United States of to-day is not the United States I knew fifteen years ago, when I lived in Washington.' French officers and members of the Government who come here express themselves even more strongly than do the British. The British newspapers to-day publish translations of ridicule of the United States from German papers."

To the President

London,
January 5, 1916.

DEAR MR. PRESIDENT:

I wish—an impossible thing of course—that some sort of guidance could be given to the American correspondents of the English newspapers. Almost every day they telegraph about the visits of the Austrian Chargé or the German Ambassador to the State Department to assure Mr. Lansing that their governments will of course make a satisfactory explanation of the latest torpedo-act in the Mediterranean or to "take one further step in reaching a satisfactory understanding about the *Lusilania*." They usually go on to say also that more notes are in preparation to Germany or to Austria. The impression made upon the European mind is that the German and Austrian officials in Washington are leading the Administration on

---
[1] The Marquis Imperiali.

to endless discussion, endless notes, endless hesitation. Nobody in Europe regards their pledges or promises as worth anything at all: the *Arabic* follows the *Lusitania*, the *Hesperian* follows the *Arabic*, the *Persia* follows the *Ancona*. "Still conferences and notes continue," these people say, "proving that the American Government, which took so proper and high a stand in the *Lusitania* notes, is paralyzed—in a word is hoodwinked and 'worked' by the Germans." And so long as these diplomatic representatives are permitted to remain in the United States, "to explain," "to parley" and to declare that the destruction of American lives and property is disavowed by their governments, atrocities on sea and land will of course continue; and they feel that our Government, by keeping these German and Austrian representatives in Washington, condones and encourages them and their governments.

This is a temperate and even restrained statement of the English feeling and (as far as I can make out) of the whole European feeling.

It has been said here that every important journal published in neutral or allied European countries, daily, weekly, or monthly, which deals with public affairs, has expressed a loss of respect for the United States Government and that most of them make continuous severe criticisms (with surprise and regret) of our failure by action to live up to the level of our *Lusitania* notes. I had (judiciously) two American journalists, resident here— men of judgment and character—to inquire how true this declaration is. After talking with neutral and allied journalists here and with men whose business it is to read the journals of the Continent, they reported that this declaration is substantially true—that the whole European press (outside Germany and its allies) uses the same tone toward our Government that the English press uses—to-day, disappointment verging on contempt; and many of them explain our keeping diplomatic intercourse with Germany by saying that we are afraid of the German vote, or of civil war, or that the peace-at-any-price people really rule the United States and have paralyzed our power to act—even to cut off diplomatic relations with governments that have insulted and defied us.

Another (similar) declaration is that practically all men of public influence in England and in the European allied and neutral countries have publicly or privately expressed themselves to the same effect. The report that I have about this is less definite than about the newspapers, for, of course, no one can say just what proportion of men of public influence have so expressed themselves; but the number who have so expressed themselves is overwhelming.

In this Kingdom, where I can myself form some opinion more or less accurate, and where I can check or verify my opinion by various methods—I am afraid, as I have frequently already reported, that the generation now living will never wholly regain the respect for our Government that it had a year ago. I will give you three little indications of this feeling; it would be easy to write down hundreds of them:

(One) The governing class: Mr. X [a cabinet member] told Mrs. Page a few nights ago that for sentimental reasons only he would be gratified to see the United States in the war along with the Allies, but that merely sentimental reasons were not a sufficient reason for war—by no means; that he felt most grateful for the sympathetic attitude of the large mass of the American people, that he had no right to expect anything from our Government, whose neutral position was entirely proper. Then he added; "But what I can't for the life of me understand is your

Government's failure to express its disapproval of the German utter disregard of its *Lusitania* notes. After eight months, it has done nothing but write more notes. My love for America, I must confess, is offended at this inaction and—puzzled. I can't understand it. You will pardon me, I am sure."

(Two) "Middle Class" opinion: A common nickname for Americans in the financial and newspaper districts of London is "Too-prouds."

(Three) The man in the street: At one of the moving picture shows in a large theatre a little while ago they filled in an interval by throwing on the screen the picture of the monarch, or head of state, and of the flag of each of the principal nations. When the American picture appeared, there was such hissing and groaning as caused the managers hastily to move that picture off the screen.

Some time ago I wrote House of some such incidents and expressions as these; and he wrote me that they were only part and parcel of the continuous British criticism of their own Government—in other words, a part of the passing hysteria of war. This remark shows how House was living in an atmosphere of illusion.

As the matter stands to-day our Government has sunk lower, as regards British and European opinion, than it has ever been in our time, not as a part of the hysteria of war but as a result of this process of reasoning, whether it be right or wrong:

We said that we should hold the Germans to strict accountability on account of the *Lusitania*. We have not settled that yet and we still allow the German Ambassador to discuss it after the *Hesperian* and other such acts showed that his *Arabic* pledge was worthless.

The *Lusitania* grows larger and larger in European memory and imagination. It looks as if it would become the great type of war atrocities and barbarities. I have seen pictures of the drowned women and children used even on Christmas cards. And there is documentary proof in our hands that the warning, which was really an advance announcement, of that disaster was paid for by the German Ambassador and charged to his Government. It is the *Lusitania* that has caused European opinion to regard our foreign policy as weak. It is not the wish for us to go to war. No such general wish exists.

I do not know, Mr. President, who else, if anybody, puts these facts before you with this complete frankness. But I can do no less and do my duty.

No Englishman—except two who were quite intimate friends—has spoken to me about our Government for months, but I detect all the time a tone of pity and grief in their studied courtesy and in their avoidance of the subject. And they talk with every other American in this Kingdom. It is often made unpleasant for Americans in the clubs and in the pursuit of their regular business and occupations; and it is always our inaction about the *Lusitania*. Our controversy with the British Government causes little feeling and that is a sort of echo of the *Lusitania*. They feel that we have not lived up to our promises and professions.

That is the whole story.

Believe me always heartily,

WALTER H. PAGE.

This dismissal of Dumba and of the Attachés has had little more effect on opinion here than the dismissal of the Turkish Ambassador.[1] Sending these was regarded as

---

[1]Rustem Bey, the Turkish Ambassador to the United States, was sent home early in the war, for publishing indiscreet newspaper and magazine articles.

merely kicking the dogs of the man who had stolen our sheep.

VI

One of the reasons why Page felt so intensely about American policy at this time was his conviction that the severance of diplomatic relations, in the latter part of 1915, or the early part of 1916, in itself would have brought the European War to an end. This was a conviction from which he never departed. Count Bernstorff was industriously creating the impression in the United States that his dismissal would immediately cause war between Germany and the United States, and there is little doubt that the Administration accepted this point of view. But Page believed that this was nothing but Prussian bluff. The severance of diplomatic relations at that time, in Page's opinion, would have convinced the Germans of the hopelessness of their cause. In spite of the British blockade, Germany was drawing enormous quantities of food supplies from the United States, and without these supplies she could not maintain indefinitely her resistance. The severance of diplomatic relations would naturally have been accompanied by an embargo suspending trade between the United States and the Fatherland. Moreover, the consideration that was mainly leading Germany to hope for success was the belief that she could embroil the United States and Great Britain over the blockade. A break with Germany would of course mean an end to that manœuvre. Page regarded all Mr. Wilson's attempts to make peace in 1914 and early 1915—before the *Lusitania*—as mistakes, for reasons that have already been set forth. Now, however, he believed that the President had a real opportunity to end the war and the unparalleled suffering which it was causing. The mere dismissal of Bernstorff, in the Ambassador's opinion, would accomplish this result.

In a cablegram sent to the President on February 15, 1916, he made this plain.

To the President

February 15, 7 P. M.

The Cabinet has directed the Censor to suppress, as far as he can with prudence, comment which is unfavourable to the United States. He has taken this action because the public feeling against the Administration is constantly increasing. Because the *Lusitania* controversy has been going on so long, and because the Germans are using it in their renewed U-boat campaign, the opinion of this country has reached a point where only prompt action can bring a turn in the tide. Therefore my loyalty to you would not be complete if I should refrain from sending, in the most respectful terms, the solemn conviction which I hold about our opportunity and our duty.

If you immediately refuse to have further parley or to yield one jot or tittle of your original *Lusitania* notes, and if you at once break diplomatic relations with the German Empire, and then declare the most vigorous embargo of the Central Powers, you will quickly end the war. There will be an immediate collapse in German credit. If there are any Allies who are wavering, such action will hold them in line. Certain European neutrals—Sweden, Rumania, Greece, and others—will put up a firm resistance to Germanic influences and certain of them will take part with Great Britain and France. There will be an end at once to the German propaganda, which is now worldwide. The moral weight of our country will be a determining influence and bring an early peace. The credit you will receive for such a decision will make you immortal and even the people of Germany will be forever grateful.

It is my conviction that we would not be called upon to fire a gun or to lose one human life.

Above all, such an action will settle the whole question of permanent peace. The absolute and grateful loyalty of the whole British Empire, of the British Fleet, and of all the Allied countries will be ours. The great English-speaking nations will be able to control the details of the peace and this without any formal alliance. There will be an incalculable saving of human life and of treasure. Such an act will make it possible for Germany to give in honourably and with good grace because the whole world will be against her. Her bankrupt and blockaded people will bring such pressure to bear that the decision will be hastened.

The sympathies of the American people will be brought in line with the Administration.

If we settle the *Lusitania* question by compromising in any way your original demands, or if we permit it to drag on longer, America can have no part in bringing the war to an end. The current of allied opinion will run so strongly against the Administration that no censorship and no friendly interference by an allied government can stem the distrust of our Government which is now so strong in Europe.

We shall gain by any further delay only a dangerous, thankless, and opulent isolation. The *Lusitania* is the turning point in our history. The time to act is now.

PAGE.

CHAPTER XV

THE AMBASSADOR AND THE LAWYERS

REFERENCES in the foregoing letters show that Page was still having his troubles over the blockade. In the latter part of 1915, indeed, the negotiations with Sir Edward Grey on this subject had reached their second stage. The failure of Washington to force upon Great Britain an entirely new code of naval warfare—the Declaration of London—has already been described. This failure had left both the British Foreign Office and the American State Department in an unsatisfactory frame of mind. The Foreign Office regarded Washington with suspicion, for the American attempt to compel Great Britain to adopt a code of naval warfare which was exceedingly unfavourable to that country and exceedingly favourable to Germany, was susceptible of a sinister interpretation. The British rejection of these overtures, on the other hand, had evidently irritated the international lawyers at Washington. Mr. Lansing now abandoned his efforts to revolutionize maritime warfare and confined himself to specific protests and complaints. His communications to the London Embassy dealt chiefly with particular ships and cargoes. Yet his persistence in regarding all these problems from a strictly legalistic point of view Page regarded as indicating a restricted sense of statesmanship.

53

To Edward M. House

London, August 4, 1915.

MY DEAR HOUSE:

. . . The lawyer-way in which the Department goes on in its dealings with Great Britain is losing us the only great international friendship that we have any chance of keeping or that is worth having. Whatever real principle we have to uphold with Great Britain— that's all right. I refer only to the continuous series of nagging incidents—always criticism, criticism, criticism of small points—points that we have to yield at last, and never anything constructive. I'll illustrate what I mean by a few incidents that I can recall from memory. If I looked up the record, I should find a very, very much larger list.

(1) We insisted and insisted and insisted, not once but half a dozen times, at the very beginning of the war, on England's adoption of the Declaration of London entire in spite of the fact that Parliament had distinctly declined to adopt it. Of course we had to give in—after we had produced a distinctly unfriendly atmosphere and much feeling.

(2) We denied the British right to put copper on the contraband list—much to their annoyance. Of course we had at last to acquiesce. They were within their rights.

(3) We protested against bringing ships into port to examine them. Of course we had to give in—after producing irritation.

(4) We made a great fuss about stopped telegrams. We have no case at all; but, even after acknowledging that we have no case, every pouch continues to bring telegrams with the request that I ask an explanation why

they were stopped. Such explanations are practically refused. I have 500 telegrams. Periodically I wire the state of the case and ask for more specific instructions. I never get an answer to these requests. But the Department continues to send the telegrams! We confessedly have no case here; and this method can produce nothing but irritation.

I could extend this list to 100 examples—of mere lawyer-like methods—mere useless technicalities and objections which it is obvious in the beginning cannot be maintained. A similar method is now going on about cotton. Now this is not the way Sir Edward Grey takes up business. It's not the way I've done business all my life, nor that you have, nor other frank men who mean what they say and do not say things they do not mean. The constant continuation of this method is throwing away the real regard and confidence of the British Government and of the British public—very fast, too.

I sometimes wish there were not a lawyer in the world. I heard the President say once that it took him twenty years to recover from his legal habit of mind. Well, his Administration is suffering from it to a degree that is pathetic and that will leave bad results for 100 years.

I suspect that in spite of all the fuss we have made we shall at last come to acknowledge the British blockade; for it is pretty nearly parallel to the United States blockade of the South during our Civil War. The only difference is—they can't make the blockade of the Baltic against the traffic from the Scandinavian neutral states effective. That's a good technical objection; but, since practically all the traffic between those States and Germany is in our products, much of the real force of it is lost.

If a protest is made against cotton being made contraband—it'll amount to nothing and give only irritation. It will only play into Hoke Smith-German hands and accomplish nothing here.   We make as much fuss about points which we have silently to yield later as about a real principle.   Hence they all say that the State Department is merely captious, and they pay less and less attention to it and care less and less for American opinion— if only they can continue to get munitions.   We are reducing English regard to this purely mercenary basis. . . .

We are—under lawyers' quibbling—drifting apart very rapidly, to our complete isolation from the sympathy of the whole world.

Yours forever sincerely,

W. H. P.

Page refers in this letter to the "blockade"; this was the term which the British Government itself used to describe its restrictive measures against German commerce, and it rapidly passed into common speech.   Yet the truth is that Great Britain never declared an actual blockade against Germany.   A realization of this fact will clear up much that is obscure in the naval warfare of the next two years.   At the beginning of the Civil War, President Lincoln laid an interdict on all the ports of the Confederacy; the ships of all nations were forbidden entering or leaving them: any ship which attempted to evade this restriction, and was captured doing so, was confiscated, with its cargo.   That was a blockade, as the term has always been understood.   A blockade, it is well to keep in mind, is a procedure which aims at completely closing the blockaded country from all commercial intercourse with the world.   A blockading navy, if the blockade is

---

[1]Senator Hoke Smith, of Georgia, was at this time—and afterward—conducting a bitter campaign against the British blockade and advocating an embargo as a retaliation.

successful, or "effective," converts the whole country into a beleaguered fortress, just as an army, surrounding a single town, prevents goods and people from entering or leaving it. Precisely as it is the purpose of a besieging army to starve a particular city or territory into submission, so it is the aim of a blockading fleet to enforce the same treatment on the nation as a whole. It is also essential to keep in mind that the question of contraband has nothing to do with a blockade, for, under this drastic method of making warfare, everything is contraband. Contraband is a term applied to cargoes, such as rifles, machine guns, and the like, which are needed in the prosecution of war.

That a belligerent nation has the right to intercept such munitions on the way to its enemy has been admitted for centuries. Differences of opinion have raged only as to the extent to which this right could be carried—the particular articles, that is, that constituted contraband, and the methods adopted in exercising it. But the important point to be kept in mind is that where there is a blockade, there is no contraband list—for everything automatically becomes contraband. The seizure of contraband on the high seas is a war measure which is availed of only in cases in which the blockade has not been established.

Great Britain, when she declared war on Germany, did not follow President Lincoln's example and lay the whole of the German coast under interdict. Perhaps one reason for this inaction was a desire not unduly to offend neutrals, especially the United States; but the more impelling motive was geographical. The fact is that a blockade of the German seacoast would accomplish little in the way of keeping materials out of Germany. A glance at the map of northwestern Europe will make this fact clear. In the first place the seacoast of Germany is a small affair. In the North Sea the German coast is a little indentation, not more than two hundred miles long, wedged in between the longer coastlines of Holland and Denmark; in the Baltic it is somewhat more extensive, but the entrances to this sea are so circuitous and treacherous that the suggestion of a blockade here is not a practicable one. The greatest ports of Germany are located on this little North Sea coastline or on its rivers—Hamburg and Bremen. It might therefore be assumed that any nation which successfully blockaded these North Sea ports would have strangled the commerce of Germany. That is far from being the case. The point is that the political boundaries of Germany are simply fictions, when economic considerations are involved. Holland, on the west, and Denmark, on the north, are as much a part of the German transportation system as though these two countries were parts of the German Empire. Their territories and the territories of Germany are contiguous; the railroad and the canal systems of Germany, Holland, and Denmark are practically one. Such ports as Rotterdam, Amsterdam, and Copenhagen are just as useful to Germany for purposes of commerce as are Hamburg and Bremen, and, in fact, a special commercial arrangement with Rotterdam has made that city practically a port of Germany since 1868. These considerations show how ineffective would be a blockade of the German coast which did not also comprehend the coast of Holland and Denmark. Germany could still conduct her commerce through these neighbouring countries. And at this point the great difficulty arose. A blockade is an act of war and can be applied only to a country upon which war has been declared. Great Britain had declared war on Germany and could therefore legally close her ports; she had not declared war on Holland and Denmark, and therefore could not use the same measure against those friendly countries. Consequently the blockade was useless to Great Britain; and so, in the first six months of the war, the Admiralty fell back upon the milder system of declaring certain articles contraband of war and seizing ships that were suspected of carrying them to Germany.

A geographical accident had apparently largely destroyed the usefulness of the British fleet and had guaranteed Germany an unending supply of those foodstuffs without which she could not maintain her resistance for any extended period. Was Great Britain called upon to accept this situation and to deny herself the use of the blockade in this, the greatest struggle in her history? Unless the British fleet could stop cargoes which were really destined to Germany but which were bound for neutral ports, Great Britain could not win the war; if the British fleet could intercept such cargoes, then the chances strongly favoured victory. The experts of the Foreign Office searched the history of blockades and found something which resembled a precedent in the practices of the American Navy during the Civil War. In that conflict Nassau, in the Bahamas, and Matamoros, in Mexico, played a part not unlike that played by Rotterdam and Copenhagen in the recent struggle. These were both neutral ports and therefore outside the jurisdiction of the United States, just as Rotterdam and Copenhagen were outside the jurisdiction of Great Britain. They were the ports of powers with which the United States was at peace, and therefore they could not be blockaded, just as Amsterdam and Copenhagen were ports of powers with which Great Britain was now at peace.

Trade from Great Britain to the Bahamas and Mexico was ostensibly trade from one neutral port to another neutral port in the same sense as was trade from the United States to Holland and Denmark. Yet the fact is that the "neutrality" of this trade, in the Civil War, from Great Britain to the Bahamas and Mexico, was the most transparent subterfuge; such trade was not "neutral" in the slightest degree. It consisted almost entirely of contraband of war and was intended for the armies of the Confederate States, then in arms against the Federal Government. What is the reason, our Government asked, that these gentle and unwarlike inhabitants of the Bahamas have so suddenly developed such an enormous appetite for percussion caps, rifles, cannon, and other instruments of warfare? The answer, of course, lay upon the surface; the cargoes were intended for reshipment into the Southern States, and they were, in fact, immediately so reshipped. The American Government, which has always regarded realities as more important than logic, brushed aside the consideration that this trade was conducted through neutral ports, unhesitatingly seized these ships and condemned both the ships and their cargoes. Its action was without legal precedent, but our American courts devised a new principle of international law to cover the case—that of "continuous voyage" or "ultimate destination." Under this new doctrine it was maintained that cargoes of contraband could be seized anywhere upon the high seas, even though they were going from one neutral port to another, if it could be demonstrated that this contraband was really on its way to the enemy. The mere fact that it was transshipped at an intermediate neutral port was not important; the important point was the "ultimate destination." British shippers naturally raged over these decisions, but they met with little sympathy from their own government. Great Britain filed no protest against the doctrine of "continuous voyage," but recognized its fundamental soundness, and since 1865 this doctrine has been a part of international law.

Great Britain's good sense in acquiescing in our Civil War practices now met its reward; for these decisions of American courts proved a godsend in her hour of trial. The one neutral from which trouble was anticipated was the United States. What better way to meet this situation than to base British maritime warfare upon the decisions of American courts? What more ideal solution of the problem than to make Chief Justice Chase, of the United States Supreme Court, really the author of the British "blockade" against Germany? The policy of the British Foreign Office was to use the sea power of Great Britain to crush the enemy, but to do it in a way that would not alienate American sympathy and American support; clearly the one way in which both these ends could be attained was to frame these war measures upon the pronouncements of American prize courts. In a broad sense this is precisely what Sir Edward Grey now proceeded to do. There was a difference, of course, which Great Britain's enemies in the American Senate—such men as Senator Hoke Smith, of Georgia, and Senator Thomas Walsh, of Montana—proceeded to point out; but it was a difference of degree. Great Britain based her blockade measures upon the American principle of "ultimate destination," but it was necessary considerably to extend that doctrine in order to meet the necessities of the new situation. President Lincoln had applied this principle to absolute contraband, such as powder, shells, rifles, and other munitions of war. Great Britain now proceeded to apply it to that nebulous class of commodities known as "conditional contraband," the chief of which was foodstuffs. If the United States, while a war was pending, could evolve the idea of "ultimate destination" and apply it to absolute contraband, could not Great Britain, while another war was pending, carry it one degree further and make it include conditional contraband? Thus reasoned the British Foreign Office. To this Mr. Lansing replied that to stop foodstuffs on the way to Germany through a neutral port was simply to blockade a neutral port, and that this was something utterly without precedent. Seizing contraband is not an act of war against the nation whose ships are seized; blockading a port is an act of war; what right therefore had Great Britain to adopt measures against Holland, Denmark, and Sweden which virtually amounted to a blockade?

This is the reason why Great Britain, in the pronouncement of March 1, 1915, and the Order in Council of March 11, 1915, did not describe these measures as a "blockade." President Wilson described his attack on Mexico in 1914 as "measures short of war," and now someone referred to the British restrictions on neutral commerce as "measures short of blockade." The British sought another escape from their predicament by justifying this proceeding, not on the general principles of warfare, but on the ground of reprisal. Germany declared her submarine warfare on merchant ships on February 4, 1915; Great Britain replied with her announcement of March 1st, in which she declared her intention of preventing "commodities of any kind from reaching or leaving Germany." The British advanced this procedure as a retaliation for the illegal warfare which Germany had declared on merchant shipping, both that of the enemy and of neutrals. "The British and French governments will therefore hold themselves free to detain and take into port ships carrying goods of presumed enemy destination, ownership, and origin." This sentence accurately describes the purposes of a blockade—to cut the enemy off from all commercial

Col. Edward M. House.   From a painting by P. A. Laszlo

The Rt. Hon. Herbert Henry Asquith, Prime Minister
of Great Britain, 1908–1916

relations with the outside world; yet the procedure Great
Britain now proposed to follow was not that of a blockade.
When this interdict is classically laid, any ship that attempts to run the lines is penalized with confiscation,
along with its cargo; but such a penalty was not to be
exacted in the present instance. Great Britain now proposed to purchase cargoes of conditional contraband discovered on seized ships and return the ships themselves to
their owners, and this soon became the established practice. Not only did the Foreign Office purchase all cotton
which was seized on its way to Germany, but it took measures to maintain the price in the markets of the world.
In the succeeding months Southern statesmen in both
Houses of Congress railed against the British seizure of
their great staple, yet the fact was that cotton was all this
time steadily advancing in price. When Senator Hoke
Smith made a long speech advocating an embargo on the
shipment of munitions as a punishment to Great Britain
for stopping American cotton on the way to Germany,
the acute John Sharp Williams, of Mississippi, arose in the
Senate and completely annihilated the Georgia politician
by demonstrating how the Southern planters were growing
rich out of the war.

That the so-called "blockade" situation was a tortuous
one must be apparent from this attempt to set forth the
salient facts. The basic point was that there could be no
blockade of Germany unless the neutral ports of contiguous countries were also blockaded, and Great Britain
believed that she had found a precedent for doing this in
the operations of the American Navy in the Civil War.
But it is obvious that the situation was one which would
provide a great feast for the lawyers. That Page sympathized with this British determination to keep foodstuffs out of Germany, his correspondence shows. Day

after day the "protests" from Washington rained upon his desk. The history of our foreign relations for 1915 and 1916 is largely made up of an interminable correspondence dealing with seized cargoes, and the routine of the Embassy was an unending nightmare of "demands," "complaints," "precedents," "cases," "notes," "detentions" of Chicago meats, of Southern cotton, and the like. The American Embassy in London contains hundreds of volumes of correspondence which took place during Page's incumbency; more material has accumulated for those five years than for the preceding century and a quarter of the Government's existence. The greater part of this mass deals with intercepted cargoes.

The following memorandum, part of which was incorporated in a letter to the President, gives a fair idea of the atmosphere that prevailed in London while this correspondence was engaging the Ambassador's mind:

The truth is, in their present depressed mood, the United States is forgotten—everything's forgotten but the one great matter in hand. For the moment at least, the English do not care what we do or what we think or whether we exist—except those critics of things-in-general who use us as a target since they must take a crack at somebody. And I simply cannot describe the curious effect that is produced on men here by the apparent utter lack of understanding in the United States of the phase the war has now entered and of the mood that this phase has brought. I pick up an American paper eight days old and read solemn evidence to show that the British Government is interrupting our trade in order to advance its own at our expense, whereas the truth is that the British Government hasn't given six seconds' thought in six months to anybody's trade—not even its own.

When I am asked to inquire why Pfister and Schmidt's telegram from New York to Schimmelpfenig and Johann in Holland was stopped (the reason is reasonably obvious), I try to picture to myself the British Minister in Washington making inquiry of our Government on the day after Bull Run, why the sailing boat loaded with persimmon blocks to make golf clubs is delayed in Hampton Roads.

I think I have neither heard nor read anything from the United States in three months that didn't seem so remote as to suggest the captain of the sailing ship from Hongkong who turned up at Southampton in February and had not even heard that there was a war. All day long I see and hear women who come to ask if I can make inquiry about their sons and husbands, "dead or missing," with an interval given to a description of a man half of whose body was splashed against a brick wall last night on the Strand when a Zeppelin bomb tore up the street and made projectiles of the pavement; as I walk to and from the Embassy the Park is full of wounded and their nurses; every man I see tells me of a new death; every member of the Government talks about military events or of Balkan venality; the man behind the counter at the cigar store reads me part of a letter just come from his son, telling how he advanced over a pile of dead Germans and one of them grunted and turned under his feet—they (the English alone) are spending $25,000,000 a day to keep this march going over dead Germans; then comes a telegram predicting blue ruin for American importers and a cheerless Christmas for American children if a cargo of German toys be not quickly released at Rotterdam, and I dimly recall the benevolent unction with which American children last Christmas sent a shipload of toys to this side of the world—many of them for German children —to the tune of "God bless us all"—do you wonder we often have to pinch ourselves to find out if we are we; and what year of the Lord is it? What *is* the vital thing— the killing of fifty people last night by a Zeppelin within sight of St. Paul's on one side and of Westminster Abbey on the other, or is it making representations to Sir Edward Grey, who has hardly slept for a week because his despatches from Sofia, Athens, Belgrade, and Salonika come at all hours, each possibly reporting on which side a new government may throw its army—to decide perhaps the fate of the canal leading to Asia, the vast British Asiatic empire at stake—is it making representations to Sir Edward while his mind is thus occupied, that it is of the greatest importance to the United States Government that a particular German who is somewhere in this Kingdom shall be permitted to go to the United States because he knows how to dye sealskins and our sealskins are yet undyed and the winter is coming? There will be no new sealskins here, for every man and woman must give half his income to keep the cigarman's son marching over dead Germans, some of whom grunt and turn under his feet. Dumba is at Falmouth to-day and gets just two lines in the newspapers. Nothing and nobody gets three lines unless he or it in some way furthers the war. Every morning the Washington despatches say that Mr. Lansing is about to send a long note to England. England won't read it till there comes a lull in the fighting or in the breathless diplomatic struggle with the Balkans. London and the Government are now in much the same mood that Washington and Lincoln's administration were in after Lee had crossed the Potomac on his way to Gettysburg. Northcliffe, the Lord of Yellow Journals, but an uncommonly brilliant fellow, has taken to his bed from sheer nervous worry. "The revelations that are imminent," says he, "will shake the world—the incom-

petence of the Government, the losses along the Dardanelles, the throwing away of British chances in the Balkans, perhaps the actual defeat of the Allies." I regard
Lord Northcliffe less as an entity than as a symptom.
But he is always very friendly to us and he knows the
United States better than any Englishman that I know
except Bryce. He and Bryce are both much concerned
about our Note's coming just "at this most distressing
time." "If it come when we are calmer, no matter; but
now it cannot receive attention and many will feel that
the United States has hit on a most unhappy moment—
almost a cruel moment—to remind us of our sins."—
That's the substance of what they say.

Overwork, or perhaps mainly the indescribable strain
on the nerves and vitality of men, caused by this experience, for which in fact men are not built, puts one of
our staff after another in bed. None has been seriously
sick: the malady takes some form of "grip." On the
whole we've been pretty lucky in spite of this almost
regular temporary breakdown of one man after another.
I've so far escaped. But I am grieved to hear that
Whitlock is abed—"no physical ailment whatever—just
worn out," his doctor says. I have tried to induce him
and his wife to come here and make me a visit; but one
characteristic of this war-malady is the conviction of the
victim that he is somehow necessary to hold the world
together. About twice a week I get to the golf links and
take the risk of the world's falling apart and thus escape
both illness and its illusions.

"I cannot begin to express my deep anxiety and even
uneasiness about the relations of these two great governments and peoples," Page wrote about this time.
"The friendship of the United States and Great Britain

is all that now holds the world together. It is the greatest asset of civilization left. All the cargoes of copper and oil in the world are not worth as much to the world. Yet when a shipper's cargo is held up he does not think of civilization and of the future of mankind and of free government; he thinks only of his cargo and of the in- dignity that he imagines has been done him; and what is the American Government for if not to protect his rights? Of course he's right; but there must be somebody some- where who sees things in their right proportion. The man with an injury rushes to the Department of State— quite properly. He is in a mood to bring England to book. Now comes the critical stage in the journey of his complaint. The State Department hurries it on to me— very properly; every man's right must be guarded and de- fended—a right to get his cargo to market, a right to get on a steamer at Queenstown, a right to have his censored telegram returned, any kind of a right, if he have a right. Then the Department, not wittingly, I know, but hu- manly, almost inevitably, in the great rush of overwork, sends his 'demands' to me, catching much of his tone and apparently insisting on the removal of his grievance as a right, without knowing all the facts in the case. The telegrams that come to me are full of 'protests' and 'demands'—protest and demand this, protest and demand that. A man from Mars who should read my book of telegrams received during the last two months would find it difficult to explain how the two governments have kept at peace. It is this serious treatment of trifling griev- ances which makes us feel here that the exactions and dis- locations and necessary disturbances of this war are not understood at home.

"I assure you (and there are plenty of facts to prove it) that this Government (both for unselfish and selfish reasons) puts a higher value on our friendship than on any similar thing in the world. They will go—they are going—the full length to keep it. But, in proportion to our tendency to nag them about little things will the value set on our friendship diminish and will their confidence in our sincerity decline."

The note which Lord Bryce and Lord Northcliffe so dreaded reached the London Embassy in October, 1915. The State Department had spent nearly six months in preparing it; it was the American answer to the so-called blockade established by the Order in Council of the preceding March. Evidently its contents fulfilled the worst forebodings:

To Edward M. House

London, November 12, 1915.

DEAR HOUSE:

I have a great respect for the British Navy. Admiral Jellicoe now has under his command 3,000 ships of all sorts—far and away the biggest fleet, I think, that was ever assembled. For the first time since the ocean was poured out, one navy practically commands all the seas: nothing sails except by its grace. It is this fleet of course that will win the war. The beginning of the end—however far off yet the end may be—is already visible by reason of the economic pressure on Germany. But for this fleet, by the way, London would be in ruins, all its treasure looted; every French seacoast city and the Italian peninsula would be as Belgium and Poland are; and thousands of English women would be violated—just as dead French girls are found in many German trenches that have been taken in France. Hence I greatly respect the British fleet.

We have a good navy, too, for its size, and a naval personnel as good as any afloat. I hear—with much joy—that we are going to make our navy bigger—as much bigger (God save the mark!) as Bryan will permit.

Now, whatever the future bring, since any fighting enterprise that may ever be thrust on us will be just and justified, we must see to it that we win, as doubtless we shall and as hitherto we always have won. We must be dead sure of winning. Well, whatever fight may be thrust on us by anybody, anywhere, at any time, for any reason—if it only be generally understood beforehand that our fleet and the British fleet shoot the same language, there'll be no fight thrust upon us. The biggest bully in the world wouldn't dare kick the sorriest dog we have.

Here, therefore, is a Peace Programme for you—the only basis for a permanent peace in the world. There's no further good in having venerable children build houses of sand at The Hague; there's no further good in peace organizations or protective leagues to enforce peace. We had as well get down to facts. So far as ensuring peace is concerned the biggest fact in the world is the British fleet. The next biggest fact is the American fleet, because of itself and still more because of the vast reserve power of the United States which it implies. If these two fleets perfectly understand one another about the undesirability of wars of aggression, there'll be no more big wars as long as this understanding continues. Such an understanding calls for no treaty—it calls only for courtesy.

And there is no other peace-basis worth talking about—by men who know how the world is governed.

Since I have lived here I have spent my days and nights, my poor brain, and my small fortune all most freely and gladly to get some understanding of the men who rule this Kingdom, and of the women and the customs and the traditions that rule these men—to get their trick of thought, the play of their ideals, the working of their imagination, the springs of their instincts. It is impossible for any man to know just how well he himself does such a difficult task—how accurately he is coming to understand the sources and character of a people's actions. Yet, at the worst, I do know something about the British: I know enough to make very sure of the soundness of my conclusion that they are necessary to us and we to them. Else God would have permitted the world to be peopled in some other way. And when we see that the world will be saved by such an artificial combination as England and Russia and France and Japan and Serbia, it calls for no great wisdom to see the natural way whereby it must be saved in the future.

For this reason every day that I have lived here it has been my conscious aim to do what I could to bring about a condition that shall make sure of this—that, whenever we may have need of the British fleet to protect our shores or to prevent an aggressive war anywhere, it shall be ours by a natural impulse and necessity—even without the asking.

I have found out that the first step toward that end is courtesy; that the second step is courtesy, and the third step—such a fine and high courtesy (which includes courage) as the President showed in the Panama tolls controversy. We have—we and the British—common aims and character. Only a continuous and sincere courtesy—over periods of strain as well as of calm—is necessary for as complete an understanding as will be required for the automatic guidance of the world in peaceful ways.

Now, a difference is come between us—the sort of difference that handled as between friends would serve only to bind us together with a sturdier respect. We

send a long lawyer's Note, not discourteous but wholly
uncourteous, which is far worse. I am writing now only
of the manner of the Note, not of its matter. There is
not a courteous word, nor a friendly phrase, nor a kindly
turn in it, not an allusion even to an old acquaintance, to
say nothing of an old friendship, not a word of thanks for
courtesies or favours done us, not a hint of sympathy in
the difficulties of the time. There is nothing in its tone
to show that it came from an American to an Englishman:
it might have been from a Hottentot to a Fiji-Islander.

I am almost sure—I'll say quite sure—that this un-
courteous manner is far more important than its endless
matter. It has greatly hurt our friends, the real men of
the Kingdom. It has made the masses angry—which is
of far less importance than the severe sorrow that our
discourtesy of manner has brought to our friends—I fear
to all considerate and thoughtful Englishmen.

Let me illustrate: When the Panama tolls controversy
arose, Taft ceased to speak the language of the natural
man and lapsed into lawyer's courthouse zigzagging mutterings. Knox wrote a letter to the British Government
that would have made an enemy of the most affectionate
twin brother—all mere legal twists and turns, as agreeable
as a pocketful of screws. Then various bovine "international lawyers" wrote books about it. I read them and
became more and more confused the further I went: you
always do. It took me some time to recover from this
word-drunk debauch and to find my own natural intelligence again, the common sense that I was born with.
Then I saw that the whole thing went wrong from the place
where that Knox legal note came in. Congressmen in the
backwoods quoted cryptic passages from it, thought they
were saying something, and proceeded to make their
audiences believe that somehow England had hit us with

a club—or would have hit us but for Knox. That pure discourtesy kept us apart from English sympathy for something like two years.

Then the President took it up. He threw the legal twaddle into the gutter. He put the whole question in a ten-minutes' speech to Congress, full of clearness and fairness and high courtesy. It won even the rural Congressmen. It was read in every capital and the men who conduct every government looked up and said, "This is a real man, a brave man, a just man." You will recall what Sir Edward Grey said to me: "The President has taught us all a lesson and set us all a high example in the noblest courtesy."

This one act brought these two nations closer together than they had ever been since we became an independent nation. It was an act of courtesy. . . .

My dear House, suppose the postman some morning were to leave at your door a thing of thirty-five heads and three appendices, and you discovered that it came from an old friend whom you had long known and greatly valued—this vast mass of legal stuff, without a word or a turn of courtesy in it—what would you do? He had a grievance, your old friend had. Friends often have. But instead of explaining it to you, he had gone and had his lawyers send this many-headed, much-appendiced ton of stuff. It wasn't by that method that you found your way from Austin, Texas, to your present eminence and wisdom. Nor was that the way our friend found his way from a little law-office in Atlanta, where I first saw him, to the White House.

More and more I am struck with this—that governments are human. They are not remote abstractions, nor impersonal institutions. Men conduct them; and they do not cease to be men. A man is made up of six parts of human nature and four parts of facts and other things—a little reason, some prejudice, much provincialism, and of the particular fur or skin that suits his habitat. When you wish to win a man to do what *you* want him to do, you take along a few well-established facts, some reasoning and such-like, but you take along also three or four or five parts of human nature—kindliness, courtesy, and such things—sympathy and a human touch.

If a man be six parts human and four parts of other things, a government, especially a democracy, is seven, or eight, or nine parts human nature. It's the most human thing I know. The best way to manage governments and nations—so long as they are disposed to be friendly— is the way we manage one another. I have a confirmation of this in the following comment which came to me to-day. It was made by a friendly member of Parliament.

"The President himself dealt with Germany. Even in his severity he paid the Germans the compliment of a most courteous tone in his Note. But in dealing with us he seems to have called in the lawyers of German importers and Chicago pork-packers. I miss the high Presidential courtesy that we had come to expect from Mr. Wilson."

An American banker here has told me of the experience of an American financial salesman in the city the day after our Note was published. His business is to make calls on bankers and other financial men, to sell them securities. He is a man of good address who is popular with his clients. The first man he called on, on that day, said: "I don't wish to be offensive to you. But I have only one way to show my feeling of indignation toward the United States, and that is, to have nothing more to do with Americans."

The next man said: "No, nothing to-day, I thank you. No—nor to-morrow either; nor the next day. Good morning."

After four or five such greetings, the fellow gave it up and is now doing nothing.

I don't attach much importance to such an incident as this, except as it gives a hint of the general feeling. These financial men probably haven't even read our Note. Few people have. But they have all read the short and sharp newspaper summary which preceded it in the English papers. But what such an incident does indicate is the prevalence of a state of public feeling which would prevent the Government from yielding any of our demands even if the Government so wished. It has now been nearly a week since the Note was published. I have seen most of the neutral ministers. Before the Note came they expressed great eagerness to see it: it would champion their cause. Since it came not one of them has mentioned it to me. The Secretary of one of them remarked, after being invited to express himself: "It is too—too—long!" And, although I have seen most of the Cabinet this week, not a man mentioned it to me. People seem studiously to avoid it, lest they give offense.

I have, however, got one little satisfaction. An American—a half-expatriated loafer who talks "art"—you know the intellectually affected and degenerate type—screwed his courage up and told me that he felt ashamed of his country. I remarked that I felt sure the feeling was mutual. That, I confess, made me feel better.

As nearly as I can make out, the highwater mark of English good-feeling toward us in all our history was after the President's Panama tolls courtesy. The low-water mark, since the Civil War, I am sure, is now. The Cleveland Venezuela message came at a time of no nervous strain and did, I think, produce no long-lasting effect. A part of the present feeling is due to the English conviction that we have been taken in by the Germans in the submarine controversy, but a large part is due to the lack of courtesy in this last Note—the manner in which it was written even more than its matter. As regards its matter, I have often been over what I conceive to be the main points with Sir Edward Grey—very frankly and without the least offense. He has said: "We may have to arbitrate these things," as he might say, "We had better take a cab because it is raining." It is easily possible—or it was—to discuss anything with this Government without offense. I have, in fact, stood up before Sir Edward's fire and accused him of stealing a large part of the earth's surface, and we were just as good friends afterward as before. But I never drew a lawyer's indictment of him as a land-thief: that's different.

I suppose no two peoples or governments ever quite understand one another. Perhaps they never will. That is too much to hope for. But when one government writes to another it ought to write (as men do) with some reference to the personality of the other and to their previous relations, since governments are more human than men. Of course I don't know who wrote the Note. Hence I can talk about it freely to you without implying criticism of anybody in particular. But the man who wrote it never saw the British Government and wouldn't know it if he met it in the road. To him it is a mere legal entity, a wicked, impersonal institution against which he has the task of drawing an indictment—not the task of trying to persuade it to confess the propriety of a certain course of conduct. In his view, it is a wicked enemy to start with —like the Louisiana lottery of a previous generation or the Standard Oil Company of our time.

One would have thought, since we were six months in preparing it, that a draft of the Note would have been sent to the man on the ground whom our Government keeps in London to study the situation at first hand and to make the best judgment he can about the most effective methods of approach on delicate and difficult matters. If that had been done, I should have suggested a courteous short Note saying that we are obliged to set forth such and such views about marine law and the rights of neutrals, to His Majesty's Government; and that the contention of the United States Government was herewith sent—etc., etc.—Then this identical Note (with certain court-house, strong, shirt-sleeve adjectives left out) could have come without arousing any feeling whatsoever. Of course I have no personal vanity in saying this to you. I am sure I outgrew that foible many years ago. But such a use of an ambassador—of any ambassador—is obviously one of the best and most natural uses he could be put to; and all governments but ours do put their ambassadors to such a use: that's what they have 'em for.

Per contra: a telegram has just come in saying that a certain Lichtenstein in New York had a lot of goods stopped by the British Government, which (by an arrangement made with their attorney here) agreed to buy them at a certain price: will I go and find out why the Government hasn't yet paid Lichtenstein and when he may expect his money? Is it an ambassadorial duty to collect a private bill for Lichtenstein, in a bargain with which our Government has had nothing to do? I have telegraphed the Department, quite calmly, that I don't think it is. I venture to say no ambassador ever had such a request as that before from his Government.

My dear House, I often wonder if my years of work here—the kind of high good work I've tried to do—have not been thrown away. I've tried to take and to busy myself with a long-range view of great subjects. The British Empire and the United States will be here long after we are dead, and their relations will continue to be one of the most important matters—perhaps the most important matter—in the world. Well, now think of Lichtenstein's bill!

To get back where I started—I fear, therefore, that, when I next meet the Admiral of the Grand Fleet (with whom I used to discuss everything quite freely before he sailed away to the war), he may forget to mention that we may have his 3,000 ships at our need.

Since this present difference is in danger of losing the healing influence of a kindly touch—has become an un-courteous monster of 35 heads and 3 appendices—I see no early end of it. The British Foreign Office has a lot of lawyers in its great back offices. They and our lawyers will now butt and rebut as long as a goat of them is left alive on either side. The two governments—the two human, kindly groups—have retired: they don't touch, on this matter, now. The lawyers will have the time of their lives, each smelling the blood of the other.

If more notes must come—as the English papers report over and over again every morning and every afternoon— the President might do much by writing a brief, human document to accompany the Appendices. If it be done courteously, we can accuse them of stealing sheep and of dyeing the skins to conceal the theft—without provoking the slightest bad feeling; and, in the end, they'll pay another *Alabama* award without complaint and frame the check and show it to future ambassadors as Sir Edward shows the *Alabama* check to me sometimes.

And it'll be a lasting shame (and may bring other Great Wars) if lawyers are now permitted to tear the garments with which Peace ought to be clothed as soon as she can escape from her present rags and tatters.

Yours always heartily,

W. H. P.

P. S. My dear House: Since I have—in weeks and months past—both telegraphed and written the Department (and I presume the President has seen what I've sent) about the feeling here, I've written this letter to you and not to the President nor Lansing. I will not run the risk of seeming to complain—nor even of seeming to seem to complain. But if you think it wise to send or show this letter to the President, I'm willing you should. This job was botched: there's no doubt about that. We shall not recover for many a long, long year. The identical indictment could have been drawn with admirable temper and the way laid down for arbitration and for keeping our interpretation of the law and precedents intact—all done in a way that would have given no offense.

The feeling runs higher and higher every day—goes deeper and spreads wider.

Now on top of it comes the *Ancona*.[1] The English press, practically unanimously, makes sneering remarks about our Government. After six months it has got no results from the *Lusitania* controversy, which Bernstorff is allowed to prolong in secret session while factories are blown up, ships supplied with bombs, and all manner of outrages go on (by Germans) in the United States. The English simply can't understand why Bernstorff is allowed to stay. They predict that nothing will come of the *Ancona* case, nor of any other case. Nobody wants us to get into the war—nobody who counts—but they are

---

[1]Torpedoed off Sardinia on Nov. 7, 1915, by the Austrians. There was a large loss of life, including many Americans.

losing respect for us because we seem to them to submit to anything.

We've simply dropped out. No English person ever mentions our Government to me. But they talk to one another all the time about the political anæmia of the United States Government. They think that Bernstorff has the State Department afraid of him and that the Pacifists dominate opinion—the Pacifists-at-any-price. I no longer even have a chance to explain any of these things to anybody I know.

It isn't the old question we used to discuss of our having no friend in the world when the war ends. It's gone far further than that. It is now whether the United States Government need be respected by anybody.

W. H. P.

CHAPTER XVI

DARK DAYS FOR THE ALLIES

To Edward M. House

June 30, 1915.

MY DEAR HOUSE:

There's a distinct wave of depression here—perhaps I'd better say a period of setbacks has come. So far as we can find out only the Germans are doing anything in the war on land. The position in France is essentially the same as it was in November, only the Germans are much more strongly entrenched. Their great plenty of machine guns enables them to use fewer men and to kill more than the Allies. The Russians also lack ammunition and are yielding more and more territory. The Allies —so you hear now—will do well if they get their little army away from the Dardanelles before the German-Turks eat 'em alive, and no Balkan state comes in to help the Allies. Italy makes progress—slowly, of course, over almost impassable mountains—etc., etc. Most of this doleful recital I think is true; and I find more and more men here who have lost hope of seeing an end of the war in less than two or three years, and more and more who fear that the Germans will never be forced out of Belgium. And the era of the giant aeroplane seems about to come—a machine that can carry several tons and several men and go great distances—two engines, two propellers, and the like. It isn't at all impossible, I am told, that these machines may be the things that will at last end the war—possibly, but I doubt it.

81

At any rate, it is true that a great wave of discouragement is come. All these events and more seem to prove to my mind the rather dismal failure the Liberal Government made—a failure really to grasp the problem. It was a dead failure. Of course they are waking up now, when they are faced with a certain dread lest many soldiers prefer frankly to die rather than spend another winter in practically the same trenches. You hear rumours, too, of great impending military scandals—God knows whether there be any truth in them or not.

In a word, while no Englishman gives up or will ever give up—that's all rot—the job he has in hand is not going well. He's got to spit on his hands and buckle up his belt two holes tighter yet. And I haven't seen a man for a month who dares hope for an end of the fight within any time that he can foresee.

I had a talk to-day with the Russian Ambassador.[1] He wished to know how matters stood between the United States and Great Britain. I said to him: "I'll give you a task if you have leisure. Set to and help me hurry up your distinguished Ally in dealing with our shipping troubles."

The old man laughed—that seemed a huge joke to him; he threw up his hands and exclaimed—"My God! He is slow about his own business—has always been slow—can't be anything else."

After more such banter, the nigger in his wood-pile poked his head out: "Is there any danger," he asked, "that munitions may be stopped?"

The Germans have been preparing northern France for German occupation. No French are left there, of course, except women and children and old men. They must be fed or starved or deported. The Germans put them on

---

[1] Count Beckendorff.

trains—a whole village at a time—and run them to the Swiss frontier. Of course the Swiss pass them on into France. The French have their own and—the Germans will have northern France without any French population, if this process goes on long enough.

The mere bang! bang! frightful era of the war is passed. The Germans are settling down to permanent business with their great organizing machine. Of course they talk about the freedom of the seas and such mush-mush; of course they'd like to have Paris and rob it of enough money to pay what the war has cost them, and London, too. But what they really want for keeps is seacoast— Belgium and as much of the French coast as they can win. That's really what they are out gunning for. Of course, somehow at some time they mean to get Holland, too, and Denmark, if they really need it. Then they'll have a very respectable seacoast—the thing that they chiefly lack now.

More and more people are getting their nerves knocked out. I went to a big hospital on Sunday, twenty-five miles out of London. They showed me an enormous, muscular Tommy sitting by himself in a chair under the trees. He had had a slight wound which quickly got well. But his speech was gone. That came back, too, later. But then he wouldn't talk and he'd insist on going off by himself. He's just knocked out—you can't find out just how much gumption he has left. That's what the war did for him: it stupefied him. Well, it's stupefied lots of folks who have never seen a trench. That's what's happened. Of all the men who started in with the game, I verily believe that Lloyd George is holding up best. He organized British finance. Now he's organizing British industry.

It's got hot in London—hotter than I've ever known

it. It gets lonelier (more people going away) and sadder
—more wounded coming back and more visible sorrow.
We seem to be settling down to something that is more
or less like Paris—so far less, but it may become more and
more like it. And the confident note of an earlier period
is accompanied by a dull undertone of much less cheerfulness. The end is—in the lap of the gods.

W. H. P.

To Arthur W. Page

American Embassy, London,
July 25, 1915.

DEAR ARTHUR:

. . . Many men here are very active in their
thought about the future relations of the United States
and Great Britain. Will the war bring or leave them
closer together? If the German machine be completely
smashed (and it may not be completely smashed) the
Japanese danger will remain. I do not know how to
estimate that danger accurately. But there is such a
danger. And, if the German wild beast ever come to life
again, there's an eternal chance of trouble with it. For
defensive purposes it may become of the very first importance that the whole English-speaking world should
stand together—not in entangling alliance, but with a
much clearer understanding than we have ever yet had.
I'll indicate to you some of my cogitations on this subject by trying to repeat what I told Philip Kerr[1] a fortnight ago—one Sunday in the country. I can write this
to you without seeming to parade my own opinions.—
Kerr is one of "The Round Table," perhaps the best
group of men here for the real study and free discussion
of large political subjects. Their quarterly, *The Round*

---

[1]Afterward private secretary to Premier Lloyd George.

Table, is the best review, I dare say, in the world. Kerr is red hot for a close and perfect understanding between Great Britain and the United States. I told him that, since Great Britain had only about forty per cent. of the white English-speaking people and the United States had about sixty per cent., I hoped in his natural history that the tail didn't wag the dog. I went on:

"You now have the advantage of us in your aggregation of three centuries of accumulated wealth—the spoil of all the world—and in the talent that you have developed for conserving it and adding to it and in the institutions you have built up to perpetuate it—your merchant ships, your insurance, your world-wide banking, your mortgages on all new lands; but isn't this the only advantage you have? This advantage will pass. You are now shooting away millions and millions, and you will have a debt that is bound to burden industry. On our side, we have a more recently mixed race than yours; you've begun to inbreed. We have also (and therefore) more adaptability, a greater keenness of mind in our masses; we are Old-World men set free—free of classes and traditions and all that they connote. Your so-called democracy is far behind ours. Your aristocracy and your privileges necessarily bring a social and economic burden. Half your people look backward.

"Your leadership rests on your wealth and on the power that you've built on your wealth."

When he asked me how we were to come closer together—"closer together, with your old-time distrust of us and with your remoteness?"—I stopped him at "remoteness."

"That's the reason," I said. "Your idea of our 'remoteness.' 'Remoteness' from what? From you? Are you not betraying the only real difficulty of a closer sympathy by assuming that you are the centre of the world? When you bring yourself to think of the British Empire as a part of the American Union—mind you, I am not saying that you would be formally admitted—but when you are yourselves in close enough sympathy with us to wish to be admitted, the chief difficulty of a real union of thought will be gone. You recall Lord Rosebery's speech in which he pictured the capital of the British Empire being moved to Washington if the American Colonies had been retained under the Crown? Well, it was the Crown that was the trouble, and the capital of English-speaking folk has been so moved and you still remain 'remote.' Drop 'remote' from your vocabulary and your thought and we'll actually be closer together."

It's an enormous problem—just how to bring these countries closer together. Perhaps nothing can do it but some great common danger or some great common adventure. But this is one of the problems of your lifetime. England can't get itself clean loose from the continent nor from continental mediævalism; and with that we can have nothing to do. Men like Kerr think that somehow a great push toward democracy here will be given by the war. I don't quite see how. So far the aristocracy have made perhaps the best showing in defense of English liberty. They are paying the bills of the war; they have sent their sons; these sons have died like men; and their parents never whimper. It's a fine breed for such great uses as these. There was a fine incident in the House of Lords the other day, which gave the lie to the talk that one used to hear here about "degeneracy." Somebody made a perfectly innocent proposal to complete a list of peers and peers' sons who had fallen in the war—a thing that will, of course, be done, just as a similar list will be compiled of the House of Commons, of Oxford and Cambridge Universities. But one peer after another objected vigorously lest such a list appear immodest. "We are but doing our duty. Let the matter rest there."

In a time like this the aristocracy proves its worth. In fact, all aristocracies grew chiefly out of wars, and perhaps they are better for wars than a real democracy. Here, you see, you run into one of those contradictions in life and history which make the world so hard to change. . . .

You know there are some reasons why peace, whenever it may come, will bring problems as bad as the problems of the war itself. I can think of no worse task than the long conferences of the Allies with their conflicting interests and ambitions. Then must come their conferences with the enemy. Then there are sure to be other conferences to try to make peace secure. And, of course, many are going to be dissatisfied and disappointed, and perhaps out of these disappointments other wars may come. The world will not take up its knitting and sit quietly by the fire for many a year to come. . . .

Affectionately,

W. H. P.

One happiness came to Mr. and Mrs. Page in the midst of all these war alarums. On August 4, 1915, their only daughter, Katharine, was married to Mr. Charles G. Loring, of Boston, Massachusetts. The occasion gave the King an opportunity of showing the high regard in which Page and his family were held. It had been planned that the wedding should take place in Westminster Abbey, but the King very courteously offered Miss Page the Royal chapel in St. James's Palace. This was a distinguished compliment, as it was the first time that any marriage, in which both bride and bridegroom were foreigners, had ever been celebrated in this building, which for centuries has been the scene of royal weddings. The special place which his daughter had always held in the Ambassador's affections is apparent in the many letters that now followed her to her new home in the United States. The unique use Page made of the initials of his daughter's name was characteristic.

To Mrs. Charles G. Loring

London, September 1, 1915.

My dear K. A. P-tain:

Here's a joke on your mother and Frank: We three (and Smith) went up to Broadway in the car, to stay there a little while and then to go on into Wales, etc. The hotel is an old curiosity shop; you sit on Elizabethan chairs by a Queen Anne table, on a drunken floor, and look at the pewter platters on the wall or do your best to look at them, for the ancient windows admit hardly any light. "Oh! lovely," cries Frank; and then he and your mother make out in the half-darkness a perfectly wonderful copper mug on the mantelpiece; and you go out and come in the ramshackle door (stooping every time) after you've felt all about for the rusty old iron latch, and then you step down two steps (or fall), presently to step up two more. Well, for dinner we had six kinds of meat and two meat pies and potatoes and currants! My dinner was a potato. I'm old and infirm and I have many ailments, but I'm not so bad off as to be able to live on a potato a day. And since we were having a vacation, I didn't see the point. So I came home where I have seven courses for dinner, all good; and Mrs. Leggett took my place in the car. That carnivorous company went on. They've got to eat six kinds of meat and two meat pies and—currants! I haven't. Your mother calls me up on the phone every morning—me, who am living here in luxury, seven courses at every dinner—and asks anxiously, "And how *are* you, dear?" I answer: " Prime, and how are *you*?" We are all enjoying ourselves, you see, and I don't have to eat six kinds of meat and two meat pies and—currants! They do; and may Heaven save 'em and get 'em home safe!

It's lovely in London now—fine, shining days and showers at night and Ranelagh beautiful, and few people here; but I don't deny its loneliness—somewhat. Yet sleep is good, and easy and long. I have neither an ocean voyage nor six kinds of meat and two meat pies and currants. I congratulate myself and write to you and mother.

You'll land to-morrow or next day—good; I congratulate you. Salute the good land for me and present my respectful compliments to vegetables that have taste and fruit that is not sour—to the sunshine, in fact, and to everything that ripens and sweetens in its glow.

And you're now (when this reaches you) fixing up your home—your *own* home, dear Kitty. Bless your dear life, you left a home here—wasn't it a good and nice one?—left it very lonely for the man who has loved you twenty-four years and been made happy by your presence. But he'll love you twenty-five more and on and on—always. So you haven't lost that—nor can you. And it's very fit and right that you should build your own nest; that adds another happy home, you see. And I'm very sure it will be very happy always. Whatever I can do to make it so, now or ever, you have only to say. But —your mother took your photograph with her and got it out of the bag and put it on the bureau as soon as she went to her room—a photograph taken when you were a little girl.

Hodson[1] came up to see me to-day and with tears of gratitude in his voice told me of the present that you and Chud had made him. He is very genuinely pleased. As for the rest, life goes on as usual.

I laugh as I think of all your new aunts and cousins looking you over and wondering if you'll fit, and then saying to one another as they go to bed: "She is lovely—isn't she?" I could tell 'em a thing or two if I had a whack at 'em.

And you'll soon have all your pretty things in place in your pretty home, and a lot more that I haven't seen. I'll see 'em all before many years—and you, too! Tell me, did Chud get you a dinner book? Keep your record of things: you'll enjoy it in later years. And you'll have a nice time this autumn—your new kinsfolk, your new friends and old and Boston and Cambridge. If you run across Mr. Mifflin, William Roscoe Thayer, James Ford Rhodes, President Eliot—these are my particular old friends whose names occur at the moment.

My love to you and Chud too,

Affectionately,

W. H. P.

The task of being "German Ambassador to Great Britain" was evidently not without its irritations.

To Arthur W. Page

September 15, 1915.

DEAR ARTHUR:

Yesterday was my German day. When the boy came up to my room, I told him I had some official calls to make.

---

[1] A messenger in the American Embassy.

"Therefore get out my oldest and worst suit." He looked much confused; and when I got up both my worst and best suits were laid out. Evidently he thought he must have misunderstood me. I asked your mother if she was ready to go down to breakfast. "Yes."—"Well, then I'll leave you." She grunted something and when we both got down she asked: "What *did* you say to me upstairs?" I replied: "I regard the incident as closed." She looked a sort of pitying look at me and a minute or two later asked: "What on earth is the matter with you? Can't you hear at all?" I replied: "No. Therefore let's talk." She gave it up, but looked at me again to make sure I was all there.

I stopped at the barber shop, badly needing a shave. The barber got his brush and razor ready. I said: "Cut my hair." He didn't talk for a few minutes, evidently engaged in deep thought.

When I got to my office, a case was brought to me of a runaway American who was caught trying to send news to Germany. "Very good," said I, "now let it be made evident that it shall appear therefore that his innocence having been duly established he shall be shot."

"What, sir?"

"That since it must be evident that his guilt is genuine therefore see that he be acquitted and then shot."

Laughlin and Bell and Stabler were seen in an earnest conference in the next room for nearly half an hour.

Shoecraft brought me a letter. "This is the most courteous complaint about the French passport bureau we have yet had. I thought you'd like to see this lady's letter. She says she knows you."

"Do not answer it, then."

He went off and conferred with the others.

Hodson spoke of the dog he sold to Frank. "Yes,"

said I, "since he was a very nice dog, therefore he was worthless."

"Sir?"

And he went off after looking back at me in a queer way.

The day went on in that fashion. When I came out to go to lunch, the stairs down led upward and I found myself, therefore, stepping out of the roof on to the sidewalk—the house upside down. Smith looked puzzled. "Home, sir?"

"No. Go the other way." After he had driven two or three blocks, I told him to turn again and go the other way—home!

Your mother said almost as soon as I got into the door—"What *was* the matter with you this morning?"

"Oh, nothing. You forget that I am the German Ambassador."

Now this whole narrative is a lie. Nothing in it occurred. If it were otherwise it wouldn't be German.

Affectionately,

W. H. P.

To Mrs. Charles G. Loring

London, 6 Grosvenor Square.
Sunday, September 19, 1915.

MY DEAR KITTY:

You never had a finer autumnal day in the land of the free than this day has been in this old kingdom—fresh and fair; and so your mother said to herself and me: "Let's go out to the Laughlins' to lunch," and we went. There never was a prettier drive. We found out among other things that you pleased Mrs. Laughlin very much by your letter. Her garden changes every week or so, and it never was lovelier than it is now.—Then we came back home and dined alone. Well, since we can't have

you and Chud and Frank, I don't care if we do dine
alone sometimes for some time to come. Your mother's
monstrous good company, and sometimes three is a
crowd. And now is a good time to be alone. London
never was so dull or deserted since I've known it, nor
ever so depressed. The military (land) operations are
not cheerful; the hospitals are all full; I see more wounded
soldiers by far than at any previous time; the Zeppelins
came somewhere to this island every night for a week—
one of them, on the night of the big raid, was visible from
our square for fifteen or twenty minutes—in general it is
a dull and depressing time. I have thought that since
you were determined to run off with a young fellow, you
chose a pretty good time to go away. I'm afraid there'll
be no more of what we call "fun" in this town as long
as we stay here.

Worse yet: in spite of the Coalition Government and
everybody's wish to get on smoothly and to do nothing
but to push the war, since Parliament convened there's
been a great row, which doesn't get less. The labour
men give trouble; people blame the politicians: Lloyd
George is saving the country, say some; Lloyd George
ought to be hanged, say others. Down with Northcliffe!
They seem likely to burn him at the stake—except those
who contend that he has saved the nation. Some maintain that the cabinet is too big—twenty-two. More say
that it has no leadership. If you favour conscription,
you are a traitor: if you don't favour it, you are pro-
German. It's the same sort of old quarrel they had before the war, only it is about more subjects. In fact,
nobody seems very clearly to know what it's about.
Meantime the Government is spending money at a rate
that nobody ever dreamed of before. Three million
pounds a day—some days five million. The Germans

meantime are taking Russia; the Allies are not taking the Dardanelles; in France the old deadlock continues. Boston at its worst must be far more cheerful than this.

Affectionately and with my love to Chud,

W. H. P.

To the President

London, September 26, 1915.

DEAR MR. PRESIDENT:

The suppression of facts about the military situation is more rigorous than ever since the military facts have become so discouraging. The volume of pretty well authenticated news that I used to hear privately has become sensibly diminished. Rumours that reach me by the back door, in all sorts of indirect ways, are not fewer, but fewer of them are credible. There is great confusion, great fear, very great depression—far greater, I think, than England has felt, certainly since the Napoleonic scare and probably since the threat of the Armada. Nobody, I think, supposes that England herself will be conquered: confidence in the navy is supreme. But the fear of a practical defeat of the Allies on the continent is become general. Russia may have to pay a huge indemnity, going far to reimburse Germany for the cost of the war; Belgium may be permanently held unless Germany receive an indemnity to evacuate, and her seaports may be held anyhow; the Germans may reach Constantinople before the Allies, and Germany may thus hold, when the war ends, an open way to the East; and France may have to pay a large sum to regain her northern territory now held by the Germans. These are not the convictions of men here, but they have distinctly become the fears; and many men's mind are beginning to adjust themselves to the possible end of the war, as a draw, with these results. Of course such an

Herbert C. Hoover, in 1914

principle it is the same fight that we have made, in our domestic field, during recent decades. Now the same fight has come on a far larger scale than men ever dreamed of before.

It isn't, therefore, for merely doctrinal reasons that we are concerned for the spread of democracy nor merely because a democracy is the only scheme of organization yet wrought out that keeps the door of opportunity open and invites all men to their fullest development. But we are interested in it because under no other system can the world be made an even reasonably safe place to live in. For autocracies only wage aggressive wars. Aggressive autocracies, especially military autocracies, must be softened down by peace (and they have never been so softened) or destroyed by war. The All-Highest doctrine of Germany today is the same as the Taxation-without-Representation of George III — only more virulent, stronger, and further-reaching. Only by its end can the German people recover and build up their character and take the permanent peace in the world that they — thus changed — will be entitled to. They will either reduce Europe to the vassalage of a military autocracy, which may then overrun the whole world or drench it in blood, or they must through stages of Liberalism work their way towards some approach to a democracy; and there is no doubt which event is impending. The Liberal idea will win this struggle, and Europe will be out of danger of a

A facsimile page from the Ambassador's letter of November 24, 1916, resigning his Ambassadorship

end would be a real German victory and—another war as soon as enough men grow up to fight it.

When the more cheerful part of public opinion, especially when any member of the Government, affects to laugh at these fears, the people say: "Well, make known the facts that you base your hope on. Precisely how many men have volunteered? Is the voluntary system a success or has it reached its limit? Precisely what is the situation in the Dardanelles? Are the allied armies strong enough to make a big drive to break through the German line in France? Have they big guns and ammunition enough? What are the facts about the chance in the Dardanelles? What have we done with reference to the Balkan States?" Thus an angry and ominous political situation is arising. The censorship on war news apparently becomes severer, and the general fear spreads and deepens. The air, of course, becomes heavily charged with such rumours as these: that if the Government continue its policy of secrecy, Lloyd George will resign, seeing no hope of a real victory: that, if he do resign, his resignation will disrupt the Government—cause a sort of earthquake; that the Government will probably fall and Lloyd George will be asked to form another one, since he is, as the public sees it, the most active and efficient man in political life; that, if all the Balkan States fail the Allies, Sir Edward Grey will be reckoned a failure and must resign; and you even now hear talk of Mr. Balfour's succeeding him.

It is impossible to say what basis there is for these and other such rumours, but they show the general very serious depression and dissatisfaction. Of that there is no doubt. Nor is there any doubt about grave differences in the Cabinet about conscription nor of grave fear in the public mind about the action of labour unions in hindering the utmost production of ammunition, nor of the increasing feeling that the Prime Minister doesn't lead the nation. Except Lloyd George and the Chancellor of the Exchequer[1] the Cabinet seems to suffer a sort of paralysis. Lord Kitchener's speech in the House of Lords, explaining the military situation, reads like a series of month-old bulletins and was a great disappointment. Mr. Asquith's corresponding speech in the House seemed to lack complete frankness. The nation feels that it is being kept in the dark, and all the military information that it gets is discouraging. Sir Edward Grey, as philosophic and enduring a man as I know, seems much more depressed than I have ever known him to be; Bryce is very very far from cheerful; Plunkett,[2] whom also you know, is in the dumps—it's hard to find a cheerful or a hopeful man.

The secrecy of official life has become so great and successful that prophecy of political changes must be mere guess work. But, unless good news come from the Dardanelles in particular, I have a feeling that Asquith may resign—be forced out by the gradual pressure of public opinion; that Lloyd George will become Prime Minister, and that (probably) Sir Edward Grey may resign. Yet I cannot take the prevailing military discouragement at its face value. The last half million men and the last million pounds will decide the contest, and the Allies will have these. This very depression strengthens the nation's resolution to a degree that they for the moment forget. The blockade and the armies in the field will wear Germany down—not absolutely conquer her, but wear her down—probably in another year.

In the meantime our prestige (if that be the right word), in British judgment, is gone. As they regard it, we have

[1]The Rt. Hon. Reginald McKenna.

[2]Sir Horace Plunkett.

permitted the Germans to kill our citizens, to carry on a worldwide underhand propaganda from our country (as well as in it), for which they have made no apology and no reparation but only vague assurances for the future now that their submarine fleet has been almost destroyed. They think that we are credulous to the point of simplicity to accept any assurances that Bernstorff may give—in a word, that the peace-at-any-price sentiment so dominates American opinion and the American Government that we will submit to any indignity or insult—that we will learn the Germans' real character when it is too late to save our honour or dignity. There is no doubt of the definiteness or depth of this opinion.

And I am afraid that this feeling will show itself in our future dealings with this government. The public opinion of the nation as well as the Government accepts their blockade as justified as well as necessary. They will not yield on that point, and they will regard our protests as really inspired by German influence—thus far at least: that the German propaganda has organized and encouraged the commercial objection in the United States, and that this propaganda and the peace-at-any-price sentiment demand a stiff controversy with England to offset the stiff controversy with Germany; and, after all, they ask, what does a stiff controversy with the United States amount to? I had no idea that English opinion could so quickly become practically indifferent as to what the United States thinks or does. And as nearly as I can make it out, there is not a general wish that we should go to war. The prevalent feeling is not a selfish wish for military help. In fact they think that, by the making of munitions, by the taking of loans, and by the sale of food we can help them more than by military and naval action.

Their feeling is based on their disappointment at our submitting to what they regard as German dallying with us and to German insults.   They believe that, if we had sent Bernstorff home when his government made its unsatisfactory reply to our first *Lusitania* note, Germany would at once have "come down"; opportunist Balkan States would have come to the help of the Allies; Holland and perhaps the Scandinavian States would have got some consideration at Berlin for their losses by torpedoes; that more attention would have been paid by Turkey to our protest against the wholesale massacre of the Armenians; and that a better settlement with Japan about Pacific islands and Pacific influence would have been possible for the English at the end of the war.   Since, they argue, nobody is now afraid of the United States, her moral influence is impaired at every capital; and I now frequently hear the opinion that, if the war lasts another year and the Germans get less and less use of the United States as a base of general propaganda in all neutral countries, especially all American countries, they are likely themselves to declare war on us as a mere defiance of the whole world and with the hope of stirring up internal trouble for our government by the activity of the Germans and the Irish in the United States, which may hinder munitions and food and loans to the Allies.

I need not remark that the English judgment of the Germans is hardly judicial.   But they reply to this that every nation has to learn the real, incredible character of the Prussian by its own unhappy experience.   France had so to learn it, and England, Russia, and Belgium; and we (the United States), they say, fail to profit in time by the experience of these.   After the Germans have used us to the utmost in peace, they will force us into war—or even flatly declare war on us when they think they can thus cause more embarrassment to the Allies, and when they conclude that the time is come to make sure that no great nation shall emerge from the war with a clear commercial advantage over the others; and in the meantime they will prove to the world by playing with us that a democracy is necessarily pacific and hence (in their view) contemptible. I felt warranted the other day to remark to Lord Bryce on the unfairness of much of the English judgment of us (he is very sad and a good deal depressed). "Yes," he said, "I have despaired of one people's ever really understanding another even when the two are as closely related and as friendly as the Americans and the English."

You were kind enough to inquire about my health in your last note. If I could live up to the popular conception here of my labours and responsibilities and delicate duties (which is most flattering and greatly exaggerated), I should be only a walking shadow of a man. But I am most inappreciately well. I imagine that in some year to come, I may enjoy a vacation, but I could not enjoy it now. Besides since civilization has gone backward several centuries, I suppose I've gone back with it to a time when men knew no such thing as a vacation. (Let's forgive House for his kindly, mistaken solicitude.) The truth is, I often feel that I do not know myself—body or soul, boots or breeches. This experience is making us all here different from the men we were—but in just what respects it is hard to tell. We are not within hearing of the guns (except the guns that shoot at Zeppelins when they come); but the war crowds itself in on us sensibly more and more. There are more wounded soldiers on the streets and in the parks. More and more families one knows lose their sons, more and more women their husbands. Death is so common that it seems a little thing.

Four persons have come to my house to-day (Sunday) in the hope that I may find their missing kinsmen, and two more have appealed to me on the telephone and two more still have sent me notes. Since I began this letter, Mrs. Page insisted on my going out on the edge of the city to see an old friend of many years who has just lost both his sons and whose prospective son-in-law is at home wounded. The first thing he said was: "Tell me, what is America going to do?" As we drove back, we made a call on a household whose nephew is "missing."—"Can't you possibly help us hear definitely about him?"

This sort of thing all day every day must have some effect on any man. Then—yesterday morning gave promise of a calm, clear day. I never know what sensational experience awaits me around the next corner. Then there was put on my desk the first page of a reputable weekly paper which was filled with an open letter to me written by the editor and signed. After the usual description of my multitudinous and delicate duties, I was called on to insist that my government should protest against Zeppelin raids on London because a bomb might kill me! Humour doesn't bubble much now on this side the world, for the censor had forbidden the publication of this open letter lest it should possibly cause American-German trouble! Then the American correspondents came in to verify a report that a news agency is said to have had that I was deluged with threatening letters!— More widows, more mothers looking for lost sons! . . . Once in a while—far less often than if I lived in a sane and normal world—I get a few hours off and go to a lonely golf club. Alas! there is seldom anybody there but now and then a pair of girls and now and then a pair of old fellows who have played golf for a century. Yet back in

London in the War Office I hear they indulge in disrespectful hilarity at the poor game I play. Now how do they know? (You'd better look to your score with Grayson: the English have spies in America. A major-general in their spy-service department told Mrs. Page that they knew all about Archibald[1] before he got on the ship in New York.)

All this I send you not because it is of the slightest permanent importance (except the English judgment of us) but because it will prove, if you need proof, that the world is gone mad. Everything depends on fighting power and on nothing else. A victory will save the Government. Even distinctly hopeful military news will. And English depression will vanish with a turn of the military tide. If it had been Bernstorff instead of Dumba—*that* would have affected even the English judgment of us. Tyrrell[2] remarked to me—did I write you? "Think of the freaks of sheer, blind Luck; a man of considerable ability like Dumba caught for taking a risk that an idiot would have avoided, and a fool like Bernstorff escaping!" Then he added: "I hope Bernstorff will be left. No other human being could serve the English as well as he is serving them." So, you see, even in his depression the Englishman has some humour left—e. g., when that old sea dog Lord Fisher heard that Mr. Balfour was to become First Lord of the Admiralty, he cried out: "Damn it! he won't do: Arthur Balfour is too much of a gentleman." So John Bull is now, after all, rather pathetic—depressed as he has not been depressed for at least a hundred years. The nobility and the common man are doing their whole duty, dying on the Bosphorus or in France without

---

[1] It was Archibald's intercepted baggage that furnished the documents which caused Dumba's dismissal.

[2] Sir William Tyrrell, private secretary to Sir Edward Grey.

a murmur, or facing an insurrection in India; but the labour union man and the commercial class are holding back and hindering a victory. And there is no great national leader.

Sincerely yours,

WALTER H. PAGE.

CHAPTER XVII

CHRISTMAS IN ENGLAND, 1915

To Edward M. House

London, December 7, 1915.

MY DEAR HOUSE:

I hear you are stroking down the Tammany tiger—an easier job t.an I have with the British lion. You can find out exactly who your tiger is, you know the house he lives in, the liquor he drinks, the company he goes with. The British lion isn't so easy to find. At times in English history he has dwelt in Downing Street—not so now. So far as our struggle with him is concerned, he's all over the Kingdom; for he is public opinion. The governing crowd in usual times and on usual subjects can here overrun public opinion—can make it, turn it, down it, dodge it. But it isn't so now—as it affects us. Every mother's son of 'em has made up his mind that Germany must and shall be starved out, and even Sir Edward's scalp isn't safe when they suspect that he wishes to be lenient in that matter. They keep trying to drive him out, on two counts: (1) he lets goods out of Germany for the United States "and thereby handicaps the fleet"; and (2) he failed in the Balkans. Sir Edward is too much of a gentleman for this business of rough-riding over all neutral rights and for bribing those Balkan bandits.

I went to see him to-day about the *Hocking*, etc. He asked me: "Do *you know* that the ships of this line are really owned, in good faith, by Americans?"

"I'll answer your question," said I, "if I may then ask

you one. No, I don't know of my own knowledge. Now, *do you know* that they are *not* owned by Americans?"

He had to confess that he, of his own knowledge, didn't know.

"Then," I said, "for the relief of us both, I pray you hurry up your prize court."

When we'd got done quarrelling about ships and I started to go, he asked me how I liked Wordsworth's war poems. "The best of all war poems," said he, "because they don't glorify war but have to do with its philosophy." Then he told me that some friend of his had just got out a little volume of these war poems selected from Wordsworth; "and I'm going to send you a copy."

"Just in time," said I, "for I have a copy of 'The Life and Letters of John Hay'[1] that I'm sending to you."

He's coming to dine with me in a night or two: he'll do anything but discuss our Note with me. And he's the only member of the Government who, I think, would like to meet our views; and he can't. To use the language of Lowell about the campaign of Governor Kent—these British are hell-bent on starving the Germans out, and neutrals have mighty few rights till that job's done.

The worst of it is that the job won't be done for a very long time. I've been making a sort of systematic round of the Cabinet to see what these fellows think about things in general at this stage of the game. Bonar Law (the Colonies) tells me that the news from the Balkans is worse than the public or the newspapers know, and that still worse news will come. Germany will have it all her own way in that quarter.

"And take Egypt and the canal?"

"I didn't say *that*," he replied. But he showed that he fears even that.

---

[1] By William Roscoe Thayer, published in 1915.

I could go on with a dozen of 'em; but I sat down to write you a Christmas letter, and nothing else. The best news I have for you is not news at all, but I conceive it to be one of the best hopes of the future. In spite of Irishmen past, present, and to come; in spite of Germans, whose fuss will soon be over; in spite of lawyers, who (if left alone) would bankrupt empires as their clients and think they'd won a victory; I'm going to leave things here in a year and a half so that, if wise men wish to lay a plan for keeping the peace of the world, all they need to do will be to say first to Uncle Sam: "This fellow or that must understand that he can't break loose like a wild beast." If Uncle Sam agrees (and has a real navy himself), he'll wink at John Bull, and John will follow after. You see our blackleg tail-twisters have the whole thing backward. They say we truckle to the British. My plan is to lead the British—not for us to go to them but to have them come to us. We have three white men to every two white men in their whole Empire; and, when peace comes, we'll be fairly started on the road to become as rich as the war will leave them. There are four clubs in London which have no other purpose than this; and the best review[1] in the world exists chiefly for this purpose. All we need to do is to be courteous (we can do what we like if we do it courteously). Our manners, our politicians, and our newspapers are all that keep the English-speaking white man, under our lead, from ruling the world, without any treaty or entangling alliance whatsoever. If, when you went to Berlin to talk to your gentle and timid friend, the Emperor, about disarmament before the war—if about 200 American dreadnaughts and cruisers, with real grog on 'em, had come over to make a friendly call, in the North Sea, on the 300 English dread-

---

[1] The Ambassador had in mind *The Round Table*.

naughts and cruisers—just a friendly call, admirals on admirals—the "Star-Spangled Banner" and "God Save the King"—and if General Bell, from the Philippines, had happened in London just when Kitchener happened to be home from Egypt—*then, there wouldn't have been this war now.* Nothing need have been said—no treaty, no alliance, nothing. For then 100 or more British naval ships would have joined the Panama naval procession and any possible enemy would have seen that combined fleet clean across the Pacific.

Now this may all be a mere Christmas fancy—a mere yarn about what might have been—because we wouldn't have sent ships here in our old mood; the crew would have missed one Sunday School. But it's *this kind* of thing that does the trick. But this means the practice of courtesy, and we haven't acquired the habit. Two years or more ago the training ships from Annapolis with the cadets aboard anchored down the Thames and stayed several weeks and let the boys loose in England. They go on such a voyage every two years to some country, you know. The English didn't know that fact and they took the visit as a special compliment. Their old admirals were all greatly pleased, and I hear talk about that yet. We ought to have two or three of our rear-admirals here on their fleet now. Symington, of course, is a good fellow; but he's a mere commander and attaché—not an admiral—in other words, not any particular compliment or courtesy to the British Navy. (As soon as the war began, a Japanese admiral turned up here and he is here now.) We sent over two army captains as military observers. The Russians sent a brigadier-general. We ought to have sent General Wood. You see the difference? There was no courtesy in our method. It would be the easiest and prettiest job in the world to swallow the whole British organization, lock, stock, and barrel—King, Primate, Cabinet, Lords, and Commons, feathers and all, and to make 'em follow our *courteous* lead anywhere. The President had them in this mood when the war started and for a long time after—till the *Lusitania* seemed to be forgotten and till the lawyers began to write his Notes. He can get 'em back, after the war ends, by several acts of courtesy—if we could get into the habit of doing such things as sending generals and admirals as compliments to them. The British Empire is ruled by a wily use of courtesies and decorations. If I had the President himself to do the correspondence, if I had three or four fine generals and admirals and a good bishop or two, a thoroughbred senator or two and now and then a Supreme Court Justice to come on proper errands and be engineered here in the right way—we could do or say anything we liked and they'd do whatever we'd say. I'd undertake to underwrite the whole English-speaking world to keep peace, under our leadership. Instead whereof, every move we now make is to *follow* them or to *drive* them. The latter is impossible, and the former is unbecoming to us.

But to return to Christmas.—I could go on writing for a week in this off-hand, slap-dash way, saying wise things flippantly. But Christmas—that's the thing now. Christmas! What bloody irony it is on this side the world! Still there will be many pleasant and touching things done. An Englishman came in to see me the other day and asked if I'd send $1,000 to Gerard[1] to use in making the English prisoners in Germany as happy as possible on Christmas Day—only I must never tell anybody who did it. A lady came on the same errand—for the British

---

[1]James W. Gerard, American Ambassador to Germany, and, as such, in charge of British interests in Germany.

prisoners in Turkey, and with a less but still a generous sum. The heroism, the generosity, the endurance and self-restraint and courtesy of these people would melt a pyramid to tears. Of course there are yellow dogs among 'em, here and there; but the genuine, thoroughbred English man or woman is the real thing—one of the realest things in this world. So polite are they that not a single English person has yet mentioned our Note to me—not one.

But every one I've met for two days has mentioned the sending of Von Papen and Boy-Ed[1] home—not that they expect us to get into the war, but because they regard this action as maintaining our self-respect.

Nor do they neglect other things because of the war. I went to the annual dinner of the Scottish Corporation the other night—an organization which for 251 years has looked after Scotchmen stranded in London; and they collected $20,000 then and there. There's a good deal of Christmas in 'em yet. One fellow in a little patriotic speech said that the Government is spending twenty-five million dollars a day to whip the Germans.—"Cheap work, very cheap work. We can spend twice that if necessary. Why, gentlemen, we haven't exhausted our pocket-change yet."

Somehow I keep getting away from Christmas. It doesn't stay put. It'll be a memorable one here for its sorrows and for its grim determination—an empty chair at every English table. But nowhere in the world will it be different except in the small neutral states here and in the lands on your side the world.

How many Christmases the war may last, nobody's wise enough to know. That depends absolutely on

---

[1]The German military and naval attachés, whose persistent and outrageous violation of American laws led to their dismissal by President Wilson.

Germany. The Allies announced their terms ten months
ago, and nothing has yet happened to make them change
them. That would leave the Germans with Germany and
a secure peace—no obliteration or any other wild nonsense, but only a secure peace. Let 'em go back home,
pay for the damage they've done, and then stay there.
I do hope that the actual fighting will be ended by Christmas of next year. Of course it *may* end with dramatic
suddenness at any time, this being the only way, perhaps,
for the Kaiser to save his throne. Or it may go on for
two or three years. My guess is that it'll end next year—
a guess subject to revision, of course, by events that can't
be foreseen.

But as I said before—to come back to Christmas. Mrs.
Page and I send you and Mrs. House our affectionate good
wishes and the hope that you keep very well and very
happy in your happy, prosperous hemisphere. We do,
I thank you. We haven't been better for years—never
before so busy, never, I think, so free from care. We get
plenty to eat (such as it is in this tasteless wet zone), at a
high cost, of course; we have comfortable beds and shoes
(we spend all our time in these two things, you know);
we have good company, enough to do (!!), no grievances
nor ailments, no ill-will, no disappointments, a keen
interest in some big things—all the chips are blue, you
know; we don't feel ready for halos, nor for other uncomfortable honours; we deserve less than we get and
are content with what the gods send. This, I take it, is
all that Martin[1] would call a comfortable mood for
Christmas; and we are old enough and tough enough to
have thick armour against trouble. When Worry knocks
at the door, the butler tells him we're not at home.

And I see the most interesting work in the world cut

---

[1] E. S. Martin, Editor of *Life*.

out for me for the next twenty-five or thirty years—to get such courtesy into our dealings with these our kinsmen here, public and private—as will cause them to follow us in all the developments of democracy and—in keeping the peace of the world secure.   I can't impress it on you strongly enough that the English-speaking folk have got to set the pace and keep this world in order.   Nobody else is equal to the job.   In all our dealings with the British, public and private, we allow it to be assumed that *they* lead: they don't.   *We* lead.   They'll follow, if we do really lead and are courteous to them.   If we hold back, the Irishman rears up and says we are surrendering to the English!   Suppose we go ahead and the English surrender to us, what can your Irishmen do then?   Or your German?   The British Navy is a pretty good sort of dog to have to trot under your wagon.   If we are willing to have ten years of thoughtful good manners, I tell you Jellicoe will eat out of your hand.

Therefore, cheer up!   It's not at all improbable that Ford[1] and his cargo of cranks, if they get across the ocean, may strike a German mine in the North Sea.   Then they'll die happy, as martyrs; and the rest of us will live happy, and it'll be a Merry Christmas for everybody.

Our love to Mrs. House.

Always heartily yours,

W. H. P.

To Frank N. Doubleday and Others

London, Christmas, 1915.

Dear D. P. & Co.

   . . . Now, since we're talking about the war, let me deliver my opinion and leave the subject.   They're

---

[1]Mr. Henry Ford at this time was getting together his famous peace ship, which was to sail to Europe " to get the boys out of the trenches by Christmas."

killing one another all right; you needn't have any doubt about that—so many thousand every day, whether there's any battle or not.   When there's "nothing to report" from France, that means the regular 5,000 casualties that happen every day.   There isn't any way of getting rid of men that has been forgotten or neglected.   Women and children, too, of course, starve in Serbia and Poland and are massacred in Turkey.   England, though she has by very much the largest army she ever had, has the smallest of all the big armies and yet I don't know a family that had men of fighting age which hasn't lost one or more members.   And the worst is to come.   But you never hear a complaint.   Poor Mr. Dent,[1] for instance (two sons dead), says: "It's all right.   England must be saved."

And this Kingdom alone, as you know, is spending twenty-five million dollars a day.   The big loan placed in the United States[2] would last but twenty days!   If this pace of slaughter and of spending go on long enough, there won't be any men or any money left on this side the world.   Yet there will be both left, of course; for somehow things never quite go to the ultimate smash that seems to come.   Read the history of the French Revolution.   How did the French nation survive?

It will go on, unless some unexpected dramatic military event end it, for something like another year at least— many say for two years more, and some, three years more.   It'll stop, of course, whenever Germany will propose terms that the Allies can consider—or something near such terms; and it won't stop before.   By blockade pressure and by fighting, the Allies are gradually wearing the Germans out.   We can see here the gradual pressure

---

[1] J. M. Dent, the London publisher.

[2] $500,000,000.

of events in that direction. My guess is that they won't go into a third winter.

Well, dear gentlemen, however you may feel about it, that's enough for me. My day—every day—is divided into these parts: (1) two to three hours listening to Americans or their agents here whose cargoes are stopped, to sorrowing American parents whose boys have run away and gone into the English Army, to nurses and doctors and shell makers who wish to go to France, to bereaved English men and women whose sons are "missing": can I have them found in Germany? (2) to answering letters about these same cheerful subjects; (3) to going over cases and documents prepared about all these sorts of troubles and forty other sorts, by the eight or ten secretaries of the Embassy, and a conference with every one of them; (4) the reading of two books of telegrams, one incoming, the other outgoing, and the preparation of a lot of answers; (5) going to the Foreign Office, not every day but often, to discuss more troubles there; (6) home to dinner at 8 o'clock—at home or somewhere else, and there is more talk about the war or about the political troubles. That for a regular daily routine for pretty nearly a year and a half! As I say, if anybody is keeping the war up for my entertainment, he now has my permission to stop. No time to read, no time to write, little time to think, little or no time to see the people you most wish to see, I often don't know the day of the week or of the month: it's a sort of life in the trenches, without the immediate physical danger. Then I have my cabinet meetings, my financial reports (money we spend for four governments: I had till recently about a million dollars subject to my check); then the commission for the relief of Belgium; then the Ambassadors and Ministers of the other neutral states— our task is worse than war!

Well, praise God for sleep. I get from seven to nine hours a night, unbroken; and I don't take Armageddon to bed with me.

I don't mind telling *you* (nobody else) that the more I see just how great statesmen work and manage great governments—the more I see of them at close range— whether in Washington or London or Berlin or Vienna or Constantinople (for these are *my* Capitals), the more I admire the methods of the Long Island farmers. Boys, I swear I could take our crowd and do a better job than many of these great men do. I have to spend a lot of time to correct their moves before the other fellow finds out the mistake. For instance I know I spent $2,000 in telegrams before I could make the German Government understand the British military age, and the British Government understand the German military age, for exchanging prisoners who had lost two legs or arms or both eyes; and I've had to send a man to Berlin to get a financial report from one man on one floor of a building there and to take it to another man on the floor above. Just yesterday I was reminded that I had made eighteen requests for the same information of the British Government, when the nineteenth request for it came from Washington; and I have now telegraphed that same thing nineteen times since the war began. Of course everybody's worked to death. But something else ails a lot of 'em all the way from Constantinople to London. Leaving out common gutter lying (and there's much of it) the sheer stupidity of governments is amazing. They are all so human, so mighty human! I wouldn't be a government for any earthly consideration. I'd rather be a brindled dog and trot under the wagon.

But it has been an inexpressibly interesting experience to find all this out for myself. There's a sort of weary satisfaction in feeling that you've seen too much of them to be fooled by 'em any more. And, although most men now engaged in this game of government are mere common mortals with most of the common mortal weaknesses, now and then a really big man does stumble into the business. I have my doubts whether a really big man ever deliberately goes into it. And most of the men who the crowd for the moment thinks are big men don't really turn out so. It's a game like bull fighting. The bull is likely to kill you—pretty sure to do so if you keep at the business long enough; but in the meantime you have some exciting experiences and the applause of the audience. When you get killed, they forget you—immediately. There are two rather big men in this Government, and you wouldn't guess in three rounds who they are. But in general the war hasn't so far developed very big men in any country. Else we are yet too close to them to recognize their greatness. Joffre seems to have great stuff in him; and (I assure you) you needn't ever laugh at a Frenchman again. They are a great people. As for the British, there was never such a race. It's odd—I hear that it happens just now to be the fashion in the United States to say that the British are not doing their share. There never was a greater slander. They absolutely hold the Seven Seas. They have caught about seventy submarines and some of them are now destroying German ships in the Baltic Sea. They've sent to France by several times the largest army that any people ever sent over the sea. They are financing most of their allies and they have turned this whole island into gun and shell factories. They made a great mistake at the Dardanelles and they are slower than death to change their set methods. But no family in the land, from charcoal burners to dukes, hesitates one moment to send its sons into the army.

When the news comes of their death, they never whimper. When you come right down to hard facts, the courage and the endurance of the British and the French excel anything ever before seen on this planet. All the old stories of bravery from Homer down are outdone every day by these people. I see these British at close range, full-dress and undress; and I've got to know a lot of 'em as well as we can ever come to know anybody after we get grown. There is simply no end to the silly sides of their character. But, when the real trial comes, they don't flinch; and (except the thoroughbred American) there are no such men in the world.

A seven-foot Kansas lawyer (Kansas all over him) came to see me yesterday. He came here a month ago on some legal business. He told me yesterday that he had always despised Englishmen. He's seen a few with stud-horse clothes and white spats and monocles on who had gone through Kansas to shoot in the Rocky Mountains. He couldn't understand 'em and he didn't like 'em. "So infernally uppish," said he.

"Well, what do you think of 'em now?"

"The very best people in the world," said he. I think he has a notion of enlisting!

You're still publishing books, I hear. That's a good occupation. I'd like to be doing it myself. But I can't even get time to read 'em now.

But, as you know, nobody's writing anything but war books—from Kipling to Hall Caine. Poor Kipling!—his boy's dead. I have no doubt of it. I've had all the German hospitals and prison camps searched for him in vain. These writing men and women, by the way, are as true blue and as thoroughbred as any other class. I can never forget Maurice Hewlett's brave behaviour when he thought that his flying corps son had been killed by the

Germans or drowned at sea. He's no prig, but a real man. And the women are as fine as the men. . . .

To go back to books: Of course nobody can tell what effect the war will have on the writing of them, nor what sort of new writers may come up. You may be sure that everything is stirred to its profoundest depths and will be stirred still more. Some old stagers will be laid on the shelf; that's certain. What sort of new ones will come? I asked H. G. Wells this question. He has promised to think it out and tell me. He has the power to guess some things very well. I'll put that question to Conrad when I next see him.

Does anybody in the United States take the Prime Minister, Mr. Asquith, to be a great man? His wife is a brilliant woman; and she has kept a diary ever since he became Prime Minister; and he now has passed the longest single term in English history. Mr. Dent thinks he's the biggest man alive, and Dent has some mighty good instincts.

Talk about troubles! Think of poor Northcliffe. He thinks he's saved the nation from its miserable government, and the government now openly abuses him in the House of Commons. Northcliffe puts on his brass knuckles and turns the *Times* building upside down and sets all the *Daily Mail* machine guns going, and has to go to bed to rest his nerves, while the row spreads and deepens. The Government keeps hell in the prayer-book because without it they wouldn't know what to do with Northcliffe; and Northcliffe is just as sure that he has saved England as he is sure the Duke of Wellington did.

To come back to the war. (We always do.) Since I wrote the first part of this letter, I spent an evening with a member of the Cabinet and he told me so much had military news, which they prevent the papers from publishing or even hearing, that to-night I almost share this man's opinion that the war will last till 1918. That isn't impossible. If that happens the offer that I heard a noble old buck make to a group of ladies the other night may be accepted. This old codger is about seventy-five, ruddy and saucy yet. "My dear ladies," said he, "if the war goes on and on we shall have no young men left. A double duty will fall on the old fellows. I shall be ready, when the need comes, to take four extra wives, and I daresay there are others of my generation who are as patriotic as I am."

All of which is only my long-winded, round-about diplomatic way of wishing you every one and every one of yours and all the folk in the office, their assigns, superiors, dependents, companions in labour—all, everyone and sundry, the happiest of Christmases; and when you take stock of your manifold blessings, don't forget to be thankful for the Atlantic Ocean. That's the best asset of safety that we have.

Affectionately yours,

W. H. P.

To Mrs. Charles G. Loring

6 Grosvenor Square,

London, December 7, 1915.

DEAR KITTY:

This is my Christmas letter to you and Chud—a poor thing, but the best I have to give you. At least it carries my love, dear, and my wishes that every Christmas under your own roof will be happier than the preceding one. Since your starting point is on the high level of your first Christmas in your own home—that's a good wish: isn't it?

I'm beginning to think a good deal of your mother and me. Here we are left alone by every one of you—in a foreign land; and, contrary to all predictions that any of you would have made about us four or five years ago, we're faring pretty well, thank you, and not on the edge of dying of loneliness at all. I tell you, I think we're pretty brave and hardy.

We're even capable of becoming cocky and saucy to every one of you. Be careful, then.

You see if you have a war to live with you don't necessarily need children: you'll have strife enough without 'em. We'll console ourselves with such reflections as these.

And the truth is—at least about me—that there isn't time to think of what you haven't got. Of course, I'm working, as always, to soften the relations between these two governments. So far, in spite of the pretty deep latent feeling on both sides—far worse than it ought to be and far worse than I wish it were—I'm working all the time to keep things as smooth as possible. Happily, nobody can prove it, but I believe it, that there is now and there has been all along more danger of a serious misunderstanding than anybody has known. The Germans have, of course, worked in 1000 ways to cause misunderstanding between England and the United States. Then, of course, there has been constant danger in the English bull-headed insularity which sees nothing but the Englishman's immediate need, and in the English slowness. Add to these causes the American ignorance of war and of European conditions. It has been a God's mercy for us that we have so far had a man like Sir Edward Grey in his post. And in my post, while there might well have been a better man, this much at least has been lucky—that I do have a consciousness of English history and of our common origin and some sense of the inevitable destiny of the great English-speaking race—so that, when we have come to sharp corners in the road, I have known that whatever happen we must travel in the right general direction—have known that no temporary difference must be allowed to assume a permanent quality. I have thought several times that we had passed the worst possible place, and then a still worse one would appear. It does look now as if we had faced most of the worst difficulties that can come, but I am not sure what Congress may do or provoke. If we outlast Congress, we shall be safe. Now to come through this enormous war even with no worse feeling than already exists between the two countries—that'll be a big thing to have done. But it's work like the work of the English fleet. Nobody can prove that Jellicoe has been a great admiral. Yet the fleet has done the whole job more successfully than if it had had sea-fights and lost a part of their ships.

Our Note has left a great deal of bad feeling—suppressed, but existent. A part of it was inevitable and (I'd say) even necessary. But we put in a lot of things that seem to me to be merely disputatious, and we didn't write it in the best form. It corresponds to what you once called *suburban:* do you remember? Not thoroughbred. But we'll get over even that, especially if the Administration and the courts continue to bring the Germans to book who are insulting our dignity and destroying our property and killing Americans. If we can satisfactorily settle the *Lusitania* trouble, the whole outlook will be very good.

Your mother and I are hearing much interesting political talk. We dined last night with Mr. Bonar Law. Sir Edward Carson was there. To-day we lunched with Lady P.—the other side, you see. There are fundamental differences continually arising. They thought a few weeks ago that they had the Prime Minister's scalp. He proved too nimble for them. Now one person after another says to you: "Kitchener doesn't deserve the reverence the people give him." More and more folks say he's hard to work with—is domineering and selfish. Nobody seems really to know him; and there are some signs that there may be a row about him.

We've heard nothing from Harold in quite a little while. We have, you know, three of our footmen in the war. Allen was wounded at Loos—a flesh, bullet-wound. He's about well now and is soon going back. Leslie is in the trenches and a postal card came from him the other day. The third one, Philip, is a prisoner in Germany. Your mother sent him a lot of things, but we've never heard whether he received them or not. The general strain—military, political, financial—gets greater. The streets are darker than ever. The number of wounded increases rapidly. More houses are turned into hospitals. The Manchesters', next door, is a hospital now. And everybody fears worse days are to come. But they have no nerves, these English. They grit their teeth, but they go on bravely, enduring everything. We run into experiences every day that melt you, and the heroic things we hear outnumber and outdo all the stories in all the books.

I keep forgetting Xmas, Kitty, and this is my Xmas letter. You needn't put it in your stocking, but you'd really better burn it up. It would be the ruination of the world if my frank comments got loose. It's for you and Chud only. You may fill your stocking full of the best wishes you ever received—enough to fill the polar bear skin. And I send you both my love.

W. H. P.

To Ralph W., Arthur W., and Frank C. Page[1]

London, Christmas, 1915.

DEAR BOYS: R. W. P., A. W. P., F. C. P.

A Merry Christmas to you! Good cheer, good company, good food, good fires, good golf. I suppose (though the Lord only knows) that I'll have to be here another Christmas; but another after that? Not on your life!

I think I'm as cheerful and hopeful as I ever was, but this experience here and the war have caused my general confidence in the orderly progress of civilization somewhat to readjust itself. I think that any man who looks over the world and who knows something of the history of human society—I mean any American who really believes in democracy and in human progress—is somewhat saddened to see the exceeding slowness of that progress. In the early days of our Republic hopeful Americans held the opinion that the other countries of the world would follow our example; that is to say, would educate the people, would give the masses a chance to become real men, would make their governments and institutions serve the people, would dispense with kings and gross privileges and become free. Well, they haven't done it. France is nominally a republic, but the masses of its people are far, far backward. Switzerland *is* a republic, but a very small one. Denmark is a very free state, in spite of its monarchical form of government. In South America they think they have republics, but they haven't the slightest idea of the real education and freedom of the people. Practically, therefore, the United States and the self-governing British colonies are the only really free countries of much importance in the whole world—

---

[1] The Ambassador's sons.

these and this Kingdom. Our example hasn't been followed. In Europe, Germany and Russia in particular have monarchs who are in absolute command. Thus on both sides the world, so far as government and the danger of war are concerned, there hasn't been very much real progress in five hundred years.

This is a little disappointing. And it means, of course, that we are likely to have periodical earthquakes like this present one till some radical change come. Republics have their faults, no doubt. But they have at least this virtue: that no country where the people really have the control of their government is likely to start out deliberately on any war of conquest—is not likely to run amuck—and will not regard its population as mere food for shell and powder.

Nor do I believe that our example of our government has, relatively to our strength and wealth and population, as much influence in the world as we had one hundred years ago. Our people have no foreign consciousness and I know that our government knows almost nothing about European affairs; nor do our people know. As regards foreign affairs our government lacks proper machinery. Take this as an illustration: The President wrote vigorous and proper notes about the *Lusitania* and took a firm stand with Germany. Germany has paid no attention to the *Lusitania* outrage. Yet (as I understand it) the people will not run the risk of war—or the Administration thinks they will not—and hence the President can do nothing to make his threat good. Therefore we stand in a ridiculous situation; and nobody cares how many notes we write. I don't know that the President could have done differently—unless, before he sent the *Lusitania* notes, he had called Congress together and submitted his notes to Congress. But, as the matter stands, the Germans are merely encouraged to blow up factories and practically to carry on war in the United States, because they know we can (or will) do nothing. Mere notes break nobody's skin.

We don't seem to have any machinery to bring any influence to bear on foreign governments or on foreign opinion; and, this being so, it is little wonder that the rest of the world does not follow our republican example.

And this sort of impotence in influence has curious effects at home. For example, the ship-purchase bill, as it was at the last session of Congress, was an economic crime. See what has happened: We have waked up to the fact that we must have a big navy. Well, a navy is of no far-fighting value unless we have auxiliary ships and a lot of 'em. Admiral Jellicoe has 3,000 ships under his command; and he couldn't keep his fleet on the job if he didn't have them. Most of them are commandeered merchant, passenger, and fishing ships. Now we haven't merchant, passenger, and fishing ships to commandeer. We've got to build and buy auxiliary ships to our navy. This, to my mind, makes the new ship-purchase bill, or something like it, necessary. Else our navy, when it comes to the scratch, will be of no fighting value, however big it be. It's the price we've got to pay for not having built up a merchant marine. And we haven't built up a merchant marine because we've had no foreign consciousness. While our Irishmen have been leading us to twist the Lion's tail, we've been depending almost wholly on English ships—and, in late years, on German ships. You can't cross the ocean yet in a decent American ship. You see, we've declared our independence; and, so far as individual development goes, we've worked it out. But the governmental machinery for maintaining it and for making it visible to the world—we've simply neglected to build it or to shape it. Hence the President's notes hurt nobody and accomplish nothing; nor could our navy put up a real fight, for lack of colliers and supply ships. It's the same way all around the horizon. And these are the reasons we haven't made our democracy impress the world more.

A democracy is not a quick-trigger war-engine and can't be made into one. When the quick-trigger engines get to work, they forget that a democracy does not consider fighting the first duty of man. You can bend your energies to peaceful pursuits or you can bend them to war. It's hard to do both at the same time. The Germans are the only people who have done both at the same time; and even they didn't get their navy big enough for their needs.

When the infernal thing's over—that'll be a glad day; and the European world won't really know what it has cost in men and money and loss of standards till it is over. . . .

Affectionately,

W. H. P.

To Walter H. Page, Jr.[1]

London, Christmas, 1915.

SIR:

For your first Christmas, I have the honour to send you my most affectionate greetings; and in wishing you all good health, I take the liberty humbly to indicate some of the favours of fortune that I am pleased to think I enjoy in common with you.

First—I hear with pleasure that you are quite well content with yourself—not because of a reasoned conviction of your own worth, which would be mere vanity and un-

---

[1]The Ambassador's infant grandson, son of Arthur W. Page.

worthy of you, but by reason of a philosophical disposition.   It is too early for you to bother over problems of
self-improvement—as for me it is too late; wherefore we
are alike in the calm of our self-content.   What others
may think or say about us is a subject of the smallest
concern to us.   Therefore they generally speak well of
us; for there is little satisfaction in speaking ill of men
who care nothing for your opinion of them.   Then, too,
we are content to be where we happen to be—a fact that
we did not order in the beginning and need not now
concern ourselves about.   Consider the eternal coming
and going of folk.   On every road many are travelling
one way and an equal number are travelling the other way.
It is obvious that, if they were all content to remain at
the places whence they set forth, the distribution of the
population would be the same.   Why therefore move
hither and yon at the cost of much time and labour and
money, since nothing is accomplished thereby?   We
spare ourselves by being content to remain where we are.
We thereby have the more time for reflection.   Nor can
we help observing with a smile that all persons who have
good reasons to see us themselves make the necessary
journey after they discover that we remain fixed.

Again, people about us are continually doing this service and that for some other people—running errands,
mending fences, bearing messages, building, and tearing
down; and they all demand equal service in return.   Thus
a large part of mankind keeps itself in constant motion
like bubbles of water racing around a pool at the foot of a
water-fall—or like rabbits hurrying into their warrens
and immediately hurrying out again.   Whereas, while
these antics amuse and sadden us, we for the most part
remain where we are.   Hence our wants are few; they
are generally most courteously supplied without our ask-

ing; or, if we happen to be momentarily forgotten, we can quickly secure anything in the neighbourhood by a little judicious squalling. Why, then, should we whirl as bubbles or scurry as rabbits? Our conquering self-possession gives a masterful charm to life that the victims of perpetual locomotion never seem to attain.

You have discovered, and my experience confirms yours, that a perpetual self-consciousness brings most of the misery of the world. Men see others who are richer than they; or more famous, or more fortunate—so they think; and they become envious. You have not reached the period of such empty vanity, and I have long passed it. Let us, therefore, make our mutual vows not to be disturbed by the good luck or the good graces of others, but to continue, instead, to contemplate the contented cat on the rug and the unenvious sky that hangs over all alike.

This mood will continue to keep our lives simple. Consider our diet. Could anything be simpler or better? We are not even tempted by the poisonous victuals wherewith mankind destroys itself. The very first sound law of life is to look to the belly; for it is what goes into a man that ruins him. By avoiding murderous food, we may hope to become centenarians. And why not? The golden streets will not be torn up and we need be in no indecent haste to travel even on them. The satisfactions of this life are just beginning for us; and we shall be wise to endure this world for as long a period as possible.

And sleep is good—long sleep and often; and your age and mine permit us to indulge in it without the sneers of the lark or the cock or the dawn.

I pray you, sir, therefore, accept my homage as the philosopher that you are and my assurance of that high

esteem indicated by my faithful imitation of your virtues.
I am,

    With the most distinguished consideration,
    With the sincerest esteem, and
    With the most affectionate good wishes,

Sir,

Your proud,

Humble,

Obedient

GRANDDADDY.

To Master Walter Hines Page,
   On Christmas, 1915.

CHAPTER XVIII

A PERPLEXED AMBASSADOR

THE beginning of the new year saw no improvement in German-American relations. Germany and Austria continued to violate the pledge given by Bernstorff after the sinking of the *Arabic*—if that shifty statement could be regarded as a "pledge." On November 7, 1915, the Austrians sank the *Ancona,* in the Mediterranean, drowning American citizens under conditions of particular atrocity, and submarine attacks on merchant ships, without the "warning" or attempt to save passengers and crew which Bernstorff had promised, took place nearly every day. On March 24, 1916, the *Sussex* was torpedoed in the British channel, again without warning. As this ship carried American passengers, its destruction brought the submarine situation to a crisis; President Wilson sent what was practically an ultimatum to Germany, demanding that it "immediately declare and effect an abandonment of its present methods of warfare against passenger and freight carrying vessels," declaring that, unless it did so, the United States would sever diplomatic relations with the German Empire. In reply, Germany apparently backed down and gave the promise the President had demanded. However, it coupled this concession with an expression of its expectation that the United States would compel Great Britain to observe international law in the blockade. As this latter statement might be interpreted as a qualification of its surrender, the incident hardly ended satisfactorily.

To Arthur W. Page

Bournemouth
May 22, 1916.

DEAR ARTHUR:

I stick on the back of this sheet a letter that Sydney Brooks wrote from New York (May 1st) to the *Daily Mail*. He formulates a question that we have many times asked ourselves and that, in one way or other, comes into everybody's mind here. Of course the common fellow in Jonesville who has given most of his time and energy to earning a living for his wife and children has no foreign consciousness, whether his Jonesville be in the United States or in England or in France or in Zanzibar. The real question is, *Do* these fellows in Jonesville make up the United States? or has there been such a lack of prompt leadership as to make all the Jonesville people confused? It's hard for me to judge at this distance just how far the President has led and just how far he has waited and been pushed along. Suppose he had stood on the front steps every morning before breakfast for a month after the *Lusitania* went down and had called to the people in the same tone that he used in his note to Germany—had sounded a bugle call—would we have felt as we now feel? What would the men in Jonesville have done then? Would they have got their old guns down from over the doors? Or do they so want peace and so think that they can have peace always that they've lost their spine? Have they really been Bryanized, Fordized, Janeaddamsized, Sundayschooled, and Chautauquaed into supine creatures to whom the United States and the ideals of the Fathers mean nothing? Who think a German is as good as an Englishman? Who have no particular aims or aspirations for our country and for democracy? When T. R. was in the White House he surely was an active fellow. He called us to exercise ourselves every morning. He bawled "Patriotism" loudly. We surely thought we were awake during those strenuous years. Were we really awake or did we only look upon him and his antics as a sort of good show? All that time Bryan was peace-a-footing and prince-of-peacing. Now did he really have the minds of the people or did T. R.?

If we've really gone to sleep and if the United States stands for nothing but personal comfort and commercialism to our own people, what a job you and the patriotic men of your generation have cut out for you!

My own conviction (which I don't set great store by) is that our isolation and prosperity have not gone so far in softening us as it seems. They've gone a good way, no doubt; but I think that even the Jonesville people yet feel their Americanism. What they need is—leadership. Their Congressmen are poor, timid, pork-barrel creatures. Their governors are in training for the Senate. The Vice-President reads no official literature of the war, "because then I might have a conviction about it and that wouldn't be neutral." And so on. If the people had a *real* leadership, I believe they'd wake up even in Jonesville.

Well, let's let these things go for the moment. How's the Ambassador?[1] And the Ambassador's mother and sister? They're nice folks of whom and from whom I hear far too little. Give 'em my love. I don't want you to rear a fighting family. But these kids won't and mustn't grow up peace-cranks—not that anybody objects to peace, but I do despise and distrust a crank, a crank about anything. That's the lesson we've got to learn from these troubled times. First, let cranks alone—the other side of the street is good enough for them. Then,

---

[1] A playful reference to the Ambassador's infant grandson, Walter H. Page, Jr.

if they persist, I see nothing to do but to kill 'em, and that's troublesome and inconvenient.

But, as I was saying, bless the babies. I can't begin to tell you how very much I long to see them, to make their acquaintance, to chuckle 'em and punch 'em and see 'em laugh, and to see just what sort of kids they be.

I've written you how in my opinion there's no country in the world fit for a modern gentleman and man-of-character to live in except (1) the United States and (2) this island. And this island is chiefly valuable for the breed of men—the right stock. They become more valuable to the world after they go away from home. But the right blood's here. This island's breed is the best there is. An Englishman or a Scotchman is the best ancestor in this world, many as his shortcomings are. Some Englishman asked me one night in what, I thought, the Englishman appeared at his best. I said, "As an ancestor to Americans!" And this is the fundamental reason why we (two peoples) belong close together. Reasons that flow from these are such as follows: (1) The race is the sea-mastering race and the navy-managing race and the ocean-carrying race; (2) the race is the literary race, (3) the exploring and settling and colonizing race, (4) the race to whom fair play appeals, and (5) that insists on individual development.

Your mother having read these two days 1,734 pages of memoirs of the Coke family, one of whose members wrote the great law commentaries, another carried pro-American votes in Parliament in our Revolutionary times, refused peerages, defied kings and—begad! here they are now, living in the same great house and saying and doing what they darn please—we know this generation of 'em!— well, your mother having read these two big volumes about the old ones and told me 175 good stories out of

these books, bless her soul! she's gone to sleep in a big chair
on the other side of the table.   Well she may, she walked
for two hours this morning over hills and cliffs and through
pine woods and along the beach.   I guess I'd better wake
her up and get her to go to bed—as the properer thing to
do at this time o'night, viz. 11.   My golf this afternoon
was too bad to confess.   But I must say that a 650 and
a 730 yard hole argues the audacity of some fellow and the
despair of many more.   Nature made a lot of obstructions
there and Man made more.   It must be seven or eight
miles around that course!   It's almost a three hour task
to follow my slow ball around it.   I suggested we play
with howitzers instead of clubs.   Good night!

W. H. P.

To Frank N. Doubleday and Others

Royal Bath and East Cliff Hotel,
Bournemouth, May 29, 1916.

Dear D. P. & Co.:

I always have it in mind to write you letters; but there's
no chance in my trenches in London; and, since I have
not been out of London for nearly two years—since the
war began—only an occasional half day and a night—till
now—naturally I've concocted no letter.   I've been down
here a week—a week of sunshine, praise God—and people are not after me every ten minutes, or Governments
either; and my most admirable and efficient staff (now
grown to one hundred people) permit few letters and
telegrams to reach me.   There never was a little rest more
grateful.   The quiet sea out my window shows no sign of
crawling submarines; and, in general, it's as quiet and
peaceful here as in Garden City itself.

I'm on the home-stretch now in all my thoughts and
plans.   Three of my four years are gone, and the fourth

will quickly pass. That's not only the limit of my leave, but it's quite enough for me. I shouldn't care to live through another such experience, if the chance should ever come to me. It has changed my whole life and my whole outlook on life; and, perhaps, you'd like to hear some impressions that it has made upon me.

The first impression—perhaps the strongest—is a loss of permanent interest in Europe, especially all Europe outside of this Kingdom. I have never had the illusion that Europe had many things that we needed to learn. The chief lesson that it has had, in my judgment, is the lesson of the art of living—the comforts and the courtesies of life, the refinements and the pleasures of conversation and of courteous conduct. The upper classes have this to teach us; and we need and can learn much from them. But this seems to me all—or practically all. What we care most for are individual character, individual development, and a fair chance for every human being. Character, of course, the English have—immense character, colossal character. But even they have not the dimmest conception of what we mean by a fair chance for every human being—not the slightest. In one thousand years they *may* learn it from us. Now on the continent, the only important Nation that has any character worth mentioning is the French. Of course the little nations— some of them—have character, such as Holland, Switzerland, Sweden, etc. But these are all. The others are simply rotten. In giving a free chance to every human creature, we've nothing to learn from anybody. In character, I bow down to the English and Scotch; I respect the Frenchman highly and admire his good taste. But, for our needs and from our point of view, the English can teach us only two great lessons—character and the art of living (if you are rich).

The idea that we were brought up on, therefore, that Europe is the home of civilization in general—nonsense! It's a periodical slaughter-pen, with all the vices that this implies. I'd as lief live in the Chicago stock-yards. There they kill beeves and pigs. Here they kill men and (incidentally) women and children. I should no more think of encouraging or being happy over a child of mine becoming a European of any Nation than I should be happy over his fall from Grace in any other way.

Our form of government and our scheme of society— God knows they need improving—are yet so immeasurably superior, as systems, to anything on this side the world that no comparison need be made.

My first strong impression, then, is not that Europe is "effete"—that isn't it. It is mediæval—far back toward the Dark Ages, much of it yet uncivilized, held back by *inertia* when not held back by worse things. The caste system is a constant burden almost as heavy as war itself and often quite as cruel.

The next impression I have is, that, during the thousand years that will be required for Europe to attain real (modern) civilization, wars will come as wars have always come in the past. The different countries and peoples and governments will not and cannot learn the lesson of federation and coöperation so long as a large mass of their people have no voice and no knowledge except of their particular business. Compare the miles of railway in proportion to population with the same proportion in the United States—or the telephones, or the use of the mails, or of bank checks; or make any other practical measure you like. Every time, you'll come back to the discouraging fact that the masses in Europe are driven as cattle. So long as this is true, of course, they'll be driven periodically into wars. So many countries, so many races, so many languages all within so small an area as Europe positively invite deadly differences. If railroads had been invented before each people had developed its own separate language, Europe could somehow have been coördinated, linked up, federated, made to look at life somewhat in the same way. As it is, wars will be bred here periodically for about another thousand years. The devil of this state of things is that they may not always be able to keep their wars at home.

For me, then, except England and the smaller exceptions that I have mentioned, Europe will cut no big figure in my life. In all the humanities, we are a thousand years ahead of any people here. So also in the adaptabilities and the conveniences of life, in its versatilities and in its enjoyments. Most folk are stolid and sad or dull on this side of the world. Else how could they take their kings and silly ceremonies seriously?

Now to more immediate and definite impressions. I have for a year had the conviction that we ought to get into the war—into the economic war—for the following among many reasons.

1. That's the only way to shorten it. We could cause Germany's credit (such as she has) instantly to collapse, and we could hasten her hard times at home which would induce a surrender.

2. That's the only way we can have any real or important influence in adjusting whatever arrangements can be made to secure peace.

3. That's the best way we can inspire complete respect for us in the minds of other nations and thereby, perhaps, save ourselves from some wars in the future.

4. That's the best way we can assert our own character—our Americanism, and forever get rid of all kinds of hyphens.

5. That's the only way we shall ever get a real and sensible preparedness, which will be of enormous educational value even if no military use should ever be made of our preparation.

6. That's the only way American consciousness will ever get back to the self-sacrificing and patriotic point of view of the Fathers of the Republic.

7. That's the best way to emancipate ourselves from cranks.

8. That's the only way we'll ever awaken in our whole people a foreign consciousness that will enable us to assert our natural influence in the world—political, financial, social, commercial—the best way to make the rest of the world our customers and friends and followers.

All the foregoing I have fired at the Great White Chief for a year by telegraph and by mail; and I have never fired it anywhere else till now.   Be very quiet, then.

No man with whom I have talked or whose writings I have read seems to me to have an adequate conception of the colossal changes that the war is bringing and will bring.   Of course, I do not mean to imply that I have any adequate conception.   Nobody can yet grasp it.   The loss of (say) ten million men from production of work or wares or children; what a changed world that fact alone will make!   The presence in all Europe of (perhaps) fifteen or twenty million more women than men will upset the whole balance of society as regards the sexes.   The loss of most of the accumulated capital of Europe and the vast burdens of debt for the future to pay will change the financial relations of the whole world.   From these two great losses—men and money—God knows the many kinds of changes that will come.   Women are doing and will continue to do many kinds of work hitherto done by men.

Of course there are some great gains. Many a flabby or abject fellow will come out of the war a real man: he'll be nobody's slave thereafter. The criminal luxury of the rich will not assert itself again for a time. The unparalleled addition to the world's heroic deeds will be to the good of mankind, as the unparalleled suffering has eclipsed all records. The survivors will be in an heroic mood for the rest of their lives. In general, life will start on a new plane and a lot of old stupid habits and old party quarrels and class prejudices will disappear. To get Europe going again will call for new resolution and a new sort of effort. Nobody can yet see what far-reaching effects it will have on government.

If I could make the English and Scotch over, I could greatly improve them. I'd cut out the Englishman's arrogance and key him up to a quicker gait. Lord! he's a slow beast. But he's worked out the germ and the beginning of all real freedom, and he has character. He knows how to conserve and to use wealth. He's a great John Bull, after all. And as for commanding the sea, for war or trade, you may properly bow down to him and pay him homage. The war will, I think, quicken him up. It will lessen his arrogance—to *us*, at least. I think it will make him stronger and humbler. And, whatever his virtues and his faults, he's the only Great Power we can go hand in hand with. . . .

These kinds of things have been going on now nearly two years, and not till these ten days down here have I had time or chance or a free mind to think them over; and now there's nothing in particular to think—nothing but just to go on, doing these 40,000 things (and they take a new turn every day) the best I can, without the slightest regard to consequences. I've long ago passed the place where, having acted squarely according to my best judgment, I can afford to pay the slightest attention to what anybody thinks. I see men thrown on the scrap heap every day. Many of them deserve it, but a good many do not. In the abnormal state of mind that everybody has, there are inevitable innocent misunderstandings, which are as fatal as criminal mistakes. The diplomatic service is peculiarly exposed to misunderstandings: and, take the whole diplomatic service of all nations as shown up by this great strain, it hasn't stood the test very well. I haven't the respect for it that I had when I started. Yet, God knows, I have a keen sympathy for it. I've seen some of 'em displaced; some of 'em lie down; some of 'em die.

As I've got closer and closer to big men, as a rule they shrink up. They are very much like the rest of us—many of 'em more so. Human nature is stripped in these times of most of its disguises, and men have to stand and be judged as a rule by their real qualities. Among all the men in high place here, Sir Edward Grey stands out in my mind bigger, not smaller, than he stood in the beginning. He's a square, honourable gentleman, if there is one in this world. And it is he, of course, with whom I have had all my troubles. It's been a truly great experience to work and to quarrel with such a man. We've kept the best friendship—a constantly ripening one. There are others like him—only smaller.

Yet they are all in turn set upon by the press or public opinion and hounded like criminals. They try (somebody tries) to drive 'em out of office every once in a while. If there's anything I'm afraid of, it's the newspapers. The correspondents are as thick as flies in summer—all hunting sensations—especially the yellow American press. I play the game with these fellows always squarely, sometimes I fear indiscreetly. But what is discretion? That's the hardest question of all. We have regular meetings. I tell 'em everything I can—always on the condition that I'm kept out of the papers. If they'll never mention me, I'll do everything possible for them. Absolute silence of the newspapers (as far as I can affect it) is the first rule of safety. So far as I know, we've done fairly well; but always in proportion to silence. I don't want any publicity. I don't want any glory. I don't want any office. I don't want nothin'—but to do this job squarely, to get out of this scrape, to go off somewhere in the sunshine and to see if I can slip back into my old self and see the world sane again. Yet I'm immensely proud that I have had the chance to do some good—to keep our record straight—as far as I can, and to be of what service I can to these heroic people.

Out of it all, one conviction and one purpose grows and becomes clearer. The world isn't yet half-organized. In the United States we've lived in a good deal of a fool's paradise. The world isn't half so safe a place as we supposed. Until steamships and telegraphs brought the nations all close together, of course we could enjoy our isolation. We can't do so any longer. One mad fool in Berlin has turned the whole earth topsy-turvy. We'd forgotten what our forefathers learned—the deadly dangers of real monarchs and of castes and classes. There are a lot of 'em left in the world yet. We've grown rich and—weak; we've let cranks and old women shape our ideas. We've let our politicians remain provincial and ignorant.

And believe me, dear D. P. & Co. with affectionate greeting to every one of you and to every one of yours, collectively and singly,

Yours heartily,

W. H. P.

*Memorandum written after attending the service at
St. Paul's in memory of Lord Kitchener.*[1]

American Embassy, London.

There were two Kitcheners, as every informed person
knows—(1) the popular hero and (2) the Cabinet Minister
with whom it was impossible for his associates to get along.
He made his administrative career as an autocrat dealing
with dependent and inferior peoples. This experience
fixed his habits and made it impossible for him to do team
work or to delegate work or even to inform his associates
of what he had done or was doing. While, therefore, his
name raised a great army, he was in many ways a hindrance in the Cabinet. First one thing and then another
was taken out of his hands—ordnance, munitions, war
plans. When he went to Gallipoli, some persons pre-
dicted that he would never come back. There was a hot
meeting of the Cabinet at which he was asked to go to
Russia, to make a sort of return visit for the visit that important Russians had made here, and to link up Russia's
military plans with the plans of the Western Allies. He
is said to have remarked that he was going only because he
had been ordered to go. There was a hope and a feeling
again that he might not come back till after the war.

Now just how much truth there is in all this, one has
to guess; but undoubtedly a good deal. He did much in
raising the army, but his name did more. What an extraordinary situation! The great hero of the Nation an
impossible man to work with. The Cabinet could not
tell the truth about him: the people would not believe it
and would make the Cabinet suffer. Moreover, such a
row would have given comfort to the enemy. Kitchener,

---

[1] Drowned on the *Hampshire*, June 5, 1916, off the coast of Scotland.

on his part, could not afford to have an open quarrel.
The only solution was to induce him to go away for a long
time. Both sides saw that. Such thoughts were in
everybody's mind while the impressive funeral service was
said and sung in St. Paul's. The Great Hero, who had
failed, was celebrated of course as a Great Hero—quite
truly and yet far from true. For him his death came at
a lucky time: his work was done.

There is even a rumour, which I don't for a moment
believe, that he is alive on the Orkney Islands and prefers to disappear there till the war ends. This is fantastic, and it was doubtless suggested by the story that
he did disappear for several years while he was a young
officer.

I could not help noticing, when I saw all the Cabinet
together at the Cathedral, how much older many of them
look than they looked two years ago. Sir Edward Grey,
Mr. Asquith, Mr. Balfour, who is really an old man,
Lloyd George—each of these seems ten years older. And
so does the King. The men in responsible places who are
not broken by the war will be bent. General French,
since his retirement to command of the forces in England,
seems much older. So common is this quick aging that
Lady Jellicoe, who went to Scotland to see her husband
after the big naval battle, wrote to Mrs. Page in a sort of
rhapsody and with evident surprise that the Admiral
really did not seem older! The weight of this thing is so
prodigious that it is changing all men who have to do with
it. Men and women (who do not wear mourning) mention the death of their sons in a way that a stranger might
mistake for indifference. And it has a curious effect on
marriages. Apparently every young fellow who gets a
week's leave from the trenches comes home and marries
and. of course, goes straight back—especially the young

officers. You see weddings all day as you pass the favourite churches; and already the land is full of young widows.

To Edwin A. Alderman[1]

Embassy of the U. S. A., London,
June 22, 1916.

MY DEAR ED ALDERMAN:

I shall not forget how good you were to take time to write me a word about the meeting of the Board—*the* Board: there's no other one in that class—at Hampton,[2] and I did most heartily appreciate the knowledge that you all remembered me. Alas! it's a long, long time ago when we all met—so long ago that to me it seems a part of a former incarnation. These three years—especially these two years of the war—have changed my whole outlook on life and foreshortened all that came before. I know I shall never link back to many things (and alas! too, to many people) that once seemed important and surely were interesting. Life in these trenches (five warring or quarrelling governments mining and sapping under me and shooting over me)—two years of universal ambassadorship in this hell are enough—enough I say, even for a man who doesn't run away from responsibilities or weary of toil. And God knows how it has changed me and is changing me: I sometimes wonder, as a merely intellectual and quite impersonal curiosity.

Strangely enough I keep pretty well—very well, in fact. Perhaps I've learned how to live more wisely than I knew in the old days; perhaps again, I owe it to my old grandfather who lived (and enjoyed) ninety-four years. I

[1]President of the University of Virginia.

[2]Hampton Institute, at Hampton, Va.

have walked ten miles to-day and I sit down as the clock strikes eleven (p. m.) to write this letter.

You will recall more clearly than I certain horrible, catastrophic, universal-ruin passages in Revelation— monsters swallowing the universe, blood and fire and clouds and an eternal crash, rolling ruin enveloping all things— well, all that's come. There are, perhaps, ten million men dead of this war and, perhaps, one hundred million persons to whom death would be a blessing. Add to these as many millions more whose views of life are so distorted that blank idiocy would be a better mental outlook, and you'll get a hint (and only a hint) of what the continent has already become—a bankrupt slaughter-house inhabited by unmated women. We have talked of "problems" in our day. We never had a problem; for the worst task we ever saw was a mere blithe pastime compared with what these women and the few men that will remain here must face. The hills about Verdun are not blown to pieces worse than the whole social structure and intellectual and spiritual life of Europe. I wonder that anybody is sane.

Now we have swung into a period and a state of mind wherein all this seems normal. A lady said to me at a dinner party (think of a dinner party at all!), "Oh, how I shall miss the war when it ends! Life without it will surely be dull and tame. What can we talk about? Will the old subjects ever interest us again?" I said, "Let's you and me try and see." So we talked about books—not war books—old country houses that we both knew, gardens and gold and what not; and in fifteen minutes we swung back to the war before we were aware.

I get out of it, as the days rush by, certain fundamental convictions, which seem to me not only true—true beyond any possible cavil—truer than any other political things are true—and far more important than any other contemporary facts whatsoever in any branch of endeavour, but better worth while than anything else that men now living may try to further:

1.   The cure for democracy is more democracy. The danger to the world lies in autocrats and autocracies and privileged classes; and these things have everywhere been dangerous and always will be. There's no security in any part of the world where people cannot think of a government without a king, and there never will be. You cannot conceive of a democracy that will unprovoked set out on a career of conquest. If all our religious missionary zeal and cash could be turned into convincing Europe of this simple and obvious fact, the longest step would be taken for human advancement that has been taken since 1776. If Carnegie, or, after he is gone, his Peace People could see this, his Trust might possibly do some good.

2.   As the world stands, the United States and Great Britain must work together and stand together to keep the predatory nations in order. A League to Enforce Peace and the President's idea of disentangling alliances are all in the right direction, but vague and general and cumbersome, a sort of bastard children of Neutrality. *The* thing, the *only* thing is—a perfect understanding between the English-speaking peoples. That's necessary, and that's all that's necessary. We must boldly take the lead in that. I frankly tell my friends here that the English have got to throw away their damned arrogance and their insularity and that we Americans have got to throw away our provincial ignorance ("What is abroad to us?"), hang our Irish agitators and shoot our hyphenates and bring up our children with reverence for English history and in the awe of English literature. This is the only job now in the world worth the whole zeal and

energy of all first-class, thoroughbred English-speaking men. *We* must lead. We are natural leaders. The English must be driven to lead. Item: We must get their lads into our universities, ours into theirs. They don't know how to do it, except the little driblet of Rhodes men. Think this out, remembering what fools we've been about exchange professors with Germany! How much good could Fons Smith[1] do in a thousand years, on such an errand as he went on to Berlin? And the English don't know *how* to do it. They are childish (in some things) beyond belief. An Oxford or Cambridge man never thinks of going back to his university except about twice a lifetime when his college formally asks him to come and dine. Then he dines as docilely as a scared Freshman. I am a D. C. L. of Oxford. I know a lot of their faculty. They are hospitality itself. But I've never yet found out one important fact about the university. They never tell me. I've been down at Cambridge time and again and stayed with the Master of one of the colleges. I can no more get at what they do and how they do it than I could get at the real meaning of a service in a Buddhist Temple. I have spent a good deal of time with Lord Rayleigh, who is the Chancellor of Cambridge University. He never goes there. If he were to enter the town, all the men in the university would have to stop their work, get on their parade-day gowns, line-up by precedent and rank and go to meet him and go through days of ceremony and incantations. I think the old man has been there once in five years. Now this mediævalism must go—or be modified. You fellers who have universities must work a real alliance—a big job here. But to go on.

[1]C. Alphonso Smith, Professor of English, U. S. Naval Academy; Roosevelt Professor at Berlin, 1910-11.

The best informed English opinion is ripe for a complete working understanding with us. We've got to work up our end—get rid of our ignorance of foreign affairs, our shirt-sleeve, complaining kind of diplomacy, our sport of twisting the lion's tail and such things and fall to and bring the English out. It's the *one* race in this world that's got the guts.

Hear this in confirmation: I suppose 1,000 English women have been to see me—as a last hope—to ask me to have inquiries made in Germany about their "missing" sons or husbands, generally sons. They are of every class and rank and kind, from marchioness to scrub-woman. Every one tells her story with the same dignity of grief, the same marvellous self-restraint, the same courtesy and deference and sorrowful pride. Not one has whimpered—but one. And it turned out that she was a Belgian. It's the breed. Spartan mothers were theatrical and pinchbeck compared to these women.

I know a lady of title, very well to do, who for a year got up at 5:30 and drove herself in her own automobile from her home in London to Woolwich where she worked all day long in a shell factory as a volunteer and got home at 8 o'clock at night. At the end of a year they wanted her to work in a London place where they keep the records of the Woolwich work. "Think of it," said she, as she shook her enormous diamond ear-rings as I sat next to her at dinner one Sunday night not long ago, "think of it—what an easy time I now have. I don't have to start till half-past seven and I get home at half-past six!"

I could fill forty pages with stories like these. This very Sunday I went to see a bedridden old lady who sent me word that she had something to tell me. Here it was: An English flying man's machine got out of order and he had to descend in German territory. The Germans captured him and his machine. They ordered him to take two of their flying men in his machine to show them a particular place in the English lines. He declined. "Very well, we'll shoot you, then." At last he consented. The three started. The Englishman quietly strapped himself in. There were no straps for the two Germans. The Englishman looped-the-loop. The Germans fell out. The Englishman flew back home. "My son has been to see me from France. He told me that. He knows the man"—thus said the old lady and thanked me for coming to hear it! She didn't know that the story has been printed.

But the real question is, "How are you?" Do you keep strong? Able, without weariness, to keep up your good work? I heartily hope so, old man. Take good care of yourself—very.

My love to Mrs. Alderman. Please don't quote me—yet. I have to be very silent publicly about everything. After March 4th, I shall again be free.

Yours always faithfully,
W. H. P.

CHAPTER XIX

WASHINGTON IN THE SUMMER OF 1916

I

IN JULY Page received a cablegram summoning him to Washington. This message did not explain why his presence was desired, nor on this point was Page ever definitely enlightened, though there were more or less vague statements that a "change of atmosphere" might better enable the Ambassador to understand the problems which were then engrossing the State Department.

The President had now only a single aim in view. From the date of the so-called *Sussex* "pledge," May 4, 1916, until the resumption of submarine warfare on February 1, 1917, Mr. Wilson devoted all his energies to bringing the warring powers together and establishing peace. More than one motive was inspiring the President in this determination. That this policy accorded with his own idealistic tendencies is true, and that he aspired to a position in history as the great "peace maker" is probably the fact, but he had also more immediate and practical purposes in mind. Above all, Mr. Wilson was bent on keeping the United States out of the war; he knew that there was only one certain way of preserving peace in this country, and that was by bringing the war itself to an end. "An early peace is all that can prevent the Germans from driving us at last into the war," Page wrote at about this time; and this single sentence gives the key to the President's activities for the succeeding nine months. The negotiations over the *Sussex* had taught

Mr. Wilson this truth. He understood that the pledge which the German Government had made was only a conditional one; that the submarine campaign had been suspended only for the purpose of giving the United States a breathing spell during which it could persuade Great Britain and France to make peace.

"I repeat my proposal," Bernstorff cabled his government on April 26,[1] "to suspend the submarine war at least for the period of negotiations. This would remove all danger of a breach [with the United States] and also enable Wilson to continue his labours in his great plan of bringing about a peace based upon the freedom of the seas—i. e., that for the future trade shall be free from all interference in time of war. According to the assurances which Wilson, through House, has given me, he would in that case take in hand measures directly against England. He is, however, of the opinion that it would be easier to bring about peace than to cause England to abandon the blockade. This last could only be brought about by war and it is well known that the means of war are lacking here. A prohibition of exports as a weapon against the blockade is not possible as the prevailing prosperity would suffer by it.

"The inquiries made by House have led Wilson to believe that our enemies would not be unwilling to consider peace. In view of the present condition of affairs, I repeat that there is only one possible course, namely, that Your Excellency [Von Jagow] empower me to declare that we will enter into negotiations with the United States touching the conduct of the submarine war while the negotiations are proceeding. This would give us the advantage that the submarine war, being over Mr.

---

[1]This is quoted from a hitherto unpublished despatch of Bernstorff's to Berlin which is found among Page's papers.

Wilson's head, like the sword of Damocles, would compel him at once to take in hand the task of mediation."

This dispatch seems sufficiently to explain all the happenings of the summer and winter of 1916–1917. It was sent to Berlin on April 26th; the German Government gave the *Sussex* "pledge" on May 4th, eight days afterward. In this reply Germany declared that she would now expect Mr. Wilson to bring pressure upon Great Britain to secure a mitigation or suspension of the British blockade, and to this Mr. Wilson promptly and energetically replied that he regarded the German promise as an unconditional one and that the Government of the United States "cannot for a moment entertain, much less discuss, a suggestion that respect by German naval authorities for the rights of citizens of the United States upon the high seas should in any way or in the slightest degree be made contingent upon the conduct of any other government affecting the rights of neutrals and non-combatants. Responsibility in such matters is single not joint; absolute not relative."

This reply gave satisfaction to both the United States and the countries of the Allies, and Page himself regarded it as a master stroke. "The more I think of it," he wrote on May 17th, "the better the strategy of the President appears, in his latest (and last) note to Germany. They laid a trap for him and he caught them in their own trap. The Germans had tried to 'put it up' to the President to commit the first unfriendly act. He now 'puts it up' to them. And this is at last bound to end the controversy if they sink another ship unlawfully. The French see this clearly and so do the best English, and it has produced a most favourable impression. The future? The German angling for peace will prove futile. They'll have another fit of fury Whether they will again become reckless or commit 'mistakes' with their submarines will depend partly on their fury, partly on their fear to make a breach with the United States, but mainly on the state of their submarine fleet. How many have the English caught and destroyed? That's the main question, after all. The English view may not be fair to them. But nobody here believes that they will long abstain from the luxury of crime."

It is thus apparent that when the Germans practically demanded, as a price of their abstention from indiscriminate submarine warfare, that Mr. Wilson should move against Great Britain in the matter of the blockade, they realized the futility of any such step, and that what they really expected to obtain was the presidential mediation for peace. President Wilson at once began to move in this direction. On May 27th, three weeks after the *Sussex* "pledge," he made an address in Washington before the League to Enforce Peace, which was intended to lay the basis for his approaching negotiations. It was in this speech that he made the statement that the United States was "not concerned with the causes and the objects" of the war. "The obscure fountains from which its stupendous flood has burst forth we are not interested to search for or to explain." This was another of those unfortunate sentences which made the President such an unsympathetic figure in the estimation of the Allies and seemed to indicate to them that he had no appreciation of the nature of the struggle. Though this attitude of non-partisanship, of equal balance between the accusations of the Allies and Germany, was intended to make the President acceptable as a mediator, the practical result was exactly the reverse, for Allied statesmen turned from Wilson as soon as those sentences appeared in print. The fact that this same oration specified the "freedom of the seas" as one of the foundation rocks of the proposed new settlement only accentuated this unfavourable attitude.

This then was clearly the "atmosphere" which prevailed in Washington at the time that Page was summoned home. But Page's letters of this period indicate how little sympathy he entertained for such negotiations. "It is quite apparent," he had recently written to Colonel House, "that nobody in Washington understands the war. Come over and find out." Extracts from a letter which he wrote to his brother, Mr. Henry A. Page, of Aberdeen, North Carolina, are especially interesting when placed side by side with the President's statements of this particular time. These passages show that a two years' close observation of the Prussians in action had not changed Page's opinion of their motives or of their methods; in 1916, as in 1914, Page could see in this struggle nothing but a colossal buccaneering expedition on the part of Germany. "As I look at it," he wrote, "our dilly-dallying is likely to get us into war. The Germans want somebody to rob—to pay their great military bills. They've robbed Belgium and are still robbing it of every penny they can lay their hands on. They robbed Poland and Serbia—two very poor countries which didn't have much. They set out to rob France and have so far been stopped from getting to Paris. If they got to Paris there wouldn't be thirty cents' worth of movable property there in a week, and they'd levy fines of millions of francs a day. Their military scheme and teaching and open purpose is to make somebody pay for their vast military outlay of the last forty years. They must do that or go bankrupt. Now it looks as if they would go bankrupt. But in a little while they may be able to bombard New York and demand

billions of dollars to refrain from destroying the city.
That's the richest place left to spoil.

"Now they say that—quite openly and quite frankly.
Now if we keep 'neutral' to a highwayman—what do we
get for our pains? That's the mistake we are making.
If we had sent Bernstorff home the day after the *Lusitania*
was sunk and recalled Gerard and begun to train an army
we'd have had no more trouble with them. But since
they have found out that they can keep us discussing
things forever and a day, they will keep us discussing
things till they are ready. We are very simple; and we'll
get shot for it yet. . . .

"The prestige and fear of the United States has gone
down, down, down—disappeared; and we are regarded as
'discussors,' incapable of action, scared to death of war.
That's all the invitation that robbers, whose chief business is war, want—all the invitation they need. These
devils are out for robbery—and you don't seem to believe
it in the United States: that's the queer thing. This
neutrality business makes us an easy mark. As soon as
they took a town in Belgium, they asked for all the money
in the town, all the food, all the movable property; and
they've levied a tax every month since on every town and
made the town government borrow the money to pay it.
If a child in a town makes a disrespectful remark, they fine
the town an extra $1,000. They haven't got enough so
far to keep them going flush; and they won't unless they
get Paris—which they can't do now. If they got London,
they'd be rich; they wouldn't leave a shilling and they'd
make all the rich English get all the money they own
abroad. This is the reason that Frenchmen and Englishmen prefer to be killed by the 100,000. In the country
over which their army has passed a crow would die of
starvation and no human being has ten cents of real

money.   The Belgian Commission is spending more than 100 million dollars a year to keep the Belgians alive—only because they are robbed every day.   They have a rich country and could support themselves but for these robbers.   That's the meaning of the whole thing.   And yet we treat them as if they were honourable people.   It's only a question of time and of power when they will attack us, or the Canal, or South America.   Everybody on this side the world knows that.   And they are 'yielding' to keep us out of this war so that England will not help us when they (the Germans) get ready to attack America.

"There is the strangest infatuation in the United States with Peace—the strangest illusion about our safety without preparation."

Several letters to Colonel House show the state of the British mind on the subject of the President's peace proposals:

To Edward M. House

Royal Bath and East Cliff Hotel,
Bournemouth,
23 May, 1916.

DEAR HOUSE:

The motor trip that the Houses, the Wallaces, and the Pages took about a year ago was the last trip (three days) that I had had out of London; and I'd got pretty tired. The *China* case having been settled (and settled as we wanted it), I thought it a good time to try to get away for a week.   So here Mrs. Page and I are—very much to my benefit.   I've spent a beautiful week out of doors, on this seashore; and I have only about ten per cent. of the fatal diseases that I had a week ago.   That is to say, I'm as sound as a dollar and feel like a fighting cock.

Sir Edward was fine about the *China*[1] case.   He never disputed the principle of the inviolability of American ships on the high seas; but the Admiralty maintained that some of these men are officers in the German Army and are now receiving officers' pay.   I think that that is probably true.   Nevertheless, the Admiralty had bungled the case badly and Sir Edward simply rode over them.   They have a fine quarrel among themselves and we got all we wanted and asked for.

Of course, I can't make out the Germans but I am afraid some huge deviltry is yet coming.   When the English say that the Germans must give up their militarism, I doubt if the Germans yet know what they mean.   They talk about conquered territory—Belgium, Poland, and the rest.   It hasn't entered their heads that they've got to give up their armies and their military system.   When this does get into their heads, if it ever do, I think they may so swell with rage at this "insult" that they may break loose in one last desperate effort, ignoring the United States, defying the universe, running amuck.   Of course it would be foolhardy to predict this, but the fear of it keeps coming into my mind.   The fear is the more persistent because, if the worst comes to them, the military caste and perhaps the dynasty itself will prefer to die in one last terrific onslaught rather than to make a peace on terms which will require the practical extinction of their supreme power. This, I conceive, is the really great danger that yet awaits the world—if the Allies hold together till defeat and famine drive the Germans to the utmost desperation.

In the meantime, the Allies still holding together as

[1] The *China* case was a kind of *Trent* case reversed.   In 1861 the American ship *San Jacinto* stopped the British vessel *Trent* and took off Mason and Slidell, Confederate commissioners to Great Britain.   Similarly a British ship, in 1916, stopped an American ship, the *China*, and removed several German subjects. As the British quickly saw the analogy, and made suitable amends, the old excitement over the *Trent* was not duplicated in the recent war.

they are, there's no peace yet in the British and French minds. They're after the militarism of Prussia—not territory or other gains; and they seem likely to get it, as much by the blockade as by victories on land. Do you remember how in the Franco-Prussian War, Bismarck refused to deal with the French Emperor? He demanded that representatives of the French people should deal with him. He got what he asked for and that was the last of the French Emperor. Neither the French nor the English have forgotten that. You will recall that the Germans starved Paris into submission. Neither the French nor the English have forgotten that. These two leaves out of the Germans' own book of forty-five years ago—these two and no more—*may* be forced on the Germans themselves. They are both quite legitimate, too. You can read a recollection of both these events between the lines of the interviews that Sir Edward and Mr. Balfour recently gave to American newspapers.

There is nothing but admiration here for the strategy of the President's last note to Germany. That was the cleverest play made by anybody since the war began— clever beyond praise. Now he's "got 'em." But nobody here doubts that they will say, sooner or later, that the United States, not having forced the breaking of the British blockade, has not kept its bargain—that's what they'll *say*—and it is in order again to run amuck. This is what the English think—provided the Germans have enough submarines left to keep up real damage. By that time, too, it will be clear to the Germans that the President can't bring peace so long as only one side wishes peace. The Germans seem to have counted much on the Irish uprising, which came to pass at all only because of the customary English stupid bungling; and the net result has been only to put the mass of the Irish on their mettle to show that they are not Sinn Feiners. The final upshot will be to strengthen the British Army. God surely is good to this bungling British Government. Wind and wave and the will of High Heaven seem to work for them. I begin to understand their stupidity and their arrogance. If your enemies are such fools in psychological tactics and Heaven is with you, why take the trouble to be alert? And why be modest? Whatever the reason, these English are now more cocky and confident than they've been before since the war began. They are beginning to see results. The only question seems to be to hold the Allies together, and they seem to be doing that. In fact, the battle of Verdun has cemented them. They now have visible proof that the German Army is on the wane. And they have trustworthy evidence that the blockade is telling severely on the Germans. Nobody, I think, expects to thrash 'em to a frazzle; but the almost universal opinion here is that the hold of militarism will be shaken loose. And the German High Canal Navy—what's to become of that? Von Tirpitz is down and out, but there are thousands of Germans, I hear, who complain of their naval inactivity. But God only knows the future— I don't. I think that I do well if I keep track of the present. . . .

My kindest regards to Mrs. House,

Yours very heartily,
W. H. P.

To Edward M. House

London, 25 May, 1916.

DEAR HOUSE:

No utterance by anybody has so stirred the people of this kingdom for many months as Sir Edward Grey's impromptu speech last night in the House of Commons about Peace, when he called the German Chancellor a first-class liar. I sent you to-day a clipping from one of the morning papers. Every paper I pick up compliments Sir Edward. Everyone says, "We must fight to a finish." The more sensational press intimates that any Englishman who uses the word "peace" ought to be shot. You have never seen such a rally as that which has taken place in response to Sir Edward's cry. In the first place, as you know, he is the most gentle of all the Cabinet, the last man to get on a "war-rampage," the least belligerent and rambunctious of the whole lot. When he felt moved to say that there can be no peace till the German military despotism is broken, everybody from one end of the Kingdom to the other seems to have thrown up his hat and applauded. Except the half-dozen peace-cranks in the House (Bryan sort of men) you can't find a man, woman, child, or dog that isn't fired with the determination to see the war through. The continued talk about peace which is reported directly and indirectly from Germany—coming from Switzerland, from Rome, from Washington—has made the English and the French very angry: no, "angry" isn't quite the right word. It has made them very determined. They feel insulted by the impudence of the Germans, who, since they know they are bound to lose, seem to be turning heaven and earth to induce neutrals to take their view of peace. People are asking here, "If they are victorious, why doesn't their fleet come out of the canal and take the seas, and again open their commerce? Why do they whimper about the blockade when they will not even risk a warship to break it?" You'll recall how the talk here used to be that the English wouldn't wake up. You wouldn't know 'em now. Your bulldog has got his grip and even thunder doesn't disturb him.

Incidentally, all the old criticism of Sir Edward Grey seems to have been forgotten. You hear nothing but praise of him now. I am told that he spoke his impromptu speech last night with great fire and at once left the House. His speech has caused a greater stir than the Irish rebellion, showing that every Englishman feels that Sir Edward said precisely what every man feels.

The Germans have apparently overdone and overworked their premature peace efforts and have made things worse for them. They've overplayed their hand.

In fact, I see no end of the war. The Allies are not going to quit prematurely. They won't even discuss the subject yet with one another, and the Germans, by their peace-talk of the sort that they inspire, simply postpone the day when the Allies will take the subject up.

All the while, too, the Allies work closer and closer together. They'll soon be doing even their diplomatic work with neutrals, as a unit—England and France as one nation, and (on great subjects) Russia and Italy also with them.

I've talked lately not only with Sir Edward but with nearly half the other members of the Cabinet, and they are all keyed up to the same tune. The press of both parties, too, are (for once) wholly agreed: Liberal and Conservative papers alike hold the same war-creed.

Sincerely yours,
WALTER H. PAGE.

Before leaving for Washington Page discussed the situation personally with Sir Edward Grey and Lord Bryce. He has left memoranda of both interviews.

Notes of a Private and Informal Conversation with Sir Edward Grey, at his residence, on July 27, 1916, when I called to say good-bye before sailing on leave to the United States

. . . Sir Edward Grey went on to say quite frankly that two thoughts expressed in a speech by the President some months ago had had a very serious influence on British opinion. One thought was that the causes or objects of the war were of no concern to him, and the other was his (at least implied) endorsement of "the freedom of the seas," which the President did not define.

Concerning the first thought, he understood of course that a neutral President could not say that he favoured one side or the other: everybody understood that and nobody expected him to take sides. But when the President said that the objects of the war did not concern him, that was taken by British public opinion as meaning a condemnation of the British cause, and it produced deep feeling.

Concerning the "freedom of the seas," he believed that the first use of the phrase was made by Colonel House (on his return from one of his visits to Berlin),[1] but the public now regarded it as a German invention and it meant to the British mind a policy which would render British supremacy at sea of little value in time of war; and public opinion resented this. He knew perfectly well that at a convenient time new rules must be made governing the conduct of war at sea and on the land, too. But the German idea of "the freedom of the seas" ("freedom" was needed on land also) is repulsive to the British mind.

He mentioned these things because they had produced

---

[1]See Chapter XIII, page 434.

in many minds an unwillingness, he feared, to use the good offices of the President whenever any mediatorial service might be done by a neutral. The tendency of these remarks was certainly in that direction. Yet Sir Edward carefully abstained from expressing such an unwillingness on his own part, and the inference from his tone and manner, as well as from his habitual attitude, is that he feels no unwillingness to use the President's good office, if occasion should arise.

I asked what he meant by "mediatorial"—the President's offering his services or good offices on his own initiative? He said—No, not that. But the Germans might express to the President their willingness or even their definite wish to have an armistice, on certain terms, to discuss conditions of peace coupled with an intimation that he might sound the Allies. He did not expect the President to act on his own initiative, but at the request or at least at the suggestion of the German Government, he might conceivably sound the Allies—especially, he added, "since I am informed that the notion is wide-spread in America that the war will end inconclusively—as a draw." He smiled and remarked, as an aside, that he didn't think that this notion was held by any considerable group of people in any other country, certainly not in Great Britain.

In further talk on this subject he said that none of the Allies could mention peace or discuss peace till France should express such a wish; for it is the very vitals of France that have received and are receiving the shock of such an assault as was never before launched against any nation. Unless France was ready to quit, none of France's Allies could mention peace, and France showed no mood to quit. Least of all could the English make or receive any such suggestion at least till her new great army had done its best; for until lately the severest fighting had not been done by the British, whose army had practically been held in reserve. There had for a long time been a perfect understanding between Joffre and Haig—that the English would wait to begin their offensive till the moment arrived when it best suited the French.

The impression that I got from this part of the conversation was that Sir Edward hoped that I might convey to the President (as, of course, he could not) Sir Edward's idea of the effect of these parts of the President's speech on feeling in England toward him. Nowhere in the conversation did he make any request of me. Any one, overhearing it, might have supposed it to be a conversation between two men, with no object beyond expressing their views. But, of course, he hoped and meant that I should, in my own way, make known to the President what he said. He did not say that the President's good offices, when the time should come, would be unwelcome to him or to his government; and he meant, I am sure, to convey only the fear that by these assertions the President had planted an objection to his good offices in a large section of British opinion.

Among the conditions of peace that Sir Edward himself personally would like to see imposed (he had not yet discussed the subject with any of his colleagues in the Government) was this: that the German Government should agree to submit to an impartial (neutral) commission or court the question, Who began the war and who is responsible for it? The German Chancellor and other high German officials have put it about and continue to put it about that England is responsible, and doubtless the German people at least believe it. All the governments concerned must (this is his idea) submit to the tribunal all its documents and other evidence bearing on the subject; and of course the finding of the tribunal must be published.

Then he talked a good deal about the idea that lies behind the League for Enforcing Peace—in a sympathetic mood. He went on to point out how such a league—with force behind it—would at any one of three stages have prevented this war—(1) When England proposed a conference to France, Germany, Italy, and Russia, all agreed to it but Germany. Germany alone prevented a discussion. If the League to Enforce Peace had included England, France, Italy, and Russia—there would have been no war; for Germany would have seen at once that they would all be against her. (2) Later, when the Czar sent the Kaiser a personal telegram proposing to submit their differences to some tribunal, a League to Enforce Peace would have prevented war. And (3) when the question of the invasion of Belgium came up, every signatory to the treaty guaranteeing Belgium's integrity gave assurance of keeping the treaty—but Germany, and Germany gave an evasive answer. A league would again have prevented a war—or put all the military force of all its members against Germany.

Throughout the conversation, which lasted about an hour, Sir Edward said more than once, as he has often said to me, that he hoped we should be able to keep the friction between our governments at the minimum. He would regard it as the greatest calamity if the ill-feeling that various events have stirred up in sections of public opinion on each side should increase or should become permanent. His constant wish and effort were to lessen and if possible to remove all misunderstandings.

Lord Bryce was one of the Englishmen with whom Page was especially inclined to discuss pending problems.

Notes on a conversation with Lord Bryce,
July 31, 1916

Lord Bryce spoke of the President's declaration that we were not concerned with the causes or objects of the war and he said that that remark had caused much talk—all, as he thought, on a misunderstanding of Mr. Wilson's meaning. "He meant, I take it, only that he did not propose at that time to discuss the causes or the objects of the war; and it is a pity that his sentence was capable of being interpreted to mean something else; and the sentence was published and discussed here apart from its context—a most unfair proceeding. I can imagine that the President and his friends may be much annoyed by this improper interpretation."

I remarked that the body of the speech in which this remark occurred might have been written in Downing Street, so friendly was it to the Allies.

"Quite, quite," said he.

This was at dinner, Lady Bryce and Mrs. Page and he and I only being present.

When he and I went into the library he talked more than an hour.

"And what about this blacklist?" he asked. I told him. He had been in France for a week and did not know just what had been done. He said that that seemed to him a mistake. "The Government doesn't know America—neither does the British public. Neither does the American Government (*no* American government) know the British. Hence your government writes too many notes—all governments are likely to write too many notes. Everybody gets tired of seeing them and they lose their effect."

He mentioned the blockade and said that it had become quite effective—wonderfully effective, in fact; and he implied that he did not see why we now failed to recognize it. Our refusal to recognize it had caused and doubtless is now causing such ill-feeling as exists in England.

Then he talked long about peace and how it would probably be arranged. He judged, from letters that he receives from the United States as well as from Americans who come over here, that there was an expectation in America that the President would be called in at the peace settlement and that some persons even expected him to offer mediation. He did not see how that could be. He knew no precedent for such a proceeding. The President might, of course, on the definite request of either side, make a definite inquiry of the other side; but such a course would be, in effect, merely the transmission of an inquiry.

But after peace was made and the time came to set up a League for Enforcing Peace, or some such machinery, of course the United States would be and would have to be a party to that if it were to succeed. He reminded me that a little group of men here, of whom he was one, early in the war sketched substantially the same plan that the American League to Enforce Peace has worked out. It had not seemed advisable to have any general public discussion of it in England till the war should end: nobody had time now to give to it.

As he knew no precedent for belligerents to call in a third party when they met to end a war, so he knew no precedent for any outside government to protest against the invasion of a country by a Power that had signed a treaty to guarantee the integrity of the invaded country—no precedent, that is to say, for the United States to protest against the invasion of Belgium. "That precedent," I said, "was found in Hysteria."

Lord Bryce, who had just returned from a visit to the British headquarters in France, hardly dared hope for the end of the war till next year; and the intervening time between now and the end would be a time, he feared, of renewed atrocities and increasing hatred. He cited the killing of Captain Fryatt of the *Brussels* and the forcible deportation of young women from Lille and other towns in the provinces of France occupied by the Germans.

The most definite idea that he had touching American-British relations was the fear that the anti-British feeling in the United States would become stronger and would outlast the war. "It is organized," he said. "The disaffected Germans and the disaffected Irish are interested in keeping it up." He asked what effect I thought the Presidential campaign would have on this feeling. He seemed to have a fear that somehow the campaign would give an occasion for stirring it up even more.

"Good-bye. Give my regards to all my American friends; and I'm proud to say there are a good many of them."

One episode that was greatly stirring both Great Britain and the United States at this time was the trial of Sir Roger Casement, the Irish leader who had left Wilhelmshaven for Ireland in a German submarine and who had been captured at Tralee in the act of landing arms and munitions for an Irish insurrection. Casement's subsequent trial and conviction on a charge of high treason had inspired a movement in his favour from Irish-Americans, the final outcome of which was that the Senate, in early August, passed a resolution asking the British Government for clemency and stipulating that this resolution should be presented to the Foreign Office. Page was then on the ocean bound for the United States and the delicate task of presenting this document to Sir Edward Grey fell upon Mr. Laughlin, who was now Chargé d'affaires. Mr. Laughlin is a diplomat of great experience, but this responsibility at first seemed to be something of a poser even for him. He had received explicit instructions from Washington to present this resolution, and the one thing above all which a diplomatic officer must do is to carry out the orders of his government, but Mr. Laughlin well knew that, should he present this paper in the usual manner, the Foreign Secretary might decline to receive it; he might regard it as an interference with matters that exclusively concerned the sovereign state. Mr. Laughlin, however, has a technique all his own, and, in accordance with this, he asked for an interview with Sir Edward Grey to discuss a matter of routine business. However, the Chargé d'affaires carried the Casement resolution tucked away in an inside pocket when he made his call.

Like Mr. Page, Mr. Laughlin was on the friendliest terms with Sir Edward Grey, and, after the particular piece of business had been transacted, the two men, as usual, fell into casual conversation. Casement then loomed large in the daily press, and the activities of the American Senate had likewise caused some commotion in London. In round-about fashion Mr. Laughlin was able to lead Sir Edward to make some reference to the Casement case.

"I see the Senate has passed a resolution asking clemency," said the Foreign Secretary—exactly the remark which the American wished to elicit.

"Yes," was the reply. "By the way, I happen to have a copy of the resolution with me. May I give it to you?"

"Yes, I should like to have it."

The Foreign Secretary read it over with deliberation.

"This is a very interesting document," he said, when he

had finished. "Would you have any objection if I showed it to the Prime Minister?"

Of course that was precisely what Mr. Laughlin did wish, and he replied that this was the desire of his government. The purpose of his visit had been accomplished, and he was able to cable Washington that its instructions had been carried out and that the Casement resolution had been presented to the British Government. Simultaneously with his communication, however, he reported also that the execution of Roger Casement had taken place. In fact, it was being carried out at the time of the interview. This incident lends point to Page's memorandum of the last interview which he had before leaving England.

August 1st. I lunched with Mr. Asquith. One does not usually bring away much from his conversations, and he did not say much to-day worth recording. But he showed a very eager interest in the Presidential campaign, and he confessed that he felt some anxiety about the anti-British feeling in the United States. This led him to tell me that he could not in good conscience interfere with Casement's execution, in spite of the shoals of telegrams that he was receiving from the United States. This man, said he, visited Irish prisoners in German camps and tried to seduce them to take up arms against Great Britain— their own country. When they refused, the Germans removed them to the worst places in their Empire and, as a result, some of them died. Then Casement came to Ireland in a German man-of-war (a submarine) accompanied by a ship loaded with guns. "In all good conscience to my country and to my responsibilities I cannot interfere." He hoped that thoughtful opinion in the United States would see this whole matter in a fair and just way.

I asked him about anti-American feeling in Great Britain. He said: "Do not let that unduly disturb you. At bottom we understand you. At bottom the two people surely understand one another and have unbreakable bonds of sympathy. No serious breach is conceivable." He went on quite earnestly: "Mr. Page, after any policy or plan is thought out on its merits my next thought always is how it may affect our relations with the United States. That is always a fundamental consideration."

I ventured to say that if he would keep our relations smooth on the surface, I'd guarantee their stability at the bottom. It's the surface that rolls high at times, and the danger is there. Keep the surface smooth and the bottom will take care of itself.

Then he asked about Mexico, as he usually has when I have talked with him. I gave him as good a report as I could, reminding him of the great change in the attitude of all Latin-America caused by the President's patient policy with Mexico. When he said, "Mexico is a bad problem," I couldn't resist the impulse to reply: "When Mexico troubles you, think of—Ireland. As there are persons in England who concern themselves with Mexico, so there are persons in the United States who concern themselves about Ireland. Ireland and Mexico have each given trouble for two centuries. Yet these people talk about them as if they could remove all trouble in a month."

"Quite true," he said, and smiled himself into silence. Then he talked about more or less frivolous subjects; and, as always, he asked about Mr. Bryan and Mr. Roosevelt, "alike now, I suppose, in their present obscure plight." I told him I was going from his house to the House of Lords to see Sir Edward Grey metamorphosed into Viscount Grey of Fallodon.

"The very stupidest of the many stupid ceremonies that we have," said he—very truly.

He spoke of my "onerous duties" and so on and so on— tut, tut! talk that gets nowhere. But he did say, quite' sincerely, I think, that my frankness called forth frankness and avoided misunderstanding; for he has said that to other people about me.

Such is the Prime Minister of Great Britain in this supreme crisis in English history, a remarkable man, of an abnormally quick mind, pretty nearly a great man, but now a spent force, at once nimble and weary. History may call him Great. If it do, he will owe this judgment to the war, with the conduct of which his name will be forever associated.

II

Mr. and Mrs. Page's homecoming was a tragedy. They sailed from Liverpool on August 3rd, and reached New York on the evening of August 11th. But sad news awaited them upon the dock. About two months previously their youngest son, Frank, had been married to Miss Katherine Sefton, of Auburn, N. Y., and the young couple had settled down in Garden City, Long Island. That was the summer when the epidemic of infantile paralysis swept over the larger part of the United States. The young bride was stricken; the case was unusually rapid and unusually severe; at the moment of the Pages' arrival, they were informed that there was practically no hope; and Mrs. Frank Page died at two o'clock on the afternoon of the following day. The Pages had always been a particularly united and happy family; this was the first time that they had suffered from any domestic sorrow of this kind, and the Ambassador was so affected that it was with difficulty that he could summon himself for the task that lay ahead.

In a few days, however, he left for Washington. He has

himself described his experience at the Capital in words that must inevitably take their place in history. To appreciate properly the picture which Page gives, it must be remembered that the city and the officialdom which he portrays are the same city and the same men who six months afterward declared war on Germany. When Page reached Washington, the Presidential campaign was in full swing, with Mr. Wilson as the Democratic candidate and Mr. Charles E. Hughes as the Republican. But another crisis was absorbing the nation's attention: the railway unions, comprising practically all the 2,000,000 railway employees in the United States, were threatening to strike—ostensibly for an eight-hour day, in reality for higher wages.

Mr. Page's memorandum of his visit to Washington in August, 1916

The President was very courteous to me, in his way. He invited me to luncheon the day after I arrived. Present: the President, Mrs. Wilson, Miss Bones, Tom Bolling, his brother-in-law, and I. The conversation was general and in the main jocular. Not a word about England, not a word about a foreign policy or foreign relations.

He explained that the threatened railway strike engaged his whole mind. I asked to have a talk with him when his mind should be free. Would I not go off and rest and come back?—I preferred to do my minor errands with the Department, but I should hold myself at his convenience and at his command.

Two weeks passed. Another invitation to lunch. Sharp, the Ambassador to France, had arrived. He, too, was invited. Present: the President, Mrs. Wilson, Mrs.

Wallace, the Misses Smith of New Orleans, Miss Bones, Sharp, and I. Not one word about foreign affairs.

After luncheon, the whole party drove to the Capitol, where the President addressed Congress on the strike, proposing legislation to prevent it and to forestall similar strikes. It is a simple ceremony and somewhat impressive. The Senators occupy the front seats in the House, the Speaker presides and the President of the Senate sits on his right. An escorting committee is sent out to bring the President in. He walks to the clerk's or reader's desk below the presiding officer's, turns and shakes hands with them both and then proceeds to read his speech, very clearly and audibly. Some passages were applauded. When he had done, he again shook hands with the presiding officer and went out, preceded and followed by the White House escort. I sat in the Presidential (or diplomatic?) gallery with the White House party, higgledy-piggledy.

The speech ended, the President drove to the White House with his escort in his car. The crowds in the corridors and about the doors waited and crowded to see Mrs. Wilson, quite respectful but without order or discipline. We had to push our way through them. Now and then a policeman at a distance would yell loudly, "Make way there!"

When we reached the White House, I asked the doorman if the President had arrived.

"Yes."

"Does he expect me to go in and say good-bye?"

"No."

Thus he had no idea of talking with me now, if ever. Not at lunch nor after did he suggest a conversation about American-British affairs or say anything about my seeing him again.

This threatened strike does hold his whole mind—

bothers him greatly. It seems doubtful if he can avert a general strike. The Republicans are trying "to put him in a political hole," and they say he, too, is playing politics. Whoever be to blame for it, it is true that politics is in the game. Nobody seems to foresee who will make capital out of it. Surely I can't.

There's no social sense at the White House. The President has at his table family connections only—and they say few or no distinguished men and women are invited, except the regular notables at the set dinners—the diplomatic, the judiciary, and the like. His table is his private family affair—nothing more. It is very hard to understand why so intellectual a man doesn't have notable men about him. It's the college professor's village habit, I dare say. But it's a great misfortune. This is one way in which Mr. Wilson shuts out the world and lives too much alone. feeding only on knowledge and subjects that he has already acquired and not getting new views or fresh suggestions from men and women.

He sees almost nobody except members of Congress for whom he sends for special conferences, and he usually sees these in his office. The railroad presidents and men he met in formal conference—no social touch.

A member of his Cabinet told me that Mr. Wilson had shown confidence in him, given him a wide range of action in his own Department and that he relies on his judgment. This Cabinet member of course attends the routine state dinners and receptions, as a matter of required duty. But as for any social recognition of his existence—he had never received a hint or nod. Nor does any member of the Cabinet (except, no doubt, Mr. McAdoo, his son-in-law). There is no social sense nor reason in this. In fact, it works to a very decided disadvantage to the President and to the Nation.

By the way, that a notable man in our educational life could form such a habit does not speak well for our educational life.

What an unspeakably lamentable loss of opportunity! This is the more remarkable and lamentable because the President is a charming personality, an uncommonly good talker, a man who could easily make personal friends of all the world. He does his own thinking, untouched by other men's ideas. He receives nothing from the outside. His domestic life is spent with his own, nobody else, except House occasionally. His contact with his own Cabinet is a business man's contact with his business associates and kind—at his office.

He declined to see Cameron Forbes[1] on his return from the Philippines.

The sadness of this mistake!

Another result is—the President doesn't hear the frank truth about the men about him. He gives nobody a chance to tell him. Hence he has several heavy encumbrances in his official family.

The influence of this lone-hand way of playing the game extends very far. The members of the Cabinet do not seem to have the habit of frankness with one another. Each lives and works in a water-tight compartment. I sat at luncheon (at a hotel) with Lansing, Secretary of State; Lane, Secretary of the Interior; Gregory, Attorney-General; Baker, Secretary of War; Daniels, Secretary of the Navy; and Sharp, Ambassador to France; and all the talk was jocular or semi-jocular, and personal—mere cheap chaff. Not a question was asked either of the Ambassador to France or of the Ambassador to Great Britain about the war or about our foreign relations. The

---

[1] Mr. Forbes had been Governor-General of the Philippines from 1909 to 1913. His work had been extraordinarily successful.

war wasn't mentioned. Sharp and I might have come from Bungtown and Jonesville and not from France and England. We were not encouraged to talk—the local personal joke held the time and conversation. This astounding fact must be the result of this lone-hand, watertight compartment method and—of the neutrality suppression of men. The Vice-President confessed to his neighbour at a Gridiron dinner that he had read none of the White Papers, or Orange Papers, etc., of the bel'igerent governments—confessed this with pride--lest he should form an opinion and cease to be neutral! Miss X, a member of the President's household, said to Mrs. Y, the day we lunched there, that she had made a remark privately to Sharp showing her admiration of the French.

"Was that a violation of neutrality?" she asked in all seriousness.

I can see it in no other way but this: the President suppressed free thought and free speech when he insisted upon personal neutrality. He held back the deliberate and spontaneous thought and speech of the people except the pro-Germans, who saw their chance and improved it! The mass of the American people found themselves forbidden to think or talk, and this forbidding had a sufficient effect to make them take refuge in indifference. It's the President's job. He's our leader. He'll attend to this matter. We must not embarrass him. On this easy cushion of non-responsibility the great masses fell back at their intellectual and moral ease—softened, isolated, lulled.

That wasn't leadership in a democracy. Right here is the President's vast failure. From it there is now no escape unless the Germans commit more submarine crimes. They have kept the United States for their own exploiting after the war. They have thus had a real triumph of us.

I have talked in Washington with few men who showed any clear conception of the difference between the Germans and the British. To the minds of these people and high Government officials, German and English are alike foreign nations who are now foolishly engaged in war. Two of the men who look upon the thing differently are Houston[1] and Logan Waller Page.[2] In fact, there is no realization of the war in Washington. Secretary Houston has a proper perspective of the situation. He would have done precisely what I recommended—paved the way for claims and let the English take their course. "International law" is no strict code and it's all shot to pieces anyhow.

The Secretary [of State] betrayed not the slightest curiosity about our relations with Great Britain. I saw him several times—(1) in his office; (2) at his house; (3) at the French Ambassador's; (4) at Wallace's; (5) at his office; (6) at Crozier's[3]—this during my first stay in Washington. The only remark he made was that I'd find a different atmosphere in Washington from the atmosphere in London. Truly. All the rest of his talk was about "cases." Would I see Senator Owen? Would I see Congressman Sherley? Would I take up this "case" and that? His mind ran on "cases."

Well, at Y's, when I was almost in despair, I rammed down him a sort of general statement of the situation as I saw it; at least, I made a start. But soon he stopped me and ran off at a tangent on some historical statement I had made, showing that his mind was not at all on the real subject, the large subject. When I returned to Washington, and he had read my interviews with Grey, Asquith,

---

[1]Secretary of Agriculture.

[2]In charge of government road building, a distant relative of the Ambassador.

[3]Major General William Crozier, U. S. A., Chief of Ordnance.

and Bryce,[1] and my own statement, he still said nothing, but he ceased to talk of "cases." At my final interview he said that he had had difficulty in preventing Congress from making the retaliatory resolution mandatory. He had tried to keep it back till the very end of the session, etc.

This does not quite correspond with what the President told me—that the State Department asked for this retaliatory resolution.

I made specific suggestions in my statement to the President and to Lansing. They have (yet) said nothing about them. I fancy they will not. I have found nowhere any policy—only "cases."

I proposed to Baker and Daniels that they send a General and an Admiral as attachés to London. They both agreed. Daniels later told me that Baker mentioned it to the President and he "stepped on the suggestion with both feet." I did not bring it up. In the Franco-Prussian War of 1870, both General McClellan (or Sheridan?[2]) and General Forsythe were sent to the German Army. Our military ideas have shrunk since then!

I find at this date (a month before the Presidential election), the greatest tangle and uncertainty of political opinion that I have ever observed in our country. The President, in spite of his unparalleled leadership and authority in domestic policy, is by no means certain of election. He has the open hostility of the Germans—all very well, if he had got the fruits of a real hostility to them; but they have, in many ways, directed his foreign policy. He has lost the silent confidence of many men upon whose conscience this great question weighs heavily. If he be defeated he will owe his defeat to the loss of con-

---

[1] See Chapter XIX, pages 160–164.

[2] It was General Sheridan.

fidence in his leadership on this great subject. His opponent has put forth no clear-cut opinion. He plays a silent game on the German "issue." Yet he will command the support of many patriotic men merely as a lack of confidence in the President.

Nor do I see any end of the results of this fundamental error. In the economic and political readjustment of the world we shall be "out of the game," in any event—unless we are yet forced into the war by Hughes's election or by the renewal of the indiscriminate use of submarines by the Germans.

There is a great lesson in this lamentable failure of the President really to lead the Nation. The United States stands for democracy and free opinion as it stands for nothing else and as no other nation stands for it. Now when democracy and free opinion are at stake as they have not before been, we take a "neutral" stand—we throw away our very birthright. We may talk of "humanity" all we like: we have missed the largest chance that ever came to help the large cause that brought us into being as a Nation. . . .

And the people, sitting on the comfortable seats of neutrality upon which the President has pushed them back, are grateful for Peace, not having taken the trouble to think out what Peace has cost us and cost the world —except so many as have felt the uncomfortable stirrings of the national conscience.

There is not a man in our State Department or in our Government who has ever met any prominent statesmen in any European Government—except the third Assistant Secretary of State, who has no authority in forming policies; there is not a man who knows the atmosphere of Europe. Yet when I proposed that one of the under Secretaries should go to England on a visit of a few weeks for observation, the objection arose that such a visit would not be "neutral."

III

The extraordinary feature of this experience was that Page had been officially summoned home, presumably to discuss the European situation, and that neither the President nor the State Department apparently had the slightest interest in his visit.

"The President," Page wrote to Mr. Laughlin, "dominates the whole show in a most extraordinary way. The men about him (and he sees them only on 'business') are very nearly all very, very small fry, or worse—the narrowest twopenny lot I've ever come across. He has no real companions. Nobody talks to him freely and frankly. I've never known quite such a condition in American life." Perhaps the President had no desire to discuss inconvenient matters with his Ambassador to Great Britain, but Page was certainly determined to have an interview with the President. "I'm not going back to London," he wrote Mr. Laughlin, "till the President has said something to me or at least till I have said something to him. I am now going down to Garden City and New York till the President send for me; or, if he do not send for me, I'm going to his house and sit on his front steps till he come out!" Page had brought from England one of the medals which the Germans had struck in honour of the *Lusitania* sinking, and one reason why he particularly wished to see the President alone was to show him this memento.

Another reason was that in early September Page had received important news from London concerning the move which Germany was making for peace and the attitude of Great Britain in this matter. The several plans which

Germany had had under consideration had now taken the form of a definite determination to ask for an armistice before winter set in. A letter from Mr. Laughlin, Chargé d'affaires in Page's absence, tells the story.

From Irwin Laughlin

Embassy of the United States of America.
London, August 30, 1916.

DEAR MR. PAGE:

For some little time past I have heard persistent rumours, which indeed are more than rumours, since they have come from important sources, of an approaching movement by Germany toward an early armistice. They have been so circumstantial and so closely connected—in prospect—with the President, that I have examined them with particular attention and I shall try to give you the results, and my conclusions, with the recommendation that you take the matter up directly with the President and the Secretary of State. I have been a little at a loss to decide how to communicate what I have learned to the Government in Washington, for the present conditions make it impossible to set down what I want to say in an official despatch, but the fortunate accident of your being in the United States gives me the safe opportunity I want, and so I send my information to you, and by the pouch, as time is of less importance than secrecy.

There seems to be no doubt that Germany is casting about for an opportunity to effect an armistice, if possible before the winter closes in. She hopes it may result in peace—a peace more or less favourable to her, of course—but even if such a result should fail of accomplishment she would have gained a breathing space; have secured an opportunity to improve her strategic position in a military sense, perhaps by shortening her line in Flanders; have stiffened the resistance of her people; and probably have influenced a certain body of neutral opinion not only in her favour but against her antagonists.

I shall not try to mention the various sources from which the threads that compose this fabric have been drawn, but I finally fastened on X of the Admiralty as a man with whom I could talk profitably and confidentially, and he told me positively that his information showed that Germany was looking in the direction I have indicated, and that she would soon approach the President on the subject—even if she had not already taken the first steps toward preparing her advance to him.

I asked X if he thought it well for me to broach the subject to Lord Grey and he suggested that I first consult Y, which I did. The latter seemed very wary at the outset, but he warmed up at last and in the course of the conversation told me he had reliable information that when Bethmann-Hollweg went to Munich just before the beginning of the allied offensive in the west in June he told the King of Bavaria that he was confident the Allies would be obliged to begin overtures for peace next October; adding that if they didn't Germany would have to do so. The King, it appears, asked him how Germany could approach the Allies if it proved to be advisable and he replied: "Through our good friend Wilson."

I asked Y if the King of Spain's good offices would not be enlisted jointly with those of the President in attempting to arrange an armistice, but he thought not, and said that the King of Spain was very well aware that the Allies would not consider anything short of definite peace proposals from Germany and that His Majesty knew the moment for them had not arrived. I then finally asked him point blank if he thought the Germans would approach the President for an armistice, and, if so, when.

He said he was inclined to think they might do so perhaps about October. On my asking him if he was disposed to let me communicate his opinion privately to the Government in Washington he replied after some hesitation that he had no objection, but he quickly added that I must make it clear at the same time that the British Government would not listen to any such proposals.

These conversations took place during the course of last week, and on Sunday—the 27th—I invited the Spanish Ambassador to luncheon at Tangley when I was able to get him to confirm what Y had said of his Sovereign's attitude and opinions.

I may mention for what it is worth that on Hoover's last trip to Germany he was told by Bullock, of the Philadelphia *Ledger*, that Zimmermann of the Berlin Foreign Office had told him that the Germans had intended in June to take steps for an armistice which were prevented by the preparations for the allied offensive in the west.

Y was very emphatic in what he said of the attitude of his government and the British people toward continuing the war to an absolutely conclusive end, and I was much impressed. He said among other things that the execution of Captain Fryatt had had a markedly perceptible effect in hardening British public opinion against Germany and fixing the determination to fight to a relentless finish. This corresponds exactly with my own observations.

I leave this letter entirely in your hands. You will know what use to make of it. It is meant as an official communication in everything but the usual form from which I have departed for reasons I need not explain further.

I look forward eagerly to your return,

Very sincerely yours,
IRWIN LAUGHLIN.

Page waited five weeks before he succeeded in obtaining his interview with Mr. Wilson.

To the President

The New Willard, Washington, D. C.
Thursday, September 21, 1916.

DEAR MR. PRESIDENT:

While I am waiting for a convenient time to come when you will see me for a conference and report, I send you notes on conversations with Lord Grey and Lord Bryce.[1] They are, in effect, though of course not in form, messages to you.

The situation between our government and Great Britain seems to me most alarming; and (let me add) easily removable, if I can get the ear of anybody in authority. But I find here only an atmosphere of suspicion— unwarranted by facts and easily dissipated by straight and simple friendly methods. I am sure of this.

I have, besides, a most important and confidential message for you from the British Government which they prefer should be orally delivered.

And I have written out a statement of my own study of the situation and of certain proposals which, I think, if they commend themselves to you, will go far to remove this dangerous tension. I hope to go over them with you at your convenience.

Yours faithfully,
WALTER H. PAGE.

The situation was alarming for more reasons than the determination of Germany to force the peace issue. The State Department was especially irritated at this time

---

[1] See Chapter XIX, pages 160 and 164.

over the blockade. Among the "trade advisers" there was a conviction, which all Page's explanations had not destroyed, that Great Britain was using the blockade as a means of destroying American commerce and securing America's customers for herself. Great Britain's regulations on the blacklist and "bunker coal" had intensified this feeling. In both these latter questions Page regarded the British actions as tactless and unjust; he had had many sharp discussions at the Foreign Office concerning them, but had not made much headway in his efforts to obtain their abandonment. The purpose of the "blacklist" was to strike at neutral firms with German affiliations which were trading with Germany. The Trading with the Enemy Act provided that such firms could not trade with Great Britain; that British vessels must refuse to accept their cargoes, and that any neutral ship which accepted such cargoes would be denied bunker coal at British ports. Under this law the Ministry of Blockade issued a "blacklist" of more than 1,000 proscribed exporting houses in the United States. So great was the indignation against this boycott in the United States that Congress, in early September, had passed a retaliatory act; this gave the President the authority at any time to place an embargo upon the exports to the United States of countries which discriminated against American firms and also to deny clearance to ships which refused to accept American cargoes. The two countries indeed seemed to be hastening toward a crisis.

Page's urgent letter to Mr. Wilson brought a telegram from Mr. Tumulty inviting the Ambassador to spend the next evening and night with the President at Shadow Lawn, the seaside house on the New Jersey coast in which Mr. Wilson was spending the summer. Mr. Wilson received his old friend with great courtesy and listened

quietly and with apparent interest to all that he had to say.
The written statement to which Page refers in his letter
told the story of Anglo-American relations from the time
of the Panama tolls repeal up to the time of Page's visit
to Shadow Lawn. Quotations have already been made
from it in preceding chapters, and the ideas which it
contains have abundantly appeared in letters already
printed. The document was an eloquent plea for American coöperation with the Allies—for the dismissal of
Bernstorff, for the adoption of a manly attitude toward
Germany, and for the vindication of a high type of Americanism.

Page showed the President the *Lusitania* medal, but
that did not especially impress him. "The President said to me," wrote Page in reference to this visit,
"that when the war began he and all the men he met
were in hearty sympathy with the Allies; but that now
the sentiment toward England had greatly changed.
He saw no one who was not vexed and irritated by the
arbitrary English course. That is, I fear, true—that
he sees no one but has a complaint. So does the Secretary of State, and the Trade Bureau and all the rest
in Washington. But in Boston, in New York, and in
the South and in Auburn, N. Y., I saw no one whose
sympathy with the Allies had undergone any fundamental change. I saw men who felt vexed at such an
act as the blacklist, but that was merely vexation, not
a fundamental change of feeling. Of course, there
came to see me men who had 'cases.' Now these are
the only kind of men, I fear, whom the Government at
Washington sees—these and the members of Congress
whom the Germans have scared or have 'put up' to
scare the Government—who are 'twisting the lion's tail,'
in a word."

"The President said," wrote Page immediately after coming from Shadow Lawn, "'Tell those gentlemen for me'—and then followed a homily to the effect that a damage done to any American citizen is a damage to him, etc. He described the war as a result of many causes, some of long origin. He spoke of England's having the earth and of Germany wanting it. Of course, he said, the German system is directly opposed to everything American. But I do not gather that he thought that this carried any very great moral reprehensibility.

"He said that he wouldn't do anything with the retaliatory act till after election lest it might seem that he was playing politics. But he hinted that if there were continued provocation afterward (in case he were elected) he would. He added that one of the worst provocations was the long English delay in answering our Notes. Was this delay due to fear or shame? He evidently felt that such a delay showed contempt. He spoke of the Bryan treaty.[1] But on no question had the British 'locked horns' with us—on no question had they come to a clear issue so that the matter might be referred to the Commission."

Page delivered his oral message about the German determination to obtain an armistice. This was to the effect that Great Britain would not grant it. Page intimated that Britain would be offended if the President proposed it.

"If an armistice, no," answered Mr. Wilson. "That's a military matter and is none of my business. But if they propose an armistice looking toward peace—yes, I shall be glad."

---

[1] The treaty between the United States and Great Britain, adopted through the urgency of Mr. Bryan, providing for the arbitration of disputes between the two countries.

The experience was an exceedingly trying one for both men. The discussion showed how far apart were the President and his Ambassador on practically every issue connected with the crisis. Naturally the President's reference to the causes of the war—that there were many causes, some of them of long persistence, and that Great Britain's domination of the "earth" was one of them— conflicted with the judgment of a man who attributed the origin of the struggle to German aggression. The President's statement that American sympathy for the Allies had now changed to irritation, and the tolerant attitude toward Germany which Mr. Wilson displayed, affected Page with the profoundest discouragement. The President's intimation that he would advance Germany's request for an armistice, if it looked toward peace—this in reply to Page's message that Great Britain would not receive such a proposal in a kindly spirit— seemed to lay the basis of further misunderstandings. The interview was a disheartening one for Page. Many people whom the Ambassador met in the course of this visit still retain memories of his fervour in what had now become with him a sacred cause. With many friends and officials he discussed the European situation almost like a man inspired. The present writer recalls two long conversations with Page at this time: the recollection of his brilliant verbal portraiture, his description of the determination of Englishmen, his admiration for the heroic sacrifice of Englishwomen, remain as about the most vivid memories of a life-time. And now the Ambassador had brought this same eloquence to the President's ear at Shadow Lawn. It was in this interview that Page had hoped to show Mr. Wilson the real merits of the situation, and persuade him to adopt the course to which the national honour and safety pointed; he talked long and eloquently, painting the whole European tragedy with that intensity and readiness of utterance and that moral conviction which had so moved all others with whom he had come into contact during this memorable visit to the United States; but Mr. Wilson was utterly cold, utterly unresponsive, interested only in ending the war. The talk lasted for a whole morning; its nature may be assumed from the many letters already printed; but Page's voice, when it attempted to fire the conscience of the President, proved as ineffective as his pen. However, there was nothing rasping or contentious about the interview. The two men discussed everything with the utmost calmness and without the slightest indications of ill-nature. Both men had in mind their long association, both inevitably recalled the hopes with which they had begun their official relationship three years before, at that time neither having the faintest intimation of the tremendous problems that were to draw them asunder. Mr. Wilson at this meeting did not impress his Ambassador as a perverse character, but as an extremely pathetic one. Page came away with no vexation or anger, but with a real feeling for a much suffering and a much perplexed statesman. The fact that the President's life was so solitary, and that he seemed to be so completely out of touch with men and with the living thoughts of the world, appealed strongly to Page's sympathies. "I think he is the loneliest man I have ever known," Page remarked to his son Frank after coming away from this visit.

Page felt this at the time, for, as he rose to say good-bye to the President, he put his hand upon his shoulder. At this Mr. Wilson's eyes filled with tears and he gave Page an affectionate good-bye. The two men never met again.

CHAPTER XX
"PEACE WITHOUT VICTORY"

"OF ONE thing I am sure," Page wrote to his wife from Washington, while waiting to see President Wilson. "We wish to come home March 4th at midnight and to go about our proper business. There's nothing here that I would for the world be mixed up with. As soon as I can escape with dignity I shall make my bow and exit. . . . But I am not unhappy or hopeless for the long run. They'll find out the truth some day, paying, I fear, a heavy penalty for delay. But the visit here has confirmed me in our previous conclusions—that if we can carry the load until March 4th, midnight, we shall be grateful that we have pulled through."

Soon after President Wilson's reëlection, therefore, Page sent his resignation to Washington. The above quotation shows that he intended this to be more than a "courtesy resignation," a term traditionally applied to the kind of leave-takings which Ambassadors usually send on the formation of a new administration, or at the beginning of a new Presidential term, for the purpose of giving the President the opportunity of reorganizing his official family. Page believed that his work in London had been finished, that he had done everything in his power to make Mr. Wilson see the situation in its true light and that he had not succeeded. He therefore wished to give up his post and come home. This explains the fact that his resignation did not consist of the half dozen perfunctory lines which most diplomatic officers find sufficient on such an occasion, but took the form of a review of the reasons why the United States should align itself on the side of the Allies.

To the President

London, November 24, 1916.

DEAR MR. PRESIDENT:

We have all known for many years that the rich and populous and organized states in which the big cities are do not constitute the political United States. But, I confess, I hardly expected so soon to see this fact proclaimed at the ballot-box. To me that's the surprise of the election. And your popular majority as well as your clear majority in the Electoral College is a great personal triumph for you. And you have remade the ancient and demoralized Democratic party. Four years ago it consisted of a protest and of the wreck wrought by Mr. Bryan's long captaincy. This rebirth, with a popular majority, is an historical achievement—of your own.

You have relaid the foundation and reset the pillars of a party that may enjoy a long supremacy for domestic reasons. Now, if you will permit me to say so, from my somewhat distant view (four years make a long period of absence) the big party task is to build up a clearer and more positive foreign policy. We are in the world and we've got to choose what active part we shall play in it—I fear rather quickly. I have the conviction, as you know, that this whole round globe now hangs as a ripe apple for our plucking, if we use the right ladder while the chance lasts. I do not mean that we want or could get the apple for ourselves, but that we can see to it that it is put to proper uses. What we have to do, in my judgment, is to go back to our political fathers for our clue. If my long-time memory be good, they were sure that their establishment of a great free Republic would soon be imitated by European peoples—that democracies would take the place of autocracies in all so-called civilized countries; for that was the form that the fight took in their day against organized Privilege. But for one reason or another—in our life-time partly because we chose so completely to isolate ourselves—the democratic idea took root in Europe with disappointing slowness. It is, for instance, now perhaps for the first time, in a thoroughgoing way, within sight in this Kingdom. The dream of the American Fathers, therefore, is not yet come true. They fought against organized Privilege exerted from over the sea. In principle it is the same fight that we have made, in our domestic field, during recent decades. Now the same fight has come on a far larger scale than men ever dreamed of before.

It isn't, therefore, for merely doctrinal reasons that we are concerned for the spread of democracy nor merely because a democracy is the only scheme of organization yet wrought out that keeps the door of opportunity open and invites all men to their fullest development. But we are interested in it because under no other system can the world be made an even reasonably safe place to live in. For only autocracies wage aggressive wars. Aggressive autocracies, especially military autocracies, must be softened down by peace (and they have never been so softened) or destroyed by war. The All-Highest doctrine of Germany to-day is the same as the Taxation-without-Representation of George III—only more virulent, stronger, and farther-reaching. Only by its end can the German people recover and build up their character and take the permanent place in the world that they—thus changed—will be entitled to. They will either reduce Europe to the vassalage of a military autocracy, which may then overrun the whole world or drench it in blood, or they must through stages of Liberalism work their way toward some approach to a democracy; and there is no doubt which event is impending. The Liberal idea will win this struggle, and Europe will be out of danger of a general assault on free institutions till some other autocracy which has a military caste try the same Napoleonic game. The defeat of Germany, therefore, will make for the spread of the doctrine of our Fathers and our doctrine yet.

An interesting book might be made of concrete evidences of the natural antipathy that the present German autocracy has for successful democracy and hence for us. A new instance has just come to me. My son, Arthur, who succeeded to most of my activities at home, has been over here for a month and he has just come from a visit to France. In Paris he had a long conversation with Delcassé, who told him that the Kaiser himself once made a proposal to him to join in producing "the complete isolation" of the United States. What the Kaiser meant was that if the great Powers of Europe would hold off, he would put the Monroe Doctrine to the test and smash it.

The great tide of the world will, by reason of the war, now flow toward democracy—at present, alas! a tide of blood. For a century democracies and Liberal governments have kept themselves too much isolated, trusting prematurely and too simply to international law and treaties and Hague conventions. These things have never been respected, except as springes to catch woodcock, where the Divine Right held sway. The outgrowing or the overthrow of the Divine Right is a condition precedent to the effectiveness of international law and treaties.

It has seemed to me, looking at the subject only with reference to our country's duty and safety, that somehow and at some early time our championship of democracy must lead us to redeclare our faith and to show that we believe in our historic creed. Then we may escape falling away from the Liberal forces of the Old World and escape the suspicion of indifference to the great scheme of government which was set up by our fathers' giving their blood for it. I see no other way for us to take the best and biggest opportunity that has ever come to prove true to our faith as well as to secure our own safety and the safety of the world. Only some sort of active and open identification with the Allies can put us in effective protest against the assassins of the Armenians and the assassins of Belgium, Poland, and Serbia, and in a friendly attitude to the German people themselves, as distinguished from their military rulers. This is the attitude surely that our fathers would have wished us to take—and would have expected us to take—and that our children will be proud of us for taking; for it is our proper historic attitude, whether looked at from the past or looked back at from the future. There can be no historic approval of neutrality for years, while the world is bleeding to death.

The complete severance of relations, diplomatic at first and later possibly economic as well, with the Turks and the Germans, would probably not cost us a man in battle nor any considerable treasure; for the moral effect of withdrawing even our formal approval of their conduct—at least our passive acquiescence—would be—that the Germans would see that practically all the Liberal world stands against their system, and the war would end before we should need to or could put an army in the field. The Liberal Germans are themselves beginning to see that it is not they, but the German system, that is the object of attack because it is *the* dangerous thing in the world. Maximilian Harden presents this view in his

Berlin paper.   He says in effect that Germany must get rid of its predatory feudalism.   That was all that was the matter with George III.

Among the practical results of such action by us would, I believe, be the following:

1.   The early ending of the war and the saving of, perhaps, millions of lives and of incalculable treasure;

2.   The establishment in Germany of some form of more liberal government;

3.   A league to enforce peace, ready-made, under our guidance—i.e., the Allies and ourselves;

4.   The sympathetic coöperation and the moral force of every Allied Government in dealing with Mexico:

5.   The acceptance—and even documentary approval— of every Allied Government of the Monroe Doctrine;

6.   The warding off and no doubt the final prevention of danger from Japan, and, most of all, the impressive and memorable spectacle of our Great Democracy thus putting an end to this colossal crime, merely from the impulse and necessity to keep our own ideals and to lead the world right on.   We should do for Europe on a large scale essentially what we did for Cuba on a small scale and thereby usher in a new era in human history.

I write thus freely, Mr. President, because at no time can I write in any other way and because I am sure that all these things can quickly be brought to pass under your strong leadership.   The United States would stand, as no other nation has ever stood in the world—predominant and unselfish—on the highest ideals ever reached in human government.   It is a vision as splendid as the Holy Grael.   Nor have I a shadow of doubt of the eager and faithful following of our people, who would thereby reëstablish once for all our weakened nationality.   We are made of the stuff that our Fathers were made of.

And I write this now for the additional reason that I am within sight of the early end of my service here. When you called me I answered, not only because you did me great honour and laid a definite patriotic duty on me, but because also of my personal loyalty to you and my pride in helping forward the great principles in which we both believe. But I understood then (and I am sure the subject lay in your mind in the same way) that my service would be for four years at the most. I made all my arrangements, professional and domestic, on this supposition. I shall, therefore, be ready to lay down my work here on March 4th or as soon thereafter as meets your pleasure.

I am more than proud of the confidence that you have shown in me. To it I am indebted for the opportunity I have had to give such public service to my country as I could, as well as for the most profitable experience of my life. A proper and sympathetic understanding between the two English-speaking worlds seems to me the most important duty of far-seeing men in either country. It has taken such a profound hold on me that I shall, in whatever way I can, work for its complete realization as long as I can work for anything.

I am, Mr. President, most faithfully and gratefully yours,

WALTER H. PAGE.

This letter was written at a time when President Wilson was exerting his best energies to bring about peace. The Presidential campaign had caused him to postpone these efforts, for he believed that neither Germany nor Great Britain could take seriously the activities of a President whose own political position was insecure. At the time Page's letter was received, the President was thinking only of a peace based upon a stalemate; it was then his apparent conviction that both sides to the struggle were about equally in the wrong and that a decisive victory of either would not be a good thing for the world.　Yet it is interesting to compare this letter with the famous speech which the President made six months afterward when he asked Congress to declare the existence of a state of war with Germany.　Practically all the important reasons which Mr. Wilson then advanced for this declaration are found in Page's letter of the preceding November.　That autocracies are a constant menace to world peace, that the United States owes it to its democratic tradition to take up arms against the enemy of free government, that in doing this, it was not making war upon the German people, but upon its imperialistic masters—these were the arguments which Page laid before the President in his letter of resignation, and these were the leading ideas in Mr. Wilson's address of April 2nd.　There are even sentences in Page's communication which seem to foreshadow Mr. Wilson's assertion that "The world must be made safe for democracy."　This letter in itself sufficiently makes it clear that Page's correspondence, irritating in its later phases as it may have been, strongly influenced Mr. Wilson in his final determination on war.

On one point, indeed, Colonel House afterward called the Ambassador to account.　When America was preparing to raise armies by the millions and to spend its treasure by the billions, he reminded Page of his statement that the severance of diplomatic relations "would probably not cost us a man in battle nor any considerable treasure."　Page's statement in this November letter merely reiterated a conviction which for more than a year he had been forcing upon the President and Colonel House—that the dismissal of Bernstorff would not necessarily imply war with Germany, but that it would in itself be enough to bring the war to an end. On this point Page never changed his mind, as is evident from the letter which he wrote to Colonel House when this matter was called to his attention:

To Edward M. House

London, June 29, 1917.

MY DEAR HOUSE:

I never put any particular value on my own prophecies nor on anybody else's. I have therefore no pride as a prophet. Yet I do think that I hit it off accurately a year or a year and a half ago when I said that we could then have ended the war without any appreciable cost. And these are my reasons:

If we had then come in and absolutely prevented supplies from reaching Germany, as we are now about to do, the war would then have been much sooner ended than it can now be ended:

(1) Our supplies enabled her to go on.

(2) She got time in this way to build her great submarine fleet. She went at it the day she promised the President to reform.

(3) She got time and strength to overrun Rumania whence she got food and oil; and continues to get it.

(4) During this time Russia fell down as a military force and gave her more time, more armies for France and more supplies. Russian guns have been sold to the Germans.

If a year and a half ago we had starved her out, it would have been over before any of these things happened. This delay is what will cost us billions and billions and men and men.

And it cost us one thing more. During the neutrality

period we were as eager to get goods to the little neutral states which were in large measure undoubtedly bound to Germany as we are now eager to keep them out. Grey, who was and is our best friend, and who was unwilling to quarrel with us more than he was obliged to, was thrown out of office and his career ended because the blockade, owing to his consideration for us, was not tight enough. Our delay caused his fall.

But most of all, it gave the Germans time (and to some extent material) to build their present fleet of submarines. They were at work on them all the while and according to the best opinion here they continue to build them faster than the British destroy them; and the submarines are destroying more merchant ships than all the shipbuilding docks of all the world are now turning out. This is the most serious aspect of the war—by far the most serious. I am trying to get our Government to send over hundreds of improvised destroyers—armed tugs, yachts, etc., etc. Admiral Sims and the British Admiralty have fears that unless such help come the full fruits of the war may never be gathered by the Allies—that some sort of a compromise peace may have to be made.

It is, therefore, true that the year and a half we waited after the *Lusitania* will prove to be the most costly year and a half in our history; and for once at least my old prophecy was quite a good guess. But that water has flowed over the dam and it is worth mentioning now only because you challenged me. . . .

That part of Page's letter which refers to his retirement had a curious history. It was practically a resignation and therefore called for an immediate reply, but Mr. Wilson did not even acknowledge its receipt. For two months the Ambassador was left in the dark as to the attitude of Washington. Finally, in the latter part of January, 1917, Page wrote urgently to Mr. Lansing, asking him to bring the matter to the President's attention. On February 5, 1917, Mr. Lansing's reply was received. "The President," he said, "under extreme pressure of the present situation, has been unable to consider your communication in regard to your resignation. He desires me to inform you that he hopes that, at the present time, you will not press to be relieved from service; that he realizes that he is asking you to make a personal sacrifice, but he believes that you will appreciate the importance, in the crisis which has developed, that no change should be made. I hardly need to add my personal hope that you will put aside any thought of resigning your post for the present."

At this time, of course, any idea of retiring was out of the question. The President had dismissed Bernstorff and there was every likelihood that the country would soon be at war. Page would have regarded his retirement at this crisis as little less than the desertion of his post. Moreover, since Mr. Wilson had adopted the policy which the Ambassador had been urging for nearly two years, and had sent Bernstorff home, any logical excuse that may have existed for his resignation existed no longer. Mr. Wilson had now adopted a course which Page could enthusiastically support.

"I am happy to serve here at any sacrifice"—such was his reply to Mr. Lansing—"until after the end of the war, and I am making my arrangements to stay for this period."

The months that intervened between the Presidential election and the declaration of war were especially difficult for the American Embassy in London. Page had informed the President, in the course of his interview of September 22nd, how unfavourably Great Britain re-

garded his efforts in the direction of peace; he had in
fact delivered a message from the Foreign Office that
any Presidential attempt to "mediate" would be rejected
by the Allies. Yet his earnest representation on this
point had produced no effect upon Mr. Wilson. The
pressure which Germany was bringing to bear upon Washington was apparently irresistible. Count Bernstorff's
memoirs, with their accompanying documents, have revealed the intensity of the German efforts during this
period; the most startling fact revealed by the German
Ambassador is that the Kaiser, on October 9th, notified
the President, almost in so many words, that, unless he
promptly moved in the direction of peace, the German
Government "would be forced to regain the freedom of
action which it has reserved to itself in the note of May
4th last."[1]   It is unlikely that the annals of diplomacy
contain many documents so cool and insolent as this one.
It was a notification from the Kaiser to the President that
the so-called "*Sussex* pledge" was not regarded as an
unconditional one by the Imperial Government; that it
was given merely to furnish Mr. Wilson an opportunity to
bring the war to an end; and that unless the Presidential
attempt to accomplish this were successful, there would be
a resumption of the indiscriminate submarine campaign.
The curious developments of the next two months are
now a familiar story.   Possibly because the British Government had notified him, through Page, that his proffer of
mediation would be unacceptable, Mr. Wilson moved
cautiously and slowly, and Germany became impatient.
The successful campaign against Rumania, resulting in the
capture of Bucharest on December 6th, and the new vista
which it opened to Germany of large food supplies,
strengthened the Teutonic purpose.   Perhaps Germany,

[1] "My Three Years in America," by Count Bernstorff, p. 294.

with her characteristic lack of finesse, imagined that her
own open efforts would lend emphasis to Mr. Wilson's
pacific exertions. At any rate, on December 12th, just as
Mr. Wilson was preparing to launch his own campaign for
mediation, Germany herself approached her enemies with a
proposal for a peace conference. A few days afterward
Page, as the representative of Germany, called at the Foreign Office to deliver the large white envelope which contained the Kaiser's "peace proposal." In delivering this to
Lord Robert Cecil, who was acting as Foreign Secretary
in the temporary absence of Mr. Balfour, Page emphasized
the fact that the American Government entirely disasso-
ciated itself from its contents and that he was acting
merely in his capacity of "German Ambassador." Two
communications from Lord Robert to Sir Cecil Spring
Rice, British Ambassador at Washington, tell the story
and also reveal that it was almost impossible for Page,
even when engaged in an official proceeding, to conceal
his contempt for the whole enterprise:

Lord R. Cecil to Sir C. Spring Rice

Foreign Office,
December 18, 1916.

SIR:

The American Ambassador came to see me this morning
and presented to me the German note containing what is
called in it the "offer of peace." He explained that he
did so on instructions of his Government as representing
the German Government, and not in any way as representing their own opinions. He also explained that the
note must be regarded as coming from the four Central
Powers, and as being addressed to all the Entente Powers
who were represented by the United States.

He then read to me a telegram from his Government,

but declined to leave me a copy of it. The first part of the telegram explained that the Government of the United States would deeply appreciate a confidential intimation of the response to be made to the German note and that they would themselves have certain representations to make to the Entente Powers, to which they urgently begged the closest consideration. The telegram went on to explain that the Government of the United States had had it in mind for some time past to make such representations on behalf of neutral nations and humanity, and that it must not be thought that they were prompted by the Governments of the Central Powers. They wished us to understand that the note of the Central Powers created a good opportunity for making the American representations, but was not the cause of such representations being made.

I replied that I could of course say nothing to him on such an important matter without consulting my colleagues.

I am, etc.,

ROBERT CECIL.

Lord R. Cecil to Sir C. Spring Rice

Foreign Office,
19 December, 1916.

SIR:

The American Ambassador came to see me this afternoon.

I asked him whether he could tell me why his government were anxious to have confidential information as to the nature of our response to the German peace note.

He replied that he did not know, but he imagined it was to enable them to frame the representations of which he had spoken to me.

I then told him that we had asked the French to draft a reply, and that it would then be considered by the Allies, and in all probability an identic note would be presented in answer to the German note. I thought it probable that we should express our view that it was impossible to deal with the German offer, since it contained no specific proposals.

He said that he quite understood this, and that we should in fact reply that it was an offer "to buy a pig in a poke" which we were not prepared to accept. He added that he thought his Government would fully anticipate a reply in this sense, and he himself obviously approved it.

Then, speaking quite seriously, he said that he had heard people in London treating the German offer with derision, but that no doubt the belligerent governments would treat it seriously.

I said that it was certainly a serious thing, and no doubt would be treated seriously.

I asked him if he knew what would be contained in the proposed representations from his government.

He said that he did not; but as he understood that they were to be made to all the belligerents, he did not think that they could be much more than a pious aspiration for peace; since that was the only thing that was equally applicable to the Germans and to us.

As he was leaving he suggested that the German note might be published in our press.

I am, etc.,
Robert Cecil.

This so-called German "peace proposal" began with the statement that the war "had been forced" upon Germany, contained the usual reference to the military might of the Central Powers, and declared that the Fatherland was fighting for "the honour and liberty of national evolution." It is therefore not surprising that Lord Robert received it somewhat sardonically, especially as the communication contained no specific proposals, but merely a vague suggestion of "negotiations." But another spectacular performance now drove the German manœuvre out of everybody's mind. That President Wilson resented this German interference with his own plans is well known; he did not drop them, however, but on December 18th, he sent his long-contemplated peace communication to all the warring Powers. His appeal took the form of asking that they state the objects for which they were fighting, the Presidential belief evidently being that, if they did this, a common meeting ground might possibly be found. The suggestion that the Allied war aims were not public property, despite the fact that British statesmen had been broadly proclaiming them for three years, caused a momentary irritation in England, but this was not a serious matter, especially as the British Cabinet quickly saw that this request gave them a position of advantage over Germany, which had always refused to make public the terms on which it would end the war. The main substance in this Presidential approach, therefore, would have produced no ill-feeling; as usual, it was a few parenthetical phrases— phrases which were not essential to the main argument— which set the allied countries seething with indignation. The President, this section of his note ran, "takes the liberty of calling attention to the fact that the objects which the statesmen of the belligerents on both sides have in mind in this war, are virtually the same, as stated in general terms to their own people and to the world. Each side desires to make the rights and privileges of weak peoples and small states as secure against aggression and denial in the future as the rights and privileges of the great and powerful states now at war." This idea was elaborated in several sentences of a similar strain, the general purport of the whole passage being that there was little to choose between the combatants, inasmuch as both were apparently fighting for about the same things. Mr. Wilson's purpose in this paragraph is not obscure; he was making his long expected appearance as a mediator, and he evidently believed that it was essential to this rôle that he should not seem to be prejudiced in favour of either side, but should hold the balance impartially between them.

It is true that a minute reading indicates that Mr. Wilson was merely quoting, or attempting to paraphrase, the statements of the leaders of both sides, but there is such a thing as quoting with approval, and no explanation could convince the British public that the ruler of the greatest neutral nation had not declared that the Allies and the Central Powers stood morally upon the same level. The popular indignation which this caused in Great Britain was so intense that it alarmed the British authorities. The publication of this note in the British press was withheld for several hours, in order to give the Government an opportunity to control the expression of editorial opinion; otherwise it was feared that this would be so unrestrained in its bitterness that relations with the United States might be imperilled. The messages which the London correspondents were permitted to send to the United States were carefully censored for the same reason. The dispatch sent by the Associated Press was the product of a long struggle between the Foreign Office and its London correspondent. The representatives spent half an hour considering whether the American correspondents could cable their country that the note had been received in

England with "surprise and irritation." After much discussion it was decided that "irritation" could not be used, and the message of the Associated Press, after undergoing this careful editing by the Foreign Office, was a weak and ridiculous description of the high state of excitement which prevailed in Great Britain. The fact that the British Foreign Office should have given all this trouble over the expressions sent to American newspapers and should even have spent half an hour debating whether a particular word should be used, almost pathetically illustrates the great care taken by the British Government not to influence American opinion against the Allies.

The Government took the same precautions with its own press in England. When the note was finally released the Foreign Office explicitly directed the London newspapers to comment with the utmost caution and in no case to question the President's sincerity. Most of them acquiesced in these instructions by maintaining silence. There was only one London newspaper, the *Westminster Gazette*, which made even a faint-hearted attempt to explain away the President's statement. From the first day of the war the British people had declared that President Wilson did not understand the issues at stake; and they now declared that this note confirmed their worst forebodings. The comments of the man-in-the-street were unprintable, but more serious than these was the impression which Mr. Wilson's dubious remarks made upon those Englishmen who had always been especially friendly to the United States and who had even defended the President in previous crises. Lord Bryce, who had accepted philosophically the Presidential statement that the United States was not "concerned with the causes" of the war, could not regard so indulgently this latest judgment of Great Britain and Germany. "Bryce came to see me in a state of great depression," wrote Page. "He has sent Mr. Wilson a personal letter on this matter." Northcliffe commanded his newspapers, the *Times* and the *Daily Mail*, to discuss the note in a judicial spirit, but he himself told Mr. Page that "everybody is as angry as hell." When someone attempted to discuss the Wilson note with Mr. Asquith, he brushed the subject away with a despairing gesture. "Don't talk to me about it," he said. "It is most disheartening." But the one man in England who was perhaps the most affected was King George. A man who had attended luncheon at Buckingham Palace on December 21st gave Page a description of the royal distress. The King, expressing his surprise and dismay that Mr. Wilson should think that Englishmen were fighting for the same things in this war as the Germans, broke down.

The world only now understands the dreadful prospect which was opening before Europe at the moment when this Presidential note added a new cause for general despondency. Rumania had collapsed, the first inkling of the Russian revolution had been obtained, the British well knew that the submarine warfare was to be resumed, and British finances were also in a desperate plight. More and more it was becoming evident to the British statesmen that they needed the intervention of the United States. This is the reason why they could not destroy the chances of American help by taking official offense even at what Page, in a communication to the Secretary of State, did not hesitate to call President Wilson's "insulting words"; and hence their determination to silence the press and to give no outward expression of what they felt. Page's interview with Lord Robert Cecil on December 26th, while the

Presidential communication was lying on his desk, discloses the real emotions of Englishmen. Apparently Page's frank cables concerning the reception of this paragraph had caused a certain interest in the State Department; at least the Ambassador was instructed to call at the Foreign Office and explain that the interpretation which had been commonly put upon the President's words was not the one which he had intended. At the same time Page was instructed to request the British Foreign Office, in case its reply were "favourable," not to publish it, but to communicate it secretly to the American Government. The purpose of this request is a little obscure; possibly it was the President's plan to use such a favourable reply to force Germany likewise to display an acquiescent mood. The object of Page's call was to present this disclaimer.

Lord Robert Cecil, the son of the late Lord Salisbury, —that same Lord Salisbury whose combats with Secretary Blaine and Secretary Olney form piquant chapters in British-American history—is one of the most able and respected of British statesmen. In his earlier life Lord Salisbury had been somewhat overbearing in his attitude toward the United States; in his later years, however, perhaps owing to the influence of his nephew, Mr. Balfour, his manner had changed. In his attitude toward the United States Lord Robert Cecil reflected only the later phases of his father's career. To this country and to its peaceful ideals he had always been extremely sympathetic, and to Page especially he had never manifested anything but cordiality. Yet it was evident, as Page came into his office this morning, that to Lord Robert, as to every member of the Government, the President's note, with its equivocal phrases, had been a terrible shock. His manner was extremely courteous, as always, but he made no attempt to conceal his feelings. Ordinarily Lord Robert did not wear his emotions on the surface; but he took occasion on this visit to tell Page how greatly the President's communication had grieved him.

"The President," he said, "has seemed to pass judgment on the allied cause by putting it on the same level as the German. I am deeply hurt."

Page conveyed Mr. Lansing's message that no such inference was justified. But this was not reassuring.

"Moreover," Lord Robert added, "there is one sentence in the note—that in which the President says that the position of neutrals is becoming intolerable—that seems almost a veiled threat."

Page hastened to assure Lord Robert that no threat was intended.

Lord Robert's manner became increasingly serious.

"There is nothing that the American Government or any other human power can do," he remarked slowly and solemnly, "which will bring this war to a close before the Allies have spent their utmost force to secure a victory. A failure to secure such a victory will leave the world at the mercy of the most arrogant and the bloodiest tyranny that has ever been organized. It is far better to die in an effort to defeat that tyranny than to perish under its success."

On any occasion Lord Robert is an impressive or at least a striking and unusual figure; he is tall, lank, and ungainly, almost Lincolnesque in the carelessness of his apparel and the exceeding awkwardness of his postures and manners. His angular features, sharp nose, pale face, and dark hair suggest the strain of asceticism, almost of fanaticism, which runs in the present generation of his family. And the deep sincerity and power of his words on this occasion made an impression which Page never forgot; they transformed the British statesman into an eloquent, almost an heroic figure. If we are to understand the full tragedy of this moment we must remember that, incredible as it now seems, there was a fear in British officialdom that the United States might not only not pursue a course favourable to the Allies, but that it might even throw its support to Germany. The fear, of course, was baseless; any suggestion of such a policy in the United States would have destroyed any official who had brought it forward; but Lord Robert knew and Page knew that there were insidious influences at work at that time, both in the United States and in Great Britain, which looked in this direction. A group of Americans, whom Page used to refer to as "peace spies," were associated with English pacifists, for the purpose of bringing about peace on almost any terms. These "peace spies" had worked out a programme all their own. The purpose was to compel Great Britain to accept the German terms for ending the war. Unless she did accept them, then it was intended that the American Government should place an embargo on the shipment of foodstuffs and munitions to the Allies. There is little question that the United States, by taking such action, could have ended the war almost instantaneously. Should the food of her people and the great quantities of munitions which were coming from this country be suddenly cut off, there is little likelihood that Great Britain could have long survived. The possibility that an embargo might shut out these supplies had hung over the heads of British statesmen ever since the war began; they knew that the possession of this mighty power made the United States the potential dictator of events; and the fear that it might be used had never ceased to influence their thoughts or their actions. Even while this interview was taking place, certain anti-British forces in the United States, such as Senator Hoke Smith of Georgia, were urging action of this kind.

"I have always been almost a Pacifist," Lord Robert continued. "No man has ever hated war worse than I. No man has ever had a more earnest faith that war can be abolished. But European civilization has been murderously assaulted and there is nothing now to do but to defeat this desperate enemy or to perish in the effort. I had hoped that the United States understood what is at stake."

Lord Robert went on:

"I will go so far as to say that if the United States will come into the war it will decide which will win, freedom or organized tyranny. If the United States shall help the Germans, civilization will perish and it will be necessary to build it up slowly again—if indeed it will ever appear again. If the United States will help the Allies, civilization will triumph."[1]

As to the proposal that the British terms should be conveyed confidentially to Mr. Wilson, Lord Robert said that that would be a difficult thing to do. The President's note had been published, and it therefore seemed necessary that the reply should also be given to the press. This was the procedure that was ultimately adopted.

Startling as was the sensation caused by the President's December note, it was mild compared with that which was now to come. Page naturally sent prompt reports of all these conversations to the President and likewise kept him completely informed as to the state of public feeling, but his best exertions apparently did not immediately affect the Wilson policy. The overwhelming fact is that

---

[1]This narrative is based upon memoranda made by Page.

the President's mind was fixed on a determination to compel the warring powers to make peace and in this way to keep the United States out of the conflict. Even the disturbance caused by his note of December 18th did not make him pause in this peace campaign. To that note the British sent a manly and definite reply, drafted by Mr. Balfour, giving in detail precisely the terms upon which the Allies would compose their differences with the Central Powers. The Germans sent a reply consisting of ten or a dozen lines, which did not give their terms, but merely asked again for a conference. Events were now moving with the utmost rapidity. On January 9th, a council of German military chieftains was held at Pless; in this it was decided to resume unrestricted submarine warfare. On January 16th the Zimmermann-Mexico telegram was intercepted; this informed Bernstorff, among other things, that this decision had been made. On January 16th, at nine o'clock in the morning, the American Embassy in London began receiving a long cipher despatch from Washington. The preamble announced that the despatch contained a copy of an address which the President proposed to deliver before the Senate "in a few days." Page was directed to have copies of the address "secretly prepared" and to hand them to the British Foreign Office and to newspapers of the type of the *Nation*, the *Daily News*, and the *Manchester Guardian*— all three newspapers well known for their Pacifist tendencies. As the speech approached its end, this sentence appeared: "It must be a peace without victory." The words greatly puzzled the secretary in charge, for they seemed almost meaningless. Suspecting that an error had been made in transmission, the secretary directed the code room to cable Washington for a verification of the cipher groups. Very soon the answer was received; there had been no mistake; the Presidential words were precisely those which had been first received: "Peace without victory." The slips were then taken to Page, who read the document, especially these fateful syllables, with a consternation which he made no effort to conceal. He immediately wrote a cable to President Wilson, telling him of the deplorable effect this sentence would produce and imploring him to cut it out of his speech—with what success the world now knows.

An astonishing feature of this episode is that Page had recently explained to the Foreign Office, in obedience to instructions from Washington, that Mr. Wilson's December note should not be interpreted as placing the Allies and the Central Powers on the same moral level. Now Mr. Wilson, in this "peace without victory" phrase, had repeated practically the same idea in another form. On the day the speech was received at the Embassy, about a week before it was delivered in the Senate, Page made the following memorandum:

The President's address to the Senate, which was received to-day (January 16th),[1] shows that he thinks he can play peace-maker. He does not at all understand, (or, if he do, so much the worse for him) that the Entente Powers, especially Great Britain and France, cannot make "peace without victory." If they do, they will become vassals of Germany. In a word, the President does not know the Germans; and he is, unconsciously, under their influence in his thought. His speech plays into their hands.

This address will give great offense in England, since it puts each side in the war on the same moral level.

I immediately saw the grave danger to our relations with

---

[1] It was delivered and published on January 22nd.

Great Britain by the Peace-without-Victory plan; and I telegraphed the President, venturing to advise him to omit that phrase—with no result.

Afterward Page added this to the above:

Compare this Senate speech with his speech in April calling for war: Just when and how did the President come to see the true nature of the German? What made him change from Peace-Maker to War-Maker? The Zimmermann telegram, or the February U-boat renewal of warfare? Had he been so credulous as to believe the German promise? This promise had been continuously and repeatedly broken.

Or was it the pressure of public opinion, the growing impatience of the people that pushed him in?

This distressing peace-move—utterly out of touch with the facts of the origin of the war or of its conduct or of the mood and necessities of Great Britain—a remote, academic deliverance, while Great Britain and France were fighting for their very lives—made a profoundly dejected feeling; and it made my place and work more uncomfortable than ever. "Peace without victory" brought us to the very depths of European disfavour.

CHAPTER XXI

THE UNITED STATES AT WAR

I

THE United States broke off diplomatic relations with Germany on February 3, 1917. The occasion was a memorable one in the American Embassy in London, not unrelieved by a touch of the ridiculous. All day long a nervous and rather weary company had waited in the Ambassador's room for the decisive word from Washington. Mr. and Mrs. Page, Mr. and Mrs. Laughlin, Mr. Shoecraft, the Ambassador's secretary, sat there hour after hour, hardly speaking to one another in their tense excitement, waiting for the news that would inform them that Bernstorff's course had been run and that their country had taken its decision on the side of the Allies. Finally, at nine o'clock in the evening, the front door bell rang. Mr. Shoecraft excitedly left the room; half way downstairs he met Admiral William Reginald Hall, the head of the British Naval Intelligence, who was hurrying up to the Ambassador. Admiral Hall, as he spied Mr. Shoecraft, stopped abruptly and uttered just two words:

"Thank God!"

He then went into the Ambassador's room and read a secret code message which he had just received from Captain Gaunt, the British naval attaché at Washington. It was as follows:

"Bernstorff has just been given his passports. I shall probably get drunk to-night!"

It was in this way that Page first learned that the long tension had passed.

Page well understood that the dismissal of Bernstorff at that time meant war with the Central Empires. Had this dismissal taken place in 1915, after the sinking of the *Lusitania*, or in 1916, after the sinking of the *Sussex*, Page believed that a simple break in relations would in itself have brought the war to an early end. But by February, 1917, things had gone too far. For Germany had now decided to stake everything upon the chance of winning a quick victory with the submarine. Our policy had persuaded the Kaiser's advisers that America would not intervene; and the likelihood of rapidly starving Great Britain was so great—indeed the Germans had reduced the situation to a mathematical calculation of success—that an American declaration of war seemed to Berlin to be a matter of no particular importance. The American Ambassador in London regarded Bernstorff's dismissal much more seriously. It justified the interpretations of events which he had been sending to Mr. Wilson, Colonel House, and others for nearly three years. If Page had been inclined to take satisfaction in the fulfilment of his own prophecies, Germany's disregard of her promises and the American declaration of war would have seemed an ample justification of his course as ambassador.

But Page had little time for such vain communings. "All that water," as he now wrote, "has flowed over the dam." Occasionally his mind would revert to the dreadful period of "neutrality," but in the main his activities, mental and physical, were devoted to the future. A letter addressed to his son Arthur shows how quickly and how sympathetically he was adjusting himself to the new prospect. His mind was now occupied with ships, food, armies, warfare on submarines, and the approaching resettlement of the world. How completely he foresaw the part that the United States must play in the actual waging of hostilities, and to what an extent he himself was responsible for the policies that ultimately prevailed, appears in this letter:

To Arthur W. Page

25 March, 1917, London.

DEAR ARTHUR:

It's very hard, not to say impossible, to write in these swiftly moving days. Anything written to-day is out of date to-morrow—even if it be not wrong to start with. The impression becomes stronger here every day that we shall go into the war "with both feet"—that the people have pushed the President over in spite of his vision of the Great Peacemaker, and that, being pushed over, his idea now will be to show how he led them into a glorious war in defense of democracy. That's my reading of the situation, and I hope I am not wrong. At any rate, ever since the call of Congress for April 2nd, I have been telegraphing tons of information and plans that can be of use only if we go to war. Habitually they never acknowledge the receipt of anything at Washington. I don't know, therefore, whether they like these pieces of information or not. I have my staff of twenty-five good men getting all sorts of warlike information; and I have just organized twenty-five or thirty more—the best business Americans in London—who are also at work. I am trying to get the Government at Washington to send over a committee of conference—a General, an Admiral, a Reserve Board man, etc., etc. If they do half the things that I recommend we'll be in at the final lickin' big, and will save our souls yet.

There's lots of human nature in this world. A note is

now sometimes heard here in undertone (Northcliffe strikes it)—that they don't want the Americans in the war. This means that if we come in just as the Allies finish the job we'll get credit, in part, for the victory, which we did little to win! But that's a minor note. The great mass of people do want us in, quick, hard, and strong—our money and our guns and our ships.

A gift of a billion dollars[1] to France will fix Franco-American history all right for several centuries. Push it through. Such a gift could come to this Kingdom also but for the British stupidity about the Irish for three hundred years. A big loan to Great Britain at a low rate of interest will do the work here.

My mind keeps constantly on the effect of the war and especially of our action on our own country. Of course that is the most important end of the thing for us. I hope that—

1. It will break up and tear away our isolation;

2. It will unhorse our cranks and soft-brains.

3. It will make us less promiscuously hospitable to every kind of immigrant;

4. It will reëstablish in our minds and conscience and policy our true historic genesis, background, kindred, and destiny—i. e., kill the Irish and the German influence.

5. It will revive our real manhood—put the mollycoddles in disgrace, as idiots and dandies are;

6. It will make our politics frank and manly by restoring our true nationality;

7. It will make us again a great sea-faring people. It is this that has given Great Britain its long lead in the world;

8. Break up our feminized education—make a boy a

---

[1]At this time the proposal of such a gift found much popular favour. However, the plan was not carried through.

vigorous animal and make our education rest on a whole-some physical basis;

9. Bring men of a higher type into our political life.

We need waking up and shaking up and invigorating as much as the Germans need taking down.

There is no danger of "militarism" in any harmful sense among any English race or in any democracy.

By George! all these things open an interesting outlook and series of tasks—don't they?

My staff and I are asking everybody what the Ameri-cans can best do to help the cause along. The views are not startling, but they are interesting.

Jellicoe: More ships, merchant ships, any kind of ships, and take over the patrol of the American side of the Atlantic and release the British cruisers there.

Balfour: American credits in the United States big enough to keep up the rate of exchange.

Bonar Law: Same thing.

The military men: An expeditionary force, no matter how small, for the effect of the American Flag in Europe. If one regiment marched through London and Paris and took the Flag to the front, that would be worth the win-ning of a battle.

Think of the vast increase of territory and power Great Britain will have—her colonies drawn closer than ever, the German colonies, or most of them, taken over by her, Bag-dad hers—what a way Germany chose to lessen the Brit-ish Empire! And these gains of territory will be made, as most of her gains have been, not by any prearranged, set plan, but as by-products of action for some other purpose. The only people who have made a deliberate plan to con-quer the earth—now living—are the Germans. And from first to last the additions to the British Empire have been made because she has been a first-class maritime power.

And that's the way she has made her trade and her money, too.

On top of this the President speculates about the danger of the white man losing his supremacy because a few million men get killed! The truth is every country that is playing a big part in the war was overpopulated. There will be a considerable productive loss because the killed men were, as a rule, the best men; but the white man's control of the world hasn't depended on any few million of males. This speculation is far up in the clouds. If Russia and Germany really be liberated from social and political and industrial autocracy, this liberation will bring into play far more power than all the men killed in the war could have had under the pre-war régime. I observe this with every year of my observation—there's no substitute for common-sense.

The big results of the war will, after all, be the freedom and the stimulation of men in these weary Old-World lands—in Russia, Germany itself, and in England. In five or ten years (or sooner, alas!) the dead will be forgotten.

If you wish to make a picture of the world as it will be when the war ends, you must conjure up such scenes as these—human bones along the Russian highways where the great retreat took place and all that such a sight denotes; Poland literally starved; Serbia, blasted and burned and starved; Armenia butchered; the horrible tragedy of Gallipoli, where the best soldiers in the world were sacrificed to politicians' policies; Austria and Germany starved and whipped but liberalized—perhaps no king in either country; Belgium—belgiumized; northern France the same and worse; more productive Frenchmen killed in proportion to the population perhaps than any other country will have lost; Great Britain—most of her best men gone or maimed; colossal debts; several Teutonic countries bankrupt; every atrocity conceivable committed somewhere—a hell-swept great continent having endured more suffering in three years than in the preceding three hundred. Then, ten years later, most of this suffering a mere memory; governments reorganized and liberalized; men made more efficient by this strenuous three years' work; the fields got back their bloom, and life going on much as it did before—with this chief difference—some kings have gone and many privileges have been abolished. The lessons are two—(1) that no government can successfully set out and conquer the world; and (2) that the hold that privilege holders acquire costs more to dislodge than any one could ever have guessed. That's the sum of it. Kings and privilege mongers, of course, have held the parts of the world separate from one another. They fatten on provincialism, which is mistaken for patriotism. As they lose their grip, human sympathy has its natural play between nations, and civilization has a chance. With any Emperor of Germany left the war will have been half in vain.

If we (the U. S. A.) cultivate the manly qualities and throw off our cranks and read our own history and be true to our traditions and blood and get some political vigour; then if we emancipate ourselves from the isolation theory and from the landlubber theory—get into the world and build ships, ships, ships, ships, and run them to the ends of the seas, we can dominate the world in trade and in political thought.

You know I have moments when it occurs to me that perhaps I'd better give whatever working years I may have to telling this story—the story of the larger meaning of the war. There's no bigger theme—never was one so big.

Affectionately,

W. H. P.

On April 1st, the day before President Wilson made his great address before Congress requesting that body to declare the existence of a state of war with Germany, Page committed to paper a few paragraphs which summed up his final judgment of President Wilson's foreign policy for the preceding two and a half years.

Embassy of the United States of America,
April 1, 1917.

In these last days, before the United States is forced into war—by the people's insistence—the preceding course of events becomes even clearer than it was before; and it has been as clear all the time as the nose on a man's face.

The President began by refusing to understand the meaning of the war.   To him it seemed a quarrel to settle economic rivalries between Germany and England.   He said to me last September[1] that there were many causes why Germany went to war.   He showed a great degree of toleration for Germany; and he was, during the whole morning that I talked with him, complaining of England. The controversies we had with England were, of course, mere by-products of the conflict.   But to him they seemed as important as the controversy we had with Germany.   In the beginning he had made—as far as it was possible—neutrality a positive quality of mind.   He would not move from that position.

That was his first error of judgment.   And by insisting on this he soothed the people—sat them down in comfortable chairs and said, "Now stay there."   He really suppressed speech and thought.

The second error he made was in thinking that he could

---

[1]At the meeting of Page and the President at Shadow Lawn, September 22, 1916.   See Chapter XIX.

Walter H. Page, at the time of America's entry into the war,
April, 1917

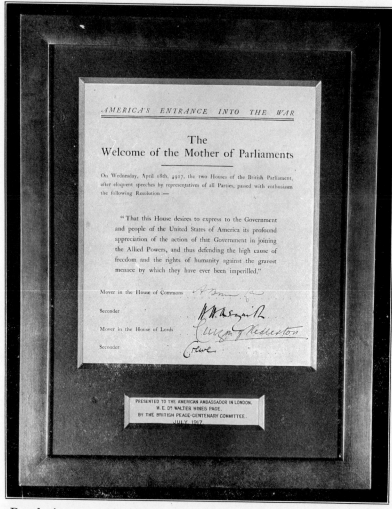

Resolution passed by the two Houses of Parliament, April 18, 1917, on America's entry into the war

play a great part as peacemaker—come and give a blessing to these erring children. This was strong in his hopes and ambitions. There was a condescension in this attitude that was offensive.

He shut himself up with these two ideas and engaged in what he called "thought." The air currents of the world never ventilated his mind.

This inactive position he has kept as long as public sentiment permitted. He seems no longer to regard himself nor to speak as a leader—only as the mouthpiece of public opinion after opinion has run over him.

He has not breathed a spirit into the people: he has encouraged them to supineness. He is *not* a leader, but rather a stubborn phrasemaker.

And now events and the aroused people seem to have brought the President to the necessary point of action; and even now he may act timidly.

"One thing pleases me," Page wrote to his son Arthur, "I never lost faith in the American people. It is now clear that I was right in feeling that they would have gladly come in any time after the *Lusitania* crime, Middle West in the front, and that the German hasn't made any real impression on the American nation. He was made a bug-a-boo and worked for all he was worth by Bernstorff; and that's the whole story. We are as Anglo-Saxon as we ever were. If Hughes had had sense and courage enough to say: 'I'm for war, war to save our honour and to save democracy,' he would now be President. If Wilson had said that, Hughes would have carried no important states in the Union. The suppressed people would have risen to either of them. That's God's truth as I believe it. The real United States is made up of you and Frank and the Page boys at Aberdeen and of the 10,000,000 other young fellows who are ready to do the job and who instinctively see the whole truth of the situation. But of course what the people would not have done under certain conditions—that water also has flowed over the dam; and I mention it only because I have resolutely kept my faith in the people and there has been nothing in recent events that has shaken it."

Two letters which Page wrote on this same April 1st are interesting in that they outline almost completely the war policy that was finally carried out:

To Frank N. Doubleday

Embassy of the United States of America,
April 1, 1917.

DEAR EFFENDI:

Here's the programme:

(1) Our navy in immediate action in whatever way a conference with the British shows we can best help.

(2) A small expeditionary force to France immediately—as large as we can quickly make ready, if only 10,000 men—as proof that we are ready to do some fighting.

(3) A large expeditionary force as soon as the men can be organized and equipped. They can be trained into an effective army in France in about one fourth of the time that they could be trained anywhere else.

(4) A large loan to the Allies at a low rate of interest.

(5) Ships, ships, ships—troop ships, food ships, munition ships, auxiliary ships to the navy, wooden ships, steel ships, little ships, big ships, ships, ships, ships without number or end.

(6) A clear-cut expression of the moral issue involved

in the war. Every social and political ideal that we stand for is at stake. If we value democracy in the world, this is the chance to further it or—to bring it into utter disrepute. After Russia must come Germany and Austria; and then the King-business will pretty nearly be put out of commission.

(7) We must go to war in dead earnest. We must sign the Allies' agreement not to make a separate peace, and we must stay in to the end. Then the end will be very greatly hastened.

It's been four years ago to-day since I was first asked to come here. God knows I've done my poor best to save our country and to help. It'll be four years in the middle of May since I sailed. I shall still do my best. I'll not be able to start back by May 15th, but I have a feeling, if we do our whole duty in the United States, that the end may not be very many months off. And how long off it may be may depend to a considerable degree on our action.

We are faring very well on army rations. None of us will live to see another time when so many big things are at stake nor another time when our country can play so large or important a part in saving the world. Hold up your end. I'm doing my best here.

I think of you engaged in the peaceful work of instructing the people, and I think of the garden and crocuses and the smell of early spring in the air and the earth and—push on; I'll be with you before we grow much older or get much grayer; and a great and prosperous and peaceful time will lie before us. Pity me and hold up your end for real American participation. Get together? Yes; but the way to get together is to get in!

Affectionately,

W. H. P.

To David F. Houston[1]

Embassy of the United States of America,
April 1, 1917.

DEAR HOUSTON:

The Administration can save itself from becoming a black blot on American history only by vigorous action— acts such as these:

Putting our navy to work—vigorous work—wherever and however is wisest.   I have received the Government's promise to send an Admiral here at once for a conference. We must work out with the British Navy a programme whereby we can best help; and we must carry it without hesitancy or delay.

Sending over an expeditionary military force immediately—a small one, but as large as we can, as an earnest of a larger one to come.   This immediate small one will have a good moral effect; and we need all the moral reinstatement that we can get in the estimation of the world; our moral stock is lower than, I fear, any of you at home can possibly realize.   As for a larger expeditionary force later—even that ought to be sent quite early.   It can and must spend some time in training in France, whatever its training beforehand may have been.   All the military men agree that soldiers in France back of the line can be trained in at least half the time that they can be trained anywhere else.   The officers at once take their turn in the trenches, and the progress that they and their men make in close proximity to the fighting is one of the remarkable discoveries of the war.   The British Army was so trained and all the colonial forces.   Two or three or four hundred thousand Americans could be sent over as soon almost as they are organized and equipped—provided transports

[1]Secretary of Agriculture in President Wilson's Cabinet.

and a continuous supply of food and munition ships can be got. They can be trained into fighting men—into an effective army—in about one third of the time that would be required at home.

I suppose, of course, we shall make at once a large loan to the Allies at a low rate of interest. That is most important, but that alone will not save us. We must also *fight*.

All the ships we can get—build, requisition, or confiscate —are needed immediately

Navy, army, money, ships—these are the first things, but by no means all. We must make some expression of a conviction that there is a moral question of right and wrong involved in this war—a question of humanity, a question of democracy. So far we have (officially) spoken only of the wrongs done to our ships and citizens. Deep wrongs have been done to all our moral ideas, to our ideals. We have sunk very low in European opinion because we do not seem to know even yet that a German victory would be less desirable than (say) a Zulu victory of the world.

We must go in with the Allies, not begin a mere single fight against submarines. We must sign the pact of London—not make a separate peace.

We mustn't longer spin dreams about peace, nor leagues to enforce peace, nor the Freedom of the Seas. These things are mere intellectual diversions of minds out of contact with realities. Every political and social ideal we have is at stake. If we make them secure, we'll save Europe from destruction and save ourselves, too.

I pray for vigour and decision and clear-cut resolute action.

(1) The Navy—full strength, no "grapejuice" action.

(2) An immediate expeditionary force.

(3) A larger expeditionary force very soon.

(4) A large loan at a low interest.

(5) Ships, ships, ships.

(6) A clear-cut expression of the moral issue. Thus (and only thus) can we swing into a new era, with a world born again.

Yours in strictest confidence,

W. H. P.

A memorandum, written on April 3rd, the day after President Wilson advised Congress to declare a state of war with Germany:

The Day

When I went to see Mr. Balfour to-day he shook my hand warmly and said: "It's a great day for the world." And so has everybody said, in one way or another, that I have met to-day.

The President's speech did not appear in the morning papers—only a very brief summary in one or two of them; but the meaning of it was clear. The fact that the House of Representatives organized itself in one day and that the President addressed Congress on the evening of that day told the story. The noon papers had the President's speech in full; and everybody applauds.

My "Cabinet" meeting this morning was unusually interesting; and the whole group has never before been so delighted. I spoke of the suggestive, constructive work we have already done in making reports on various war preparations and activities of this kingdom. "Now we have greater need than ever, every man to do constructive work—to think of plans to serve. We are in this excellent strategical position in the capital of the greatest belligerent—a position which I thank my stars, the President, and all the powers that be for giving us. We can each strive to justify our existence."

Few visitors called; but enthusiastic letters have begun to come in.

Nearly the whole afternoon was spent with Mr. Balfour and Lord Robert Cecil. Mr. Balfour had a long list of subjects. Could we help in (1)—(2)—(3)?— Every once in a while he stopped his enumeration of subjects long enough to tell me how the action of the United States had moved him.

To Lord Robert I said: "I pray you, give the Black List a decent burial: It's dead now, but through no act of yours. It insulted every American because you did not see that it was insulting: that's the discouraging fact to me." He thanked me earnestly. He'll think about that.

II

These jottings give only a faint impression of the change which the American action wrought in Page. The strain which he had undergone for twenty-nine months had been intense; it had had the most unfortunate effect upon his health; and the sudden lifting might have produced that reaction for the worse which is not unusual after critical experiences of this kind. But the gratification which Page felt in the fact that the American spirit had justified his confidence gave him almost a certain exuberance of contentment. Londoners who saw him at that time describe him as acting like a man from whose shoulders a tremendous weight had suddenly been removed. For more than two years Page had been compelled, officially at least, to assume a "neutrality" with which he had never had the slightest sympathy, but the necessity for this mask now no longer existed. A well-known Englishman happened to meet Page leaving his house in Grosvenor Square the day after the Declaration of War. He stopped and shook the Ambassador's hand.

"Thank God," the Englishman said, "that there is one hypocrite less in London to-day."

"What do you mean?" asked Page.

"I mean you. Pretending all this time that you were neutral! That isn't necessary any longer."

"You are right!" the Ambassador answered as he walked on with a laugh and a wave of the hand.

A few days after the Washington Declaration, the American Luncheon Club held a feast in honour of the event. This organization had a membership of representative American business men in London, but its behaviour during the war had not been based upon Mr. Wilson's idea of neutrality. Indeed its tables had so constantly rung with denunciations of the *Lusitania* notes that all members of the American Embassy, from Page down, had found it necessary to refrain from attending its proceedings. When Page arose to address his compatriots on this occasion, therefore, he began with the significant words, "I am glad to be back with you *again*," and the mingled laughter and cheers with which this remark was received indicated that his hearers had caught the point.

The change took place not only in Page, but in London and the whole of Great Britain. An England that had been saying harsh things of the United States for nearly two years now suddenly changed its attitude. Both houses of Parliament held commemorative sessions in honour of America's participation; in the Commons Mr. Lloyd George, Mr. Asquith, and other leaders welcomed their new allies, and in the Upper Chamber Lord Curzon, Lord

Bryce, the Archbishop of Canterbury, and others similarly voiced their admiration. The Stars and Stripes almost instantaneously broke out on private dwellings, shops, hotels, and theatres; street hucksters did a thriving business selling rosettes of the American colours, which even the most stodgy Englishmen did not disdain to wear in their buttonholes; wherever there was a band or an orchestra, the Star Spangled Banner acquired a sudden popularity; and the day even came when the American and the British flags flew side by side over the Houses of Parliament—the first occasion in history that any other than the British standard had received this honour. The editorial outgivings of the British press on America's entrance form a literature all their own. The theatres and the music halls, which had found in "notes" and "nootrality" an endless theme of entertainment for their patrons, now sounded Americanism as their most popular refrain. Churches and cathedrals gave special services in honour of American intervention, and the King and the President began to figure side by the side in the prayer book. The estimation in which President Wilson was held changed overnight. All the phrases that had so grieved Englishmen were instantaneously forgotten. The President's address before Congress was praised as one of the most eloquent and statesmanlike utterances in history. Special editions of this heartening document had a rapid sale; it was read in school houses, churches, and at public gatherings, and it became a most influential force in uplifting the hopes of the Allies and inspiring them to renewed activities. Americans everywhere, in the streets, at dinner tables, and in general social intercourse, could feel the new atmosphere of respect and admiration which had suddenly become their country's portion. The first American troops that passed through London—a company of en-

gineers, an especially fine body of men—aroused a popular enthusiasm which was almost unprecedented in a
capital not celebrated for its emotional displays. Page
himself records one particularly touching indication of the
feeling for Americans which was now universal. "The
increasing number of Americans who come through England," he wrote, "most of them on their way to France,
but some of them also to serve in England, give much
pleasure to the British public—nurses, doctors, railway
engineers, sawmill units, etc. The sight of every American uniform pleases London. The other morning a group
of American nurses gathered with the usual crowd in front
of Buckingham Palace while the Guards band played inside the gates. Man after man as they passed them and
saw their uniforms lifted their hats."

The Ambassador's mail likewise underwent a complete
transformation. His correspondence of the preceding
two years, enormous in its extent, had contained much
that would have disturbed a man who could easily get
excited over trifles, but this aspect of his work never
caused Page the slightest unhappiness. Almost every
crank in England who disliked the American policy had
seemed to feel it his duty to express his opinions to the
American Ambassador. These letters, at times sorrowful, at others abusive, even occasionally threatening, varying in their style from cultivated English to the grossest
illiteracy, now written in red ink to emphasize their bitterness, now printed in large block letters to preserve their
anonymity, aroused in Page only a temporary amusement.
But the letters that began to pour in upon him after our
Declaration, many of them from the highest placed men
and women in the Kingdom, brought out more vividly
than anything else the changed position of his country.
Sonnets and verses rained upon the Embassy, most of

them pretty bad as poetry, but all of them commendable for their admiring and friendly spirit. Of all these letters those that came from the steadfast friends of America perhaps gave Page the greatest satisfaction. "You will have been pleased at the universal tribute paid to the spirit as well as to the lofty and impressive terms of the President's speech," wrote Lord Bryce. "Nothing finer in our time, few things so fine." But probably the letter which gave Page the greatest pleasure was that which came from the statesman whose courtesy and broad outlook had eased the Ambassador's task in the old neutrality days. In 1916, Sir Edward Grey—now become Viscount Grey of Fallodon—had resigned office, forced out, Page says in one of his letters, mainly because he had refused to push the blockade to a point where it might produce a break with the United States. He had spent the larger part of the time since that event at his country place in Northumberland, along the streams and the forests which had always given him his greatest pleasure, attempting to recover something of the health that he had lost in the ten years which he had spent as head of the British Foreign Office and bearing with characteristic cheerfulness and fortitude the tragedy of a gradually failing eyesight. The American Declaration of War now came to Lord Grey as the complete justification of his policy. The mainspring of that policy, as already explained, had been a determination to keep the friendship of the United States, and so shape events that the support of this country would ultimately be cast on the side of the Allies. And now the great occasion for which he had prepared had come, and in Grey's mind this signified more than a help to England in soldiers and ships; it meant bringing together the two branches of a common race for the promotion of common ideals.

From Viscount Grey of Fallodon

Rosehall Post Office,
Sutherland,
April 8, 1917.

DEAR MR. PAGE:

This is a line that needs no answer to express my congratulations on President Wilson's address. I can't express adequately all that I feel. Great gratitude and great hope are in my heart. I hope now that some great and abiding good to the world will yet be wrought out of all this welter of evil. Recent events in Russia, too, stimulate this hope: they are a good in themselves, but not the power for good in this war that a great and firmly established free country like the United States can be. The President's address and the way it has been followed up in your country is a splendid instance of great action finely inspired. I glow with admiration.

Yours sincerely,
GREY OF FALLODON

One Englishman who was especially touched by the action of the United States was His Majesty the King. Few men had watched the course of America during the war with more intelligent interest than the head of the British royal house. Page had had many interviews with King George at Buckingham Palace and at Windsor, and his notes contain many appreciative remarks on the King's high character and conscientious devotion to his duties. That Page in general did not believe in kings and emperors as institutions his letters reveal; yet even so profound a Republican as he recognized sterling character, whether in a crowned head or in a humble citizen, and he had seen enough of King George to respect him. Moreover, the peculiar limitations of the British monarchy certainly gave it an unusual position and even saved it from much of the criticism that was fairly lavished upon such nations as Germany and Austria. Page especially admired King George's frankness in recognizing these limitations and his readiness to accommodate himself to the British Constitution. On most occasions, when these two men met, their intercourse was certainly friendly or at least not formidable. After all formalities had been exchanged, the King would frequently draw the Ambassador aside; the two would retire to the smoking room, and there, over their cigars, discuss a variety of matters—submarines, international politics, the Irish question and the like. His Majesty was not averse even to bringing up the advantages of the democratic and the monarchical system. The King and Ambassador would chat, as Page himself would say, like "two human beings"; King George is an emphatic and vivacious talker, fond of emphasizing his remarks by pounding the table; he has the liveliest sense of humour, and enjoys nothing quite so much as a good story. Page found that, on the subject of the Germans, the King entertained especially robust views. "They are my kinsmen," he would say, "but I am ashamed of them."

Probably most Englishmen, in the early days of the war, preferred that the United States should not engage in hostilities; even after the *Lusitania*, the majority in all likelihood held this view. There are indications, however, that King George favoured American participation. A few days after the *Lusitania* sinking, Page had an audience for the purpose of presenting a medal sent by certain societies in New Orleans. Neither man was thinking much about medals that morning. The thoughts uppermost in their minds, as in the minds of most Americans and

Englishmen, were the *Lusitania* and the action that the United States was likely to take concerning it. After the formalities of presentation, the King asked Page to sit down and talked with him for more than half an hour. "He said that Germany was evidently trying to force the United States into the war; that he had no doubt we would soon be in it and that, for his part, he would welcome us heartily. The King also said he had reliable information from Germany, that the Emperor had wished to return a conciliatory answer to our *Lusitania* note, but that Admiral von Tirpitz had prevented it, even going so far as to 'threaten' the Kaiser. It appears that the Admiral insisted that the submarine was the only weapon the Germans could use with effect against England and that they could not afford to give it up. He was violent and the Kaiser finally yielded."[1]

The statement from the King at that crisis, that he would "heartily welcome the United States into the war," was interpreted by the Ambassador as amounting practically to an invitation—and certainly as expressing a wish that such an intervention should take place.

That the American participation would rejoice King George could therefore be taken for granted. Soon after this event, the Ambassador and Mrs. Page were invited to spend the night at Windsor.

"I arrived during the middle of the afternoon," writes Page, "and he sent for me to talk with him in his office.

"'I've a good story on you,' said he. 'You Americans have a queer use of the word "some," to express mere bigness or emphasis. We are taking that use of the word from you over here. Well, an American and an Englishman were riding in the same railway compartment. The

---

[1] The quotation is from a memorandum of the conversation made by one of the secretaries of the American Embassy.

American read his paper diligently—all the details of a big battle. When he got done, he put the paper down and said: "Some fight!" "And some don't!" said the Englishman.'

"And the King roared. 'A good one on you!'

"'The trouble with that joke, sir,' I ventured to reply, 'is that it's out of date.'

"He was in a very gay mood, surely because of our entry into the war. After the dinner—there were no guests except Mrs. Page and me, the members of his household, of course, being present—he became even familiar in the smoking room. He talked about himself and his position as king. 'Knowing the difficulties of a limited monarch, I thank heaven I am spared being an absolute one.'

"He went on to enumerate the large number of things he was obliged to do, for example, to sign the death warrant of every condemned man—and the little real power that he had—not at all in a tone of complaint, but as a merely impersonal explanation.

"Just how much power—perhaps 'influence' is a better word—the King has, depends on his personality. The influence of the throne—and of him on the throne, being a wholly thoughtful, industrious, and conscientious man— is very great—greatest of all in keeping the vested interests of the aristocratic social structure secure.

"Earlier than this visit to Windsor he sent for me to go to Buckingham Palace very soon after we declared war. He went over the whole course of events—and asked me many questions. After I had risen and said 'good-bye' and was about to bow myself out the door, he ran toward me and waving his hand cried out, 'Ah—Ah!—we knew where *you* stood all the time.'

"When General Pershing came along on his way to France, the King summoned us to luncheon. The luncheon was eaten (here, as everywhere, strict war rations are observed) to a flow of general talk, with the Queen, Princess Mary, and one of the young Princes. When they had gone from the luncheon room, the King, General Pershing, and I stood smoking by the window; and the King at once launched into talk about guns, rifles, ammunition, and the American place in the battle line. Would our place be with the British or with the French or between the two?

"General Pershing made a diplomatic reply. So far as he knew the President hadn't yet made a final decision, but there was a feeling that, since we were helping the British at sea, perhaps we ought to help the French on land.

"Then the King expressed the earnest hope that our guns and ammunition would match either the British or the French. Else if we happened to run out of ammunition we could not borrow from anybody. He thought it most unfortunate that the British and French guns and rifles were of different calibres."

To Arthur W. Page

Brighton, England,
April 28, 1917.

DEAR ARTHUR:
. . . Well, the British have given us a very good welcome into the war. They are not very skillful at such a task: they do not know how to say "Welcome" very vociferously. But they have said it to the very best of their ability. My speeches (which I send you, with some comment) were very well received indeed. Simple and obvious as they were, they meant a good deal of work.

I cannot conceal nor can I express my gratification that we are in the war. I shall always wonder but never find out what influence I had in driving the President over. All I know is that my letters and telegrams for nearly two years—especially for the last twelve months—have put before him every reason that anybody has expressed why we should come in—in season and out of season. And there is no new reason—only more reason of the same old sort—why we should have come in now than there was why we should have come in a year ago. I suspect that the pressure of the press and of public opinion really became too strong for him. And, of course, the Peace-Dream blew up—was torpedoed, mined, shot, captured, and killed. I trust, too, much enlightenment will be furnished by the two Commissions now in Washington.[1] Yet it's comical to think of the attitude of the poor old Department last September and its attitude now. But thank God for it! Every day now brings a confession of the blank idiocy of its former course and its long argument! Never mind that, so long as we are now right.

I have such a sense of relief that I almost feel that my job is now done. Yet, I dare say, my most important work is still to come.

The more I try to reach some sort of rational judgment about the war, the more I find myself at sea. It does look as if the very crisis is near. And there can be no doubt now—not even, I hope, in the United States—about the necessity of a clear and decisive victory, nor about punishment. All the devastation of Northern France, which outbarbarizes barbarism, all the ships sunk, including hospital ships, must be paid for; that's all. There'll be famine in Europe whenever it end. Not only must these destructions be paid for, but the Hohenzollerns and all they stand for must go. Trust your Frenchman for that, if nobody else!

[1] The British and French Commissions, headed by Mr. Balfour and M. Viviani.

If Europe had the food wasted in the United States, it would make the difference between sustenance and famine. By the way, the submarine has made every nation a danger zone except those few that have self-feeding continents, such as ours. It can bring famine to any other kind of a country.

You are now out in the country again—good. Give Mollie my love and help her with the garden. I envy you the fresh green things to eat. Little Mollie, kiss her for granddaddy. The Ambassador, I suppose, waxes even sturdier, and I'm glad to hear that A. W. P., Jr., is picking up. Get him fed right at all costs. If Frank stays at home and Ralph and his family come up, you'll all have a fine summer. We've the very first hint of summer we've had, and it's cheerful to see the sky and to feel the sunshine.

Affectionately,

W. H. P.

To Frank N. Doubleday

American Embassy,
London, May 3, 1917.

DEAR EFFENDI:

I aim this at you. It may hit a German submarine. But we've got to take our chances in these days of risk. Your letter from the tropics—a letter from you from any place is as scarce as peace!—gave me a pleasant thrill and reminder of a previous state of existence, a long way back in the past. I wonder if, on your side the ocean you are living at the rate of a century a year, as we are here? Here in bountiful England we are living on rations. I spent a night with the King a fortnight ago, and he gave us only so much bread, one egg apiece, and—lemonade. We are to begin bread tickets next week. All this is per-

fectly healthful and wholesome and as much as I ever eat.
But the hard part of it is that it's necessary. We haven't
more than six weeks' food supply and the submarines
sunk eighty-eight ships—237,000 tons—last week. These
English do not publish these harrowing facts, and nobody
knows them but a few official people. And they are destroying the submarines at a most beggarly slow rate.
They work far out at sea—100 to 200 miles—and it's as
hard to find them as it would be to find whales. The simple truth is we are in a dangerous plight. If they could
stop this submarine warfare, the war would pretty quickly
be won, for the Germans are in a far worse plight for food
and materials and they are getting much the worst of it
on land. The war would be won this summer or autumn
if the submarine could be put out of business. If it isn't,
the Germans may use this success to keep their spirits up
and go on till next year.

We (the United States) have about 40 destroyers. We
are sending over 6! I'm doing my best to persuade the
Government at Washington to send every one we have.
But, since the British conceal the facts from their own
press and the people and from all the world, the full pressure of the situation is hard to exert on Washington. Our
Admiral (Sims) and I are trying our best, and we are
spending enough on cables to build a destroyer. All this,
you must, of course, regard as a dark secret; but it's a
devilish black secret.

I don't mean that there's any danger of losing the war.
Even if the British armies have to have their food cut
down and people here go hungry, they'll win; but the
winning may be a long time off. Nothing but their continued success can keep the Germans going. Their people are war-weary and hungry. Austria is knocked out
and is starving. Turkey is done up but can go on living

on nothing, but not fighting much more. When peace comes, there'll be a general famine, on the continent at least, and no ships to haul food. This side of the world will have to start life all over again—with insufficient men to carry things on and innumerable maimed men who'll have (more or less) to be cared for. The horror of the whole thing nobody realizes. We've all got used to it here; and nobody clearly remembers just what the world was like in peace times; those times were so far away. All this I write not to fill you with horrors but to prove that I speak the literal truth when I say that it seems a hundred years since I had before heard from you.

Just how all this affects a man, no man can accurately tell. Of how much use I'll be when I can get home, I don't know. Sometimes I think that I shall be of vastly greater use than ever. Plans and publishing ambitions pop up in my mind at times which look good and promising. I see books and series of books. I see most useful magazine stuff. Then, before I can think anything out to a clear plan or conclusion, the ever-increasing official duties and responsibilities here knock everything else out of my head, perhaps for a whole month. It's a literal fact that many a month I do not have an hour to do with as I please nor to think about what I please, from the time I wake up till I go to bed. In spite of twenty-four secretaries (the best fellows that ever were and the best staff that any Embassy ever had in the world) more and more work comes to me. I thank Heaven we no longer have the interests of Germany, Austria, and Turkey to look after; but with our coming into the war, work in general has increased enormously. I have to spend very much more time with the different departments of the British Government on war plans and such like things. They have welcomed us in very handsomely; and one form of their welcome is consulting with me about—navy plans, war plans, loans of billions, ships, censorship, secret service—everything you ever heard of. At first it seemed a little comical for the admirals and generals and the Governor of the Bank of England to come and ask for advice. But when I gave it and it worked out well, I went on and, after all, the thing's easier than it looks. With a little practice you can give these fellows several points in the game and play a pretty good hand. They don't know half as much as you might suppose they'd know. All these years of lecturing the State Department and the President got my hand in! The whole game is far easier than any small business. You always play with blue chips better than you play with white ones.

This country and these people are not the country and the people they were three years ago. They are very different. They are much more democratic, far less cocksure, far less haughty, far humbler. The man at the head of the army rose from the ranks. The Prime Minister is a poor Welsh schoolteacher's son, without early education. The man who controls all British shipping began life as a shipping "clark," at ten shillings a week. Yet the Lords and Ladies, too, have shown that they were made of the real stuff. This experience is making England over again. There never was a more interesting thing to watch and to be part of.

There are about twenty American organizations here— big, little, rag-tag, and bobtail. When we declared war, every one of 'em proceeded to prepare for some sort of celebration. There would have been an epidemic of Fourth-of-July oratory all over the town—before we'd done anything—Americans spouting over the edges and killing Kruger with their mouths. I got representatives of 'em all together and proposed that we hold our tongues

till we'd won the war—then we can take London. And
to give one occasion when we might all assemble and dedicate ourselves to this present grim business, I arranged for
an American Dedicatory Service at St. Paul's Cathedral.
The royal family came, the Government came, the Allied
diplomats came, my Lords and Ladies came, one hundred
wounded American (Canadian) soldiers came—the pick
of the Kingdom; my Navy and Army staff went in full
uniform, the Stars and Stripes hung before the altar, a
double brass band played the Star Spangled Banner and
the Battle Hymn of the Republic, and an American bishop
(Brent) preached a red-hot American sermon, the Archbishop of Canterbury delivered the benediction; and (for
the first time in English history) a foreign flag (the Stars
and Stripes) flew over the Houses of Parliament. It was
the biggest occasion, so they say, that St. Paul's ever had.
And there's been no spilling of American oratory since!
If you had published a shilling edition of the words and
music of the Star Spangled Banner and the Battle Hymn
you could have sent a cargo of 'em here and sold them.
There isn't paper enough in this Kingdom to get out an
edition here.

Give my love to all the Doubledays and to all the fellows
in the shop, and (I wonder if you will) try your hand at
another letter.   You write very legibly these days!

Sincerely yours,

WALTER H. PAGE.

"Curiously enough," Page wrote about this time, "these
most exciting days of the war are among the most barren
of exciting topics for private correspondence. The 'atmosphere' here is unchanging—to us—and the British are
turning their best side to us continuously. They are
increasingly appreciative, and they see more and more

clearly that our coming into the war is all that saved them
from a virtual defeat—I mean the public sees this more
and more clearly, for, of course, the Government has
known it from the beginning.   I even find a sort of mor-
bid fear lest they do not sufficiently show their appreciation.   The Archbishop last night asked me in an apprehensive tone whether the American Government and
public felt that the British did not sufficiently show their
gratitude.   I told him that we did not come into the war
to win compliments but to whip the enemy, and that we
wanted all the help the British can give: that's the main
thing; and that thereafter of course we liked appreciation,
but that expressions of appreciation had not been lacking.
Mr. Balfour and Sir Edward Carson also spoke to me
yesterday much in the same tone as the Archbishop of
Canterbury.

"Try to think out any line of action that one will, or
any future sequence of events or any plan touching the
war, one runs into the question whether the British are
doing the best that could be done or are merely plugging
away.   They are, as a people, slow and unimaginative,
given to over-much self-criticism; but they eternally hold
on to a task or to a policy.   Yet the question forever
arises whether they show imagination, to say nothing of
genius, and whether the waste of a slow, plodding policy
is the necessary price of victory.

"Of course such a question is easy to ask and it is easy
to give dogmatic answers.   But it isn't easy to give an
answer based on facts.   Our General Lassiter,[1] for instance—a man of sound judgment—has in general been
less hopeful of the military situation in France than most
of the British officers.   But he is just now returned from
the front, much cheered and encouraged.   'Lassiter,' I

[1] American military attaché in London.

asked, 'have the British in France or has any man among them what we call genius, or even wide vision; or are they merely plodding along at a mechanical task?' His answer was, 'We don't see genius till it has done its job. It is a mechanical task—yes, that's the nature of the struggle—and they surely do it with intelligence and spirit. There is waste. There is waste in all wars. But I come back much more encouraged.'

"The same sort of questions and answers are asked and given continuously about naval action. Every discussion of the possibility of attacking the German naval bases ends without a plan. So also with preventing the submarines from coming out. These subjects have been continuously under discussion by a long series of men who have studied them; and the total effect so far has been to leave them among the impossible tasks. So far as I can ascertain all naval men among the Allies agree that these things can't be done.

"Here again—Is this a merely routine professional opinion—a merely traditional opinion—or is it a lack of imagination? The question will not down. Yet it is impossible to get facts to combat it. What are the limits of the practicable?

"Mr. Balfour told me yesterday his personal conviction about the German colonies, which, he said, he had not discussed with his associates in the Cabinet. His firm opinion is that they ought not to be returned to the Germans, first for the sake of humanity. 'The natives—the Africans especially—have been so barbarously treated and so immorally that it would be inhuman to permit the Germans to rule and degrade them further. But Heaven forbid that we should still further enlarge the British Empire. As a practical matter I do not care to do that. Besides, we should incur the criticism of fighting in order to get more territory, and that was not and is not our aim. If the United States will help us, my wish is that these German Colonies that we have taken, especially in Africa, should be "internationalized." There are great difficulties in such a plan, but they are not insuperable if the great Powers of the Allies will agree upon it.' And much more to the same effect. The parts of Asiatic Turkey that the British have taken, he thought, might be treated in the same way."

CHAPTER XXII

THE BALFOUR MISSION TO THE UNITED STATES

I

PAGE now took up a subject which had been near his heart for a long time. He believed that one of the most serious causes of Anglo-American misunderstanding was the fact that the leading statesmen of the two countries had never had any personal contact with one another. At one time, as this correspondence shows, the Ambassador had even hoped that President Wilson himself might cross the ocean and make the British people an official visit. The proposal, however, was made before the European war broke out, the occasion which Page had in mind being the dedication of Sulgrave Manor, the old English home of the Washington family, as a perpetual memorial to the racial bonds and common ideals uniting the two countries. The President found it impossible to act upon this suggestion and the outbreak of war made the likelihood of such a visit still more remote. Page had made one unsuccessful attempt to bring the American State Department and the British Foreign Office into personal contact. At the moment when American irritation had been most keen over the blockade and the blacklist, Page had persuaded the Foreign Office to invite to England Mr. Frank L. Polk, at that time Counsellor of the Department; the Ambassador believed that a few conversations between such an intelligent gentleman as Mr. Polk and the British statesmen would smooth out all the points which were then making things so difficult. Unfortunately the pressure of work at Washington prevented Mr. Polk from accepting Sir Edward Grey's invitation.

But now a greater necessity for close personal association had arisen. The United States had entered the war, and this declaration had practically made this country an ally of Great Britain and France. The British Government wished to send a distinguished commission to the United States, for two reasons: first, to show its appreciation of the stand which America had taken, and secondly, to discuss plans for coöperation in the common task. Great Britain frankly admitted that it had made many mistakes in the preceding three years—mistakes naval, military, political, and economic; it would welcome an opportunity to display these errors to Washington, which might naturally hope to profit from them. As soon as his country was in the war, Page took up this suggestion with the Foreign Office. There was of course one man who was preëminently fitted, by experience, position, and personal qualities, to head such a commission; on this point there was no discussion. Mr. Balfour was now in his seventieth year; his activities in British politics dated back to the times of Disraeli; his position in Great Britain had become as near that of an "elder statesman" as is tolerable under the Anglo-Saxon system. By this time Page had established the friendliest possible relations with this distinguished man. Mr. Balfour had become Foreign Secretary in December, 1916, in succession to Lord Grey. Greatly as Page regretted the resignation of Grey, he was much gratified that Mr. Balfour had been selected to succeed him. Mr. Balfour's record for twenty-five years had been one of consistent friendliness toward the United States. When President Cleveland's Venezuelan message, in 1896, had precipitated a crisis in the relations of the two countries, it was Mr. Balfour's influence which was especially potent in causing Great Britain to modify its attitude and to accept the American demand for arbitration. That action not only amicably settled the Venezuelan question; it marked the beginning of a better feeling between the English-speaking countries and laid the basis for that policy of benevolent neutrality which Great Britain had maintained toward the United States in the Spanish War. The excellent spirit which Mr. Balfour had shown at this crisis he had manifested on many occasions since. In the criticisms of the United States during the *Lusitania* troubles Mr. Balfour had never taken part. The era of "neutrality" had not ruffled the confidence which he had always felt in the United States. During all this time the most conspicuous dinner tables of London had rung with criticisms of American policy; the fact was well known, however, that Mr. Balfour had never sympathized with these reproaches; even when he was not in office, no unfriendly word concerning the United States had ever escaped his lips. His feeling toward this country was well shown in a letter which he wrote Page, in reply to one congratulating him on his seventieth birthday. "I have now lived a long life," said Mr. Balfour, "and most of my energies have been expended in political work, but if I have been fortunate enough to contribute, even in the smallest degree, to drawing closer the bonds that unite our two countries, I shall have done something compared with which all else that I may have attempted counts in my eyes as nothing."

Page's letters and notes contain many references to Mr. Balfour's kindly spirit. On the day following the dismissal of Bernstorff the American Ambassador lunched with the Foreign Secretary at No. 4 Carlton Gardens.

"Mr. Balfour," Page reported to Washington, "gave expression to the hearty admiration which he entertained for the President's handling of a difficult task. He said that never for a moment had he doubted the President's wisdom in the course he was pursuing. He had the profoundest admiration for the manner in which he had promptly broken with Germany after receiving Germany's latest note. Nor had he ever entertained the slightest question of the American people's ready loyalty to their Government or to their high ideals. One of his intellectual pleasures, he added, had long been contemplation of the United States as it is and, even more, as its influence in the world will broaden. 'The world,' said Mr. Balfour, 'will more and more turn on the Great Republic as on a pivot.'"

Occasionally Mr. Balfour's discussion of the United States would take a more pensive turn. A memorandum which Page wrote a few weeks after the above touches another point:

March 27, 1917.

I had a most interesting conversation with Mr. Balfour this afternoon. "It's sad to me," said he, "that we are so unpopular, so much more unpopular than the French, in your country. Why is it? The old school books?"

I doubted the school-book influence.

"Certainly their influence is not the main cause. It is the organized Irish. Then it's the effect of the very fact that the Irish question is not settled. You've had that problem at your very door for 300 years. What's the matter that you don't solve it?"

"Yes, yes,"—he saw it. But the plaintive tone of such a man asking such a question was significant and interesting and—sad.

Then I told him the curious fact that a British Government made up of twenty individuals, every one of whom is most friendly to the United States, will, when they act together as a Government, do the most offensive things. I mentioned the blacklist; I mentioned certain complaints that I then held in my hand—of Americans here who are told by the British Government that they must turn over to the British Government's agent in New York their American securities which they hold in America!

There's a sort of imperious, arrogant, Tory action that comes natural to the English Government, even when not natural to the individual Englishman.

On April 5th, the day before the United States formally declared war, Page notified Washington that the British Government wished Mr. Balfour to go to the United States as the head of a Commission to confer with our Government. "Mr. Balfour is chosen for this mission," Page reported, "not only because he is Secretary of State for Foreign Affairs, but because he is personally the most distinguished member of the Government." Page tells the story in more detail in a letter to Mr. Polk, at that time Counsellor of the State Department.

To Frank L. Polk

London, May 3, 1917.

DEAR MR. POLK:

. . . Mr. Balfour accurately represents British character, British opinion, and the British attitude. Nobody who knows him and knows British character and the British attitude ever doubted that. I know his whole tribe, his home-life, his family connections, his friends; and, of course, since he became Foreign Secretary, I've come to know him intimately. When the question first came up here of his going, of course I welcomed it enthusiastically. About that time during a two-hour conversation he asked me why the British were so unpopular in the United States. Among other reasons I told him that our official people on both sides steadfastly refused to visit one another and to become acquainted. Neither he nor Lord Grey, nor Mr. Asquith, nor Mr. Lloyd George, had ever been to the United States, nor any other important British statesman in recent times, and not a single member of the Administration was personally known to a single member of the British Government. "I'll go," said he, "if you are perfectly sure my going will be agreeable to the President." He himself recalled the fact, during one of our several conversations just before he left, that you had not come when he and Lord Grey had invited you. If you had come, by the way, this era of a better understanding would have begun then, and half our old troubles would then have been removed. Keeping away from one another is the best of all methods of keeping all old misunderstandings alive and of making new ones.

I have no doubt that Mr. Balfour's visit will cause visits of many first-class British statesmen during the war or soon afterward. That's all we need to bring about a perfect understanding.

You may remember how I tried to get an official report about the behaviour of the *Benham*,[1] and how, in the absence of that, Lord Beresford made a disagreeable speech about our Navy in the House of Lords, and how, when

---

[1] The reference is to the attack made in October, 1916, by the German Submarine *U*-53, off Nantucket on several British ships. An erroneous newspaper account said that the *Benham*, an American destroyer, had moved in a way that facilitated the operations of the German submarine. This caused great bitterness in England, until Page showed the Admiralty a report from the Navy Department proving that the story was false.

months later you sent me Roosevelt's[1] letter, Lord Beresford expressed regret to me and said that he would explain
in another speech. I hadn't seen the old fellow for a long
time till a fortnight ago. He greeted me cheerily, and I
said, "I don't think I ought to shake hands with you till
you retract what you said about our navy." He insisted
on my dining with him. He invited Admiral Sims also,
and those two sailors had a jolly evening of it. Sims's
coming has straightened out all that naval misunderstanding and more. He is of immense help to them and
to us. But I'm going to make old Beresford's life a burden till he gets up in the Lords and takes that speech back
—publicly. He's really all right; but it's just as well to
keep the records right. The proceedings of the House of
Lords are handsomely bound and go into every gentleman's library. I have seen two centuries of them in
many a house.

We can now begin a distinctly New Era in the world's
history and in its management if we rise to the occasion:
there's not a shadow of doubt about that. And the
United States can play a part bigger than we have yet
dreamed of if we prove big enough to lead the British and
the French instead of listening to Irish and Germans.
Neither England nor France is a democracy—far from it.
We can make them both democracies and develop their
whole people instead of about 10 per cent. of their
people. We have simply to conduct our affairs by a large
national policy and not by the complaints of our really
non-American people. See how a declaration of war has
cleared the atmosphere!

We're happy yet, on rations. There are no potatoes.
We have meatless days. Good wheat meantime is sunk

---

[1]This, of course, is Franklin D. Roosevelt, Assistant Secretary of the Navy in
1917.

The Rt. Hon. David Lloyd George, Chancellor of
the Exchequer, 1908–1915, Minister of Munitions,
1915–1916, Prime Minister of Great Britain, 1916-1922

The Rt. Hon. Arthur James Balfour (now the Earl of Balfour)
Secretary of State for Foreign Affairs, 1916–1919

every day.   The submarine must be knocked out.   Else
the earth will be ruled by the German bayonet and natural
living will be *verboten*.   We'll all have to goose-step as the
Crown Prince orders or—be shot.   I see they now propose
that the United States shall pay the big war indemnity
in raw materials to the value of hundreds of billions of
dollars!   Not just yet, I guess!

As we get reports of what you are doing, it's most cheerful.   I assure you, God has yet made nothing or nobody
equal to the American people; and I don't think He ever
will or can.

Sincerely yours,

WALTER H. PAGE.

One of the curious developments of this Balfour Mission
was a request from President Wilson that Great Britain
should take some decisive step for the permanent settlement of the Irish question.   "The President," this message ran, "wishes that, when you next meet the Prime
Minister, you would explain to him that only one circumstance now appears to stand in the way of perfect
coöperation with Great Britain.   All Americans who
are not immediately connected with Germany by blood
ties find their one difficulty in the failure of Great Britain
so far to establish a satisfactory form of self-government in
Ireland.   In the recent debates in Congress on the War
Resolution, this sentiment was especially manifest.   It
came out in the speeches of those enemies of the Declaration who were not Irish themselves nor representatives of
sections in which Irish voters possessed great influence—
notably members from the Southern States.

"If the American people were once convinced that there
was a likelihood that the Irish question would soon be
settled, great enthusiasm and satisfaction would result

and it would also strengthen the coöperation which we are now about to organize between the United States and Great Britain. Say this in unofficial terms to Mr. Lloyd George, but impress upon him its very great significance. If the British Government should act successfully on this matter, our American citizens of Irish descent and to a great extent the German sympathizers who have made common cause with the Irish, would join hands in the great common cause."

To the President

London, May 4, 1917.

DEAR MR. PRESIDENT:

. . . It is a remarkable commentary on the insularity of the British and on our studied isolation that till Mr. Balfour went over not a member of this Government had ever met a member of our Administration! Quite half our misunderstandings were due to this. If I had the making of the laws of the two governments, I'd have a statutory requirement that at least one visit a year by high official persons should be made either way. We should never have had a blacklist, etc., if that had been done. When I tried the quite humble task of getting Polk to come and the excuse was made that he couldn't be spared from his desk—Mr. President, I fear we haven't half enough responsible official persons in our Government. I should say that no man even of Polk's rank ought to have a desk: just as well give him a mill-stone. Even I try not to have a desk: else I'd never get anything of importance done; for I find that talks and conferences in my office and in the government offices and wherever else I can find out things take all my waking hours. The Foreign Office here has about five high position men to every one in the State Department. God sparing me,

I'm going one of these days to prepare a paper for our Foreign Affairs Committee on the Waste of Having too Few High Grade Men in the Department of State; a Plea for Five Assistant Secretaries for Every One Now Existing and for Provision for International Visits by Them.

Here's an ancient and mouldy precedent that needs shattering—for the coming of our country into its proper station and influence in the world.

I am sure that Mr. Balfour's visit has turned out as well as I hoped, and my hopes were high. He is one of the most interesting men that I've ever had the honour to know intimately—he and Lord Grey. Mr. Balfour is a Tory, of course; and in general I don't like Tories, yet liberal he surely is—a sort of high-toned Scotch democrat. I have studied him with increasing charm and interest. Not infrequently when I am in his office just before luncheon he says, "Come, walk over and we'll have lunch with the family." He's a bachelor. One sister lives with him. Another (Lady Rayleigh, the wife of the great chemist and Chancellor of Cambridge University) frequently visits him. Either of those ladies could rule this Empire. Then there are nieces and cousins always about—people of rare cultivation, every one of 'em. One of those girls confirmed the story that "Uncle Arthur" one day concluded that the niblick was something more than a humble necessity of a bad golfer —that it had positive virtues of its own and had suffered centuries of neglect. He, therefore, proceeded to play with the niblick only, till he proved his case and showed that it is a club entitled to the highest respect.

A fierce old Liberal fighter in Parliamentary warfare, who entered politics about the time Mr. Balfour did, told me this story the other day. "I've watched Balfour, for about forty years as a cat watches a rat. I hate his party. I hated him till I learned better, for I hated that whole Salisbury crowd. They wanted to Cecil everything. But I'll tell you, Sir, apropos of his visit to your country, that in all those years he has never spoken of the United States except with high respect and often with deep affection. I should have caught him, if he had."

I went with him to a college in London one afternoon where he delivered a lecture on Dryden, to prove that poetry can carry a certain cargo of argument but that argument can't raise the smallest flight of poetry. Dry as it sounds, it was as good a literary performance as I recall I ever heard.

At his "family" luncheon, I've found Lord Milner or Lord Lansdowne, or some literary man who had come in to find out from Lady Rayleigh how to conduct the Empire or to write a great book; and the modest old chemical Lord sits silent most of the time and now and then breaks loose to confound them all with a pat joke. This is a vigorous family, these Balfours. There's one of them (a cousin of some sort, I think, of the Foreign Secretary) who is a Lord of much of Scotland, about as tall as Ben Nevis is high—a giant of a man. One of his sons was killed early in the war and one was missing— whether dead or not he did not know. Mrs. Page expressed her hope one day to the old man that he had had news from his missing son. "No, no," said he simply, "and me lady is awearying."

We've been lucky, Mr. President, in these days of immortal horrors and of difficulties between two governments that did not know one another—uncommonly lucky, in the large chances that politics gives for grave errors, to have had two such men in the Foreign Office here as Lord Grey and Mr. Balfour. There are men who were

mentioned for this post that would have driven us mad—
or to war with them. I'm afraid I've almost outgrown
my living hero worship. There isn't worshipful material
enough lying around in the world to keep a vigorous reverence in practice. But these two gentlemen by birth
and culture have at least sometimes seemed of heroic size
to me. It has meant much to know them well. I shall
always be grateful to them, for in their quiet, forceful
way they helped me much to establish right relations
with these people—which, pray God, I hope to retain
through whatever new trials we may yet encounter. For
it will fall to us yet to loose and to free the British, and a
Briton set free is an American. That's all you can do for
a man or for a nation of men.

These Foreign Secretaries are not only men of much
greater cultivation than their Prime Ministers but of
greater moral force. But I've come to like Lloyd George
very much. He'd never deliver a lecture on Dryden, and
he doesn't even play a good game of golf; but he has what
both Lord Grey and Mr. Balfour lack—a touch of genius
—whatever that is—not the kind that takes infinite pains,
but the kind that acts as an electric light flashed in the
dark. He said to me the other day that experts have
nearly been the death of him. "The Government has
experts, experts, experts, everywhere. In any department where things are not going well, I have found boards
and committees and boards of experts. But in one department at least I've found a substitute for them. I let
twenty experts go and I put in one Man, and things
began to move at once. Do you know any real Men?
When you hear of any, won't you let me know?"

A little while ago he dined with me, and, after dinner, I
took him to a corner of the drawing room and delivered
your message to him about Ireland. "God knows, I'm try-

ing," he replied. "Tell the President that. And tell him to talk to Balfour." Presently he broke out—"Madmen, madmen—I never saw any such task," and he pointed across the room to Sir Edward Carson, his First Lord of the Admiralty—"Madmen." "But the President's right. We've got to settle it and we've got to settle it now." Carson and Jellicoe came across the room and sat down with us. "I've been telling the Ambassador, Carson, that we've got to settle the Irish question now—in spite of you."

"I'll tell you something else we've got to settle now," said Carson. "Else it'll settle us. That's the submarines. The press and public are working up a calculated and concerted attack on Jellicoe and me, and, if they get us, they'll get you. It's an attack on the Government made on the Admiralty. Prime Minister," said this Ulster pirate whose civil war didn't come off only because the big war was begun—"Prime Minister, it may be a fierce attack. Get ready for it." Well, it has been developing ever since. But I can't for the life of me guess at the possible results of an English Parliamentary attack on a government. It's like a baseball man watching a game of cricket. He can't see when the player is out or why, or what caused it. Of course, the submarine *may* torpedo Lloyd George and his Government. It looks very like it may overturn the Admiralty, as Gallipoli did. If this public finds out the whole truth, it will demand somebody's head. But I'm only a baseball man; cricket is beyond me.

But Lloyd George will outlive the war as an active force, whatever happen to him in the meantime. He's too heavily charged with electricity to stop activity. The war has ended a good many careers that seemed to have long promise. It is ending more every day. But there is only one Lloyd George, and, whatever else he lack, he doesn't lack life.

I heard all the speeches in both Houses on the resolution of appreciation of our coming into the war—Bonar Law's, Asquith's (one of the best), Dillon's, a Labour man's, and, in the Lords, Curzon's, Crewe's, the Archbishop's (who delivered in the course of his remarks a benediction on me) and Bryce's (almost the best of all). It wasn't "oratory," but it was well said and well meant. They know how badly they need help and they do mean to be as good to us as their benignant insularity will permit. They are changing. I can't describe the great difference that the war has made in them. They'll almost become docile in a little more time.

And we came in in the nick of time for them—in very truth. If we hadn't, their exchange would have gone down soon and they know it. I shall never forget the afternoon I spent with Mr. Balfour and Mr. Bonar Law on that subject. They saw blue ruin without our financial help. And now, if we can save them from submarines, those that know will know how vital our help was. Again, the submarine is the great and grave and perhaps the only danger now. If that can be scotched, I believe the whole Teutonic military structure would soon tumble. If not, the Germans may go on as long as they can feed their army, allowing their people to starve.

Of course, you know, we're on rations now—yet we suffer no inconvenience on that score. But these queer people (they *are* the most amusing and confusing and contradictory of all God's creatures, these English, whose possibilities are infinite and whose actualities, in many ways, are pitiful)—these queer people are fiercely pursuing food-economy by discussing in the newspapers whether a hen consumes more food than she produces, and whether what dogs eat contains enough human food to justify the shooting of every one in the Kingdom. That's the way we are coming down to humble fare. But nothing can quite starve a people who all live near the sea which yields fish enough near shore to feed them wastefully.

All along this South shore, where I am to-day,[1] I see the Stars and Stripes; and everywhere there is a demand for the words and music of the Battle Hymn of the Republic and the Star Spangled Banner.

This our-new-Ally business is bringing me a lot of amusing troubles. Theatres offer me boxes, universities offer me degrees, hospitals solicit visits from me, clubs offer me dinners—I'll have to get a new private secretary or two well-trained to say "No" politely, else I shall not have my work done. But all that will presently wear away as everything wears away (quickly, too) in the grim face of this bloody monster of war which is consuming men as a prairie fire consumes blades of grass. There's a family that lives around the corner from this hotel. One son is in the trenches, another is in a madhouse from shell-shock, a third coming home wounded the other day was barely rescued when a torpedo sunk a hospital ship and may lose his reason. I suppose I saw one hundred men this afternoon on a single mile of beach who had lost both legs. Through the wall from my house in London is a hospital. A young Texan has been there, whose legs are gone at the thighs and one arm at the elbow. God pity us for not having organized the world better than this! We'll do it, yet, Mr. President—*you'll* do it; and thank God for you. If we do not organize Europe

---

[1] This letter is dated London and was probably begun there. It is evident, however, that the latter part was written at Brighton, where the Ambassador was taking a brief holiday.

and make another such catastrophe impossible, life will not be worth being born into except to the few whose days happen to fall between recurring devastations of the world.

Yours sincerely,

WALTER H. PAGE.

"I hope that the English people," Colonel House wrote to Page about this time, "realize how successful Mr. Balfour's visit to America really was. There is no man they could have sent who could have done it better. He and the President got along marvellously well. The three of us dined and spent the evening together and it was delightful to see how sympathetic their minds were."

A letter from Mr. Polk also discloses the impression which Mr. Balfour made upon Washington:

From Frank L. Polk

Washington, May 25, 1917.

MY DEAR MR. PAGE:

I just want to get off a line to catch the pouch.

You probably know what a wonderful success the British Mission has been, but I do not think you can realize what a deep impression they have made on all of us. Mr. Balfour really won the affection of us all, and I do not know when I was more sorry to have a man leave than I was to have him go last night. He expressed himself as having been very much impressed with his reception and the way he was treated. He was most fair in all discussions, and I think has a better understanding of our point of view. I had the good fortune of being present at the financial and the diplomatic conferences, and I think we all felt that we were dealing with a sympathetic friend.

He and the President got on tremendously. The best evidence of that was the fact that the President went up to Congress and sat in the gallery while Mr. Balfour addressed the House. This is without precedent.

The difficult problem of course was the blacklist and bunkering agreement, but I think we are by that. The important thing now is for the British to make all the concessions possible in connection with the release of goods in Rotterdam and the release of goods in Prize Court, though the cases have not been begun. Of course I mean cases of merely suspicion rather than where there is evidence of wrongdoing.

The sending of the destroyers and troops abroad is going to do a great deal toward impressing our people with the fact that we really are in the war. I do not think it is thoroughly borne home on the majority yet what a serious road we have chosen.

With warm regards,

Yours faithfully,

FRANK L. POLK.

Mr. Polk's reference to the blacklist recalls an episode which in itself illustrates the changed character of the relations that had now been established between the American and the British governments. Mr. Balfour discussed shipping problems for the most part with Mr. Polk, under whose jurisdiction these matters fell. As one of these conferences was approaching its end Mr. Balfour slightly coughed, uttered an " er, " and gave other indications that he was about to touch upon a ticklish question.

"Before I go," he said, "there—er—is one subject I would—er—like to say something about."

Mr. Polk at once grasped what was coming.

"I know what you have in mind," said Mr. Polk in his

characteristically quick way. "You want us to apply your blacklist to neutrals."

In other words, the British hoped that the United States, now that it was in the war, would adopt against South America and other offenders those same discriminations which this country had so fiercely objected to, when it was itself a neutral.

The British statesman gave Mr. Polk one of his most winning smiles and nodded.

"Mr. Balfour," said Mr. Polk, "it took Great Britain three years to reach a point where it was prepared to violate all the laws of blockade. You will find that it will take us only two months to become as great criminals as you are!"

Mr. Balfour is usually not explosive in his manifestations of mirth, but his laughter, in reply to this statement, was almost uproarious. And the State Department was as good as its word. It immediately forgot all the elaborate "notes" and "protests" which it had been addressing to Great Britain. It became more inexorable than Great Britain had ever been in keeping foodstuffs out of neutral countries that were contiguous to Germany. Up to the time the United States entered the war, Germany, in spite of the watchful British fleet, had been obtaining large supplies from the United States through Holland, Denmark, and the Scandinavian peninsula. But the United States now immediately closed these leaks. In the main this country adopted a policy of "rationing"; that is, it would furnish the little nations adjoining Germany precisely the amount of food which they needed for their own consumption. This policy was one of the chief influences in undermining the German people and forcing their surrender. The American Government extended likewise the blacklist to South America and other countries, and, in doing so, it bettered the instruction of Great Britain herself.

Though the whole story of the blockade thus seems finally to have ended in a joke, the whole proceeding has its serious side. The United States had been posing for three years as the champion of neutral rights; the point of view of Washington had been that there was a great principle at stake. If such a principle were involved, it was certainly present in just the same degree after the United States became belligerent as in the days when we were neutrals. The lofty ideals by which the Administration had professed to be guided should have still controlled its actions; the mere fact that we, as a belligerent, could obtain certain advantages would hardly have justified a great and high-minded nation in abandoning its principles. Yet abandon them we did from the day that we declared war. We became just as remorseless in disregarding the rights of small states as Great Britain—according to our numerous blockade notes—had been. Possibly, therefore, Mr. Balfour's mirth was not merely sympathetic or humorous; it perhaps echoed his discovery that our position for three years had really been nothing but a sham; that the State Department had been forcing points in which it did not really believe, or in which it did not believe when American interests were involved. At any rate, this ending of our long argument with Great Britain was a splendid justification for Page; his contention had always been that the preservation of civilization was more important than the technicalities of the international lawyers. And now the Wilson Administration, by throwing into the waste basket all the finespun theories with which it had been embarrassing the Allied cause since August 4, 1914, accepted—and accepted joyously—his point of view.

II

One of the first things which Mr. Balfour did, on his arrival in Washington, was personally to explain to President Wilson about the so-called "secret treaties." The "secret treaty" that especially preyed upon Mr. Wilson's mind, and which led to a famous episode at the Versailles Conference, was that which had been made with Italy in 1915, as consideration for Italy's participation in the war. Mr. Balfour, in telling the President of these territorial arrangements with Italy, naturally did not criticise his ally, but it was evident that he regarded the matter as something about which the United States should be informed.

"This is the sort of thing you have to do when you are engaged in a war," he explained, and then he gave Mr. Wilson the details.

Probably the most important information which Mr. Balfour and the French and Italian Commissions brought to Washington was the desperate situation of the Allied cause. On that point not one of the visiting statesmen or military and naval advisers made the slightest attempt at concealment. Mr. Balfour emphasized the seriousness of the crisis in one of his earliest talks with Mr. McAdoo, Secretary of the Treasury. The British statesman was especially interested in the financial situation and he therefore took up this matter at an early date with the Treasury Department.

"Mr. Balfour," said Mr. McAdoo, "before we make any plans of financial assistance it is absolutely necessary that we know precisely where we stand. The all-important thing is the question as to how long the war is likely to last. If it is only to last a few months, it is evident that we need to make very different arrangements than if it is to last several years. Just what must we make provision for? Let us assume that the United States goes in with all its men and resources—that we dedicate all our money, our manufacturing plants, our army, our navy, everything we have got, to bringing the war to an end. How long will it take?"

Mr. Balfour replied that it would be necessary to consult his naval and military advisers before he answered that question. He said that he would return in a day or two and make an explicit statement. He did so and his answer was this: Under these circumstances—that the United States should make war to the full limit of its power, in men and resources—the war could not be ended until the summer or the autumn of 1919. Mr. McAdoo put the same question in the same form to the French and Italian Missions and obtained precisely the same answer.

Page's papers show that Mr. Balfour, in the early stages of American participation, regarded the financial situation as the thing which chiefly threatened the success of the Allied cause. So much greater emphasis has been laid upon the submarine warfare that this may at first seem rather a misreading of Great Britain's peril. Yet the fact is that the high rate of exchange and the depredatory U-boat represented almost identically the same danger. The prospect that so darkened the horizon in the spring of 1917 was the possible isolation of Great Britain. England's weakness, as always, consisted in the fact that she was an island, that she could not feed herself with her own resources and that she had only about six weeks' supply of food ahead of her at any one time. If Germany could cut the lines of communication and so prevent essential supplies from reaching British ports, the population of Great Britain could be starved into surrender in a very brief time, France would be over-whelmed, and the triumph of the Prussian cause would be complete. That the success of the German submarine campaign would accomplish this result was a fact that the popular mind readily grasped. What it did not so clearly see, however, was that the financial collapse of Great Britain would cut these lines of communication quite as effectually as the submarine itself. The British were practically dependent for their existence upon the food brought from the United States, just as the Allied armies were largely dependent upon the steel which came from the great industrial plants of this country. If Great Britain could not find the money with which to purchase these supplies, it is quite apparent that they could not be shipped. The collapse of British credit therefore would have produced the isolation of the British Isles and led to a British surrender, just as effectively as would the success of the German submarine campaign.

As soon as Bernstorff was sent home, therefore, and the participation of this country in the war became extremely probable, Mr. Balfour took up the financial question with Page.

Cablegram to the President

March 5, 1917.

The inquiries which I have made here about financial conditions disclose an international situation which is most alarming to the financial and industrial outlook of the United States. England has not only to pay her own war bills, but is obliged to finance her Allies as well. Up to the present time she has done these tasks out of her own capital. But she cannot continue her present exten-sive purchases in the United States without shipping gold as payment for them, and there are two reasons why she cannot make large shipments of gold. In the first place, both England and France must keep the larger part of the gold they have to maintain issues of their paper at par; and, in the second place, the German U-boat has made the shipping of gold a dangerous procedure even if they had it to ship. There is therefore a pressing danger that the Franco-American and Anglo-American exchange will be greatly disturbed; the inevitable consequence will be that orders by all the Allied Governments will be reduced to the lowest possible amount and that trans-Atlantic trade will practically come to an end. The result of such a stoppage will be a panic in the United States. The world will therefore be divided into two hemispheres, one of them, our own, will have the gold and the commodities: the other, Great Britain and Europe, will need these commodities, but it will have no money with which to pay for them. Moreover, it will have practically no commodities of its own to exchange for them. The financial and commercial result will be almost as bad for the United States as for Europe. We shall soon reach this condition unless we take quick action to prevent it. Great Britain and France must have a credit in the United States which will be large enough to prevent the collapse of world trade and the whole financial structure of Europe.

If the United States declare war against Germany, the greatest help we could give Great Britain and its Allies would be such a credit. If we should adopt this policy, an excellent plan would be for our Government to make a large investment in a Franco-British loan. Another plan would be to guarantee such a loan. A great advantage would be that all the money would be kept in the United States. We could keep on with our trade and increase it, till the war ends, and after the war Europe would purchase food and an enormous supply of materials with which to reëquip her peace industries. We should thus reap the profit of an uninterrupted and perhaps an enlarging trade over a number of years and we should hold their securities in payment.

On the other hand, if we keep nearly all the gold and Europe cannot pay for reëstablishing its economic life, there may be a world-wide panic for an indefinite period.

Of course we cannot extend such a credit unless we go to war with Germany. But is there no way in which our Government might immediately and indirectly help the establishment in the United States of a large Franco-British credit without violating armed neutrality? I do not know enough about our own reserve bank law to form an opinion. But these banks would avert such a danger if they were able to establish such a credit. Danger for us is more real and imminent, I think, than the public on either side the Atlantic understands. If it be not averted before its manifestations become apparent, it will then be too late to save the day.

The pressure of this approaching crisis, I am certain, has gone beyond the ability of the Morgan financial agency for the British and French governments. The financial necessities of the Allies are too great and urgent for any private agency to handle, for every such agency has to encounter business rivalries and sectional antagonisms.

It is not improbable that the only way of maintaining our present preëminent trade position and averting a panic is by declaring war on Germany. The submarine has added the last item to the danger of a financial world crash. There is now an uncertainty about our being drawn into the war; no more considerable credits can be privately placed in the United States. In the meantime a collapse may come.

PAGE.

Urgent as this message was, it really understated the desperate condition of British and Allied finances. That the warring powers were extremely pressed for money has long been known; but Page's papers reveal for the first time the fact that they were facing the prospect of bankruptcy itself. "The whole Allied combination on this side the ocean are very much nearer the end of their financial resources," he wrote in July, "than anybody has guessed or imagined. We only can save them. . . . The submarines are steadily winning the war. Pershing and his army have bucked up the French for the moment. But for his coming there was more or less danger of a revolution in Paris and of serious defection in the army. Everybody here fears that the French will fail before another winter of the trenches. Yet—the Germans must be still worse off."

The matter that was chiefly pressing at the time of the Balfour visit was the fact that the British balances in the New York banks were in a serious condition. It should always be remembered, however, that Great Britain was financing not only herself, but her Allies, and that the difficult condition in which she now found herself was caused by the not too considerate demands of the nations with which she was allied in the war. Thus by April 6, 1917, Great Britain had overdrawn her account with J. P. Morgan to the extent of $400,000,000 and had no cash available with which to meet this overdraft. This obligation had been incurred in the purchase of supplies, both for Great Britain and the allied governments; and securities, largely British owned stocks and bonds, had been deposited to protect the bankers. The money was now coming due; if the obligations were not met, the credit of Great Britain in this country would reach the vanishing point. Though at first there was a slight misunderstanding about this matter, the American Government finally paid this over-draft out of the proceeds of the first Liberty Loan. This act saved the credit of the allied countries; it was, of course, only the beginning of the financial support that America brought to the allied cause; the advances that were afterward furnished from the American Treasury made possible the purchases of food and supplies in enormous quantities. The first danger that threatened, the isolation and starvation of Great Britain, was therefore overcome. It was the joint product of Page's work in London and that of the Balfour Commission in the United States.

III

Until these financial arrangements had been made there was no certainty that the supplies which were so essential to victory would ever leave the United States; this obstruction at the source had now been removed. But the greater difficulty still remained. The German submarines were lying off the waters south and west of Ireland ready to sink the supply ships as soon as they entered the prohibited zone. Mr. Balfour and his associates were working also on this problem in Washington; and, at the same time, Page and Admiral Sims and the British Admiralty were bending all their energies in London to obtain immediate coöperation.

A remark which Mr. Balfour afterward made to Admiral Sims shows the frightful nature of the problem which was confronting Great Britain at that time.

"That was a terrible week we spent at sea in that voyage to the United States," Mr. Balfour said. "We knew that the German submarine campaign was succeeding. Their submarines were destroying our shipping and we

had no means of preventing it.   I could not help thinking
that we were facing the defeat of Great Britain."

Page's papers show that as early as February 25th he
understood in a general way the disheartening proportions of the German success.   "It is a momentous crisis,"
he wrote at that time.   "The submarines are destroying
shipping at an appalling rate."   Yet it was not until
Admiral Sims arrived in London, on April 9th, that the
Ambassador learned all the details.   In sending the Admiral to England the Navy Department had acted on an
earnest recommendation from Page.   The fact that the
American Navy was inadequately represented in the
British capital had long been a matter of embarrassment
to him.   The ability and personal qualifications of our
attachés had been unquestioned; but none of them during
the war had been men of high rank, and this in itself
proved to be a constant impediment to their success.
While America was represented by Commanders, Japan,
Italy, and France had all sent Admirals to London.
Page's repeated requests for an American Admiral had so
far met with no response, but the probability that this
country would become involved in the war now gave new
point to his representations.   In the latter part of March,
Page renewed his request in still more urgent form, and
this time the President and the Navy Department responded favourably.   The result was that, on April 9th,
three days after the American declaration of war, Admiral Sims and his flag-lieutenant, Commander Babcock,
presented themselves at the American Embassy.   There
was little in the appearance of these men to suggest a violent naval demonstration against Germany.   Both wore
civilian dress, their instructions having commanded them
not to bring uniforms; both were travelling under assumed
names, and both had no more definite orders than to in-

vestigate the naval situation and cable the results to Washington. In spite of these attempts at secrecy, the British had learned that Admiral Sims was on the way; they rejoiced not only in this fact, but in the fact that Sims had been chosen, for there was no American naval officer whose professional reputation stood so high in the British Navy or who was so personally acceptable to British officialdom and the British public. The Admiralty therefore met Admiral Sims at Liverpool, brought him to London in a special train, and, a few hours after his arrival, gave him the innermost secrets on the submarine situation—secrets which were so dangerous that not all the members of the British Cabinet had been let into them.

Page welcomed Admiral Sims with a cordiality which that experienced sea veteran still gratefully remembers. He at once turned over to him two rooms in the Embassy. "You can have everything we've got," the Ambassador said. "If necessary to give you room, we'll turn the whole Embassy force out into the street." The two men had not previously met, but in an instant they became close friends. A common sympathy and a common enthusiasm were greatly needed at that crisis. As soon as Admiral Sims had finished his interview with Admiral Jellicoe, he immediately sought out the Ambassador and laid all the facts before him. Germany was winning the war. Great Britain had only six weeks' food supply on hand, and the submarines were sinking the ships at a rate which, unless the depredations should be checked, meant an early and unconditional surrender of the British Empire. Only the help of the United States could prevent this calamity.

Page, of course, was aghast: the facts and figures Admiral Sims gave him disclosed a situation which was even more desperate than he had imagined. He advised the Admiral to cable the whole story immediately to Washington. Admiral Sims at first had some difficulty in obtaining the Admiralty's consent to doing this, and the reason was the one with which Page had long been familiar —the fear, altogether too justified, that the news would "leak" out of Washington. Of course there was no suspicion in British naval circles of the good faith of the Washington officials, but important facts had been sent so many times under the seal of the strictest secrecy and had then found their way into the newspapers that there was a deep distrust of American discretion. Certainly no greater damage could have been done the allied cause at that time than to have the Germans learn how successfully their submarine campaign was progressing. The question was referred to the Imperial War Council and its consent obtained. The report, however, was sent to the Navy Department in the British naval code, and decoded in the British Embassy in Washington.

Admiral Sims's message gave all the facts about the submarine situation, and concluded with the recommendation that the United States should assemble all floating craft that could be used in the anti-submarine warfare, destroyers, tugs, yachts, light cruisers, and similar vessels, and send them immediately to Queenstown, where they would do valuable service in convoying merchant vessels and destroying the U-boats. At that time the American Navy had between fifty and sixty destroyers that were patrolling the American coast; these could have been despatched, almost immediately, to the scene of operations; but, in response to this request, the Department sent six to Queentown.

The next few months were very unhappy ones for Admiral Sims. He was the representative in London of one of the world's greatest naval powers, participating in the greatest war that had ever enlisted its energies, yet his constant appeals for warships elicited the most inadequate response, his well-reasoned recommendations for meeting the crisis were frequently unanswered and at other times were met with counter-proposals so childish that they seemed almost to have originated in the brains of newspaper amateurs, and his urgent pictures of a civilization rapidly going to wreck were apparently looked upon with suspicion as the utterances of a man who had been completely led astray by British guile. To give a fair idea of Washington's neglect during this period it is only necessary to point out that, for four months, Admiral Sims occupied the two rooms in the Embassy directly above Page's, with Commander Babcock as his only aid. Sims's repeated requests to Secretary Daniels for an additional staff went unheeded. Had it not been for the Admiral's constant daily association with Page and the comfort and encouragement which the Ambassador gave him, this experience would have been almost unbearable. In the latter part of April, the Admiral's appeals to Washington having apparently fallen on deaf ears, he asked Page to second his efforts. The Admiral and Commander Babcock wrote another message, and drove in a motor car to Brighton, where Page was taking a little rest. The Admiral did not know just how strong a statement the Ambassador would care to sponsor, and so he did not make this representation as emphatic as the judgment of both men would have preferred.

The Admiral handed Page the paper, saying that he had prepared it with the hope that the Ambassador would sign it and send it directly to President Wilson.

"It is quite apparent," Admiral Sims said, "that the Department doesn't believe what I have been saying. Or they don't believe what the British are saying. They think that England is exaggerating the peril for reasons of its own. They think I am hopelessly pro-British and that I am being used. But if you'll take it up directly with the President, then they may be convinced."

Page put on his spectacles, took the paper, and read it through. Then, looking over the rim of his glasses in his characteristic way, he leaned toward Admiral Sims and said:

"Admiral, it isn't half strong enough! I think I can write a better despatch than that, myself! At least let me try."

He immediately took a pen and paper and in a few minutes he had written his own version which he gave the Admiral to read. The latter was delighted with it and in a brief time it was on its way to Washington.

From: Ambassador Page.
To: Secretary of State.
Sent: 27 April, 1917.

Very confidential for Secretary and President

There is reason for the greatest alarm about the issue of the war caused by the increasing success of the German submarines. I have it from official sources that during the week ending 22nd April, 88 ships of 237,000 tons, allied and neutral, were lost. The number of vessels unsuccessfully attacked indicated a great increase in the number of submarines in action.

This means practically a million tons lost every month till the shorter days of autumn come. By that time the sea will be about clear of shipping. Most of the ships are sunk to the westward and southward of Ireland. The British have in that area every available anti-submarine craft, but their force is so insufficient that they hardly discourage the submarines.

The British transport of troops and supplies is already strained to the utmost, and the maintenance of the armies in the field is threatened.   There is food enough here to last the civil population only not more than six weeks or two months.

Whatever help the United States may render at any time in the future, or in any theatre of the war, our help is now more seriously needed in this submarine area for the sake of all the Allies than it can ever be needed again, or anywhere else.

After talking over this critical situation with the Prime Minister and other members of the Government, I cannot refrain from most strongly recommending the immediate sending over of every destroyer and all other craft that can be of anti-submarine use.   This seems to me the sharpest crisis of the war, and the most dangerous situation for the Allies that has arisen or could arise.

If enough submarines can be destroyed in the next two or three months, the war will be won, and if we can contribute effective help immediately, it will be won directly by our aid.   I cannot exaggerate the pressing and increasing danger of this situation.   Thirty or more destroyers and other similar craft sent by us immediately would very likely be decisive.

There is no time to be lost.

(Signed) PAGE.

This cablegram had a certain effect.   The reply came from Washington that "eventually" thirty-six destroyers would be sent.

Page's letters of this period are full of the same subject.

To the President

London, May 4, 1917.

DEAR MR. PRESIDENT:

The submarines have become a very grave danger. The loss of British and allied tonnage increases with the longer and brighter days—as I telegraphed you, 237,000 tons last week; and the worst of it is, the British are not destroying them. The Admiralty publishes a weekly report which, though true, is not the whole truth. It is known in official circles here that the Germans are turning out at least two a week—some say three; and the British are not destroying them as fast as new ones are turned out. If merely the present situation continue, the war will pretty soon become a contest of endurance under hunger, with an increasing proportion of starvation. Germany is yet much the worse off, but it will be easily possible for Great Britain to suffer to the danger point next winter or earlier unless some decided change be wrought in this situation.

The greatest help, I hope, can come from us—our destroyers and similar armed craft—provided we can send enough of them quickly. The area to be watched is so big that many submarine hunters are needed. Early in the war the submarines worked near shore. There are very many more of them now and their range is one hundred miles, or even two hundred, at sea.

The public is becoming very restive with its half-information, and it is more and more loudly demanding all the facts. There are already angry threats to change the personnel of the Admiralty; there is even talk of turning out the Government. "We must have results, we must have results." I hear confidentially that Jellicoe has threatened to resign unless the Salonica expedition is brought back: to feed and equip that force requires too many ships.

And there are other troubles impending. Norway has lost so many of her ships that she dare not send what are left to sea. Unarmed they'll all perish. If she arm them, Germany will declare war against her. There is a plan on foot for the British to charter these Norwegian ships and to arm them, taking the risk of German war against Norway. If war come (as it is expected) England must then defend Norway the best she can. And *then England may ask for our big ships to help in these waters.* All this is yet in the future, but possibly not far in the future.

For the present the only anti-submarine help is the help we may be able to give to patrol the wide area off Ireland. If we had one hundred destroyers to send, the job there could, I am told, be quickly done. A third of that number will help mightily. At the present rate of destruction more than four million tons will be sunk before the summer is gone.

Such is this dire submarine danger. The English thought that they controlled the sea; the Germans, that they were invincible on land. Each side is losing where it thought itself strongest.

Admiral Sims is of the greatest help imaginable. Of course, I gave him an office in one of our Embassy buildings, and the Admiralty has given him an office also with them. He spends much of his time there, and they have opened all doors and all desks and drawers to him. He strikes me (and the English so regard him) as a man of admirable judgment—unexcitable and indefatigable. I hope we'll soon send a general over, to whom the War Department will act similarly. Hoover, too, must have a good man here as, I dare say, he has already made known. These will cover the Navy, the Army, Food, and Shipping.

Perhaps a Censor and an Intelligence (Secret Service) group ought to come. I mean these for permanent—at least indefinite—service. Exchange visits by a Congressional Committee (such as the French and British make) and by high official persons such as members of your Cabinet (such also as the French and British make)— you will have got ideas about these from Mr. Balfour.

W. H. P.

In the latter part of June Admiral Sims went to Queenstown. Admiral Bayly, who directed the operation of the anti-submarine forces there, had gone away for a brief rest, and Admiral Sims had taken over the command of both the British and American forces at that point. This experience gave Admiral Sims a first-hand picture of a really deplorable situation. The crisis was so desperate that he made another appeal to Page.

From Admiral William S. Sims

Admiralty House, Queenstown,
June 25, 1917.

MY DEAR MR. PAGE:

I enclose herewith a letter on the submarine situation.[1]

I think I have made it plain therein that the Allies are losing the war; that it will be already lost when the loss of shipping reaches the point where fully adequate supplies cannot be maintained on the various battle fronts.

I cannot understand why our Government should hesitate to send the necessary anti-submarine craft to this side.

There are at least seventeen more destroyers employed on our Atlantic coast, *where there is no war*, not to mention numerous other very useful anti-submarine craft, including sea-going tugs, etc.

---

[1] This was a long document describing conditions in great detail.

Can you not do something to bring our Government to an understanding of how very serious the situation is?

Would it not be well to send another telegram to Mr. Lansing and the President, and also send them the enclosed correspondence?

I am sending this by mail because I may be somewhat delayed in returning to London.

Very sincerely yours,

WM. S. SIMS.

Page immediately acted on this suggestion.

Most confidential for the Secretary of State and President only

Sims sends me by special messenger from Queenstown the most alarming reports of the submarine situation which are confirmed by the Admiralty here. He says that the war will be won or lost in this submarine zone within a few months. Time is of the essence of the problem, and anti-submarine craft which cannot be assembled in the submarine zone almost immediately may come too late. There is, therefore, a possibility that this war may become a war between Germany and the United States alone. Help is far more urgently and quickly needed in this submarine zone than anywhere else in the whole war area.

PAGE.

The United States had now been in the war for three months and only twenty-eight of the sixty destroyers which were available had been sent into the field. Yet this latest message of Page produced no effect, and, when Admiral Sims returned from Queenstown, the two men, almost in despair, consulted as to the step which they should take next. What was the matter? Was it that

Washington did not care to get into the naval war with its full strength, or was it that it simply refused to believe the representations of its Admiral and its Ambassador? Admiral Sims and Page went over the whole situation and came to the conclusion that Washington regarded them both as so pro-British that their reports were subject to suspicion. Just as Page had found that the State Department, and its "trade advisers," had believed that the British were using the blockade as a means of destroying American trade for the benefit of Britain, so now he believed that Mr. Daniels and Admiral Benson, the Chief of Naval Operations, evidently thought that Great Britain was attempting to lure American warships into European waters, to undergo the risk of protecting British commerce, while British warships were kept safely in harbour. Page suggested that there was now only one thing left to do, and that was to request the British Government itself to make a statement to President Wilson that would substantiate his own messages.

"Whatever else they think of the British in Washington," he said, "they know one thing—and that is that a British statesman like Mr. Balfour will not lie."

Mr. Balfour by this time had returned from America. The fact that he had established these splendid personal relations with Mr. Wilson, and that he had impressed the American public so deeply with his sincerity and fine purpose, made him especially valuable for this particular appeal. Page and Admiral Sims therefore went to the Foreign Office and laid all the facts before him. Their own statements, Page informed the Foreign Secretary, were evidently regarded as hysterical and biased by an unreasoning friendliness to Great Britain. If Mr. Balfour would say the same things over his own signature, then they would not be disbelieved.

Mr. Balfour gladly consented. He called in Admiral Jellicoe and asked him to draft a despatch, so that all the technical facts would be completely accurate. He also consulted with Sir Edward Carson, the First Lord of the Admiralty. Then Mr. Balfour put the document in its final shape and signed it. It was as follows:

Mr. Balfour to the President

June 30, 1917.

The forces at present at the disposal of the British Admiralty are not adequate to protect shipping from submarine attack in the danger zone round the British Islands. Consequently shipping is being sunk at a greater rate than it can be replaced by new tonnage of British origin.

The time will come when, if the present rate of loss continues, the available shipping, apart from American contribution, will be insufficient to bring to this country sufficient foodstuffs and other essentials, including oil fuel. The situation in regard to our Allies, France, and Italy, is much the same.

Consequently, it is absolutely necessary to add to our forces as a first step, pending the adoption or completion of measures which will, it is hoped, eventually lead to the destruction of enemy submarines at a rate sufficient to ensure safety of our sea communications.

The United States is the only allied country in a position to help. The pressing need is for armed small craft of every kind available in the area where commerce concentrates near the British and French coasts. Destroyers, submarines, gunboats, yachts, trawlers, and tugs would all give invaluable help, and if sent in sufficient numbers would undoubtedly save a situation which is manifestly critical. But they are required now and in as great numbers as possible. There is no time for delay.

The present method of submarine attack is almost entirely by torpedo with the submarine submerged. The gun defense of merchant ships keeps the submarine below the surface but does no more; offensively against a submerged submarine it is useless, and the large majority of the ships torpedoed never see the attacking submarine until the torpedo has hit the ship.[1]

The present remedy is, therefore, to prevent the submarine from using its periscope for fear of attack by bomb or ram from small craft, and this method of defense for the shipping and offense against the submarine requires small craft in very large numbers.

The introduction of the convoy system, provided there are sufficient destroyers to form an adequate screen to the convoy, will, it is hoped, minimize losses when it is working, and the provision of new offensive measures is progressing; but for the next few months there is only one safeguard, viz., the immediate addition to patrols of every small vessel that can possibly be sent to European waters.

Page, moreover, kept up his own appeal:

Cablegram to the President

July 5th.

Strictly confidential to the President and the Secretary

The British Cabinet is engaging in a threatening controversy about the attitude which they should take toward the submarine peril. There is a faction in the Admiralty which possesses the indisputable facts and which takes

---

[1]The Navy Department had taken the position that arming merchantmen was the best protection against the submarine. This statement was intended to refute this belief.

a very disheartening view of the situation. This group insists that the Cabinet should make a confession at least to us of the full extent of the danger and that it should give more information to the public. The public does not feel great alarm simply because it has been kept in too great ignorance. But the political faction is so far the stronger. It attempts to minimize the facts, and, probably for political reasons, it refuses to give these discouraging facts wide publicity. The politicians urge that it is necessary to conceal the full facts from the Germans. They also see great danger in throwing the public into a panic.

Mr. Lloyd George is always optimistic and he is too much inclined to yield his judgment to political motives. In his recent address in Glasgow he gave the public a comforting impression of the situation. But the facts do not warrant the impression which he gave.

This dispute among the political factions is most unfortunate and it may cause an explosion of public feeling at any time. Changes in the Cabinet may come in consequence. If the British public knew all the facts or if the American people knew them, the present British Government would probably fall. It is therefore not only the submarine situation which is full of danger. The political situation is in a dangerous state also.

PAGE.

To Arthur W. Page

Wilsford Manor, Salisbury,
July 8, 1917.

DEAR ARTHUR:

Since admirals and generals began to come from home, they and the war have taken my time so completely, day and night, that I haven't lately written you many things that I should like to tell you. I'll try here—a house of a friend of ours where the only other guest besides your mother and me is Edward Grey. This is the first time I've seen him since he left office. Let me take certain big subjects in order and come to smaller things later:

1. The German submarines are succeeding to a degree that the public knows nothing about. These two things are true: (a) The Germans are building submarines faster than the English sink them. In this way, therefore, they are steadily gaining. (b) The submarines are sinking freight ships faster than freight ships are being built by the whole world. In this way, too, then, the Germans are succeeding. Now if this goes on long enough, the Allies' game is up. For instance, they have lately sunk so many fuel oil ships, that this country may very soon be in a perilous condition—even the Grand Fleet may not have enough fuel. Of course the chance is that oil ships will not continue to fall victims to the U-boats and we shall get enough through to replenish the stock. But this illustrates the danger, and it is a very grave danger.

The best remedy so far worked out is the destroyer. The submarines avoid destroyers and they sink very, very few ships that are convoyed. If we had destroyers enough to patrol the whole approach (for, say, 250 miles) to England, the safety of the sea would be very greatly increased; and if we had enough to patrol and to convoy every ship going and coming, the damage would be reduced to a minimum. The Admiral and I are trying our best to get our Government to send over 500 improvised destroyers—yachts, ocean-going tugs—any kind of swift craft that can be armed. Five hundred such little boats might end the war in a few months; for the Germans are keeping the spirit of their people and of their army up by their submarine success. If that success were stopped they'd have no other cry half so effective. If they could see this in Washington as we see it, they'd do it and do it not halfway but with a vengeance. If they don't do it, the war may be indefinitely prolonged and a wholly satisfactory peace may never be made. The submarine is the most formidable thing the war has produced—by far —and it gives the German the only earthly chance he has to win. And he *may* substantially win by it yet. That's what the British conceal. In fact, half of them do not see it or believe it. But nothing is truer, or plainer. One hundred thousand submarine chasers next year may be worth far less than 500 would be worth now, for next year see how few ships may be left! The mere arming of ships is not enough. Nearly all that are sunk are armed. The submarine now carries a little periscope and a big one, each painted the colour of the sea. You can't see a little periscope except in an ocean as smooth as glass. It isn't bigger than a coffee cup. The submarine thus sinks its victims without ever emerging or ever being seen. As things now stand, the Germans are winning the war, and they are winning it on the sea; that's the queer and the most discouraging fact. My own opinion is that all the facts ought to be published to all the world. Let the Germans get all the joy they can out of the confession. No matter, if the Government and the people of the United States knew all the facts, we'd have 1,000 improvised destroyers (yachts, tugs, etc., etc.) armed and over here very quickly. Then the tide would turn.

Then there'd be nothing to fear in the long run. For the military authorities all agree that the German Army is inferior to the British and French and will be whipped. That may take a long time yet; but of the result nobody who knows seems to have any doubt—unless the French get tired and stop. They have periods of great war weariness and there is real danger that they may quit and make a separate peace. General Pershing's presence has made the situation safe for the moment. But in a little while something else spectacular and hopeful may be required to keep them in line.

Such is an accurate picture of the war as it is now, and it is a dangerous situation.

2. The next grave danger is financial. The European Allies have so bled the English for money that the English would by this time probably have been on a paper money basis (and of course all the Allies as well) if we had not come to their financial aid. And we've got to keep our financial aid going to them to prevent this disastrous result. That wouldn't at once end the war, if they had all abandoned specie payments; but it would be a frightfully severe blow and it might later bring defeat. That is a real danger. And the Government at Washington, I fear, does not know the full extent of the danger. They think that the English are disposed to lie down on them. They don't realize the cost of the war. This Government has bared all this vast skeleton to me; but I fear that Washington imagines that part of it is a deliberate scare. It's a very real danger.

Now, certain detached items:

Sims is the idol of the British Admiralty and he is doing his job just as well as any man could with the tools and the chance that he has. He has made the very best of the chance and he has completely won the confidence and admiration of this side of the world.

Pershing made an admirable impression here, and in France he has simply set them wild with joy. His coming and his little army have been worth what a real army will be worth later. It is well he came to keep the French in line.

The army of doctors and nurses have had a similar effect.

Even the New England saw-mill units have caused a furor of enthusiasm. They came with absolute Yankee completeness of organization—with duplicate parts of all their machinery, tents, cooks, pots, and pans, and everything ship-shape. The only question they asked was: "Say, where the hell are them trees you want sawed up?" That's the way to do a job! Yankee stock is made high here by such things as that.

We're getting a crowd of Yankee lecturers on the United States to go up and down this Kingdom. There's the greatest imaginable curiosity to hear about the United States in all kinds of society from munition workers to universities. I got the British Government to write Buttrick[1] to come as its guest, and the Rockefeller Boards rose to the occasion. He'll probably be along presently. If he hasn't already sailed when you get this, see him and tell him to make arrangements to have pictures sent over to him to illustrate his lectures. Who else could come to do this sort of a job?

I am myself busier than I have ever been. The kind of work the Embassy now has to do is very different from the work of the days of neutrality. It continues to increase—especially the work that I have to do myself. But it's all pleasant now. We are trying to help and no longer to hinder. To save my life I don't see how the Washington crowd can look at themselves in a mirror and keep their faces straight. Yesterday they were bent on sending everything into European neutral states. The foundations of civilization would give way if neutral trade were interfered with. Now, nothing must go in except on a ration basis. Yesterday it must be a peace without victory. Now it must be a complete victory, every man

---

[1] Dr. Wallace Buttrick, President of the General Education Board, who was sent at this time to deliver lectures throughout Great Britain on the United States.

and every dollar thrown in, else no peace is worth having. I don't complain. I only rejoice. But I'm glad that kind of a rapid change is not a part of my record. The German was the same beast yesterday that he is to-day; and it makes a simple-minded, straight-minded man like me wonder which attitude was the (or is the) attitude of real conviction. But this doesn't bother me now as a real problem—only as a speculation. What we call History will, I presume, in time work this out. But History is often a kind of lie. But never mind that. The only duty of mankind now is to win. Other things can wait.

I walked over to Stonehenge and back (about six miles) with Lord Grey (Sir Edward, you know) and we, like everybody else, fell to talking about when the war may end. We know as well as anybody and no better than anybody else. I have very different moods about it—no convictions. It seems to me to depend, as things now are, more on the submarines than on anything else. If we could effectually discourage them so that the Germans would have to withdraw them and could no more keep up the spirit of their people by stories of the imminent starvation of England, I have a feeling that the hunger and the war weariness of the German people would lead them to force an end. But, the more they are called on to suffer the more patriotic do they think themselves and they *may* go on till they drop dead in their tracks.

What I am really afraid of is that the Germans may, before winter, offer all that the Western Allies most want —the restoration of Belgium and France, the return of Alsace-Lorraine, etc., in the West and the surrender of the Colonies—provided Austria is not dismembered. That would virtually leave them the chance to work out their Middle Europe scheme and ultimately there'd probably have to be another war over that question. That's the real eventuality to be feared—a German defeat in the West but a German victory in the Southeast. Everybody in Europe is so war weary that such a plan *may* succeed.

On the other hand, what Hoover and Northcliffe fear may come true—that the Germans are going to keep up the struggle for years—till their armies are practically obliterated, as Lee's army was. If the Allies were actually to kill (not merely wound, but actually kill) 5,000 Germans a day for 300 days a year, it would take about four years to obliterate the whole German Army. There is the bare possibility, therefore, of a long struggle yet. But I can't believe it. My dominant mood these days is an end within a very few months after the submarines are knocked out. Send over, therefore, 1,000 improvised destroyers the next two months, and I'll promise peace by Christmas. Otherwise I can make no promises. That's all that Lord Grey and I know, and surely we are two wise men. What, therefore, is the use in writing any more about this?

The chief necessity that grows upon me is that all the facts must be brought out that show the kinship in blood and ideals of the two great English-speaking nations. We were actually coming to believe ourselves that we were part German and Slovene and Pole and What-not, instead of essentially being Scotch and English. Hence the unspeakable impudence of your German who spoke of eliminating the Anglo-Saxon element from American life! The truth should be forcibly and convincingly told and repeated to the end of the chapter, and our national life should proceed on its natural historic lines, with its proper historic outlook and background. We can do something to bring this about.

Affectionately,

W. H. P.

The labour of getting the American Navy into the war was evidently at first a difficult one, but the determination of Page and Admiral Sims triumphed, and, by August and September, our energies were fully engaged. And the American Navy made a record that will stand everlastingly to its glory. Without its help the German submarines could never have been overcome.

CHAPTER XXIII

PAGE—THE MAN

THE entrance of America into the war, followed by the successful promotion of the Balfour visit, brought a period of quiet into Page's life. These events represented for him a personal triumph; there were many things still to be done, it is true, and Page, as always, was active in advancing the interests that were nearest his heart; yet the mighty relief that followed the American declaration was the kind that one experiences after accomplishing the greatest task of a lifetime. Page's letters have contained many references to the sense of moral isolation which his country's policy had forced upon him; he probably exaggerated his feeling that there was a tendency to avoid him; this was merely a reflection of his own inclination to keep away from all but the official people. He now had more leisure and certainly more interest in cultivating the friends that he had made in Great Britain. For the fact is that, during all these engrossing years, Page had been more than an Ambassador; by the time the United States entered the war he had attained an assured personal position in the life of the British capital. He had long since demonstrated his qualifications for a post, which, in the distinction of the men who have occupied it, has few parallels in diplomacy. The scholarly Lowell, the courtly Bayard, the companionable Hay, the ever-humorous Choate, had set a standard for American Ambassadors which had made the place a difficult one for their successors. Though Page had characteristics in common with all these men, his personality had its own distinctive tang; and it was something new to the political and social life of London. And the British capital, which is extremely exacting and even merciless in its demands upon its important personages, had found it vastly entertaining. "I didn't know there could be anything so American as Page except Mark Twain," a British literary man once remarked; and it was probably this strong American quality, this directness and even breeziness of speech and of method, this absence of affectation, this almost openly expressed contempt for finesse and even for tradition, combined with those other traits which we like to think of as American—an upright purpose, a desire to serve not only his own country but mankind—which made the British public look upon Page as one of the most attractive and useful figures in a war-torn Europe.

There was a certain ruggedness in Page's exterior which the British regarded as distinctly in keeping with this American flavour. The Ambassador was not a handsome man. To one who had heard much of the liveliness of his conversation and presence a first impression was likely to be disappointing. His figure at this time was tall, gaunt, and lean—and he steadily lost weight during his service in England; his head was finely shaped—it was large, with a high forehead, his thin gray hair rather increasing its intellectual aspect; and his big frank brown eyes reflected that keen zest for life, that unsleeping interest in everything about him, that ever-working intelligence and sympathy which were the man's predominant traits. But a very large nose at first rather lessened the pleasing effects of his other features, and a rather weather-beaten, corrugated face gave a preliminary suggestion of roughness. Yet Page had only to begin talking and the impression immediately changed. "He puts his mind to yours," Dr. Johnson said, describing the sympathetic qualities of a friend, and the same was true of Page. Half a dozen sentences, spoken in his quick, soft, and ingratiating accents, accompanied by the most genial smile, at once converted the listener into a friend. Few men have ever lived who more quickly responded to this human relationship. The Ambassador, at the simple approach of a human being, became as a man transformed. Tired though he might be, low in spirits as he not infrequently was, the press of a human hand at once changed him into an animated and radiating companion. This responsiveness deceived all his friends in the days of his last illness. His intimates who dropped in to see Page invariably went away much encouraged and spread optimistic reports about his progress. A few minutes' conversation with Page would deceive even his physicians. The explanation was a simple one: the human presence had an electric effect upon him, and it is a revealing sidelight on Page's character that almost any man or woman could produce this result. As an editor, the readiness with which he would listen to suggestions from the humblest source was a constant astonishment to his associates. The office boy had as accessible an approach to Page as had his partners. He never treated an idea, even a grotesque one, with contempt; he always had time to discuss it, to argue it out, and no one ever left his presence thinking that he had made an absurd proposal. Thus Page had a profound respect for a human being simply because he was a human being; the mere fact that a man, woman, or child lived and breathed, had his virtues and his failings, constituted in Page's imagination a tremendous fact. He could not wound such a living creature any more than he could wound a flower or a tree; consequently he treated every person as an important member of the universe. Not infrequently, indeed, he stormed at public men, but his thunder, after all, was not very terrifying; his remarks about such personages as Mr. Bryan merely reflected his indignation at their policies and their influence but did not indicate any feeling against the victims themselves. Page said "Good morning" to his doorman with the same deference that he showed to Sir Edward Grey, and there was not a little stenographer in the building whose joys and sorrows did not arouse in him the most friendly interest. Some of the most affecting letters written about Page, indeed, have come from these daily associates of more humble station. "We so often speak of Mr. Page," writes one of the Embassy staff—"Findlater, Short, and Frederick"—these were all English servants at the Embassy; "we all loved him equally, and hardly a day passes that something does not remind us of him, and I often fancy that I hear his laugh, so full of kindness and love of life." And the impression left on those in high position was the same. "I have seen ladies representing all that is most worldly in Mayfair," writes Mr. Ellery Sedgwick, the editor of the *Atlantic Monthly*, "start at the sudden thought of Page's illness, their eyes glistening with tears."

Perhaps what gave most charm to this human side was the fact that Page was fundamentally such a scholarly man. This was the aspect which especially delighted his English friends. He preached democracy and Americanism with an emphasis that almost suggested the backwoodsman—the many ideas on these subjects that appear in his letters Page never hesitated to set forth with all due resonance at London dinner tables—yet he phrased his creed in language that was little less than literary style, and illuminated it with illustrations and a philosophy that were the product of the most exhaustive reading. "Your Ambassador has taught us something that we did not know before," an English friend remarked to an American. "That is that a man can be a democrat and a man of culture at the same time." The Greek and Latin authors had been Page's companions from the days when, as the holder of the Greek Fellowship at Johns Hopkins, he had been a favourite pupil of Basil L. Gildersleeve. British statesmen who had been trained at Balliol, in the days when Greek was the indispensable ear-mark of a gentleman, could thus meet their American associate on the most sympathetic terms. Page likewise spoke a brand of idiomatic English which immediately put him in a class by himself. He regarded words as sacred things. He used them, in his writing or in his speech, with the utmost care and discrimination; yet this did not result in a halting or stilted style; he spoke with the utmost ease, going rapidly from thought to thought, choosing invariably the one needful word, lighting up the whole with whimsicalities all his own, occasionally emphasizing a good point by looking downward and glancing over his eyeglasses, perhaps, if he knew his companion intimately, now and then giving him a monitory tap on the knee. Page, in fact, was a great and incessant talker; hardly anything delighted him more than a companionable exchange of ideas and impressions; he was seldom so busy that he would not push aside his papers for a chat; and he would talk with almost any one, on almost any subject—his secretaries, his stenographers, his office boys, and any crank who succeeded in getting by the doorman—for, in spite of his lively warnings against the breed, Page did really love cranks and took a collector's joy in uncovering new types. Page's voice was normally quiet; though he had spent all his early life in the South, the characteristic

Southern accents were ordinarily not observable; yet his
intonation had a certain gentleness that was probably an
inheritance of his Southern breeding. Thus, when he
first began talking, his words would ripple along quietly
and rapidly; a characteristic pose was to sit calmly, with
one knee thrown over the other, his hands folded; as his
interest increased, however, he would get up, perhaps
walk across the room, or stand before the fireplace, his
hands behind his back; a large cigar, sometimes unlighted,
at other times emitting huge clouds of smoke, would
oscillate from one side of his mouth to the other; his talk
would grow in earnestness, his voice grow louder, his
words come faster and faster, until finally they would
gush forth in a mighty torrent.

All Page's personal traits are explained by that one
characteristic which tempered all others, his sense of
humour. That Page was above all a serious-minded man
his letters show; yet his spirits were constantly alert for
the amusing, the grotesque, and the contradictory; like
all men who are really serious and alive to the pathos of
existence, he loved a hearty laugh, especially as he found
it a relief from the gloom that filled his every waking
moment in England. Page himself regarded this ability
to smile as an indispensable attribute to a well-rounded
life. "No man can be a gentleman," he once declared,
"who does not have a sense of humour." Only he who
possessed this gift, Page believed, had an imaginative
insight into the failings and the virtues of his brothers;
only he could have a tolerant attitude toward the stupidities of his fellows, to say nothing of his own. And humour
with him assumed various shades; now it would flash in
an epigram, or smile indulgently at a passing human
weakness; now and then it would break out into genial
mockery; occasionally it would manifest itself as sheer

horse-play; and less frequently it would become sardonic or even savage. It was in this latter spirit that he once described a trio of Washington statesmen, whose influence he abhorred as, "three minds that occupy a single vacuum." He once convulsed a Scottish audience by describing the national motto of Scotland—and doing so with a broad burr in his voice that seemed almost to mark the speaker a native to the heath—as "Liber-r-ty, fra-a-ternity and f-r-r-u-gality." The policy of his country occasioned many awkward moments which, thanks to his talent for amiable raillery, he usually succeeded in rendering harmless. Not infrequently Page's fellow guests at the dinner table would think the American attitude toward Germany a not inappropriate topic for small talk. "Mr. Page," remarked an exaltedly titled lady in a conversational pause, "when is your country going to get into the war?" The more discreet members of the company gasped, but Page was not disturbed. "Please give us at least ninety days," he answered, and an exceedingly disagreeable situation was thus relieved by general laughter.

On another occasion his repudiation of this flippant spirit took a more solemn and even more effective form. The time was a few days before the United States had declared war. Bernstorff had been dismissed; events were rapidly rushing toward the great climax; yet the behaviour of the Washington Administration was still inspiring much caustic criticism. The Pages were present at one of the few dinners which they attended in the course of this crisis; certain smart and tactless guests did not seem to regard their presence as a bar to many gibes against the American policy. Page sat through it all impassive, never betraying the slightest resentment.

Presently the ladies withdrew. Page found himself sitting next to Mr. Harold Nicolson, an important official

in the Foreign Office.   It so happened that Mr. Nicolson
and Page were the only two members of the company who
were the possessors of a great secret which made ineffably
silly all the chatter that had taken place during the dinner; this was that the United States had decided on war
against Germany and would issue the declaration in a
few days.

"Well, Mr. Nicolson," said Page, "I think that you
and I will drink a glass of wine together."

The two men quietly lifted their glasses and drank the
silent toast.   Neither made the slightest reference to the
forthcoming event.   Perhaps the other men present were
a little mystified, but in a few days they understood what
it had meant, and also learned how effectively they had
been rebuked.

"Is it any wonder," says Mr. Nicolson, telling this
story, "that I think that Mr. Page is perhaps the greatest
gentleman I have ever known?   He has only one possible
competitor for this distinction—and that is Arthur Balfour."

The English newspapers took delight in printing Page's
aphorisms, and several anecdotes that came from America
afforded them especial joy.   One went back to the days
when the Ambassador was editor of the *Atlantic Monthly*.
A woman contributor had sent him a story; like most
literary novices she believed that editors usually rejected
the manuscripts of unknown writers without reading them.
She therefore set a trap for Page by pasting together certain sheets.   The manuscript came back promptly, and,
as the prospective contributor had hoped, these sheets
had not been disturbed.   These particular sections had
certainly not been read.   The angry author triumphantly
wrote to Page, explaining how she had caught him and
denouncing the whole editorial tribe as humbugs.   "Dear

Madam," Page immediately wrote in reply, "when I break an egg at breakfast, I do not have to eat the whole of it to find out that it is bad." Page's treatment of authors, however, was by no means so acrimonious as this little note might imply. Indeed, the urbanity and consideration shown in his correspondence with writers had long been a tradition in American letters. The remark of O. Henry in this regard promises to become immortal: "Page could reject a story with a letter that was so complimentary," he said, "and make everybody feel so happy that you could take it to a bank and borrow money on it."

Another anecdote reminiscent of his editorial days was his retort to S. S. McClure, the editor of *McClure's Magazine*.

"Page," said Mr. McClure, "there are only three great editors in the United States."

"Who's the third one, Sam?" asked Page.

Plenty of stories, illustrating Page's quickness and aptness in retort, have gathered about his name in England. Many of them indicate a mere spirit of boyish fun. Early in his Ambassadorship he was spending a few days at Stratford-on-Avon, his hostess being an American woman who had beautifully restored an Elizabethan house; the garden contained a mulberry tree which she liked to think had been planted by Shakespeare himself. The dignitaries of Stratford, learning that the American Ambassador had reached town, asked permission to wait upon him; the Lord Mayor, who headed the procession, made an excellent speech, to which Page appropriately replied, and several hundred people were solemnly presented. After the party had left Page turned to his hostess:

"Have they all gone?"

"Yes."

"All?"

"Yes."

"Are you sure?"

"Yes."

"Then let's take hands and dance around the mulberry tree!"

Page was as good as his word; he danced as gaily as the youngest member of the party, to the singing of the old English song.

The great service in St. Paul's Cathedral, in commemoration of America's entry into the war, has already been described. A number of wounded Americans, boys whose zeal for the Allies had led them to enlist in the Canadian Army, were conspicuous participants in this celebration. After the solemn religious ceremonies, the Ambassador and these young men betook themselves for lunch to a well-known London restaurant. In an interval of the conversation one of the Americans turned to Page.

"Mr. Ambassador, there was just one thing wrong with that service."

"What was that?"

"We wanted to yell, and we couldn't."

"Then why don't you yell now?"

The boy jumped on a chair and began waving his napkin. "The Ambassador says we may yell," he cried. "Let's yell!"

"And so," said Page, telling the story, "they yelled for five minutes and I yelled with them. We all felt better in consequence."

This geniality, this disposition not to take life too solemnly, sometimes lightened up the sombre atmosphere of the Foreign Office itself. "Mr. Balfour went on a sort of mild rampage yesterday," Page records. "The British and American navies had come to an arrangement whereby the Brazilian ships that are coming over to help us fight should join the American unit, not the British, as was at first proposed. Washington telegraphed me that the British Minister at Rio was blocking the game by standing out for the first British idea—that the Brazilian ships should join the British. It turned out in the conversation that the British Minister had not been informed of the British-American naval arrangement. Mr. Balfour sent for Lord Hardinge. He called in one of the private secretaries. Was such a thing ever heard of?

"'Did you ever know,' said the indignant Mr. Balfour, turning to me, 'of such a thing as a minister not even being informed of his Government's decisions?' 'Yes,' I said, 'if I ransack my memory diligently, I think I could find such cases.' The meeting went into laughter!"

Evidently the troubles which Page was having with his own State Department were not unfamiliar to British officialdom.

Page's letters sufficiently reveal his fondness for Sir Edward Grey and the splendid relations that existed between them. The sympathetic chords which the two men struck upon their first meeting only grew stronger with time. A single episode brings out the bonds that drew them together. It took place at a time when the tension over the blockade was especially threatening. One afternoon Page asked for a formal interview; he had received another exceedingly disagreeable protest from Washington, with instructions to push the matter to a decision; the Ambassador left his Embassy with a grave expression upon his face; his associates were especially worried over the outcome. So critical did the situation seem that the most important secretaries gathered in the Ambassador's room, awaiting his return, their nerves strung almost to the breaking point. An hour went by and nothing was heard from Page; another hour slowly passed and still the Ambassador did not return. The faces of the assembled staff lengthened as the minutes went by; what was the Ambassador doing at the Foreign Office? So protracted an interview could portend only evil; already, in the minds of these nervous young men, ultimatums were flying between the United States and Great Britain, and even war might be hanging in the balance. Another hour drew out its weary length; the room became dark, dinner time was approaching, and still Page failed to make his appearance. At last, when his distracted subordinates were almost prepared to go in search of their chief, the Ambassador walked jauntily in, smiling and apparently carefree. What had happened? What was to be done about the detained ships?

"What ships?" asked Page, and then suddenly he remembered. "Oh, yes—those." That was all right; Sir Edward had at once promised to release them; it had all been settled in a few minutes.

"Then why were you so long?"

The truth came out: Sir Edward and Page had quickly turned from intercepted cargoes to the more congenial subject of Wordsworth, Tennyson, and other favourite poets, and the rest of the afternoon had been consumed in discussing this really important business.

Perhaps Page was not so great a story-teller as many Americans, but he excelled in a type of yarn that especially delights Englishmen, for it is the kind that is native to the American soil. He possessed an inexhaustible stock of Negro anecdotes, and he had the gift of bringing them out at precisely the right point. There was one which the Archbishop of York never tired of repeating. Soon after America entered the war, the Archbishop asked Page how long his country was "in for." "I can best answer that by telling you a story," said Page. "There were two Negroes who had just been sentenced to prison terms. As they were being taken away in the carriage placed at their disposal by the United States Government, one said to the other, 'Sam, how long is you in fo'?' 'I guess dat it's a yeah or two yeahs,' said Sam. 'How long is you in fo'?' 'I guess it's from now on,' said the other darky." "From now on," remarked the Archbishop, telling this story. "What could more eloquently have described America's attitude toward the war?"

The mention of the Archbishop suggests another of Page's talents—the aptness of his letters of introduction. In the spring of 1918 the Archbishop, at the earnest recommendation of Page and Mr. Balfour, came to the United States. Page prepared the way by letters to several distinguished Americans, of which this one, to Theodore Roosevelt, is a fair sample:

To Theodore Roosevelt

London, January 16, 1918.

DEAR MR. ROOSEVELT:

The Archbishop of York goes to the United States to make some observations of us and of our ways and to deliver addresses—on the invitation of some one of our church organizations; a fortunate event for us and, I have ventured to tell him, for him also.

During his brief stay in our country, I wish him to make your acquaintance, and I have given him a card of introduction to you, and thus I humbly serve you both.

The Archbishop is a man and a brother, a humble, learned, earnest, companionable fellow, with most charming manners and an attractive personality, a good friend of mine, which argues much for him and (I think) implies also something in my behalf. You will enjoy him.

I am, dear Mr. Roosevelt,

Sincerely yours,

WALTER H. PAGE.

Greatly as Page loved England he never ceased to preach his Americanism. That he preferred his own country to any other and that he believed that it was its greatest destiny to teach its institutions to the rest of the world, Page's letters show; yet this was with him no cheap spread-eagleism; it was a definite philosophy which the Ambassador had completely thought out. He never hesitated to express his democratic opinions in any company, and only once or twice were there any signs that these ideas jarred a little in certain strongholds of conservatism. Even in the darkest period of American neutrality Page's faith in the American people remained complete. After this country had entered the war and the apparent slowness of the Washington Administration had raised certain questionings, Page never doubted that the people themselves, however irresolute and lukewarm their representatives might be, would force the issue to its only logical end. Even so friendly a man as Mr. Balfour once voiced a popular apprehension that the United States might not get into the war with all its strength or might withdraw prematurely. This was in the early period of our participation. "Who is going to stop the American people and how?" Page quickly replied. "I think that was a good answer," he said, as he looked back at the episode in the summer of 1918, when hundreds of thousands of Americans were landing in France every month. A scrap of his writing records a discussion at a dinner party on this question: "If you could have a month in any time and any country, what time and what country would you choose?" The majority voted for England in the time of Elizabeth, but Page's preference was for Athens in the days of Pericles. Then came a far more interesting debate: "If you could spend a second lifetime when and where would you choose to spend it?" On this Page had not a moment's hesitation: "In the future and in the U. S. A.!" and he upheld his point with such persuasiveness that he carried the whole gathering with him. His love of anything suggesting America came out on all occasions. One of his English hostesses once captivated him by serving corn bread at a luncheon. "The American Ambassador and corn bread!" he exclaimed with all the delight of a schoolboy. Again he was invited, with another distinguished American, to serve as godfather at the christening of the daughter of an American woman who had married an Englishman. When the ceremony was finished he leaned over the font toward his fellow godfather. "Born on July 4th," he exclaimed, "of an American mother! And we two Yankee godfathers! We'll see that this child is taught the Constitution of the United States!"

One day an American duchess came into Page's office.

"I am going home for a little visit and I want a passport," she said.

"But you don't get a passport here," Page replied. "You must go to the Foreign Office."

His visitor was indignant.

"Not at all," she answered. "I am an American: you know that I am; you knew my father. I want an American passport."

Page patiently explained the citizenship and naturalization laws and finally convinced his caller that she was now a British subject and must have a British passport. As this American duchess left the room he shook at her a menacing forefinger.

"Don't tell me," was the Ambassador's parting shot, "that you thought that you could have your Duke and Uncle Sam, too!"

The judgments which Page passed on men and things were quick and they were not infrequently wise. One of these judgments had historic consequences the end of which cannot even yet be foreseen. On the outbreak of hostilities, as already related, an American Relief Committee was organized in London to look out for the interests of stranded Americans. Page kept a close eye on its operations, and soon his attention was attracted by the noiseless efficiency of an American engineer of whom he had already caught a few fleeting glimpses in the period of peace. After he had finished his work with the American Committee, Mr. Herbert C. Hoover began to make his arrangements to leave for the United States. His private affairs had been disorganized; he had already sent his family home, and his one ambition was to get on the first ship sailing for the United States The idea of Belgian relief, or of feeding starving people anywhere, had never occurred to him. At this moment an American, Mr. Millard K. Shaler, came from Brussels and gave the most harrowing account of conditions in Belgium. Mr. Hoover took Mr. Shaler to Page, who immediately became sympathetic. The Ambassador arranged an interview between Mr. Hoover and Sir Edward Grey, who likewise showed great interest and promised government support. Soon afterward three Belgians arrived and described the situation as immediately alarming: Brussels had only food enough to feed the people for thirty-six hours; after that, unless help were forthcoming, the greatest distress would set in. Five men—Page, the three Belgians, and Mr. Hoover—at once got together at the American Embassy. Upon the result of that meeting hung the fate of millions of people. Who before had ever undertaken a scheme for feeding an entire nation for an indefinite period? That there were great obstacles in the way all five men knew; the British Admiralty in particular were strongly opposed; there was a fear that the food, if it could be acquired and sent to Belgium, would find its way to the German Army. Unless the British Government could be persuaded that this could be prevented, the enterprise would fail at the start. How could it be done?

"There is only one way," said Page. "Some government must give its guarantee that this food will get to the Belgian people." "And, of course," he added, "there is only one government that can do that. It must be the American Government."

Mr. Hoover pointed out that any such guarantee involved the management of transportation; only by controlling the railroads could the American Government make sure that this food would reach its destination.

And that, added Page, involved a director—some one man who could take charge of the whole enterprise. Who should it be?

Then Page turned quickly to the young American.

"Hoover, you're It!"

Mr. Hoover made no reply; he neither accepted nor rejected the proposal. He merely glanced at the clock, then got up and silently left the room. In a few minutes he returned and entered again into the discussion.

"Hoover, why did you get up and leave us so abruptly?" asked Page, a little puzzled over this behaviour.

"I saw by the clock," came the answer—and it was a story that Page was fond of telling, as illustrating the rapidity with which Mr. Hoover worked—"that there was an hour left before the Exchange closed in New York. So I went out and cabled, buying several millions of bushels of wheat—for the Belgians, of course."

For what is usually known as "society" Page had little inclination. Yet for social intercourse on a more genuine plane he had real gifts. Had he enjoyed better health, week ends in the country would have afforded him welcome entertainment. He also liked dinner parties but indulged in them very moderately. He was a member of many London clubs but he seldom visited any of them. There were a number of organizations, however, which he regularly attended. The Society of Dilettanti, a company of distinguished men interested in promoting the arts and improving the public taste, which has been continuously in existence since 1736, enrolling in each generation the greatest painters and writers of the time, elected Page to membership. He greatly enjoyed its dinners in the Banquet Hall of the Grafton Gallery. "Last night," he writes, describing his initial appearance, "I attended my first Dilettanti dinner and was inducted, much as a new Peer is inducted into the House of Lords. Lord Mersey in the chair—in a red robe. These gay old dogs have had a fine time of it for nearly 200 years—good wine, high food, fine satisfaction. The oldest dining society in the Kingdom. The blue blood old Briton has the art of enjoying himself reduced to a very fine point indeed." Another gathering whose meetings he seldom missed was that of the Kinsmen, an informal club of literary men who met occasionally for food and converse in the Trocadero Restaurant. Here Page would meet such congenial souls as Sir James Barrie and Sir Arthur Pinero, all of whom retain lively memories of Page at these gatherings. "He was one of the most lovable characters I have ever had the good fortune to encounter," says Sir Arthur Pinero, recalling these occasions. "In what special quality or qualities lay the secret of his charm and influence? Surely in his simplicity and transparent honesty, and in the possession of a disposition which, without the smallest loss of dignity, was responsive and affectionate. Distinguished American Ambassadors will come and go, and will in their turn win esteem and admiration. But none, I venture to say, will efface the recollection of Walter Page from the minds of those who were privileged to gain his friendship."

One aspect of Page that remains fixed in the memory of his associates is his unwearied industry with the pen. His official communications and his ordinary correspondence Page dictated; but his personal letters he wrote with his own hand. He himself deplored the stenographer as a deterrent to good writing; the habit of dictating, he argued, led to wordiness and general looseness of thought. Practically all the letters published in these volumes were therefore the painstaking work of Page's own pen. His handwriting was so beautiful and clear that, in his editorial days, the printers much preferred it as "copy" to typewritten matter. This habit is especially surprising in view of the Ambassador's enormous epistolary output. It must be remembered that the letters included in the present book are only a selection from the vast number that he wrote during his five years in England; many of these letters fill twenty and thirty pages of script; the labour involved in turning them out, day after day, seems fairly astounding. Yet with Page this was a labour of love. All through his Ambassadorship he seemed hardly contented unless he had a pen in his hand. As his secretaries would glance into his room, there they would see the Ambassador bending over his desk—writing, writing, eternally writing; sometimes he would call them in, and read what he had written, never hesitating to tear up the paper if their unfavourable criticisms seemed to him well taken. The Ambassador kept a desk also in his bedroom, and here his most important correspondence was attended to. Page's all-night self-communings before his wood fire have already been described, and he had another nocturnal occupation that was similarly absorbing. Many a night, after returning late from his office or from dinner, he would put on his dressing gown, sit at his bedroom desk, and start pouring forth his inmost thoughts in letters to the President, Colonel House, or some other correspondent. His pen flew over the paper with the utmost rapidity and the Ambassador would sometimes keep at his writing until two or three o'clock in the morning. There is a frequently expressed fear that letter writing is an art of the past; that the intervention of the stenographer has destroyed its spontaneity; yet it is evident that in Page the present generation has a letter writer of the old-fashioned kind, for he did all his writing with his own hand and under circumstances that would assure the utmost freshness and vividness to the result.

An occasional game of golf, which he played badly, a trip now and then to rural England—these were Page's only relaxations from his duties. Though he was not especially fond of leaving his own house, he was always delighted when visitors came to him. And the American Embassy, during the five years from 1913 to 1918, extended a hospitality which was fittingly democratic in its quality but which gradually drew within its doors all that was finest in the intellect and character of England. Page himself attributed the popularity of his house to his wife. Mrs. Page certainly embodied the traits most desirable in the Ambassadress of a great Republic. A woman of cultivation, a tireless reader, a close observer of people and events and a shrewd commentator upon them, she also had an unobtrusive dignity, a penetrating sympathy, and a capacity for human association, which, while more restrained and more placid than that of her husband, made her a helpful companion for a sorely burdened man. The American Embassy under Mr. and Mrs. Page was not one of London's smart houses as that word is commonly understood in this great capital. But No. 6 Grosvenor Square, in the spaciousness of its rooms, the simple beauty of its furnishings, and especially in its complete absence of ostentation, made it the worthy abiding place of an American Ambassador. And the people who congregated there were precisely the kind that appeal to the educated American. "I didn't know I was getting into an assembly of immortals," exclaimed Mr. Hugh Wallace, when he dropped in one Thursday afternoon for tea, and found himself foregathered with Sir Edward Grey, Henry James, John Sargent, and other men of the same type. It was this kind of person who most naturally gravitated to the Page establishment, not the ultra-fashionable, the merely rich, or the many titled. The formal functions which the position demanded the Pages scrupulously gave; but the affairs which Page most enjoyed and which have left the most lasting remembrances upon his guests were the informal meetings with his chosen favourites, for the most part literary men. Here Page's sheer brilliancy of conversation showed at its best. Lord Bryce, Sir John Simon, John Morley, the inevitable companions, Henry James

and John Sargent—"What things have I seen done at
the Mermaid"; and certainly these gatherings of wits and
savants furnished as near an approach to its Elizabethan
prototype as London could then present.

Besides his official activities Page performed great services to the two countries by his speeches. The demands
of this kind on an American Ambassador are always numerous, but Page's position was an exceptional one; it was
his fortune to represent America at a time when his own
country and Great Britain were allies in a great war. He
could therefore have spent practically all his time in speaking had he been so disposed. Of the hundreds of invitations received he was able to accept only a few, but most
of these occasions became memorable ones. In any spectacular sense Page was not an orator; he rather despised
the grand manner, with its flourishes and its tricks; the
name of public speaker probably best describes his talents
on the platform. Here his style was earnest and conversational: his speech flowed with the utmost readiness;
it was invariably quiet and restrained; he was never aiming
at big effects, but his words always went home. Of the
series of speeches that stand to his credit in England probably the one that will be longest remembered is that
delivered at Plymouth on August 4, 1917, the third anniversary of the war. This not only reviewed the common history of the two nations for three hundred years,
and suggested a programme for making the bonds tighter
yet, but it brought the British public practical assurances as to America's intentions in the conflict. Up to
that time there had been much vagueness and doubt; no
official voice had spoken the clear word for the United
States; the British public did not know what to expect
from their kinsmen overseas. But after Page's Plymouth
speech the people of Great Britain looked forward with

complete confidence to the coöperation of the two countries and to the inevitable triumph of this coöperation.

To Arthur W. Page

Knebworth House, Knebworth,
August 11, 1917.

DEAR ARTHUR:

First of all, these three years have made me tired. I
suppose there's no doubt about that, if there were any
scientific way of measuring it. While of course the strain
now is nothing like what it was during the days of neutrality, there's yet some strain.

I went down to Plymouth to make a speech on the anniversary of the beginning of the war—went to tell them
in the west of England something about relations with
the United States and something about what the United
States is doing in the war. It turned out to be a great
success. The Mayor met me at the train; there was a
military company, the Star Spangled Banner and real
American applause. All the way through the town the
streets were lined with all the inhabitants and more—
apparently millions of 'em. They made the most of it for
five solid days.

On the morning of August 4th the Mayor gave me an
official luncheon. Thence we went to the esplanade facing the sea, where soldiers and sailors were lined up for
half a mile. The American Flag was flung loose, the Star
Spangled Banner broke forth from the band, and all the
people in that part of the world were there gathered to see
the show. After all this salute the Mayor took me to the
stand and he and I made speeches, and the background
was a group of dozens of admirals and generals and many
smaller fry. Then I reviewed the troops; then they
marched by me and in an hour or two the show was over.

Then the bowling club—the same club and the same green as when Drake left the game to sail out to meet the Armada.

Then a solemn service in the big church, where the prayers were written and the hymns selected with reference to our part in the war.

Then, of course, a dinner party. At eight o'clock at night, the Guildhall, an enormous town hall, was packed with people and I made my speech at 'em. A copy (somewhat less good than the version I gave them) goes to you, along with a leader from the *Times*. They were vociferously grateful for any assuring word about the United States. It's strange how very little the provincial Englander knows about what we have done and mean to do. They took the speech finely, and I have had good letters about it from all sorts of people in every part of the Kingdom.

Then followed five days of luncheons and dinners and garden parties—and (what I set out to say) I got back to London last night dead tired. To-day your mother and I came here—about twenty-five miles from London—for a fortnight.

This is Bulwer-Lytton's house—a fine old English place hired this year by Lady Strafford, whom your mother is visiting for a fortnight or more, and they let me come along, too. They have given me the big library, as good a room as I want—with as bad pens as they can find in the Kingdom.

Your mother is tired, too. Since the American Red Cross was organized here, she has added to her committee and hospitals. But she keeps well and very vigorous. A fortnight here will set her up. She enjoyed Plymouth very much in spite of the continual rush, and it was a rush.

What the United States is doing looks good and large at

Lord Robert Cecil, Minister of Blockade, 1916–18, Assistant Secretary of State for Foreign Affairs, 1918

General John J. Pershing, Commander-in-Chief of the American
Expeditionary Force in the Great War

this distance. The gratitude here is unbounded; but I detect a feeling here and there of wonder whether we are going to keep up this activity to the end.

I sometimes feel that the German collapse *may* come next winter. Their internal troubles and the lack of sufficient food and raw materials do increase. The breaking point may be reached before another summer. I wish I could prove it or even certainly predict it. But it is at least conceivable. Alas, no one can *prove* anything about the war. The conditions have no precedents. The sum of human misery and suffering is simply incalculable, as is the loss of life; and the gradual and general brutalization goes on and on and on far past any preceding horrors.

With all my love to you and Mollie and the trio,

W. H. P.

And so for five busy and devastating years Page did his work. The stupidities of Washington might drive him to desperation, ill-health might increase his periods of despondency, the misunderstandings that he occasionally had with the British Government might add to his discouragements, but a naturally optimistic and humorous temperament overcame all obstacles, and did its part in bringing about that united effort which ended in victory. And that it was a great part, the story of his Ambassadorship abundantly proves. Page was not the soldier working in the blood and slime of Flanders, nor the sea fighter spending day and night around the foggy coast of Ireland, nor the statesman bending parliaments to his will and manipulating nations and peoples in the mighty game whose stake was civilization itself. But history will indeed be ungrateful if it ever forget the gaunt and pensive figure, clad in a dressing gown, sitting long into the morning before the smouldering fire at 6 Grosvenor Square, seeking to find some way to persuade a reluctant and hesitating President to lead his country in the defense of liberty and determined that, so far as he could accomplish it, the nation should play a part in the great assize that was in keeping with its traditions and its instincts.

CHAPTER XXIV

A RESPITE AT ST. IVES

To Edward M. House

Knebworth House
Sunday, September, [sic] 1917.

DEAR HOUSE:

. . . By far the most important peace plan or utterance is the President's extraordinary answer to the Pope.[1] His flat and convincing refusal to take the word of the present rulers of Germany as of any value has had more effect here than any other utterance and it is, so far, the best contribution we have made to the war. The best evidence that I can get shows also that it has had more effect in Germany than anything else that has been said by anybody. That hit the bull's-eye with perfect accuracy; and it has been accepted here as *the* war aim and *the* war condition. So far as I can make out it is working in Germany toward peace with more effect than any other deliverance made by anybody. And it steadied the already unshakable resolution here amazingly.

I can get any information here of course without danger of the slightest publicity—an important point, because even the mention of peace now is dangerous. All the world, under this long strain, is more or less off the normal,

---

[1] On August 1, 1917, Pope Benedict XV sent a letter to the Powers urging them to bring the war to an end and outlining possible terms of settlement. On August 29th President Wilson sent his historic reply. This declared, in memorable language, that the Hohenzollern dynasty was unworthy of confidence and that the United States would have no negotiations with its representatives. It inferentially took the stand that the Kaiser must abdicate, or be deposed, and the German autocracy destroyed, as part of the conditions of peace.

and all my work—even routine work—is done with the profoundest secrecy: it has to be.

Our energetic war preparations call forth universal admiration and gratitude here on all sides and nerve up the British and hearten them more than I know how to explain. There is an eager and even pathetic curiosity to hear all the details, to hear, in fact, anything about the United States; and what the British do not know about the United States would fill the British Museum. They do know, however, that they would soon have been obliged to make an unsatisfactory peace if we hadn't come in when we did and they freely say so. The little feeling of jealousy that we should come in and win the war at the end has, I think, been forgotten, swallowed up in their genuine gratitude.

Sincerely yours,

WALTER H. PAGE.

To Arthur W. Page

American Embassy,
London, Sept. 3, 1917.

DEAR ARTHUR:

. . . The President has sent Admiral Mayo over to study the naval situation. So far as I can learn the feeling at Washington is that the British Navy has done nothing. Why, it hasn't attacked the German naval bases and destroyed the German navy and ended the war! Why not? I have a feeling that Mayo will supplement and support Sims in his report. Then gradually the naval men at Washington may begin to understand and they may get the important facts into the President's head. Meantime the submarine work of the Germans continues to win the war, although the government and the people here and in the United States appear not to believe it.

They are still destroying seventy-five British ships a month besides an additional (smaller) number of allied and neutral ships. And all the world together is not turning out seventy-five ships a month; nor are we all destroying submarines as fast as the Germans are turning *them* out. Yet all the politicians are putting on a cheerful countenance about it because the Germans are not starving England out and are not just now sinking passenger ships. They may begin this again at any time. They have come within a few feet of torpedoing two of our American liners. The submarine *is* the war yet, but nobody seems disposed to believe it. They'll probably wake up with a great shock some day—or the war may possibly end before the destruction of ships becomes positively fatal.

The President's letter to the Pope gives him the moral and actual leadership now. The Hohenzollerns must go. Somehow the subjects and governments of these Old World kingdoms have not hitherto laid emphasis on this. There's still a divinity that doth hedge a king in most European minds. To me this is the very queerest thing in the whole world. What again if Germany, Austria, Spain should follow Russia? Whether they do or not crowns will not henceforth be so popular. There is an unbounded enthusiasm here for the President's letter and for the President in general.

In spite of certain details which it seems impossible to make understood on the Potomac, the whole American preparation and enthusiasm seem from this distance to be very fine. The *people* seem in earnest. When I read about tax bills, about the food regulation and a thousand other such things, I am greatly gratified. And it proves that we were right when we said that during the days of neutrality the people were held back. It all looks exceedingly good from this distance, and it makes me homesick.

To Frank N. Doubleday

American Embassy.

[Undated, but written about October 1, 1917]

DEAR EFFENDI:

. . . The enormous war work and war help that everybody seems to be doing in the United States is heartily appreciated here—most heartily. The English eat out of our hands. You can see American uniforms every day in London. Every ship brings them. Everybody's thrilled to see them. The Americans here have great houses opened as officers' clubs, and scrumptious huts for men where countesses and other high ladies hand out sandwiches and serve ice cream and ginger beer. Our two admirals are most popular with all classes, from royalty down. English soldiers salute our officers in the street and old gentlemen take off their hats when they meet nurses with the American Red Cross uniform. My Embassy now occupies four buildings for offices, more than half of them military and naval. And my own staff, proper, is the biggest in the world and keeps growing. When I go, in a little while, to receive the Freedom of the City of Edinburgh, I shall carry an Admiral or a General as my aide!

That's the way we keep a stiff upper lip.

And Good Lord! it's tiresome. Peace? We'd all give our lives for the right sort of peace, and never move an eyelid. But only the wrong sort has yet come within reach. The other sort is coming, however; for these present German contortions are the beginning of the end. But the weariness of it, and the tragedy and the cost. No human creature was ever as tired as I am. Yet I keep well and keep going and keep working all my waking

hours. When it ends, I shall collapse and go home and
have to rest a while. So at least I feel now. And, if I
outlive the work and the danger and the weariness, I'll
praise God for that. And it doesn't let up a single day.
And I'm no worse off than everybody else.

So this over-weary world goes, dear Effendi; but the
longest day shades at last down to twilight and rest; and
so this will be. And poor old Europe will then not be
worth while for the rest of our lives—a vast grave and
ruin where unmated women will mourn and starvation
will remain for years to come.

God bless us.

Sincerely yours, with my love to all the boys,

W. H. P.

To Frank N. Doubleday

London, November 9, 1917.

DEAR EFFENDI:

. . . This infernal thing drags its slow length along
so that we cannot see even a day ahead, not to say a week,
or a year. If any man here allowed the horrors of it to
dwell on his mind he would go mad, so we have to skip
over these things somewhat lightly and try to keep the
long, definite aim in our thoughts and to work away distracted as little as possible by the butchery and by the
starvation that is making this side of the world a shambles
and a wilderness. There is hardly a country on the Continent where people are not literally starving to death,
and in many of them by hundreds of thousands; and this
state of things is going to continue for a good many years
after the war. God knows we (I mean the American
people) are doing everything we can to alleviate it but
there is so much more to be done than any group of forces
can possibly do, that I have a feeling that we have hardly

touched the borders of the great problem itself. Of course here in London we are away from all that. In spite of the rations we get quite enough to eat and it's as good as it is usually in England, but we have no right to complain. Of course we are subject to air raids, and the wise air people here think that early next spring we are going to be bombarded with thousands of aeroplanes, and with new kinds of bombs and gases in a well-organized effort to try actually to destroy London. Possibly that will come; we must simply take our chance, every man sticking to his job. Already the slate shingles on my roof have been broken, and bricks have been knocked down my chimney; the skylight was hit and glass fell down all through the halls, and the nose of a shrapnel shell, weighing eight pounds, fell just in front of my doorway and rolled in my area. This is the sort of thing we incidentally get, not of course from the enemy directly, but from the British guns in London which shoot these things at German aeroplanes. What goes up must come down. Between our own defences and the enemy, God knows which will kill us first!

In spite of all this I put my innocent head on my pillow every night and get a good night's sleep after the bombing is done, and I thank Heaven that nothing interrupts my sleep. This, and a little walking, which is all I get time to do in these foggy days, constitute my life outdoors and precious little of it is outdoors.

Then on every block that I know of in London there is a hospital or supply place and the ambulances are bringing the poor fellows in all the time. We don't get any gasolene to ride so we have to walk. We don't get any white bread so we have to eat stuff made of flour and corn meal ground so fine that it isn't good. While everybody gets a little thinner, the universal opinion is that they also get a little better, and nobody is going to die here of hunger.

We feel a little more cheerful about the submarines than we did some time ago. For some reason they are not getting so many ships. One reason, I am glad to believe, is that they are getting caught themselves. If I could remember all the stories that I hear of good fighting with the submarines I could keep you up two nights when I get home, but in these days one big thing after another crowds so in men's minds that the Lord knows if, when I get home, I shall remember anything.

Always heartily yours,
W. H. P.

To the President

London, December 3, 1917.

DEAR MR. PRESIDENT:

. . . Some of the British military men in London are not hopeful of an early end of the war nor even cheerful about the result. They are afraid of the war-weariness that overcame Russia and gave Italy a setback. They say the military task, though long and slow and hard, can be done if everybody will pull together and keep at the job without weariness—*be done by our help.* But they have fits of fear of France. They are discouraged by the greater part of Lord Lansdowne's letter.[1] I myself do not set great value on this military feeling in London, for the British generals in France do not share it. Lord French once said to me and General Robertson, too, that when they feel despondent in London, they go to the front and get cheered up. But it does seem to be a long job. Evidently the Germans mean to fight to the last man

---

[1] On November 29, 1917, the London *Daily Telegraph* published a letter from the Marquis of Lansdowne, which declared that the war had lasted too long and suggested that the British restate their war aims. This letter was severely condemned by the British press and by practically all representative British statesmen. It produced a most lamentable impression in the United States also.

unless they can succeed in inducing the Allies to meet them to talk it over without naming their terms in advance. That is what Lord Lansdowne favours, and no public out-giving by any prominent man in England has called forth such a storm of protest since the war began. I think I see the genesis of his thought, and it is this: there is nothing in his letter and there was nothing in the half dozen or more rather long conversations that I have had with him on other subjects to show that he has the slightest conception of democracy as a social creed or as a political system. He is, I think, the most complete aristocrat that I have ever met. He doesn't see the war at all as a struggle between democracy and its opposite. He sees it merely as a struggle between Germany and the Allies; and inferentially he is perfectly willing the Kaiser should remain in power. He is of course a patriotic man and a man of great cultivation. But he doesn't see the deeper meaning of the conflict. Add to this defect of under-standing, a long period of bad health and a lasting de-pression because of the loss of his son, and his call to the war-weary ceases to be a surprise.

I am, dear Mr. President,

Sincerely yours,

WALTER H. PAGE.

To Arthur W. Page

American Embassy,
London, December 23, 1917.

DEAR ARTHUR:

I sent you a Christmas cable yesterday for everybody. That's about all I can send in these days of slow mail and restricted shipping and enormously high prices; and you gave all the girls each $100 for me, for the babies and them-selves? That'll show 'em that at least we haven't forgotten them.   Forgotten?   Your mother and I are always talking of the glad day when we can go home and live among them.   We get as homesick as small boys their first month at a boarding school.   Do you remember the day I left you at Lawrenceville, a forlorn and lonely kid?— It's like that.

A wave of depression hangs over the land like a London fog.   And everybody on this tired-out side of the world shows a disposition to lean too heavily on us—to depend on us so completely that the fear arises that they may unconsciously relax their own utmost efforts when we begin to fight.   Yet they can't in the least afford to relax, and, when the time comes, I dare say they will not.   Yet the plain truth is, the French may give out next year for lack of men.   I do not mean that they will quit, but that their fighting strength will have passed its maximum and that they will be able to play only a sort of second part. Except the British and the French, there's no nation in Europe worth a tinker's damn when you come to the real scratch.   The whole continent is rotten or tyrannical or yellow-dog.   I wouldn't give Long Island or Moore County for the whole of continental Europe, with its kings and itching palms.

. . . Waves of depression and of hope—if not of elation—come and go.   I am told, and I think truly, that waves of weariness come in London far oftener and more depressingly than anywhere else in the Kingdom.   There is no sign nor fear that the British will give up; they'll hold on till the end.   Winston Churchill said to me last night: "We can hold on till next year.   But after 1918, it'll be your fight.   We'll have to depend on you."   I told him that such a remark might well be accepted in some quarters as a British surrender.   Then he came up to the scratch: "Surrender? Never."   But I fear we need—in some practical and non-ostentatious way—now and then to remind all these European folk that we get no particular encouragement by being unduly leaned on.

It is, however, the weariest Christmas in all British annals, certainly since the Napoleonic wars. The untoward event after the British advance toward Cambrai caused the retirement of six British generals and deepened the depression here. Still I can see it now passing. Even a little victory will bring back a wave of cheerfulness.

Depression or elation show equally the undue strain that British nerves are under. I dare say nobody is entirely normal. News of many sorts can now be circulated only by word of mouth. The queerest stories are whispered about and find at least temporary credence. For instance: The report has been going around that the revolution that took place in Portugal the other day was caused by the Germans (likely enough); that it was a monarchical movement and that the Germans were going to put the King back on the throne as soon as the war ended. Sensation-mongers appear at every old-woman's knitting circle. And all this has an effect on conduct. Two young wives of noble officers now in France have just run away with two other young noblemen—to the scandal of a large part of good society in London. It is universally said that the morals of more hitherto good people are wrecked by the strain put upon women by the absence of their husbands than was ever before heard of. Everybody is overworked. Fewer people are literally truthful than ever before. Men and women break down and fall out of working ranks continuously. The number of men in the government who have disappeared from public view is amazing, the number that would like to disappear is still greater—from sheer overstrain. The Prime Minister is tired. Bonar Law in a long conference that Crosby and I had with him yesterday wearily ran all round a circle rather than hit a plain proposition with a clear decision. Mr. Balfour has kept his house from overwork a few days every recent week. I lunched with Mr. Asquith yesterday; even he seemed jaded; and Mrs. Asquith assured me that "everything is going to the devil damned fast." Some conspicuous men who have always been sober have taken to drink. The very few public dinners that are held are served with ostentatious meagreness to escape criticism. I attended one last week at which there was no bread, no butter, no sugar served. All of which doesn't mean that the world here is going to the bad—only that it moves backward and forward by emotions; and this is normally a most unemotional race. Overwork and the loss of sons and friends—the list of the lost grows—always make an abnormal strain. The churches are fuller than ever before. So, too, are the "parlours" of the fortune-tellers. So also the theatres—in the effort to forget one's self. There are afternoon dances for young officers at home on leave: the curtains are drawn and the music is muffled. More marriages take place—blind and maimed, as well as the young fellows just going to France—than were ever celebrated in any year within men's memory. Verse-writing is rampant. I have received enough odes and sonnets celebrating the Great Republic and the Great President to fill a folio volume. Several American Y. M. C. A. workers lately turned rampant Pacifists and had to be sent home. Colonial soldiers and now and then an American sailor turn up at our Y. M. C. A. huts as full as a goat and swear after the event that they never did such a thing before. Emotions and strain everywhere!

Affectionately,

W. H. P.

In March Page, a very weary man—as these letters indicate—took a brief holiday at St. Ives, on the coast of Cornwall. As he gazed out on the Atlantic, the yearning for home, for the sandhills and the pine trees of North Carolina, again took possession of his soul. Yet it is evident, from a miscellaneous group of letters written at this time, that his mind revelled in a variety of subjects, ranging all the way from British food and vegetables to the settlement of the war and from secret diplomacy to literary style.

To Mrs. Charles G. Loring

St. Ives, Cornwall, March 3, 1918.

DEAR KITTY:

Your mother of course needed a rest away from London after the influenza got done with her; and I discovered that I had gone stale. So she and I and the golf clubs came here yesterday—as near to the sunlit land of Uncle Sam as you can well get on this island. We look across the ocean—at least out into it—in your direction, but I must confess that Labrador is not in sight. The place is all right, the hotel uncommonly good, but it's Greenlandish in its temperature—a very cold wind blowing. The golf clubs lean up against the wall and curse the weather. But we are away from the hordes of people and will have a little quiet here. It's as quiet as any far-off place by the sea, and it's clean. London is the dirtiest town in the world.

By the way that picture of Chud came (by Col. Honey) along with Alice Page's adorable little photograph. As for the wee chick, I see how you are already beginning to get a lot of fun with her. And you'll have more and more as she gets bigger. Give her my love and see what she'll say. You won't get so lonesome, dear Kitty, with little Alice; and I can't keep from thinking as well as hoping that the war will not go on as long as it sometimes seems that it must. The utter collapse of Russia has given Germany a vast victory on that side and it may turn out that this will make an earlier peace possible than would otherwise have come. And the Germans may be—in fact, *must* be, very short of some of the essentials of war in their metals or in cotton. They are in a worse internal plight than has been made known, I am sure. I can't keep from hoping that peace may come this year. Of course, my guess may be wrong; but everything I hear points in the direction of my timid prediction.

> Bless you and little Alice,
> Affectionately,
> W. H. P.

Page's oldest son was building a house and laying out a garden at Pinehurst, North Carolina, a fact which explains the horticultural and gastronomical suggestions contained in the following letter:

To Ralph W. Page

> Tregenna Castle Hotel,
> St. Ives, Cornwall, England,
> March 4, 1918.

DEAR RALPH:
　Asparagus
　Celery
　Tomatoes
　Butter Beans
　Peas
　Sweet Corn
　Sweet Potatoes

Squash—the sort you cook in the rind
Cantaloupe
Peanuts
Egg Plant
Figs
Peaches
Pecans
Scuppernongs
Peanut-bacon, in glass jars
Razor-back hams, divinely cured
Raspberries
Strawberries
etc. etc. etc. etc.

You see, having starved here for five years, my mind, as soon as it gets free, runs on these things and my mouth waters. All the foregoing things that grow can be put up in pretty glass jars, too.

Add cream, fresh butter, buttermilk, fresh eggs. Only one of all the things on page one grows with any flavour here at all—strawberries; and only one or two more grow at all. Darned if I don't have to confront Cabbage every day. I haven't yet surrendered, and I never shall unless the Germans get us. Cabbage and Germans belong together: God made 'em both the same stinking day.

Now get a bang-up gardener no matter what he costs. Get him started. Put it up to him to start toward the foregoing programme, to be reached in (say) three years —two if possible. He must learn to grow these things absolutely better than they are now grown anywhere on earth. He must get the best seed. He must get muck out of the swamp, manure from somewhere, etc. etc. He must have the supreme flavour in each thing. Let him take room enough for each—plenty of room. He doesn't want much room for any one thing, but good spaces between.

This will be the making of the world. Talk about fairs? If he fails to get every prize he must pay a fine for every one that goes to anybody else.

How we'll live! I can live on these things and nothing else. But (just to match this home outfit) I'll order tea from Japan, ripe olives from California, grape fruit and oranges from Florida. Then poor folks will hang around, hoping to be invited to dinner!

Plant a few fig trees now; and pecans? Any good?

The world is going to come pretty close to starvation not only during the war but for five or perhaps ten years afterward. An acre or two *done right*—divinely right— will save us. An acre or two on my land in Moore County —no king can live half so well if the ground be got ready this spring and such a start made as one natural-born gardener can make. The old Russian I had in Garden City was no slouch. Do you remember his little patch back of the house? That far, far, far excelled anything in all Europe. And you'll recall that we jarred 'em and had good things all winter.

This St. Ives is the finest spot in England that I've ever seen. To-day has been as good as any March day you ever had in North Carolina—a fine air, clear sunshine, a beautiful sea—looking out toward the United States; and this country grows—the best golf links that I've ever seen in the world, and nothing else worth speaking of but —tin. Tin mines are all about here. Tin and golf are good crops in their way, but they don't feed the belly of man. As matters stand the only people that have fit things to eat now in all Europe are the American troops in France, and their food comes out of tins chiefly. Ach! Heaven! In these islands man is amphibious and carnivorous. It rains every day and meat, meat, meat is the only human idea of food. God bless us, one acre of the Sandhills is worth a vast estate of tin mines and golf links to feed the innards of

Yours affectionately,

W. H. P.

P. S. And cornfield peas, of just the right rankness, cooked with just the right dryness.

When I become a citizen of the Sandhills I propose to induce some benevolent lover of good food to give substantial prizes to the best grower of each of these things and to the best cook of each and to the person who serves each of them most daintily.

We can can and glass jar these things and let none be put on the market without the approval of an expert employed by the community. Then we can get a reputation for Sandhill Food and charge double price.

W. H. P.

To Arthur W. Page

St. Ives, Cornwall,
England, March 8, 1918.

DEAR ARTHUR:

Your letter, written from the University Club, is just come. It makes a very distinct impression on my mind which my own conclusions and fears have long confirmed. Let me put it at its worst and in very bald terms: The Great White Chief is at bottom pacifist, has always been so and is so now. Of course I do not mean a pacifist at any price, certainly not a cowardly pacifist. But (looked at theoretically) war is, of course, an absurd way of settling any quarrel, an irrational way. Men and nations are wasteful, cruel, pigheaded fools to indulge in it. Quite true. But war is also the only means of adding to a nation's territory the territory of other nations which they do not wish to sell or to give up—the robbers' only way to get more space or to get booty. This last explains this war. Every Hohenzollern (except the present Emperor's father, who reigned only a few months) since Frederick the Great has added to Prussian and German area of rule. Every one, therefore, as he comes to the throne, feels an obligation to make his addition to the Empire. For this the wars of Prussia with Austria, with Denmark, with France were brought on. They succeeded and won the additions that old William I made to the Empire. Now William II must make *his* addition. He prepared for more than forty years; the nation prepared before he came to the throne and his whole reign has been given to making sure that he was ready. It's a robber's raid. Of course, the German case has been put so as to direct attention from this bald fact.

Now the philosophical pacifists—I don't mean the cowardly, yellow-dog ones—have never quite seen the war in this aspect. They regard it as a dispute about something—about trade, about more seaboard, about this or that, whereas it is only a robber's adventure. They want other people's property. They want money, treasure, land, indemnities, minerals, raw materials; and they set out to take them.

Now confusing this character of the war with some sort of rational dispute about something, the pacifists try in every way to stop it, so that the "issue" may be reasoned out, debated, discussed, negotiated. Surely the President tried to reach peace—tried **as** hard and as long as the people would allow him. The Germans argued away time with him while they got their submarine fleet built. Then they carried out the programme they had always had in mind and had never thought of abandoning. Now they wish to gain more time, to slacken the efforts of the Allies, if possible to separate them by asking for "discussions"—peace by "negotiation." When you are about to kill the robber, he cries out, "For God's sake, let's discuss the question between us. We can come to terms."—Now here's where the danger comes from the philosophical pacifist—from any man who does not clearly understand the nature of the war and of the enemy. To discuss the difference between us is so very reasonable in sound—so very reasonable in fact if there were a discussable difference. It is a programme that would always be in order except with a burglar or a robber.

The yet imperfect understanding of the war and of the nature of the German in the United States, especially at Washington—more especially in the White House—herein lies the danger.

. . . This little rest down here is a success. The weather is a disappointment—windy and cold. But to be away from London and away from folks—that's much. Shoecraft is very good.[1] He sends us next to nothing. Almost all we've got is an invitation to lunch with Their Majesties and they've been good enough to put that off. It's a far-off country, very fine, I'm sure in summer, and with most beautiful golf links. The hill is now so windy that no sane man can play there.

We're enjoying the mere quiet. And your mother is quite well again.

Affectionately,

W. H. P.

---

[1] Eugene C. Shoecraft, the Ambassador's secretary.

To Mrs. Charles G. Loring

St. Ives, Cornwall,
March 10, 1918.

DEAR KITTY:

A week here. No news. Shoecraft says we've missed nothing in London. What we came for we've got: your mother's quite well. She climbs these high hills quite spryly. We've had a remarkable week in this respect— we haven't carried on a conversation with any human being but ourselves. I don't think any such thing has ever happened before. I can stand a week, perhaps a fortnight of this now. But I don't care for it for any long period. At the bottom of this high and steep hill is the quaintest little town I ever saw. There are some streets so narrow that when a donkey cart comes along the urchins all have to run to the next corner or into doors. There is no sidewalk, of course; and the donkey cart takes the whole room between the houses. Artists take to the town, and they have funny little studios down by the water front in tiny houses built of stone in pieces big enough to construct a tidewater front. Imagine stone walls made of stone, each weighing tons, built into little houses about as big as your little back garden! There's one fellow here (an artist) whom I used to know in New York, so small has the world become!

On another hill behind us is a triangular stone monument to John Knill. He was once mayor of the town. When he died in 1782, he left money to the town. If the town is to keep the money (as it has) the Mayor must once in every five years form a procession and march up to this monument. There ten girls, natives of the town, and two widows must dance around the monument to the playing of a fiddle and a drum, the girls dressed in white. This ceremony has gone on, once in five years, all this time and the town has old Knill's money!

Your mother and I—though we are neither girls nor widows—danced around it this morning, wondering what sort of curmudgeon old John Knill was.

Don't you see how easily we fall into an idle mood?

Well, here's a photograph of little Alice looking up at me from the table where I write—a good, sweet face she has.

And you'll never get another letter from me in a time and from a place whereof there is so little to tell.

Affectionately, dear Kitty,

W. H. P.

To Ralph W. Page

Tregenna Castle Hotel,
St. Ives, Cornwall,
March 12, 1918.

MY DEAR RALPH:

Arthur has sent me Gardiner's 37-page sketch of American-British Concords and Discords—a remarkable sketch; and he has reminded me that your summer plan is to elaborate (into a popular style) your sketch of the same subject. You and Gardiner went over the same ground, each in a very good fashion. That's a fascinating task, and it opens up a wholly new vista of our History and of Anglo-Saxon, democratic history. Much lies ahead of that. And all this puts it in my mind to write you a little discourse on *style*. Gardiner has no style. He put his facts down much as he would have noted on a blue print the facts about an engineering project that he sketched. The style of your article, which has much to be said for it as a magazine article, is not the best style for a book.

Now, this whole question of style—well, it's the gist of good writing. There's no really effective writing without it. Especially is this true of historical writing. Look at X Y Z's writings. He knows his American history and has written much on it. He's written it as an Ohio blacksmith shoes a horse—not a touch of literary value in it all; all dry as dust—as dry as old Bancroft.

Style is good breeding—and art—in writing. It consists of the arrangement of your matter, first; then, more, of the gait; the manner and the manners of your expressing it. Work every group of facts, naturally and logically grouped to begin with, into a climax. Work every group up as a sculptor works out his idea or a painter, each group complete in itself. Throw out any superfluous facts or any merely minor facts that prevent the orderly working up of the group—that prevent or mar the effect you wish to present.

Then, when you've got a group thus presented, go over what you've made of it, to make sure you've used your material and its arrangement to the best effect, taking away merely extraneous or superfluous or distracting facts, here and there adding concrete illustrations—putting in a convincing detail here, and there a touch of colour.

Then go over it for your vocabulary. See that you use no word in a different meaning than it was used 100 years ago and will be used 100 years hence. You wish to use only the permanent words—words, too, that will be understood to carry the same meaning to English readers in every part of the world. Your vocabulary must be chosen from the permanent, solid, stable parts of the language.

Then see that no sentence contains a hint of obscurity. Then go over the words you use to see if they be the best. Don't fall into merely current phrases. If you have a long word, see if a native short one can be put in its place which will be more natural and stronger. Avoid a Latin vocabulary and use a plain English one—short words instead of long ones.

Most of all, use *idioms*—English idioms of force. Say an agreement was "come to." Don't say it was "consummated." For the difference between idioms and a Latin style, compare Lincoln with George Washington. One's always interesting and convincing. The other is dull in spite of all his good sense. How most folk do misuse and waste words!

Freeman went too far in his use of one-syllable words. It became an affectation. But he is the only man I can think of that ever did go too far in that direction. X— would have written a great history if he had had the natural use of idioms. As it is, he has good sense and no style; and his book isn't half so interesting as it would have been if he had some style—some proper value of short, clear-cut words that mean only one thing and that leave no vagueness.

You'll get a good style if you practice it. It is in your blood and temperament and way of saying things. But it's a high art and must be laboriously cultivated.

Yours affectionately,
W. H. P.

This glimpse of a changing and chastened England appears in a letter of this period:

The disposition shown by an endless number of such incidents is something more than a disposition of gratitude of a people helped when they are hard pressed. All these things show the changed and changing Englishman. It has already come to him that he may be weaker than he had thought himself and that he may need friends more than he had once imagined; and, if he must have helpers and friends, he'd rather have his own kinsmen. He's a queer "cuss," this Englishman. But he isn't a liar nor a coward nor any sort of "a yellow dog." He's true, and he never runs—a possible hero any day, and, when heroic, modest and quiet and graceful. The trouble with him has been that he got great world power too easily. In the times when he exploited the world for his own enrichment, there were no other successful exploiters. It became an easy game to him. He organized sea traffic and sea power. Of course he became rich—far, far richer than anybody else, and, therefore, content with himself. He has, therefore, kept much of his mediæval impedimenta, his dukes and marquesses and all that they imply—his outworn ceremonies and his mediæval disregard of his social inferiors. Nothing is well done in this Kingdom for the big public, but only for the classes. The railway stations have no warm waiting rooms. The people pace the platform till the train comes, and milord sits snugly wrapt up in his carriage till his footman announces the approach of the train. And occasional discontent is relieved by emigration to the Colonies. If any man becomes weary of his restrictions he may go to Australia and become a gentleman. The remarkable loyalty of the Colonies has in it something of a servant's devotion to his old master.

Now this trying time of war and the threat and danger of extinction are bringing—have in fact already brought —the conviction that many changes must come. The first sensible talk about popular education ever heard here is just now beginning. Many a gentleman has made up his mind to try to do with less than seventeen servants for the rest of his life since he now *has* to do with less. Privilege, on which so large a part of life here rests, is already pretty well shot to pieces. A lot of old baggage will never be recovered after this war: that's certain. During a little after-dinner speech in a club not long ago I indulged in a pleasantry about excessive impedimenta. Lord Derby, Minister of War and a bluff and honest aristocrat, sat near me and he whispered to me—"That's me." "Yes," I said, "that's you," and the group about us made merry at the jest. The meaning of this is, they now joke about what was the most solemn thing in life three years ago.

None of this conveys the idea I am trying to explain—the change in the English point of view and outlook—a half century's change in less than three years, radical and fundamental change, too. The mother of the Duke of X came to see me this afternoon, hobbling on her sticks and feeble, to tell me of a radiant letter she had received from her granddaughter who has been in Washington visiting the Spring Rices. "It's all very wonderful," said the venerable lady, "and my granddaughter actually heard the President make a speech!" Now, knowing this lady and knowing her son, the Duke, and knowing how this girl, his daughter, has been brought up, I dare swear that three years ago not one of them would have crossed the street to hear any President that ever lived. They've simply become different people. They were very genuine before. They are very genuine now.

It is this steadfastness in them that gives me sound hope for the future. They don't forget sympathy or help or friendship. Our going into the war has eliminated the Japanese question. It has shifted the virtual control of the world to English-speaking peoples. It will bring into the best European minds the American ideal of service.

It will, in fact, give us the lead and make the English in the long run our willing followers and allies. I don't mean that we shall always have plain sailing. But I do mean that the direction of events for the next fifty or one hundred years has now been determined.

Yet Page found one stolid opposition to his attempts to establish the friendliest relations between the two peoples. That offish attitude of the Washington Administration, to which reference has already been made, did not soften with the progress of events. Another experience now again brought out President Wilson's coldness toward his allies. About this time many rather queer Americans —some of the "international" breed—were coming to England on more or less official missions. Page was somewhat humiliated by these excursions; he knew that his country possessed an almost unlimited supply of vivid speakers, filled with zeal for the allied cause, whose influence, if they could be induced to cross the Atlantic, would put new spirit into the British. The idea of having a number of distinguished Americans come to England and tell the British public about the United States and especially about the American preparations for war, was one that now occupied his thoughts. In June, 1917, he wrote his old friend Dr. Wallace Buttrick, extending an invitation to visit Great Britain as a guest of the British Government. Dr. Buttrick made a great success; his speeches drew large crowds and proved a source of inspiration to the British masses. So successful were they, indeed, that the British Government desired that other Americans of similar type should come and spread the message. In November, therefore, Dr. Buttrick returned to the United States for the purpose of organizing such a committee. Among the eminent Americans whom he per-

suaded to give several months of their time to this work
of heartening our British allies were Mr. George E. Vincent,
President of the Rockefeller Foundation, Mr. Harry Pratt
Judson, President of Chicago University, Mr. Charles
R. Van Hise, President of the University of Wisconsin,
Mr. Edwin A. Alderman, President of the University of
Virginia, Mr. Harry Emerson Fosdick, and Bishop Law-
rence of Massachusetts. It was certainly a distinguished
group, but it was the gentleman selected to be its head
that gave it almost transcendent importance in the eyes
of the British Government. This was ex-President William H. Taft. The British lay greater emphasis upon
official rank than do Americans, and the fact that an ex-
President of the United States was to head this delegation
made it almost an historic event. Mr. Taft was exceedingly busy, but he expressed his willingness to give up all
his engagements for several months and to devote his
energies to enlightening the British public about America
and its purposes in the war. An official invitation was
sent him from London and accepted.

Inasmuch as Mr. Taft was an ex-President and a
representative of the political party opposed to the one
in power, he thought it only courteous that he call upon
Mr. Wilson, explain the purpose of his mission, and obtain
his approval. He therefore had an interview with the
President at the White House; the date was December 12,
1917. As soon as Mr. Wilson heard of the proposed visit
to Great Britain he showed signs of irritation. He at
once declared that it met with his strongest disapproval.
When Mr. Taft remarked that the result of such an enterprise would be to draw Great Britain and the United States
more closely together, Mr. Wilson replied that he seriously
questioned the desirability of drawing the two countries
any more closely together than they already were. He

was opposed to putting the United States in a position of seeming in any way to be involved with British policy. There were divergencies of purpose, he said, and there were features of the British policy in this war of which he heartily disapproved. The motives of the United States in this war, the President continued, "were unselfish, but the motives of Great Britain seemed to him to be of a less unselfish character." Mr. Wilson cited the treaty between Great Britain and Italy as a sample of British statesmanship which he regarded as proving this contention. The President's reference to this Italian treaty has considerable historic value; there has been much discussion as to when the President first learned of its existence, but it is apparent from this conversation with ex-President Taft that he must have known about it on December 12, 1917, for President Wilson based his criticism of British policy largely upon this Italian convention.[1]

The President showed more and more feeling about the matter as the discussion continued. "There are too many Englishmen," he said, "in this country and in Washington now and I have asked the British Ambassador to have some of them sent home."

Mr. Wilson referred to the jealousy of France at the close relations which were apparently developing between Great Britain and the United States. This was another reason, he thought, why it was unwise to make the bonds between them any tighter. He also called Mr. Taft's attention to the fact that there were certain elements in the United States which were opposed to Great Britain— this evidently being a reference to the Germans and the

---

[1] As related in Chapter XXII, page 267, President Wilson was informed of the so-called "secret treaties" by Mr. Balfour, in the course of his memorable visit to the White House.

Irish—and he therefore believed that any conspicuous attempts to increase the friendliness of the two countries for each other would arouse antagonism and resentment.'

As Mr. Taft was leaving he informed Mr. Wilson that the plan for his visit and that of the other speakers had originated with the American Ambassador to Great Britain. This, however, did not improve the President's temper.

"Page," said the President, "is really an Englishman and I have to discount whatever he says about the situation in Great Britain."

And then he added, "I think you ought not to go, and the same applies to the other members of the party. I would like you to make my attitude on this question known to those having the matter in charge."

Despite this rebuff Dr. Buttrick and Mr. Taft were reluctant to give up the plan. An appeal was therefore made to Colonel House. Colonel House at once said that the proposed visit was an excellent thing and that he would make a personal appeal to Mr. Wilson in the hope of changing his mind. A few days afterward Colonel House called up Dr. Buttrick and informed him that he had not succeeded. "I am sorry," wrote Colonel House to Page, "that the Buttrick speaking programme has turned out as it has. The President was decidedly opposed to it and referred to it with some feeling."

CHAPTER XXV

GETTING THE AMERICAN TROOPS TO FRANCE

A GROUP of letters, written at this time, touch upon a variety of topics which were then engaging the interest of all countries:

To Arthur W. Page

London, January 19, 1918.

DEAR ARTHUR:

While your letter is still fresh in my mind I dictate the following in answer to your question about Palestine.

It has not been settled—and cannot be, I fancy, until the Peace Conference—precisely what the British will do with Palestine, but I have what I think is a correct idea of their general attitude on the subject. First, of course, they do not propose to allow it to go back into Turkish hands; and the same can be said also of Armenia and possibly of Mesopotamia. Their idea of the future of Palestine is that whoever shall manage the country, or however it shall be managed, the Jews shall have the same chance as anybody else. Of course that's quite an advance for the Jews there, but their idea is not that the Jews should have command of other populations there or control over them—not in the least. My guess at the English wish, which I have every reason to believe is the right guess, is that they would wish to have Palestine internationalized, whatever that means. That is to say, that it should have control of its own local affairs and be a free country but that some great Power, or number of Powers, should see to it that none of the races that live there should be allowed to impose upon the other races. I don't know just how such a guarantee can be given by the great Powers or such a responsibility assumed except by an agreement among two or three of them, or barely possibly by the English keeping control themselves; but the control by the English after the war of the former German colonies will put such a large task on them that they will not be particularly eager to extend the area of their responsibility elsewhere. Of course a difficult problem will come up also about Constantinople and the Dardanelles. The Dardanelles must be internationalized.

I have never been able to consider the Zionist movement seriously. It is a mere religious sentiment which will express itself in action by very few people. I have asked a number of Jews at various times who are in favour of the Zionist movement if they themselves are going there. They always say no. The movement, therefore, has fixed itself in my mind as a Jewish movement in which no Jew that you can lay your hands on will ever take part but who wants other Jews to take part in it. Of course there might be a flocking to Palestine of Jews from Russia and the adjoining countries where they are not happy, but I think the thing is chiefly a sentiment and nothing else. Morgenthau[1] is dead right. I agree with him *in toto*. I do not think anybody in the United States need be the least concerned about the Zionist movement because there isn't a single Jew in our country such a fool as to go to Palestine when he can stay in the United States. The whole thing is a sentimental, religious, more or less

---

[1] Mr. Henry Morgenthau, American Ambassador to Turkey, 1913–16, an American of Jewish origin who opposed the Zionist movement as un-American and deceptive.

Admiral William Sowden Sims, Commander of American naval
forces operating in European waters during the Great War

A silver model of the *Mayflower*, the farewell gift of the Plymouth
Council to Mr. Page

unnatural and fantastic idea and I don't think will ever trouble so practical a people as we and our Jews are.

The following memorandum is dated February 10, 1918:

General Bliss[1] has made a profound and the best possible impression here by his wisdom and his tact. The British have a deep respect for him and for his opinions, and in inspiring and keeping high confidence in us he is worth an army in himself. I have seen much of him and found out a good deal about his methods. He is simplicity and directness itself. Although he is as active and energetic as a boy, he spends some time by himself to think things out and even to say them to himself to see how his conclusions strike the ear as well as the mind. He has been staying here at the house of one of our resident officers. At times he goes to his room and sits long by the fire and argues his point—out loud—oblivious to everything else. More than once when he was so engaged one of his officers has knocked at the door and gone in and laid telegrams on the table beside him and gone out without his having known of the officer's entrance. Then he comes out and tries his conclusion on someone who enjoys his confidence. And then he stands by it and when the time comes delivers it slowly and with precision; and there he is; and those who hear him see that he has thought the matter out on all sides and finally.

Our various establishments in London have now become big—the Embassy proper, the Naval and Army Headquarters, the Red Cross, the War Trade Board's representatives, and now (forthwith) the Shipping Board, besides Mr. Crosby of the Treasury. The volume of work is

---

[1]American member of the Supreme War Council. Afterward member of the American Commission to Negotiate Peace.

enormous and it goes smoothly, except for the somewhat halting Army Headquarters, the high personnel of which is now undergoing a change; and that will now be all right. I regularly make the rounds of all the Government Departments with which we deal to learn if they find our men and methods effective, and the rounds of all our centres of activity to find whether there be any friction with the British. The whole machine moves very well. For neither side hesitates to come to me whenever they strike even small snags. All our people are at work on serious tasks and (so far as I know) there are now none of those despicable creatures here who used during our neutrality days to come from the United States on peace errands and what-not to spy on the Embassy and me (their inquiries and their correspondence were catalogued by the police). I have been amazed at the activity of some of them whose doings I have since been informed of.

We now pay this tribute to the submarines—that we have entered the period of compulsory rations. There is enough to eat in spite of the food that has gone to feed the fishes. But no machinery of distribution to a whole population can be uniformly effective. The British worker with his hands is a greedy feeder and a sturdy growler and there will be trouble. But I know no reason to apprehend serious trouble.

The utter break-up of Russia and the German present occupation of so much of the Empire as she wants have had a contrary effect on two sections of opinion here, as I interpret the British mind. On the undoubtedly enormously dominant section of opinion these events have only stiffened resolution. They say that Germany now *must* be whipped to a finish. Else she will have doubled her empire and will hold the peoples of her new territory as vassals without regard to their wishes and the war lord caste will be more firmly seated than ever before. If her armies be literally whipped she'll have to submit to the Allies' terms, which will dislodge her from overlordship over these new unwilling subjects—and she can be dislodged in no other way. This probably means a long war, now that after a time she can get raw materials for war later and food from Rumania and the Ukraine, etc. This will mean a fight in France and Belgium till a decisive victory is won and the present exultant German will is broken.

The minority section of public opinion—as I judge a small minority—has the feeling that such an out-and-out military victory cannot be won or is not worth the price; and that the enemies of Germany, allowing her to keep her Eastern accretions, must make the best terms they can in the East; that there's no use in running the risk of Italy's defeat and defection before some sort of bargain could be made about Belgium, Alsace-Lorraine, and Serbia. Of course this plan would leave the German warlordship intact and would bring no sort of assurance of a prolonged peace. It would, too, leave European Russia at least to German mercy, and would leave the Baltic and the Black Seas practically wholly under German influence. As for the people of Russia, there seems small chance for them in this second contingency. The only way to save them is to win a decisive victory.

As matters stand to-day Lord Lansdowne and his friends (how numerous they are nobody knows) are the loudest spokesmen for such a peace as can be made. But it is talked much of in Asquith circles that the time may come when this policy will be led by Mr. Asquith, in a form somewhat modified from the Lansdowne formula. Mr. Asquith has up to this time patriotically supported the government and he himself has said nothing in public which could warrant linking his name with an early peace-seeking policy. But his friends openly and incessantly predict that he will, at a favourable moment, take this cue. I myself can hardly believe it. Political victory in Great Britain doesn't now lie in that direction.

The dominant section of opinion is much grieved at Russia's surrender, but they refuse to be discouraged by it. They recall how Napoleon overran most of Europe, and the French held practically none of his conquests after his fall.

Such real political danger as exists here—if any exists, of which I am not quite sure—comes not only now mainly of this split in public opinion but also and to a greater degree from the personal enemies of the present government. Lloyd George is kept in power because he is the most energetic man in sight—by far. Many who support him do not like him nor trust him—except that nobody doubts his supreme earnestness to win the war. On all other subjects he has enemies of old and he makes new ones. His intense and superb energy has saved him in two notable crises. His dismissal of Sir William Robertson[1] has been accepted in the interest of greater unity of military control, but it was a dangerous rapids that he shot, for he didn't do it tactfully. Yet there's a certain danger to the present powers in the feeling that some of them are wearing out. Parliament itself—an old one now—is thought to have gone stale. Bonar Law is over-worked and tired; Balfour is often said to be too philosophical and languid; but, when this feeling seems in danger of taking definite shape, he makes a clearer statement than anybody else and catches on his feet. The man of new energy, not yet fagged, is Geddes,[2] whose frankness carries conviction.

---

[1] Sir Henry Wilson had recently succeeded Sir William Robertson as Chief of the Imperial General Staff.

[2] First Lord of the Admiralty.

To the President

London, March 17, 1918.

DEAR MR. PRESIDENT:

The rather impatient and unappreciative remarks made by the Prime Minister before a large meeting of preachers of the "free" churches about a League of Nations reminds me to write you about the state of British opinion on that subject. What Lloyd George said to these preachers is regrettable because it showed a certain impatience of mind from which he sometimes suffers; but it is only fair to him to say that his remarks that day did not express a settled opinion. For on more than one previous occasion he has spoken of the subject in a wholly different tone— much more appreciatively. On that particular day he had in mind only the overwhelming necessity to win the war— other things, *all* other things must wait. In a way this is his constant mood—the mood to make everybody feel that the only present duty is to win the war. He has been accused of almost every defect in the calendar except of slackness about the war. Nobody has ever doubted his earnestness nor his energy about *that*. And the universal confidence in his energy and earnestness is what keeps him in office. Nobody sees any other man who can push and inspire as well as he does. It would be a mistake, therefore, to pay too much heed to any particular utterance of this electrical creature of moods, on any subject.

Nevertheless, he hasn't thought out the project of a league to enforce peace further than to see the difficulties. He sees that such a league might mean, in theory at least, the giving over in some possible crisis the command of the British Fleet to an officer of some other nationality. That's unthinkable to any red-blooded son of these islands. Seeing a theoretical possibility even of raising such a question, the British mind stops and refuses to go further—refuses in most cases even to inquire seriously whether any such contingency is ever likely to come.

The British Grand Fleet, in fact, is a subject that stands alone in power and value and in difficulties. It classifies itself with nothing else. Since over and over again it has saved these islands from invasion when nothing else could have saved them and since during this war in particular it has saved the world from German conquest—as every Englishman believes—it lies in their reverence and their gratitude and their abiding convictions as a necessary and perpetual shield so long as Great Britain shall endure. If the Germans are thrashed to a frazzle (and we haven't altogether done that yet) and we set about putting the world in order, when we come to discuss Disarmament, the British Fleet will be the most difficult item in the world to dispose of. It is not only a Fact, with a great and saving history, it is also a sacred Tradition and an Article of Faith.

The first reason, therefore, why the British general mind has not firmly got hold on a league is the instinctive fear that the formation of any league may in some conceivable way affect the Grand Fleet. Another reason is the general inability of a somewhat slow public opinion to take hold on more than one subject at a time or more than one urgent part of one subject. The One Subject, of course, is winning the war. Since everything else depends on that, everything else must wait on that.

The League, therefore, has not taken hold on the public imagination here as it has in the United States. The large mass of the people have not thought seriously about it: it has not been strongly and persistently presented to the mass of the people. There is no popular or general organization to promote it. There is even, here and there, condemnation of the idea. The (London) *Morning Post*, for example, goes out of its way once in a while to show the wickedness of the idea because, so it argues, it will involve the sacrifice, more or less, of nationality. But the *Morning Post* is impervious to new ideas and is above all things critical in its activities and very seldom constructive. The typical Tory mind in general sees no good in the idea. The typical Tory mind is the insular mind.

On the other hand, the League idea is understood as a necessity and heartily approved by two powerful sections of public opinion—(1) the group of public men who have given attention to it, such as Bryce, Lord Robert Cecil, and the like, and (2) some of the best and strongest leaders of Labour. There is good reason to hope that whenever a fight and an agitation is made for a League these two sections of public opinion will win; but an agitation and a fight must come. Lord Bryce, in the intervals of his work as chairman of a committee to make a plan for the reorganization of the House of Lords, which, he remarked to me the other day, "involves as much labour as a Government Department," has fits of impatience about pushing a campaign for a league, and so have a few other men. They ask me if it be not possible to have good American public speakers come here—privately, of course, and in no way connected with our Government nor speaking for it—to explain the American movement for a League in order to arouse a public sentiment on the subject.

Thus the case stands at present.

Truth and error alike and odd admixtures of them come in waves over this censored land where one can seldom determine what is true, before the event, from the newspapers. "News" travels by word of mouth, and information that one can depend on is got by personal inquiry from sources that can be trusted.

There is a curious wave of fear just now about what Labour may do, and the common gossip has it that there is grave danger in the situation. I can find no basis for such a fear. I have talked with labour leaders and I have talked with members of the government who know most about the subject. There is not a satisfactory situation—there has not been since the war began. There has been a continuous series of labour "crises," and there have been a good many embarrassing strikes, all of which have first been hushed up and settled—at least postponed. One cause of continuous trouble has been the notion held by the Unions, sometimes right and sometimes wrong, that the employers were making abnormal profits and that they were not getting their due share. There have been and are also other causes of trouble. It was a continuous quarrel even in peace times. But I can find no especial cause of fear now. Many of the Unions have had such advances of wages that the Government has been severely criticized for giving in. Just lately a large wing of the Labour Party put forth its war aims which—with relatively unimportant exceptions—coincide with the best declarations made by the Government's own spokesmen.

Of course, no prudent man would venture to make dogmatic predictions. There have been times when for brief intervals any one would have been tempted to fear that these quarrels might cause an unsatisfactory conclusion of the war. But the undoubted patriotism of the British workman has every time saved the situation. While a danger point does lie here, there is no reason to be more fearful now than at any preceding time when no especial trouble was brewing. This wave of gossip and fear has no right to sweep over the country now.

Labour hopes and expects and is preparing to win the next General Election—whether with good reason or not

I cannot guess. But most men expect it to win the Government at some time—most of them *after* the war. I recall that Lord Grey once said to me, before the war began, that a general political success of the Labour Party was soon to be expected.

Another wave which, I hear, has swept over Rome as well as London is a wave of early peace expectation. The British newspapers have lately been encouraging this by mysterious phrases. Some men here of good sense and sound judgment think that this is the result of the so-called German "peace offensive," which makes the present the most dangerous period of the war.

W. H. P.

To David F. Houston[1]

London, March 23, 1918.

My dear Houston:

It is very kind of you indeed to write so generously about the British visitors who are invading our sacred premises, such as the Archbishop of York, and it is good to hear from you anyhow about any subject and I needn't say that it is quite a rare experience also. I wish you would take a little of your abundant leisure and devote it to good letters to me.

And in some one of your letters tell me this.—The British send over men of this class that you have written about to see us, but they invite over here—and we permit to come—cranks on prohibition, experts in the investigation of crime, short-haired women who wish to see how British babies are reared, peace cranks and freaks of other kinds.[2] Our Government apparently won't let plain,

---

[1] Secretary of Agriculture.
[2] See Chapter XXIV.

honest, normal civilians come over, but if a fellow comes along who wants to investigate some monstrosity then one half of the Senate, one half of the House of Representatives, and a number of the executive offices of the Government give him the most cordial letters. Now there are many things, of course, that I don't know, but it has been my fate to have a pretty extensive acquaintance with cranks of every description in the United States. I don't think there is any breed of them that didn't haunt my office while I was an editor. Now I am surely punished for all my past sins by having those fellows descend on me here. I know them, nearly all, from past experience and now just for the sake of keeping the world as quiet as possible I have to give them time here far out of proportion to their value.

Now, out of your great wisdom, I wish you would explain to me why the deuce we let all this crew come over here instead of sending a shipload of perfectly normal, dignified, and right-minded gentlemen. These thug reformers!—Baker will be here in a day or two and if I can remember it I am going to suggest to him that he round them all up and put them in the trenches in France where those of them who have so far escaped the gallows ought to be put.

I am much obliged to have the illuminating statement about our crops. I am going to show it to certain gentlemen here who will be much cheered by it. By gracious, you ought to hear their appreciation of what we are doing! We are not doing it for the sake of their appreciation, but if we were out to win it we could not do it better. Down at bottom the Englishman is a good fellow. He has his faults but he doesn't get tired and he doesn't suffer spasms of emotion.

Give my love to Mrs. Houston, and do sit down and

write me a good long letter—a whole series of them, in fact.

Believe me, always most heartily yours,

WALTER HINES PAGE.

To Frank L. Polk

London, March 22, 1918.

DEAR MR. POLK:

You are good enough to mention the fact that the Embassy has some sort of grievance against the Department. Of course it has, and you are, possibly, the only man that can remove it. It is this: You don't come here to see the war and this government and these people who are again saving the world as we are now saving them. I thank Heaven and the Administration for Secretary Baker's visit. It is a dramatic moment in the history of the race, of democracy, and of the world. The State Department has the duty to deal with foreign affairs—the especial duty—and yet no man in the State Department has been here since the war began. This doesn't look pretty and it won't look pretty when the much over-worked "future historian" writes it down in a book. Remove that grievance.

The most interesting thing going on in the world to-day —a thing that in History will transcend the war and be reckoned its greatest gain—is the high leadership of the President in formulating the struggle, in putting its aims high, and in taking the democratic lead in the world, a lead that will make the world over—and in taking the democratic lead of the English-speaking folk. Next most impressive to that is to watch the British response to that lead. Already they have doubled the number of their voters, and even more important definite steps in Democracy will be taken. My aim—and it's the only way to save the world—is to lead the British in this direction. They are the most easily teachable people in our way of thinking and of doing. Of course everybody who works toward such an aim provokes the cry from a lot of fools among us who accuse him of toadying to the English and of "accepting the conventional English conclusion." They had as well talk of missionaries to India accepting Confucius or Buddha. Their fleet has saved us four or five times. It's about time we were saving them from this bloody Thing that we call Europe, for our sake and for theirs.

The bloody Thing will get us all if we don't fight our level best; and it's only by *our* help that we'll be saved. That clearly gives us the leadership. Everybody sees that. Everybody acknowledges it. The President authoritatively speaks it—speaks leadership on a higher level than it was ever spoken before to the whole world. As soon as we get this fighting job over, the world procession toward freedom—our kind of freedom—will begin under our lead. This being so, can't you delegate the writing of telegrams about "facilitating the license to ship poppy seed to McKesson and Robbins," and come over and see big world-forces at work?

I cannot express my satisfaction at Secretary Baker's visit. It was historic—the first member of the Cabinet, I think, who ever came here while he held office. He made a great impression and received a hearty welcome.

That's the only grievance I can at the moment unload on you. We're passing out of our old era of isolation. These benighted heathen on this island whom we'll yet save (since they are well worth saving) will be with us as

we need them in future years and centuries.   Come, help
us heighten this fine spirit.

Always heartily yours,

WALTER HINES PAGE.

P. S. You'd see how big our country looks from a distance.   It's gigantic, I assure you.

The above letter was written on what was perhaps the
darkest day of the whole war.   The German attack on
the Western Front, which had been long expected, had
now been launched, and, at the moment that Page was
penning this cheery note to Mr. Polk, the German armies
had broken through the British defenses, had pushed their
lines forty miles ahead, and, in the judgment of many
military men, had Paris almost certainly within their
grasp.   A great German gun, placed about seventy miles
from the French capital, was dropping shells upon the
apparently doomed city.   This attack had been regarded
as inevitable since the collapse of Russia, which had enabled the Germans to concentrate practically all their
armies on the Western Front.

The world does not yet fully comprehend the devastating effect of this apparently successful attack upon
the allied morale.   British statesmen and British soldiers
made no attempt to conceal from official Americans the
desperate state of affairs.   It was the expectation that
the Germans might reach Calais and thence invade England. The War Office discussed these probabilities most
freely with Colonel Slocum, the American military attaché.
The simple fact was that both the French and the British
armies were practically bled white.

"For God's sake, get your men over!" they urged General Slocum.   "You have got to finish it."

Page was writing urgently to President Wilson to the same purpose. Send the men and send them at once. "I pray God," were his solemn words to Mr. Wilson, "that you will not be too late!"

One propitious event had taken place at the same time as the opening of the great German offensive. Mr. Newton D. Baker, the American Secretary of War, had left quietly for France in late February, 1918, and had reached the Western Front in time to obtain a first-hand sight of the great March drive. No visit in history has ever been better timed, and no event could have better played into Page's hands. He had been urging Washington to send all available forces to France at the earliest possible date; he knew, as probably few other men knew, the extent to which the Allies were depending upon American troops to give the final blow to Germany; and the arrival of Secretary Baker at the scene of action gave him the opportunity to make a personal appeal. Page immediately communicated with the Secretary and persuaded him to come at once to London for a consultation with British military and political leaders. The Secretary spent only three days in London, but the visit, brief as it was, had historic consequences. He had many consultations with the British military men; he entered into their plans with enthusiasm; he himself received many ideas that afterward took shape in action, and the British Government obtained from him first-hand information as to the progress of the American Army and the American determination to coöperate to the last man and the last dollar. "Baker went straight back to France," Page wrote to his son Arthur, "and our whole coöperation began."

Page gave a dinner to Mr. Baker at the Embassy on March 23rd—two days after the great March drive had begun. This occasion gave the visitor a memorable glimpse of the British temperament. Mr. Lloyd George, Mr. Balfour, Lord Derby, the War Secretary, General Biddle, of the United States Army, and Admiral Sims were the Ambassador's guests. Though the mighty issues then overhanging the world were not ignored in the conversation the atmosphere hardly suggested that the existence of the British Empire, indeed that of civilization itself, was that very night hanging in the balance. Possibly it was the general sombreness of events that caused these British statesmen to find a certain relief in jocular small talk and reminiscence. For the larger part of the evening not a word was said about the progress of the German armies in France. Mr. Lloyd George and Mr. Balfour, seated on opposite sides of the table, apparently found relaxation in reviewing their political careers and especially their old-time political battles. They would laughingly recall occasions when, in American parlance, they had put each other "in a hole"; the exigencies of war had now made these two men colleagues in the same government, but the twenty years preceding 1914 they had spent in political antagonism. Page's guests on this occasion learned much political history of the early twentieth century, and the mutual confessions of Mr. Lloyd George and Mr. Balfour gave these two men an insight into each others' motives and manœuvres which was almost as revealing. "Yes, you caught me that time," Mr. Lloyd George would say, and then he would counter with an episode of a political battle in which he had got the better of Mr. Balfour. The whole talk was lively and bantering, and accompanied with much laughter; and all this time shells from that long-distance gun were dropping at fifteen minute intervals upon the devoted women and children of Paris and the Germans were every hour driving the British back in disorder. At times the conversation took a more philosophic

turn. Would the men present like to go back twenty-
five years and live their lives all over again? The practically unanimous decision of every man was that he would
not wish to do so.

All this, of course, was merely on the surface; despite
the laughter and the banter, there was only one thing which
engrossed the Ambassador's guests, although there were
not many references to it. That was the struggle which
was then taking place in France. At intervals Mr. Lloyd
George would send one of the guests, evidently a secretary, from the room. The latter, on his return, would
whisper something in the Prime Minister's ear, but more
frequently he would merely shake his head. Evidently
he had been sent to obtain the latest news of the
battle.

At one point the Prime Minister did refer to the great
things taking place in France.

"This battle means one thing," he said. "That is a
generalissimo."

"Why couldn't you have taken this step long ago?"
Admiral Sims asked Mr. Lloyd George.

The answer came like a flash.

"If the cabinet two weeks ago had suggested placing
the British Army under a foreign general, it would have
fallen. Every cabinet in Europe would also have fallen,
had it suggested such a thing."

Memorandum on Secretary Baker's visit

Secretary Baker's visit here, brief as it was, gave the
heartiest satisfaction. So far as I know, he is the first
member of an American Cabinet who ever came to England while he held office, as Mr. Balfour was the first
member of a British Cabinet who ever went to the United
States while he held office. The great governments of

the English-speaking folk have surely dealt with one another with mighty elongated tongs. Governments of democracies are not exactly instruments of precision. But they are at least human. But personal and human neglect of one another by these two governments over so long a period is an astonishing fact in our history. The wonder is that we haven't had more than two wars. And it is no wonder that the ignorance of Englishmen about America and the American ignorance of England are monumental, stupendous, amazing, passing understanding. I have on my mantelpiece a statuette of Benjamin Franklin, an excellent and unmistakable likeness which was made here during his lifetime; and the inscription burnt on its base is *Geo. Washington.* It serves me many a good turn with my English friends. I use it as a measure of their ignorance of us. Of course this is a mere little error of a statuette-maker, an error, moreover, of a hundred years ago. But it tells the story of to-day also. If I had to name the largest and most indelible impression that has been made on me during my five years' work here, I should say the ignorance and aloofness of the two peoples—not an ignorance of big essential facts but of personalities and temperaments—such as never occur except between men who had never seen one another.

But I was writing about Mr. Baker's visit and I've got a long way from that. I doubt if he knows himself what gratification it gave; for these men here have spoken to me about it as they could not speak to him.

Here is an odd fact: For sixty years, so far as I know, members of the Administration have had personal acquaintance with some of the men in power in Salvador, Costa Rica, Venezuela, Peru, etc., etc., and members of the British Government have had personal acquaintance with some men in authority in Portugal, Serbia, Montenegro and Monte Carlo; but during this time (with the single exception of John Hay) I think no member of any Administration had a real personal acquaintance while he held office with any member of the British Government while he held office, and vice versa—till Mr. Balfour's visit. Suspicion grows out of ignorance. The longer I live here the more astonished I become at the fundamental ignorance of the British about us and of our fundamental ignorance about them. So colossal is this ignorance that every American sent here is supposed to be taken in, to become Anglophile; and often when one undertakes to enlighten Englishmen about the United States one becomes aware of a feeling inside the English of unbelief, as if he said, "Oh, well! you are one of those queer people who believe in republican government." All this is simply amazing. Poor Admiral Sims sometimes has a sort of mania, a delusion that nobody at Washington trusts his judgment because he said seven or eight years ago that he liked the English. Yet every naval officer who comes here, I understand, shares his views about practically every important naval problem or question. I don't deserve the compliment (it's a very high one) that some of my secretaries sometimes pay me when they say that I am the only man they know who tries to tell the whole truth to our Government in favour of the Englishman as well as against him. It is certain that American public opinion is universally supposed to suspect any American who tries to do anything with the British lion except to twist his tail—a supposition that I never believed to be true.—But it is true that the mutual ignorance is as high as the Andes and as deep as the ocean. Personal acquaintance removes it and nothing else will.

To Arthur W. Page

American Embassy,
London, April 7, 1918.

DEAR ARTHUR:

I daresay you remember this epic:

Old Morgan's wife made butter and cheese;
Old Morgan drank the whey.
There came a wind from West to East
And blew Old Morgan away.

I'm Old Morgan and your mother got ashamed of my wheyness and made the doctor prescribe cream for me. There's never been such a luxury, and anybody who supposes that I am now going to get fat and have my cream stopped simply doesn't know me. So, you see why I'm intent on shredded wheat biscuits. That's about the best form of real wheat that will keep. And there's no getting real wheat-stuff, pure and simple, in any other form.

There's no use in talking about starving people—except perhaps in India and China. White men can live on anything. The English could fight a century on cabbage and Brussels sprouts. I've given up hope of starving the Germans. A gut of dogmeat or horse flesh and a potato will keep them in fighting trim forever. I've read daily for two years of impending starvation across the Rhine; but I never even now hear of any dead ones from hunger. Cold steel or lead is the only fatal dose for them.

Therefore I know that shredded wheat will carry me through.

You'll see, I hope, from the clippings that I enclose that I'm not done for yet anyhow. Two speeches a day is no small stunt; and I did it again yesterday—hand running; and I went out to dinner afterward. It was a notable occasion—this celebration of the anniversary of our coming into the war.[1]

Nobody here knows definitely just what to fear from the big battle; but everybody fears more or less. It's a critical time—very. I am told that that long-range gunning of Paris is the worst form of frightfulness yet tried. The shells do not kill a great many people. But their falling every fifteen minutes gets on people's nerves and they can't sleep. I hear they are leaving Paris in great numbers. Since the big battle began and the Germans have needed all their planes and more in France, they've let London alone. But nobody knows when they will begin again.

Nobody knows any future thing about the war, and everybody faces a fear.

Secretary Baker stayed with me the two days and three nights he was here. He made a good impression but he received a better one. He now knows something about the war. I had at dinner to meet him:

Lloyd George, Prime Minister.
Balfour, Foreign Secretary.
The Chief of Staff.
Lord Derby, War Secretary.
General Biddle, U. S. A., in command in London.
Admiral Sims, U. S. N.

The talk was to the point—good and earnest. Baker went straight back to France and our *whole* coöperation began. With the first group of four he had conferences besides for two days. His coming was an admirable move.

Yours affectionately,

W. H. P.

---

[1]This meeting, on April 6, 1918, was held at the Mansion House. Page and Mr. Balfour were the chief speakers.

To Ralph W. Page

London, April 13, 1918.

DEAR RALPH:

Your cheery letters about entertaining governors, planting trees and shrubbery and your mother's little orchard give us much pleasure. The Southern Pines paper brings news of very great damage to the peach crop. I hope it is much exaggerated. Is it?

We haven't any news here, and I send you my weekly note only to keep my record clear. The great battle—no one talks or thinks of anything else. We have suffered and still suffer a good deal of fear and anxiety, with real reason, too. But the military men are reassuring. Yet I don't know just how far to trust their judgment or to share their hopes. Certainly this is the most dangerous situation that modern civilization was ever put in. If we can keep them from winning any *great* objective, like Paris or a channel port, we ought to end the war this year. If not, either they win or at the least prolong the war indefinitely. It's a hazardous and trying time.

There were never such casualties on either side as now. Such a bloody business cannot keep up all summer. But before everybody is killed or a decisive conclusion is reached, the armies will, no doubt, dig themselves in and take a period of comparative rest. People here see and feel the great danger. But the extra effort now *may* come too late. Still we keep up good hope. The British are hard to whip. They never give up. And as for the French army, I always remember Verdun and keep my courage up.

The wounded are coming over by the thousand. We are incomparably busy and in great anxiety about the result (though still pretty firm in the belief that the Germans will lose), and luckily we keep very well.

Affectionately,

W. H. P.

To Ralph W. Page

London, April 7, 1918.

DEAR RALPH:

There used to be a country parson down in Wake County who, when other subjects were talked out, always took up the pleasing topic of saving your soul. That's the way your mother and I do—with the subject of going home. We talk over the battle, we talk over the boys, we talk over military and naval problems, we discuss the weather and all the babies, and then take up politics, and talk over the gossip of the wiseacres; but we seldom finish a conversation without discussing going home. And we reach just about as clear a conclusion on our topic as the country parson reached on his. I've had the doctors going over me (or rather your mother has) as an expert accountant goes over your books; and I tried to bribe them to say that I oughtn't to continue my arduous duties here longer. They wouldn't say any such thing. Thus that device failed—dead. It looks as if I were destined for a green old age and no martyr business at all.

All this is disappointing; and I don't see what to do but to go on. I can't keep from hoping that the big battle may throw some light on the subject; but there's no telling when the big battle will end. Nothing ends—that's the trouble. I sometimes feel that the war may never end, that it may last as the Napoleonic Wars did, for 20 years; and before that time we'll all have guns that shoot 100 miles. We can stay at home and indefinitely bombard the enemy across the Rhine—have an endless battle at long range.

So, we stick to it, and give the peach trees time to grow up.

We had a big day in London yesterday—the anniversary of our entry into the war. I send you some newspaper clippings about it.

The next best news is that we have a little actual sunshine—a very rare thing—and some of the weather is now almost decent. . . .

Affectionately,

W. H. P.

CHAPTER XXVI

LAST DAYS IN ENGLAND

IN SPITE of the encouraging tone of the foregoing letters, everything was not well with Page. All through the winter of 1917–1918 his associates at the Embassy had noticed a change for the worse in his health. He seemed to be growing thinner; his face was daily becoming more haggard; he tired easily, and, after walking the short distance from his house to his Embassy, he would drop listlessly into his chair. His general bearing was that of a man who was physically and nervously exhausted. It was hoped that the holiday at St. Ives would help him; that he greatly enjoyed that visit, especially the westward —homeward—outlook on the Atlantic which it gave him, his letters clearly show; there was a temporary improvement also in his health, but only a temporary one. The last great effort which he made in the interest of the common cause was Secretary Baker's visit; the activities which this entailed wearied him, but the pleasure he obtained from the resultant increase in the American participation made the experience one of the most profitable of his life. Indeed, Page's last few months in England, though full of sad memories for his friends, contained little but satisfaction for himself. He still spent many a lonely evening by his fire, but his thoughts were now far more pleasurable than in the old *Lusitania* days. The one absorbing subject of contemplation now was that America was "in." His country had justified his deep confidence. The American Navy had played a determining part in defeating the

374

submarine, and American shipyards were turning out merchant ships faster than the Germans were destroying them. American troops were reaching France at a rate which necessarily meant the early collapse of the German Empire. Page's own family had responded to the call and this in itself was a cause of great contentment to a sick and weary man. The Ambassador's youngest son, Frank, had obtained a commission and was serving in France; his son-in-law, Charles G. Loring, was also on the Western Front; while from North Carolina Page's youngest brother Frank and two nephews had sailed for the open battle line. The bravery and success of the American troops did not surprise the Ambassador but they made his last days in England very happy.

Indeed, every day had some delightful experience for Page. The performance of the Americans at Cantigny especially cheered him. The day after this battle he and Mrs. Page entertained Mr. Lloyd George and other guests at lunch. The Prime Minister came bounding into the room with his characteristic enthusiasm, rushed up to Mrs. Page with both hands outstretched and shook hands joyously.

"Congratulations!" he exclaimed. "The Americans have done it! They have met the Prussian guard and defeated them!"

Mr. Lloyd George was as exuberant over the achievement as a child.

This was now the kind of experience that had become Page's daily routine. Lively as were his spirits, however, his physical frame was giving way. In fact Page, though he did not know it at the time, was suffering from a specific disease—nephritis; and its course, after Christmas of 1917, became rapid. His old friend, Dr. Wallace Buttrick, had noted the change for the worse and had attempted to persuade him to go home.

"Quit your job, Page," he urged. "You have other big tasks waiting you at home. Why don't you go back?"

"No—no—not now."

"But, Page," urged Dr. Buttrick, "you are going to lay down your life."

"I have only one life to lay down," was the reply. "I can't quit now."

To Mary E. Page[1]

London, May 12, 1918.

DEAR MARY:

You'll have to take this big paper and this paint brush pen—it's all the pen these blunt British have. This is to tell you how very welcome your letter to Alice is—how *very* welcome, for nobody writes us the family news and nothing is so much appreciated. I'll try to call the shorter roll of us in the same way:

After a miserable winter we, too, are having the rare experience of a little sunshine in this dark, damp world of London. The constant confinement in the city and *in the house* (that's the worst of it—no outdoor life or fresh air) has played hob with my digestion. It's not bad, but it's troublesome, and for some time I've had the feeling of being one half well. It occurred to me the other day that I hadn't had leave from my work for four years, except my short visit home nearly two years ago. I asked for two months off, and I've got it. We are going down by the shore where there is fresh air and where I can live outdoors and get some exercise. We have a house that we can get there and be comfortable. To get away from London

---

[1]Of Aberdeen, N. C., the Ambassador's sister.

when the weather promises to be good, and to get away from people seemed a joyous prospect. I can, at any time I must, come to London in two hours.

The job's too important to give up at this juncture. This, then, is the way we can keep it going. I've no such hard task now as I had during the years of our neutrality, which, praise God! I somehow survived, though I am now suffering more or less from the physical effects of that strain. Yet, since I have had the good fortune to win the confidence of this Government and these people, I feel that I ought to keep on now until some more or less natural time to change comes.

Alice keeps remarkably well—since her influenza late in the winter; but a rest away from London is really needed as much by her as by me. They work her to death. In a little while she is to go, by the invitation of the Government and the consent of the King, to christen a new British warship at Newcastle. It will be named the "Eagle." Meantime I'll be trying to get outdoor life at Sandwich.

Yesterday a regiment of our National Army marched through the streets of London and were reviewed by the King and me; and the town made a great day of it. While there is an undercurrent of complaint in certain sections of English opinion because we didn't come into the war sooner, there is a very general and very genuine appreciation of everything we have done and of all that we do. Nothing could be heartier than the welcome given our men here yesterday. Nor could any men have made a braver or better showing than they made. They made us all swell with pride.

They are coming over now, as you know, in great quantities. There were about 8,000 landed here last week and about 30,000 more are expected this week. I think that many more go direct to France than come through England. On their way through England they do not come to London. Only twice have we had them here, yesterday and one day last summer when we had a parade of a regiment of engineers. For the *army* London is on a sidetrack—is an out of the way place. For our navy, of course, it's the European headquarters, since Admiral Sims has his headquarters here. We thus see a good many of our sailors who are allowed to come to London on leave. A few days ago I had a talk with a little bunch of them who came from one of our superdreadnaughts in the North Sea. They had just returned from a patrol across to the coast of Norway. "Bad luck, bad luck," they said, "on none of our long patrol trips have we seen a single Hun ship!"

About the war, you know as much as I know. There is a general confidence that the Allies will hold the Germans in their forthcoming effort to get to Calais or to Paris. Yet there is an undercurrent of fear. Nobody knows just how to feel about it. Probably another prodigious onslaught will be made before you receive this letter. It seems to me that we can make no intelligent guess until this German effort is finished in France—no guess about the future. If the Germans get the French ports (Calais, for example) the war will go on indefinitely. If they are held back, it *may* end next autumn or winter —partly because of starvation in Germany and partly because the Germans will have to confess that they can't whip our armies in France. But, even then, since they have all Russia to draw on, they may keep going for a long time. One man's guess is as good as another's.

One sad thing is certain: we shall at once begin to have heavy American casualties. Our Red Cross and our army here are getting hospitals ready for such American wounded as are brought over to England—the parts of our army that are fighting with the British.

We have a lot of miserable politics here which interfere with the public feeling. The British politician is a worse yellow dog than the American—at times he is, at least; and we have just been going through such a time. Another such time will soon come about the Irish.

Well, we have an unending quantity of work and wear —no very acute bothers but a continuous strain, the strain of actual work, of uneasiness, of seeing people, of uncertainty, of great expense, of doubt and fear at times, of inability to make any plans—all which is only the common lot now all over the world, except that most persons have up to this time suffered incomparably worse than we. And there's nothing to do but to go on and on and on and to keep going with the stoutest hearts we can keep up till the end do at last come. But the Germans now (as the rest of us) are fighting for their lives. They are desperate and their leaders care nothing for human life.

The Embassy now is a good deal bigger than the whole State Department ever was in times of peace. I have three buildings for offices, and a part of our civil force occupies two other buildings. Even a general supervision of so large a force is in itself a pretty big job. The army and the Navy have each about the same space as the Embassy proper. Besides, our people have huts and inns and clubs and hospitals all over the town. Even though there be fewer vexing problems than there were while we were neutral, there is not less work—on the contrary, more. Nor will there be an end to it for a very long time—long after my time here. The settling of the war and the beginning of peace activities, whenever these come, will involve a great volume of work. But I've no ambition to have these things in hand. As soon as a natural time of relief shall come, I'll go and be happier in my going than you or anybody else can guess.

Now we go to get my digestion stiffened up for another long tug—unless the Germans proceed forthwith to knock us out—which they cannot do.

With my love to everybody on the Hill,

Affectionately yours,

W. H. P.

Mr. and Mrs. Waldorf Astor—since become Viscount and Viscountess Astor—had offered the Pages the use of their beautiful seaside house at Sandwich, Kent, and it was the proposed vacation here to which Page refers in this letter. He obtained a six weeks' leave of absence and almost the last letters which Page wrote from England are dated from this place. These letters have all the qualities of Page at his best: but the handwriting is a sad reminder of the change that was progressively taking place in his physical condition. It is still a clear and beautiful script, but there are signs of a less steady hand than the one that had written the vigorous papers of the preceding four years.

Memorandum

Sandwich, Kent, Sunday, 19 May, 1918.

We're at Rest Harrow and it's a fine, sunny early spring Carolina day. The big German drive has evidently begun its second phase. We hear the guns distinctly. We see the coast-guard aeroplanes at almost any time o' day. What is the mood about the big battle?

The soldiers—British and French—have confidence in their ability to hold the Germans back from the Channel and from Paris. Yet can one rely on the judgment of soldiers? They have the job in hand and of course they believe in themselves. While one does not like in the least to discount their judgment and their hopefulness, for my part I am not *quite* so sure of their ability to make sound judgments as I wish I were. The chances are in favour of their success; but—suppose they should have to yield and give up Calais and other Channel ports? Well, they've prepared for it as best they can. They have made provision for commandeering most of the hotels in London that are not yet taken over—for hospitals for the wounded now in France.

And the war would take on a new phase. Whatever should become of the British and American armies, the Germans would be no nearer having England than they now are. They would not have command of the sea. The combined British and American fleets could keep every German ship off the ocean and continue the blockade by sea—indefinitely; and, if the peoples of the two countries hold fast, a victory would be won at last—at sea.

To Ralph W. Page

Rest Harrow, Sandwich, Kent.
May 19, 1918.

DEAR RALPH:

I felt very proud yesterday when I read T. R.'s good word in the *Outlook* about your book.[1] If I had written what he said myself—I mean, if I had written what *I* think of the book—I should have said this very thing. And there is one thing more I should have said, viz.:—All your life and all my life, we have cultivated the opinion at home that we had nothing to do with the rest of the

[1] "Dramatic Moments in American Diplomacy," by Ralph W. Page, 1918.

world, nothing to do with Europe in particular—and in
our political life our hayseed spokesmen have said this
over and over again till many people, perhaps most people,
came really to believe that it was true. Now this aloofness, this utterly detached attitude, was a pure invention
of the shirt-sleeve statesman at home. I have long concluded, for other reasons as well as for this, that these men
are the most ignorant men in the whole world; more ignorant—because they are viciously ignorant—than the Negro
boys who act as caddies at Pinehurst; more ignorant than
the inmates of the Morganton Asylum; more ignorant
than sheep or rabbits or idiots. They have been the
chief hindrances of our country—worse than traitors, in
effect. It is they, in fact, who kept our people ignorant
of the Germans, ignorant of the English, ignorant of our
own history, ignorant of ourselves. Now your book,
without mentioning the subject, shows this important
fact clearly, by showing that our aloofness has all been a
fiction. *We've been in the world—and right in the middle
of the world—the whole time.*

And our public consciousness of this fact has enormously
slipped back. Take Franklin, Madison, Monroe, Jefferson; take Hay, Root—and then consider some of our
present representatives! One good result of the war and
of our being in it will be the restoration of our foreign consciousness. Every one of the half million, or three million,
soldiers who go to France will know more about foreign
affairs than all Congress knew two years ago.

A stay of nearly five years in London (five years ago
to-day I was on the ship coming here) with no absence
long enough to give any real rest, have got my digestion
wrong. I've therefore got a real leave for two months.
Your mother and I have a beautiful house here that has
been lent to us, right on the Channel where there's nothing

worth bombing and where as much sunshine and warmth come as come anywhere in England. We got here last night and to-day is as fine an early spring day as you ever had in the Sandhills. I shall golf and try to find me an old horse to ride, and I'll stay out in the sunshine and try to get the inside machinery going all right. We may have a few interruptions, but I hope not many, if the Germans leave us alone. Your mother has got to go to Newcastle to christen a new British warship—a compliment the Admiralty pays her "to bind the two nations closer together" etc. etc. And I've got to go to Cambridge to receive an LL. D. for the President. Only such things are allowed to interrupt us. And we are very much hoping to see Frank here.

We are in sound of the battle. We hear the big guns whenever we go outdoors. A few miles down the beach is a rifle range and we hear the practice there. Almost any time of day we can hear aeroplanes which (I presume) belong to the coast guard. There's no danger of forgetting the war, therefore, unless we become stone deaf. But this decent air and sunshine are blessings of the highest kind. I never became so **tired** of anything since I had the measles as I've become of London.

My Lord! it sounded last night as if we had jumped from the frying pan into the fire. Just as we were about to go to bed the big gun on the beach—just outside the fence around our yard—about 50 yards from the house, began its thundering belch—five times in quick succession, rattling the windows and shaking the very foundation of things. Then after a pause of a few minutes, another round of five shots. Then the other guns all along the beach took up the chorus—farther off—and the inland guns followed. They are planted all the way to London —ninety miles. For about two hours we had this roar and racket. There was an air raid on, and there were supposed to be twenty-five or thirty German planes on their way to London. I hear that it was the worst raid that London has had. Two of them were brought down —that's the only good piece of news I've heard about it. Well, we are not supposed to be in danger. They fly over us on the way to bigger game. At any rate I'll take the risk for this air and sunshine. Trenches and barbed wire run all along the beach—I suppose to help in case of an invasion. But an invasion is impossible in my judgment. Holy Moses! what a world!—the cannon in the big battle in France roaring in our ears all the time, this cannon at our door likely to begin action any night and all the rest along the beach and on the way to London, and this is what we call rest! The world is upside down, all crazy, all murderous; but we've got to stop this barbaric assault, whatever the cost.

Ray Stannard Baker is spending a few days with us, much to our pleasure.

With love to Leila and the babies,

Yours affectionately,

W. H. P.

To Arthur W. Page

Rest Harrow, Sandwich Beach,
Sandwich, Kent, England.
May 20, 1918.

DEAR ARTHUR:

. . . I can't get quite to the bottom of the anti-English feeling at Washington. God knows, this people have their faults. Their social system and much else here is mediæval. I could write several volumes in criticism of them. So I could also in criticism of anybody else.

But Jefferson's[1] letter is as true to-day as it was when he wrote it. One may or may not have a lot of sentiment about it; but, without sentiment, it's mere common sense, mere prudence, the mere instinct of safety to keep close to Great Britain, to have a decent respect for the good qualities of these people and of this government. Certainly it is a mere perversity—lost time—lost motion, lost everything—to cherish a dislike and a distrust of them —a thing that I cannot wholly understand. While we are, I fear, going to have trade troubles and controversies, my feeling is, on the whole, in spite of the attitude of our official life, that an increasing number of our people are waking up to what England has done and is and may be depended on to do. Isn't that true?

We've no news here. We see nobody who knows anything. I am far from strong—the old stomach got tired and I must gradually coax it back to work. That's practically my sole business now for a time, and it's a slow process. But it's coming along and relief from seeing hordes of people is as good as medicine.

Affectionately,

W. H. P.

To the President

Sandwich, May 24, 1918.

DEAR MR. PRESIDENT:

Your speeches have a cumulative effect in cheering up the British. As you see, if you look over the mass of newspaper clippings that I send to the Department, or have them looked over, the British press of all parties and

[1] The reference is to a letter written in 1823 by Thomas Jefferson to President Monroe at the time when the Holy Alliance was threatening the independence of South America. "With Great Britain," Jefferson wrote, "we should most sedulously cherish a cordial friendship and nothing would tend more to knit our affections than to be fighting once more, side by side, in the same cause."

shades of opinion constantly quote them approvingly and gratefully. They have a cumulative effect, too, in clearing the atmosphere. Take, for instance, your declaration in New York about standing by Russia. All the allied governments in Europe wish to stand by Russia, but their pressing business with the war, near at hand, causes them in a way to forget Russia; and certainly the British public, all intent on the German "drive" in France had in a sense forgotten Russia. You woke them up. And your "Why set a limit to the American Army?" has had a cheering effect. As leader and spokesman of the enemies of Germany—by far the best trumpet-call spokesman and the strongest leader—your speeches are worth an army in France and more, for they keep the proper moral elevation. All this is gratefully recognized here. Public opinion toward us is wholesome and you have a "good press" in this Kingdom. In this larger matter, all is well. The English faults are the failings of the smaller men—about smaller matters—not of the large men nor of the public, about large matters.

In private, too, thoughtful Englishmen by their fears pay us high tribute. I hear more and more constantly such an opinion as this: "You see, when the war is over, you Americans will have much the largest merchant fleet. You will have much the largest share of money, and England and France and all the rest of the world will owe you money. You will have a large share of essential raw materials. You will have the machinery for marine insurance and for foreign banking. You will have much the largest volume of productive labour. And you will know the world as you have never known it before. What then is going to become of British trade?"

The best answer I can give is: "Adopt American methods of manufacture, and the devil take the hindmost. There will be for a long time plenty for everybody to do; and let us make sure that we both play the game fairly: that's the chief matter to look out for." That's what I most fear in the decades following the end of the war—trade clashes.

The Englishman's pride will be hurt. I recall a speech made to me by the friendliest of the British—Mr. Balfour himself: "I confess that as an Englishman it hurts my pride to have to borrow so much even from you. But I will say that I'd rather be in your debt than in anybody else's."

To Edward M. House

May 27, 1918.

MY DEAR HOUSE:

. . . I can write in the same spirit of the Labour Group which left for home last week. Nobody has been here from our side who had a better influence than they. They emphatically stuck by their instructions and took pleasure, against the blandishments of certain British Socialists, in declaring against any meeting with anybody from the enemy countries to discuss "peace-by-negotiation" or anything else till the enemy is whipped. They made admirable speeches and proved admirable representatives of the bone and sinew of American manhood. They had dead-earnestness and good-humour and hard horse-sense.

This sort of visit is all to the good. Great good they do, too, in the present English curiosity to see and hear the right sort of frank, candid Americans. Nobody who hasn't been here lately can form an idea of the eagerness of all classes to hear and learn about the United States. There never was, and maybe never will be again, such a chance to inform the British and—to help them toward a right understanding of the United States and our people.

We are not half using the opportunity. There seems to be a feeling on your side the ocean that we oughtn't to send men here to "lecture" the British. No typical, earnest, sound American who has been here has "lectured" the British. They have all simply told facts and instructed them and won their gratitude and removed misconceptions. For instance, I have twenty inquiries a week about Dr. Buttrick. He went about quietly during his visit here and talked to university audiences and to working-men's meetings and he captured and fascinated every man he met. He simply told them American facts, explained the American spirit and aims and left a grateful memory everywhere. Buttrick cost our Government nothing: he paid his own way. But if he had cost as much as a regiment it would have been well spent. The people who heard him, read American utterances, American history, American news in a new light. And most of his talk was with little groups of men, much of it even in private conversation. He did no orating or "lecturing." A hundred such men, if we had them, would do more for a perfect understanding with the British people than anything else whatsoever could do.

Yours sincerely,

WALTER H. PAGE.

To Arthur W. Page

Sandwich, May 27, 1918.

DEAR ARTHUR:

. . . I do get tired—my Lord! how tired!—not of the work but of the confinement, of the useless things I have to spend time on, of the bad digestion that has overtaken me, of London, of the weather, of absence from you all—of the general breaking up of the world, of this mad slaughter of men. But, after all, this is the common lot now and I am grateful for a chance to do what I can. That's the true way to look at it.

. . . Worry? I don't worry about anything except the war in general and this mad world so threatened by these devil barbarians. And I have a feeling that, when we get a few thousand flying machines, we'll put an end to that, alas! with the loss of many of our brave boys. I hear the guns across the channel as I write—an unceasing boom! boom! boom! That's what takes the stuff out of me and gets my inside machinery wrong. Still, I'm gradually getting even that back to normal. Golf and the poets are fine medicine. I read Keats the other day, with entire forgetfulness of the guns. Here we have a comfortable house, our own servants (as many as we need), a beautiful calm sea, a perfect air and for the present ideal weather. There's nobody down here but Scottish soldiers. We've struck up a pleasant acquaintance with them; and some of the fellows from the Embassy come down week ends. Only the murderous guns keep their eternal roar.

Thanks, thanks, a thousand thanks, old man. It'll all work out right.

. . . I look at it in this way: all's well that ends well. We are now doing our duty. That's enough. These things don't bother me, because doing our duty now is worth a million years of past errors and shortcomings.

Your mother's well and spry—very, and the best company in the world. We're having a great time.

Bully for the kids! Kiss 'em for me and Mollie too.

Affectionately,
W. H. P.

Make Shoecraft tell you everything. He's one of the best boys and truest in the world.

To Ralph W. Page

Rest Harrow, Sandwich, Kent.
June 7, 1918.

MY DEAR RALPH:

. . . I have all along cherished an expectation of two things—(1) That when we did get an American Army by conscription, if it should remain at war long enough to learn the game, it would become the best army that the world ever saw, for the simple reason that its ranks would contain more capable men than any other country has ever produced. The proof of this comes at once. Even our new and raw troops have astonished the veterans of the French and British armies and (I have no doubt) of the German Army also. It'll be our men who will whip the Germans, and there are nobody else's men who could do it. We've already saved the Entente from collapse by our money. We'll save the day again by our fighting men. That is to say, we'll save the world, thank God; and I fear it couldn't have been saved in any other way. (2) Since the people by their mood command and compel efficiency, the most efficient people will at last (as recent events show) get at the concrete jobs, in spite of anybody's preferences or philosophy. And this seems at last to be taking place. What we have suffered and shall suffer is not failure but delays and delays and bunglings. But they've got to end by the sheer pressure of the people's earnestness. These two things, then, are all to the good.

I get the morning papers here at noon. And to-day I am all alone. Your mother went early on her journey to launch a British battleship. I haven't had a soul to speak to all day but my servants. At noon, therefore, I was rather eager for the papers. I saw at a glance that a submarine is at work off the New Jersey coast! It's an awful thing for the innocent victims, to be drowned. But their deaths have done us a greater service than 100 times as many lives lost in battle. If anybody lacked earnestness about the war, I venture to guess that he doesn't lack it any longer. If the fools would now only shell some innocent town on the coast, the journey to Berlin would be shortened.

If the Germans had practised a chivalrous humanity in their war for conquest, they'd have won it. Nothing on earth can now save them; for the world isn't big enough to hold them and civilized people. Nor is there any room for pacifists till this grim business is done.

Affectionately,
W. H. P.

The last piece of writing from Sandwich is the following memorandum: ·

Sandwich, Kent.
June 10, 1918.

The Germans continue to gain ground in France—more slowly, but still they gain. The French and British papers now give space to plans for the final defense—the desperate defense—of Paris. The Germans are only forty miles away. Slocum, military attaché, thinks they will get it and he reports the same opinion at the War Office— because the Germans have taken such a large number of guns and so much ammunition. Some of these guns were meant for the American troops, and they cannot now be replaced in time if the German advance continues. But I do not know enough facts at first hand to form an opinion. But, if Paris be taken, the war will go on a long time —unless the English-speaking rulers make a compromise. And, then, in another form—and forms—it'll go on indefinitely.—There has been no more perilous or uncertain or anxious time than now.

The United States too late, too late, too late: what if it should turn out so?

But it did not turn out so. Even while Page was penning these lines great events were taking place in France and the American troops were having a large share in them. In June the Americans stopped the German troops at Belleau Wood—a battle which proved the mettle of these fresh levies not only for the benefit of the Germans but of the Allies as well. Thus Page had the great satisfaction of returning to London while the city was ringing with the praise of these achievements. He found that the atmosphere had materially changed since he had last been in the British capital; when he had left for Sandwich there had been a general expectation that the Germans would get Paris or the Channel ports; now, however, there was every confidence of victory. Greatly as Page rejoiced over the new prospect, however, the fight at Belleau Wood brought him his last great sorrow. His nephew, Allison M. Page, of Aberdeen, North Carolina, the son of his youngest brother, Frank, lost his life in that engagement. At first the young man was reported "missing"; the investigation set afoot by the Ambassador for some time brought no definite information. One of the most pathetic of Page's papers is a brief note addressed by him to Allison Page, asking him for news: "It's been a long time since we heard from you," Page wrote his nephew. "Write how it goes with you. Affectionately, Uncle Wat." After travelling over a considerable part of France, this note found its way back to the Embassy. The boy—he was only 19—had been killed in action near Belleau Wood, on June 25th, while leading his detachment in an attack on a machine gun. Citations and decorations for gallantry in action were given posthumously by General Pershing, Marshal Pétain, Major-General Omar Bundy, and Major-General John A. LeJeune.

And now the shadows began to close in rapidly on Page. In early July Major Frank C. Page, the Ambassador's youngest son, came over from France. A brief glance at his father convinced him that he was dying. By this time the Ambassador had ceased to go to the Chancery, but was transacting the most imperative business propped up in a chair at home. His mind was possessed by two yearnings: one was to remain in London until the end of the war, the other was to get back to his childhood home in North Carolina. Young Page urged his father to resign, but the weary invalid insisted on sticking to his post. On this point it seemed impossible to move him. Knowing that his brother Arthur had great influence with his father, Frank Page cabled, asking him to come to England immediately. Arthur took the first boat, reaching London late in July.

The Ambassador's two sons then gently pressed upon their father the fact that he must resign. Weak as he was, the Ambassador was still obdurate.

"No," he said. "It's quitting on the job. I must see the war through. I can't quit until it's over."

But Sir William Osler, Page's physician and devoted friend, exercised his professional authority and insisted on the resignation. Finally Page consented.

To the President

American Embassy, London,
August 1, 1918.

My dear Mr. President:

I have been struggling for a number of months against the necessity to write you this note; for my doctors now advise me to give up all work for a period—my London doctor says for six months. I have a progressive digestive trouble which does not yield to the usual treatment. It's the war, five London winters, and the unceasing labour which is now the common lot. I am ashamed to say that these have brought me to something near a breakdown. I have had Sir William Osler as well as two distinguished London physicians for several months. The digestive trouble has brought other ills in its train; and I am assured that they will yield to freedom from responsibility and complete rest for a time in a dry, warm climate and that they are not likely to yield to anything else.

I see nothing else to do then but to bow to the inevitable and to ask you to be kind enough to relieve me and to accept my resignation to take effect as soon as I can go to Washington and make a somewhat extended report on the work here, which, I hope, will be of some use to the Department; and I ought to go as soon as possible—say, in September. I cannot tell you how great my disappointment is that this request has become necessary.

If the world and its work were so organized that we could do what we should like to do, I should like a leave of absence till winter be broken and then to take up my duties here again till the war end. But that, of course, is impracticable. And it is now a better time to change Ambassadors than at any time since the war began. My five years' service has had two main phases—the difficult period of our neutrality and the far easier period since we came into the war. But when the war ends, I fear that there will be again more or less troublesome tasks arising out of commercial difficulties.

But for any reasonable period the Embassy's work fortunately can now go on perfectly well with Mr. Laughlin as Chargé—until my successor can get here. The Foreign Office like him, he is *persona grata* to all other Departments of the Government, and he has had a long experience; and he is most conscientious and capable. And the organization is in excellent condition.

I venture to ask you to have a cable message sent to me (to be deciphered by me alone). It will require quite a little time to pack up and to get away.

I send this, Mr. President, with more regret than I can express and only after a struggle of more than six months to avoid it.

Yours sincerely,

WALTER H. PAGE.

Arthur Page took his father to Banff, in Scotland, for a little rest in preparation for the voyage. From this place came Page's last letter to his wife:

To Mrs. Page

Duff House, Banff, Scotland.
Sunday, September 2, 1918.

MY DEAR:

. . . I've put the period of our life in London, in my mind, as closed. That epoch is ended. And I am glad. It was time it ended. My job (*that* job) is done. From the letters that Shoecraft has sent me and from what the papers say, I think I couldn't have ended it more happily —or at a better time. I find myself thinking of the winter down South—of a Thanksgiving Day dinner for the older folks of our family, of a Christmas tree for the kids, of frolics of all sorts, of Rest, of some writing (perhaps not much), going over my papers with Ralph—that's what he wants, you know; etc., etc., etc.——

And I've got to eat more. *I* myself come into my thinking and planning in only two ways—(1) I'm going to have a suit like old Lord N.'s and (2) I'm going to get all the good things to eat that there are!

Meantime, my dear, how are you? Don't you let this getting ready wear you out. Let something go undone rather. Work Miss Latimer and the boys and the moving and packing men, and Petherick and the servants. Take it very easy yourself.

Nine and a half more days here—may they speed swiftly. Comfortable as I am, I'm mortal tired of being away from you—dead tired.

Praise God it's only $9\frac{1}{2}$ days. If it were $9\frac{3}{4}$, I should not stand it, but break for home prematurely.

Yours, dear Allie, with all my love,

W. H. P.

On August 24th came the President's reply:

I have received your communication of August 1st. It caused me great regret that the condition of your health makes it necessary for you to resign. Under the circumstances I do not feel I have the right to insist on such a sacrifice as your remaining in London. Your resignation is therefore accepted. As you request it will take effect when you report to Washington. Accept my congratulations that you have no reason to fear a permanent impairment of your health and that you can resign knowing that you have performed your difficult duties with distinguished success.

WOODROW WILSON.

The news of Page's resignation inspired tributes from the British press and from British public men such as have been bestowed upon few Americans. The London *Times* headed its leader "A Great Ambassador" and this note,

was echoed in all sections of Great Britain. The part of
Page's career which Englishmen chiefly recalled was his
attitude during the period of neutrality. This, the newspapers declared, was Page's great contribution to the cause.
The fact that it had had such far-reaching influences on history was the one especially insisted on. His conciliatory
and skillful behaviour had kept the United States and Great
Britain friends at a time when a less tactful ambassador
might easily have made them enemies; the result was that,
when the time came, the United States could join forces
against the common enemy, with results that were then
daily unfolding on the battlefields of France. "I really
believe," wrote the Marquess of Crewe, "that there were
several occasions when we might have made it finally impossible for America to join us in the war; that these
passed by may have been partly due to some glimmering
of common sense on our part, with Grey as its main exponent; but it was more largely owing to your patience and
courtesy and to the certainty which the Foreign Office
always enjoyed that its action would be set before the
Secretary of State in as favourable a light as it conscien-
tiously could be." That, then, was Page's contribution to
the statesmanship of this crisis—that of holding the two
countries together so that, when the time came, the
United States could join the Allies. A mass of private
letters, all breathing the same sentiment, began to pour in
on Page. There was hardly an illustrious name in Great
Britain that was not represented among these leave-takings. As illustrating the character and spirit animating
them, the following selections are made:

From the King

The information communicated to me yesterday
through Mr. Laughlin of Your Excellency's resignation of

the Post of Ambassador and the cause of this step fill me with the keenest regret. During your term of office in days of peace and of war your influence has done much to strengthen the ties of friendship and good-will which unite the two English-speaking nations of the world. I trust your health will soon be restored and that we may have the pleasure of seeing you and Mrs. Page before your departure.

GEORGE R. I.

From the Prime Minister

10, Downing Street, Whitehall, S. W. 1
30th August, 1918.

MY DEAR AMBASSADOR:

It is with the deepest regret that my colleagues and I have received the news that you have been forced by ill health to resign your office and that the President has consented to your relinquishing your ambassadorial duties. We are sorry that you are leaving us, all the more because your tenure of office has coincided with one of the greatest epochs in the history of our two countries and of the world, and because your influence and counsel throughout this difficult time have been of the utmost value to us all.

The power for good or evil which can be exerted by the occupant of your high position is at all times necessarily very great. That our peoples are now fighting side by side in the cause of human freedom and that they are manifesting an ever growing feeling of cordiality to one another is largely attributable to the exceptional wisdom and good-will with which you have discharged your duties. For the part you have played during the past five years in bringing about this happy result we owe you our lasting gratitude.

May I add that while you have always firmly presented the point of view of your own country, you have succeeded in winning, not only the respect and admiration of official circles, but the confidence, and I can say without hesitation, the affection of all sections of our people? It will be with universal regret that they will learn that, owing to the strain of the great responsibilities you have borne, you are no longer to remain among us. I earnestly trust that a well-earned rest will speedily restore you to complete health, and that you have many years of public service still in store for you.

I should like also to say how much we shall miss Mrs. Page. She has won a real place in all our hearts. Through her unfailing tact, her genuine kindliness, and her unvarying readiness to respond to any call upon her time and energy, she has greatly contributed to the success of your ambassadorship.

Ever sincerely,
D. LLOYD GEORGE.

From Viscount Grey of Fallodon

Glen Innerleithen, Scotland,
September 2, 1918.

DEAR MR. PAGE:

I have been out of touch with current events for a few days, but yesterday I read the two articles in the *Times* on your retirement. I am very grieved to think that you are going. There was not a word of eulogy in the *Times* articles that was not under- rather than over-stated, and reflecting thus I thought how rare it is in public life to have an occasion that justifies the best that can be said. But it is so now, and I am filled with deep regret that you are going and with deep gratitude that you came to us and were here when the war broke out and subsequently. If the United States had been represented here by any one less decided as to the right and wrong of the war and less firm and courageous than yourself, the whole of the relations between your country and ours would have been in peril. And if the two countries had gone apart instead of coming together the whole fate of the world would be very different from what I hope it will now be.

I have often thought that the forces behind public affairs are so tremendous that individuals have little real, even when much apparent, influence upon the course of events. But in the early years of the war I think everything might have gone wrong if it had not been that certain men of strong moral conviction were in certain places. And you were preëminently one of these. President Wilson I am sure was another, though I know him only through you and Colonel House and his own public utterances. Even so your influence must have counted in his action, by your friendship with him as well as by the fact of your being the channel through which communications passed between him and us.

I cannot adequately express what it was to me personally in the dark days of 1914, 1915, and 1916 to know how you felt about the great issues involved in the war.

I go to Fallodon at the end of this week and come to London the first week of September—if you and Mrs. Page have not left by then I hope I may see you. I long to do so before you go. I wish you may recover perfect health. My eyesight continues to fail and I shall soon be absolutely dependent upon other eyes for reading print. Otherwise I feel as well as a schoolboy, but it is depressing to be so well and yet so crippled in sight.

Please do not trouble to answer this letter—you must have too many letters of the kind to be able to reply to them separately—but if there is a chance of my seeing

you before you go please let me have a message to say
when and where.

Yours sincerely,

GREY OF F.

A few months before his resignation Page had received
a letter from Theodore Roosevelt, who was more familiar
than most Americans with Page's work in London. This
summed up what will be probably the judgment of history
upon his ambassadorship. The letter was in reply to one
written to the Ex-President, asking him to show hospitality to the Archbishop of York,[1] who was about to visit the
United States.

(Office of the Metropolitan Magazine)
342 Fourth Ave., New York,
March 1st, 1918.

MY DEAR MR. AMBASSADOR:

I am very much pleased with your letter, and as soon
as the Archbishop arrives, he will be addressed by me
with all his titles, and I will get him to lunch with me or
dine with me, or do anything else he wishes! I shall do it
for his own sake, and still more, my dear fellow, I shall do
it for the sake of the Ambassador who has represented
America in London during these trying years as no other
Ambassador in London has ever represented us, with the
exception of Charles Francis Adams, during the Civil
War.

Faithfully yours,

THEODORE ROOSEVELT.

The seriousness of Page's condition was not understood
in London; consequently there were many attempts to do

---

[1] See Vol. II, page 307.

him honour in which he was unable to participate.   Custom demands that a retiring Ambassador shall go to
Windsor Castle to dine and to sleep; but King George,
who was very solicitous about Page's health, offered to
spare the Ambassador this trip and to come himself to
London for this leave-taking.   However, Page insisted on
carrying out the usual programme; but the visit greatly
tired him and he found it impossible personally to take
part in any further official farewells.   The last ceremony
was a visit from the Lord Mayor and Council of Plymouth,
who came to the Ambassador's house in September to present the freedom of the city.   Ever since Page's speech of
August 4, 1917, Plymouth had been planning to do him this
honour; when the Council heard that the Ambassador's
health would make it impossible for him to visit Plymouth,
they asked if they might not come to London.   The proceeding was most impressive and touching and the Ambassador's five-minute speech, the last one which he made in
England, had all his old earnestness and mental power,
though the physical weakness of the man saddened everybody present.   The Lord Mayor presented the freedom
of the ancient borough in a temporary holder, explaining
that a more permanent receptacle would follow the Ambassador to America.   When this arrived, it proved to be
a beautiful silver model of the *Mayflower*.   Certainly
there could have been no more appropriate farewell gift
to Page from the English town whose name so closely
links the old country with the United States.

The last scene took place at Waterloo Station.   Sir
Arthur Walsh came representing the King, while Mr.
Balfour, Lord Robert Cecil, and other ministers represented the cabinet.   The Government had provided a
special railway carriage, and this was stationed at a convenient place as Page's motor drew up.   So weak was

the Ambassador that it was with difficulty that his companions, the ever devoted Mr. Laughlin, on one side, and Page's secretary, Mr. Shoecraft, on the other, succeeded in supporting him to his chair. Mr. Balfour, Lord Robert Cecil and the others then entered the carriage, and, with all that sympathetic dignity in which Englishmen of this type excel, said a few gracious and affectionate words of good-bye. They all stood, with uncovered heads, as the train slowly pulled out of the station, and caught their final glimpse of Page as he smiled at them and faintly waved his hand.

Perhaps the man most affected by this leave-taking was Mr. Balfour. He knew, as did the others, that that frail and emaciated figure had been one of the greatest friends that Britain had had at the most dreadful crisis in her history. He has many times told of this parting scene at Waterloo Station and always with emotion.

"I loved that man," he once said to an American friend, recalling this event. "I almost wept when he left England."

CHAPTER XXVII
THE END

PAGE came home only to die. In fact, at one time it seemed improbable that he would live to reach the United States. The voyage of the *Olympic*, on which he sailed, was literally a race with death. The great-hearted Captain, Sir Bertram Hayes, hearing of the Ambassador's yearning to reach his North Carolina home, put the highest pressure upon his ship, which almost leaped through the waves. But for a considerable part of the trip Page was too ill to have much consciousness of his surroundings. At times he was delirious; once more he lived over the long period of "neutrality"; again he was discussing intercepted cargoes and "notes" with Sir Edward Grey; from this his mind would revert to his English literary friends, and then again he was a boy in North Carolina. The *Olympic* reached New York more than a day ahead of schedule; Page was carried down the gangplank on a stretcher, propped up with pillows; and since he was too weak then to be taken to his Southern home, he was placed temporarily in St. Luke's Hospital. Page arrived on a beautiful sunshiny October day; Fifth Avenue had changed its name in honour of the new Liberty Loan and had become the "Avenue of the Allies"; each block, from Forty-second Street north, was decorated with the colours of one of the nations engaged in the battle against Germany; the street was full of Red Cross workers and other picturesquely clad enthusiasts selling Liberty Bonds; in its animated beauty and in its inspiring significance it formed an appropriate setting for Page's home-coming.

The American air seemed to act like a tonic on Page; in a short time he showed such improvement that his recovery seemed not impossible. So far as his spirits and his mind were concerned, he became his old familiar self. He was able to see several of his old friends, he read the newspapers and discussed the international situation with his customary liveliness. With the assistance of his daughter, Mrs. Loring, he even kept track of his correspondence. Evidently the serious nature of his illness was not understood, for invitations to speak poured in from all quarters. Most of these letters Mrs. Loring answered, but there was one that Page insisted on attending to himself. The City of Cleveland was organizing some kind of a meeting dedicated to closer relations with Great Britain, and the Mayor wrote Page asking him to speak. The last thing which Page wrote with his own hand was his reply to this invitation; and it is an impressive fact that his final written word should have dealt with the subject that had been so close to his heart for the preceding five years.

To Harry L. Davis, Mayor of Cleveland, Ohio

I deeply regret my health will not permit me to attend any public function for some time to come; for I deeply appreciate your invitation on behalf of the City of Cleveland for the meeting on December 7th, and have a profound sympathy with its purpose to bring the two great English-speaking worlds as close together as possible, so that each shall thoroughly understand the courage and sacrifice and ideals of the other. This is the greatest political task of the future. For such a complete and lasting understanding is the only basis for the continued progress of civilization. I am proud to be associated in your thought, Mr. Mayor, with so fitting and happy an occasion, and only physical inability could cause absence.

Sincerely,

WALTER H. PAGE.

Page's improvement was only temporary; a day or two after this letter was written he began to sink rapidly; it was therefore decided to grant his strongest wish and take him to North Carolina. He arrived in Pinehurst on December 12th, so weak that his son Frank had to carry him in his arms from the train.

"Well, Frank," said Page, with a slightly triumphant smile, "I did get here after all, didn't I?"

He lingered for a few days and died, at eight o'clock in the evening, on December 21st, in his sixty-fourth year. He suffered no pain. He was buried in the Page family plot in the Bethesda Cemetery near Aberdeen.

He was as much of a war casualty as was his nephew Allison Page, who lost his life with his face to the German machine guns in Belleau Wood.

THE END

APPENDIX

PAGE was not methodical in keeping diaries. His documents, however, reveal that he took many praiseworthy resolutions in this direction. They include a large number of bulky books, each labelled "Diary" and inscribed with the year whose events were to be recorded. The outlook is a promising one; but when the books are opened they reveal only fragmentary good intentions. Entries are kept up for a few days, and then the work comes to an end. These volumes contain many scraps of interesting writing, however, which are worth preserving; some of them are herewith presented in haphazard fashion, with no attempt at order in subject matter.

1913

PETHERICK

PETHERICK: may he be immortal; for he is a man who has made of a humble task a high calling; and without knowing it he has caused a man of a high calling to degrade it to a mean level. Now Petherick is a humble Englishman, whose father many years ago enjoyed the distinction of carrying the mail pouch to and from the post office for the American Embassy in London. As father, so son. Petherick succeeded Petherick. In this remote period (*the* Petherick must now be 60) Governments had "despatch agents," men who distributed mail and whatnot, sent it on from capital to capital—were a sort of general "forwarding" factotums. The office is really out of date now. Telegraph companies, express companies, railway companies, the excellent mail service and the like out-despatch any conceivable agent—except Petherick. Petherick has qualities that defy change, such as an unfailing courtesy, a genuine joy in serving his fellows, the very genius of helpfulness. Well, since a governmental office once established acquires qualities of perpetuity, three United States despatch agents have survived the development of modern communication, one in London, one in New York, and the third (I think) in San Francisco. At any rate, the London agent remains.

Now in the beginning the London despatch agent was a mail messenger (as I understand) for the Embassy. He still takes the pouch to the post office, and brings it back. In ordinary times, that's all he does for the Embassy, for which his salary of about * * * is paid by the State Department—too high a salary for the labour done, but none too high for the trustworthy qualities required. If this had been all that Petherick did, he would probably have long ago gone to the scrap heap. It is one mark of a man of genius that he always makes his job. So Petherick. The American Navy came into being and parts of it come to this side of the world. Naval officers need help when they come ashore. Petherick was always on hand with despatches and mail for them, and Petherick was a handy man. Did the Captain want a cab? Petherick had one waiting. Did the Captain want rooms? Such-and-such a hotel was the proper one for him. Rooms were engaged. Did the Captain's wife need a maid? Petherick had thought of that, too. Then a Secretary from some continental legation wished to know a good London tailor.

He sought Petherick. An American Ambassador from the continent came to London. London yielded Petherick for his guidance and his wants. Petherick became omnipresent, universally useful—an American institution in fact. A naval officer who had been in Asiatic waters was steaming westward to the Mediterranean. His wife and three babies came to London, where she was to meet her husband, who was to spend several weeks here. A telegram to Petherick: they needed to do nothing else. When the lady arrived a furnished flat, a maid and a nurse and a cook and toys awaited her. When her husband arrived, a pair of boots awaited him from the same last that his last pair had been made on, in London, five years before. At some thoughtful moment $1,000 was added to Petherick's salary by the Navy Department; and a few years ago a handsome present was made to Petherick by the United States Naval Officers all over the world.

But Petherick, with all his virtues, is merely an Englishman, and it is not usual for an Englishman to hold a $3,000 office under appointment from the United States Government. The office of despatch agent, therefore, has been nominally held by an American citizen in London. This American citizen for a good many years has been Mr. Crane, a barrister, who simply turns over the salary to Petherick; and all the world, except the Secretary of State, knows that Petherick is Petherick and there is none other but him.

Now comes the story: Mr. Bryan, looking around the world for offices for his henchmen, finds that one Crane has been despatch agent in London for many years, and he writes me a personal and confidential letter, asking if this be not a good office for some Democrat!

I tell the story to the Naval Attaché! He becomes

riotous. He'll have to employ half a dozen clerks to do for the Navy ill what Petherick does well with ease, if he's removed. Life would not be worth living anyhow. I uncover Petherick to the Secretary and show him in his glory. It must be said to the Secretary's credit that he has said nothing more about it. Petherick, let us hope, will live forever. The Secretary's petty-spoils mind now works on grand plans for Peace, holy Peace, having unsuccessfully attacked poor Petherick. And Petherick knows nothing about it and never dreams of an enemy in all the world, and in all naval and diplomatic life he has only fast friends. If Mr. Bryan had removed him, he might have made a temporary friend of one Democrat from Oklahoma, and lasting enemies of all that Democrat's rivals and of the whole naval and diplomatic service.

November, 1914.

We have to get away from it—or try to—a minute at a time; and the comic gods sometimes help us. Squier[1] has a junior officer here to hold his desk down when he's gone. He's a West Point Lieutenant with a German name. His study is ordnance. A new kind of bomb gives him the same sort of joy that a new species would have given Darwin. He was over in France—where the armies had passed to and from Paris—and one day he found an unexploded German bomb of a new sort. The thing weighed half a ton or thereabouts, and it was loaded. Somehow he got it to London—I never did hear how. He wrapped it in blankets and put it under his bed. He went out of town to study some other infernal contraption and the police found this thing under his bed. The War Office took it and began to look for him—to shoot him, the

---

[1]Colonel (now Major General) George O. Squier, Military Attaché at the American Embassy.

bomb-harbouring German! They soon discovered, of course, that he was one of our men and an officer in the United States Army. Then I heard of it for the first time. Here came a profuse letter of apology from the Government; they had not known the owner was one of my attachés. Pardon, pardon—a thousand apologies. But while this letter was being delivered to me one of the under-secretaries of the Government was asking one of our secretaries, "In Heaven's name, what's the Ambassador going to do about it? We have no right to molest the property of one of your attachés, but this man's room is less than 100 yards from Westminster Abbey: it might blow up half of London. We can't give the thing back to him!" They had taken it to the Duck Pond, wherever that is. About that time the Lieutenant came back. His pet bomb gone—what was I going to do about it?

The fellow actually wanted to bring it to his office in the Embassy!

"Look here, Lieutenant, besides the possibility of blow-up this building and killing every mother's son of us, consider the scandal of the American Embassy in London blown up by a German bomb. That would go down in the school histories of the United States. Don't you see?" No, he didn't see instantly—he does so love a bomb! I had to threaten to disown him and let him be shot before he was content to go and tell them to unload it—he *would* have it, unloaded, if not loaded.

Well, I had to write half a dozen letters before the thing was done for. He thinks me a chicken-livered old coward and I know much more about him than I knew before; and we are at peace. The newspapers never got the story, but his friends about town still laugh at him for trying first to blow up Westminister Abbey and then his own Ambassador. He was at my house at dinner the other night and one of the ladies asked him: "Lieutenant, have you any darling little pet lyddite cartridges in your pocket?" Think of a young fellow who just loves bombs! Has loaded bombs for pets! How I misspent my youth!

February, 1915.

This is among the day's stories: The British took a ship that had a cargo of 100,000 busts of Von Hindenburg—filled with copper.

Another: When Frederick Watts was painting Lord Minto he found it hard to make the portrait please him. When he was told that Lord Minto liked it and Lady Minto didn't and that So-and-So praised it, he exclaimed: "I don't care a d—n what anyone thinks about it—except a fellow named Sargent."

And the King said (about the wedding[1]): "I have the regulation of the dress to be worn at all functions in the Chapel Royal. I, therefore, declare that the American Ambassador may have any dress worn that he pleases!"

E. M. House went to Paris this morning, having no peace message from this Kingdom whatever. This kind of talk here now was spoken of by the Prime Minister the other day "as the twittering of a sparrow in a tumult that shakes the world."

Lady P. remarked to me to-day, as many persons do, that I am very fortunate to be Ambassador here at this particular time. Perhaps; but it isn't easy to point out precisely wherein the good fortune consists. This much is certain: it is surely a hazardous occupation now. Henry James remarked, too, that nobody could afford to miss the experience of being here—nobody who could be here. Perhaps true, again; but I confess to enough shock and horror to keep me from being so very sure of that. Yet

[1] The wedding of Mr. Page's daughter at the Chapel Royal.

no other phenomenon is more noticeable than the wish of every sort of an American to be here. I sometimes wonder whether the really well-balanced American does. Most of them are of the overwrought and excitable kinds.

A conservative lady, quite conscientious, was taken down to dinner by Winston Churchill. Said she, to be quite frank and fair: "Mr. Churchill, I must tell you that I don't like your politics. Yet we must get on together. You may say, if you like, that this is merely a matter of personal taste with me, as I might not like your—well, your moustache." "I see no reason, Madam, why you should come in contact with either."

My talk with Bonar Law: He was disposed to believe that if England had declared at once that she would go to war with Germany if France was attacked, there would have been no war. Well, would English opinion, before Belgium was attacked, have supported a government which made such a declaration?

Mr. Bonar Law thinks that President Wilson ought to have protested about Belgium.

He didn't agree with me that much good human material goes to waste in this Kingdom for lack of opportunity. (That's the Conservative in him.)

Friday, April 30, 1915.

Sir Edward Grey came to tea to talk with Mr. House and me—little talk of the main subject (peace), which is not yet ripe by a great deal. Sir Edward said the Germans had poisoned wells in South Africa. They have lately used deadly gases in France. The key to their mind says Sir Edward, is this—they attribute to other folk what they are thinking of doing themselves.

While Sir Edward was here John Sargent came in and brought Katharine the charcoal portrait of her that he

had made—his present to her for her and Chud to give'
to W. A. W. P.[1] and me. A very graceful and beautiful
thing for him to do.

April 30, 1915.

Concerning Peace: The German civil authorities want
peace and so does one faction of the military party.
But how can they save their face? They have made
their people believe that they are at once the perse-
cuted and the victorious. If they stop, how can
they explain their stopping? The people might rend
them. The ingenious loophole discovered by House is—
mere moonshine, viz., the freedom of the seas in war.
That is a one-sided proposition unless they couple with
it the freedom of the land in war also, which is nonsense.
Nothing can be done, then, until some unfavourable military event brings a new mind to the Germans. Peace
talk, therefore, is yet mere moonshine. House has been
to Berlin, from London, thence to Paris, then back to
London again—from Nowhere (as far as peace is concerned) to Nowhere again.

May 3, 1915.

Why doesn't the President make himself more accessible? Dismiss X and get a bigger man? Take his cabinet
members really into his confidence? Everybody who
comes here makes these complaints of him!

We dined to-night at Y's. Professor M. was there, etc.
He says we've got to have polygamy in Europe after the
war to keep the race up.

Friday, May 21, 1915.

Last night the Italian Parliament voted to give the
Government war-powers; and this means immediate war,

---

[1]Mrs. Page.

on the side of the Allies. There are now eight nations fighting against Germany, Austria, and Turkey; viz., Great Britain, France, Russia, Italy, Japan, Belgium, Serbia, Montenegro. And it looks much as if the United States will be forced in by Germany.

The British Government is wrestling with a very grave internal disruption—to make a Coalition Government. The only portfolios that seem absolutely secure are the Prime Minister's and the Foreign Secretary's (Sir Edward Grey's)—for which latter, many thanks. The two-fold trouble is—(1) a difference between Churchill (First Lord of the Admiralty) and Lord Fisher—about the Dardanelles campaign and (I dare say) other things, and (2) Lord Kitchener's failure to secure ammunition—"to organize the industries of the Kingdom." Some even declare K. of K. (they now say Kitchener of Kaos) is a general colossal failure. But the prevailing opinion is that his raising of the new army has been good work but that he has failed with the task of procuring munitions. As for Churchill, he's too restless and erratic and dictatorial and fussy and he runs about too much. I talked with him at dinner last night at his mother's. He slips far down in his chair and swears and be-dams and by-Gods his assertions. But his energy does interest one. An impromptu meeting in the Stock Exchange to-day voted confidence in K. of K. and burned up a copy of the *Daily Mail*, which this morning had a severe editorial about him.

Washington, having sent a severe note to Germany, is now upbraided for not sending another to England, to match and pair it. That's largely German influence, but also the Chicago packers and the cotton men. These latter have easy grievances, like the Irish. The delays of the British Government are exasperating, but they are really not so bad now as they have been. Still, the President can be influenced by the criticism that he must hit one side every time he hits the other, else he's not neutral! I am working by every device to help the situation and to prevent another note. I proposed to-day to Sir Edward Grey that his Government make an immediate advance payment on the cotton that it proposes to buy.

Unless Joffre be a man of genius—of which there are some indications—and unless French also possibly have some claim to this distinction and *perhaps* the Grand Duke Nikolas, there doesn't yet seem to be a great man brought forth by the war. In civil life, Sir Edward Grey vomes to a high measure. As we yet see it from this English corner of the world, no other statesman now ranks with him.

March 20, 1916.

I am sure I have the best secret service that could be got by any neutral. I am often amazed at its efficiency. It is good because it is not a secret—certainly not a spy service at all. It is all aboveboard and it is all done by men of high honour and good character—I mean the Embassy staff. Counting the attachés there are about twenty good men, every one of whom moves in a somewhat different circle from any other one. Every one cultivates his group of English folk, in and out of official life, and his group in the diplomatic corps. There isn't a week but every man of them sees his particular sources of information—at their offices, at the Embassy, at luncheon, at dinner, at the clubs—everywhere. We all take every possible occasion to serve our friends and they serve us. The result is, I verily believe, that we hear more than any other group in London. These young fellows are all keen as razors. They know when to be silent, too; and they are trusted as they deserve to be. Of course I see them, singly or in pairs, every day in the regular conduct of the work of the Embassy; and once a week we all meet together and go over everything that properly comes before so large a "cabinet" meeting. Thus some of us are on confidential terms with somebody in every department of the Government, with somebody in every other Embassy and Legation, with all the newspapers and correspondents—even with the censors. And the wives of those that are married are abler than their husbands. They are most attractive young women—welcome everywhere—and indefatigable. Mrs. Page has them spend one afternoon a week with her, rolling bandages; and that regular meeting always yields something else. They come to my house Thursday afternoons, too, when people always drop in to tea—visitors from other countries, resident Americans, English—everybody—sometimes one hundred.

Nobody in this company is a "Spy"—God forbid! I know no more honourable or attractive group of ladies and gentlemen. Yet can conceive of no organization of spies who could find out as many things. And the loyalty of them all! Somebody now and then prefaces a revelation with the declaration, "This is in strict confidence—absolutely nobody is to hear it." The answer is—"Yes, only, you know, I have no secrets from the Ambassador: no member of his staff can ever have."—Of course, we get some fun along with our tragedies. If I can find time, for instance, I am going to write out for House's amusement a verbatim report of every conversation that he held in London. It has all come to me—from what he said to the King down; and it all tallies with what House himself told me. He went over it all himself to me the other day at luncheon.—I not only believe—I am sure—that in this way I do get a correct judgment of public feeling and public opinion, from Cabinet Ministers to stock-brokers.

December 11, 1916.

The new Government is quite as friendly to us in its intentions as the old, and much more energetic. The old Government was a spent force. Mr. Balfour is an agreeable man to deal with, with a will to keep our sympathy, unless the dire need of ships forces him to unpleasantness. The Prime Minister is—American in his ways. Lord Robert has the old Cecil in him, and he's going to maintain the blockade at any cost that he can justify to himself and to public opinion, and the public opinion is with him. They are all eager to have American approval—much more eager, I think, than a large section of public opinion, which has almost ceased to care what Americans think or do. The more we talk about peace, the more they think about war. There is no vindictiveness in the English. They do not care to do hurt to the German people: they regard them as misguided and misled. But no power on earth can stop the British till the German military caste is broken—that leadership which attacked Belgium and France and would destroy England. Balfour, Lloyd George, the people, the army and the navy are at one in this matter, every labouring man, everybody, except a little handful of Quakers and professors and Noel Buxton. I think I know and see all the peace men. They feel that they can talk to me with safety. They send me their pamphlets and documents. I think that all of them have now become warlike but three, and one of them is a woman. If you meet a woman you know on the street and express a sympathy on the loss of her second son, she will say to you, "Yes, he died in defence of his country. My third son will go next week. They all die to save us." Doubtless she sheds tears in private. But her eyes are dry in public. She has discarded her luxuries to put money in the war loan. Say "Peace" to her? She would insult you.

May 10, 1917.

We dined at Lambeth Palace. There was Lord Morley, whom I had not seen since his long illness—much reduced in flesh, and quite feeble and old-looking. But his mind and speech were most alert. He spoke of Cobden favouring the Confederate States because the constitution of the Confederacy provided for free trade. But one day Bright informed Cobden that he was making the mistake of his life. Thereafter Cobden came over to the Union side. This, Morley heard direct from Bright.

The Archbishop spoke in high praise of Charnwood's Lincoln—was surprised at its excellence, etc.

Geoffrey Robinson[1] asked who wrote the *Quarterly* articles in favour of the Confederacy all through the war —was it Lord Salisbury? Nobody knew.

The widow of the former Archbishop Benson was there —the mother of all the Bensons, Hugh, A. C., etc., etc.— a remarkable old lady, who talked much in admiration of Balfour.

The Bishop of—Winchester(?)—was curious to know whether the people in the United States really understood the Irish question—the two-nation, two-religion aspect of the case. I had to say no!

There is an orphan asylum founded by some preceding Archbishop, by the sea. The danger of bombardment raised the question of safety. The Archbishop ordered all the children (40) to be sent to Lambeth Palace. We dined in a small dining room: "The children," Mrs. David-

[1]Editor of the London *Times*.

son explained, "have the big dining room." Each child has a lady as patroness or protector who "adopts" her, i.e., sees that she is looked after, etc. Some of the ladies who now do this were themselves orphans!

At prayers as usual at 10 o'clock in the chapel where prayers have been held every night—for how many centuries?

At lunch to-day at Mr. Asquith's—Lord Lansdowne there; took much interest in the Knapp farm work while I briefly explained.

Lord Morley said to Mrs. Page he had become almost a Tolstoyan—Human progress hasn't done much for mankind's happiness, etc. Look at the war—by a "progressive" nation. Now the mistake here is born of a class-society, a society that rests on privilege. "Progress," *has* done everything (1) in liberating men's minds and spirits in the United States. This is the real gain; (2) in arraying all the world *against* Germany.

Tuesday, January 22, 1918.

Some days bring a bunch of interesting things or men. Then there sometimes come relatively dull days—not often, however. To-day came:

General Tasker H. Bliss, Chief-of-Staff, now 64—the wisest (so I judge) of our military men, a rather wonderful old chap. He's on his way to Paris as a member of the Supreme War Council at Versailles. The big question he has struck is: Shall American troops be put into the British and French lines, in small groups, to fill up the gaps in those armies? The British have persuaded him that it is a military necessity. If it were less than a necessity, it would, of course, be wrong—i.e., it would cut across our national pride, force our men under another flag, etc. It is not proposed to deprive Pershing of his command nor even of his army. The plan is to bring over troops that would not otherwise now come and to lend these to the British and French armies, and to let Pershing go on with his army as if this hadn't been done. Bliss is inclined to grant this request on condition the British bring these men over, equip and feed them, etc. He came in to ask me to send a telegram for him to-morrow to the President, making this recommendation. But on reflection he decided to wait till he had seen and heard the French also, who desire the same thing as the British.

General Bliss is staying with Major Warburton; and Warburton gave me some interesting glimpses of him. A telegram came for the General. Warburton thought that he was out of the house and he decided to take it himself to the General's room. He opened the door. There sat the General by the fire talking to himself, wrapped in thought. Warburton walked to the middle of the room. The old man didn't see him. He decided not to disturb him, for he was rehearsing what he proposed to say to the Secretary of State for War or to the Prime Minister—getting his ears as well as his mind used to it. Warburton put the telegram on the table near the General, went out, and wasn't discovered.

Several nights, he sat by the fire with Warburton and began to talk, again rehearsing to himself some important conclusions that he had reached. Every once in a while he'd look up at Warburton and say: "Now, what do you think of that?"

That's an amazing good way to get your thought clear and your plans well laid out. I've done it myself.

I went home and Kipling and Carrie[1] were at lunch with us. Kipling said: "I'll tell you, your coming into the war made a new earth for me." He is on a committee to see

---

[1] Mrs. Kipling.

that British graves are properly marked and he talked much about it. I could not help thinking that in the back of his mind there was all the time thought of his own dead boy, John.

Then in the afternoon Major Drain brought the copy of a contract between the United States Government and the British to build together 1500 tanks ($7,500,000). We took it to the Foreign Office and Mr. Balfour and I signed it. Drain thinks that the tanks are capable of much development and he wishes our army after the war to keep on studying and experimenting with and improving such machines of destruction. Nobody knows what may come of it.

Then I dined at W. W. Astor's (Jr.) There were Balfour, Lord Salisbury, General and Lady Robertson, Mrs. Lyttleton and Philip Kerr.

During the afternoon Captain Amundsen, Arctic explorer came in, on his way from Norway to France as the guest of our Government, whereafter he will go to the United States and talk to Scandinavian people there.

That's a pretty good kind of a full day.

April, 19, 1918.

Bell,[1] and Mrs. Bell during the air raid took their little girl (Evangeline, aged three) to the cellar. They told her they went to the cellar to hear the big fire crackers. After a bomb fell that shook all Chelsea, Evangeline clapped her hands in glee. "Oh, mummy, what a *big* fire cracker!"

---

[1]Mr. Edward Bell, Second Secretary of the American Embassy.

INDEX

INDEX

Grey, Sir Edward, credentials presented to, I 135; high regard for, I 150; his fairness facilitates diplomatic business, I 155; talks with on Mexican situation, I 184, 185, 188, 199; informed as to Carden's activities, I 219, 220; asked to meet Colonel House at luncheon, I 245; note to Sir C. Spring Rice on Wilson's address to Congress on Tolls Bill, I 254; criticized for "bowing too low to the Americans," I 261; depressed at extent of Anglophobia in the United States, I 266; evinces satisfaction at clearing up of problems, I 285; weeps as he informs Page of ultimatum to Germany, I 309, 315; "subservience" to American interests, I 364; accepts Declaration of London with modifications, I 384; joking over serious affairs, I 390; welcomes Page's solution of the *Dacia* tangle, I 394; letter to Sir Cecil Spring Rice regarding Speyer-Straus peace proposal, I 408; states war could be ended more quickly if America ceased protests against seizure of contraband, I 421; talk on detained shipping and Wordsworth poems, II 103; "a God's mercy for a man like him at his post," II 118; aged by the war, II 141; satisfactory settlement of the *China* case, II 155; speech in House of Commons on Peace, II 157; nothing but praise heard of him, II 159; memorandum of conversation with, on conditions of peace, II 160; receives Senate Resolution asking clemency for Sir Roger Casement, II 167; forced to resign, because he refused to push the blockade and risk break with America, II 233; guest with Mr. and Mrs. Page at Wilsford Manor, II 288; walk to Stonehenge with, II 292; serious blockade questions give way to talks on poets, II 305; promises government support of Belgian Relief plan, II 310; frequent visitor at the Embassy, II 315

Letters from: congratulations on Wilson's address to Congress advising declaration of war, II 234; expressing grief at Page's departure and citing his great help, II 400

Haldane, Viscount, at Thanksgiving Dinner of the American Society, I 213; discussion with Von Tirpitz as to relative sizes of navies, I 278; knew that Germany intended war, II 35
Hall, Admiral William Reginald, brings news of Bernstorff's dismissal, II 215
Hanning, Mrs. Robert, sister of Thomas Carlyle, I 60
Harcourt, Right Honourable Lewis, eulogizes work of International Health Board, I 101
Harden, Maximilian, says Germany must get rid of its predatory feudalism, II 193
Harper & Brothers, difficulties of, I 64
Harrow, visit to, and talk to schoolboys, I 17

Harvey, George, succeeds Page as editor of Harper's, I 66
Hay, John, understanding of Hay-Pauncefote Treaty, I 242; accused of Anglomania while Ambassador, I 257
Hays, Sir Bertram, captain of the *Olympic*, races ship to hasten Page's homecoming, II 404
Hearst, William Randolph, used by Germans in their peace propaganda, I 410, 411
Hearst papers, antagonism of, I 149, 256, 264, 286
Hesperian, submarined in violation of Bernstorff's pledges, II 30
Hewlett, Maurice, his son among the missing, II 115
Home Rule Bill, Carson threatens resistance to, I 137; "division" in House of Lords, I 138
Hookworm eradication, efforts in, I 98
Hoover, Charles L., war relief work while American Consul at Carlsbad, I 334
Hoover, Herbert C., relief work at beginning of war, I 333; selected by Page for Belgian Relief post, II 310
House, Colonel Edward M., wires Page to come North, expecting to offer Secretaryship of Interior, I 118; transmits offer of Ambassadorship, I 130; on Cowdray and Carden, I 218, 220; meets Sir Edward Grey to talk over Panama Tolls question, I 246; mission to the Kaiser a disappointment, I 289; no success in France, I 297; fancied security in England, thinks his mission unnecessary, I 298; telegrams, to and from Wilson on proffering good offices to avert war, I 317, 318; declares bill admitting foreign ships to American registry "full of lurking dangers," I 392; declares America will declare war on Germany after *Lusitania* sinking, II 2; sees "Too proud to fight" poster in London, II 6; recommends Page's appointment as Secretary of State, II 11; fails to alter Wilson's opposition to Taft Committee visiting England, I 348

Letters from: reporting progress in Panama Tolls matter, I 253; plans to visit Kaiser and bring about naval holiday between nations, I 277; cites further plans for visiting Germany, I 281; respecting proposed trip to Germany, I 285, 286, en route, I 288; note from Berlin, I 296; from Paris, I 297; on the outbreak of the war, I 299; transmitting Wilson's warning to adhere more strictly to neutrality, I 362; explains the toning down of demands that Declaration of London be adhered to, I 378; on German peace proposals, and giving his ideas for a settlement, I 413; proposing that Wilson start peace parleys, I 416; thinks Germany ready for peace proposals, I 424, 425; decides to visit combatants in interests